D1247199

THE ENGLISH VERSIONS OF
# THE SHIP OF FOOLS

PLATE I.—Title-page of the German original, 1494.
See §§ 359 and 367.

# THE ENGLISH VERSIONS OF
# THE SHIP OF FOOLS

## A CONTRIBUTION TO THE HISTORY OF THE EARLY FRENCH RENAISSANCE IN ENGLAND

BY

FR. AURELIUS POMPEN, O.F.M.

*WITH 4 PLATES*

1967

**OCTAGON BOOKS, INC.**

*New York*

Originally published 1925 by Longmans, Green and Co.

*Reprinted 1967*
*by special arrangement with Fr. Aurelius Pompen, O.F.M.*

OCTAGON BOOKS, INC.
175 Fifth Avenue
New York, N. Y. 10010

Library of Congress Catalog Card Number: 67-20302

831.9003
p788e

*Printed in U.S.A. by*
NOBLE OFFSET PRINTERS, INC.
NEW YORK 3, N. Y.

# PREFATORY NOTE

THIS work could not have been written without much friendly co-operation and assistance. From the officials of the Bibliothèque Nationale at Paris and of the British Museum in London I have experienced the greatest kindness and consideration. Those are the two libraries where the bulk of the material was collected. But I owe debts of gratitude also to the Amsterdamsche Universiteitsbibliotheek, to the Koninklijke Bibliotheek at The Hague, to the Stadtsbibliothek at Aix-la-Chapelle, and to the Bibliothèque Royale at Brussels.—Individual assistance was given me by the Franciscans at Argenteuil and Woodford Green, and three friends kindly undertook to read through my manuscript before it was printed. Thus I was able to profit by the extensive knowledge of English literature of Professor Swaen and by the bibliographical erudition and acumen of F. Bonaventura Kruitwagen, while it is due to an M.A. of the London University, F. Conrad Walmsley, that my English is no worse than it is.—My principal obligations I have acknowledged in the notes, but several friends to whom I owe helpful suggestions or services could not very well be explicitly mentioned. They go unnamed, but they shall not be unremembered, and I hope that all will accept this general expression of gratitude.

FR. AURELIUS POMPEN, O.F.M.

Heerlen, 8 December 1924.

**METHODIST COLLEGE LIBRARY**
Fayetteville, N. C.

38041

# TABLE OF CONTENTS

## LIST OF ILLUSTRATIONS

# LIST OF WORKS CONSULTED[1]

ALDEN, R. M.—The Rise of Formal Satire in England under classical influence. (Publications of the Univ. of Pennsylvania.) Philadelphia 1899.

ALLEN, P. S.—Opus Epistolarum Des. Erasmi Roterodami I. 1906.

ALLUT, M. P.—Etude biographique et bibliographique sur Symphorien Champier. Lyon 1859.

BELOW, G. VON.—Die Ursachen der Reformation. (Historische Bibliothek 38.) 1917.

BEZOLD, FR. VON.—Aus Mittelalter und Renaissance. München 1918.

BMC.=Catalogue of books printed in the 15th century now in the British Museum. 1908 etc.

BOBERTAG, Dr. J.—Sebastian Brant's Narrenschiff. (Deutsche National-Litteratur Bd. 16.) n.d.

BÖCKING, ED.—Ulrichi Hutteni equitis Operum Supplementum. Epistolae Obscurorum Virorum. Lipsiae 1864.

BOGGIS, R. J. E.—A History of the Diocese of Exeter. Exeter 1922.

BRANT, SEB.—Varia Carmina. Basel 1498. Brit. Mus. 166. e. 2.

BRIE, F. W. D.—Skelton Studien, in Englische Studien 37. 1907.

BURCKHARDT, JAC.—Die Kultur der Renaissance in Italien. 13te Aufl. Neudruck W. Goetz. Stuttgart 1922.

BURDACH, K.—Reformation Renaissance Humanismus. Berlin 1918.

BURGER, K.—The printers and publishers of the 15th century. 1902.

Cambridge History of English Literature III. 1918.

CHATELAIN, H.—Recherches sur le Vers Français au XVe siècle. Paris 1908.

CHAUCER, G.—The Complete Works of Geoffrey Chaucer. Ed. W. W. Skeat. Oxford 1894 etc.

CHEVALIER, U.—Répertoire des Sources Historiques du Moyen Age. Bio-Bibliographie. Paris 1877–86. Topo-Bibliographie 1903.

CLAUDIN, H.—Histoire de l'imprimerie en France au 15e et au 16e siècles. Paris 1900 etc.

COPINGER, W. A.—Supplement to Hain's Repertorium Bibliographicum. London 1895–1902.

DALHEIMER, V.—Die Sprache Alexander Barclay's in the Ship of Folys of the Worlde. Dissertation Zürich 1899.

D'ARGENTRÉ, C. DU PLESSIS.—Collectio Judiciorum de novis Erroribus. Paris 1728.

DEDEKIND, FR.—Grobianus verdeutscht von Kaspar Scheidt. Abdruck der ersten Ausgabe 1551. Neudrucke deutscher Litteraturwerke. Halle 1882. (Introd. signed by G. Milchsack.)

DICHTEN.—Veelderhande Geneuchlijcke—uitg. Maatschappij der Nederl. Letterk. Leiden 1899.

DNB.=Dictionary of National Biography.

---

[1] This list does not include the works and editions that form the real subject of this study, nor all the works that have been used only for an occasional reference. Of the first there is an account in Part III (pp. 14–19) ; of the second the full titles are in the notes. Nor have encyclopedias and dictionaries been inserted such as Ducange, Godefroy, Grimm, Kirchenlexicon, Catholic Encyclopedia, etc., except to explain some special abbreviations.

Douce, Fr.—Illustrations of Shakespeare. London 1807.

Duff, E. Gordon.—Fifteenth Century English Books. (Illustrated Monographs 18.) 1917.

Duhem, P.—Les Précurseurs Parisiens de Galilée. (Etudes sur Leonard de Vinci III.) 1913.

Dyce, A.—The Poetical Works of John Skelton. London 1843 ; Boston 1856.

Eckhardt, E.—Die lustige Person im älteren englischen Drama. Palaestra XVI. 1902.

Epistolae Obscurorum Virorum. See Böcking.

Erasmus. See Allen.

Flögel, K. F.—Geschichte des Grotesk-Komischen hrsg. M. Bauer. München 1914.

Fraustadt, F.—Ueber das Verhältnis von Barclay's Ship of Fools zur lateinischen, französischen und deutschen Quelle. Dissertation Breslau. 1894.

Gasquet, F. A.—The Eve of the Reformation. 1900.

Gasquet, F. A.—Henry VIII and the English Monasteries. 1906.

Goedeke, K.—Das Narrenschiff von Sebastian Brant. (Deutsche Dichter des 16ten Jahrhunderts, vol. 7.) Leipzig 1872.

Goedeke, K.—Grundrisz zur Geschichte der Deutschen Dichtung. I. Dresden 1884.

Grube, Dr. K.—Des Augustinerpropstes Johannes Busch Chronicon Windesheimense und Liber de reformatione monasteriorum. (Geschichtsquellen der Provinz Sachsen 19.) 1886.

Guy, H.—Histoire de la Poésie Française au XVIe Siècle I. L'école des rhétoriqueurs. 1910.

Hain, L.—Repertorium bibliographicum. Stuttgart 1826–38.

Hain-Copinger.—Supplement to Hain's Repertorium Bibliographicum. London 1895.

Hamon, A.—Un grand Rhétoriqueur Poitevin, Jean Bouchet (1476–1557 ?). 1901.

Hazlitt, W. C.—Remains of the Early Popular Poetry of England. 1866.

Hehle, Dr.—Der schwäbische Humanist Jacob Locher Philomusus (1471–1528), eine kultur- und literarhistorische Skizze. Programm. kgl. Gymnasium in Ehingen I (1873), II (1874) Nachträge (1875).

Hemmerlin, Felix.—Varie oblectationis Opuscula et tractatus ; ed. S. Brant. n.d. BMC. I. 172. Hain 8424. Brit. Mus. IB. 2562.

Herford, Ch. H.—Studies in the literary Relations of England and Germany in the sixteenth century. 1886.

Hub, I.—Die komische und humoristische Literatur der deutschen Prosaisten des 16ten Jahrhunderts. I. Nürnberg 1856.

Huizinga, J.—Herfsttij der Middeleeuwen, 2e druk. Haarlem 1921.

Izacke, R.—Antiquities of the City of Exeter, 3rd ed. 1731.

Jamieson, T. H.—The Ship of Fools translated by Alexander Barclay. Edinburgh 1874.

Janssen-Pastor.—Geschichte des deutschen Volkes seit dem Ausgang des Mittelalters, I. 19. und 20. Auflage, durch L. von Pastor. 1913.

Jongh, H. de.—L'ancienne Faculté de Théologie de Louvain au premier siècle de son existence (1432–1540). Louvain 1911.

Junghans, H. A.—Seb. Brant's Narrenschiff.—Universal Bibliothek, Leipzig, 899, 900. 1877.

Jusserand, J. J.—A Literary History of the English People. 1906.

Kalff, Dr. G.—Westeuropeesche Letterkunde. Groningen 1923, 1924.

Knepper, Dr. J.—Nationaler Gedanke und Kaiseridee bei den elsässischen Humanisten (Erläuterungen u. Ergänzungen I). 1898.

Knepper, Dr. J.—Jakob Wimpfeling 1450–1528. (Erläuterungen III.) 1902.

Koelbing, A.—Zur Charakteristik John Skeltons. 1904.

Lea, H. C.—History of the Inquisition of the Middle Ages II. New York 1906.

Leach, A. F.—The Schools of Medieval England. (The Antiquary's Books.) n.d. (c. 1912.)

Lehmann, P.—Die Parodie im Mittelalter. München 1922.

Lupton, J. H.—A Life of John Colet, D.D. New ed. Bell. 1909.

LYTE, H. C. MAXWELL.—A History of the University of Oxford from the earliest times to the year 1530. 1886.

MACFARLANE, J.—Antoine Vérard. Illustrated Monographs Bibliographical Society VII. 1900.

MESTWERDT, P.—Die Anfänge des Erasmus Humanismus und ' Devotio Moderna.' (Studien zur Kultur und Gesch. der Reformation II.) 1917.

MORLEY, HENRY.—English Writers. An Attempt towards a History of English Literature, VII. From Caxton to Coverdale. 1891.

MULLINGER, J. B.—The University of Cambridge from the earliest times to the Royal Injunctions of 1535. 1873.

MUTHER, R.—Die Deutsche Bücherillustration der Gothik und Frührenaissance, 1460–1530, I. München 1884.

NED.=New English Dictionary, ed. Sir J. A. H. Murray and others. 1888–1924.

OLIVER, G.—Historic Collections relating to the Monasteries in Devon. Exeter 1820.

OLIVER, G.—Ecclesiastical Antiquities in Devon. Exeter 1840.

OLIVER, G.—Monasticon Diocesis Exoniensis. Exeter 1846.

OLIVER, G.—Lives of the Bishops of Exeter. Exeter 1861.

OULMONT, CH.—La Poésie morale, politique et dramatique à la veille de la Renaissance. Pierre Gringore. (Bibliothèque du XVe siècle XIV.) 1911.

PASTOR. See JANSSEN.

PEDDIE, R. A.—Conspectus Incunabulorum. An index catalogue of Fifteenth Century Books. 1910–1914.

PELLECHET, M.—Catalogue général des incunables des bibliothèques publiques de France. 1897 etc.

PETIT DE JULLEVILLE, L.—Les Comédiens en France au moyen âge. 1885.

PETIT DE JULLEVILLE, L.—La Comédie et les mœurs en France au moyen âge. 1886.

PICOT, E.—Recueil général des Sotties (Société des anciens textes français) I. 1902.

PLANCHÉ, J. R.—A Cyclopaedia of Costume. 1876, 1879.

POLLARD, A. W.—Introduction to The Castell of Labour transl. from the French of Pierre Gringore by Al. Barclay. Roxburghe Club, 1905.

POLLARD, A. F.—The Reign of Henry VII from contemporary sources. 1913, 1914.

PRANTL, C.—Geschichte der Logik im Abendlande. Leipzig 1855–1870.

PROCTOR, R. G. C.—An index to the early printed books in the British Museum. 1898–1906.

RAMSAY, R. L., ed.—Magnyfycence. A moral play by John Skelton. Early Engl. Text Soc., Extra Series 98. 1906 (issued in 1908).

RASHDALL, HASTINGS, M.A.—The Universities of Europe in the Middle Ages. I. 1895.

REICHLING, D.—Das Doctrinale des Alexander de Villa Dei.—Monumenta Germaniae Paedagogica XI. 1893.

REISSERT, O.—Die Eklogen des Alexander Barclay in Neuphilologische Beiträge 54. (Hanover 1886.) 14–31.

RENAUDET, A.—Préréforme et Humanisme à Paris pendant les premières guerres d'Italie (1494–1517).—Biblioth. de l'Inst. franç. de Florence (Univ. de Grenoble) 1re série, tome VI. 1916.

RENOUARD, PH.—Bibliographie des Impressions et des Œuvres de Josse Badius Ascensius, Imprimeur et Humaniste, 1462–1535. 1908.

REY, A.—Skelton's satirical poems in their relation to Lydgate's Order of Fools, Cock Lorell's Bote, and Barclay's Ship of Fools. Dissert. Bern 1899.

RÜHL, E.—Grobianus in England.—Palaestra XXXVIII. 1904.

SAMOUILLAN, A.—Olivier Maillard, sa Prédication et son temps. Toulouse 1891.

SANDYS, J. E.—A History of Classical Scholarship, II. 1908.

SCHMIDT, CH.—Histoire littéraire de l'Alsace à la fin du XVe et au commencement du XVIe siècle. 1879.

SCHREIBER, W. L.—Manuel de l'amateur de la gravure sur bois et sur métal au XVe siècle. 1891–1911.

SCHULTZ, A.—Deutsches Leben im XIV. und XV. Jahrhundert. Wien 1892.

SEEBOHM, FR.—The Oxford Reformers John Colet, Erasmus and Thomas More. 1887.

SEIFERT, J.—Alexander Barclay's Ship of Fools. Programm Oberrealschule Brünn. 1884.

SMITH, PRESERVED.—Erasmus. A study of his life, ideals and place in history. New York 1923.

STINTZING, R.—Geschichte der populären Literatur des Römisch–kanonischen Rechts in Deutschland. Leipzig 1867.

SÜPFLE, TH.—Geschichte des deutschen Kultur-einflusses auf Frankreich. I. Gotha 1886.

THÜMMEL, A.—Studien über John Skelton. 1905.

THUSANE, L.—Roberti Gaguini Epistole et Orationes. Bibl. litt. de la Renaissance II. 1904.

TILLEY, A.—The dawn of the French Renaissance. 1918.

WARTON, TH.—The History of English Poetry, III. 1824.

WEISBACH, W.—Die Baseler Buchillustration des XV. Jahrhunderts.—Studien zur Deutschen Kunstgeschichte VIII. Strassburg 1896.

WEISBACH, W.—Der Meister der Bergmannschen Officin. Studien zur Deutschen Kunstgeschichte VI. Strassburg 1896.

WOERMANN, K.—Geschichte der Kunst aller Zeiten und Völker, IV. 1919.

WOLTERS, M.—Beziehungen zwischen Holzschnitt und Text bei Sebastian Brant. etc. Dissert. Strassburg 1917.

WRIGHT, TH.—A History of Caricature and Grotesque in Literature and Art. 1865.

WRIGHT, TH.—A History of domestic Manners and Sentiments in England during the Middle Ages. 1862.

ZAPF, G. W.—Jakob Locher genannt Philomusus in biographisch- und litterarischer Hinsicht. Nürnberg 1803.

ZARNCKE, F.—Sebastian Brant's Narrenschiff. Leipzig 1854.

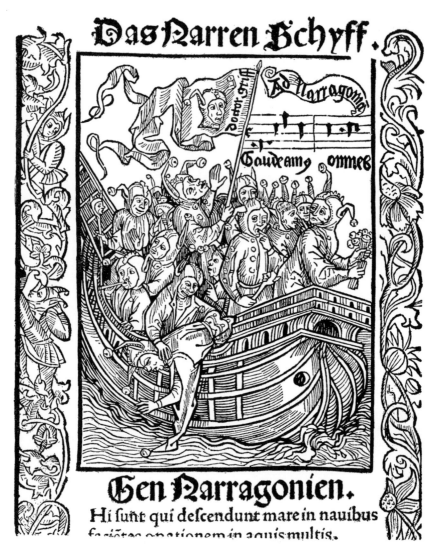

PLATE II.—Back of the title-page of the German original, 1494.
See §§ 359 and 367.

# THE ENGLISH VERSIONS

OF

# THE SHIP OF FOOLS

## I

### INTRODUCTION

1.—The Ship of Fools is one of the most famous books ever written. Some historians have even gone so far as to describe it as powerfully influencing the course of historical events. The author of the article on 'The Eve of the Reformation' in the CAMBRIDGE MODERN HISTORY,[1] Henry Charles Lea, writes of it as follows :

'There was no product of humanistic literature . . . which so aided in paving the way for the Reformation, as the NARRENSCHIFF, or SHIP OF FOOLS, the work of a layman, Sebastian Brant, Chancellor (City clerk) of Strassburg. Countless editions and numerous translations of this work, first printed in Basel in 1494, showed how exactly it responded to the popular tendencies, and how wide and lasting was its influence. One of the foremost preachers of the day, Geiler von Kaisersberg, used its several chapters or sections as texts for a series of sermons at Strassburg, in 1498, and the opinions of the poet lost none of their significance in the expositions of the preacher. The work forms a singularly instructive document for the intellectual and moral history of the period. Brant satirizes all the follies and weaknesses of man ; those of the clergy are of course included and, though no special attention is devoted to them, the manner in which they are handled shows how completely the priesthood had forfeited popular respect. But the important feature of the work is the deep moral earnestness which pervades its jest and satire ; man is exhorted never to lose sight of his salvation, and the future life is represented as the goal to which his efforts are to be directed. With all this, the Church is never referred to as the means through which the pardon of sin and the grace of God are to be attained ; confession is alluded to in passing once or twice, but not the intercession of the Virgin and saints, and there is no intimation that the offices of the Church are essential. The lesson is taught that man deals directly with God and is responsible to Him alone. Most significant is the remark that many a mass is celebrated which had better have been left unsung, for God does not accept a sacrifice sinfully offered in sin. Wisdom is the one thing for which man should strive,—wisdom being obedience to God and a virtuous life, while the examples cited are almost exclusively drawn

[1] Vol. i (1902), p. 683.

from classic paganism—Hercules, Pythagoras, Socrates, Plato, Penelope, Virgil—though the references to Scripture show adequate acquaintance with Holy Writ. As the embodiment of humanistic teaching through which Germany, unlike Italy, aspired to moral elevation as well as to classical training, the *Narrenschiff* holds the highest place alike for comprehensiveness and effectiveness.'

2.—This quotation may justify the choice of subject,—in more than one sense. For Professor Lea would never have written these words if the Ship of Fools had been really known in England. The correction of all his mistakes would be somewhat controversial, but if the reader will turn back to this quotation after he has read my book, he will probably find that nearly every sentence needs serious revision.

Only one error of fact must be corrected here, for Sebastian Brant, the German author, did not go back to Strassburg, his native town, until 1500 ; when he wrote the Ship of Fools he was a Professor of Law in the University of Basel.

3.—Not with the German version, however, is my concern, but with the English. And here I am convinced that I am penetrating into partly unexplored regions. Watson's translation has found no modern editor, perhaps it might be said no modern reader. Even the writers of the NEW ENGLISH DICTIONARY have overlooked it. F. Brie in 1907 [1] was the first to draw attention to its importance, and his opinion that it might be worth while to compare the English with its French original is partly responsible for its inclusion in this study. Only three or four copies are known to exist,[2] but the very rarity of the book, of which Wynkyn de Worde gave at least two editions, and which must have been spread over the country in more than a thousand copies, is a proof of its former popularity. The most popular books always become the rarest in course of time, because the public reads them to rags.

4.—Barclay's translation is somewhat better known, for the original edition of the year 1509 was beautifully reprinted half a century ago. The editor, T. H. Jamieson, Keeper of the Advocates' Library at Edinburgh, could write of it with little exaggeration [3] : ' Barclay's Ship of Fools is not only important as a picture of the English life and popular feeling of his time, it is, both in style and vocabulary, a most valuable and remarkable monument of the English language. . . . In the long barren tract between Chaucer and Spenser, the Ship of Fools stands all but alone as a popular poem, and the continuance of this popularity for a century and more [4] is no doubt to be

---

[1] Englische Studien xxxvi (1907), 18.

[2] There is one in Paris, one in the Bodleian, and one in the British Museum. Jamieson, p. ci, mentions a fourth, in the library of the Roxburghe Club, bought for £64.

[3] Jamieson xx–xxii.

[4] This indication of the period probably rests on the fact that in the seventeenth century there appeared a little popular tract of four leaves with the same title (but nothing else) as Barclay's version (London : J. W. for J. Clark, n.d., probably about 1650), and that Sir Aston Cokayne in an address ' To my learned friend, Mr. Thomas Bancroft, upon his Book of Satires,' was able to mention Barclay among the great Satirists of all time. Quotation in Jamieson lxxxv.

attributed as much to the use of the language of the " coming time " as to the popularity of the subject. In more recent times, however, Barclay has, probably in part, from accidental circumstances, come to be relegated to a position among the English classics, those authors whom everyone speaks of but few read. . . . As a graphic and comprehensive picture of the social condition of pre-Reformation England, as an important influence in the formation of our modern English tongue, and as a rich and unique exhibition of early art . . . this medieval picture-poem is of unrivalled interest.'

Judging from what has been published since 1874, Barclay is still among 'those authors whom everyone speaks of but few read,' so that Jamieson's edition does not seem to have attained its object. Barclay's contemporary, Skelton, has recently been studied again and again. But on Barclay's work only two little German dissertations have appeared, and, except perhaps some reviews in 1875,[1] no article seems to have been written in any of the great periodicals, English, Continental or American.—Barclay is in many respects superior to Skelton, and yet his comparative neglect is not very amazing ; for a rogue is more interesting than a preacher. And besides, Dyce's edition of Skelton's works is to be had everywhere, while Jamieson's Barclay is a somewhat peculiar and exclusive production.[2]

5.—My book is mainly an attempt to bring both Barclay and Watson somewhat nearer to the student of English Literature, and correctly to apprise their historical and literary value. I shall not try to analyse their influence on contemporary or later writers. The students of Skelton have often quoted Barclay,—though with no great success,—as a source from which that Poet Laureate may have derived his ideas and expressions. And very competent critics have shown how important a factor the general plan and conception of Barclay's version has been for the development of satire, of the English drama and of the novel.[3] But nothing has been done yet—as far as I know—for the correct interpretation of the text itself. In how far is it original ? What is new in it and what is old ? What are the literary merits of the various chapters ? What is the historical significance of the more concrete ideas expressed in it ? These are the questions to which I have tried to find an answer.

6.—At the same time I have endeavoured to throw some light on the methods of the old translators. Since there is a German text by Brant, a Latin text by Locher, one French text by Riviere, one by Drouyn, and one by an anonymous translator whom I have called, after the publisher, the Marnef-translator, and finally the two English versions, the subject offered exceptional opportunities for such a study. They had all to be compared, because the German, the Latin and the three French versions,

---

[1] I have really seen only one : The Nation (New York) xxi (1875), 359 sq. It is somewhat disconcerting to read there : ' Mr. Jamieson is well-nigh a perfect editor. His researches can have overpassed very little, if anything, touching Barclay to remunerate future explorers.'

[2] See further § 17. Antiquarians sell it for no less than £3.

[3] Herford 338 sqq. ; Alden 17 sqq. ; Ramsay lxxxix ; A. W. Ward in DNB.

which preceded the English, might all have influenced the English versions. As the Marnef-translator, however, soon proved not to have been even known to the English translators or their models, I have quoted him only for some unusually interesting passages.—It was hardly thought necessary to give many literal quotations from the German original, though in itself the most important of all. It was published with full critical and bibliographical apparatus by Professor Friedrich Zarncke as early as 1854. For this reason I could also refrain from making any comments upon Brant's ideas. But as the old Alsatian dialect presents a great many linguistic difficulties which can only be understood by constant reference to Zarncke's notes, the reader may perhaps welcome a summary in intelligible English of the more important chapters.

7.—These summaries were indispensable for my third purpose. I have no prejudice upon the subject. When I began my study I had no doubt that Barclay made his translation from the German or at least under German influence, as all the handbooks of English Literature have it. I thought that Professor C. H. Herford had quite correctly made the Ship of Fools the *pièce de résistance* of his STUDIES IN THE LITERARY RELATIONS OF ENGLAND AND GERMANY IN THE SIXTEENTH CENTURY (Cambridge 1886), and that Arthur Koelbing, Ph.D., Freiburg im Breisgau, when writing his article on Barclay and Skelton in THE CAMBRIDGE HISTORY OF LITERATURE, III (first edition, 1908 ; new impression, 1918), was fully justified in adding to it the sub-title *Early German Influences on English Literature*. Only gradually, when personally comparing one chapter after the other, did it dawn upon me that a legend had been created,—without malice prepense of course. Barclay himself has led all the earlier critics, from Warton [1] downwards, by the nose. They have all believed that he really 'translated out of Laten, French and Doche into Englysse.' [2] And this was enough to prove German influence. Not till 1894 [3] did anyone investigate Barclay's relation to his sources. Feodor Fraustadt at Breslau produced a very clever little pamphlet. But the writer had to work under several disadvantages. For the Latin he had no other copy at his disposal than the last (1572) edition ; for the

---

[1] The History of English Poetry (1st ed. 1774–1781 ; new ed., R. Price, 1824), iii, 74.

[2] Argument (K). See § 341.

[3] Herford, 341 *note*, mentions a pamphlet by J. Seifert, 'Alexander Barclay's Ship of Fools.'—Fraustadt has traced it to a *Brünner Schulprogramm* 1884. It has cost me no end of trouble to get a copy of it. It is not in any public library in Holland, nor at Bonn, Cologne, Aix-la-Chapelle, Brussels, Paris, nor even in the British Museum. A friend of mine, the Rev. Ananias Beunen, at Fulda, wrote to the libraries of Berlin, Leipzig, Munich, Heidelberg, Breslau, Brünn—all in vain; at last he discovered it in the University Library of Vienna. When I had read it, I thought of the ' two grains of wheat hid in two bundles of chaff ; you shall seek all day ere you find them ; and when you have them, they are not worth the search.' It contains the bold statement that Barclay did not understand German, but its many inaccuracies prove that the author must have written more from vague impressions than from accurate knowledge. Fraustadt (p. 45) could easily refute nearly all its assertions.

English only Jamieson's reprint.  Now Locher's translation can only be accurately valued from the original Basel editions.  And Jamieson's reprint is worthless from the point of view of literary criticism.[1] Secondly, Fraustadt had very little space.  For the title announces three parts, but when he has finished the first part (Barclay's relation to the Latin) on p. 42, he says that he has no space to spare for the rest.  He can only summarize his second part (Barclay's relation to the French) in three pages, and a refutation of the many errors in Seifert's essay takes the place of what had to be the third part, Barclay's relation to the German.  He formulates, however, the general result of his study in the words which Koelbing has translated for the Cambridge History (l.c. p. 59) : ' Careful comparison has shown that Barclay follows chiefly the Latin version, but that he made use of the French version by Pierre Riviere (Paris 1497), which was founded on Locher also, and that he used at the same time, though in a much less degree, the German original.'— I am not aware that anyone has ever taken up the subject again.  The ' German influence ' remained an established fact in all the Histories of English Literature.  The correction of this universal mistake is the third purpose of my book.

This minor purpose, however, has not been developed at the expense of the objective character of the work.  The exposition of texts still remains its principal purpose.

8.—A sketch of the Early French Renaissance would have been too subjective and one-sided, for it would naturally have been made to suit my purpose.  And it would always have been incomplete.  A good summary was given by Arthur Tilley in THE DAWN OF THE FRENCH RENAISSANCE in 1918, and A. Renaudet devoted a most exhaustive study to the period under consideration in his admirable volume PRÉRÉFORME ET HUMANISME À PARIS PENDANT LES PREMIÈRES GUERRES D'ITALIE (1494–1517), published in 1916.

9.—I am painfully conscious of one great defect in my book.  There is no unity in it, nor equality of treatment.

This is partly due to the subject itself.  A synthetical view is only safe after a careful analysis has been made.  And when the subject is a collection of disconnected sermons—the Ship of Fools is hardly anything else—the analysis necessarily becomes disconnected itself.  Only two English critics, to my knowledge, have tried to give a connected summary of the whole.  But Professor Herford took only the German text,[2] and even there he seems to have looked more at the titles and the pictures than at the text itself.[3]  Henry Morley[4] used Barclay's translation and must have read the whole.  But almost half his summary is devoted to the Introduction and the Prologue, and at the end he

---

[1] See below §17.

[2] Literary Relations 333–338 ; he includes the chapters omitted by Locher and the translators, e.g. chapters 74 and 75.

[3] The subject of chapter 25 is said to be ' dishonest borrowing,' of ch. 75 ' outlay of precious hours with the gun,' of ch. 79 ' rough oppressors like the knights,' etc.  The real subject is described below in §§ 94, 289, 199.

[4] English Writers vii (1891), 95–103.

confesses : ' A full classification would be nothing less than the outline of a complete system of ethics.'—For the chapters that really matter, I have tried to be complete, and I have sacrificed unity to completeness.

A selection from the one hundred and odd chapters might have made my book more interesting for the general reader but would have impaired its critical value in a point of vital importance. I should have given a one-sided view and left the subject where it was ; for it would not have been unnecessary for later critics to go through the same labours again. In the most difficult part of my work, the comparison of the different versions, I felt it my duty to be exhaustive and, if possible, to say the last word on the subject.

There is also a more personal aspect of the case, which I hope critics will not entirely overlook. The majority of the texts used for this study are in the British Museum, and, together, nowhere else in the world, while the unique copy of Watson's first edition is only in the Bibliothèque Nationale at Paris. So I had to work in two different places, and I had only a very limited time at my disposal. I had to make the most both of my time and of my opportunities.

A premature critic of my work has expressed the fear that it would be a scientific Wembley. I am afraid that I have to put up with this criticism. The material proved to be so overwhelming that I could only arrange it in a great many side-shows. Fortunately there was no necessity to group it all in a Palace of Industry, as one of the texts has also provided entertainment in the Amusements Park.

## II

## METHODS AND BOOKS

10.—The German NARRENSCHIFF written by Sebastian Brant, then a Professor of Law at Basel, was produced for the first time in the town where the author lived, in the year 1494. It is a splendidly printed book with beautiful woodcuts. A second, enlarged, edition appeared from the same Basel press the following year, while in the meantime two pirated editions had been issued at Reutlingen and Nuremberg and a free imitation at Strassburg. There were a great many other editions, but from the 1495 edition James Locher, called Philomusus, a Professor of Rhetoric and Poetry at the Friburg University, made what he called a translation *in latinum traducta eloquium*, with an original contribution by Brant on the Beghards, and with hundreds of quotations to indicate the sources. It appeared from the same Basel press on the 1st of March 1497, with the woodcuts of the original. Five months later, on the 1st of August, a second edition was called for, and Brant himself contributed to it a long appendix, called *De corrupto ordine vivendi pereuntibus*, and on the margin of the woodcuts it was provided with texts and quotations, aptly illustrating the contents of each chapter. On the 1st of March of the following year, 1498, appeared a third edition, in which the work took its final form, enlarged as it was with one forgotten chapter and an *Egloga* of a Bologna student, Thomas Beccadelli.

11.—But before this third edition was printed, the work had become famous in France. One of the principal publishers in Paris, Geoffroy de Marnef, brought out a reprint of the second edition on the 8th of March 1498, including everything, even the eulogies on the original Basel printer, with his device (Nihil sine causa) and name, but at the end he added a little poem by Robert Gaguin, *De fatuo mundano*. A printer at Lyons, Jacques Sacon, reprinted in his turn the work of his Parisian colleague on the 28th of June of the same year.—These two French editions had been preceded, and perhaps partly called for, by a French paraphrase in verse which had been published anonymously by the joint firm of Jean Phillippes Mansteuer and Geoffroy de Marnef in 1497, universally ascribed to one Pierre Riviere. The year 1498 saw not only the two Latin editions in France, but also a new French version. 'Maistre Jehan Drouyn, bachelier es loix et en decret,' was responsible for it ; it professed to be a prose-paraphrase of the verse-paraphrase written by the anonymous Pierre Riviere. It was printed at Lyons by Guillaume Balsarin, and met with so great a success that it had to be reprinted the following year,

1499. Paris and Lyons seemed to be competing with each other in their admiration for the Ship of Fools.

12.—A sort of appendix for the special benefit of the fair sex was written by Jodocus Badius Ascensius in Latin. He sent the MS. to Jean Drouyn to have it translated into French. De Marnef published the NEF DES FOLLES probably in 1498 and had to reprint it within a very short time, even before the original Latin could appear in 1500. This extraordinary success encouraged him to bring out in 1499 an entirely new translation in prose from Locher's Latin, ' selon la lettre ' says the Prologue. The author is unknown and no one has ever made a guess at his identity. I have, therefore, called him the Marnef-translator. It continued to be the rage for a long time. Badius wrote his own NAVIS STULTIFERA in Latin in 1505, but it had little in common with Brant or Locher except the title and the woodcuts.[1] Guy Marchand, who for the nonce called himself Guido Coopman, published even a Dutch version in 1500, DER ZOTTEN ENDE DER NARREN SCIP, and its success continued for more than a century. But these fall outside the scope of this study. For they had certainly nothing to do with the English versions.[2]

13.—As a basis for the following study I have used Locher's third Basel-edition, after having compared it carefully with the first and the second editions, and with the two editions issued in France.[3]

Of Riviere's verse-paraphrase only one edition seems to be extant, so that this part of my study offered no difficulties. The only difficulty here was to answer the question : Has Barclay really used Riviere ? There is nothing to go upon but his own words in the Prologue (I) that he has used a French translation by ' another, whose name to me is unknowen.' Since Zarncke, it has always been assumed that this must mean the (anonymous) Riviere. But Zarncke did not know of the existence of the Marnef-translator.[4] So the possibility had to be considered, that he and not Riviere had influenced the English translation. Therefore all the passages in which Barclay deviates from the Latin have been compared with both these versions.[5] This comparison has made it abundantly clear that Riviere and no one else was in fact used by Barclay.

14.—The reason why the unknown author has been identified with

---

[1] It is quite customary to say that Badius made a translation of the *Narrenschiff*, and even a better one than Locher's. He did nothing of the sort, as can be seen from Badius's own bibliographer, Ph. Renouard (i. 160).

[2] Badius is sometimes mentioned as having influenced Barclay, but this is simply due to a statement made by Zarncke (p. 242) in 1854, when the newer bibliographical facilities were not yet available.

[3] They are all in the British Museum, though only the first Basel-edition is mentioned in the BMC. iii, 795. Locher's third edition was kindly placed at my disposal by the Franciscan Monastery Library, Woerden.

[4] He thought the reference given by Brunet, Manuel du Libraire i, 447, valueless (p. 233).

[5] In the beginning I thought that I should have to content myself with a later edition (Lyon 1529), for in France there are only two copies of the original edition, one in Marseille and one in Toulouse. Afterwards, however, I found a copy in the British Museum.

Pierre Riviere may be of some interest to many readers. All biblio-graphers simply copy the name from each other, and Zarncke (p. 219) expressly says that he is relying only on the authority of Van Praet.

The information probably goes back, in the first instance, to Dreux du Radier, who wrote a BIBLIOTHÈQUE HISTORIQUE ET CRITIQUE DU POITOU in 1754. This author refers (i. 424 sq.) to M. l'Abbé Goujet, BIBLIOTHÈQUE FRANÇOISE OU HISTOIRE DE LA LITTÉRATURE FRANÇOISE. In the eleventh volume of this work, published in 1747, it appears (on p. 332) that he knows Pierre Riviere only from *Dame Rhetorique* and from Jean Bouchet, and he quotes: 'La Rhetorique parlant à Pierre Gervaise, dit :

> Congnois-tu point Maistre Pierre Riviere
> Ton compaignon, qui sçeut lart et manière
> De bien rimer, et tant bien translata
> *La nef des fols* ; puis en rime dicta
> Ung euvre gent pour son esprit esbattre
> Ou bien au long parla de vertuz quatre.'[1]

Then follow some extracts from Bouchet. But the whole passage may be quoted from the original because of its special interest and importance. It is taken from J. BOUCHET, LES GÉNÉALOGIES, EFFIGIES ET EPI-TAPHES DES ROYS DE FRANCE . . . AVEC PLUSIEURS AULTRES OPUSCULES, published at Poictiers, 1545. On feuillet 78 there occurs Epitaphe 49 :

> *Epitaphe de feu maistre Pierre Riviere natif de Poictiers,*
> *qui traduict en Francois la nef des folz, et fut grand legislateur.*

> Icy dessoubz ces pierres et quartiers
> Gist le corps mort d'un enfant de Poictiers
> Qu'on appeloit maistre Pierre Riviere
> Qui luy vivant feit chose singuliere
> C'est qu'il traduit de Latin en Francois
> La nef des Foulz, que commencé i'avois
> L'an qu'il mourut il feit meilleure chose
> Ce fust ung livre en vers, ainsi en prose
> Intitule des vertuz le recueil,
> Qui entre gens scavans eu bon acueil
> Car il estoit en ung tresorné style
> Combien qu'il fut subtil et difficile
> Et s'il estoit bon vulgaire orateur
> Encores fut meilleur interpreteur
> Des droictz civilz, sa principalle estude
> Estoit des loix par grand sollicitude
> En son ieune aage il fut fort studieux
> A Dieu devot, aux gens tres gratieulx
> Humble et courtois, et de bonne nature,
> Prisé de tous pour sa literature.

---

[1] The last lines probably refer to another work of his, mentioned by Dreux du Radier, l.c. 'L'année de sa mort, qui fut l'an 1499, il publia un autre Ouvrage Moral mêlé de vers et de prose, intitulé le Cercueil (? Recueil) des Vertus. Bouchet le préfère à la traduction de la Nef des Fous.' See Bouchet's Epitaph. Is it a translation of Mancini's *De Quatuor Virtutibus* translated by Barclay under the title *The Myrrour of Good Maners* and by an anonymous author for Wynkyn de Worde ?—See Jamieson, cv sq.

> Et sur le poinct qu'il s'attendoit florir
> Comme advocat, il va ieune mourir,
> Lors qu'il devoit espouse avoir et prendre
> La mort le vint supplanter et surprendre
> Ce fut au pere et mere grand ennuy
> Veu qu'ilz n'avoient filz ne fille que luy,
> Et qu'au droit poinct que de leur esperaunce
> Attendoient fruict, en veirent deffaillance
> Ce fut l'an mil quatre vingt quatre cens
> Et dix et neuf.  Priez tous de bon sens
> Qui passerez par cest saincte place
> Que Dieu pardon a son pauvre ame face.

15.—This is a touching little picture of the 'enfant de Poictiers' with whom we shall have repeatedly to occupy ourselves.  For there can be no doubt that the subject of this epitaph is identical with the author of the verse-paraphrase that appeared in 1497.  At the conclusion of the *Prologue du translateur* (H) he begs the readers ' que benignement pardonnent au translateur *qui est ieune.*'  But the most decisive argument I find in the rhymes.  Bouchet's ideal rhymes are Riviere's ideal rhymes.—Thomas Sibilet in his well-known ART POËTIQUE FRANÇOIS of 1548, in which the ideals of the Grands Rhétoriqueurs are formulated, says: ' Tu peux rymer bien et deuëment le simple contre le composé, combien que aucuns veuillent soutenir le contraire, mais sans apparence de raison . . . Mais aussi regarde bien, que tu ne tombes de la en une faute, qui est de mettre un mot rymant contre soy-mesme.  Si d'aventure nestoit diversifié par signification ou partie d'oraison.' [1]—We have examples of both cases in the above quotation, *prendre : surprendre ; cens : sens.* But this Epitaph is not really in his best style.  Among the EPISTRES MORALES ET FAMILIERES DU TRAVERSEUR (Poictiers, 1545) there is in the *Deuxieme Partie, ep.* 107 (the pages are not numbered) an *Epistre de l'acteur . . . ou il parle d'aulcunes reigles de rime.* If anywhere the author will here try to set a good example.  And here are his first six lines :

> Indigne suis, purpure senateur
> Prudent seigneur, eloquent orateur,
> De ton epistre a moy par toy transmise
> Encores plus de la louange y mise
> De moy, qui suis un petit palatin
> Fort esloigne de tout orné latin. *etc.*

I think that these lines suffice to show that Auguste Hamon [2] does not express himself adequately, when, commenting upon Sibilet's words, he says : ' Jean Bouchet use largement de cette liberté, il en abuse même ' and ' Presque toujours les mots semblables que Jean Bouchet fait rimer entre eux different et par le sens et par l'analyse.'—It is not a question of use or abuse, it is a principle, it is an ideal.  And it is exactly the same ideal which we find in Riviere.  In his best passages he is always trying to rhyme a word with its own compound, or with itself in another sense.

---

[1] In the edition of Benoist Rigaud (Lyon 1576), 51 sq.
[2] Un grand rhétoriqueur Poitevin, Jean Bouchet, 324 sq.

I need not give many examples to prove this. They occur in every chapter. Here are two examples taken at random.

From chapter 53 :

> Engendriez a qui te maintient
> Lenvieux lequel en main tient
> Le dart vironne de meschief
> Pour a chacun donner meschief
> Sans les laisser en nul repos
> Ains travailler en tous propos.

And from chapter 106 :

> Et si le saige prent quelque heurt
> Et que soudainement il meurt
> Pour mort ne sensuit que pardonne
> Dieu a luy et que pardon donne
> Car quant mondains sont departis
> De ce monde a lautre et partis
> Pour y aller sachez et certes
> Que selon les grans bien et sertes
> Seront de la retribuez *etc.*

Surely, the man who wrote this must have belonged to the circle of Jean Bouchet. And if Jean Bouchet says that Pierre Riviere translated La Nef des Folz, no reasonable doubt is possible.

16.—Watson translated ' out of Frensh,' he says. And Zarncke (p. 242) already pointed out that the translation literally followed Drouyn. There are two editions of Drouyn. I compared them in the Bibliothèque Nationale, and found only small deviations. But where there is a real deviation of a few words, Watson follows the second edition and not the first.[1]

Of Watson's first edition there is but one copy in the world. It is a vellum copy in the Bibliothèque Nationale.[2] Copious extracts were made from every chapter, and compared with the text of the second edition in the British Museum [3]; they were found to be in every respect the same. As the greater part of this work was written in London, the second edition has been quoted freely, where the extracts from the first were

---

[1] See below, § 344. My conclusion is just the opposite of what Zarncke, p. 242, says. He appeals to a communication from Dr. C. Bursian, who had based his opinion ' on a comparison of the woodcuts.' But the woodcuts in the first and in the second edition are identical.

[2] Vélin 2368. The Bibliothèque Nationale is rich in vellum copies of the Ship of Fools. It has a vellum copy of the Paris edition of Locher, 1498 (Vélin 2367), with all the woodcuts richly hand-coloured ; the name and mark of the printer, De Marnef, at the end, have been obliterated. Probably the work of Vérard. There are two vellum copies of Riviere, Vélins 608 and 607 ; in both the woodcuts have been painted over by miniatures, which (in 607) seem real little masterpieces of their kind. In these copies Vérard has also obliterated the name of the printer. On the unscrupulous practices of Vérard see John Macfarlane, Antoine Vérard (Bibliographical Society vii, London 1900), xxvii. Number 607 once belonged to King Louis XII, annotates Van Praet, Catalogue des livres imprimés sur vélin de la bibliothèque du roi, iv (1822), 231. Some of its miniatures are reproduced in A. Claudin, ii, 227–231.

[3] C. 57, e. 12. The pages have been cut down rather badly, but the text has not suffered. The last leaf is supplied in facsimile, probably from the copy in the Bodleian, which I have not seen. For one real difference between the first and the second edition see below, § 230.

deficient. Where there was any doubt as to the identity of the two, it has been mentioned in a note.

17.—Barclay's text also presented some difficulties, for it was less accessible than it might seem. It was reprinted, beautifully, by T. H. Jamieson in 1874. But he has done for Barclay almost the opposite of what Zarncke did for Brant. Zarncke's edition is full of learning and criticism and contains a wealth of illustration from contemporary works, but all in a very unattractive form, in small type on bad paper. Jamieson produces two splendid quarto volumes on hand-made paper, with only four stanzas on every page. But he has omitted everything that is of any critical value for the text.[1] He has not only omitted Locher's Latin text, which he found in the original edition,—this would have been pardonable, if only for considerations of space in such a splendidly got-up edition ;—but he has also dropped all Barclay's marginal notes when they are Latin. And the poet must have attached great importance to them, for he mentions these notes in his *Argument* (K) and they often serve to indicate original passages (*Additio auctoris. Addicio Alexandri Barclay* etc.). Of all these there is nothing in Jamieson. But he has given the woodcuts. Not, however, the woodcuts from Barclay's own edition, nor from the Latin edition used by Barclay, but from the Basel edition of 1497, facsimiled by Mr. J. J. Reid,[2] undoubtedly with great care and fidelity. The result is a splendid edition fit for the shelves of a rich man's library, but useless for the work-desk of a poor student. One great advantage, however, the book has : it gives a faithful reprint of the English text. And in a great many instances the quotations could be taken from it.[3] This had to be done especially because the beautiful copy of the first edition in the British Museum is preserved in one of the show cases and the superintendent does not like to have it taken away for any length of time. Hardly anything of importance, however, can have been missed.

18.—The importance has always been judged from the point of view of historical and literary and linguistic criticism,—not from that of bibliographical description. Hence two liberties have been taken with Barclay's text : *u* and *v* and capital letters have been used in accordance with modern usage ; and a punctuation has been introduced to bring out the meaning.—Locher's and Riviere's and Drouyn's and Watson's text, which have never been edited in modern times, are reproduced just as they are, with the exception only of *u* and *v*.

19.—A very simple system of quotation has been chosen. The

---

[1] His introduction, however, with a ' Notice of the Life and Writings of Alexander Barclay,' also published separately in the same year, is valuable for a biography of Barclay, and the bibliographical description of the works (xcvii–cix) is very careful and complete.

At the end of the second volume he has given a glossary of difficult words of eight pages (339–346). But the most difficult words are all wrongly interpreted. It serves, however, a useful purpose by indicating some variations between the first and the second editions.

[2] Jamieson, vi.

[3] A copy had been graciously put at my disposal by the Amsterdam University Library.

chapters of the Ship of Fools, which come to more than a hundred, are not numbered in the German, nor in the Latin nor in the French. Watson has numbered them in his own way, 'Coopman' in a different way, Badius in a third way. A passage, therefore, can only be indicated by folios and pages. This makes comparison extremely difficult and is apt to lead to confusion. The New English Dictionary, in quoting from Barclay, sometimes gives the folios of Cawood's edition in 1570, sometimes the volume and pages of Jamieson's reprint. Fraustadt quotes the Latin text by referring to the pages of a late edition, and when he compares Locher, Riviere, and Barclay, it looks like a logarithmic table. Surely it is desirable to take one uniform standard. This standard can be no other than the one critical edition that exists, Zarncke's German original. Here all the chapters have been numbered, and even the lines have been marked. His numbers have been adopted and carried through in the other texts. For the new contributions, which are not in the German original, names had to be invented ; and they are called A, B, C, *etc.* when they occur in the beginning, and a, b, c, *etc.* when at the end. Besides, the stanzas of Barclay's translation have been numbered from 1 to 1975. To prevent confusion and to make reference easy, so that even the quotations in the New English Dictionary can be traced in any edition, all the numbers and indications have been affixed to the comparative table in the Appendix. I hope that this method will meet with the approval of scholars, as I am sure it will cause the least difficulty to the general reader.

## III

## A FULL LIST OF THE DIFFERENT VERSIONS AND EDITIONS OF THE SHIP OF FOOLS

20.—Of the GERMAN TEXT the following editions are known :

1  1494  Basel. Bergman.  4°.
         Zarncke XCIX.  Hain * 3736.
2  1494  Reutlingen.  4°.
         Zarncke CIV.  Hain 3738.
3  1494  Nuremberg. Wagner.  8°.
         Zarncke CV.  BMC. ii, 464 sq.  HC. 3737.
4  1494  Augsburg. Schönsperger.  8°.
         Zarncke LXXXI from Aretins Neuem Lit. Anzeiger 1807, 200.  Hain
         3739.  Schreiber 3558.
5  1494  Strassburg. Grüninger.  4°, *interpolated edition.*[1]
         Zarncke LXXXII sqq.  CVI.  Hain 3743.
6  1495  Augsburg. Schönsperger.  4°, *interpolated edition.*
         Zarncke LXXXVI.  CVIII.  Hain 3744.
7  1495  Basel. Bergman.  4°.
         Zarncke CI.  Hain 3740.
8  1497  Strassburg.  4°.
         Hain 3741.  Burger 326.  Schreiber 3564.  Not mentioned by
         Zarncke.
9  1498  Augsburg. Schönsperger.  4°, *interpolated edition.*
         Zarncke LXXXVI.  CVIII.  BMC. ii, 372.  HC. * 3745.
10 1499  Basel. Bergman.  4°.
         Zarncke CI.  BMC. iii, 797.  HC. 3742.
11 1506  Basel. Bergman, (probably Lamparter).  4°.
         Zarncke LXXX.  CII.
12 1509  Basel. Lamparter.  4°.
         Zarncke LXXX.  CII.
13 1512  Strassburg. Hupffuff.  4°.
         Zarncke LXXX.  CIII.  Proctor II, 10032.

Since Brant's death in 1521 the *Narrenschiff* became public property, and the publishers changed the dialect and interpolated it, as the occasion seemed to require.  Zarncke LXXXVII sqq., CVI sqq., describes the following versions :

14 1531  Augsburg. Stayner.  4°. (' Ain nützlich Büchlein ' by H. Hörburger.)
         cf. Zarncke CIX.
15 1540  Strassburg. Cammerlander.  4°. (' Das klein Narren schiff.')
         Zarncke CX.

---

[1] Perhaps by John Pauli, O.F.M., who afterwards became Guardian of the Friary at Strassburg.  Zarncke LXXXVI ; Schmidt, i, 377.

16   1545   Strassburg. Cammerlander. 4°. (' Der Narren Spiegel. Das grosz Narrenschiff.')
Zarncke CX.

17   1549   Strassburg. Rihel. 4°. (' Der Narren Spiegel. Das grosz Narrenschiff.')
Zarncke CX.

18   1553   Frankfort. Gülfferichen. 8°.
Zarncke CXI.

19   1555   Frankfort. Gülfferichen. 8°.
Zarncke CXI.

20   1560   Frankfort. Han. 8°.
Zarncke CXII.

21   1563   Zürich. Froschower.
See Zarncke XCI, who has to rely on L. Meister in Beyträgen zur Gesch. der teutschen Sprache. London 1777, 8.1, 252 sqq.

22   1564   Strassburg. Rihel. 4°. (' Das grosz Narrenschiff.')
Zarncke CXI.

23   1566   Frankfort. Hanen Erben. 8°.
Zarncke CXII.

24   1567   Frankfort. Doubtful.
Zarncke XCIII.

25   1574   Basel. Heinricpetri. 8°. (' Weltspiegel'—with a German translation of Geiler's sermons.)
Zarncke CXIII.

26   1625   Frankfort. De Zetter. 8°. (' Der Narrenzunfft.')
Zarncke CXIV.

27   1629   [Frankfort.] 4°. (' Hasen-Jacht'—2nd ed. ; in the first edition (1593) Brant's work had not been inserted. Both pretended to be printed ' zu Haszleben.')
Zarncke CXIVv.

28 c.1670   Freystadt (= Augsburg ?). in fol. (' Narrenspiegel' with engravings by Merian).
Zarncke CXV. XCVI. sq.

This is the last popular edition known.

Modern editions were produced :

29   1839   by A. W. Strobel. Quedlinburg. 8°. Severely criticised by Zarncke.

30   1845   by J. Scheible. Stuttgart. 8°. The first volume of ' Das Kloster Weltlich und Geistlich ' reproduces the 1574 Basel edition.

31   1854   by Friedrich Zarncke. Leipzig. 8°. Standard edition.

32   1872   by K. Goedeke. Leipzig. 8°. (7th vol. of ' Deutsche Dichter des 16. Jahrhunderts.')

33   1872   by K. Simrock. Berlin. 8°. A modernized edition with reproduction of the old woodcuts. The author calls it ' ein Hausschatz zur Ergötzung und Erbauung erneuert ' ! The edition has amused German critics. See C. Schmidt, i, 316.

34   1877   by H. Junghans. Leipzig. 12°. Modernized for Reclam's Universal-Bibliothek 899–900.

35 c.1880   by F. Bobertag. Berlin. 8°. (16th vol. of ' Deutsche National-Litteratur.')

36   1913   by H. Koegler. Basel. 4°. A facsimile reproduction of the first (1494) edition for the ' Gesellschaft der Bibliophilen.'

37   1913   by Fr. Schultz (?) A facsimile reproduction. Quoted by M. Wolters and in Brockhaus. No copy in Bibl. Nat. nor in British Museum.

21.—The LOW GERMAN translation is probably the only one directly from the German.

1   1497   Lübeck. The Poppy Printer (Matth. Brandis ?). 4°. ' Dat narren schyp.' Unique copy in the Brit. Mus. See BMC. ii, 559. Two

pages reproduced in Publ. of the Type Facsimile Society 1903.a.—
Zarncke (XCVIII and 205) thought it was lost. See his essay in
Haupt's Zeitschrift für deutsche Altertumskunde IX, 380 sqq. The
new edition, promised by H. Brandes (see below Schröder's edition,
p. iii), does not seem to have appeared.

2  1519  Rostock. Lud. Diez. 4°. 'Dat nye schip van Narragonien.'
         (' vorlenget . . mit velen kortwiligen spröke.')
         Zarncke XCIX. Extracts 205 sqq. and in notes.
3  1892  Schwerin. 8°.
         A reprint of the second (1519) edition by C. Schröder.


22.—More than with the German original we shall have to deal with
Locher's LATIN VERSION.

The title-page of the first edition has 'Stultifera Navis' at the top.
Below a woodcut (125 × 65) representing a ship of fools with the inscription above ' navis stultorum ' and on the ship ' 1497.' Then :
' Narragonice profectionis numquam satis laudata Navis : per Sebastianum Brant : vernaculo vulgarique sermone et rhythmo, pro cunctorum
mortalium fatuitatis semitas effugere cupientium directione, speculo,
commodoque et salute : proque inertis ignaveque stultitie perpetua
infamia, execratione, et confutatione, nuper fabricata : Atque iam-
pridem per Jacobum Locher, cognomento Philomusum : Suevum : in
latinum traducta eloquium : et per Sebastianum Brant : Denuo seduloque
revisa : felici exorditur principio.—1497.—Nihil sine causa.' [1] The last
chapters have the following arrangement :

Fol. cxxxviii v. Navis socialis mechanicorum. Large woodcut.
  ,,   cxxxix r. Socialis navis mechanicorum. Text.
  ,,   cxl r. De singularitate. Woodcut : a bird-nesting fool. Text ends
             on fol. cxlii v.
  ,,   cxlii r. Epistola Jacobi locher. Text ends on fol. cxliiii r.
  ,,   cxliiii v. Ad numeros suos. Text ends on following page.
  ,,   cxlv v. Finis stultifere navis. Finis Narragonice navis per Sebastianum
             Brant vulgari sermone theutonico quondam fabricate : atque iam
             pridem per Iacobum locher cognomento philomusum in latinum
             traducte : perque pretactum Sebastianum Brant denuo revise :
             aptissimisque concordantiis et suppletionibus exornate :    In
             laudatissima Germanie urbe Basiliensi, nuper opera et promotione
             Johannis Bergman de Olpe Anno salutis nostre millesimo
             quadringentesimo nonagesimo septimo. Kalendis Martiis. Vale
             inclyte Lector.
             Bergmann's device.
  ,,   cxlvi. Registrum stultifere Navis.


23.—The title-page of the second Basel edition is the same as that of
the first as far as the words ' denuo seduloque revisa.' Then follows
' et nova quadam exactaque emendatione elimata atque superadditis
quibusdam novis admirandisque fatuorum generibus suppleta : foelici

---

[1] The device of the printer, Bergman. In the German editions : Nüt on ursach.

exorditur principio. 1497. Nihil sine causa. Io. de Olpe.' Contains some more marginal notes. A great many by the side of the woodcuts.—The last chapters have a different arrangement :

Fol. cxxxviii *v*. Navis socialis mechanicorum. Text.

„ cxxxix *v*. Epistola Jacobi Locher. Concludes on fol. cxl *v*.

„ cxli *r*. Ad numeros suos.

„ cxlii *r*. De singularitate. Woodcut : a wise man and a fool. Text ends on fol. cxliiii *v*.

„ cxlv *r*. De corrupto ordine. Woodcut.

„ cxlv *v*. Quod ordinatio causa fuerit destructionis omnium rerum. Text ends on fol. clv *v*.

„ clvi *r*. Epigramma Thome beccadelli.

„ clvi *v*. Finis, as in first edition as far as ' exornate.' Then follows : ' Et nova quadam exactaque emendatione elimate. Atque superadditis quibusdam novis admirandisque fatuorum generibus supplete : In laudatissima Germanie urbe Basiliensi : nuper opera et promotione Johannis Bergman de Olpe. Anno salutis nostre M.CCCCXCVII. Kl. Augusti.'

„ clvii *r*. Registrum.

24.—The third Basel edition has the same title as the second. There are hardly any deviations in the text or the notes. Only towards the end the order of the first edition has been restored and some new additions made :

Fol. cxxxviii *v*. Navis socialis mechanicorum. With the woodcut, which had dropped out in the second edition.

„ cxl *r*. De singularitate. Woodcut : a wise man and a fool. The marginal notes which accompanied the woodcut in the second edition are left out.

„ cxliii. Epistola.

„ cxliiii *v*. Ad numeros suos.

„ cxlv *v*. *Unnumbered*. De Fatuis sagittariis.

„ cxlvii *v*. *Unnumbered*. Egloga thomae beccadelli. Text ends on fol. cxlviiii *v*, *unnumbered*. Then follows :

„ cxlv. De Corrupto ordine, just as in the second edition. These last pages, including the Registrum, have been taken over unchanged from the second edition, except the date (M.CCCCXCVIII. Kl. Martii), so that the Register does not agree with the text.

25.—Like the German Narrenschiff, the Navis Stultifera was published also in several pirated editions. The following is a complete list in chronological order :

1   1497   1 March. Basel. Bergman. 4°.
           Hain-Copinger 3746. BMC. III, 795 sq.   Pellechet 2820.

2   1497   1 April. Augsburg. Schönsperger. 4°.
           Hain *3748. BMC. II, 370. Schreiber 3569.

3   1497   1 June. Strassburg. Grüninger. 4°.
           Hain *3749. BMC. I, 112. Pellechet 2821.

4  1497  [Nuremberg.  Wagner-Stuchs.] 8°.  BMC. 471.  Wrongly mentioned
        by Hain *3747 as Basel 1497.  Also at the Hague K.B. (Holtrop
        150).
        A reprint, mostly page for page of the 1st ed., Bergman's colophon
        *etc.* being reproduced without alteration.  The woodcuts are those of
        Wagner's German ed. of 1494, except the frontispiece and three
        others, which are copies of cuts added to Bergman's edition.

5  1497  1 August.  Basel.  Bergman.  4°.
        Hain-Copinger *3750.  Pellechet 2822.  Bibl. Mazarine 937.  Brit.
        Mus. IA 37945.  Not in BMC.

6  1498  8 March.  Paris.  De Marnef.  4°.
        Hain-Copinger 3753.  Pellechet 2824.  Brit. Mus. IA 40953.
        Reproduces the second Basel edition, not, as Zarncke 210 says, the
        first.  The colophon is the same as far as ' suppletae.'  Then follows :
        ' In laudatissima urbe Parisiensi nuper opera et promotione Gofridi
        de marnef.  Anno salutis nostre. M.CCCC.XCVIII die VIII Martii.'—
        At the end after the Registrum a poem ' De Fatuo Mundano '(h).

7  1498  (Misprinted 1488)
        28 June.  Zachoni.  4°.
        Hain-Copinger 3752.  Pellechet 2825.  Brit. Mus. IA 42173.
        Reproduces the second Basel (or rather the Paris) edition, with the
        poem De Fatuo Mundano.  Only the end of the colophon has been
        changed and becomes more sober : ' impressum per iacobum Zachoni
        de romano Anno domini. M.CCCC.LXXXVIII. die. XXVIII. mensis
        Iunii.'

8  1498  1 March.  Basel.  Bergman.  4°.
        Woerden P 356.  Brit. Mus. IA 37947 (not in BMC.).  Hain *3751.
        Pellechet 2823.

9  1572  Basel.  Heinricpetri.  8°.
        Schmidt, II, 344.  Bibl. Nat. Rés. Yh 102.  Brit. Mus. 11511, a. 5.

26.—Of the FRENCH versified paraphrase by RIVIERE only one
edition is known :

1  1497  Paris.  Jean Phillippes Mansteuer and Geoffrey de Marnef.  in-fol.
        Pellechet II, 2827.  Brussels, Bibl. Royale B 563.  Brit. Mus. IB 11342
        (and two others).
        The real printer is Jean Lambert.  See A. Claudin, Hist. de
        l'imprimerie en France, II, 227.  Here on pp. 228–231 reproductions
        of some of the miniatures on the vellum copy of the Bibliothèque
        Nationale.  See above, note to § 16.
        Parts of Riviere's paraphrase appeared :
2  After 1532 [1]  Paris.  Janot.  4°.  (' Le grand nauffraige des folz.').  Brit.
        Mus. 242, l. 28.

27.—DROUYN'S PROSE VERSION of this verse-paraphrase had
more success :

1  1498  Lyon.  Balsarin.  in-fol.
        Pellechet 2828.  Bibl. Nat. Rés. Yh 2.
2  1499  Lyon.  Balsarin.  in-fol.
        Pellechet 2830.  Bibl. Nat. Rés. Yh 3.  Brit. Mus. IB 41795.

---

[1] There is no date, but the title-page says : ' On les vend a Paris en la rue
neufve nostre dame a lenseigne sainct Jehan baptiste pres saincte Geneviefve des
ardens par Denys Janot.'  Janot, who married Jeanne de Marnef, had his press at
several other places, before he moved in 1532 to the ' rue neufve Nostre Dame, a
l'enseigne Sainct Jehan Baptiste.'  See H. Omont, Catalogue des éditions françaises
de Denys Janot (Mém. Soc. de l'Hist. de Paris et de l'Ile-de-France, XXV, 1898),
p. 12.  The work is still in Janot's Catalogue of the year 1544, No. 111.  See ib.
pp. 20 and 28.  Cf. Renouard, Imprimeurs Parisiens (Paris 1898), p. 191.

3   1579   Lyon.   Jean D'Ogerolles.  in-fol.  (' reveue nouvellement et corrigee
en infiniz lieux ').
BM. 86, f. 21.

28.—The work of the MARNEF-TRANSLATOR ' selon la lettre '
had also a longer life and deserved it better :

1   1499   Paris.   De Marnef.   in-fol.
Pellechet 2829.   Brit. Mus. IB 40278.
2   1529   Paris.   Le Noir.[1]   4°.
Bibl. Nat. Rés. Yh 59.
3   1530   Lyon.   Juste.   4°.
Bibl. Nat. Rés. p. Y [2] 281.   Brit. Mus. 637, g. 33.

29.—I shall not give a list of the different editions of Badius' *Navis
Stultifera*, or rather *Navis Stultiferae Collectanea* as the second edition
is called.   First because there is a complete list in Renouard II, 81–87,
and secondly because it is no translation at all, and I could not give
anything like an exhaustive list of all the imitations of the Ship of Fools.
For this reason I must also leave out—though with some regret—the
version ' vut den latijne ende walsche in duytsche verstelt ' by Guido
Coopman, of which there is a fine copy in the Bibliothèque Nationale.[2]

30.—Of BARCLAY'S ENGLISH TRANSLATION two old editions
are known :

1   1509   London.   Pynson.   in-fol.   ' The Shyp of Folys of the Worlde.'
Full description in Jamieson xcviii.
2   1570   London.   Cawood.   in-fol.   ' Stultifera Navis . .  The Ship of Fools
. . with divers other works . . very profitable and fruitfull for
all men.'
Jamieson xcix.

And a modern reprint by Jamieson :

3   1874   Edinburgh.   Paterson.   4°, two vols.

31.—The two editions of WATSON'S WORK followed each other
more rapidly :

1   1509   Westminster.   Wynkyn de Worde.   4°.   ' The Shyppe of Fooles (of
this worlde).[3]
Bibl. Nat. Vélins 2, 368.   Van Praet, IV (1822), p. 232 (n. 346).
2   1517   Westminster.   Wynkyn de Worde.   4°.   ' The grete Shyppe of Fooles
of this worlde.'
Jamieson ci.   Brit. Mus. C. 57, e. 12.

---

[1] The colophon gives the printer as Denis Ianot, ' devant lhostel dieu, a lenseigne
de la Corne de cerf.'   But the title says ' On les vend a paris en la rue sainct
Jaques a lenseigne de la Rose blanche couronne.'   According to Renouard, Imprimeurs Parisiens, l.c., this is the address of Philippe Le Noir in 1529.
[2] Rés. Yh 64.   Later editions (1504, 1548, 1584, 1610, 1635) in the British
Museum and the Bodleian.   I do not think they have been studied yet.
[3] The title calls it ' The Shyppe of fooles,' the prologue ' the grete shyppe of
fooles of this worlde,' and the colophon ' the shyppe of fooles of this worlde.'

IV

## CHAPTERS RELATING TO THE SEVEN DEADLY SINS

32.—It is rather difficult and even risky to arrange the numerous chapters of the Ship of Fools into categories. But something of the kind has to be done if only to bring a little order or at least the appearance of order into the discussion of the different versions, and to place the intrinsically important chapters as near to each other as possible. In true medieval fashion those chapters, the main subject of which can in some way be reduced to any one of the Deadly Sins, may be taken first and in the same order as they are found in Langland and in Chaucer.— Brant, however, has not given them the first place, perhaps he has not even thought of them, so that it is quite by accident that we can find them all more or less explicitly mentioned.

33.—The first of them is PRIDE, but only towards the middle of the book are some chapters devoted to satirizing its different aspects. SELF-COMPLACENCY is the subject of chapter 54, in which Brant sharply rebukes unwillingness to accept correction and advice from others, and insists on the nothingness and worthlessness of man, winding up with some apt quotations from Ecclesiasticus. Locher omits these quotations but paraphrases the rest very clearly.—Barclay in his turn paraphrases Locher. His best idiomatic expression occurs towards the end :

> (771)   Better it is to endure, thoughe it be not lyght,
> To suffer a wyse man the sharply to repreve,
> Than a flaterynge fole to clawe the by the sleve.

Riviere also follows Locher without any striking deviations—Drouyn, however, feels himself inspired by the picture to an ' invitation ' that has not the least bearing upon the subject of the chapter. Part of it is in Watson : ' Impacyent fooles playenge on instrumentes, brynge hether your harpes and lutes,' but Drouyn speaks of ' harpes, leucz, fleustes et psalterions simbales, trompettes, clairons, fleches arcz arbelestes et couleurines,' thus exhausting probably his whole stock of knowledge of musical instruments. Watson omits all this and a great deal more in the first part of his translation, so that his meaning is often rather difficult or quite impossible to follow without the help of the French. Towards the end, when he has realized that the following chapter can begin in its proper place, he feels more at ease, and he speaks of ' a florysshed rose that endureth but a lytell whyle ' to render the French ' la rose flourie qui peu dure.'

34.—A similar subject is spoken of in the chapter (60) on VANITY, where Locher follows Brant more closely, and criticizes chiefly the self-complacency with which men as well as women constantly regard themselves in a looking-glass. The Roman Emperor, Otho, Pygmalion and Narcissus are quoted as examples. The other translations have nothing remarkable to offer, except that Riviere splits up Locher's (or rather Juvenal's) 'Pathici gestamen Othonis' into two different personages (wisely enough with a query) :

> Que diray de patricius
> Que diray ie dothonius (!)

Barclay follows Locher faithfully, only adding some details about women's dress, quite different from Riviere's additions.

> (868)   The wanton mayde may for hirself ordayne
> Hir call, hir coyfe, and suche conceytis newe
> As broches, fyletes [1] and oyntmentis soverayne
> And clothynge of dyvers colour and of hewe.

I wonder if the author has been able to read the last line so as to retain anything like metre or rhythm. Perhaps he thought the rhyme sufficient to save his poetry.

35.—Another aspect of Pride is developed in chapter 76, which treats of BOASTING. Locher has condensed Brant's double chapter into a single one, sadly mutilating it by leaving out the most picturesque details. But he has retained the two or three leading ideas, viz. that some men pride themselves on knightly deeds which they have never performed, or on noble descent on the sole ground of their great wealth, while others proudly assume the name of Doctors without having gone through a proper course of study.

There are two lines in Locher with geographical names. He mentions a knight's boast

> Me solyme videre sacre Memphitica tellus,
> Gallia bellipotens : marticoleque Gete.

The ' Getae ' are a hobby for Locher but a crux for his translators. Riviere makes of it :

> Sicque mon nom est haulte et digne
> En Solime et toute sa gent
> En Memphiticque refulgent
> Et en la trespuissante gaule
> Gecte et la terre marticole
> Et plusieurs aultres nations,

---

[1] Call = caul, a kind of close-fitting cap worn by women. The word occurs in Chaucer, but that it was made of very costly material in the early sixteenth century appears from *Tottel's Miscellany* (Arber's reprint, p. 201) : ' On her head a caule of gold she ware.' It occurs still in Hakluyt ; but in Shakespeare's time it must have been out of fashion. See NED.—*Coyfe* or *coif* is, presumably, something similar. About the middle of the fifteenth century it is mentioned in *Merlin*, XXVII, 507, and in the beginning of the sixteenth century it is known to Douglas as an ornament—Aeneis, IV, iv, 19 : ' Hir brycht tressis envolupit war and wound intill a kuafe [ed. 1710 queif] of fyne gold wyrin threid.'—A *fylet* or *fillet* is a head band, used especially ' for a maydens heed, a *fronteau*,' says Palsgrave in 1530. And from the *Paston Letters* No. 568, II, 298, ' She would fayne have a new felet,' it appears that it must have been somewhat elaborate.—NED.

which Drouyn changes into 'en la trespuissante france et en la terre marticole et plussieurs aultres nations,' quietly omitting the incomprehensible ' Gecte ' and by a slight change making ' Marticole ' a country. This is faithfully rendered by Watson ' and in france, and in the londe of marticole, and dyvers other regyons and countrees.' The patriotic Englishman only skips the flattering adjective before ' France.' He does the same in another place where Drouyn has a remarkable addition to Riviere's text.

Riviere had simply paraphrased Locher :

> Pour reciter a desarroy
> Que de celui il est issu
> Comme de Romulus a sceu
> Ou dung aultre grant et saige homme.

Drouyn has something more to say :

> Et dira quil est descendu de luy, comme de Romulus, ou de Jason, comme dient aulcuns que le duc de Bourgogne est descendu a cause quil porte pour son ordre la toison et les fusis.   Comme le trescrestien et tresiluestre roy de France porte en son ordre Monsieur Sainct Michel et les coquilles.

The House of Burgundy and its Golden Fleece was of course very famous in France, but Watson is not aware of any anomaly and he translates :

> . . . Wyll saye that he is descended from hym.  As of Romulus or of Jason. As some wyll saye that the Duke of Burgoyne is descended by cause that he bereth for his ordre the golden fleece, and the fuze to smyte fyre with.[1]   And as the kynge of France [no adjectives !] bereth in his ordre saynt Myghell, and the shelles.

36.—Of all this there is nothing in Barclay.  He follows Locher only ; but cleverly evades the difficulties :

> (1116)   Lo, sayth a fole, I have be longe in warre
> In straunge countrees and far beyonde the se ;
> To dyvers nations my dedys knowen ar,
> Both Spayne and Egypt and Fraunce spekes of me ;
> In so many countrees in warrys have I be,
> That all the people of Est, West, North and South
> My name and laudys have onely in theyr mouth.

He also speaks of ' Doctours come from strange costis ' (1117).  But one hit, quite peculiar to him, is perhaps rather personal :

> (1111)   Some other crowned as Poetis Lawreat,
> And other as Doctours expert in medycyne.

We shall meet with more such allusions.

37.—VAINGLORY is the subject of chapter 92.  As this chapter is rather important from the point of view of comparative criticism, a more detailed account of it must be given.

Vainglory, says Brant, is like lighting a fire on a thatched roof, like building on a rainbow, or supporting a vault on a fir tree (1–10).   Many pride themselves on

---

[1] The *fusils* or fire-stones used in the badge of the Golden Fleece were evidently not familiar to the English author or his readers.

their study at foreign Universities : Bologna, Pavia, Paris, Siena, Rome,[1] Orleans, besides Strassburg[2] (11–18). As if they could not find plenty of schools and books in their own country (19–26). But they value no learning if it does not come from Athens ; they can find everything in Germany but they want only wine and idleness (27–34). All learning is vain, if acquired for pride or for the love of money (35–40). The vanity of women leads many into the traps of the devil (41–48). Through the counsel of Balaam, the children of Israel were deceived by the Madianite women : Num. xxxi. 16 (49–52). Judith seduced Holofernes, Jezabel Jehu (53–56). Do not allow yourself to be enticed by the face of women, for women are always trying to make fools of men (57–66). Think of Bersabee and Dina (67–70). A humble woman is worthy of praise, a vain one can never be pleased and will subdue the strongest man by her subtlety (71–84). Pride will have a fall as Lucifer had (85–88), and will complain too late : what was the good of it ? (89–96). Pride drove the angels out of heaven, Adam out of Eden, it drives man to hell (97–110). It drove out Agar, killed Pharao and Core, built the foolish tower of Babel and brought the angel's punishment on Herod (111–122). God humbles the proud and exhalts the humble (123–124).

38.—Locher substitutes his own introduction for lines 1–10 ; in 11–18 he mentions only Bologna. He skips 19–26 and takes only some ideas from 27–40, to which he adds eight long lines to describe the fall of Lucifer. Then he speaks of women ; paraphrasing a little part of 41–48 ; he omits 49–52, 57–66 ; he takes the two examples of 67–70 and then stops translating anything of the rest. To fill out his page he picks out only a few references : first from 123–124, then the fall of Lucifer from 85–88, and finally from 111–122 he takes the name Core but adds the names of his companions Dathan and Abiron and concludes with telling their story.

Riviere paraphrases this text with his usual verbosity. The only concrete addition I can find is that he adds one French name to Locher's Bologna, which he represents as ' panonie cite saige '

> Et lautre a couru en gresnobles
> En argive et es aultres pais.

Drouyn did not know what this could mean, and so after corrupting the name of Bologna still further by making it into *Pavonye*, he continues : ' Laultre a courru en france, en picardie, et en languedoc, ou en aultres pays.'—Watson does not like to mention French names ; there could be no harm in ' Pavonye the wyse cyte,' but then he deviates from his text : ' The other hathe ronnen in fraunce, in Spayne and in other places where as he is hated.'—Neither Drouyn nor Watson seems to have given any thought to the subject in hand.

39.—Barclay's version is the best of all. The same Latin paraphrase of a selection of Brant's ideas is apparently his only source throughout

---

[1] No doubt Rome is meant by ' inn der Sapientz ' (15), though Zarncke does not mention it.

[2]           Und den roraffen gesähen heth
          Und Meter pyrr de Conniget (17 sq.).

The *Roraffen* was a well-known grotesque figure in Strassburg Minster. *Maître Pierre de Coignet* was a similar figure in the Notre Dame at Paris.—The second allusion has been explained by G. Paris in *Revue Critique* 1873, 20. See Schmidt I. 300.—The Universities mentioned by Brant are those mainly visited by German students (Zarncke, 435).

the chapter, but he makes it into a full sermon of twenty-two stanzas.
They are all in good straightforward English but hardly worth quoting.
The best line is perhaps :

> (1403)  The noblest hertis by this vyce ar acloyed,

a weak anticipation of Milton's ' last infirmity of noble mind ' (Lyc. 71).
*Germania* is of course changed into ' Englonde ' (1409), and two real
names are added to Locher's *Bononia*.

> (1407)  Lo, sayth a fole, attached with this vyce,
> I have ben norsshed at the Unyversyte
> In dyvers contrees and stodyes of great pryce,
> Both in these partyes and eke beyonde the se :
> At Bonony, Parys and Padway have I be ;
> Wherfore I ought to have preemynence
> And the chefe place with lawde and reverence.

The Universities of Paris and Padua were among those specially
frequented by English students at that time.[1]

At the end of the chapter, as of almost all other chapters, there is
an original Envoy, containing an admonition.  It here inculcates the
necessity of humility :

> (1424)  For pryde is the rote of all unhappynes,
> Supporter of vyce, and enmy to vertue ;
> Therfore it is sayd—and true it is doutles—
> That pryde goth before but shame do it ensue.

40.—The last line must have been a common proverb at the time,
for it occurs also in the well-known *Treatyse of a Galaunt*, which was so
popular that Wynkyn de Worde printed no fewer than three editions of it
during the reign of Henry VIII.  This interesting poem must have been
written by a moralist of Barclay's stamp ; it laments the pride, avarice
and ambition of the new-fledged courtier and his love of quarrelling.[2]
It is written in the usual Chaucerian stanza with the refrain :

> Englonde may wayle, that ever it came here.

For the unknown author, just as Barclay,[3] sought the origin of all English
pride in France, and his most emphatic warning is expressed in the same
words as Barclay had used :

> Pryde goth before, and shame cometh behynde.[4]

41.—Barclay formulated it a little more solemnly, and found in it
the inspiration for a sermon in four stanzas, all in octaves, and all ending
(with what little alteration the construction required) with the same
line :

> Pryde goeth before and shame doth ensue.

---

[1] John Free, Linacre, De Selling, Latimer, Pace, Tunstall, *etc.*  See J. H.
Lupton, A Life of John Colet (1909), 46 ;  Maxwell Lyte, 386, 389 ;  Allen, I, 438,
445.
[2] Cambr. Hist. III, 98.          [3] See § 276.
[4] The poem has been published by J. O. Halliwell (London 1860), where the
quotation occurs on p. 23, and by W. C. Hazlitt, Remains of Early Popular Poetry
I (1866), 146 sqq.  Quotation on p. 160.

This little piece of rhetoric bears the title of *An Exclamacion ayenst Pryde*. Pride is a venom to destroy

> (1425) So many Kynges, so many a great estate.

It drove Lucifer out of heaven and made all mankind miserable

> (1426) Tyll Ave for Eve had made a recompence.

The pride of those that built 'Babylon' was punished and the king transformed 'unto a brute bestes shape'; and also Agar was punished for her pride (1427);

> (1428) But shortly to drawe me to a conclusyon :
> Thou hast made thousandes to ende in care and wo ;
> By the had Moab payne and confusion,
> Holofernes, Aman, Nichanor and Pharao,
> Balthasar, Antiochus, Herode and many mo
> In the Olde Testament and also in the Newe.
> But shortly to speke and farther nat to go :
> Pryde goeth before and shame doth ensue.

This stiff clumsy production is accompanied by some marginal notes indicating the biblical passages in Genesis, Judith, Macchabees and Acts. The names mentioned belong to the usual stock-in-trade of a sermon on Pride, so that they would hardly deserve any special notice, were it not that some of them were exactly those omitted by Locher from the original text. The sin of Eden, Babylon (Babel), Agar, Herod, Pharao are in Brant's German and not in Locher nor in Riviere. So it is very likely that these names have really been taken from the German. If so, this haphazard picking out of some proper names is the strongest proof imaginable that the author did not understand a word of German and was barely able to extricate from the German text some familiar names printed in capital letters.

42.—FLATTERY is the reflection of Pride, and the very idiomatic chapter (100) which Brant devotes to it has been rendered by Locher in very smooth Latin. The vice of courtiers is criticized in it.—The French translations do not offer many remarkable deviations. Only where Locher says that to those flatterers 'Jam datur insignis locus' Riviere makes of it :

> Au moyen de quoy au plus noble
> Lieu fust il de Constantinoble.

But this eccentricity has been skipped by Drouyn and so does not appear in Watson's version ; Barclay[1] gives a little more point to Locher's smoothness :

> (1579) They are fals flaterers, fyllyd full of gyle
> And fowle corrupcion, as is a botche or byle.

The alliteration shows that he follows his own inspiration. Those 'faynynge flaterers' are so false

> (1583) That if theyr mayster say that the crowe is whyte
> They say the same, and have therin delyte.

---

[1] Herford 355 and Rey 51 think that this chapter is the direct prototype of Skelton's Bowge of Court. Ramsay lxxxiii sq. is probably more correct in tracing its influence in Skelton's Magnyfycence.

Taking a hint from Locher's ' ad flatus ventorum obducere pallam ' [1] Barclay insists :

> (1585)    No man in court shall nowe a lyvynge fynde,
>         Without that he can bowe to every wynde ;

and he elaborates the fable vigorously in the next stanza :

> (1586)    The tre that bowyth to no wynde that doth blowe,
>         In stormes and tempest is in moste jeoperdy
>         And often with sodayne blastis overthrowe ;
>         Therfore these flaterers to eche wynde aply ;
>         And he that can upholde his mayster's lye
>         With *ye* and *nay*, and helpe him if he tryp,
>         Obteyneth nowe grettest honour and worshyp.

43.—THE SELF-OPINIONATED are rebuked in chapter 36.

They are sure to be scratched with thorns ; they will go astray whence they cannot return and will fall into irretrievable ruin. Such people, who would not be taught better, have become heretics out of sheer pride. Climbing trees for high birds' nests they have fallen shamefully ; unpiloted ships come to wreck and ruin ; those who would not listen to Noë all perished ; Core and his followers were swallowed by the earth.—He who will always follow his own ideas, would not hesitate to rend the coat without seam (of the Church). But whosoever would be free from deceitful fools must put wax in his ears as Ulysses did against the Sirens.

It may be due to a mere oversight or to a more deliberate action : but Locher has left out this chapter. The consequence is that *all* the so-called translators of the Narrenschiff have done the same ! Neither Riviere nor Barclay nor Badius nor the Guido-Coopman translator seems to know of the existence of this chapter.—The woodcut represents a bird-nesting fool falling out of a tree ; it may have been the wish to preserve this picture that led to the insertion and perhaps even to the composition of Gaguin's *De fatuo mundano*.[2]

44.—LECHERY is the second of the Deadly Sins and more than one chapter is devoted to it. First of all comes chapter 13. In Brant this is a double chapter, mainly showing the wickedness of lechery in a long list of more than thirty classical and half a dozen biblical examples. Locher has entirely changed this chapter. He leaves out nearly all the examples, retaining only the story of Troy, of Phaedra and of Messalina, and adding Marcus Antonius, Cleopatra and Julia, and a description of the power of love partly adapted from Ovid. But at the end there is a noteworthy addition by Brant himself, as we are expressly informed by a marginal note :

> Addo his infames draucos, paticosque cinedos :
> Quos contra ultrices flamme leges quoque surgant :
> Horret enim humanum genus hec commertia feda :
> Obque flammivomo perierunt imbre Gomorre.

---

[1] Cf. the Dutch expression : ' de huik naar de wind hangen.'
[2] See chap. h in § 130.

The most original part of Barclay's version of this chapter [1] is in the Envoy :

(235)    For many of them so folowys in this way
         That they sell theyr soules and bodys to go gay.

(236)    The graceless galantes and the apprentyce pore,
         Though they nought have, themselfe they set nought by,
         Without they be acquaynted with some hore
         Of Westmynster or some other place of rybawdry ;
         Than fall they to murder theft and robery ;
         For were nat proude clothynge and also flesshely lust,
         All the feters and gyves of Englande shulde rust.

45.—In a great many details, however, the English deviates from the Latin in this chapter, but all these deviations are also to be found in Riviere's French paraphrase. This proves that Barclay must here have taken the Frenchman as his principal guide. In the beginning Riviere imitates Locher so faithfully that it is difficult to see from which of the two Barclay's stanzas 222 and 223 have been taken. The following stanza, however, is more like the French, for it turns Locher's dependent clause into an exclamation just as Riviere does. Stanzas 225–228, telling the story of Troy and of Cleopatra, are evidently from Riviere, although the first part is elaborated a little more. ' Theyr cyte brent ' is ' leur cite mise en feu,' and ' this one pleasour ' seems an echo of ' pour une plaisance mondaine.' The ' two hundred shyppes ' are not in Locher but in Riviere just as the two forcible lines :

(228)    For two serpentis that venemus were and fell
         Were set to the brestis of fayre Cleopatray.

This is only a less sentimental rendering of :

       Et par deux serpens fit tirer
       Quelle mist lors a ses deux mamelles
       Si resplendissantes et belles
       Dont le sang de son pauvre corps
       Dont en pleurs et tres grans discors
       Sans comfort avoir ne demy
       Mourut illec pres son amy.[2]

The Ovidian description of the power of love in stanzas 229 and 230 is almost the same in Riviere and Locher. Stanzas 231 and 232 mention Phaedra and ' Ypolitus ' and ' Phasyphe ' and Nero and Messalina with nearly all the expressions taken from Riviere, though Barclay has

---

[1] Jamieson xliv calls Barclay's description of the passion of love ' so graphical that it is difficult to imagine our priestly moralist a total stranger to its powers.'— This description, however, is nothing but a mere translation, almost word for word, of Locher's and Riviere's half-Ovidian insertion.—Ramsay lxxxii also seems to attach too much importance to it.

[2] Drouyn turns the beginning of this story into ' Cleopatre se fit mener près Marcus Anthonius par deux serpens quelle mist ' etc. Watson makes the absurdity a little more apparent : ' Cleopatra made herselfe to be transported unto the cyte of Alexandre besyde her lover Marcus Antonyus by two serpents that she put to her pappes ' etc.

condensed the stories even more than Locher.[1]—Stanza 233, however, is different.

> What shall I wryte the dedys vicious
> Of Julia or hir cruell offence ?
> What shall I wryte the inconvenyence
> Whiche came by Davythys [2] cursed avowtry,
> Syth that the Bybyll it shewyth openly ?

This cannot possibly have been derived from the French, as neither Julia nor David appears in it. So Barclay must have returned to Locher, where he really found Julia :

> Non tot abortivis foedasset Iulia romam.

He may not have known what this meant, but a marginal note *Iulia* drew attention to it, and this note, omitted by Riviere, is also in Barclay. He probably supplied the name of David of his own accord. The mentioning of this name in connexion with adultery must have come quite natural to a churchman who knew something of the Bible.[3]

The last stanza, corresponding to Brant's own addition, runs as follows :

> (234)  What shall I wryte the grevous forfayture
> Of Sodom and Gomor, syns the Bybyll doth tell
> Of their synnes agaynst God and nature,
> For whiche they sanke alyve downe into hell ?
> Thus it aperith what punysshement cruell
> Our Lorde hath taken both in the olde law and newe
> For this synne, whiche sholde us move it to eschewe.

This is very weak and very vague, vaguer than Brant, vaguer also than Riviere, who, like Drouyn and Watson, renders the serious warning with all due impressiveness. As the first line, however, resembles Riviere's expression ' plains de forfaicture ' the French seems to have been used as a source, and the vagueness must have been intentional, probably because the subject did not appeal to the clerical translator.

46.—Chapter 50 treats of LECHERY under a different aspect. Brant compares her to a prostitute that sits in the streets, and the fools go to her to lose their souls as oxen go to a slaughterhouse. Worldly pleasure leads to eternal damnation, as Sardanapalus experienced. Little enjoyment is bought with much sorrow or will end in bitterness, though Epicurus considered joy the highest good.

Locher paraphrasing this chapter makes the beginning much more graphical, and it is so amplified that there is no room left at the end for the reference to Epicurus.

---

[1] The story of Pasiphae is only just alluded to, but with a marginal note which appears in Barclay alone : *Pasiphae vide virgi. e.g. VI et Enei VI in princ.* Riviere tells the story in detail, and Drouyn (and Watson) supply even more particulars. But Barclay evidently thought the story too repulsive.

[2] Pynson (1509), Cawood (1570), and Jamieson all write ' Danythys,' but there can be little doubt that the *u* has been turned upside down, as also Fraustadt 50 supposes.

[3] Fraustadt 50 thinks he must have taken it from the German.

Barclay follows this version faithfully with very few original additions. There is only :

> (711)   The hoke of deth is hyd under the bayte,

and a somewhat fuller description of 'Shamefull Lust,' sitting in the street :

> (710)   Hir face anoyntyd, blasynge abrode hir here,
> Or els on hir folysshe front, enlaced hye,
> Hir smocke to garnysshyd ; so hir dysceytfull iye
> To shamfull lust a thousand doth attyce
> Of youth, whiche erst perchaunce knewe nought of vyce.

47.—Riviere has changed and amplified various details in this chapter, but none of them appear in Barclay.   Through another door, however, this chapter of Riviere's version has won a rather prominent place in the history of English Literature.   The bulk of Watson's translation is all but forgotten, but this one chapter has with two others (52 and 53) from the sixteenth century downwards, until quite recently, figured among Skelton's works.   As such it is in Dyce's edition,[1] and he took it, he says, (and this mention of his source perhaps indicates that he had some misgiving about its authenticity,) from Marshe's edition of Skelton's Works 1568.   As late as 1886 Professor Herford [2] inferred from it that at least one English parson followed the example of Geiler von Kaisersberg at Strassburg, in using the Ship of Fools for sermon matter, and in an eloquent page he tried to show how these three chapters of the *Narrenschiff* were just those that expressed the characteristic bitterness with which Skelton incessantly assails the follies of worldly station and of those who struggle for it.

As a matter of fact, however, we have only Drouyn's own mixture in clumsy English, in which, after the three filterings to which it has been subjected, the Brantian ingredient has become a negligible quantity. In the motto, copied by Drouyn, Riviere still retained the explanation of the woodcut, representing a sheep, an ox and a bird :

> Ainsi quon lye ces thoreaux
> Oyseaulx et moutons de cordeaulx.[3]

But Watson had no idea of the woodcut, and so he used a more convenient rhyme-word :

> And suffreth themselfe to be bounde
> In cordes as it were a hounde !

After the motto Drouyn begins with his usual introductory sentence, in which Watson-Skelton has only changed *satyre* into *chaptyre*, and *fines femmes* into *cautellous women*.[4]   Then paraphrasing Riviere he found the

---

[1] *The Poetical Works of John Skelton*, I (Boston 1856), 221.
[2] Herford 351 sq.
[3] Barclay (708) also makes mention of these three creatures.—Curiously enough the last line reads differently in Riviere : *Et oyseaulx de ces grans cordeaulx.*   Where did Drouyn get his *moutons* from ?   Has he corrected Riviere from the Latin as he sometimes but very rarely does ?   Or has he used another edition of Riviere ?
[4] *fin et cautelleux* are synonyms in French !

allegorical figure of Lust changed into actual women, and Locher's graphical description made even a little more pointed.  Drouyn added some touches of his own which I have italicized :

> *Celles* quon voit . . . *les cheveux pignes et acoutrez a merveilles* seant en plusieurs lieux sont equiparees aux paillardes voluptueuses qui font leurs cheveulx apparoir au front iaunes comme fin or *et faictes passer vos cheveulx quon appelle tremplettes en aucuns lieux* pour tirer ieunes hommes a vos amours.

Watson also made a little addition but of an entirely different character ; other parts of the sentence he leaves out, or transposes, so that we get :

> They theyr heer combed and trussed *in dyvers places* [1] mervayllously, be *unreasonable* fooles, for they dresse themself lyke voluptous harlottes that maketh theyr heer to appere at theyr browes yalowe as fyne golde made in lytell tresses for to drawe younge folke unto theyr love.

Riviere amplifies the story of Sardanapalus, relating e.g. that he dressed ' en habit dune propre femme.'  Drouyn altered *propre* into *pouvre*, and then Watson translated ' the whiche put hymself in the guyse of a poor woman.'  At the end Drouyn leaves Riviere rather abruptly and adds a whole sentence of his own :

> Resistez contre ce peche de luxure qui nest que infection et toute amertume en la fin qui se donne soubz espece de myel qui estaint le cueur de lhomme. *fuyes ces folles femmes qui rongent les amoureux iusque aux os, et vous seres aymes de dieu et des hommes.*

Watson probably did not understand the *myel qui estaint le cueur,* for he was not hampered by considerations of space when he translated :

> resyst agaynst that *vyle and abhomynable* sin of lecherye, the whiche is so full of enfeccion and bytternesse, for it dystayneth the soule of man, fle from the folysshe women that pylleth the lovers unto the harde bones, and ye shall be byloved of God and of the worlde.[2]

And then to think that this concoction could pass under Skelton's name ! and that it should have been considered as an independent paraphrase of the Latin [3] or even of the German [4] !

48.—Very nearly related to the preceding is chapter 33 on ADULTERY, but the relation of the various versions is different.  Brant wrote a double chapter on it, which was cut down by Locher to a single one. All the Biblical together with half a dozen of the classical examples have been left out.  Brant's very emphatic warnings to married people have all disappeared, and in their stead we get some classical commonplaces and a few classical examples with added detail, rather uninteresting on the whole.  Barclay could not make much of it.  He seems to have

---

[1] Drouyn, like Riviere, meant that those women were sitting *in divers places,* but Watson evidently referred the expression to the hair !

[2] The principal deviation of the version that figures among Skelton's works is the spelling *foolisshe* instead of *folysshe* (Dyce l.c.).

[3] This seems to be Dyce's opinion, for in a note, l.c. vol. III, 191, he writes : ' Paraphrase of three portions of Brant's Ship of Fools : see the Latin version by Locher, Stultifera Navis ed. 1497, fol. lviii.'

[4] Prof. Herford, l.c. 352, does not mention the Latin, but only the original German 'Narrenschiff.'  A. Koelbing, by his contribution to the Cambridge History of Literature, III, 61, in 1908, has made such a mistake impossible to-day.

looked in Riviere for something more important. Riviere has some additional marginal notes from Canon Law and from Seneca with an exclamation to Venus; Barclay copied them all. But the chapter itself is not much more interesting in Riviere than it was in Locher. I am inclined to think, however, that for his principal source he took Riviere. Like Riviere he represents Atreus as driven out of his realm by his brother, thus reversing the parts assigned to them by Locher, and like Riviere he turns Locher's reference to Clodius into the Story of Virginius and Claudius Appius, or as he calls him Alpius.[1] He did not forget Locher entirely though, for he retains the spelling Clodius.

The best lines are Barclay's own addition, e.g. where he addresses the ' cursyd husbonde ' :

> (509)   That thou for them thy wyfe wyll se diffamyd
> And helpe therto, ye, and the dede beholde ;
> Blame it, blynde dryvyll ! By the law so thou sholde,
> And nat therat to gygyll, laghe and jest :
> It is a lewde byrde that fyleth his owne nest.

49.—We may here also classify chapter 72 about OBSCENE LANGUAGE. One of the most telling satires in the German original, a double chapter, full of sarcasm and indignation and ironical proverbs. Famous is the very first line :

> Eyn nuwer heylig heisszt Grobian.

This new Saint, invented by Brant, became a popular figure. A felicitous name has a better chance of popularity than the best ideas. But his character was changed in so far that he became the general representative of rude and indecent behaviour. About the middle of the sixteenth century Fr. Dedekind wrote a book on courtesy entitled *Grobianus. De morum simplicitate*, which went through twenty-five editions and was translated into German in 1552, and into English by ' R. J. Gent ' in 1605, and by Roger Bull as late as 1739 with a dedication to Dean Swift.[2] It also provided material for an interlude [3] and for Dekker's *Gul's Horne Booke*, in which he sang the new Saint's ironic praises, and (as he expresses it) ' of a Dutchman fashioned a mere Englishman.' [4]

50.—But the pale image of the new Saint, which is found in the English versions, was quite innocent of all this literary progeny. Indeed long before it was put in an English dress the whole chapter had lost its virility by Locher's manipulation. It became a single chapter, and only a few of the sinewy sententious sayings of the original could be reduced

---

[1] Drouyn's version of Riviere's text appears in Watson : ' And also Vyrgynyus that dyde kepe his doughter from Alpeus, slewe her bytwene his handes before the Romayns, the whiche loved better his doughters honour than any worldly thynge. There by dyvers nowe that resemble to Claudius alpius.'

[2] The first translation was named 'The School of Slovenrie' ; the second 'The Compleat Booby.'

[3] Grobiana's Nuptials (c. 1640). Reprinted by Rühl (see next note).

[4] The principal references were given by Herford, 383–398. The subject has since been treated in full by E. Rühl, Grobianus in England, Palaestra XXXVIII (1904).

to smooth classical distichs. One of the very few things that were retained was the name, and so we can hear a faint echo of it in Barclay :

> (1075)   In our tyme nowe both woman, childe, and man
> Without nomber worshyp with humbyll reverence
> The festis abhominable of vyle Grobyan,
> With all theyr myght, honour and theyr dylygence,
> Compassynge his auters with lawdes and insence,
> With wordes and usys fowle and abhomynable.
> Such men myschevous to hym ar acceptable.

51.—This is at any rate a great deal better than Rivière, whose paraphrase is full of misunderstandings. Having no idea of an allusion to German *grob*, the Frenchman ' translates ' :

> Plusieurs gorbiens nommez . . .
> Celebrent les festes et ceaulx
> De leurs antiqs anciens peres.

and at the end :

> Ceul qui se veullent adonner
> A tels aultiers sacrifier
> *Gobrannes* et mortifier
> On les doit comme gens proscripts
> Anichiller de biens depris !

And Drouyn innocently paraphrases : ' Plusieurs folz nommes Gorbiens sont amasses a grans monceaulx celebrans les festes de leurs anciens peres etc.' Hence we find in Watson : ' Dyvers foles named Gorbyens ben assembled together by grete hepes, halowynge the festes of theyr auncyent faders ' etc. At the end the Grobians or ' Gobrannes ' are skipped by Drouyn and Watson, but they give some graphic expressions instead, which, however, give a new significance to the chapter. Watson translates literally : ' Ye delyte you in the foule synne of glotony etynge lyke swyne, and drynkynge lyke pygyons also longe as your brethes may holde. Such folkes doynge suche sacryfyces ought to be adnychylled and dyspraysed totally.'

52.—A great deal more pretentious than any of the preceding or even than any chapter in the whole of Locher's translation is his Strife between Virtue and Lust (B). It does not belong to the original Narrenschiff at all, however, it was Locher's own invention. It would even seem that he had omitted so much of Brant's work in order to gain more space for this production of his own genius. He has hardly ever allowed more than two pages to any of Brant's chapters, but here he occupies no less than nine pages, inclusive of the three bad woodcuts which he had had made for it.—Still, good old Brant approved of it, and no doubt by way of encouragement he wrote three distichs as an introduction to the work of his disciple : ' Aspice conflictum ' etc. ' Here is Hercules' dream of the two ways.'

Locher begins with an *Epigramma* of eighteen lines to disarm criticism and to present to us noble Virtue and foul Venus. Both Rivière and Barclay (like all other translators) run Brant's introduction and Locher's Epigram into one, but Rivière skips the first six lines of the latter and works out the rest with more than usual prolixity.—Barclay skips only two or three lines, and his translation is shorter, more faithful and better. Towards the end he adds something of his own.   Speaking of Lust, he says :

> (1817)    None can be helyd that hath hir byt,
> But noble blode she most of all doth blynde,
> Which more on hir than virtue have theyr mynde.

We know that satire on noblemen was the usual ingredient of the literature of the time and need not be taken as a symptom of anything like Dickensian feeling.   Still, taken in connexion with other more out-spoken passages towards the end, these lines seem to indicate that he had some particular person in view.

53.—After the introduction Locher begins with the *Objectio Voluptatis*. He writes a ' Débat ' ; but we must not expect anything in the least resembling the *Owl and Nightingale*.   We might perhaps with more reason call it a ' Morality ' in miniature.[1]   But there is more real life in this poem than in the chapters of his *Navis*, the ' translation ' of which must have often gone against the grain with him.   They belong to a different kind of literature.   Although the didactic aim and the edifying tendency is in them both, the satire and the idea of foolishness have here disappeared altogether.   For the first time Locher catches a lyrical strain.

A detailed comparison between the Latin and its French and English imitations might be interesting, but here it is sufficient to indicate some salient points.   Locher writes all in Alexandrines and Riviere ' translates ' him in his usual serpentine octosyllabics, drawing them out into at least three times their length.   He amplifies the four lines on the dress of ' Volupte ' to no less than twenty.   His paraphrase of ' dulcissima carmina ' is interesting :

> Chanter sonner et dire aubades
> Composer rondeaulx ou ballades
> Chancons ditez et verelaiz
> De musicque ou aultres beaulx laiz.

The ' rhétoriqueur ' understands his business !   But these lines are at once followed by blasphemous nonsense.   Venus says ' Nam soror ipsa dei, cui sacra solemnia reddunt Menades ' *etc.*, and Riviere, who thinks only of his Christian God, writes :

> Mesmes il est ainsi escript
> Que la seur de dieu iesucrist (!)
> Pour laquelle on fait sacrifice
> A leglise et sacre office
> Belle blance, pollie et saine,
> Avoit ma semblance et estraine. (!!) [2]

---

[1] It is the name which Ramsay lxxxvi gives to it.

[2] Drouyn seems to have understood that this was nonsense and he skips it, simply writing ' et suis blanche et polye, au monde ny a la pareille,' which appears in Watson as : ' and am whyte and smouthe, in all the remenaunte of the worlde is not my make.'

He next blunders through some of Locher's proper names, e.g. taking
' Canopea ' as the name of a woman and changing Hammon into
Hannion ; [1] and fills out Locher's ' corpora nostra cubant ' with graphic
detail.

54.—Barclay has not only superior knowledge but also a better
poetical taste.—Hear the entrance of Lust :

> (1819)   Lo gorgays galantis, lo galantis, here am I,
>          Lo here fayre Lust, full enmy to vertue,
>          Clothyd in laurer in sygne of victory,
>          The large worlde I hole to me subdue ;

and soon he breaks into a remarkable metrical movement [2] unknown
in the rest of the book :

> (1821)   All my vesture is of golde pure,
>          My gay chaplet with stonys set,
>          With coverture of fyne asure,
>          In sylver net my here up knet,
>          Soft silk bytwene lyst it myght fret,
>          My purpyll pall overcovereth all,
>          Clere as christall, no thynge egall.

Less felicitous are the long lines of the following stanza with internal
rhymes somewhat after the manner of Chaucer's Anelida (272 sqq.,
333 sqq.).   Better is :

> (1825)   With harpe in hande alway I stande,
>          Passynge eche hour in swete pleasour ;
>          A wanton bande of every lande
>          Ar in my tour me to honour,
>          Some of valoure,[3] some bare and poure ;
>          Kynges in theyr pryde syt by my syde,
>          Every fresshe flour of swete odour
>          To them I provyde, that with me byde.

The difficulty of the ' Soror dei ' is evaded :

> (1827)   Mo men me honour for my pleasance
>          Than worshyp the mother of the hye kynge.

---

[1] Here again Drouyn is perhaps better than his model.   To quote only Watson :
' as Ammon dyde and lykewyse Numyde and Maurisia and Athas [sic !] honoured
the hevens thrughe all the regyons of Ynde.'   Riviere has only *Hannion* and *Athlas*,

> Et si voulez que plus ie die
> Toute la region *dindie* !

But in Locher we read :

> Africa me noscit : me noscit corniger Hammon
> Me Numide infrenes : colit et Maurisius atlas
> India *etc.*

And on the margin he has *Numide, Mauritania, India*.   This proves that
Drouyn has looked into the Latin original, taking *Numide* as the name of a country
and from *Maurisius* and *Mauritania* fashioning his *Maurisia* !

[2] These lines, which may have influenced Skelton's half-lines, are fully analysed
by Ramsay lxxxvii.

[3] Cawood's reading ; the 1509 ed. has *voloure*.

And no small command of language is evinced by stanzas like the
following :

> (1828)　He shall his hede cast to no drede
> 　　　　To get the mede and-lawde of warre,
> 　　　　Nor yet have nede for to take hede,
> 　　　　Howe batayles spede, but stand a farre.

> (1829)　Nor yet be bounde to care the sounde
> 　　　　Of man or grounde or trumpet shyll [1]
> 　　　　Strokes that redounde shall nat confounde
> 　　　　Nor his mynde wounde, but if he wyll.
> 　　　　Who wyll subdue hym to insue
> 　　　　My pleasours newe, that I demayne,[2]
> 　　　　I shall hym shewe way to eschewe
> 　　　　Where hardnes grewe, and to fle payne.

After these lyrical attempts he returns to his Chaucerians again.—
In his own amusing way he gets rid of Locher's proper names :

> (1833)　As Afryke, Numyde ; the other I let be,
> 　　　　I wyll nat tary theyr namys for to tell.

There is the old Barclay back again ! Though Venus is still supposed
to be speaking up to the end :

> (1840)　The tyme passyth dayly fro mankynde
> 　　　　Our dayes of lyfe longe whyle can nat indure,
> 　　　　Therfore on pleasour establysshe we our mynde,
> 　　　　For in my mynde no erthly creature
> 　　　　After this lyfe of pleasour shall be sure ;
> 　　　　Therefore be we merry the time that we ar here,
> 　　　　And passe we our tyme alway in lusty chere.

This is more prosaic than the above lyrical passages but it is also more
natural. It is the language of common sense, though with an ironical
intonation. And so we like him better. Barclay's lyricism creates
the impression of a man speaking in a falsetto voice. Now we hear
his own natural bass tones again.

55.—All in bass tones is the Answer of Virtue : (i) After a recrimina-
tion of Voluptuosite,—(ii) Virtue admits her outward beauty, but says—
(iii) it is accompanied by shame.—(iv) Thou bringest, she says, all evils,—
(v) as so many classical towns can testify,—(vi) but I bring glory,—
(vii) as Greek and Roman heroes show.—(viii) Indeed thou art foul and
I am fair.—(ix) Hence, O young men, choose me and not Voluptuosite.—
These are the leading ideas of Locher's treatise, and they are all in Barclay,
who follows him step by step. So does Riviere, only he takes a dozen
steps where Locher takes one, and sometimes trips over a difficult passage,
which Barclay never does in this chapter.

---

[1] = sonorous, resonant, shrill. A common adj. and adv. in ME. and the sixteenth
century.—NED.

[2] Anomalous spelling and application of *to demean*. A similar meaning is in
Chaucer's *House of Fame*, 959 :

> To lete a fole han governance
> Of thing that he can not demeine.

The exact shade of meaning in which it occurs here is not in the NED.

In (i) virtue calls the preceding song a ' barayne balade ' (1841) as
well she may.—Locher's

> Aebrietas tibi fida comes : Infamia pennis
> Circum te volitat, et tua castra premit

loses nothing in Barclay's

> (1843)  Thy faythfull felawe is bestyall Dronkenes,
> Thy Pursuyvant is dredfull worldly Shame,
> Fleynge about to spred abrode thy name.

A comparison with the French sets this manly language off to even better
advantage :

> Tu es de grant sobriete
> Ennemie et debriete
> Cousine et sa propre seur *etc*.

Another interesting passage occurs under (ii) :

> Te chlamydes Tyrie velant : te balteus ornat :
> Et te Sidonio purpura tincta fuco.

To Barclay this was quite straightforward :

> (1845)  Of purpyll colour of Tyre is thy mantayle,
> With precious stones beset as thycke as hayle,
> Thy gyrdyls gay, and rynges pleasant to se ;
> But what is this but worldly vanyte ?

But Rivière seems to have had a difficulty here.  He would not allow
to Venus a *balteus*, and so he wrote :

> En Lieu de baltee *trop fier*
> *Que porte le bon homme darme*
> *Le chevalier robuste et ferme*, (!)
> Tu porte drap de calminie
> De la taincture et sidonie.

By this ' correction ' the name of clothes is turned into the name of
a country, and what the participle *tincta* has been turned into I do not
know.  Something synonymous with *Sidonie* at any rate.  Through
Drouyn's paraphrase the new country of *Calminie* has crept into the
English version of Watson, who has, however, wisely left the rest alone :
' In stede of baudryke, thou werest clothe of Calmynye and bereth no
male swerde, salade,[1] spere, or other instrument of warre.'

Under (v) Barclay takes over most of Locher's names, but has at
least the good taste to omit five out of the list of sixteen.[2]  To the eight
names of part (vii) however he adds Homer.  Part (viii) he elaborates
the most, almost as much as Rivière.  Towards the end, just before
(under (ix) ) he addresses ' Ye men ' (for Barclay writes for men, Locher
only for ' juvenes ') there occurs the striking passage referred to above.

---

[1] A variant of *sallet*, occurring in Caxton's *Chron. Engl.* cclv (1482), 331 : ' He
took syr umfreys salade.'—NED.

[2] Riviere skips only one : Tarentum.

It is contained in two stanzas, which have absolutely no parallel in Latin, and which cannot have been suggested by the context :

(1872)    But thou, fals Lust and pleasour corporall,
           All men disceyvest that unto the inclyne ;
           Thou first art swete, at last more soure than gall ;
           Thou many thousandes hast brought unto ruyne ;
           And namely such as of most noble lyne
           Discendyd ar, forgettynge theyr degre,
           Defyle theyr byrth and auncyent name by the.

This is not one of the Englishman's usual grumblings against high-born people. The tone is more direct than anywhere else, almost personal. Is he aiming at some one individual ? Our suspicion is much strengthened by the following stanza, which seems to contain an allusion to certain events about whose nature we are left in the dark :

(1873)    Thou art so fyers, so hasty and cruell,
           That no wylde beste, no, nat the mighty bere
           Can have respyte within his den to dwell ;
           Thy cruell clawes so fyersly doth him tere,
           That on his skyn remayned skant a here.
           Thou sholdest his skyn, I trowe, rent of also,
           Ne had the Lyon him socoured in his wo.

Then follows immediately ' Therefoie ye men ' etc. So it would seem that some persons in particular are meant here. Who is the bere, that has lost nearly all his hair by the claws of Lust ? And who is the Lyon that socoured him ?

56.—We must turn to the third of the Deadly Sins, ENVY, to which only one chapter (53) is devoted, and a short one at that. Locher has translated it remarkably closely with hardly any important deviations, except the skipping of a few names at the end. (Saul and David l. 19, Aglauros l. 26, Esau l. 29.) He even brings out one passage in Brant more clearly :

' Der nythart, der ist noch nit dot ' says the motto, and Locher translates :

Nec dum Nithardi semen abivit atrox.

This is rather important, though not so much for our purpose. It throws a light upon the preceding woodcut, which has puzzled so many scholars and upon the German word nythart, which Professor Zarncke [1] has failed to explain, although it occurs again in chap. 77, l. 59.—From Locher we see that a proper name is meant here, and it becomes evident that we have an allusion in the text as well as in the cut to one of the heroes in the popular carnival-plays of Germany, rough rollicking farces, which were in great favour in the fifteenth and far into the sixteenth century. In the Neidhartspiele ' Neithart der ritter reich ' is the hero and the victim of a low trick, but he also rubs shoulders with no less a personage than Parzival.[2] One of his adventures was an escape in an

---

[1] P. 389.
[2] Fastnachtspiele aus dem fünfzehnten Jahrhundert (Bibliothek des litter. Vereins in Stuttgart xxviii), Stuttgart 1853, No. 21 (p. 191), No. 53 (p. 393). Cf. Creizenach i 407 sq.

empty barrel,[1] and this is of course what the woodcut represents. Locher's spelling dispels all doubt, for the same Latin form of his name is also found in the stage-direction 'Vadat Nithardus et ponat florem sub pileo et redeat.' [2]

But this has very little to do with our subject, for, as was to be expected, none of Locher's translators have understood the reference.

Barclay has translated him as well as he could, and a great deal better than Riviere and his followers. He has even tried his hand at that line in the motto which the others have simply skipped. With no great success however :

> (749)    No state in erth therfro can kepe hym sure,
> His sede encreasyth as it woulde ever endure.

57.—But we must here again pay more attention to Watson, for this is the second chapter that has long figured under the name of Skelton.—Here is Riviere's motto, copied by Drouyn :

> Les dartz de la mauldicte envie
> Sans ceulx (Dr. eulx) ne fut oncques le monde
> Avec haine vole et desuie (Dr. defuie)
> Tristesse douleur y habunde
> En envie chacun se fonde
> Ces envieux ne sont marriz
> Du mal dautruy ains en font (Dr. font grans) ris.

The first half is to be found almost literally translated in Watson, but he sacrifices the second half :

> The dartes ryght cursed of envye
> Hath reygned syth the worlde began,
> Whiche bryngeth one evedently
> In to the bandes of sathan.
> Wherfore he is a dyscrete man
> That can eschewe that evyll synne
> Where body and soule is loste ynne.

This appears under Skelton's name with only slight variants—in the third line Dyce prints *man evydently* and in the next one *bondes*.

The chapter itself opens with *Livor edax*, Barclay's 'Wastynge Envy' (750), and these two words become three lines in Riviere :

> O Envie devoratresse
> Des loyaulx cueurs dissipatresse
> Tu brisez devorez les couraiges.

Drouyn has again a sort of little prologue :

Approches vous folz envieux qui ne pouves dire nul bien de ceulx que vous hayes, venez veoir en ceste satyre et vous congnoistres le mal ou vous estes. O Enmye qui devore les meurs les hommes, dissiperesse dhonneur *etc.*

---

[1] K. Gusinde, *Neidhart mit dem Veilchen.* (Germanistische Abhandlungen, xvii, Breslau 1899, pp. 137, 192.)

[2] K. Gusinde 24. Hans Sachs also wrote a *Neidhart-spiel,* and a *Meistergesang* on the same subject, printed ib. p. 241.

This is translated in Watson's English :

> Aproche you folysshe envyous the whiche can saye no good by them that ye hate, come and se in this chapytre [1] your perverse and Evyll condycyons. O Envye that devoureth the condycyons of men, and dyssyperesse of honour, *etc.*

The variants with which this is given in Skelton's works are not worth mentioning here, the most important being that the last word but two is written *dyssypers*.

A very curious passage occurs in the middle of the chapter. Locher there gives a ' Descriptio Invidiae ex Ovidio ' and he writes :

> macies in corpore toto
> Glauca sedet : visus torvus : squalentia ora
> Scintillant.

Barclay tries to render this by :

> (755)   Envy is pale of loke and countenance,
> His body lene, of colour pale and blewe,
> His loke frowarde, his face without pleasance,
> Pyllynge lyke scalys, his wordes ay untrue,
> His iyen sparklinge with fyre ay fresshe and newe.

He seems to have connected *squalentia* not with English *squalid* but with English *scales*, ' pyllying ' being the same as MnE. ' peeling.' Certainly such a face was ' without pleasance.' But Riviere makes it a great deal worse. He knew *Glauca* only as the name of a fish, and so puts this ' name ' upon the margin and translates :

> Cest envieux est si amer
> Que le poisson semble de mer
> Glauca avec ses yeulx vers
> Qui se regarddent a travers
> De son estomac eschauffe
> Plus ardant que nest roux chauffe
> Sintillule *etc.*

which becomes in Drouyn : ' Cest envieux est plus amer que le fiel du poisson Glauca avec ses yeulx regardant de travers lestomac eschauffe sintilulle ' *etc.* Hence we find in Watson-Skelton : ' These envyous are more bytterer [double comparatives were common enough] than the galle of the fysshe Glauca, with theyr [so he refers *ses* to the subject !] eyen beholdynge a travers the stomaches chaufed syntyllousli ' [2] !

---

[1] Dyce reads *booke*. I should like to draw attention to the fact that the word *satire* is usually avoided by Watson. This seems to confirm the view that the word had not gained a footing in English yet, and that Barclay was probably the first to introduce it   (See Alden 18.)

[2] To this ' Descriptio Invidiae ' Drouyn has added something of his own. Quoting on the margin ' Versus. Qui mel in ore gerit et me retro pungere querit eius amicitiam nolo mihi sociam,' he writes : ' Estant en lieu ou mon honneur estoit, et ie cuydoye avoir aliance dune fleur, ie fuz dung dart denvie naure, en ung instant ceulx qui estoient de ma partie me tournerent le dos.' Watson translates this literally, inserting ' odyfferaunt ' before ' floure,' and ' behynde my backe ' after ' envye.' Assuming this to have been written by Skelton, critics have thought that the author was here alluding to his own intimate circumstances (Koelbing 68). For this Rector of Diss, as is well known, kept a concubine, which led him into difficulties with his superiors. It could really seem as if in these words he was ascribing the difficulties to ' Envy ' !

58 —One can hardly understand how Barclay could ever turn to Riviere for information. But even for this very chapter he must have done so. After having written

> The mount of Ethnay though it brent ever styll,
> Yet save itself it brenneth none other thynge,

a rendering of Locher's thought, far superior to Riviere's

> Il semble ethna qui a parfoy
> Elle mesme tousiours se brusle
> Et en son cueur le grant feu brut.    le
> Frere a beaucup *etc.*

after this passage there suddenly comes something about envious brothers :

> (759)    As Romulus and Remus excellent of fame
> Whiche byldyd Rome, but after envy so grewe
> Bytwene them that the one the other slewe.

> (760)    What shall I wryte of Cayne and Abell,
> How Cayne for murder suffred great payne and wo ?
> Atreus' story and Theseus cruell
> Ar unto us example hereof also.

This cannot possibly be from Locher's

> Fraterno primi maduerunt sanguine muri
> Hoc Abel atque Chayn : hoc Atreus atque Thyestes
> Ethiocles, *etc.*

He must have looked into his Riviere, where he found the story of Romulus and Remus told in almost twenty lines, where *Thyestes* was corrupted into *Theseus* in a long story of more than thirty lines.

59.—This sudden discarding of Locher, and this preference given to a guide with ' gravel in his eyes ' would almost seem a psychological problem, if the marginal note did not reveal the secret. For Riviere annotates here : *Atreus de quo loqt boca. l. de genealo. deo.* Barclay must have seen this note, although he has not copied it, and it must have impressed him so much that he looked up to Riviere as a scholar to whose authority he was ready to sacrifice Locher's most correct versions.—It is no doubt remarkable that Riviere should quote Boccaccio, and he does it repeatedly (chaps. 8, 10, 53, 64). Yet we know of no edition of *De Genealogia Deorum Gentilium* that had appeared in France before 1498. Elsewhere the work must have been popular enough. There were already at that time almost a dozen editions, but nearly all of them were printed in Italy, except one,[1] which has been assigned to a Cologne Press.[2] Riviere's quotations show that this summary of classical mythology was just then beginning to draw attention in France. And indeed, on the 9th of February 1498 Vérard published an anonymous translation under the title *Boccace de la Genealogie des Dieux.*[3]

But Riviere must have used, and misunderstood, some edition of the

---

[1] Pellechet 2464 and 2465 are probably identical.      [2] BMC. i, 234.
[3] Pellechet 2471. Hain 3325. Macfarlane 56.

Latin, for in the translation the story of Atreus and Thyestes is told quite correctly.[1]

It was no doubt Riviere's marginal note, however, that led Barclay astray. For except for the loan of a corrupt name instead of the correct one, Barclay continues to follow Locher rather than Riviere. He does mention Romulus and Remus by name, while Locher had only alluded to them, but he does not insert anything of the long stories that Riviere had introduced concerning either Romulus and Remus or Thyestes-Theseus.[2]

60.—What Riviere's stories were like we may partly see from Watson: ' He resembleth unto Ethna the whiche brenneth alwayes [literally as in Drouyn, but the point is now entirely lost]. As of Romulus and Remus his broder the whiche Romulus edefyed fyrste Rome and gave it to name Rome (et luy imposa nom romme) after his owne name [not in Drouyn]. Nevertheless they were pastours, for they establysshed lawes in the cyte.[3] And Romulus etc. . . . We rede also how Cayme slewe his owne broder by envye. Have we not ensample of Atreus, of whome his broder occupyed the parke, how wel that they were in the realme stronge and puyssaunt for to defende them. It was Thesius (sic !) that expulsed his broder out of the realme by envye, and was called agayne bycause that he had taken the parke ' etc. I shall not quote more of this nonsense. It is all verbatim as in Drouyn, whose last sentence is only less clear : ' et fut repris pour ce quil avait prins ce parc.' But Drouyn has compressed all sense out of Riviere :

> Lequel gecta par desconfort
> Son frere hors par grant envie
> Du royaulme et sans oster sa vie
> Et pource que le parc avoit pris
> Fut de son frere ainsi repris
> Banni en estrange contree
> Despuis envie rencontree
> Non content de banissement
> Soubz bon et loyal passement
> De foy il lenvoy a querir.

---

[1] No copy of the original edition is in the British Museum, but there is an edition by Jean Petit 1531, and as the quotations given by Miss Pellechet agree with the corresponding passages here, they evidently represent the same text. In lib. XII, cap. v, it says : ' Atreus regna avec son frere Thyestes sur les Peloponences. . . . Atreus avoit un velin, duquel Senecque le tragicque dit ainsi.'—This is a correct enough translation of the Latin : ' Atreus . . . una cum Thyeste fratre apud peloponesum regnavit. . . . Insuper erat apud Atreum aries de quo sic Seneca tragicus ' (quoted from the Venice edition 1472 : Pellechet 2466, BMC. v, 162).— Nothing of Riviere's ' parc ' (see quotations in text).

[2] The preference given to Riviere elsewhere may therefore be largely due to the fascination of the impressive marginal note. This is certainly true of chapters 8 and 10 and probably also of chapters 33 and 85, where Riviere has other learned references.

[3] A little less absurd in Drouyn : ' Toutes fois ilz estoient pasteurs, lequel fist des loix de la cite,' — but he has skipped a line in Riviere :

> Toutesfois ilz estoient pastours
> Si fist romulus des atours
> Et loix en la noble cite.

On comparing these texts one feels really stupefied to find that this childish production of Watson's pen has so long been considered an original work of John Skelton, and that only in 1904 the first doubts were raised by the chance discovery of a scholar, that there was something wrong with the name Theseus,[1] that even after that time another scholar maintained its authenticity [2] until the matter was finally settled in 1907 by a comparison between the so-called Skelton and the real Watson.[3]

61.—To WRATH, the fourth of the Deadly Sins, we find likewise only one chapter (35) dedicated—Brant's main ideas are all to be found in Locher's translation with only slight additions. Thus he adds to the story of Archytas that he was born ' Tarentina in urbe,' meaning **Tarentum**. Barclay translates this as well as the rest.

> (541)   Borne in the ryche Cyte namyd Tarentyne (!) [4]

To the examples of Socrates and Plato (and ' Seneca ' put in as a stop-gap) he adds that of the ' sayntis ' and of Christ and of ' saynt Laurance,' the latter being emphatically mentioned on the margin.

The most interesting passage, however, of his translation occurs in the beginning.

> (536)   This man malycious, whiche troubled is with wrath,
> Nought els soundeth but the hoorse letter R.
> Thoughe all be well, yet he none answere hath
> Save the dogges letter glowmynge with ' nar, nar.'
> Suche labour nat this mad rancour to defar,
> Nor yet this malyce to mytygate or asswage,
> But ioyeth to be drede of men for this outrage.

This is not a bad picture of a man in a rage. But that letter R is so very striking and its application here is as far as I can see so unprecedented in English literature that the question of its source forcibly obtrudes itself. Locher, quoting Persius, writes :

> Rancidulo semper ructatur in ore canina
> Littera : nec motus mitigat ille suos.

The meaning is not obvious and if Barclay had looked up Persius he would have found there little to assist him. Persius Sat. I, 109 has only ' Sonat heic de nare canina litera.' From the French translations we see the difficulty of the passage. The most literal is, of course, the Marnef-edition. ' et de sa randicule bouche est tousiours ructuee et gectee [note that these French translators, even the most ' literal,' often use two words instead of one, a thing frequently considered peculiar to

---

[1] Fr. Brie (Breslau) in *Engl. Studien* 33 (1904), 262.

[2] Arth. Koelbing, *Zur Characteristik John Skeltons* (Stuttgart 1904), 66 : ' Ich glaube trotz Brie E. St. 33, 262, nicht, dass man das *Boke of Three Fooles* Skelton absprechen kann.'

[3] Fr. Brie in *Engl. Studien* 37 (1907), 19. It does not derogate from his merits in the least to add that he has not perceived the true relation between Watson—Drouyn—Riviere—Locher—Brant.

[4] ' Tarentine la cite ' is of course also in Riviere, as well as ' the cyte of Tarentyne ' in Watson.

Caxton] *quelque lettre canine* et ne mitigue point tel fol ses mouvemens.'
Riviere thinking that *canina* had something to do with a chimney (!)
(camina) translates :

> En sa bouche parle a foison
> Mais ung mot ne dit a raison
> Ains de son courroux ist fumee
> Autant comme de cheminee
> Habundamment par le tuain !

Drouyn renders this ' Il crye et brait et ne dit pas ung mot ou il y ait
raison il est plus fumeux que nest une basse cheminee,' or as Watson's
straightforward English has it, ' He cryeth and brayeth and meketh not
one reasonable worde, he is more smokye thenne is a lowe chymney.'

It is evident that only Barclay had understood the real meaning of
the ' canina littera,' for Locher uses it to render Brant's line 5 :

> Keyn buochstab kan er dann das R.

It is just possible that Barclay had the German original before him
and that the big letter at the end of a line gave him a good hint.

But this possibility is not the only one. It is even more likely that
among the early humanists the *r* was generally known as ' the dog's
letter.' We know that it was so to a later generation. In *Romeo and
Juliet* (II, iv, 228) even the Nurse is familiar with it. Ben Jonson in his
*English Grammar* also mentions it and quotes the above-mentioned
line from Persius to corroborate his statement.[1] But it is not very
probable that either Ben Jonson or Locher derived their knowledge
directly from Persius. For the context there would not suggest it at
all, because Persius is not speaking of letters but of a real dog.[2] Ben
Jonson quotes no other authority that has anything resembling it.
Shakespeare's commentators usually quote Lucilius by the side of
Persius. The line is usually more or less corrupted, but the correct
reading : *irritata canes quam homo quam planius dicit* is so obscure [3] that
it would not have helped either Locher or Barclay or Shakespeare, even
if they had read the line. Among the early commentators of Persius
or among the grammarians of the time the ' canina litera ' must have
been a commonplace,[4] and in this way both Barclay and Locher may
have become acquainted with it.

Even the easy-going breadth of Barclay's words, quoted above,
compared with the abrupt conciseness of Brant's single line, seems to

---

[1] Ben Jonson, *Works* (ed. Giff.-Cunningham) iii, 434. In the *Alchemyst*, II, i,
he also introduces ' a dog's snarling *er* ' (ib. ii, 35). On Aubrey's statement that
Milton pronounced *r* very hard, Dryden remarked ' Litera canina, the dog-letter,
a certain sign of a satirical wit ' (D. Masson, *Milton*, vi, 679). I owe these references
to the kindness of my friend Dr. N. Zwager.

[2] Cf. *Auli Persi Flacci Saturae*, ed. J. van Wageningen (Groningen 1911), i,
9 sqq., where the Dutch translation has ' De hond aan hunne voordeur grynst u toe.'

[3] *C. Lucilii Carminum Reliquiae* rec. Fridericus Marx (Lipsiae 1904) i, 3 (second
line) ; ii, 2 : ' Quamquam quid dixerit his verbis Lucilius adhuc obscurum est.' More
to the point would be line 377 (ib. i, 26) : ' *r* non multum est, hoc cacosyntheton
atque canina si lingua dico ; nihil ad me, nomen enim illi est.'

[4] Even the old Scholiast of Persius would do : ' Canes lacessiti sic hirriunt, ut
videantur *r* litteram minitabundi exprimere ' (Van Wageningen, l.c. ii, 24).

show that the mere suggestion of a ' canina littera ' was quite sufficient to set into motion a train of ideas which was perfectly natural and self-evident.

62.—Several chapters may be grouped under the fifth of the Deadly Sins.

AVARICE is censured in chapter 3. Though too great prodigality is described as even worse than avarice, the heaping up of riches avails nothing at death. Your heirs will forget your soul. So provide for your soul first. A wise man seeks self-knowledge first and not riches. Crassus was obliged to drink liquid gold ; but Crates was wise and threw his gold away.

Locher's translation is fairly complete. Without losing much he has been able to bring the Styx and the Acheron into the introduction, and Tantalus into the body. The story of Crassus, which is stated by Brant very simply, is made a little more complete and—more obscure.

Barclay paraphrases his text rather freely ; so that instead of the Styx and Acheron we get ' infernall flodes tedyous and horryble (65).' Tantalus is left out entirely ; Crassus gets only a vague allusion, probably because the Latin was so difficult. But Locher's reference to the heirs provides material for a lively stanza on the rapacity of executors [1] :

> (68)   If thou be dampned, than art thou at thy stent [2] ;
> By thy ryches which thou here hast left behynde
> To thy executours, thou shalt small comforte fynde.

> (69)   Theyr custome is to holde fast that they have ;
> Thy pore soule shall be farthest fro theyr thought ;
> If that thy carkes be brought onys in the grave,
> And that they have thy bagges in handes cought—
> What say they than ?   ' By God the man had nought !
> Whyle he here lyvyd he was to lyberall.'
> Thus dampned is thy soule ; thy ryches cause of all.

The admonition to give alms to the poor is preceded by a curious reflection in which the author seems to have an eye on some wealthy friends of his :

> (70)   Who wyll deny but it is necessary
> Of riches for to have plenty and store ?
> To this opynyon I wyll nat say contrary,
> So it be ordred after Holy Lore ;
> Whyle thy selfe livest departe some to the pore
> With thy owne hande ; trust nat thy executours ;
> Gyve for God, and God shall sende at all houres.

63.—Of Riviere's digressions nothing appears in Barclay, although there was an alluring little note behind the name of *Tantalus*, viz. *de quo Lactant.* The digressions are to be found in Watson :

I maye name unto the Tantalus the whiche is in the goulfre of helle, he enrageth for hungre and thruste, and is in the water unto the chynne, but whan he thynketh

---

[1] See also §§ 92, 121, 205.
[2] The Chaucerian spelling *stent* (instead of MnE. *stint*) occurs also in St. 640 : Hell ' can nat suche folys theyr synnes cause to stent ' ; and St. 1183 : ' theyr mawes so fervent . . . that no drynke can it stent.'

for to drynke it avaleth [1] (leau se baisse) soo lowe that he can not drynke of it. And there is also a pere tree besyde hym upon the whiche pere tree is a pere that toucheth almost his nose, and whan he stratcheth hymselfe up (il se hausse) for to catche it, the tree ryseth up, and in this manner of wyse he enrageth for hungre and thruste.

About Crassus Riviere had translated Locher correctly enough :

> Mais dor par les parthes apres
> Fut empoisonne tout expres.

Drouyn altered *empoisonne* into *emprisonne*, and so Watson translated : ' It befell within a shorte tyme after that he was enprysoned by the Parthes, and all was for bycause of his treasour.'

The name *Crates* must have been unfamiliar to Riviere, for he changed it into *Socrates* :

> Je vous suppli que lon comtemple
> De Socrates la preudommie *etc*.

As this name was retained in the prose-version, Watson translated :

Resemble al unto Socrates, the whiche sayd that rychesse was enemy unto scyence, moyennynge of whiche [2] (au moyen de ce) he that had so moche rychesse, threwe all his goodes in to the see, in suche wyse that no body coude blame him.

64.—Chapter 17 is also connected with AVARICE. It is the old theme of how rich people are honoured for their money and the poor despised. Locher had little difficulty in putting this classical subject into classical Latin, but in the process all the dramatic abrupt ruggedness of Brant's vernacular has vanished.—Turning this Latin into English, Barclay has made it quite graphic once again. So e.g.

> Curia sola patet diti prudensque senatus
> Solus habet laudes conquirit solus honores

becomes

> (285) Suche shall be made a Sergeant or Justyce,
> And in the Court reputed of moste pryse ;
> He shall be callyd to counseyll in the lawe,
> Though that his brayne be skarsly worth a strawe.[3]

> (286) He shall be Mayre, Baylyfe or Constable,
> And he onely promotyd to honoure ;
> His maners onely reputed ar laudable,
> His dedys praysyd as grettest of valoure.

Two lines have become eight ! But prolixity is evaded by the concreteness of the expressions. In one passage he leaves his model entirely,

---

[1] *To avale*, in the meaning of *to sink down*, was common in the fifteenth and sixteenth centuries.

[2] The expression is common in Watson.

[3] Contrast with this Riviere's

> Et ara en court alliance
> Le grant senat luy est ouvert
> De louenges est tout couvert.

The word *court* in the English and the French was of course suggested by the Latin *Curia*. Fraustadt's remark (p. 43) that Barclay, under the influence of Riviere, speaks ' vom Einflusse des Reichen bei Hofe ' is a mistake.

and then, as always, he is at his best.  Enlarging upon the idea that more gifts are sent to the rich than to the poor he adds :

> (291) The wolfe etis the shepe, the great fysshe the small,
> The hare with the houndes vexed ar and frayde ;
> He that hath halfe nedes wyll have all.
> The ryche mannes pleasour can nat be denayde :
> Be the pore wroth or be he wel apayde [1]
> Fere causeth hym sende unto the ryches hous
> His mete from his owne mouth if it be delycious.

It may be doubted whether the last rhyme was anything more than an eye-rhyme in the beginning of the sixteenth century.  The chapter concludes with an Envoy, in which the ' great estatis and men of dignyte ' are exhorted to have pity on the poor.

65.—Very nearly related to the preceding is chapter 67, a rather rambling satire on different subjects, but mainly turning on the danger or the folly of AVARICE AND PRODIGALITY.  The introduction, which explains the woodcut, is very loosely connected with the rest.

Many a one is not aware that he is being made a fool of until he is flayed alive like Marsyas (1-11).  If you are rich you will have friends until they have robbed you of everything (12-20).  Wasting your goods until you are reduced to beggary is sheer folly (21-30).  Better make friends with your goods betimes (31-34).  Many fools are laughed at by other fools (35-47), and yet they imagine themselves to be witty and wise (48-64).  Many will suffer everything to obtain money ; they like gout because it is a rich man's ailment, they put up with all abuse if they are only paid for it (65-72).  No one is content with little, but ambition drives all to amassing riches (73-77).  Many have neither kith nor kin and yet they are never tired of labouring for greater wealth (78-83).  Riches are a blessing for those that use them properly and do not hoard them up for others only (84-89).  For others, however, they are like the tortures of Tantalus (90-94).

Locher reduces this double chapter to a single one.  Telling the story of Marsyas more fully he makes the introduction much longer, incorporating in it Brant's lines 35-47.  After this he uses lines 12-30 and his page is full.

Barclay paraphrasing this mutilated chapter introduces some good lines of his own as e.g.

> (1005) He loveth to be flatered and clawed by the sleve [2] ;
> That thynge that he wolde here he gladly doth beleve.

At the end he introduces a new idea.  In Stanza 1011 he prepares the transition ; after exhausting what Locher says about prodigality he adds a reason :

> (1011) For who that is of small power and degre
> And with his betters wyll in expence stryve,
> Without all dout that fole shall never thryve.

---

[1] = satisfied, pleased.
[2] St. 771 also speaks of ' a flaterynge fole to clawe the by the sleve ' ; and the flatterer occurs again in St. 1584 :

> Another hym stryketh and clawyth by the sleve.

This leads to an *Addicio Alexandri Barclay* :

> (1012)   And also folys that stryveth in the lawe
> Agaynst an estate [1] them passynge in ryches,
> Shall theyr owne flesshe unto the bonys gnawe ;
> Or he that is voyde of reason and wytles
> And dare presume by his presumptuousnes
> Agaynst a man of hye wysdome and lore,
> He shall byde a fole even as he was before.

It is this idea alone that provides material for the admonition in the last two stanzas, which being octaves, should have been marked as an Envoy. The second is the most idiomatic and characteristic :

> (1014)   And thou that art a courter or a knave
> Or a bonde chorle and all thy hole lynage,
> Thynke well : thou shalt but small profyte have
> To stryve with thy mayster come of hye parage ;
> I fynde it moste for mannys avauntage,
> Within his bondes his body to preserve,
> And not in ryches, strength, wysdome or langage
> To stryve agaynst the streme lyst he in swymmynge sterve.

With this well-sounding Alexandrine [2] Barclay concludes his addition, which has nothing to do with avarice or prodigality but which evidently embodies the popular wisdom of the time on the futility of so many lawsuits.

66.—Drouyn's prose-rendering of this chapter is rather freer than usual, so that we get some straightforward expressions in Watson :

> If thou haste ben ryche, and that thou haste yet thy coffers full of rychesse, doubte the not, for thou shalte have kynnesmen, frendes, and felowes ynoughe. And whan thy rychesse is gone, thou shalte never have frende nor kynne for the poore man hathe no frendes.

And at the end :

> Frendeshyppe is now in the purse, for who hathe no moneye hathe no frendes, and yf they were also wyse as Salamon, and have no monye they be but fooles. And yf he were a kynges sone or a prynce, and yf he have no monye nor possessyons, he shall have none honoure nor reverence.

This last sentence has no parallel in Riviere nor in Locher. It is an original reflection of Drouyn's written with regard to a particular case. For the French does not stop here. The whole sentence, which takes the place of Riviere's vague lamentations, runs as follows :

> et fust filz de roy ou de prince, on ne aura nul honneur, sy on na or nargent et possessions comme il appert du filz du roy dangleterre qui fut nomme edouard qui a este pouvre serviteur a paris, et fut recueilly du conte de flandres.

---

[1] *Estate* or *state* is used by Barclay time and again to denote a person of high rank, a noble. This seems a somewhat peculiar use of the word, for it has been overlooked by the NED. The Century Dictionary and Cyclopedia (s.v. sub 10) mentions it with an anonymous quotation from *Notes and Queries*, one from Latimer, and one from the (unrevised) Authorised Version, Mark vi, 21.

[2] One little step further, and the Monk's Tale stanza becomes a Spenserian stanza.—But there are some little steps that can only be taken by geniuses !

I do not know if Watson understood the allusion better than we do. During and after the Wars of the Roses several such stories may have been told.[1] But Watson realized that such a rumour might be discreditable to some king of England, and so he felt loyally obliged not to pass it on !

67.—The chapter on DESPISING POVERTY (83) shows various points of contact with the preceding one. Quite as an exception Locher has taken the space of a double chapter for it, just as Brant had done. So most of the ideas and examples of the original are in it, but most of the graphical details are omitted, and the classical allusions strengthened. Barclay follows him step by step and no trace of any influence of Riviere is discernible. In the true moralist's strain he gives a dark-coloured picture of the times (and of all times) :

> (1214)  All men forsaketh in this tyme to sustayne
>         The weght and burthen of godly poverte.
> (1217)  The worlde rennyth on suche chaunce nowe adayes,
>         That none by vertue riches can attayne.

The darkness is heightened by a contrast with ' the golden age,' Hesiod's immortal chimera, which kept haunting mankind all through the Middle Ages—and after, though Sir Thomas More attempted to send it as an exile to the island of ' Nowhere ' :

> (1225)  But whan the golden age the world dyd lyght
>         And rayned amonge men, than was poverte
>         Of great lawde and glory with men of eche degre.

I shall not quote more from either of these pictures as the theme is commonplace enough. Only one curious passage from the ' examples.' The Latin has :

> Paupertatis honor Tarpeias extulit arces
>   Atque urbi titulum principiumque dedit.
> Pauperibus Roma est quondam pastoribus orta.

This becomes in Barclay :

> (1236)  The worthy cyte callyd Tarpye by name
>         Of small begynnynge is nowe made excellent ;
>         Rome hath also farre spredde abrode hir fame,
>         Thoughe it were byldyd (as lerned men assent)
>         Of symple shepherdes pore and innocent.

The French translator had the same difficulty. Not the Marnef edition, however, which has quite correctly : ' Lhonneur de povrete a Romme ainsi que dit sainct Augustin [2] esleva les hautesses tarpeyennes et donna tiltre et commencement a la cite.'

---

[1] After the battle of Towton in 1461 Margaret of Anjou, the wife of Henry VI, applied to the Duke of Burgundy in behalf of her son Edward. Is this what Drouyn means ? Or does he allude to Edward IV's flight to Sluys, and his reception by Louis of Bruges in 1471 ?

[2] *Augustinus* is cited on Locher's margin.

But this is Rivicre's version :

> Avisez quel honneur bailla
> A *tarpeye* que baille a
> Son commencement et beau tiltre
> Lisez vous pas en maint epistre
> Comment Romme les beaulx pasteurs
> Ediffierent et acteurs
> Furent de celle grant cite.

Drouyn rendered this by

> Regardes quel honneur elle (pouvrete) bailla a Tarpeye. Lises vous des bons pasteurs de Romme qui edifierent et furent aucteurs de sy grant cite.

The equivalent of this is not found in Watson, who has skipped various passages in this chapter.　He only says ' By pryde is knowen how Rome is decayed.'　Had he some misgiving that his French guide was leading him astray ?　Or has only lack of space saved him ?

68.—This is perhaps the best place for the chapter on the GIVING OF ALMS AND OTHER GIFTS (96).　With the usual restrictions, we may say that Locher has rendered it rather faithfully and Barclay does not deviate from the Latin in any important detail.　The chapter is not a very interesting one.　It is mainly an elaboration of the text ' Hilarem datorem diligit Deus ' (2 Cor. ix 7).

The best part is perhaps in the Envoy where Barclay gives his personal conclusions.　He narrows the scope of the chapter but he does it forcibly, expressing this little bit of worldly wisdom in a kind of apophthegm, called by the Germans and French a Priamel.

> (1481)　Therefore consyder with thy selfe alone
> 　　　　*To whome* thou gyvest, for that is wyt and skyll ;
> 　　　　And if thou worthy and wyse fynde the person,
> 　　　　Than gyve thy gyft with glad loke and good wyll,
> (1482)　So shall they kyndnes rewardyd be agayne ;
> 　　　　But all is lost that thou dost gyve to fynde
> 　　　　Four sortis of people : [1] the first is a vylayne
> 　　　　Or chorle, for agayne thou shalt hym prove unkynde ;
> 　　　　The second a childe, for his forgetfull mynde
> 　　　　Expellyth kyndnes ; the thirde a man in age ;
> 　　　　The fourth a woman, varyable as the wynde,
> 　　　　Beynge of hir love unstable and volage.

69.—Chapter 46, which deals with RESPECTERS OF PERSONS, is also somewhat connected with Avarice.　It speaks of princes and of judges who do not distribute justice equally but allow themselves to be bribed and corrupted.　Locher has again crushed Brant's double chapter into a single one, but it still contains hints enough for a translator like Barclay to make digressions.　Corruptible judges are mentioned by Locher and by Barclay (who does not betray any influence of the French) only towards the end together with the ' examples,' where Susanna's traitors are spoken of and Andronicus and Benadad (3 Reg. xx) and

---

[1] The construction seems somewhat clumsy, but the meaning is clear.

Tryphon and Jugurtha's saying about Rome's venality (omitted by Riviere). The Latin

> Omne genus nummum veneratur

is by Barclay turned into the pun so familiar to Elizabethan writers. No man so angry, he says,

> (966)   But the holy Crosse shall mytygate his mynde,
> All men doth it great worshyp and honour.

More interesting, however, are the passages where he speaks of righteous and unrighteous kings.

> (961)   Well is that londe and ioyous may it be,
> Whiche is defendyd by such a noble estate ;
> But wo be that londe, whose crowne of Royalte
> Is gyven to a childe, whose counsell drynketh late
> Gyven to the wombe, to ryot and debate. (!)

This may remind us of Piers Plowman's ominous warnings, in reality it is little more than Ecclesiastes x 16 quoted and added to by Locher. But how powerful is Barclay's rendering as compared with the French :

> Ainsi nous celuy regnion
> Estre prince et constitue
> Roy ieune de sens destitue
> Et pour sa terre gouverner
> Car ne le saura discerner
> Et du quel ses consulle entendent
> A gormander et ne.contendent
> Qua boire plusieurs vins nocturnes
> Des gaudeamus diuturnes
> Faire *etc*.

In the prose paraphrase the word *gaudeamus* [1] is of course carefully retained : ' La terre ou il y a ieune roy ou prince nest pas heureuse [This might well be quoted to show how the thunder of a prophet may be imitated by a child's rattle] car il ne la saura gouverner. Et ses conseillers nentendent sy non a gormander beuvant vin nocturnal et en diuturnes gaudeamus.' This becomes in English :

> The londe where as is a yonge kynge or prynce is not well sured, for he cannot governe it dyscretely.   And his counsayllers entendeth not save for to ete and drynke nocturnally and in dyurtenes [*sic*] gaudeamus.

70.—It was the passage from Ecclesiastes, perhaps, which moved Barclay to conclude his chapter with a long Envoy of five stanzas in honour of his young king Henry VIII. These stanzas are all in the best manner of the *rhétoriqueurs*. All five have the same rhymes : *-ate, -ence, -ate, -ence, -ence, -ent, -ence, -ent*, with a sort of burden on

---

[1] It is not in Godefroy.   Littré knows it only as the subjunctive of a Latin word ; the NED. as the beginning of a drinking song of German students not occurring before the nineteenth century.   In reality it is the first word of the Introit of the Mass on some of the principal feast days : *Gaudeamus omnes in Domino*.   As such it occurs also on the woodcut of ch. 108.   And the notes there added to it leave no room for doubt.   It is to that music that the words are still sung in our Catholic liturgy.

'the rede Rose redolent.' There speaks a stirring patriotism out of lines like these :

> (969)  Thoughe that we Brytons be fully separate
> From all the worlde, as is sene by evydence,
> Wallyd with the se, and longe ben in debate
> By insurreccion, yet God hath made defence
> By his provysion, ordeyned us a prynce
> In all vertues most noble and excellent.
> This prynce is Harry, clene of conscience,
> Smellynge as the Rose, ay freshe and redolent.

The metre may be irregular, but the lines have a swinging rhythm which is far from unpleasant. This moralist would have made a very good court poet. I shall quote only one more stanza, the last one, to bring this out even more clearly. Only we must not read such effusions in the light of after events :

> (972)  In hym is iustyce with petye sociate,
> Upon the poor he spareth no expence,
> Nor on the Churche, after lyke maner rate,
> Promotynge men of wysdome and science,
> Servynge his Maker with love and reverence.
> Wherforè, O Englonde, be true of thy intent,
> With faythfull herte do hym obedyence,
> Thanke God, whiche hath the Rose unto the sent !

71.—We must come down from these exalted regions of overstrained language to the last of our Deadly Sins.

Chapter 16 speaks of GLUTTONY AND DRUNKENNESS. A very realistic double chapter in Brant, with one of the earliest descriptions of the *Zutrinken*-custom, which has long survived in German student-circles, and with a special paragraph against the Biersupper, a Low-German type, and a Low-German word.—Locher makes a single chapter of it, containing only the general denunciations of this vice and reproducing only two out of half a dozen ' examples.'

The French paraphrases have reintroduced a few more graphical touches. So there are some good sayings in Watson, e.g. ' Suche folkes drynketh lyke sponges and olde bootes (Comme esponges et comme vielles bottes),' or ' Sle the one and smyte the other, that is the delyte of malycyous glotons and dronkerdes,' which is even better than the French ' Tuer lung frapper lautre se delectes mauvais yvroignes.' The example of ' Thomyris natus,' an unfamiliar name, has become confused in Riviere, and hence also in Drouyn and even worse in Watson.

72.—Barclay follows only the Latin and renders it correctly as far as I can see.—But he has some notable additions at the end. First the mention of Alexander reminds him of a good story, which according to a note he has taken from *Commentator Boetii de disci. sco. Ubi infert de ebrietate,*[1]

---

[1] *De Disciplina Scholarum*, written in the thirteenth century by an unknown author, was attributed to Boethius ; it appeared under his name in a score of separate editions before 1501 (Peddie i, 115), and was very often printed as a sequel to *De Consolatione* (see e.g. Pellechet 2503–2508, 2510–2511, 2525–2526, 2528–2529, 2534, 2539–2544). In the fifteenth century it is always accompanied by a Commentary, whose author is equally unknown. Reprinted in *Patrologia Latina* 64, 1223–1238. I owe these references to F. Bon. Kruitwagen.

and which is alluded to in Newman's famous 'appeal from Philip drunk to Philip sober.' The 'conquerour myghty' playing at chess with one of his knights and drinking deeply was regularly beaten, until Alexander became furious and ordered the knight to be hanged :

(273)   Than sayde the Knyght ' by right and Equyte
        I may apele, syns ye ar thus cruell.'
        Quod Alexander : ' to whome wylt thou apell ?
(274)   ' Knowest thou any that is gretter than I ?
        Thou shalt be hanged, thou spekest treason plaine.'
        The knyght said : ' savynge your honour certaynly,
        I am no traytoure ; apele I woll certayne
        From dronken Alexander tyll he be sober agayne.'
        His lorde than herynge his desyre sounde to reason,
        Differryd the iustyce as for that tyme and season,
(275)   And than after, whan this furour was gone,
        His knyght he pardoned repentynge his blyndenes.

After this story, very well told, with something of Chaucer's sly humour, there follows a more drastic enumeration of various sorts of drunkenness. It is accompanied by a long marginal note in which two Latin poems are quoted in full, but without indication of their source. They are too long to be reproduced here, but I feel bound to copy some of Barclay's very lively lines :

(276)   Some fygthynge, some chydynge, some to other kynde
        Nought lyvynge to them selfe ; and some dotynge Johnn,
        Beynge dronke, thynketh hym as wyse as Salomon.
(277)   Some sowe dronke, swaloynge mete without mesure,
        Some mawdelayne dronke, mournynge lowdly and hye.
(278)   Some spende all that they have and more at wast
        With revell and revell dasshe ' fyll the cup Johnn,'
        Some slepe as slogardes tyll their thryft be gone.
(279)   Some dumme, and some speketh .IX. wordes at thryse.

In his Envoy he takes up Locher's last lines, to show that he does not fall into the other extreme :

(280)   Wyne ne ale hurteth no maner creature
        But sharpeth the wyt, if it be take in kynde ;
        But if it be nat, than I the ensure :
        It dulleth the brayne, blyndynge the wyt and mynde.

73.—SLOTH is the subject of chapter 97. Brant's reprovals of lazy people are rendered pretty faithfully by Locher, who leaves out only the last six lines, closing his chapter with the 'examples' of David and of Rome.

Barclay adds here and there a little of his own. Venting a common complaint he says of laziness :

(1482)  But namely servauntis them self therto aply,
        Despysynge labour, slepynge contynually.

In Stanza 1489 he quotes ' Juvenall the noble Poete ' to confirm his words—-a reference which he did not find in Locher, nor in Riviere, whose amplifications for the rest have certainly not influenced him.

His best passage is the following rendering of two lines in Locher :

> (1486)     A slouthfull creature is as unprofytable
> As smoke or dust is for a mannes iyen,
> Or as a molle or vant [1] mete and able
> For to do profyte within a garden grene ;
> For in no goodnes besyed is he sene
> Save for to slepe and watche the fyre alway,
> Besy in no thynge but in vayne sport and play.

74.—A great deal more interesting, however, is Drouyn's and Watson's treatment of this chapter. Drouyn introduces his paraphrase, as he usually does, with an introductory sentence of his own, which Watson translates,[2] making an addition typical of the plodding Englishman : 'Slouthe is one of the vylest synnes that is.' But Drouyn closes with a curious outburst. Having spoken of Rome's fall through idleness he gives a particular emphasis to Riviere's last words, saying 'ilz (les Romains) sont de present des plus bas.' Then he continues on his own account.

O France tu es maintenant flourissante en puissance honneur chevance et chevalerie. Tu as subiugue Romme Naples toutes les Ytalies et les aliez crestiens et infideles. Ta puissance est sy grande forte et pugille que iusques en Turquie sarrasinaisme et au pays Judaicque on craint ta fureur. Tu es en tous biens habondante, tu es pleine de tristesse [sic, misprint ?] car tu as les plus souffisans clercz qui soyent sur terre. Tu as le ciel, la terre, la mer qui le favorisent. Garde doncques bien etc.

It is the French patriot's pride in the laurels won by Charles VIII in the ' Italian Wars ' a couple of years before. In another chapter (99) they are also alluded to by Riviere, but nowhere have I found in him such an eloquent expression of national pride. It seems evident again that Drouyn stood nearer to political circles or to some noble family than Riviere.

But Watson must have felt uneasy when he reached this passage. The first sentence required only the substituting of another name. ' O noble Englonde, thou arte at this present tyme florysshynge in puyssaunce, honoure, rychesse and chyvalrye.' But the second sentence could not be applied to England at all ! On the contrary ! But by the clever insertion of ' in thy tyme ' he extricated himself from the difficulty and even managed to overbid Drouyn.

Thou hast subdued in thy tyme Rome, Almayne, Fraunce, Scotlonde,[3] and dyvers other regyons, ye and a grete parte of Turkye by thy chevalrous puyssance. Thy puyssance and myght is so incomparable and so pugyll that unto hethenes and Turkye thou art redoubted and fered. Thou art replete with all sapyence and wysdome. [Watson evidently knew no more what Drouyn meant with his

---

[1] I do not know what the word *vant* means here. Jamieson (346) says it is ' a winter trap for birds.' Wright's Dialect Dictionary, s.v. *Callyvan*, mentions this abbreviated form and this meaning as belonging to the East Somerset dialect.

[2] Again changing the word ' ceste satyre ' into ' this chapytre.'

[3] Flodden Field 1513 ! We must not enquire too narrowly into the other dates.— I have copied this extract from the second edition 1515, when I had no longer access to the first (1510) edition.

' tristesse ' than we do, and so he changed the whole passage.]    Thou  arte aourned
and endued with all goodly meurs and condycyons.    Thou  arte fulfylled with dyscrete habytauntes.    Thou  hast the elementes, the erthe and the see that favoureth
the.    Wherefore be well ware *etc*.

Evidently  those  old  translators  could  work  very  conscientiously.
They  would  not  skip  anything,  and  they  were  too  peaceful  to  indulge
in  angry  controversy.    But  silently  and  carefully  they  removed  the
garlands  from  the  foreign  statues  and  placidly  hung  them  in  their  own
national  sanctuary !

## V

## CHAPTERS RELATING TO SINS AGAINST GOD AND HEAVENLY THINGS

75.—Most of the chapters belonging to this category and the two following are among the least interesting in the English translation. I shall just outline the chief contents and characters of each chapter, putting together those that contain more or less similar subjects, indicate the relation of the different versions, and quote in full only such passages as are of exceptional merit or interest.

76.—Chapter 28 treats of DISAPPROVING GOD'S WORKS. Locher has turned Brant's criticism of discontented and complaining men into a panegyric of God's wisdom.—Riviere renders it faithfully, especially dwelling on God's Providence in various sorts of weather. No influence of this upon Barclay, who adds a rebuke to those who

(445)  Grutche in theyr myndes, and openly do blame
       Almyghty God, whan theyre children ar dede.

Drouyn introduces the chapter with an invitation to ' Lunatiques folz estourdiz,' which in Watson becomes ' Innocent fooles and unreasonable creatures.'

77.—Chapter 86 treats of the PROVOCATION OF GOD by men promising themselves a long life, and presuming on a death-bed repentance. In Brant a long chapter, reduced to a short one by Locher with the leading ideas retained. Riviere's versifying is faithful enough. No notable addition, except one, which we find back in Drouyn and in Watson, viz. the pessimistic statement : ' Of a thousande with grete payne cometh one to salvacyon.' [1]—Nothing of this in Barclay, who follows Locher only, but adds an eloquent appeal to God :

(1303)  Whiche to thyntent that thou sholde nat endure
        Eternall deth, sende to tourment cruell
        His onely Son, to red thy soul fro hell.

78.—Chapter 87, which rebukes the wickedness of BLASPHEMY, is of some historical interest. A very severe chapter in Brant, it has become much more pious and vague and sentimental after Locher's operation, and the examples at the end are entirely changed.

---

[1] F. Bon. Kruitwagen informs me that this same percentage is also mentioned by Servasanctus, O.F.M. (c. 1300), Summa de Pœnitentia (Lovanii, Joh. de Westfalia, c. 1485), fol. 225 b. 1.—(Hain-Copinger 14155 ; wrongly in v. Saliceto, Nic. de, Antidotarium Animae.) Some other medieval authors are even less optimistic. An echo of Maillard's sermons again ?

Riviere's rendering is weak as usual. Nor is there anything worth quoting in Drouyn, except his own addition at the end, which is literally in Watson :

> At this tyme the noblesse and gentylmen dothe nothynge but blaspheme and swere by the name of God (iurer le nom de Dieu), and sayth that it apperteyneth not to vyllaynes to swere by God, but to myne advyse no more doth it not to gentylmen to go in to paradyse.

This very good dictum with its malicious point is a reminiscence from some sermon. For it occurs almost literally in the *Sermones Quadragesimales* of the well-known Franciscan preacher Michel Menot (1440–1518) :

> les messieurs . . . sont les premiers a blasphemer en disant qu'il n'appartient pas a villain de renoncer Dieu ; aussi il ne leur appartiendra pas non plus d'entrer en paradis.[1]

The saying must have impressed itself on Drouyn's memory, for he uses it again in his own chapter f.[2]

Barclay's version of this chapter is one of the most eloquent in the whole book. It is rather remarkable that in the same year in which the ' Ship ' appeared, Stephen Hawes had his ' Conversyon of Swerers ' printed. Are we to assume that even at that time this bad habit was as repulsive to cultured people in England as it has been since ? Or did Barclay and Hawes, on the contrary, only voice the powerless protest of the Church against an offensive or even criminal habit, which had assumed abnormal proportions ? Perhaps there was something of both.[3]

Chaucer had already preached on this subject and more than once [4] had used an expression which recurs in Barclay :

> (1313)  The Lord that dyed to red them out of payne
> They have good wyll to tere his herte agayne.

This is a very free rendering of Locher's ' laceri pectoris arma petunt ' and Barclay uses it more than once.[5] Hawes' more tender but also more artificial appeal is entirely inspired by this expression, for which he quotes St. Bernard.[6] The meaning of the woodcut at the head of this chapter, which represents a ' fool ' assailing the crucifix with a spear, must have been very obvious and needs no far-fetched explanation.[7] The old saying had become a natural association of ideas.

---

[1] I take the quotation from A. Samouillan p. 218, who quotes the ed. Paris 1530, f. 159, col. 3.

[2] ' Il nappartient pas a villain de renier dieu, ny aux nobles daller en paradis.' Watson has left it out here. On this chapter see § 191.

[3] The shrewd observer who wrote the ' Italian Relations ' under Henry VII, noticed that the English were ' extremely polite in their language.' Quoted by A. F. Pollard, p. 226.

[4] e.g. C.T., C. 474, 709.          [5] In St. 1331 and earlier in St. 1135.

[6] It recurs in 13 stanzas out of the 46 of which it consists. It is used first in St. 6, and St. Bernard is quoted at the head of St. 43.—Three old editions are known, all in 4°, viz. Wynkyn de Worde 1509 ; W. Copland for R. Troye 1551 ; and J. Butler n.d.—I have used the reprint for the Abbotsford Club, Edinburgh 1865.

[7] As Zarncke gives on p. 431.

As occasions for blasphemy Barclay mentions :

> (1319)    The tables, tenys, cardis and the dyce
>          Ar chefe begynnyng of this unhappines.

One form of blasphemy seems to be quite peculiar to England, as there is no trace of it on the Continent :

> (1321)    To swere the holy Masse, that othe is nowe so vyle
>          In mouth of man, mayden, childe and wyfe.
> (1322)    But nowe eche sweryth the Mas comonly.
> (1323)    In every bargayne, in ale-house and at borde,
>          The holy Mas is ever the seconde worde.[1]

This brings Barclay's indignation to a climax :

> (1324)    And than these houndes can suche excusys fynde
>          As to theyr soules without dout ar damnable,
>          Saynge : ' it is gode to have the Masse in mynde,
>          And the name of God and his sayntis honourable ! '
>          O erytykes, O houndes abhomynable ! *etc.*

79.—Chapter 88 is on GOD'S INDIGNATION ; in Brant largely a paraphrase of biblical quotations, mainly Ecclesiasticus xxxiv 28, Ezechiel xiv 13, and perhaps Jeremias xiv and xv. Locher has left little of it all, but he gives chiefly a pessimistic enumeration of the sins of mankind and how they find their natural punishment in various disasters. Riviere tries to surpass even this pessimism. He denounces especially the priests :

> Ilz prennent seullement le tiltre
> De prestre mais cest com ung traitre ;

and his words are echoed by Drouyn and Watson. Riviere's initial words are even made sharper by Drouyn's and Watson's address to ' foolysshe preestes ' . . . ' it is but a faynt thynge (Dr. chose faincte ; R. faintise) of the preestes nowe a dayes.' Among the evils ' la triste comecte ' is mentioned by Locher,[2] Riviere and Drouyn, not however by Watson, who puts ' grete epedymes ' instead. Drouyn adds ' Nous avons playes, poulz, puces et punaises,' which is rendered by Watson, ' We have plages, lyce, fleen [3] and other venyme.'

Barclay, without a trace of Riviere's influence, mentions among ' dyvers plagis ' :

> (1341)    As pockes, pestylence, and other yll horryble ;

and instead of Locher's comet he puts :

> (1345)    And often se we tokens of ferefull punysshement
>          By sygnes and sterres of the clere fyrmament.

---

[1] This oath occurs in ' The Interlude of Health and Wealth ' (Malone Society Reprints 1907) lines 407 and 650. The fact may be of some importance for dating the play.

[2] Not by Brant. It belonged to the Latin humanistic stock-in-trade.

[3] = fleas. The OE. form of the plural, also used by Chaucer and Lydgate ; cf. NED.

80.—PRESUMPTION ON GOD'S MERCY is the subject of chapter 14 in Brant as well as in Locher. But the one is not a translation of the other. Brant's chapter is full of proverbial concrete expressions, but hardly any of them is to be found in the Latin, which insists more in general that all sins are sure to be punished sooner or later, quoting as examples : Sodom, Rome and Pharao. These generalities are also in Barclay, who inserts David among the examples (246). Fortunately he inserts also a truly English *exemplum necis Richardi tercii Anglorum regis* :

> (247)  Remember Richarde, lately kynge of price,
> In Englonde raynynge unrightwisely a whyle,
> Howe he [1] ambycion and gyleful covetyse
> With innocent blode his handes dyd defyle ;
> But howbeit that Fortune on hym dyd smyle
> Two yere or thre, yet God sende hym punysshment
> By his true servant : the rede Rose redolent.

In the eyes of a loyal subject of the Tudors Richard III reigned 'unrightwisely' of course, and defiled his hands with innocent blood, and the Battle of Bosworth was nothing but a divine punishment. So this was a good example of the fate that will overtake a presumptuous sinner and at the same time a fitting occasion to pay a little tribute of homage to the king regnant, the 'rede Rose redolent' whom the author would celebrate whenever he had an opportunity.[2]

The tradition that culminated in Shakespeare's ideal of perverse cruelty was already firmly established.

There is a short reference to actual occurrences of the time in the Envoy :

> (250)  And remember howe ye daily punysshed be
> With dyvers dyseases both uncouthe and cruel,
> And all for your synne ; but suche as escapeth free
> And styl lyve in syn may fere the peynes of helle.

This does not seem to refer in general to the continual epidemic pestilences of the time, but more in particular to such diseases as the French Pox, which are distinctly mentioned in an earlier chapter.[3]

Riviere retains all Locher's generalities, without becoming any more concrete. Nor has the chapter improved at Drouyn's hands. I need not quote more than the very last sentence of Watson's translation :

And yf that he punysshe us durynge our vycyousnesse knowe that we shall se oure selfe empesshed in the infernall pyte of helle after our dyscease.

*Empesshed* is a curious word here, but it is literally from the French : 'empeschez aux infernaulx palus denfer.' The meaning becomes clearer from Riviere :

> Saichez quenpeschez
> Nous verrons apres noz deces
> Car il nous mectra dans les seps
> Denfer *etc.*

---

[1] There is evidently some misprint here; but Cawood has the same as Pynson.
[2] See e.g. § 70.          [3] See ch. 4, St. 96, § 276.

81.—IMPROVIDENCE is a fruitful subject for Brant and no less than three chapters are devoted to it.

Chapter 12 insists upon weighing the consequences of one's actions in time, adducing the examples of Adam, Jonathan, Caesar, Nicanor and Asahel, after an ironical introduction about taking thought during or after the action, as women are apt to do. Locher omits the last example for lack of space and polishes away the irony of the introduction. So does Barclay. But his direct model for part of this chapter seems to have been Riviere again, for he brings in most of Riviere's additions :

> Et le foul plain de faitz non stables
> Ferme les huys de ses estables
> Quant les chevaulx en sont sailliz,[1]

= Barclay's

> (212)  Whan the stede is stolyn to shyt the stable dore
> Comes small pleasoure, profyte or vauntage.

The example of Jonathan seems to have been worked out partly under the influence of Riviere, although he has ' to a cyte ' (215) for ' en la cite ptolomaide.' Similarly the story of Nicanor receives some suspicious-looking additions :

> (218)  By Judas and the children of Israel,

sounds like

> Par iudas et gens disrael.

And that his head was cut off is not in Locher but in Riviere :

> Car la teste luy fut tranchee.

This loan is somewhat disguised, however, by the addition : ' as the Bybyll sheweth playne ' (218). But Barclay's version resembles Riviere more than the real Bible story (2 Mach. viii 10 sqq., xv 30 sqq.).

Towards the end Barclay speaks

> (219)  Of Goddes lawes and his commandement,

of which there is nothing in Locher, but which sounds like Riviere's ' les dispositions de dieu.'

Watson tries to lengthen the chapter by putting in synonyms and double expressions probably to fill out the page, which is to contain only the title of the following chapter.[2]

82.—A similar subject is treated in chapter 15 where Brant adduces some examples to illustrate Luke xiv 28–30.[3] The examples adduced are Nabuchodonosor, Nemrod, Lucullus, the Pyramides and the Labyrinth.—Locher omits the last two but adds Crassus. Barclay follows

---

[1] Also in Drouyn : ' Le fol plein dinpourveance quant les chevaulx sen son fouye ferment lhuys de lestable ' ; and in Watson : ' The foole full of unpurveyance shytteth the stable doore whan the horse is stolen.'

[2] That this was a favourite arrangement appears from chapters 2, 9, 12, 13, 16, 19, 23, 27, 40, 55 etc.

[3] I greatly wonder finding that Zarncke has missed this obvious reference.

him without perceptible influence from Riviere. He mentions the
'confusion of language' (256) in connexion with Nemrod's attempt,
but this was only natural and can hardly have been suggested by Riviere's
'Ou fut faicte diffusion De langues' *etc*.[1]

Interesting is Watson's expression :

> Who that wyll builde and make grete edyfyces, fayre castelles and ynnes [= de
> beaulx chasteaulx et de logis] ought for to have grete foyson of gold and sylver
> [= doit avoir or argent, Dr.],

which stands for Barclay's shorter :

> (257)   For great byldynges requyreth great rychesse.

The examples of Lucullus and Crassus are elaborated by Riviere and
his followers—where I read the curious saying in Watson that Crassus
'aroused[2] the flesshe assyryques with blode,' meaning Drouyn's and
Riviere's 'les *chars* assiricques' (L. Assyrias carras). 'Chars' looks
somewhat like 'Chair'!

83.—Chapter 70 returns to the same charge ; it inculcates the necessity
of taking precautions betimes, of making hay while the sun shines, and
winds up with the admonition of Proverbs vi 6, 'Go to the ant,
O sluggard.' A rather tame chapter tamely rendered by Locher.—No
trace of Riviere's influence on Barclay. *De naso ad fauces*, which is
skipped by the French, appears as :

> (1050)   Theyr vayne myndes to farther thynges is dull
>          Save on that whiche from hande to mouth is brought.

And the ant as :

> (1055)   Lerne, man, of the symple emet purveaunce.

This animal receives another name from Watson : 'I praye the,
take ensample at the pysmyres.'—This same word is used in the Geneva
Bible (1560). Wycliffe used the word *aunte*, but added the gloss 'ether
pissemyre' as more popular. It survives in dialects.[3] To the 'formyes,'
which are in Riviere, Drouyn added 'les mouches a myel.' Hence
Watson's 'The hony bees dothe so in lyke wyse. And by this meanes[4]
they perysshe not for hongre in the frostye wynter.' A forcible sentence
is the following translation from Drouyn, who found only hints for it
in Riviere : 'And whan indygence sowneth him, poverte calleth hym,
myschaunce foloweth hym, hongre atteyneth hym and all vyle chaunce.'

84.—Chapter 18 on the SERVING OF TWO MASTERS is largely
a paraphrase of Matth. vi 24, without, however, the application there

---

[1] Against Fraustadt 43.

[2] Aroused = arroused = to sprinkle, to moisten. A common word in the sixteenth century, and still in the beginning of the seventeenth century (NED.). I
may here mention the occurrence of the word *moyne* in the introductory sentence :
'Yf he have moyne ynoughe for to fynysshe it with (= sil a asses pour tout bien
faire).' The earliest occurrence of this word in the NED. is towards the end of
the century only.

[3] Cf. NED.

[4] The earliest occurrence of *means* with a singular construction, mentioned in
the NED., is an anonymous letter of 1512. The second instance is from 1606.

given.  Brant heaps one proverb upon the other, mainly insisting on the impossibility of being every man's friend.  Locher has omitted only the last ten lines and has not inserted any notable additions.  It is not to be wondered at that Riviere should have added the sequel at the end :

> . . . Si fort quil ayme mieulx
> En soy damnant prendre labour
> Sans prendre soulas ne secour
> Que servir a Dieu vivre en paix
> Dont pour le present ie me tais.

The last line was probably added because Riviere felt that he was trespassing !  It is more strange that Barclay should not have insisted more on this natural conclusion.  He does mention it :

> (301)   Therefore I the counseyll for thyne owne behove :
> Let go this worlde and serve thy Lorde above.

But such an addition occurring in the middle of the chapter (with another in the beginning, Stanza 297, which is also in Locher) does certainly not prove any influence from the French.[1]  Locher's

> Jam terram ignotam querit gentesque pererrat

is rendered a little more concrete by Riviere :

> Par la mer court les undes perce
> Il chemine en Grece en Perce
> Il traverse toute la gent.

A great deal more concrete and better, however, in Barclay :

> (300)   Now workynge, now musynge, now renynge, now rydynge,
> Now on see, nowe on londe, than to se agayne,
> Sometyme to Fraunce, and nowe to Flaunders or Spayne.

Best of all is his picture of him who strives to be a friend to every man :

> (304)   Oft must he stoupe, his bonet in his honde,
> His maysters backe he must oft shrape and clawe,
> His breste anoyntynge, his mynde to understonde ;
> But be it goode or bad, therafter must he drawe.
> Without he can jest, he is nat worth a strawe ;
> But in the meane tyme, beware that he none checke,
> For than layth Malyce a mylstone in his necke.

There is only a suggestion for this in Locher, and nothing more in Riviere.  One proverb in Locher appears both in Barclay and in Watson :

> (298)   And that blynde fole mad and ignorant
> That draweth thre boltis in one bowe,
> At one marke shall shote to hye or to lowe.

Or as Watson has it : ' In lykewyse he hytteth the butte veray late that bendeth many bowes,' which is literally from the French.—For the rest this chapter affords a glaring instance of how Watson tries to fill out a page in order to have the title of the following chapter at the bottom.  This mechanical result of the intimate co-operation between

---

[1] Against Fraustadt 30.

METHODIST COLLEGE LIBRARY
Fayetteville, N. C.                    38041

writer and printer has not been generally recognized and, of course, cannot be understood from a reprint, unless it be a facsimile. To impress it upon the reader I must quote at least one sentence. Here is Drouyn :

> Il ne scaurit a tout penser—ne avoir semblablement une bonne heur de repoz— soit a la messe, beuvant, mengeant—tousiours pense a ses affaires.

I have put in some dashes to make the comparison easier. Every phrase is drawn out by Watson :

> It is impossible that his sensuall wyt may comprehende, and have so many dyvers cogytacyons in an instante, and execute them as they should be—[we have only got over six little words]—he hath not one good hour of rest in a hole weke,— whether that he be at the churche herynge Masse or that he be at home at his dyner, or in the feldes, ete he or drynke he—his thoughte is ever upon his werkes that he hath to do.

85.—In two chapters a comparison is undertaken between HEAVEN AND EARTH. Chapter 43 inculcates the worthlessness of earthly life and joy as compared with eternity. Of classical allusions there are none. Locher has the same leading ideas, reserving his classicism for expressions like *Rector Olympi* and *fumantia tartara*.

No influence of Riviere upon Barclay, nor many interesting passages.[1] I only hope the reader does not begin to feel like our translator :

> (637)   My hande is wery : fayne wolde I rest a space.

Let him take courage, however, from the same consideration :

> But folys comyth to my shyp so besely,
> That to have rest they wyll graunt me no grace,
> That nede I must theyr lewdness notefy.

Something of the same kind occurs in Riviere, but both have taken the suggestion from Locher.

86.—Chapter 89 speaks of the folly of doing more for the earth than for heaven and similarly leaves out classical examples. Locher has a longer introduction and makes the avaricious man travel over *hadriacum pelagus* instead of

> In Norwegen, Pylappen landt (l. 11).

He adds the slaves of *immitis Cytherea*, and at the end he makes a somewhat hasty conclusion.

Barclay paraphrases Locher with rather more than ordinary freedom, without however showing any other influence. He skips the *Cytherea*, but, echoing in his own way the interest of the great discoveries of the time, he dilates upon sea-voyages :

> (1357)   For money man sayles the troublous se of Spayne,
> And moche of the worlde he compassyth about
> Of ieopardy and peryll without all maner dout ;

---

[1] Drouyn expands Riviere somewhat in this chapter, for no perceptible reason. And Watson follows him of course. From his translation I note the following expressions : ' gouffre infernall ' becomes *gulfre infernall* ; ' vigueur ' is translated by *rygoure* three times, so a misprint seems out of the question ; ' ingurgitez aux tenebres denfer ' is rendered by *ingurgyted in the obscurtes of helle*, surely a somewhat peculiar form of the verb and with a meaning for which the NED. does not give earlier examples than the beginning of the seventeenth century.

and so on for two more stanzas.  In this whole chapter the preacher feels himself in his element.  The excesses of dress are, however, touched upon only in two lines ; when speaking of proud people :

> (1355)   With dyvers garnamentis presentynge statelynes
> Only on clothynge bestowynge theyr ryches.

But Riviere, the young man, pounces upon this subject, which he connects with that of Cytherea.  He has a very long and rather sensual description of the insinuations of female finery, winding up with the reflection that all this

> Nest que nourriture a vers.

A fair example of that strange perversity of taste prevailing in the fifteenth century.[1]  Drouyn leaves out most of the details, and Watson has some further omissions and even drops the idea of all-consuming Death.  This is what is left :

> The women of the presente tyme prepareth theyr hedes and fayre frontes with perles and other rychesses, and paynteth theyr vysages with oyntementes.  Of the rounde pappes I wyll wryte and of the whyte brestes, polysshed lyke crystall, that they shewe for to provoke yonge men unto carnalytees.

87.—Chapter 47 treats of THE TWO WAYS : the narrow way to heaven and the broad one to hell, the latter often more difficult than the former, yet preferred by the great majority.  Brant concludes with the gloomy reflection that out of all the Israelites that escaped from Egypt only two reached the Promised Land.  Locher expands the first part of this short chapter so much that he has no room left for the last twelve lines.  Locher's version is followed by Barclay without any striking additions or expressions.  Nor is there anything remarkable in Riviere.—Drouyn mistaking the meaning of the woodcut introduces his paraphrase with an invitation to ' folz chartiers ' translated by Watson :

> Come out of woddes and of vyllages folysshe carters and labour this chapytre [Dr. venes charrier ce sentier ; Watson confuses the metaphor !], where as ye shall fynde good erthe that bereth odyferous fruyte [fruict odorant] and floure of good doctryne.

88.—Chapter 107 is a sermon on the same subject, but a double one, and so Locher has ' translated ' only half of it.  It contains that favourite subject of the early Humanists, the story of Hercules' dream which has inspired Locher's *Concertatio*, but which he alludes to here only in general terms calling Hercules *Amphytrionadem*.  Barclay follows him, skipping the unfamiliar name.  With him he criticizes those that are desirous

> (1683)   To be callyd Doctours or Maysters of degre,
> Moste clere in wysdome of the Unyversyte ;
> But these names coveyt they nat for this intent
> The christen to infourme that of wyt ar indigent,

but only out of vainglory !

> (1684)   Such walke in the way that is on the left syde,
> On rockes and clyffis and hyghe mountains of pryde.

---

[1] See Huizinga 231 sqq.

Of his own accord he adds :

> (1685)   And other with theyr wordes hye and retorycall
> Theyr sentences paynt in favour for to come
> Or therby to purchase a name of hye wysdome.

But these are the ways ' to Hellys depe donygon.'

There is nothing very remarkable in Riviere nor in Drouyn, except that he does not here prefix his favourite introductory sentence, probably because he found one handy in his model. Watson translates him closely.

89.—Chapter 106 is in Brant a paraphrase of biblical quotations tending to prove the necessity of GOOD WORKS (Math. xxv 1 sqq., 14 sqq. ; Prov. xxx 24 sqq., xxv 16 ; Wisd. iv 7 ; Psalm xlviii 11 sq. ; Matth. iii 10, vii 19). Of all these Locher has retained hardly anything, his main point being the duty of PERSEVERANCE. He does mention good works but only in general as ' fidei sacre documenta.' The law-abiding Englishman expands this into :

> (1670)   So to do good dedes it is a thynge laudable.
> As the Churche of God to support and meyntayne
> In paynge tythes to be true and verytable.

But one must persevere in this, in order to be ready ' at domys dredefull day ' (1674).—The most remarkable passage in Riviere is the motto, which is one of the best specimens of his ideal of poetic craftsmanship : [1]

> Quiconque a sa lampe remplie
> Duylle sa lumiere remplist
> Et si apres est desemplie
> Et de bien faire nacomplist
> Parce que sa vertuz nemplist
> La porte des cieulx descouverte
> Au bons ne luy sera ouverte.

Drouyn has copied this motto like the others, and so Watson had to translate it. It is an illustration of the cut, representing the Foolish Virgins, but Watson does not seem to have realized this, he inserts the cut belonging to chapter 31 in its stead, and ' translates ' :

> He the whiche hath his lampe replete
> With oyle *he maye the better se* (!)
> Also he that hathe vertues grete
> And accomplyssheth them truely
> He lyveth in grete prosperyte
> And he the whiche dothe here lyve well
> Shall never come in fyre of hell.

This is the beginning of the chapter. From its conclusion I may quote a passage to show how mechanically he executed his task. Drouyn wrote : ' Le royaulme de dieu point nous le regardons levant les yeulx. Mais regardons aux choses inferiores ' *etc.* And Watson writes : ' The realme of God we beholde nothynge with our eyen elevate. But have unto the thynges interyours ' (*sic!*) *etc.*

[1] See § 15.

90.—The duty of PERSEVERANCE is inculcated by Brant in chapter 84, where he paraphrases Luc. ix 62, Exod. xvi 3, Prov. xxvi 11, Apoc. iii 15 sqq., and quotes Lot's wife as a warning example.—Locher dilates upon the first two passages only, and so do his translators. Barclay expands the example from Exodus at more than usual length (three stanzas—1248 sqq.—to render two lines), and Locher's example of the patient not following the doctor's advice is elaborated very concretely in three run-on stanzas, of which the first is a very bold one :

(1252)   The quakynge seke in bed lyenge prostrate,
Half dede, half lyvynge, by some mortall wounde,
And of all his myghtis of manhode clene pryvate,
Can nat be hole, but if plasters be bounde
Unto his grefe to clens it by the grounde,
Purgynge it by suche playsters mundifycatyve
And than it closynge by playsters sanatyve

(1253)   And corrosyves.  Somtyme he must endure
To purge that flesshe whiche is putrefyed
Kepynge and observynge good dyet alway sure.

91.—Watson's translation of Riviere's and Drouyn's motto gives a good example of the use of the word ' whanhope ' [1] in the meaning of ' delusion,' but it need not be quoted here. What must be quoted is the end of the chapter. Riviere concludes his poetic paraphrase with a good clinching couplet :

Car dung grant bien ung seul quartier
Ne vault rien sil nest fait entier.

But Drouyn breaks off his prosifying just before this. His patient labours must have been interrupted by some such disturbance as had inspired Brant when writing chapter 62.[2] It made him so angry that suddenly the man sprang out from behind the rhetorician. Convention and tradition are forgotten, the mask is thrown to the ground, and instead of the moralizing ' bachelier es droitz ' we see before us with a thrill of surprise—the grumbling face of our next-door neighbour :

Ceulx qui font le charivary [what can he mean ?] peuvent bien estre avec les aultres qui de nuyt vont par les rues faisant sy grant bruyt quil nest homme qui puisse reposer. Ilz font commencement de leur enfer. [They must be very bad. No wonder:—] car ilz brullent chevaulx [!] et font les plus villaines puanteurs quil est possible de faire [reason enough to make a man angry !], de quoy ie me mesbahy comment on les peult souffrir que iustice ny met la main [Yes, the police ought to put a stop to that nuisance !] car de largent quilz demandent [do they ?] cest contre Dieu et raison [of course !] et se la coustume luy soeuffre, Dieu pourtant ne le permect point [that is a consolation !] et tres mal faict de telles choses souffrir.

With this querulous complaint he closes his chapter.—And Watson had to translate all this :

They the whiche reyse up perturbacyons [I wonder if he knew what Drouyn's charivaris were] may wel go with the other that gothe in the strete by nyght, makynge

---

[1] Drouyn's ' oultrecuidance,' which occurs repeatedly, is always rendered by ' whanhope.'    [2] See § 284.

suche noyse that nobody can have no reste in theyr beddes.  They make the be-
gynnynge of theyr helle, for they borne horses and maketh the moost vyllaynous
stynke that can be thought or ymagyned [so he makes it even worse] of the whiche
I am sore abasshed that the Justice setteth not handes on them, for the monye
that they take and demande is agaynst God and reason and if they be suffred here,
yet God for all that permytteth it not.   And is ryght evyll done to suffre suche
thynges, *for it were ynough to enfecte a hole countree with.*

Watson has added this parting squeeze probably to show his sympathy
with Drouyn's grievance, whatever it might have been.

## VI

## CHAPTERS RELATING TO INJUSTICE, DISHONESTY AND UNCHARITABLENESS.

92.—From the subjects treated in this category we clearly see that Brant wrote more against the ' Sins of Society ' than against the offences of real criminals. For one of the worst acts of injustice is discussed in chapter 20 on FINDING. Brant teaches here that things found must never be kept, but given back to the owner or his heirs or else to the poor. Whoever does otherwise deserves the punishment of Achan (whom he calls Achor) or even worse.—Locher translates this fairly faithfully, only skipping the mention of Achan.—Barclay somewhat mitigates the severity of Brant's (and Locher's) doctrine by omitting to speak of the case when the lawful owner is unknown.[1] For the rest he states the alternative even more pointedly than his model:

> (337) Suche folys fere no thynge everlastynge payne,
> Nor note nat, that without true restytucion
> It small avayleth to have made confessyon.

At the end he has a peculiar addition:

> (344) Here myght I touche executours in this cryme,
> Blamynge theyr dedys, dysceyte and covetyse,
> If it were nat for wastynge of my tyme ;
> For mende they wyll nat them in any wyse
> Nor leve no poyntes of theyr disceytfull gyse.
> Let them take parte of that whiche I here note
> And be partynge foles in this present bote.

In the Envoy he takes the ' executours ' to task again but in a more serious tone :

> (345) And wast here the goodes of hym that is past ;
> The soule lyeth in payne, ye take your pleasours
> With his ryches, damnynge your owne soule at the last.

93.—Chapter 93 speaks of various forms of USURY, Brant depicts them with interesting detail, but Locher leaves out the most concrete examples, summarizes the more general points and gives instead a longer

---

[1] It is in Riviere and Drouyn. Watson's version may be quoted, were it only for the curious combination of the two meanings of *ought*: ' And yf that ye knowe not hym that ought it (celuy a qui est) nor none of his heyres, ye ought for to dystrybute it among poore folkes to the prouffyte of hym that ought it (tu le dois donner pour Dieu au proffit de celuy a qui cest).'

introduction and a longer epilogue.   Locher's ideas are all in Barclay.
His comparison of Jews and Christians is all in favour of the Jews.

> (1435)  Thoughe the Jewes lyve in errour and darknes,
>         Gyven to usury, as labourynge men oft sayes,
>         Yet ar they more gyven to pytye and mekenes,
>         And almes than Christen men ar nowe adayes ;
>         In usury we ensue the Jewes wayes.

This idea of Locher's is also in Riviere, but Drouyn added some restrictions which we find translated in Watson :

> I say that the Jewes be more charytable, more iuste, and more verytable than
> they be, for al that they kepe grete usuryes and more than the crysten men, and be
> better in theyr lawe.   They be ravyishers of goodes as the Crystyens be *etc.*

94.—USURY is also the main subject of chapter 25, at least in the
translation.   In the original its trend had rather been to criticize continual borrowing and taking on credit and the delay of paying one's
debts both to God and to man, with references to Sodom and Gomorrha,
to the Fall of Jerusalem and the fate of the Ninivites.   But Locher
laid more stress on the evil of usury and on our debts to God, putting
the Ninivites instead of the Egyptians, whom he calls *Nilicolas*.

For this chapter Barclay seems to have taken Riviere as his principal
guide to no small harm of his work.   He has the same misunderstandings
of Locher's text.   He says the borrower

> (387)   To the devourynge wolfe is most lyke or semblable,

just as Riviere called him ' a lafame loup semblable.'   The following
stanza is non-committal, but then follows :

> (389)   Where they two borewed they promys to pay thre,

and the nearest approach to this is in Riviere's

> Ce debteur prive de bon sens
> Devoir pour cent escutz deux cens.

Stanza 390 is an original one without special merit.   Stanzas 391–393
are more doubtful again.   It seems that Riviere was laid aside here,
for otherwise Barclay would not have missed Riviere's theory of
interest :

> Par ce quen ce faisant vendue
> Serait lors lespace du temps
> Qui est trop enorme contemps
> Veu que le temps nest pas a vous
> Mais a Dieu qui le donne a tous
> Ainsi quil nous est necessaire,

the prose paraphrase of which appears in Watson's English :  ' God
. . . hath defended it, bycause that ye sell the space of tyme, for ye
sell the tyme the whiche is not yours but Goddes that lenneth it to you.'

Stanza 394 is again more like Riviere's version.[1]  Stanza 395 betrays even more clearly its French origin :

> Et aussi en *Nilcolas*
> Pensez quun par piteux delas
> Et par dures pugnicions
> Et griefves desolacions
> Dieu pugnit par grans malefices
> Par ce quilz furent plains de vices.

This refers to Locher's *Nilicolas*, but if Barclay had looked at the Latin he could hardly have missed the real meaning, especially as there was a marginal note referring to Exodus iii, a note which has been left out in the French version.  He now innocently ' translates '

> (395)  The rightwyse God also dyd sore chastyce
>           The Nilicolyans and them utterly destroy *etc.*[2]

Stanza 396 in its first half is almost literally from Riviere :

> Et pour revenir au propos
> Qui prent a credit de chacun
> Et diceulx nen peult payer ung
> Est ung grant foul semblable au loup
> Qui devoure tout a ung coup.

Compare with this Barclay's

> (396)  But to our purpose to retourne agayne :
>           He that ought boroweth whiche he can nat pay,
>           Of a wolf ravysshynge foloweth the trayne.

For the rest of this stanza, which is rather difficult in Riviere, he must have consulted Locher, but the following and last one is nearer Riviere again.  On the whole, therefore, we may say that this chapter is derived from Riviere.

95.—Chapter 102 enumerates VARIOUS FORMS OF DECEIT. Brant, who devotes nearly a hundred lines to the subject, makes it extremely interesting, but Locher has again applied his peculiar condensing process, because it had to become a single chapter of thirty-eight lines ; but even in this short space he indulges in so much humanistic circumlocution that I can find in it only seventeen lines of Brant and certainly not the most interesting ones, viz. the motto with six introductory lines about Alchemy and the universality of deceit, l. 13 about the corruption of wine, l. 30 about false weights and measures, ll. 44–48 about counterfeit money and hypocritical ecclesiastics, and an idea for the epilogue in ll. 85 sq. and 90.  Riviere's paraphrase does not materially differ from Locher's version.  In his usual introduction Drouyn invites the alchemists

---

[1] Barclay changed however the obvious misprint *Sobime* into *Solym*. But Drouyn had no such critical faculties, and so we still find in Watson ' the cyte of Sobyme.'

[2] It need hardly be said that Drouyn copied the name.  Here is his version in Watson's literal translation : ' Thynke upon Sodome and Gomorre where so many folkes perysshed, and on the cyte of Sobyme, the whiche cytees by theyr grete synnes perysshed pyteouslye, as Nylycolas dyde [in the singular : Dr. comme fit Nylicolas] how well that [combien que] the folke of Nylycola were blessyd of our Lorde.'

(in Watson's translation) ' to make alcumyne dyvyne.' [1]   He speaks of
' the Taverners thet medleth [Fr. brolons] the wyne, that of whyte and
rede maketh claret [Fr. le vin claret] and fylleth theyr wynes ful of
chalke [Fr. chaus], and do dyvers other evylles of whiche I wyll holde
my pease [Fr. me taire] for this present tyme,' but the words are so
literally translated from the French that they have no documentary
value.—More independent is Watson's evidence about base coin.   Drouyn
wrote :  ' Ung tas sont aussy de roigneurs descutz et daultres pieces dor
qui est grand fraude par ce quil ne poise point son point et pareillement
de largent.'  Watson brings in something of his own experience :

> There is also a grete meyne [2] of clyppers of golde and sylver and wasshers of
> monye by newe invencyons, so that the kynges coyne is gretely destroyed, for whan
> it is lyght they put it in vessel,[3] and so there is no monye styrynge, because there is
> so moche vessell.

Barclay follows Locher step by step, so that his small similarity with
Riviere in the beginning where they both change the exclamation into
an invocation must be a mere coincidence (Stanza 1604).—In his expressions, however, he is independent enough.   The Latin ' Clericus et
monachi hipocrisi falsisque laborant Mentibus ' becomes :

> (1610)   And suche as within the cloyster doth abyde
>          Fyle theyr relygion oft by the same offence,
>          Faynynge them sayntis whan they are in presence,
>          With ypocresy payntynge theyr countenance
>          So clokynge and hydynge, theyr yll mysgovernaunce.

In his description of coiners he uses some of the same technical
expressions as Watson :

> (1612)   In iniust coyne is found also abusyon
>          And disceyt, whiche doth all the worlde defyle,
>          By clyppynge and wasshynge and lyke dymynusyon.

He has a good-humoured knock at dishonest taverners :

> (1615)   But to touche a teverners hye experience :
>          Howe lyghtly the knave can brewe a bowle of wyne !
>          As who sayth that he hath the craft and scyence
>          To amende that thynge that Goddes hye prudence
>          Hath made parfyte !   But he, his owne to save,
>          By newe brewyd wyne, men bryngeth to theyr grave.

### 96.—In chapter 48 Brant laments THE DECAY OF THE GUILDS.

Craftsmen no longer understand their crafts, they are too arrogant, too hurried ;—
Apelles the painter was already rebuked for it ; shoemakers, blacksmiths, car-
penters, tailors, printers, all are affected by the same disease ; or they are stupid
and lazy and spend more than they earn, and in the market trade becomes a farce
through the wild bargaining of ' des Kollschen böttchen : Dat halff ab ' (1. 86 sq.).

Locher had at first skipped this chapter with its great variety of contents,

---

[1] In the motto Riviere calls it *alchimye* ; Drouyn *arquemye* ; Watson *alcumye* ;
Barclay speaks of *alkemy*.
[2] meinie (= OF. meiné) = a multitude.   Skelton speaks of ' a mayny of rude
villayns ' ;  Caxton of ' a great meyny of ghees.'—NED.
[3] I have not been able to find out what he means by the word *vessel*.

but eventually he decided to append it,[1] using, however, only forty lines for Brant's ninety. He gives the main ideas of the beginning as far as (not including) ' Apelles,' omits mentioning any of the different crafts, adds something about the dishonesty of merchants, and winds up by saying that it is useless to waste more words on craftsmen, because ' livor pectora cuncta trahit.'

Barclay follows this Latin extract only, although he expands the introduction and adds a well-meaning exhortation at the end [there is no real Envoy]. The best and most original saying is in Stanza 1905 :

> Where a great thynge for lytell pryce is bought
> It sygnyfyeth that it is stolen or nought.

As the large woodcut did not leave room for a motto in the original, Drouyn has copied Riviere's first six lines to serve the same purpose. They were curiously misunderstood by Watson. The French (in Riviere and Drouyn) has

> La turbe de plusieurs iniques
> Meschans malostruz mecaniques
> Qui de bras et leurs instrumens
> Gaignent leurs vivres et alimens
> Huche nostre nef et appelle
> Et les retyre tous a elle.

The word ' instrumens,' which in reality meant the tools of the various crafts, reminded Watson only of *musical* instruments, and so he translated :

> The turbe of men full of inyquyte
> As unthryfty mecanykes with many mo
> Playenge on organs by extremyte
> Getynge theyr lyvynge with playenge to and fro
> And without ony reason they call our shyppe so
> That the shyppe redowndeth all of the sowne
> Comynge in to it as they wolde cast all downe.

The rest of the chapter adheres very closely to Drouyn's letter. In the introductory sentence Watson ventures to use the word *satyre*—' Lynatyke mecanykes come and hear my satyre.' But it is far from certain that he knew it as an English word ; for he writes also : ' Such folke ought to suffre a *cathaire* syth that they lyve so falsely,' where the French

---

[1] In the first Latin edition this chapter was the very last (it is still one of the last in the others), and Brant himself added a curious appendix to it about one Nicolaus Renner, whom he calls an *acuphahus* (needle-eater, I take it), at Strassburg. Only the Marnef-translator has translated it, but it is interesting enough to be summarized here, as it has never been noticed. ' My work is finished,' Brant says, ' but you are not in my ship, O my friend Nicolaus Renner, though you make innumerable fools ; many see your mouth full of needles, you eat and drink and swallow them and bring them back again, and by this trick you deceive fools everywhere. Now and then you rise as a god to heaven and then you fall down again and celebrate your Easter by drinking deeply [*Salvator ludorum paschalium*, explains the margin]. Your mother must·have been a monkey, giving you your cheeks and your many tongues and your quick wit. I do not know if I am to place you among Frenchmen or Spaniards, among Germans or Italians. But here I shall give you a seat among the artizans of various trades, for you cannot be alone long. And I shall travel with you to the Land of Fools, and your own town [it was Brant's native town also !] will provide you with many foolish companions.'

original has : ' telles gens doyvent souffrir ung *carathaire* puisque sy faulcement vivent.'  This renders Riviere's

> Et ceulx cy pour leurs maulvais faire
> Doivent souffrir ung carathaire.

97.—Chapter 59 reproves INGRATITUDE by one continuous string of proverbial sayings, barely one-third of which can be faintly recognized in Locher, who prefers to speak of ungrateful towns.  He therefore leaves his model altogether and mentions the attitude of Rome to Camillus, of Attica to Solon, of Sparta to Lycurgus, and the ' ingrata patria ' of Scipio.  Both Barclay and Riviere follow the Latin.  There is no influence perceivable of the latter upon the former.  The proverbial character of the chapter has completely disappeared from these poetic paraphrases, but Barclay manages to add a new proverb here and there :

> (842)    He must of maners also be commendable,
> And of his speche als pleasaunt as he can ;
> For an old proverbe true and verytable
> Sayth that good lyfe and maners maketh man.

At the end he attaches a long Envoy of five octaves all ending with the same refrain :

> (851)        an olde sayde sawe :
> Who is hym that to his Maker is unkynde.

A good piece of rhetorical eloquence on man's debt of gratitude to God.

Drouyn's prose dilates somewhat on wages, and Watson translates it all slavishly (except the last part of the last sentence).  ' O toy esparte ' becomes ' O thou Esparte ' and ' Terre de actique ' (Attica) ' londe of Actyque.'  A ludicrous effect is obtained by the translation of ' Sy tu veulx avoir nourice dhonneur ne soyes ignorant de ces choses,' which Watson renders : ' Yf thou wylte have a nourryse of honour, be not ygnoraunt of her necessytees ' !

98.—Chapter 21 on FAULT-FINDING has also been greatly changed by Locher.  In Brant it is a homely paraphrase of Matth. vii and Luke iv 23, but the Latin aims at greater stateliness by introducing fine-sounding quotations from Juvenal and Cicero, and by ending with a solemn address to priests and preachers.  Barclay follows this Latin version with felicitous freedom.  His most conspicuous change is the replacing of Juvenal's classical by more ecclesiastical names.

> (327)    Many them selfe fayne as chaste as was Saynt Johnn
> And many other fayne them meke and innocent,
> Some other as iust and wyse as Salomon,
> As holy as Poule, as Job as pacyent,
> As sad as Senecke, and as obedyent
> As Abraham, and as Martyn vertuous,
> But yet is theyr lyfe full lewde and vycious.
>
> (328)    Some lokyth with an aungels countenaunce,
> Wyse, sad and sober lyke an heremyte.

The last lines are in Barclay's best style, and they are quite original, as is indeed the whole of this passage. Locher's address to preachers has also inspired his exceptionally good Envoy :

> (333)    Ye clerkes that on your shulders bere the shelde
> Unto you graunted by the Unyversyte,
> How dare ye aventure to fyght in Cristes felde
> Agaynst synne without ye clere and gyltles be ?
> Consyder the cocke and in hym shall ye se
> A great example, for with his wynges thryse
> He betyth hym selfe to wake his own bodye,
> Before he crowe to cause other wake or ryse.

Interesting is also Barclay's version of the text from St. Matthew :

> (326)    He sertaynly may well be callyd a sote
> Moche unavysed and his owne ennemy
> Whiche in a nothers iye can spye a lyttell mote
> And in his owne can nat fele nor espye
> A moche stycke.

I need not call attention to the linguistic interest of this passage. Its prose counterpart occurs in Watson as a literal translation from Drouyn : ' Suche folkes spyeth well a lytel thorne in another mannes eye, but they se not a grete beme in theyr owne eye.' This whole chapter is again slavishly translated, the French being amplified just a little here and there in order to leave the next page free for the woodcut of the following chapter. The best sentence is the description of mockers : ' Theyr noses ben wryncled and laugheth with theyr eres ' (cf. Drouyn : ' Les nez ridicule portent et rient des oreilles '). For the rest we find Drouyn's and Riviere's blundering through Locher's quotation of ' duros Catones ' and ' sanctos Metellos ' : ' good cathonystes and holy metelistes,' and he does not hesitate to anglicize ' au moyen de ce ' into ' at the moyen of this.'—The final address to the preachers is lengthened a little : ' soyes plains de vertuz affinquon ne vous puist reprendre ' becomes ' be re-plynysshed with vertues, bycause that ye preche the worde of God and to the ende that ye be not maculate nor repreved.'

99.—Chapter 29 speaks of FAULT-FINDING when the object of attack is dead. Brant criticizes this posthumous maligning very severely.[1] Locher does it very solemnly with classical and high-flown expressions so that he has to leave the third and last part untranslated. Barclay paraphrases this Latin with felicitous freedom—' Faustae salutis Pros-peritas, quae mox fluminis instar abit ' becomes :

> (450)    The tyme passeth as water in a ryvere,
> No mortall man can it revoke agayne ;
> Dethe with his dartis unwarely doth apere ;
> It is the ende of every man certayne.

And yet there are fools who speak evil of the dead man :

> (452)    Nat thynkynge that they ensue must the same daunce.

---

[1] Zarncke's (p. 358) comments on line 20 characterize the German professor of the mid-nineteenth century rather than the medieval moralist.

They say it was all his own fault :

> (453)   And that he was feble, or full of malancoly
>         Over sad or prowde, disceytfull and pope-holy.[1]

In Watson's translation of Drouyn there occurs another version of the biblical proverb that we met with in chapter 21. ' Ye se well a strawe in your broders eye, but ye se not a blocke in your owne eye ' (= Fr. ung chevron qui vous creve loeil).   He calls le trespasse ' the deed body,' and turns the last sentence upside down by inserting a negation. ' One myght suppose that he dyde it not by envye,' where Drouyn rightly has : ' On pourroit presumer quil le feroit par envye.'

100.—Chapter 69 treats of two different subjects.   The first part may be described as a paraphrase of the saying THE BITER BIT. Brant illustrates this with half a dozen proverbial sayings and with two biblical and four classical examples.   The second part is a warning against TRUSTING PEOPLE too easily.—Locher has translated the second part faithfully enough, but the first part was too proverbial. Of the examples he retains only one biblical (Aman's treatment of Mardochai) and one classical one (the steer of Perillus).   Barclay adds again some good proverbs to Locher's version.   In the first part he has :

> (1031)   One yll turne requyreth another, be thou sure.
> (1034)   To one yll turne another doth belonge.
> (1036)   And some in theyr owne snarys ar taken fast.

In the second :

> (1039)   For oft under flowres lurketh the serpent ;
>          So paynted wordes hydeth a fals intent.
> (1042)   For amonge swete herbys oft growyth stynkynge wedes.

Watson keeps to Drouyn's prose, only changing ' en ma satyre ' into ' in this chapytre.'   In the last part his translation is so literal as to become incomprehensible without a knowledge of the French, and we can even hear in it the echoes of Riviere's strained rhymes, e.g. when he mentions ' a crosse or a patubulayr or a gybet,' Drouyn's ' croix ou patibulaire ou gibet,' which had been a necessity for Riviere's rhyme :

> Ce neanmoins si fist il faire
> Pour luy croix ou patibulaire.

It is doubtful whether Watson had any English precedent for his ' Patubulayr.'   The NED. gives no such word.

101.—THE BITER BIT would probably also indicate the contents of chapter 68, in which the same story of Aman occurs.   The chapter

---

[1] ' Pope-holy,' a common ME. word, occurring also in Chaucer's *Romaunt of the Rose* (415) and meaning ' *hypocritical* ' (French *papelard*).   Skelton calls all heretics ' popeholy braynles beestes ' ; see the note in Dyce iii (1856), 195.   It is probably connected with Middle-Dutch *popelare* ; cf. Verwys-Verdam, *Middelned. Wrdb.* s.v.   Skeat (Chaucer i, 419) says it means ' holy as a pope, *hence* hypocritical' (!)

opens in Brant with quite a collection of proverbs, two of which are in Locher, and elaborated more distinctly :

> (7)    Wer wil mit jägern gon der hetz
> Wer keyglen will, der selb uff setz.

The translation of this latter proverb is worth quoting :

> Quisquis forte globo cupiat subvertere stantes :
> Erigat ille simul mox quoque pyramides.

It is no wonder that our translators could hardly guess that these solemn words were meant to describe their homely game of nine-pins !—Barclay, therefore, simply wrote :

> (1019)    So he that wyll by yll worde man overturne,
> Must holde hym sure, lyst he unwarly spurne.

Riviere felt entirely at sea and buried the incomprehensible lines under a heap of even more incomprehensible words. At least, this seems the corresponding passage :

> Ou si plusieurs gens dessemblez
> On vouloit avoir assemblez.
> Il est convenant les vocquer
> Pour ensemble les convocquer
> Et sera la gloire atassee
> Et en une turbe amassee.

Drouyn has wisely skipped these words, and so we find nothing in Watson. In the beginning there are a few good expressions. In Drouyn's 'invitation' : ' Your playe is lordes playe (ieux de seigneurs) ye wyll playe and wyll not that they playe with you.' And in the paraphrase 'Whan a fole is dronken, loke that thou playe not with hym, for then is he daungerous.'—This is probably nearer to Locher's Latin than Barclay's.

> (1017)    He is a fole also, that hath great game,
> Whan childe or dronkard blamyth one absent,
> If he can nat also indure the same.

But towards the end Watson begins to abbreviate to save room for the beginning of the following chapter, and then he writes sentences that demand French explanations, e.g.

O how Aman was angrye whan the emperour cryed [Dr. fit crier ung edit] that every man sholde honour hym, and that Mardocheus kepte it not [Dr. quil estoit doulent de Mardocheus quil nobservoit ledict], for afore his eyen he sawe every body observe it.

Barclay elaborates Aman's example in two stanzas (1027 sq.). They are not very remarkable. Better are his proverbial expressions :

> (1020)    For lyke wyll have lyke.
> (1022)    The company of folys to folys is pleasaunt,
> For it is a proverbe and an olde sayde sawe,
> That in every place lyke to lyke will drawe.

102.—Chapter 10 speaks of TRUE FRIENDSHIP and its degeneration, and of preferring the common weal to private profit.  Good examples
were set by Jonathan and David, Patroclus and Achilles, Orestes and
Pylades, Demades and Pythias,[1] Saul and his squire, Scipio and Laelius,
by Moses, Nehemias, and Tobias.  Cain serves as an example of false
friendship.  Locher omits the passage about the common weal, skips
all the biblical names and treats Scipio and Laelius as two different
cases ; but adds emphatically Theseus and Pirithous.

Barclay's translation is good commonplace and humdrum without
any striking passages.  But on comparing it with his sources we find
that he must have translated it from the French rather than from the
Latin.  Riviere seems to have done his level best when rendering this
chapter, for no less than three times does he quote Boccaccio's *De
Genealogia Deorum*, and four times Valerius Maximus.  *Barclay copies
all Riviere's notes*,—and adds a great deal more.  Hear his initial stanza :

> (179)  He that iniustyce useth and grevance
> Agaynst all reason, lawe and equyte,
> By vyolent force puttynge to utteraunce
> A symple man full of humylyte,
> Suche by his lewdnes and iniquyte
> Makyth a grave, wherin hym selfe shall lye,
> And lewdly he dyeth that lyveth cruelly.

From this we can catch only a faint echo of Locher's motto (the only
example in the book of a rhyming iambic dimeter) :

> Qui facit iniustitiam
> Exercet et potentiam
> In viro forsan humili
> Hic facit scrobem tumuli.

Not even the keenest ears, I think, would recognize in it the sound of
the German original :

> Wer unrecht, gwalt, dut einem man
> Der im nye leydes hat gethan
> Do stossend sich sunst zehen an.

But the French is audible in it almost word for word :

> Qui fait iniustice et grevance
> Contre raison et equite
> Et exerce force et puissance
> En lomme plain dumilite
> Par sa mauvaise iniquite
> La fosse du tombeau compose
> Et de bien faire ne dispose.

Riviere's motto being of course copied by Drouyn, Watson had to

---

[1] The more ' correct' names are Damon and Phintias.  See Zarncke on this
passage, p. 318.  As *Damon and Pithias* they were introduced into the English
drama by R. Edwardes' well-known school play (± 1565).

translate it too. So we may here see the two rival translators at the same task. Here is Watson's work :

> Who that doth justyce and grevaunce
> Agaynst vertue and equyte,
> And excercyseth his puyssaunce
> Upon a man with cruelty
> By his evyll inyquyte,
> Dothe the pyt of his tombe compose,
> For of vertues he hathe no lose.[1]

If we remember that Barclay had bound himself to a five-foot beat, while Watson had only the French tetrameter to imitate, the two writers suggest a race where the competitors run neck to neck until in the last two lines Barclay far outstrips his fellow.

After the motto Barclay took two stanzas (180 and 181) from Locher. In Stanza 182 he seems to return to Riviere. Stanza 183 is an original insertion :

> Alas ! Exyled is godly charyte
> Out of our royalme *etc.*

Stanza 184 and the rest are all from Riviere. Patroclus and Achilles appear with Riviere's details (Stanza 186 sq.) ; then follow Orestes and Pylades and their gruesome story, to which Locher does not even allude (Stanzas 188–190). In Stanza 191 the story is undoubtedly taken from the French ; but Barclay replaces Riviere's more ' correct ' *Damon* [2] by Locher's spelling *Dymades*. The quotation from Valerius about Lelius and ' Cipio ' in Stanza 192 is taken from Riviere, but Barclay omits the ' story longe and ample,' as he also abbreviates the Boccaccian tale of Theseus and Pirithous in Stanza 193. The last stanza (194) contains a general reflection, which is found both in Locher and in Riviere, but Barclay's version resembles the latter more than the former.—In conclusion, therefore, we may say : that chapter 10 has been translated out of Riviere, but that in two passages (Stanzas 180 and 191) it has been ' corrected ' from Locher.

Much more need not be quoted from Watson. When Drouyn summarizes Riviere's learned prolixity into nonsense, Watson simply puts the absurdities in English or half-English words. ' All is corrumped,' he says, ' for there is no more love in grece as hath ben,' which stands for ' car il nest plus de tels folz amys en grece au temps passe.' Scipio is mentioned by Locher as ' Libyae dominator et arcis Sydoniae,' whatever this means.[3] This appears in Riviere as

> Dominateur de sidoine
> Et superateur de libie.

---

[1] *lose* (< OFr. los) = renown, fame, is a common ME. word, revived by Scott in the expression ' to acquire los and fame.'

[2] Riviere :

> Que te diray ie de damon
> Et du bon pithias aussi *etc.*

Drouyn thought the expression *de damon* too poetical and simplified it to ' Nous lisons encores damon et du bon pithias,' so that Watson had to invent a new classical name : ' We rede also of Amon and of the good Pythyas.'

[3] Locher probably mixes up Scipio Africanus the elder and the younger.

Drouyn simplifies this into 'dominateur de sodomie et de libie' and so we find him promoted in English to 'Scipyon ryght excellent domynatour of Sodomye and Lybye'!

103.—Chapter 42 contains a serious warning against MOCKERY and mocking fools, quoting Nabal, Sanaballat, the boys who mocked the Prophet (Eliseus), and Semei's outrage. Locher uses practically almost two-thirds of Brant's ideas, and takes two of Brant's examples, viz. Nabal—to whose name he adds the happy interference of Abigail ; and the mocking boys—without supplying the name of the Prophet. Just before these examples he inserts a good quotation from Juvenal :

> Loripedem rectus derideat Ethiopem albus.

Barclay has rendered all this in fairly good English, showing that he understood it all. He feels quite at ease and inserts such homely phrases as :

> (626)  All folysshe mockers I purpos to repreve :
> Clawe he his backe that felyth ytche or greve.[1]

The name of the Prophet is mentioned and the translation of Juvenal's proverb is worth quoting :

> (632)  He that goeth right, stedfast, sure and fast,
> May hym well mocke that goth haltynge and lame ;
> And he that is whyte may well his scornes cast
> Agaynst a man of Ynde.

As a real curiosity appears the version of the same proverb in the French, and in the English of Watson. Riviere was of course hampered by his rhymes and so he may be forgiven for rendering

> Et plus ung boyteaux tout deffait
> Bossu lait vil et contrefait
> Democque lethiopien
> Combien quil ait assez lieu
> De laidure et de vilite.

There is no such excuse for Drouyn's 'Le boiteux bossu vil et contrefait se mocque de lethiopien,' which becomes in English 'The crepyll lame and counterfet mocketh the Ethyopyen'!—Of Locher's boys of the Prophet, Riviere has understood so little that his version is a downright joke, too good to be missed :

> Que dirons nous de ces enfans
> Plus durs que ne sont elephans
> A digne correccion prendre
> Les voions tous les iours entendre
> A plusieurs ieux et moqueries.

Drouyn changes only the rhyme word 'elephans' :—'Que dirons nous de ses (= ces) enfans plus durs que ne sont grosses pierres a prendre correction, les voyons tous les iours en noyses ieux et mocqueries.' Watson leaves out the 'grosses pierres' probably for no better reason than to make the whole chapter just a little shorter in order to have the

---

[1] A similar proverb occurs in St. 1714. See § 310.

whole motto for the following chapter on one page : ' What shall I saye unto the chyldren that be so harde to correcke, ye se them every daye in noyses, playes and mockynges.'—But the Prophet Eliseus is far indeed from this little bit of pedagogical pessimism.

104.—Chapter 7 satirizes BACKBITING, and Brant gives a graphical and sarcastic description of the way in which it is done. He considers it mainly as causing dissension among friends, and for the punishment that this vice will entail he quotes the biblical examples of Core, Absalom, Alcimus, the man who had slain Saul, and the murderers of Isboseth.

Of all this there is nothing in Locher, who translates only the title and the motto (to explain the woodcut) and then writes quite an original chapter on ideas taken from Brant's first few lines, inveighing, towards the end, against the Terentian :

Fallaces Davi : Gnatones : et parasyti.

Barclay translates this Latin sermon to convert those whose delight

Is set to sclaunder, to diffame and bacbyte.

He even retains the Latinism of *Delatore nihil peius* in :

(146)    Than a backbyter nought is more peryllous.

There are only a few original remarks interspersed in this paraphrase, as e.g.

(147)    His darte oft retourneth to his own represe,

or when he blames those that

(149)    Inclyneth theyr erys to sclander and detraccion<br>
Moche rather than they wolde to a noble sermon.

He skips the difficult Terentian names and takes Locher's last lines in Stanza 150. But he adds three more stanzas, quite original, the first of which is in his strongest style :

(151)    An olde quean that hath been nought al hyr dayes,<br>
Whiche oft hath for money hyr body let to hyre,<br>
Thynketh that al other doth folowe hyr olde wayes ;<br>
So she and hyr boul felowes syttinge by the fyre,<br>
The boule about walkynge, with theyr tunges they conspyre<br>
Agaynst goode peple to sclander them wyth shame ;<br>
Than shal the noughty doughter lerne of the bawdy dame.

The two other stanzas contain an exhortation and are probably meant as an Envoy, though not marked as such nor written in octaves.

There is not much of interest in Watson's version. In the last sentence he says to the backbiters : ' Ye ought for to be put in dure and asper pryson, there to remayne for ever without lyght, for ye be not worthy to have the lyght of lyfe.'—Riviere had spoken of ' Lumiere deternelle vie,' but Drouyn had dropped the ' eternelle.'

105.—Chapter 41 shows the other side of BACKBITING, insisting upon the necessity of letting people talk and always doing what is right.— Locher's paraphrase is fairly faithful here, the most striking deviation

being that he begins with four introductory lines which are quite original,
and that he omits the last two lines.

This is also what we find back in Barclay.  He elaborates the introduction much more fully, adding several good lines and one whole stanza,
which gives really the best expression to the idea of this chapter :

> (615)  Lyve well and wysely, than let men chat theyr fyll ;
> Wordes ar but wynde, and though it oft so fall
> That of lewde wordes comyth great hurte and yll,
> Yet byde the ende, that onely provyth all ;
> If thou canst suffer, truste well that thou shall
> Overcome thyne ennemyes better by pacience
> Than by hye wordes, rygour or vyolence.

In Watson's version I can hardly find a sentence which makes good sense.
The motto is quite original ;  because the printer had no imitation of
the original cut, explained in Riviere's and Drouyn's introductory
stanza, Watson had to invent something of his own, and he wrote :

> He is a foole ryght varyable
> The whiche wyll gyve faythe and credence
> Unto every mannes fable
> Whiche are folysshe without sence
> And knowe they be voyde of prudence
> Ever reportynge false tydynges
> Bothe at morowe and at evenynges !

106.—Chapter 101 presents us with a third aspect of BACKBITING,
for here Brant demonstrates the injustice of listening to and believing
slanderers.  The injustice is as great as attacking from behind or condemning a person without hearing his defence.  Aman slandered
Mardochai and Siba Miphiboseth (2 Kings xvi), but Alexander (Bales)
deserved glory for not believing the slanderers of Jonathan (1 Mach. x
61),[1] while Adam and Eve lost grace by their credulity.  The world is
full of falsehood and every spirit should not be believed.

Locher makes the first half of this chapter very long, so that he has
only six lines left for the second half.  Hence he omits Adam and Eve
and the rest, omits the name of Siba, and he changes Alexander Bales
into Alexander Magnus.[2]

Barclay paraphrases this Latin text without any remarkable deviations.  An original expression occurs in Stanza 1590, where he calls
backbiting ' wordes wors than knyfe,' and a humorous little addition
in Stanza 1596.  Locher said that a slandering tongue *conterit ossa viri*,
while Barclay calls it.

> Brekynge the bonys, God wot, of many one,
> Howbeit the tunge within it hath no bone.[3]

The most humorous part of Watson's translation is the assertion :
' He is reputed for dyffamed, that lepeth uppon the backe of an other

---

[1] Zarncke's reference (p. 445) is not quite correct.
[2] Yet on the margin Brant has annotated 1 Mach. x.
[3] That this was an old proverb in England appears from **Hendyng's proverb** :
' Tonge breketh bon and nath hire selve non.'

in tellynge hym his affayres, and hurteth his backe (et le blesse au dos), for there is some sore. And after the hurte (le blesse) wolde defende hym as he that hathe a sore fote, and in spekynge unto hym tredeth upon it, and asketh noo better but for to angre hym.'—The man attacked from behind is still dimly recognizable! The following sentence, however, does not go farther back than Drouyn, who after the story of Aman gave a little reflection of his own : ' The chrysten men that byleveth lyghtly and herkeneth the Jews, is in waye of dampnacyon.' The Frenchman had not meant to express such a strongly Anti-Semitic opinion, for after *les juifs* he had added ' et leur loy.' But as Watson's page was nearly full he left this out as redundant !

## VII

## CHAPTERS RELATING TO WISE AND UNWISE ACTIONS

107.—At the head of this category we may place Brant's chapter 22, which contains a DISCOURSE OF WISDOM, where the author simply puts in rhyme and metre the well-known passage from Proverbs viii.— Locher has made an honest effort to render this in classical hexameters, without too badly disguising the true meaning, so that the translators have really been able somehow to recognize its real character. Few passages are worth quoting except Barclay's original addition :

> (351)   No fole is so ryche nor hye of dignyte
> But that a wyse man pore is more worthy than he ;

and as an anti-climax Drouyn's introductory invitation, where the allegory of his title allures him into a curious combination. It is literally rendered by Watson : ' O foles . . . renne in to the grete shyppe of fooles, and ye shal here sapyence that is so humble make a general sermon in this maner that foloweth.'

108.—Resembling the preceding, but of a somewhat more worldly character is Locher's own contribution on the PRAISE OF WISDOM which he has inserted at the end of the book (chapter a). The distichs run a smooth and natural course, and Barclay hardly deviates from his Latin model, except towards the end, where instead of an Envoy he appends *A Lementacion of Barclay for the Ruyne and Fall of Wysdome.* It is a literary *tour-de-force*, more intricate even than that in chapter 92 (§ 41). For it consists of four octaves, all rhyming thus : *-es, -aunce, -es, -aunce, -aunce, -aunce, -ace, -aunce, -ace,* and every octave ending with the burden : ' Foly in hir place.' Barclay may have learned the trick from Chaucer's *Fortune* or *To Rosemunde* or *The Compleynt to Venus*, or from any of the French *rhétoriqueurs*. The tyranny of the rhyme in such productions usually reduces the ideas to platitudes. Barclay's effort is no exception to the rule. Only in one stanza does he become for a moment more lively and concrete :

> (1808)   Foule falshode hath confoundyd faythfulnes,
> The newe disgyses hath left Almayne and Fraunce
> And come to Englonde, and eche unclenlynes
> Doth lede us, wretchys ; we make no purveaunce
> Agaynst our ende, when Deth shall will his launce
> Consume this lyfe ; we may bewayle this case ;
> Our wordes ar folysshe, so is our countenaunce ;
> Thus gone is wysdome and foly in hir place.

The last line of the last stanza sounds a more hopeful note in the prayer :

> (1809)   O glorious God, direct this perturbaunce,
>          That wysdome may agayne obtayne hir place.

For literary and philological curiosities we have to look in Watson and his originals. Locher depicts Wisdom or Minerva and says of her that 'membra tegit peplo.' These three words were replaced in Barclay by a better substitute :

> (1800)   She coveryth hir hede with vale of chastyte.

Riviere requires six lines to bring out the meaning :

> Lequel de ses beaulx ornemens
> Est pare et sainctz vestemens
> Dung peuple ou drap de fin sandal
> Par tout ses membres et aval
> Et sur le chief la grant frontiere
> De mesmes devant et derriere.

I need not quote Drouyn's version, for it is literally transcribed in Watson : 'a vesture of people or clothe of fyne sendall all aboute his membres, and upon his hed the grete frontelet.' I do not know if the translator understood the word *peuple* here. The word *people* in this meaning has been without predecessor or successor in England. At least the NED. knows no such word, and has come across the anglicized form of *peplum* only in Phillips in 1658 in the form *peple*.—Better is the saying that Wisdom (in the preceding quotation *she* had become *he*, now *she* becomes merely *it*) 'it sparpleth (in French *espant* ; in Latin *spargit*) better with the fete the roses in all places.'—Here is a good ME. word (OFr. esparpeiller, MnFr. éparpiller). It has completely disappeared ; more's the pity.

109.—THE PRAISE OF THE WISE MAN is the last chapter (112) in Brant, and little more than a translation into German of a Latin poem *De viro bono*, which was then universally attributed to Virgil and as such published by Brant himself in 1502.[1] In reality it is a rather meagre summary of the principles of an honest life [2] insisting principally on a daily examination of conscience.—Locher's re-translation into Latin might have been very instructive—had he made the attempt. But he only elaborates some ideas in a dozen lines and then starts off to complain about the degeneration of the times, especially in Germany. Towards the end he returns to 'Virgil' and then concludes, offering his good wishes to his readers and to his master Brant. 'Brant venerande vale' are the last words, which show that Locher may have originally meant to finish his book here.[3] Riviere paraphrases Locher's Latin with no small degree of success in the first part ; but gradually he is carried off his feet

---

[1] The whole is printed in Zarncke 469.       [2] Schmidt ii, 305.
[3] He must have changed his mind, however, very soon, for more than ten pages were to follow, even in the first edition, and in the second edition no less than twenty-five.

by all those classical waves.　When Locher says that in heaven we shall
' Ambrosia frui ' he can only make of it :

> Goustera sachez en somme
> Apres dambrosia celle herbe.

He does not even change the allusion to Germany, and when Locher
—whose ' poetical ' name was Philomusus—offers his best wishes to
his readers, Riviere naively writes (omitting nothing but the reference
to Brant) :

> Affin que vous puissez avoir
> Del discrecion et scavoir
> Que la gracieuse priere
> Soifue doulce et tressinguliere
> Prieres ce discret philomuses
> Affin et doulcement ses muses
> Prie pour avoir auctenticque
> Don de saigesse scienticque.

With this probably well-meaning but rather obscure prayer he concludes.
Drouyn has tried to render all this in prose, evidently misunderstanding
much of it.　The English translator translates both sense and nonsense.
Of course we also get ' Almayne the vyctoryous,' and ' this herbe that
is called ambrosia.'　Just before the above-quoted conclusion, which
may have caused him as many difficulties as it does us, Drouyn leaves
Riviere, and adds a passage which shows again that he must have stood
in some relation with court-circles.　' Les roys iadis ' *etc*.　Watson
translates literally :

> The kynges somtyme had sapyence, but at this tyme they have no more, for all
> theyr dysporte is but vanytees, and defyle the holy scriptures.　Alexandre the grete
> was so well lerned that he made his cronycles hymselfe in latyn in fayre rethoryke.
> He made nothynge but that the whiche was iust and done by hym or by his men.[1]

110.—Comparing this with Barclay we turn from the dullness of a
grammatical exercise to the real though somewhat doleful monologue
of a living preacher.　We hear no more of ' this herbe ambrosia ' and
instead of ' Almayne ' we get :

> (1782)　If the noble royalme of Englonde wolde avaunce
> In our dayes men of vertue and prudence,
> Eche man rewardynge after his governaunce,
> As : the wyse with honour and rowme of excellence
> And the yll with grevous payne for theyr offence—
> Than sholde our famous laude of olde obtayned
> Nat bene decayed, oppressyd and thus distayned.

He follows Locher's version further, and even pretends to have written :

> (1785)　Lyke as my maister Brant had first devysyd.

But we get something better than this.　Locher's solemn address
to Ticio gave him a good idea.　In an early chapter of his work (of which

---

[1] Drouyn's first edition (Lyon 1498) reads : ' qui ne faisoit chose qui ne fust
iuste et faicte ' ; the second edition (Lyon 1499) adds : ' par luy ou par ses gens.'
This is one of the proofs that Watson cannot have worked from the first edition.

we shall presently give the contents) he had ridiculed the eight 'secondaries' of his College, he will now praise as a model of a 'wise man' an intimate friend of his who bore the suggestive name of *John Bisshop*. We do not know the exact position of the worthy man. We must gather all our information from the poem itself, from the Index where he is described as *Syr John Bishop of Exeter*, and from the marginal note: *Familiarem suum Johannem Bisshop de eo benemeritum commendat.* Perhaps he was an old priest of the neighbourhood. At any rate Barclay must have been on perfect terms with the good old soul and wanted to praise him, with just a little bit of good-humoured ridicule to suit the occasion. The most obvious pretext to introduce him here lay in the fact that he had often seen the author at work and had handled his manuscript, and had then gravely told his learned friend that he should have it published by the new-fashioned invention which the late Mr. Caxton had introduced, in short to have it ' put to prent.'—And so one fine day Barclay wrote :

(1788)  Wysdome shall men avaunce unto honour,
       So Barclay wyssheth, and styll shall tyll he dye
       Parfytely pray to God our Creatour
       That vertuous men and wyse may have degre,
       As they ar worthy of lawde and dygnyte,
       But namely to his frende Bysshop by name
       Before all other desyreth he the same,
(1789)  Whiche was the first oversear of this warke (!)
       And unto his frende gave his advysement
       It nat to suffer to slepe styll in the darke
       But to be publysshyd abrode and put to prent.
       To thy monycion, my Bysshop, I assent,
       Besechynge God that I that day may se
       That thy honour may prospere and augment
       So that thy name and offyce may agre !

Fancy the old man becoming a real bishop! He had often been complaining of his scanty living ; then he would have enough and to spare !

(1790)  Thy name to worshyp and honour doth accorde,
       As borne a Bysshop without a benefyce !
       Thy lyvynge small, thy name is of a Lorde !
       And though thou nowe be stryke with covetyse (!)
       That vyce shall slake in the, if thou aryse,
       As I suppose ; and lyberalyte
       Shall suche fortune for the by grace devyse
       So that thy name and offyce shall agre !

Of course there was no great chance that such a piece of good luck should ever befall the man. Barclay knew it perfectly well.

(1791)  But if that Fortune to thy goodnes envye,
       As though she wolde the nat honour to attayne,
       Yet let hir passe and hir fraylenes defye ;
       For all hir giftis ar frayle and uncertayne.
       If she nat smyle on the, but have disdayne
       The to promote to welth and dignyte :
       To olde acquayntaunce be stedfast, true and playne,
       Than shall thy goodnes and thy name agre.

Let John Bisshop console himself. All that glitters is not gold. Let every man be content with his station in life :

> (1792) Let pas the worlde for nought in it is stable.
> The greatter baylyf the sorer is his payne !
> Some men that late were callyd honorable
> Dyd theyr promosyon after sore complayne.
> No wyse man is desyrous to obtayne
> The forked cap (!) without he worthy be—
> As ar but fewe ! But be thou glad and fayne,
> That thy good name and maners may agre.

If this will not satisfy him, nothing will. Let the grumbling old man then go to heaven ! Barclay must have enjoyed the humour of his own irony :

> (1793) In this short balade I can nat comprehende
> All my full purpose that I wolde to the wryte ;
> But fayne I wolde that thou sholde sone ascende
> To hevenly worshyp and celestyall delyte,
> Than sholde I after my pore wyte . . . and respyt
> Display thy name and great kyndnes to me !
> But at this tyme no farther I indyte,
> But pray that thy name and worshyp may agre.

I need not apologize for this long quotation. It is Barclay at his best, and it has never been appreciated at its real value.

The reader will have noticed that the first stanza is a Chaucerian seven-line stanza, and the last five are octaves. The first indeed belongs to the body of the book and runs partly parallel to Locher's last distichs, while the others take the place of an Envoy.

III.—Returning to Brant's unrelenting severity we find him in chapter 8 insisting upon the necessity of TAKING ADVICE, adducing Tobias, Lot's wife, Roboam, Nabuchodonosor, Macchabeus and Achitophel as examples to imitate or to avoid.—Locher works out the introductory lines, just touches upon Tobias and Roboam, leaves out the others altogether and gives instead the stories of Pyrrhus, Hector and Nero.

Comparing the different versions we find Barclay quoting Boccaccio's *Genealogia* again, which of course he took from Riviere. So the whole chapter may be taken from the French. Indeed the larger part undoubtedly is. From Stanza 159 down to Stanza 164 we have the story of Pyrrhus,[1] that of the Trojans and of Priam (of which Locher does not speak), of Hector (where the connexion is very slight,—Barclay knew the story too well !), of Nero, of Tobias and of Roboam. In all this Riviere must have been his principal, if not his sole guide. He has, however, considerably shortened this display of pseudo-classical scholarship. A comparison with Locher's text seems to have caused him some misgivings. For the initial stanzas (154–158) and for the last two (165 sq.) I do not know which version he has taken as his model. He is as far away from the one as from the other.

---

[1] Locher's reference to Pyrrhus and Cineas is turned into the story of Pyrrhus and Orestes.

Among the passages in Riviere which he has left untranslated there is an interesting one at the beginning.　Everyone must take advice, he says :

> Soit aussi cault que fut Enee
> Aussi saige que Salomon
> Aussi puissant comme Sanson
> Aussi virtueux quil vouldra.

The three comparisons were not quite sufficient for Drouyn's taste ; and so we find in Watson's translation :

> Be he al so cautelous as ever was Enee, also wyse as Salamon, also eloquent as Tullyus, also stronge as Sampson, also dyscrete as Ovyde, also pacyent as Job, also mercyfull [Fr. misericors] as Danyell, and also fayre as Absolon, yet yf he be entached with presumpcyon *etc.*

Riviere's conclusion also is curiously enlarged upon.　Drouyn's expanded version is still further drawn out by Watson, who had plenty of space here.　But I have not space enough to quote all their nonsense.

The best specimen is too good however.　Riviere speaks of those who follow their own ideas (Latin : qui dum sectantur proprium caput) :

> Ou bien font du tout a leurs testes.

This becomes in Drouyn : ' qui veullent voller sans helles et qui font du tout a leurs testes.'　Drouyn's *helles* played a trick with Watson's imagination and he holds forth :

> that wolde flee without wynges, *theyr busshes ben so curyously decked* (!!) the whiche ben ruled and governed after theyr fantasyes and executeth none otherwyse reason than even as it cometh fyrste in theyr mynde.

112.—Two chapters deal with KEEPING SECRETS.　Chapter 39 warns against betraying one's own plans to one's enemies, particularly when they try to insinuate themselves into one's confidence.　Locher has rendered all the main ideas in Latin, only omitting the example of Nicanor and Judas Macchabeus, enlarging upon the first lines, and adding a new conclusion.　Barclay and Riviere follow Locher independently.

The most interesting passage is a ' Priamel.'　The Latin mentions four things not easily to be concealed :

> Consilium fatui, structa urbs in vertice montis,
> Actus amatoris, stramen et in crepida.

The last expression stands for the German : ' Und strow das in den schuhen lyt ' (l. 23).　A typically German custom seems to be alluded to : wearing straw in one's shoes, probably wooden shoes ![1]　The translators were not familiar with it, and so they have all changed it.[2]

---

[1] Seb. Franck, ii, 16ª, also mentions ' Strouw im schuh,' and Thomas Murner, Gr. Luth. Nar. K.⁴ : ' stro . . . in schuhen '; Geiler, ' stramen in sotulari '; Zarncke 375.

[2] Even the ' literal ' Marnef edition has not dared to leave it unchanged.　He enumerates : ' Le conseil dung fol.　La cite faicte et construicte ou hault dune montaigne.　Les faits dung amoureux.　Et la paille en *lestrain*.'—Now *estrain* is usually a mere synonym of *paille*, e.g. in Michault, *Dance aux Aveugles* : ' Et l'autre n'a ne l'estrain ne les grains.'　But the translator has probably taken the word as synonymous with *litière*, for which there are also examples.　Cf. Godefroy.

Riviere mentions the following four :

> 1. Le chemin par ou fault aller
>    Et lon voit les pas des passans.
> 2. Le secret dung homme sans sens
> 3. Une cite sur monte construite
> 4. Et le quart la folle conduite
>    Les actes les moyen et tours
>    Dung homme qui est pris damour.

The first must do duty for the straw.—Drouyn's paraphrase is found almost literally rendered in Watson : ' the waye, the secrete of a man without wytte, a cyte that is edyfyed upon a mountayne, and the folysshe conduite of a man that is expressed with love (qui est prins damours).'

Barclay keeps closest to Locher, and his little alteration is one of remarkable felicity :

> (591) The firste is the counsell of a wytles man,
> The seconde a cyte whiche byldyd is a hye
> Upon a mountayne, the thyrde we often se
> That to hyde his dedes a lover hath no skyll,
> The fourth is strawe or fethers on a wyndy hyll.

113.—Chapter 51 warns against revealing secrets in general, more especially to women. Examples are : Sampson, Amphiaraus and Achab, and the chapter concludes with a quotation from ' the prophet ' (Isaias). Nearly the whole of it is in Locher's translation, the most complete one we have come across yet. Barclay has rendered it faithfully, misunderstanding only the final quotation from the Prophet. His best passage is the following, of which the last line is strikingly original :

> (726) Thus olde storyes doth oft recorde and tell
> By theyr examples whiche they unto us gyve,[1]
> That wymen ar no kepars of councell :
> It goeth through them as water through a syve.

The French is full of misunderstandings. Drouyn adds to Samson ' sa femme Dalida ' (= Watson : ' his wyf Dalyda '). Amphiaraus appears in Riviere, in Drouyn and in Watson as Damphyaryus. But the worst is the following :

> Si Achab roy iamais promeu
> Et declaire a femme neust
> Tout son vouloir et ce quil sceut
> De nemroth en grant vitupere
> Neust souffert de mort le repere
> Ne Achab est ainsi menge
> De chiens comme ung pauvre enrage.

Drouyn makes of this : ' Sy le roy Achas (sic) neust iamais revele son secret a sa femme Iezebel, il neust iamais souffert mort par Naboth,[2]

---

[1] If any proof were still required, these lines would prove that Barclay uses only Locher and not Brant. For Locher has ' Historiae recinunt veteres ' etc., but Brant ' die gschrifft seyt.'

[2] Although the whole passage is far more absurd in Drouyn than in Riviere, this name is quite correct. It shows that he must have looked into Locher's Latin, where he found the name Naboth and also Iezabel, the I of which could be mistaken for an l.

lequel fit menger cestuy Achas aux chiens.' Poor Watson did not know
what Drouyn meant by his *lezebel*, and as he had a little space to spare
he added something here and put an adjective before Naboth and a
synonym before 'secret' and so presented the English public with his
biblical hotch-potch : ' If that the kynge Achas hadde not tolde his
counsayll and his secret unto the wyfe of Lezebell, he hadde never ben
put to dethe by the myghty Naboth, the whiche made this same Achas
be eten with dogges.'

114.—LOQUACITY is a favourite theme for satire, and in chapter 19
Brant has exercised all the sharpness of his irony on this common foible.—
Unfortunately he uses a double chapter, with the result that Locher
has elaborated only the first twenty-five lines, that is one-fourth, and
not the most interesting part, of the whole.—The translators follow
this Latin version. In his usual introductory sentence Drouyn mistakes
the meaning of the woodcut, thinking that it represents the catching
of a bird, and so he addresses the fools (in Watson's translation) : ' Ye
trappe (vous arrestez) all beestes naturall, as well byrdes as serpentes ' !

Barclay introduces several good English proverbs :

(312)   And lyghtly his folysshe bolt shall be shot out.
(313)   A worde ones spokyn revoked can nat be ;
        Therfore thy fynger lay before thy lypes.
        For a wyse mannys tunge without advysement trypes.

When those fools go to confession :

(315)   Theyr tunges ar loste and there they syt as domme.

' Silescit nec verbum ructare potest,' says Locher with less plastic force.
In Riviere this passage is still weaker, Drouyn's paraphrase does not
improve it, and as Watson again feels no need to save space, it becomes
still further diluted in English :

Whan suche folkes do go to confessyon [*se confessent*] theyr speche faylleth them,
ye in suche wyse that they can not open theyr mouthes for to declare theyr vyle and
abhomynablye synnes unto the prest [*pour dire leurs pechez* is the original for the last
eleven words].

Barclay's most delightful addition comes at the end. He draws
attention to it in a note, the pedantry of which, however, somewhat
spoils the piquancy of this passage :

(317)   But touchynge wymen, of them I wyll nought say ;
        They can nat speke, but ar as coy and styll
        As the horle wynde or clapper of a mylle.[1]

He should not have warned us : *occupatio : color retoricus* !

[1] In Cawood's edition (1570) :
        As the whirle wynde or clapper of a mylle.
The old Douay-Bible (1609), 4 Kings ii 1, also spoke of ' a hurle wind ' where modern
editions have ' a whirlwind.' It occurs also in Harvey (1573) and Sandys (1640).—
NED. Jamieson misprints *of* in this line instead of *or*, as Fraustadt 35 had already
suspected.

A passage of more general interest is found at the beginning of this chapter, in which he gives us a glimpse into his workshop :

> (310)  Ye blaberynge folys, superflue of langage,
> Come to our shyp, our ankers ar in wayde !
> By right and lawe ye may chalange a stage.
> To you of Barklay it shall nat be denayde ;
> Howe be it the charge Pynson hathe on me layde,
> With many folys our navy not to charge,
> Yet ye of dewty shall have a sympyll barge.[1]

115.—Excessive ANXIETY for worldly advancement (chapter 24) is shown to be a folly from the example of Alexander's life and death and from Diogenes' contentment in his tub.  The chapter concludes with some idiomatic expressions and a good ' Priamel.'  The ideas are nearly all in Locher, except the conclusion with its ' Priamel.'  Diogenes is called *Cynicus* (but the margin explains the meaning), and he is said to have watched ' astrorum motus.'

Riviere has understood this text better than Barclay, who grants to Diogenes an unexpected preferment :

> (380)  Wherfore Cynicus,[2] a man of great wysdome,
> Lorde grettest of Grece in londes and cytees,
> Hathe lefte great example unto all degrees ;
> For his great ryches his herte dyd never blynde,
> But worlde pompe set clene out of his mynde.

In the next stanza he does speak of the ' scyence of astronomy,' but he forgets the tub, so that he has evidently mistaken the identity of the *Cynicus*.—Riviere's more correct interpretation is found again in Watson, where we find ' Cinicus a great philosophre . . . within a tonne ful of holes, in the whiche he hadde intellygence of the movynges of the elementes and of the sterres.'  The ' oultrecuydance ' of Drouyn's introductory sentence is here rendered by ' wanhope wyl corrumpe ' with a rather curious participle.[3]  ' Satyre ' is again replaced by ' chapytre,' and Drouyn's French proverb at the end (it is not in Riviere)— ' car on dit communement lhomme propose et dieu dispose '—becomes ' for it is a comyn proverb all aboute, man doth purpose, and God doth dispose.'

116.—Chapter 34 reproves the FICKLENESS and continual longing for change of those who will never become wiser by it.  Locher elaborates the beginning so much, that he has no room left for the last dozen lines ; and instead of Brant's ' Rom, Hierusalem, Pavy ' (l. 16) and ' din hut . . . voll krützer,' alluding no doubt to the over-numerous pilgrimages

---

[1] See §§ 315, 341.

[2] The word is also taken as a proper name by Barclay in ch. 110 b, Stanza 1751.

[3] This seems at least the obvious interpretation.  The French has : ' Et sy nest pas celuy repute saige qui par oultrecuydance son cerveau tous les iours apreste ' *etc.*  The English : ' And he is not reputed over wyse that by wanhope wyl corrumpe troubleth his brayne every daye' *etc.*—One can see that Watson has room to spare.

of the time,[1] Locher speaks of ' Patavi muros . . . celsae moenia Romae
. . . Solymas . . . Assyrios lares . . . Lybien . . . Memphitica regna . . .
Pyramides . . . Attica regna.'　A problem for the translators !

Riviere makes an honest effort :

> Ils vont en estranges voiages
> Et en divers pelerinages
> En la grande cite de Romme
> Pour voir les murailles en somme
> En Solyme et Assirie
> Et en la cite de Libye
> Aux grans royaulmes memphiticques
> De piramides et actiques.

Drouyn retains this interesting collection :

> Ilz vont en plusieurs pelerinages, comme a romme pour veoir les murailles,[2]
> en solyme, assyre, lybie, au royaulmes memphilitiques, piramides, attiques.

Watson corrupts the names a little more and adds one name of his own
accord.　Why not ?

> They goo on dyvers pylgrymages, as to Rome for to se the walles, to Solyme,
> Syrye, Lybye, and to the realmes Memphytikes. Piramides. *Myryades*. Actykes.

117.—Suchlike curiosities are all discarded by Barclay, who has
here taken Locher only as a source of inspiration, and writes a chapter
which is almost entirely original.　He must have been in high spirits,
for he is lively almost from the beginning.　He gives his own original
explanation of the picture, adds a new introduction, and the whole
chapter is so full of interesting passages that one feels at a loss which
to quote as the best.

> (519)　Many of this sort wander and compase
> 　　　　All studies, the wonders of the worlde to se,
> 　　　　With unstabyll wynges fleynge from place to place ;
> 　　　　Some seyth : lawe, and some : dyvynyte !
> 　　　　But for all this byde they in one degre ;
> 　　　　And if they were asses and folys blynde before,
> 　　　　After all these syghtes yet ar they moche more.

Hear what he substitutes for the Memphitican rubbish :

> (522)　Some fle to se the wonders of Englonde,
> 　　　　Some to the court to se the maners there,
> 　　　　Some to Wallys, Holonde, to Fraunce or Irlonde,
> 　　　　To Lybye, Afryke, and besyly enquere
> 　　　　Of all merveyles, and skantly worth a here !
> 　　　　Some into Fraunce and some to Flaunders ren,
> 　　　　To se [3] the wayes and workes of cunnynge men.

---

　　[1] Pavia, F. B. Kruitwagen informs me, must have been famous for its relics and
indulgences.　For in 1505 there appeared at Pavia : ' Jac. Gualla, Sanctuarium,
Papiae antiquitatum reliquiarum sanctorum quae erant in arca Papie, indulgenti-
arum quarumlibet intra et extra civitatem ac ubi iaceat corpus beati Bernardini
de Feltro.'—The ' arca ' meant here is the *Arca di S. Agostino* of costly workmanship
and extraordinary dimensions.　See Kirchenlexicon[2], ix, 1731, i v. Pavia.
　　[2] The first edition has *miracles*.　See § 16 and 344.
　　[3] Cawood's reading ; the first edition misprints *so*.

One need not go abroad to learn ' stultas artes ' Locher had said, and this suggestion was sufficient to inspire the following piece of exquisite moralizing humour and irony :

> (525)　Laboure nat so sore to lerne to be a fole :
> 　　　　That cometh by it selfe without any other scole !
> (526)　He that is borne in Wallys or Small Brytayne,
> 　　　　To lerne to pyke and stele nedys nat go to Rome !
> 　　　　What nede we sayle to Flaunders or Almayne
> 　　　　To lerne, syns we may it lern at home !
> (527)　To passe the se to lerne Venus rybawdry
> 　　　　It is great foly ; for thou mayst lerne thy fyll
> 　　　　In shoppis, innes and sellers, ye somtyme openly
> 　　　　At saynt Martyns Westmynster or at the Tour Hyll,
> 　　　　So that I fere all London in tyme it shall fyll ;
> 　　　　For it is there kept in lyght and in darke,
> 　　　　That the pore stuys decays for lacke of warke ! [1]

118.—At the end of the chapter he makes a transition to a new idea, not in Locher :

> (530)　But more fole is he that may lerne every day
> 　　　　Without cost or laboure out of his own countrey ;
> 　　　　And whan the well of wysdome renneth by theyre dore,
> 　　　　Yet looth they the water as if that it were soure.

It sounds quite simple and serious, although there is a something in the last line which indicates that the fit of exalted spirits is not yet quite over.  Indeed, Barclay wants to prepare an occasion to have a practical joke with some friends of his.  He is going to place them into his Ship of Fools !  Here is the last stanza :

> (531)　Soft, folys, soft !  A lytell slacke your pace,
> 　　　　Till I have space you to order by degre !
> 　　　　I have eyght neyghbours that firste shall have a place
> 　　　　Within this my Shyp, for they most worthy be !
> 　　　　They may theyr lernynge receyve costeles and fre,
> 　　　　Theyr wallys abuttynge and ioynynge to the scoles ;
> 　　　　No thynge they can, yet nought wyll they lerne nor se !
> 　　　　Therfore shall they gyde this one Shyp of Foles !

A Latin title prefixed to this stanza explains whom he means by the ' eyght neyghbours,' the butts of his pleasantry !—' Alexander Barklay ad fatuos ut dent locum octo secundariis Beate Marie de Otery qui quidem prima huius ratis transtra merentur.'—There is no further explanation, except that the Register draws attention to this stanza by mentioning ' An addicion of the secundaries of Otery Saynt Mary, in Devynshyre.'  The name *Secondaries* for a particular division of ecclesiastics is quite peculiar.  The NED. seems to know the word in its technical meaning only from Barclay, and Ducange gives no satisfactory explanation of the Latin word nor sufficient quotations to bring out the real meaning.  But it becomes quite clear when we turn to the original

---

[1] Curiously enough, the last line, the best of all, has been altered in Cawood's edition into the meaningless :
　　　And as the open stues they ar set on warke.

institution at Ottery. The Bishop of Exeter, John Grandisson, had founded the College 'to the honour of Christ Jesus, the blessed Virgin Mary, St. Edward King and Confessor and all Saints,' and had given minute directions also as regards the names by which the various functionaries were to be called. They are contained in a Papal bull of 27 June 1342,[1] and there we see that the personnel of the College consisted of : 8 canonici, 8 vicarii chori, 1 presbyter parochianus, 1 presbyter matutinalis, 1 capellanus B. Mariae, 8 clerici qui secundarii dicantur, 2 clerici ecclesiae, 2 aquebajuli, 8 pueri choristae, 1 magister scholaris.

The inferior position of the *secundarii* becomes still clearer from the instruction : 'Volumus preterea quod pueri choristae dictae ecclesiae ad loca secundariorum, cum ad virilem vocem pervenerint, necnon secundarii ad gradum vicariorum prae aliis extraneis ceteris paribus admittantur.' And in the annexed *Statuta* [2] the necessary qualifications are given : 'Secundarius . . . competentis sit staturae et, voce puerili permutata, sonoritatem in voce virili, et scienciam legendi et cantandi habeat competentem.' If their voices had broken and they had acquired the art of intoning [3] and singing, they were fit for Secondaries !

The chapter is followed by a quite serious Envoy ; but that the writer had been thinking of his last humorous hit all through the rest of the chapter, appears from the amusing title, by which he can only have meant the same 'eight neighbours' : 'Of hym that nought can and nought wyll lerne, and seyth moche, lytell berynge away, I mene nat thevys.'—Nothing like it is found in any of his originals, nor are the contents of the chapter in any way elucidated by it.

119.—To learn from the MISFORTUNES OF OTHERS is the lesson inculcated by chapter 40. The examples are Hippomenes, Phaeton, Icarus and Jeroboam, and from Aesop's fables (edited by Brant himself) the stupid lobster and the cunning fox. Locher renders the German with remarkable faithfulness, omitting only Hippomenes and Jeroboam, while he elaborates Phaeton and Icarus in greater detail.

Barclay's translation follows the Latin, with some very good expressions, e.g.

> (601)   One crab blamys another for hir bacwarde pace.
> (600)   One blynde man another doth chyde and blame.

To the example of Icarus he adds in the margin by the side of Locher's reference to Ovid : 'vide Virgilium III Eney. et servium eodem loco ' ;

---

[1] G. Oliver, Monasticon Dioecesis Exoniensis (Exeter 1846) 264–268. A not quite exact extract from it is given by W. Dugdale, Monasticon Anglicanum (ed. London 1846) VI [2] (vol. viii), 1346. See also § 346.

[2] G. Oliver l.c. p. 268. Some idea of the actual relations may also be gathered from the enumeration of the various buildings in the *Incorporatio gubernatorum*, when the College was dissolved by Henry VIII : 'domos vocatos seu cognitos per nomen vel per nomina de le vikar's house, le secondarie's house, le querister's house et le scole house ' (G. Oliver l.c. p. 418).

[3] The meaning of the 'sciencia legendi,' F. B. Kruitwagen informs me, is probably the art of intonation or recitation of the liturgical text in the choir. See e.g. Denifle in Zeitschrift für Katholische Theologie 1883.

in the text, however, he introduces no alteration.   The following stanza
is distinctly marked as an ' Addicio Alexandri Barklay ' :

> (605)   We dayle se before our syght and our presence
>           What mysaventure to many one doth fall,
>           And that worthely, for theyr synne and offence ;
>           Yet are we blynde, and ar nat ware at all,
>           But in our synnes lyve unto them egall ;
>           And where by synne we se one come to shame,
>           We wyllyngly, alas, ensue the same.

No importance could be attached to this stanza, if it were not so
clearly indicated as original.   It would now seem that there is a reference
to the same case which is alluded to towards the end of chapter b.[1]

In Riviere—Drouyn—Watson I find nothing worth quoting here.
Watson expands his model again to fill the following page and translates
' ton oultrecuydance ' by ' thy grete wanhope.'

120.—Chapter 58 insists upon MINDING ONE'S OWN BUSINESS,
and, except for the last half-dozen lines, Brant's ideas are all in Locher
and his translators.   It is a short sermon (without special application)
on the text :

> (829)   For perfyte love and also charite
>           Begynneth with hym selfe.

This occurs also in Watson, but with a French ring :  ' For charyte well
ordeyned ought to begynne at hymselfe ' ( = Charite bien ordonnee
doit commencer a soymesmes).   There is another French proverb at
the end, where Drouyn has something to add to Riviere :  ' Car on dit
ung commun proverbe. qui ayme myeulx aultre que soy a la fontaine
meurt de soif ' = ' It is a comyn proverbe, that he the whiche loveth
another better than hymselfe, deyeth for thurste at the fountayne.'

Barclay adds a better one out of his own store :

> (833)   He is well worthy to have a folys pype,
>           That goth unbyddyn to rype anothers corne
>           And suffreth his owne to stande though it be rype.

121.—Chapter 78 contains a curious list of DIFFICULT POSITIONS
in which a man may find himself through his own folly, or out of which
he is not wise enough to escape.   The greater part of the list is in Locher,
though he skips a few of the most interesting items ;  his introduction
is also a great deal longer and his epilogue much shorter than in
Brant.—The most amusing of the list is in lines 19 and 20 :

> Wer lydet das in druck syn schuch
> Und inn syn frow im wynhusz such.

Only the first, alas ! is in Locher :

> Preterea in pedibus quos torquet calceus arctus.

Locher's list is in Barclay, a very good and eloquent enumeration ;

---

[1]  §§ 52, 55.

but quite serious and severe (Stanzas 1147–1151) and concluding with an ' Addicio Alexandri Barclay ' :

> (1152) These ar proude beggers and other stately folys,
> Sclanderers, lyers, and jurours of the syse,
> Phesicians and lawyers that never went to scolys,
> And fals taverners that reken one pot twyse, (!)
> Tapsters and hostlers that folowe that same gyse ;
> These ar fals offycers that lyve upon brybes,
> As excheters, officials, counstables and scribes.

Most of the persons chastized here have been or will be satirized in other chapters. To Physicians and Lawyers whole chapters (2 and 55) are devoted, Scribes get a large share of chapter 79. ' Excheters,' or as he calls them elsewhere ' executours,' have already been rebuked (§ 62), as well as false taverners (§ 95), against whom Barclay seems to bear a curious grudge. In the list the ' shoes ' also occur in two rather stiff lines :

> (1150) Moreover into my Shyp shall they ascende,
> That ar streght shoed whiche them doth sharply greve
> But yet they se nat therto, it to amende !

Barclay must have written them simply as part of his task. That narrow shoes were at that time worn in Alsace we know also from Geiler's sermons,[1] but the fashion was certainly not universal. For this we have a very interesting witness in Watson. Drouyn has been patiently prosifying Riviere, and he has reached the passage about the shoes, which is all in Riviere as it should be,—and Watson has been translating everything : ' It is they the whiche wereth shone so strayte that they rubbe of all the skynne of theyr toes, and wolde not have none other for to chose ' ; or as the Frenchman wrote : ' et ne vouldroient pas avoir mieulx.' Here he must have taken thought for a moment, or looked at his own shoes, for suddenly he exclaims : ' De telles gens naguere en france, car les souliers sont grans et larges ' ![2]—And Watson, not to be outdone by a Frenchman, changes the statement and writes more emphatically : ' Of suche folkes there is but fewe [he does not dare to say, none !] in this prosperous realme of Englonde [his patriotism is stirred !], for thanked be God, the shone is grete and large ynough ' ![3] The emphasis of this somewhat qualified statement is perhaps partly due, however, to abundance of room for this chapter, for at the end Watson

---

[1] Cf. Zarncke 423.

[2] There is an interesting article by M. Naudin on the ' Histoire des Chaussures à la Poulaine en France ' in the *Mémoires de la Société des Sciences et des Lettres de la Ville de Blois* iv (1852). The monk of St. Denis who was commissioned to write the *Chronica Caroli VI* relates that the narrow pointed shoes were cast off since the disastrous battle of Nicopoli in 1396. And, M. Naudin adds, ' pour donner un éclatant témoignage de la haine irrévocable qu'on vouait à cette chaussure, on se mit à porter des souliers qu'on nommait *becs de cane*, ayant un bec par-devant, de quatre à cinq doigts de largeur, droit et aplati, et des pantoufles si larges par le bout, qu'elles excédaient en largeur la mesure d'un bon pied. C'était une excellente satyre des souliers à la poulaine ' (p. 409).—They returned however under Francis I.

[3] Note the singular verb after the old plural *shone*. We know that Chaucer hesitated already between *shoos* and *shoon*. The form *shoon* must have gradually developed a collective or singular meaning.

attaches even a whole commonplace sentence, which is apparently used only to fill out the page.

122.—The praise of SUFFERING seems to be the theme of chapter 23, at least in Brant, but the motto and the first six lines refer rather to the FICKLENESS OF FORTUNE, and out of these first lines only has Locher spun his whole chapter.

No more of Brant is to be found in Barclay and in Riviere. The Englishman has some pithy expressions about Fortune [1]:

<blockquote>
(364) Whyle one is ladyd to, the others backe is bare,<br>
Whyle she a begger maketh in good abounde,<br>
A lorde or state she throweth to the grounde.<br>
(371) But though she smyle trust nat to hir intent,<br>
For amonge swete herbes ofte lurketh the serpent.
</blockquote>

In the Envoy there are some more :

<blockquote>
(372) None in this lyfe can byde in one degre,<br>
But somtyme hye, than after pore and lowe,<br>
Nowe nought set by, nowe in auctoryte,<br>
Nowe full, nowe voyde, as waters ebbe and flowe.
</blockquote>

He speaks of some very prosperous people that have suddenly fallen into calamity :

<blockquote>
(373) Thus it is foly to trust in fortunes grace,<br>
For whyle the se floweth and is at Burdews hye,<br>
It as fast ebbeth at some other place.
</blockquote>

It is rather striking that the tides of Bordeaux should be recalled here. Had the town some traditional fame in this respect ? Did Barclay know the town ? Or did he only mention some far-off place which most of his readers were sure to remember as having been English in the time of their fathers ? Some of Barclay's above-quoted sayings have a nearer parallel in Riviere than in Locher :

<blockquote>
Dont si lung rit lautre sen deult<br>
Si lung est riche lautre est pauvre<br>
Si lung pert et lautre recouvre<br>
A lung ouste a lautre donne<br>
Et tous ses tresors abandonne *etc.*
</blockquote>

Still, there does not seem to be any connexion between the two versions ; both draw from their own stock of popular wisdom ; and Barclay's is the better choice.

In Drouyn-Watson there is nothing worth quoting. Both authors are very prolix in this early chapter, but they give nothing but vague or absurd generalities.[2]

123.—There can be no mistaking the character of chapter 37. THE WHEEL OF FORTUNE is writ large at the head and throughout this whole chapter after Brant's most sarcastic fashion. It is the old image,

---

[1] Ramsay lxxxv finds traces of them in Skelton.

[2] In the beginning Watson translates *folz ignares* by ' incessyve fool,' an expression which recurs continually in other chapters and must have been quite familiar to the author. It is difficult to say what word he really means ; there is nothing like it in the NED.

probably first suggested by an expression in Boethius [1] which appears in Chaucer's translation : ' Thou hast bitaken thy-self to the governaunce of Fortune and forthy it behoveth thee to ben obeisaunt to the maneres of thy lady. Enforcest thou thee to aresten or withholden the swiftnesse and the sweigh of hir turninge whele ? ' [2] Brant must have often seen it in the remarkable rose-window in the transept of Basel Minster dating from about 1200.[3] But, however old the idea may be, Brant feels himself in his element here and heaps proverb upon proverb. —Two thirds of Brant's chapter are in Locher, who inserts the example of Julius Caesar, and where the German had mentioned only the first of the three fatal sisters, Clotho, the Latin gives the names only of the two others, Lachesis and Atropos. The French translators knew them well enough :

> Nos pauvres miserables vies
> Sont dens les mains des trois furies *etc.*

Drouyn has even supplied the name of the first one, but as he or his printer unfortunately changed *vies* into *vices*, Watson had an opportunity to show that the three sisters were quite strange to him : ' Our poore vyces be betwene the handes of the furyous (!), as Latbesys with her handes spynneth a threde wher as our lyves dependeth upon, to the ende that we lyve longely, Cloto holdeth the threde (la queloigne) but Atropos the cruell messenger of dethe breketh the threde. Lathesys fedeth us with hony, and maketh our poor soules to fall in to helle with the dampned.'

Barclay cannot have been very familiar with them either, as his paraphrase of the same passage in Locher shows :

> (557)    Of our short lyfe have we no certaynty,
> For Lachesys, whan that thou hast leste drede,
> Of thy lyve dayes shall shortly breke the threde.
> (558)    Atropos is egall to pore man and estate,
> Defar wyll nat deth by prayer ne request,
> No mortall man may his furour mytygate
> Nor of hym have one day longer here to rest.

He has not only assigned to Lachesis a duty which is not classically hers but he has even made of Atropos a male person ! A great deal better are his own sayings and proverbs :

> (551)    Promote a yeman, make hym a gentyl man,
> And make a baylyf of a butchers son,
> Make a squyer knyght,—yet wyll they, if they can,
> Coveyt in theyr myndes hyer promosyon.[4]

---

[1] De Consolatione, lib. ii, prosa 1.—I owe this reference to Prof. Dr. Raphael Lichtenberg, O.F.M.—Schreiber ii, 263 notes that the image is found in Boccaccio's *De Casibus* and in the Middle English metrical *Morte Arthur* (ed. G. G. Perry 1865). It became most common in the fifteenth century, and was often reproduced in woodcuts. Schreiber ii, n. 1883, 1883a, 1884, iii, 2968.—J. Knepper, Nationaler Gedanke, 92.

[2] Skeat's edition, Book ii, Prose 1, 120 sqq.

[3] It is still extant. See M. Wackernagel, Basel (Berühmte Kunststätten 57 : Leipzig 1912), 12.

[4] The ' butchers son ' naturally appealed to Skelton in his satires on Wolsey. Ramsay lxxxi finds the traces of this stanza in Magnyfycence.

(558)  It is a fowle fall to fall from erth to hell.
(559)  For who that hye clymmeth, his fall can nat be soft.
(565)  Nowe hye, nowe lowe, unstable as a flode.

124.—Two entire stanzas are marked as 'Addicio Alexandri Barklay'
and they are undoubtedly the best part of the chapter :

(555)  In stormy wyndes lowest trees ar most sure,
     And howsys surest whiche ar nat byldyd hye,
     Where as hye byldynges may no tempest endure,
     Without they be foundyd sure and stedfastly :
     So greatest men have most fere and ieopardy ;
     Better is povertye though it be harde to bere,
     Than is a hye degre in ieopardy and fere.

(556)  The hyllys ar hye, the valeys ar but lowe,
     In valeys is corne, the hyllys ar barayne ;
     On hyest places most gras doth nat ay growe,
     A mery thynge is mesure and easy to sustayne ;
     The hyest in great fere, the lowest lyve in payne,
     Yet better ly on grounde, havynge no name at all
     Than lye on a clyf ferynge alway to fall.

These are good thoughts well expressed. There is another original
passage not expressly marked as such :

(561)  Over rede Bochas and than shalt thou se playne
     The Fall of Prynces wryten ryght compendeously,
     There shalt thou se what punnysshement and payne
     Have to them fallen somtyme by theyr foly.

Of this he found nothing in Locher, nor in Riviere, who cannot
have influenced this chapter. So he is probably referring to Lydgate's
translation of *De Casibus Virorum Illustrium* of which he even quotes
the exact title, and which had been printed by Pynson in 1494.[1]

Original is also, of course, the Envoy, in no way inferior to the rest :

(566)  Labour nat, man, with to moche besy cure
     To clymme to hye, lyst thou by fortune fall ;
     For certaynly that man slepyth nat sure,
     That lyeth lows upon a narowe wall (!).
     Better somtyme to serve than for to governe all,
     For whan the net is throwen into the se,
     The grete fysshe ar taken and the pryncipall.
     Where as the small escapyth quyte and fre.

A great deal less nervous and typical is Riviere's paraphrase. Nor does
it improve by Drouyn's and Watson's recasting. Both have ample
space at their disposal : 'La roue de fortune' becomes 'dame fortunes
whele.' Sometimes Watson's liberties are instructive : 'the gretest ben
the smalest, and the leest be the moost' stands for the French more
monotonous 'les plus grans sont les moindres, et les moindres sont
les plus grans.' But his freedom of movement here allures him also into

---

[1] E. G. Duff, n. 46. Lydgate made his paraphrase not from the Latin but from
the French of Laurent Premierfait. The French translation must have been very
popular, for no fewer than six editions appeared before 1501 (Peddie i, 113).
Pynson's English edition also remained long in favour, as appears from the reprints :
Pynson 1527, Tottel 1554, and Wayland 1558 (all in the British Museum).

the most slip-shod constructions. Drouyn's addition : ' Et quant elle
a oste les biens celluy pouvre nest de nul ayme ' becomes almost incomprehensible in the English : ' And whan she hathe with drawen her goodes
they be dysdeyned of every man and is no more beleved ' (!)

125.—The danger of PROCRASTINATION in religious matters is
very seriously insisted upon in chapter 31. Locher has again left the
last third part untranslated, so that the most telling portion is lost
owing to his drawing out the introduction.—Locher's version presents no
difficulties ; so it is all in Barclay's translation, neatly expressed.
Some expressions are even better than in Locher, e.g. (484) :

> The longer tary the lesse apt shalt thou be.

The following stanza speaks of the sinner's delay to go to confession,
and on the margin Barclay copies from Riviere quotations from Canon
Law, but in the text I cannot detect any trace of influence. The ideas
are all quite simple and natural ; so they are in Riviere. Hence Drouyn
also is quite readable here, as well as his literal English translator. At
the end the Frenchman adds one sentence of his own, in which he threatens
the sinner : ' aller il te fauldra au puant habytacle avec les diables
denfer,' and in which Watson has toned down one word : ' thou must go
unto the infecte habytacle with all the devylles of helle.'—The prose
expression : ' Be it good or evyll custome taketh no newe gyse,' though
literally taken from the French, sounds a great deal better than Barclay's

> (484)  Whan costome and use is tourned to nature
> It is right harde to leve, I the ensure.

126.—A great deal more ambitious is chapter 56, in which Brant
solemnly preaches THE END OF WORLDLY POWER. Alas, it is a
double chapter ! Locher reduces the 97 lines to 38, taking Brant's first
32 lines (examples of Caesar, Darius, Xerxes, Nabuchodonosor), 66 sq.
(Alexander), 70 sq. (Cyrus), adding Croesus of his own accord, then
taking 85–89 (the end of the old monarchies) to conclude with, while he
simply leaves out Brant's favourite idea and his sacred persuasion : that
only the Holy Roman Empire would stand to the world's end (90 sqq.).—
The translators follow this meagre skeleton. Riviere has no notable
addition nor any influence on Barclay. There are some curious misunderstandings and expressions in Drouyn-Watson. Xerxes made war
on ' le royaulme datique ' (Riviere), ' Le royaulme dattique ' (Drouyn)
(= *Attica regna*), but in Watson on ' the realme of Dattyque '—Alexander
took with him to hell nothing ' que ses pacquetz vicieux ' (Riviere),
' seul fardeau vicieulx ' (Drouyn) = ' Save a fardell full of vyces and
synnes ' ! Locher had said *subibit mox latium* ; Riviere altered this
into some long-drawn-out danger to ' noz les latin.' Drouyn simplified
the danger, ' Et pour les pechez que faisons entre nous latins iay grant
doubt que ne forgeons ung marteau pour nous rompre les membres du
corps.' The French evidently felt themselves ' latins ' on account of
their language. But the Englishman shares their feelings : ' And for
the grete synnes that we commytte amonge us Latyns, I am sore aferde
that we forge a hammer for to breke our bodys withall.'

127.—Barclay has done his level best to make his scanty material as impressive as possible. With no great success however. All the stanzas of this chapter, except the first, have *ende* as their last word. This proves a convenient frame for his examples. When Locher's store is exhausted he adds by way of a finish :

> (801)   Thus shortly to speke and all to comprehende :
> All worldly thynges at last shall have an ende.

He does *not* finish yet ; he adds eight stanzas by way of Envoy, all octaves of course, and all ending with a French burden, *ce monde est choce vayne.*[1]   The leading idea is an old one ; it is the insistent question *where ?* which a real medievalist could fill with haunting poetry and to which Villon could still impart that artificial languor that appealed so strongly to the Pre-Raphaelites.   Barclay makes of it a very good but very prosaic sermon.   He surveys the whole history of the world, taking the seven ages (or *aetates*) one by one, as he is careful to add on the margin.   Of the first age he mentions Adam, Abel, Mathusala and Tubal ; of the second, Noe ; of the third, Abraham, Isaac and Jacob ; of the fourth, David and Solomon ; of the fifth and sixth, the Kings of Babylon, Jude, Israel, Samson and all the princes before Christ.   Now comes our turn,

> (806)   In this our age whiche is the last of all . . .
> Wherfore I boldly dare speke in generall
> We all shall dye : *ce monde est choce vayne.*

But then he begins again, and mentions Tully, Cato, Arystotyll, and best of all : (807) Arthur,

> The glorious Godfray, and myghty Charlemayne.

But these three names have no romantic glamour here.   They were simply the last three of the well-known ' Nine Worthies,' of whom Caxton has told us all.[2]

His questions go on with ' the Phylosophers and Poetis lawreat ' with ' great Grammaryens and pleasant oratours,' with ' other myghty conquerours.'   ' So I conclude bycause of brevyte,'—and the last lines are really the best of all—

> (809)   Strength, honour, riches, cunnynge and beautye,
> All these decay dayly, thoughe we complayne
> *Omnia fert etas*, both helth and iolyte,
> We all shall dye, *ce monde est choce vayne.*

128.—PRUDENT BEHAVIOUR IN DIFFICULTIES seems the best title for the somewhat disconnected contents of chapter 109.   Brant may have originally meant it to be a sequel to chapter 108 and a final piece of advice to all sinners and fools.[3]—But Locher has altogether

---

[1] French poets seem to have liked an English burden now and then.   Thuasne ii, 496 prints a ' Ballade de Jean Régnier ' with the Monk's Tale rhyme-scheme, and the last line of this French poem is in English :

> God and our Lady help my !

[2] See his Preface to *Malory* (ed. O. Sommer and A. Lang, 1889) i, 3.

[3] Zarncke lv.

changed the arrangement of the last chapters, and accordingly modified the character of this one. The first twelve lines are his own invention and treat of the transitoriness of worldly things. He then takes up two of Brant's ideas, viz.

> (8)   Unglück und hor, das wechszt all tag,

and the comparison of human life with a stormy sea-voyage, and how to behave in it. The first appears with an emphatic introduction as

> Quod mala sors crescat, crinis quoque nocte dieque.

The last dozen lines with the example of Alexander and Pompey are omitted.

Barclay follows this version without any influence of Riviere. He has not understood the *crinis*, of course, and simply writes :

> (1700)   An yll fortune growyth alway more and more.

But he adds another, better, proverb instead :

> (1699)   As it is wryten and sayd of many one :
> That one myshap fortuneth never alone.

Locher's fine expression

> Irrepit tacito sors metuenda pede

is rendered in fine English :

> (1701)            for dayly thou mayst se
> How ferefull fortune sodaynly crepys on the.

The following stanza, with all the ideas taken from Locher, is nevertheless probably one of the highest poetical achievements of the book :

> (1702)   Who that dare aventure or ieoparde for to rowe
> Upon the se swellynge by wawes great and hye
> In a weyke vessell, had nede that wynde sholde blowe
> Styll, soft and cawme, lyst that he fynally,
> And also his shyp, stande in great ieopardy,
> Throwyn with the flodes on the se depe and wyde,
> And drowned at the last, or rent the syde fro syde.

The metre cannot be reduced to any scheme, but the rhythmical movement of the lines is in such harmony with the ideas and feelings expressed, that Barclay must have been endowed with one precious poetical gift. Reading this passage, one cannot help regretting that the writer has allowed this rare present of the Muse to be continually buried under the careless prolixity of the preacher and the plaintive wordiness of the moralizer.—He is regularly dropping into prose again.—In the Envoy he refers to some recent events and draws a moral from them :

> (1706)   We have late sene some men promotyd hye,
> For whose sharpnes all men fered theyr name ;
> But for they toke on them than theyr degre
> Myght nat support : they fell down in great shame.[1]

---

[1] In these two lines the punctuation is the same as in the original, as the meaning and construction are not clear.

> But well myght they have contynued without blame,
> If they had kept them within theyr boundes well
> By right and iustice ; but oft full yll they frame,
> That wyll be besy with to hye thynges to mell.

He is very probably alluding here to the well-known fate of Empson
and Dudley, who during the reign of the very parsimonious king
Henry VII had gained for themselves the names of unscrupulous
extortioners, and had been put in prison shortly after the accession of
the new king.[1]

129.—Watson translates Drouyn of course, but as Wynkyn de Worde
had not got the right woodcut, the picture of chapter 23 had to be used
again, and so one of the first sentences had to be altered : ' This foole
fyndeth hymself in his house all on a fyre, and his goodes consumed '—
where the French had : ' dedens la mer tellement que sa navire rompt,
et ses voilles et mat cheent en la mer.' He then continues from his
French companion and writes the following curious nonsense : ' O thou
man, yf thou have an unfortune for all thy heed is well combed, and
that theyr brede lyce or vermyne, the prudentes say a comyn proverbe :
" If there come yl, it is never alone." ' It is literally from Drouyn and
is meant as a paraphrase of the following passage in Riviere, which is
also curious, but not nonsensical :

> O hom si infortune tavient
> Petite aucunesfois te vient
> Quelle est de mal accompaignee
> Combien que ayez teste pignee
> Si luy survient poulx et ordure
> Daventure il cherra laidure,
> Les prudens vieux et anciens *etc.*

130.—Here may be inserted the chapter on WORLDLY FOOLS (h),
as its contents are more or less related to the preceding. It has no
parallel in Locher nor in Brant—and so it is not found in Riviere—Drouyn
—Watson. But Barclay premises a Latin poem *De fatuis mundanis*,
which, as it is very short and not to be found in the ordinary editions
of Locher's text, may be quoted here :

> Dum me cura tenet sublimia forte petendi
>   Et vigil expecto det mihi digna labor
> Destituit fortuna pedem nixumque fefellit :
>   Nec potuit lapsus pes retinere gradum
> Et quia prensus erat non parvo robore ramus
>   Praecipitem effractus retulit ecce solo
> Cura : fides probitas (fueris nisi praeditus astu
>   Et vafro ingenio) parviputata iacent.

At its head stands the woodcut to be found in Locher's first edition [2]
(not in the second or third), and in Brant before chapter 36 (not

---

[1] He probably refers to the same event in his Eclogues. See Jamieson lvii.
They were executed on the 17th of August 1510.

[2] Before chapter e, ' De Singularitate.' Riviere uses the same woodcut here,
which shows that he has used the first edition. The second edition, reprinted in
France, has a new woodcut in front of chapter e, viz. a fool in conversation with a
wise man.

translated by Locher). It represents a ' fool ' falling out of a tree. On the margin Barclay annotates : ' *Scribitur in fatuum nimis mundo confidentem : et est carmen dni Roberti Gaguini.*' The insertion of this chapter has always puzzled the critics. Zarncke puts the difficulty very concisely : ' Auf welche weise erklärt sich die aufnahme dieses gedichtes des Rob. Gaguinus, welches in der Locherschen übersetzung nie gestanden zu haben scheint, dagegen in die des Badius eingang gefunden hat, welche wiederum schwerlich dem Englischen übersetzer vorlag, da er sonst nicht unterlassen haben würde sie zu erwähnen.' [1] The solution of the problem is very simple however. Barclay took the poem from the same source from which Badius had taken it, viz. *from one of the French editions of Locher's version.* In the Marnef edition of the 8th of March 1498 (Pellechet 2824) the poem is printed on a spare page at the end, behind the Registrum, and Sachon the Lyons printer copied it in the same place (Pellechet 2825). So it had already become embodied in the *Navis Stultifera* long before Badius.[2]—The striking thing, however, is that Barclay should know that it was Gaguin's work. For in neither of the two French editions do we find the name. That the Parisian Badius should be acquainted with the authorship of the poem is no wonder. But it was more difficult for a Devonshire cleric to get at the truth. This casual mentioning of the name may be taken as an indication that Barclay had been in Paris. We have other and perhaps stronger arguments for this, but all our evidence is circumstantial, so that every corroboration is welcome. In humanistic circles in Paris the smallest poetical effort of Gaguin would never be considered as a trifle hidden away in an obscure corner. He was the recognized leader of the whole movement, and it was he, perhaps, who had seen the reprint of Locher's translation through the press, and had added his poem to it by way of an Envoy.

131.—Barclay's treatment of this poem is entirely different from his method in the rest of the book. First he uses throughout this chapter a four-beat measure, which is elsewhere adopted only in one or two mottos, and in one or two stanzas of the eccentric *Concertacio* (b). Secondly he does not pretend to translate this poem, but he writes quite an original piece of verse, only inspired by the same ideas. It consists of thirteen stanzas of 7 and three stanzas of 8 lines, with the ordinary rhyme-scheme, except Stanzas 1915 and 1916 which rhyme a b a b b a a, while the three final stanzas, which may take the place of the Envoy, all end with ' thou hast bene '—rhyming with *sene* and *wene*, and once spelled *ben* and rhyming with *iyen*.—The best hypothesis to explain these irregularities is, perhaps, that the author knew it to be a more original poem and so felt himself at liberty to deviate from his usual course. There is hardly any ground for the supposition that he wrote this poem at some earlier period, e.g. during his stay abroad. For it is certainly in no way a youthful production, inferior to the rest of his work. It has equally good proverbial sayings :

[1] Zarncke 242. The Cambr. Hist. (iii, 59) refers to the same difficulty.
[2] Cf § 11, 25.

(1914)   In hyest rowmes is greattest fere.
(1916)   If one be in a rowme a hye,
         Men that ar lowe seme to him small,
         But to say trouth and veryte,
         Yet may theyr stature be egall,
         In lyke wyse though a man royall
         Despyse them lyvynge in poverte,
         Of one metall yet both they be.
(1917)   This worlde all hole goeth up and downe,
         It ebbes and flowes lyke to the se,
         Wexynge and waynynge lyke the mone,
         Nowe in welthe and in prosperyte,
         Eft in advers and frowarde poverte ;
         But that man folowes hye wysdome
         Whiche takys all thynges lyke as they come.

And a favourite idea of his, excellently expressed :

(1919)   No erthly thynge makes more debate
         Than a vyle chorle come to a state.

In the following he may well be alluding to some Empson-and-Dudley story :

(1922)   The noble fawcons ar oft opprest,
         The egle blyndyd, and byrdes small
         Ar spoyled and dryven from theyr nest,
         Whan the gredy kyte wyll rule all ;
         But if the kyte than after fall
         By advers fortune or his iniquyte,
         The fawcons may well have ioy to se.

The three final stanzas contain an admonition to those that have risen ' unto hye degre.'   They must always remember what they have been, and, curiously enough,

(1925)   To auncient blode do reverence
         Thoughe it be but of lowe degre.

This sounds as if he is again thinking of a particular case.   The true-born Englishman adds :

(1926)   Serve God thy maker above all thynge,
         And next that with thy herte and mynde
         Be true and loyall unto thy kynge
         And to his subiectis iust and kynde.

132 —Chapter 85 is a complete sermon on DEATH with most of the usual ideas in it.   A very long chapter in Brant of about 160 lines. Quite by way of exception Locher takes a double chapter for it, of about 100 lines, and skilfully elaborates in it all the main ideas of his master.

He takes the introduction (1–10) : all men must die at an uncertain time ; 17 and 18 : the contract is made :
           Arra subest : contractus habet sua jura,
being a weak version of
             Der wynkouff ist gedruncken schon
             Wir mögen nit dem kouff abston.
29–32 : Death will fight and overcome all ;   41–44 : no dignity is free from him ; 57–58 : no age (Locher speaks of ' Nestoreum evum sive Sybillinum ') ;   60–61 : the

son often dies before the father ; 65–66 : No use crying for the dead ; 71–82 : Death delivers many from a miserable life ; 88–92 : All have to join in the Dance of Death ; 97–122 : It is folly to build costly tombs, as the Mausoleum and the Pyramids of Chemnis [ = Cheops] and of Rhodope and of Amasis; 125 sq. : the souls are forgotten ; 147–150 : it is the tombs that are superfluous ; 154 sq. : prepare for your own death, for fearful is death in a state of sin.

This cleverly constructed anthology from Brant's ideas filled out and connected by Locher's own phraseology is found in Riviere and with several rearrangements in Barclay. The Englishman[1] seems to avoid the difficult ' Nestoreum evum sive Sybillinum ' and writes instead :

> (1276)   Yet he nat graunteth to any creature.
> As symple man, great Lorde or Prince soverayne,
> Of dethes hour to be stedfast and sure ;

but the Frenchman, although he puts Locher's *Nestor* on the margin, bungles through it :

> . . . et tousiours domine
> De nestreus iucque a cest aage
> Or despuis sibille la saige.

Both Riviere and Barclay dilate, of course, upon the *Danse Macabre*. In Riviere it is little more than an enumeration of those that take part in

> Une grande et terrible dance,

but there are no such forcible expressions as

> (1280)   His cruell daunce no man mortall can stent,
> (1281)   The bysshop, lorde, the pore man lyke a state
> Deth is his daunce ledyth by the sleve . . .
> He gyvys no space to man to stande or syt,
> But sue the trompe tylle he come to the pyt.

133.—Speaking of the pyramids, however, the English translator must have sought the assistance of his weaker French fellow. Most of this passage is still a fairly correct rendering of Locher.

> (1287)   One Rodopis callyd by such a name
> Byldyd such another vayne sepulture
> The riche Amasis also dyd the same

is at any rate a hundred times better than Riviere's arbitrary alteration :

> Radulphus qui en amassis
> Construit de richesse massis
> Pareillement tel oppertoyre.

But for the Chemnis' pyramid Barclay must have followed Riviere rather than Locher, from whom he had just translated the passage about Artemisia's Mausoleum.

---

[1] The German-Latin proverb is rendered quite forcibly in Stanza 1263 :
> Thy ernest is layde, the bargen must abyde.

(1285)  Chemnys also, as Dyodorus sayes,
Byldyd a speere hye and wonderous,
To bere remembraunce of his tyme and dayes.
This speere was costely, dere and sumptous,
And of quantyte so great and marveylous,
That a thousande men and .iii. hundreth fulfylde
In twenty yeres coude it skantly bylde.

(1286)  The brother of the sayd Chemnys in lyke wyse
Brought all his royalme unto povertye,
Whyle he another lyke speere dyd devyse
For his vayne tombe, so that his comonte
And other workmen after one degre
Were longe compellyd in this worke to ete
Herbys and rotis for lacke of other mete.

As this curious piece of classical lore is also of some lexicographical interest, the corresponding passages must be quoted in Latin and in French.  Locher says :

Extulit hinc Chemnis stupidam per secula cuncta
Pyramidem . . .
Millia tercentena hominum : per lustra quaterna :
(Ut diodorus ait) molem hanc vix condere possunt.
Quid quod opes pene exhausit Memphitica tellus
Quo plebem artificum solis radicibus : atque
Exiguis herbis aleret ?  quis cetera narret
Fercula ?  vix aliquis sit vel ditissimus ipse
Princeps ex nostris (nisi fallar) solveret illa.

The relation between these two texts would be hopelessly intricate, if we had not the French version :

Et a chemnis qui ce pinacle
Ediffia ou tabernacle . . .
Et si furent trois milliers
Dhommes par quatre iours entiers
A lediffice diceluy
Sicque humain navoit celuy
Quil nesbayst de sa fabricque
*Son frere demetiticque*
Lequel apres chemnis regna
En ce royaulme et si donna
Telle structure voulut faire.

In order fully to understand Locher's Latin it would be necessary to quote Brant also, but that is not necessary for our purpose.

Barclay's ' a thousande men and .iii. hundreth in twenty yeres ' is evidently from Locher.  The small mistake (Locher means 300,000) is pardonable, and is certainly not half as bad as Riviere's ' trois milliers . . . par quatre iours.'—The misunderstanding contained in the ' herbys and rotis,' which is also in the French, is again pardonable and to some extent natural.[1]  But what is quite evident is the origin of ' The brother

---

[1] If only any of the translators had been able to look at the German original the readers would not have been pulled by the nose :
(13 sqq.).  Dan er umb krut gab also vil
(Der ander kost ich schwigen will)
Keyn fursten ich so rich yetz halt
Der das alleyn mocht han bezahlt.

of the sayd Chemnis.' As there is nothing of the kind in Locher, Barclay must have taken it from the French, although he has wisely left out the name, which sounds suspiciously like ' Memphitica [fra ?]-tellus.' The marginal note dispels all doubt. Locher quotes : *Chemnis de q. diodo. li. ii.* Riviere copies this, but a few lines further on he adds without Locher's authority : *Diodoro. li. ii. De fratre chenii q. edificavit pira-midem.* It does not matter much whether Riviere has really consulted Diodorus or not.[1] But *Barclay copied both Locher's and Riviere's note on his own margin.* So that we have another instance of Barclay succumbing to the fascination of a learned-looking note. The French origin of the ' brother ' is, therefore, beyond all doubt. We may now well ask : Where did he get his ' speere ' from, and what did he mean by it ? The one question is dependent upon the other. For in itself the word is nothing but a variant of *spire,* partly influenced by *spear.* The NED. gives the meaning *pyramid* here, but quotes no other authority for this abnormal meaning than just this passage in Barclay. If it were certain that Barclay had only translated the Latin, that would have been undoubtedly the sense of the word. But as we have seen, Barclay does not exclusively translate from the Latin here, so that he may very well have put his ' speere ' to render the French ' ce pinacle.' [2] Hence the meaning given by the NED. is not sufficiently established.

After this Chemnis-incident there do not seem to have been more encounters between Barclay and Riviere in this chapter. There are several little additions in the French, but none of them have left any trace on the English.

134.—Several of these additions, however, appear in Watson's prose. None are of particular interest. Some of his translations are :

' He dothe pardone no body, for he hath his houres *amytted* ' is supposed to render ' car elle a heure limitee.'—' Be it yonge or olde, he putteth all in his cyrcle ' does not sound bad, but Watson confuses a circle with a coffin, for the French has ' en son cercueil.' [3]—' All this serveth the not of a lytell halfpenny ' has an idiomatic ring ; the French says ' tout ce ne te sert point dune petite maille.' The Chemnis story gets the following treatment : ' In lyke wyse [as Artemisia] of Chemnys that had iii. M. men werkynge on one foure days [the pyramid has disappeared altogether in order to save space !! Drouyn had at least instead of that *one* ' tabernacle qui estoit de cinquante coudees ']. His broder Demetyque that regned afther hym had almoost destroyed his people with famyne for makynge of one [tel monument], for they had but lytell herbes to theyr nourysshynge. And before they had grete

---

[1] The *Bibliotheca* of Diodorus Siculus in Poggio's Latin version seems to have been printed at Paris at an early date (Pellechet 4265). Skelton's translation of this version, preserved only in MS. 357, Corpus Christi College, Cambridge, will be edited for the Early English Text Society, says a note in Cambr. Hist. iii, 481.

[2] That the ideas about the character of a pyramid were not very clear may be proved from the explanation of the ' literal ' Marnef-version : ' Et dit Plinius en sa naturelle hystoire que piramydes estoyent *tours* faictes en egipte pour mettre le tresor des roys les plus haultes que lon pouvoit faire.' So ' pinacle ' might be used to indicate a pyramid, while Barclay could translate *pinacle* by *speere* without having the least idea of a pyramid.

[3] As an extenuating circumstance I must add that Watson had probably not seen the picture, which represents Death with a coffin on its shoulder. Wynkyn de Worde has not reproduced this cut.

hepes of rychesses in theyr possessyons.   Rodulphus and Amaphis [1] in lyke wyse '
*etc.*

At the end Drouyn and Watson add a solemn conclusion to their
sermon :

that we may reygne above in heven withe the holy sayntes, men and women [avec
les saincts et sainctes], where as domyneth, the fader, the sone, and the holy ghoost.

135.—Chapter 94 is one of bitter irony on the foolish WAITING FOR
DEAD MEN'S SHOES.   The bitterest passages have all been left out
by Locher, who translates hardly more than a dozen lines, including the
examples of Priam and Absolom, and one peculiar ' hit ' in Brant :

> Der selb den esel dut beschlagen
> Der in gön narrenberg würt tragen,

which serves as an explanation of the woodcut and which is partly
rendered by

> Narragonum in patriam te preceps ducet asellus.

The rest of the chapter is filled out by Locher with serious admonitions
about the uncertainty of death.   Neither the French nor the English
translator, of course, could understand the meaning of *Narragonum*.
So Riviere omitted it altogether, and Barclay gave his own explanation
of the ass :

> (1447)   Thy selfe shall dye, there is no remedy,
> And if thou before canst no provysion make,
> Upon his backe the dull asse shall the take
> And to our shyp the lede through fen and myre
> For this thy folysshe hope and vayne desyre.

A great part of this chapter is quite original in Barclay, and some good
sayings occur in it, as e.g.

> (1450)   Yet Deth dayly steleth slyely on the,

and especially the grimly humorous expression about those whose
wishes for a rich uncle's death are frustrated :

> (1442)   For suche as they moste gladly dede wolde have
> Etyth of that gose that graseth on theyr grave.

There is nothing of interest in Watson, nor much of sense.   For he had
to shorten this chapter and so he cut off a part from nearly every sentence.
' Kynge Pryam for all his aege, sawe all his chyldren deye before hym.
Wherfore he deyed almoost as he wente ' is supposed to render ' Nous
lisons de Priam et de ses filz lesquelz estoient fors et vaillans.   Cestuy
Priam estoit bien vieulx, mais il veit la mort de tous ses filz.'

---

[1] Drouyn in his first edition wrote ' Radulphus et Amafis,' where the *f* might
be a misprint for an *s*.   This was an improvement upon Riviere, who takes *Amassis*
as the name of a place (see quotation above).   In the second edition *Amafis* is
changed into *Amaphis*, and we get farther afield.

## VIII

## CHAPTERS RELATING TO RELIGION, THE CHURCH AND THE CLERGY

136.—The original Ship of Fools owes its fame among modern historians largely to the chapters that fall under this category. As the translations all depend upon Locher, we shall have to detail the relation between him and Brant somewhat more carefully, in order to bring out their real significance.

Extending this category as widely as possible and taking the more abstract chapters first, we may perhaps begin with chapter 11, which seems mainly to deal with CONTEMPT OF TRUE DOCTRINE. But it is rather difficult to give one name to two such heterogeneous chapters as we have before us in Brant's original and in Locher's Latin. Brant inveighs against the credulity of so many simpletons, who run for miles to see miracles, and to hear old wives' tales about hell, and who admire impostors such as

(18)   Des sackpfiffers von Nickelshusen.[1]

To all this Locher alludes only in a word or two, speaking of ' loquacitas ' and of ' nugas aniles.'—But Brant's admonition that people ought to attach more faith to the true word of God to be found in the Bible and the teaching of the Church becomes the main contents of the Latin chapter.—This is also found in Barclay without any apparent influence from Riviere. The ' nugas aniles ' are adduced as ' the tales of an old wyfe ' (197), and the idea is then enlarged upon in an original stanza :

(198)   The holy Bybyll, grounde of trouth and of lawe,
Is nowe of many abiect and nought set by,
Nor godly Scripture is nat worth an hawe ;
But talys ar lovyd grounde of rybawdry,
And many blynddyd ar so with theyr foly,
That no Scripture thynke they so true nor gode,
As is a folysshe yest of Robyn Hode.

After having thus had a fling against a very popular story of the time,[2]

[1] An allusion to the notorious case of Hans Böhme, a fanatic at Niclashausen, who was executed in 1476 (Janssen-Pastor i, 386). Thomas Murner afterwards celebrated him ironically as a predecessor of Luther : ' Die Fahrt von Niklaushausen, da ein trummen schlager auch das lutherisch Gottswort verkundet hat ' (Kirchendieb und Ketzerkalender). So does H. C. Lea ; but seriously (A History of the Inquisition ii (1906), 418–420), just as Ullmann had done (Reformatoren vor der Reformation i (Hamburg 1841), 421 sqq.).

[2] As the allusion occurs more than once, we shall have to revert to it (see § 325). I may here only remind the reader that the *Gest of Robin Hode* was printed by W. de Worde about 1510.

for the rest of the chapter he renders Locher's vague complaints about people neglecting or despising the true doctrine and instructions of the Church into English rhymes with skilful fidelity.

137.—In the same way Watson declares : 'They that be whanhope wyll not gyve credence unto the auncyent scryptures, be fooles.' *Be whanhope* here stands for Drouyn's ' par cuyder ' = Riviere's ' par trop cuider de soy.'—Like Drouyn, Watson has plenty of space, and so the ' nugas aniles ' become ' mensonges, farceries fictions et fables,' or in English, ' They desyre moore soner to rede playes, tryfles, and fables.' It is a pity he does not tell us what fables and trifles and especially plays he means. But Watson is scolding the fools : ' They ben soo unhappely molefyed, so affusked and hardened, that hygh brayenge and hye cryenge avayleth to them nothynge.' Here are some words of interest : ' Unhappely molefyed ' is Drouyn's ' tresmal amolis,' which stands for Riviere's ' tresmal rassiz.'—' Affusked ' is ' obfusquez ' both in Drouyn and Riviere.[1]—' Hygh brayenge and hye cryenge ' is an amusing description of the delivering of a sermon. It is taken literally from the French ' hault braire ne hault crier ' (Drouyn and Riviere), where it is probably an unconscious and therefore all the more exact reflection of the methods of the popular preachers of the time. We must only remember that *to bray* had no such unpleasant associations as it has to-day, and that it was used by Lydgate, Gower and Caxton of persons to indicate any shrill cry (see NED.).—Watson's conclusion may conclude this chapter, if only to show how he is expanding to fill his space. Drouyn threatens the fools with hell, ' ou sans fin tourmentez seront, et iamais clarte ne verront,' which is enforced by Watson : ' where as they shall remayne in everlastynge payne, without the seynge of ony lyght or day that ever was create.'

138.—TRUTH ABOVE ALL is the device of chapter 104.

Fools allow themselves to be intimidated from telling the truth (1–8). God protects Truth, and a wise man will cling to her even when threatened with Phalaris's brazen bull (9–16). Jonas came to harm because of his fear, but Elias was carried to heaven, and John baptized Christ because they both loved truth (17–24). Those whom you truthfully censure, will one day be grateful (25–30). Daniel would not accept Balthasar's gifts, but Balaam was punished because he had suffered himself to be bribed (31–39). Three things cannot be hidden : a city seated on a mountain, a fool, and the splendour of truth (40–49). When I began to write this work [says Brant], many wanted me to tone down many things, but I let them all talk (50–56). If I had not been able to tell the truth, 1 should never have written my book (57–60). For Truth is stronger than all her enemies, and if I had listened to them, I should have been the greatest fool of all (61–65).

Locher, reducing this chapter to 34 lines, translates only lines 25–30 ; the rest is an original treatise on the upholding of truth in the face of flattery and of violence. He takes over two of Brant's examples, viz. Phalaris's bull and John the Baptist, adding to it the sword of Damocles

---

[1] Watson is very fond of the word *affusked*, and uses it repeatedly, sometimes even without any suggestion from the French, as in chapter 95, where ' pleins de grans vices ' becomes ' affusked in vyle synnes.' The NED. knows no *affusk* nor even *offusk*, but only *offuscate* and *obfusk* and (without any example) *offusque*. See also § 160.

and a quotation from the (pseudo-)Virgilian *De Viro Bono*. Of Brant's heroic attitude, not a word. And yet the old master approved of the translation !

Barclay, paraphrasing the Latin treatise, especially applies it to those who have ' to preche the very lawe dyvyne ' (1644), and his best stanza is again largely original :

> (1647)    But for that flaterynge so many doth overcome,
> And rewardes lettyth the trouth for to apere,
> Therfore the fole that sholde say trouth, is dum,
> Hackynge his wordes, that no man may them here ;
> And if he knowe that any one is nere
> Infect and scabbyd, he dare no worde let slyp,
> But layeth his fynger anone before his lyp.

The first two lines and the last one are from Locher, the rest, and particularly the picture of the hesitating preacher in lines three and four, is Barclay's own. So is the addition in Stanza 1650 about a preacher :

> Not ferynge to touche the foly and errour
> Of Pope nor prelate, kynge ne emperour.

This self-assumed attitude of heroism is typical of the humanistic mind. Barclay assumes it again in his Envoy :

> (1654)    O precher, thou deth ought rather to endure
> Than for love, favour, fere or punysshement
> The veryte to cloke or make the trouth obscure
> Or to hyde the lawes of God omnypotent ;
> And if that any unto thy deth assent
> For prechynge trouth, receyve it paciently ;
> So hath many sayntis theyr blode and lyves spent
> Rather than they wolde hyde veryte or lye.

Such declamations may have been honestly meant, but the heroic attitude easily becomes a pose. Many Humanists have been praised for their courage, who never showed more than the pose.

139.—Even poor Watson has something of it at second hand. Riviere does not seem to have understood the allusion to Phalaris's bull very well, because Locher spoke only of ' in Siculo tauro.' He understood only that something had happened ' au pais de cecille.' Drouyn did not like to go so far afield and made a more general statement, which became in English : ' How well that for tellynge of trouthe there hath ben sene dyvers hanged and quartered. And for all that yf that ye sholde have the same punysshemente, ye ought ever to saye the trouthe.' Watson will follow his guide through thick and thin, even bearing out the statement that John the Baptiste ' fayned hym not for to correcke Herode Antypas, bycause that he helde the wyfe of Herodiades, the whiche was the broder of Horode Antypas.' This is just what Drouyn said, who meant it as a prose version of

> . . . pour le mal
> Quil faisoit de tenir la femme
> Herodiades comme infame
> Qui estoit celle de son frere.

When Drouyn speaks without Riviere's authority he is usually a little more malicious.  In this chapter he adds two sentences at the end :

Whan the doctours ben bysshoppes or have benefyces, ye shall not here them preche nor crye nomore, for trouthe in them is hydde, and maye not take the payne no more.  And on the other syde they dare not saye nothynge, lest they sholde lese theyr benefyces.

Probably an echo of the sermons of Olivier Maillard !

140.—ILL-ADVISED PRAYERS is the theme of chapter 26, at least in the translations.  Brant had treated rather of vain wishes, and devoted a double chapter to the subject.

He began with the description of Midas' foolish wish (1-11), then followed a long passage on the disadvantages of wishing for a long life (12-44), with a plastic de-scription of the infirmities of crabbed age, and of the sorrows that often attend it, as in the case of Nestor, Peleus, Laertes, Priam, Mithridates, Marius, Pompey, Croesus.  The second vain wish was for beauty (45-58), and its resulting dangers are exemplified by the fates of Helen, Lucrece, and Diana.  The third was for riches (59-64), the fourth for power, only too prone to end in misery (65-70).  Conclusion : God knows best what is good for us (71-80), we must only pray for good health and virtue (81-85), for this is better than what Hercules and Sardanapalus had (86-90), for all other wishes may tend to our own misfortune (90-94).

Locher, as is his wont, makes a single chapter of it, and he entirely alters the arrangement.  He begins with a longer introduction, then follows with Midas in six lines ; then comes the wish for riches in eight lines, in which Lycinus and Crassus and Croesus are introduced ; then the long life with  its sorrows and the examples of Peleus, of Nestor and of ' Itacusque Laertes ' ;  power is treated of in two lines, beauty in two, and the conclusion (3 lines) that we must wish for virtue and for Juvenal's ' Mens sana in corpore sano.'

Our translators had to work on this unpromising material.  Barclay dutifully fulfils his task, with a few notable alterations and additions. The first stanza (399), quoting from the Bible, at once introduces prayers in the more technical sense of the word, and the conditions of good prayers.  Stanzas 400-408 are all as in Locher.  In Stanza 409 there appear

> Peleus and Nestor and many other mo,
> As Itackes and Laertes.

Thus the adjective has been promoted to the rank of a personal proper name.  But when this difficult passage was over, Barclay felt a bit more at ease.  The following stanza, which should simply mention the vanity of worldly power, is easily the best of this chapter :

> (409)    Yet ar mo folys whiche ought repreved be,
> And they ar suche whiche styll on God doth call
> For great rowmes, offyces and great dignyte,
> No thynge intendynge to theyr grevous fall ;
> For this is dayly sene and ever shall,
> That he that coveytys hye to clym aloft,
> If he hap to fall, his fall can nat be soft.

Before dealing with Locher's conclusion he inserts a rhyming version of the Pater Noster which may be quoted as a curiosity, and of which he himself says that it is

(411)   Nere to this sentence, nor greatly doth nat vary :
       ' Our Father wiche art in heven, eternally
       Thy name be halowyd, graunt that to thy kingdome
       All we, thy servauntis, worthely may come.
(412)   In heven and erth thy wyll be done alway,
       And of thy great grace and thy benygnyte
       Our dayly brede graunt unto us this day,
       Forgyvynge our synnes and our iniquyte,
       As we forgyve them that to us detters be,
       And to avoyde temptacion thy grace unto us len,
       And us delyver from every yll.  Amen.'

After this display of rhyming skill, the conclusion follows as in Locher,[1] and after that, before the Envoy, one more stanza :

(414)   Thus sholde thou pray, thou wretche, both day and nyght,
       With herte and mynde unto thy Creatoure,
       And nought by foly to asshe[2] agaynst right
       To hurte or losse to thy frende or neyghboure
       Nor to thy fo by yllwyll or rygoure.
       But if God to thy prayers always sholde enclyne,
       Oft sholde come great sorowe to the and to all thyne.

As there is nothing of the kind in his original, Barclay must be aiming at some particular abuse.  The last two lines, which stand in rather loose connexion with what precedes, summarize the contents of his instruction, which had opened with a similar reflection in Stanza 401 where it is an echo of Locher's Latin.[3]

141.—For curiosities we must look into Watson.  Two of the best may be quoted.  First the rhyming motto.  In Drouyn he found

Qui les mains tendans et dieu prie
Sans y avoir devocion [4] *etc.*

The Englishman omits the second line, which is the essence of the whole idea, and turns the praying attitude of the first line into a remarkable posture :

Who that on handes and fete dothe praye (!)
By false dyssymulacyon,
Cryenge on God both nyght and daye,
That he wolde graunte unto hym pardon
And gyve them clene remyssyon,
They be fools that with cryenge
Thinketh to opteyne ony thynge.

---

[1] The Juvenalian expression occurs in it as :
       For helthe of soule within thy hole body.

[2] The form *ashe* normally derived from OE. *ascian* was still in common use by the side of *aske*.  This was originally a Northern form, which has gradually displaced the South-Western and West-Midland *ash, esh*.  See NED.

[3] Brant's conclusion resembles Barclay's somewhat, but cannot of course have influenced him.

[4] Drouyn copied it from Riviere, substituting only *tendans* for *estand*.

We can easily take the anacoluthon and the transition from the singular to the plural into the bargain.

The second curiosity is the story of Midas turned into a nursery tale :

> Mydas kynge of Frygye . . . requyred of the goddes to gyve hym grete habundaunce of fyne golde the whiche they uttred [1] to hym facylly,[2] therfore it behoved hym to faste (!) for all that he touched was converted in to fyne gold.

This is literally from Drouyn, who had thus prosified into nonsense Riviere's rhyming, but quite correct, version.

### 142.—Another aspect of USELESS PRAYERS is given in chapter 45 :

> Fools are always praying, says Brant, without ever making an honest endeavour to get rid of their folly (1–8).   It is like wilfully jumping in a well and then crying for help (9–14) ;  think of Empedocles throwing himself into Etna (15–20).   That is the way of people who ask for God's grace but never try to amend their lives (21–24).   They continue to behave in such a way that grace is of no avail to them (25–28).[3]   A fool's prayer is like pursuing a wind and striking a shadow.   Eccli. xxxiv 2 (29–30).   Many seek for things that would injure them (31–32).   He who does not really seek safety must bear the consequences of his own rashness (33–34).

All these ideas are in Locher's version, except lines 25–28 and 31 sq., instead of which we get the other passages more fully elaborated, especially the introduction.

This introduction is drawn out even longer by Barclay, without adding anything new.   Only at the end he insists with somewhat tottering emphasis :

> (672)     But sothly this dare I both say and prove
>           And it avowe after my sympyll skyll,
>           That never man shall syn without his wyll.

When a man has leaped into a well it is folly

> (673)              to gyve hym corde or trayne
>           Or other engyne to helpe hym up agayne.

The story of Empedocles, of which Riviere understood nothing, seems to have been perfectly familiar to Barclay, for he gives a version of the motives that prompted the action, quite deviating from Locher's supercilious allusion [4] and also from the reference in the *Ars Poetica*, from which Brant must have borrowed the idea.[5]

> (675)     He lept hedelynge into the flamynge fyre
>           Of a brennynge hyll whiche callyd is Ethnay,
>           To knowe the trouth and nature to enquyre,
>           Whether that same flame were very fyre or nay ;
>           So with his deth the trouth he dyd assay.

---

[1] A somewhat peculiar use of the word.   The French has ' ottroyerent ' (Riviere ' octroya ').

[2] Fr. facilement.   The adverbial form is common, also in Caxton.

[3] The German is very difficult here, but this seems to be the general meaning. See Zarncke 381.

[4] Stultitiae ut faceret morte sua inditium.

[5] See quotation in Zarncke 380 sq.

An original example of the danger consequent upon a rash attempt
is given in the Envoy, where he draws in two words a picture of the
effects of a popular squabble.

> (680)   For he that is sure and to a fray wyll ren,
>              May fortune come home agayne nosles or lame,
>              And so were it better for to have byd within.[1]

143.—Watson's version offers us only nonsense and curiosities. It
begins already with the woodcut, for instead of an imitation of the
original one, he has inserted that of chapter 79, probably thinking that
it might do, because it represents a man with a halter round his neck !
—The most curious passage is that about the man in the well, where
Drouyn's paraphrase is rather free. I have bracketed the expressions
that are not in Riviere :

> Ever this fole prayeth. And his herte can not tell what he demaundeth of
> God. After he letteth hymselfe fall in to the welle of his owne voluntary wyll.
> And then he cryeth (murdre I drowne myself), and that they sholde socoure
> hym hastely. And (whan he is at the botome of the water), he prayeth (sayntes
> and) sayntesses [2] that they wolde gyve hym socoure and have mynde [souvenaunce]
> on hym, saynge: ' I requyre you sende me a corde for to drawe me out of this
> danger ' (!)

144.—Chapter 44, rebuking IRREVERENCE IN CHURCH, brings
us nearer to ecclesiastical affairs. Brant satirizes the custom of those
who take with them to church their hounds and hawks, and who make
a noise with their wooden slippers, and look about for ' frow Kryemhild.' [3]
They should think of Christ driving the merchants out of the temple.
But if Christ should now drive all sinners out of His sanctuary, few
laymen, few priests even would remain behind, and yet we know that
holiness becometh the house of the Lord (Ps. xcii. 5).

Most of these ideas are in Locher, though in a different setting.
' Kryemhild ' is replaced by ' matronas ' and ' puellas.' A quotation
from John xii is inserted ' Non propter Christum, Lazarus artat eos.'
He adds that business deals and bargains are made in church, and has
no space left for mentioning the priests. The final quotation from the
Psalms becomes :

> Thura decent superos : verba prophana nihil.

---

[1] *ren* is often made to rhyme with words in -*in* ; 267: synne : renne ; 670: synne :
ren ; 1242 : ren : therin ; 1395 : therin : syn : ren. A similar case in 268 :
blynde : ende ; and also before an *n* in 97 : prynce : prudence : inconvenyence ;
1066 : pen : therin.    ME. had two forms : *rinne* by the side of *renne* ; *blende* by
the side of *blinde*.   In Stanza 1723 we really find *syn : ryn : in* ; so these are merely
orthographical variants. See Luick's explanation, Hist. Gramm. § 379, and
Untersuchungen § 385.   In Stanza 1066 the context renders a confusion of *pen* and
*pin* very probable.    For Stanza 97 I can suggest no more plausible explanation than
inaccuracy.   See V. Dalheimer.

[2] The word ' saintesse ' occurs several times in Watson, but sometimes he
hesitates, as in chapter 95, where he translates ' festes des sainctz et saintes ' by
' sayntes dayes men and women ' three times, and once by ' the dayes established
as well of God as of saintes and sayntesses,' misprinted ' ayntesses,' at least in the
second edition.—The word is not too extravagant, as it occurs also in 1449 in an
anonymous letter, and in 1509 in Fisher, and later.   See NED.

[3] This is the only allusion to a name first occurring in the romances of chivalry.
But Brant probably knew it only as a popular expression (Schmidt i, 257).

There is enough left for Barclay to hold forth to his heart's content. Some passages do present some difficulty ; especially, as it seems, the *hawks*.[1]  Brant had called them contemptuously ' hätzen ' (7) and ' den gouch ' (18) ; Locher tries to render this idea by saying ' accipiter sive velis cuculus ' ; and so Barclay was led to the statement :

> (653)   Another on his fyst a sparhauke or fawcon,
>           Or else a cokow ;

but immediately he goes on in his best original style :

> and so wastynge his shone
> Before the auters he to and fro doth wander
> With evyn as great devocyon as a gander !

Of course the Englishman knows all about hounds :

> (654)   In comys another his houndes at his tayle,
>           With lynes and leshes and other lyke baggage ;
>           His dogges barkyth, so that withouten fayle
>           The hole churche is troubled by theyr outrage.
> (655)   They make of the churche for theyr hawkes a mewe
>           And canell for theyr dogges, whiche they shall after rewe.

The wooden slippers are also rather curious.   Brant had said that people will make every possible disturbance (line 10) :

> Und schnyp, schnap, mit den holzschuh machen,

and on the picture we can see that they were thick wooden soles or pattens tied under the shoes to keep them clean.   Locher uses the word ' calopodia ' and so we get in Barclay :

> (658)   Some with theyr slippers to and fro doth prance,
>           Clappynge with their helys in church and in quere,
>           So that good people can nat the servyce here.

Watson uses the same word to render the French ' pantoufles ' : ' The other gothe not save for custome traylynge theyr feete with slyppers or patyns.'

The best part, however, is the original contribution, expressly marked as *Addicio translatoris Alexandri Barclay* :

> (659)   What shall I wryte of maydens and of wyves,
>           Of theyr roundynges [2] and ungoodly comonynge ?
>           Howe one a sclaundre craftely contryves,
>           And in the churche therof hath hyr talkynge ;
>           The other hath therto theyr erys lenynge ;
>           And than whan they all hath harde forth hir tale,
>           With great devocyon they get them to the ale !

---

[1] With Locher he says (655) :
    One tyme the hawkys bellys jenglyth hye.
Similarly in Watson : ' theyr belles at theyr fete demeanynge grete noyse.' Here is the word *to demean* in its then current use, as it occurs e.g. in Caxton, Golden Legend 407/2, ' The levys of the tres demeaned a swete sound.'
    [2] *to round*, earlier *rounen* (OE. rūnian), in the meaning of *to whisper*, was common in ME. and still occurs in Shakespeare.   The verbal substantive *rounding* (whispering, private talk) is here and in Stanza 1584 used for the first time.—NED.

The last line is so delightfully ironical that we must not spoil the impression by asking how much poetical and satirical exaggeration there is in these statements. But the author is quite serious and the priest rises in indignation against such acts of irreverence :

> (660)    Thus is the churche defylyd with vylany . . .
> And whan our Lorde is consecrate in fourme of brede,
> Therby walkes a knave, his bonet on his hede !

This last statement is somewhat qualified in the following :

> (661)    And where as the angels ar ther with reverence
> Laudynge and worshyppynge our Holy Savyour,
> These unkynde caytyfs wyll scantly hym honour.

145.—Less important are Watson's original additions, although he has several in this chapter owing to abundance of space. Whereas Drouyn simply said that ' ces malingz complices murmurent sans fin,' Watson declares : ' they wandre aboute lyke a flocke of shepe in babelynge and claterynge the one to the other.' At the end Drouyn had added some more concrete cases, which we find again in English :

> You the which have puyssaunce make theym avoyde out [1] to the ende, that the yonge men do not as they do. At the whyte freres [aux carmes], at the graye freers [cordeliers], at the frere austyys [*sic*, misprint for austyns: Fr. augustins], at the blacke freers [jacopins], in every parysshe chyrche ye shall fynde alwayes grete habundaunce of folkes that dothe nothynge but walke up and downe in devysynge af dyvers maters, and yf that the corpus domini be lyfted up, they wyll scarcely [Drouyn had not made this qualification] knele down and take of theyr cappes.

With these last three words he has left Drouyn altogether, who goes on with the humorous remark that ' leurs prieres ne sont que de quaqueter et regarder qui a le plus beau nez ' ! Watson perhaps did not think this dignified enough, and he begins to preach of his own accord :

> Alas poore fooles wheron doo ye thynke ? Knowe ye not for a trouthe, that He is the Kynge of all Kynges and Savyour of all the worlde ? . . . Wherfore leve your walkynge up and downe in the chyrche and kepe your pues [2] in praynge devoutly unto God, or elles ye put your soules in great jeopardye of perdycyon.

146.—Chapter 57 is, in Brant, quite a treatise on the mystery of PREDESTINATION, replete with popular proverbial sayings.

> Many want to argue from the Bible without having read it (1–6), they live carelessly, saying their fate is in God's hands (7–12). But God rewards no one for nothing (13–18), else nobody would work (19–26). What the reward will be, however, is His own secret (27–34), because the potter is master of his work, see Rom. ix (35–40). He knows why He has preferred Jacob to Esau (41–44), why Nabuchodonosor repented after his punishment and Pharao did not (see Decret ii.) (45–58). He might have made all roses, but even the thistles show His justice (59–64). The servant should not have grumbled because the master gave equally to his fellows

---

[1] Fr. *saillir*. The then common meaning of the word, as in Caxton's ' Eche body avoyded out of his presence.' And still in the Authorised Version, 1 Sam. xviii 11, ' David avoided out of his presence.' Cf. NED.

[2] Is Watson thinking of women only ? The word *pews*, to indicate the fixed benches for the whole congregation, is not found till the seventeenth century, according to the NED. Before that time they were used for specially distinguished families or for women only.

(see Matt. xx) (65–70).   Good people often have a miserable life on earth and bad ones prosper (71–78).   God's plans are hidden from our eyes (79–84), the solution of the problem is to be expected only in eternity (85–88).   So do your duty and trust in God's mercy (89–94).

Locher works out the first eleven lines into twenty and then, realizing that he has written already more than half of a short chapter, puts the German text aside and just lays down the general principles.   God is almighty and righteous.   He has created us all for Heaven, and if we fall into Hell, it is only through our own free guilt.   So we have no more ground to complain—and thus the very last line returns to Brant again —than the potter's vessel.   In front of this chapter—which has thus become more head than body—he translates and completes Brant's motto, adding to it from line 17 sq. :

> Devolet inque suum rictum satis assa columba.

147.—This line is essential for the explanation of the woodcut, which represents a fool riding a crab and leaning on a broken reed while a pigeon comes flying into his open mouth.   Brant's lines (17 sq.) were much clearer :

> Und wart, wo dir von hymel kunt
> Eyn brotten tub, in dynen mundt.

It is an interesting allusion to the old tales of the *Land of Cockayne* which must have arisen among the Latin-speaking vagrant Goliards of the twelfth or thirteenth century,[1] but the oldest form of which has come down to us in a Middle English poem of the early fourteenth century.

> Fur in see bi west spayne
> Is a lond ihote cokaygne.

Among its various privileges and delicacies one has remained curiously famous :

> þe gees irostid on þe spitte
> Flee to þat abbai, god hit wot,
> And grediþ ' gees al hote, al hot.' [2]

The fame of this idea is all outside England, however, and as it would seem entirely German, although there is no German version extant written before the year 1500.[3]   The allusion in Brant is unmistakable,

---

[1] The roguish poet of the *Confessio Goliae* calls himself the *abbas Cucaniensis*, and he adds : ' et consilium meum est cum bibulis et in secta Decii voluntas mea est.' Jac. Grimm, Gedichte des Mittelalters auf Friedrich I, p. 96 ; cf. Zarncke 456.

[2] The poem was printed from the Harl. MS. 913, fol. 3, by F. J. Furnivall in *Early English Poems and Lives of Saints* (Berlin 1862 ; Transactions of the Philological Society, 1858, Part II), pp. 156 sqq.   The lines quoted are 1–2 and 102–104. Modernized edition in G. Ellis, Specimens of the Early English Poets, i (1801), pp. 83 sqq., with reference to an ancient French poem on a nearly similar plan called ' Le Ordre de bel Eyse.'

[3] The two oldest German versions known are the so-called ' Meistergesang im Lindenschnidtston ' from about 1500 and ' Das Lied von dem Schlauraffen lande in dem Roten Zwinger thon,' printed at Nuremberg before 1530 (Zarncke 455) ; now reprinted in facsimile in *Zwickauer Facsimiledrucke* xiv (1912).   The Dutch version, ' Van 't Luye-lecker-landt,' which appears in *Veelderhande Geneuchlÿcke Dichten* 142– 150, seems to be closely imitated from Hans Sachs, Das Schlauraffenland (in Ph. Wackernagel, *Deutsches Lesebuch* ii [12] (Stuttgart 1852), p. 124).

and even more decisive is Geiler's description of the *terram promissionis ridiculosam et fabulosam, ubi . . . assatae columbae in ora volant hominum*.[1]—These are almost literally the words used by Locher.

In England, however, all knowledge of the old Land of Cockayne must have died out very early, and although Sir Thomas More's plan of *Utopia* is inspired by a similar idea,[2] he seems to have derived it directly from his own classical favourite Lucianus [3] to whom the medieval Goliard was also ultimately indebted.[4] No more than a vague trace is to be recognized in the sixteenth-century substitute of *Lubberland*, although Florio takes it as synonymous with its more refined predecessor.[5] As the story of the Land of Cockayne is in some way connected with the origin of the Ship of Fools,[6] this excursion is not a digression, though it serves here only to show what difficulties our translators found in their way and to interest us in the attempts they made to surmount them.

They hardly even deserve the name of attempts. Only the Marnef-translator managed to bring out the meaning by keeping literally to the Latin : ' et vollera dedans sa bouche une colombe assez rostie.' Barclay gave it up, and instead of translating he invented an original explanation of the woodcut :

> (810)  Forsoth, this fole may longe so loke in vayne,
> And on the cravys he styll shall bacwarde ryde,
> Cryenge with the dove whose flyght shall hym ay gyde.

Riviere cannot have attached much meaning to his own words :

> Criant et volle a son hullement
> La columbe ignellement.

Drouyn copied this motto of course, but unfortunately Watson felt no need to attempt a translation of this curiosity, as his printer had no woodcut available. So he could insert something quite his own, and he wrote :

> he wyll not observe
> The byddynges and commandementes
> Have he never so many rentes !

Lubberland is far away from the Land of Cockayne !

148.—There are not many interesting passages in the rest of the chapter. Barclay's paraphrase is faithful on the whole, but he observes better

---

[1] Quoted by Zarncke 457.

[2] See Schlaraffia politica. Geschichte der Dichtungen vom besten Staate (Leipzig 1892), 42 sqq.

[3] W. v. Christ, Geschichte der griechischen Literatur, 5te Aufl. von O. Stählin und W. Schmid, in Müller's Handbuch der klass. Altertumswissenschaft, vii. 2ter Teil, 2te Hälfte (München 1903), p. 580.

[4] Zarncke 455.

[5] ' Cocagna, as we say Lubberland.' Quotation in NED. s.v. lubberland. ' Cockayne ' is not mentioned by the NED. between c. 1305 (the ME. poem) and 1677 (Hobbes).

[6] See §§ 369, 370.

proportion than Locher.  Visualizing concretely he produces a picture
out of two vague Latin lines :

> (813)   Unchrafty folys whiche scantly have over sene
> Ought of Scripture, if they knowe the bokes name,
> Or els a whyle hath at the scoles bene,
> Than bende they the browys and stedfastly they wene
> In theyr conceyt that they ar passynge wyse
> For all Scripture newe commentis to devyse.

After the potter's vessel at the end he adds a chapter to insist a little
more upon the freedom of man's will :

> (823)   And whyle we lyve here on this wretchyd grounde,
> We have our reason and wyttes us to gyde
> With our fre wyll, and if no faut be founde
> In our demenour, in heven we shall abyde ;
> But if we Goddes lawes set asyde
> Howe may we hope of hym rewarde to wyn ?
> So our owne foly is moste cause of syn.

149.—In Watson's version of Drouyn's prose there seems nothing
of special interest.  He has plenty of room at his disposal ; but he does
not much improve the nonsense of his French original.  Only a few
expressions deserve notice.  Riviere's

Leurs livres revolver sen vont

which is literally Locher's ' librosque revolvunt ' had become in prose :
' vont revyre leurs livres,' which is rendered in English ' they revycyte
theyr bookes.' [1]  At the end Drouyn has appended a conclusion of
his own :

You poore folkes that are not gradued in the holy pagyne [= graduez en la
saincte pagine] put not yourselfe therin too ferre that the devyll put many errours
in your hedes [by corrupting Drouyn's conjunction he spoils the whole sentence :
' tant que le diable ne '], and then to argue with [= contre] the doctours ;  whiche
is ynoughe to lede you in the gulfre of hell, and to make you to be brente lyke an
heretyke in this worlde.

In this positive threat there may be an allusion to recent events in France
in connexion with the doctrine of predestination.  As Drouyn, however,
knew very little, if anything, of theology, he stood entirely outside the
acrimonious discussions that were continually going on about this vexed
question of Predestination.  And so it is rather difficult to guess what
he is referring to.  The contending parties at that time were rather
liberal with mutual accusations of heresy, and public opinion considered
a case of real heresy merited capital punishment.  The Louvain dispute
raised by Pierre de Rivo and Henry van Zomeren [2] had made a great

---

[1] This is the now obsolete, technical sense of *to revisit*, as it occurs in Lord
Berners' *Froissart* : ' They saye that ye have not dilygently revisyted nor oversene
the letters patentes.'—NED.

[2] A great many documents relating to this dispute are in D'Argentré, i, 2, 258–
284.  For recent studies see H. de Jongh, L'Ancienne Faculté de Théologie de
Louvain (1911), 27, 75.

stir also at Paris [1] and rumours of suchlike controversies naturally agitated the popular mind very strongly. Such disputes, together with the execution of 1491, to be mentioned later on,[2] may very well account for Drouyn's fear.

150.—Chapter 95 satirizes the NON-OBSERVANCE OF HOLY DAYS. Brant gives quite a list of shrewdly observed light occupations which people will always perform on Sundays, either personally or through their servants, instead of going to church, as they should. He further mentions drinking habits, games of cards and backgammon, and other unlawful pastimes, perpetrated by Christians more than by the Jews described in the Bible.—Locher may have read something of this chapter before writing his own, but he has certainly not looked into his original when 'translating.' His work is in the first half full of high-flown commonplaces, but not one occupation is mentioned in detail, and the second half is almost entirely about the excesses of eating and drinking, and here only can we catch a slight echo of one or two lines in Brant. So the French and English translations also mostly turn on drinking, and Barclay has many picturesque lines here:

> (1460)  The holy day we fyle with eche unlefull thynge,
>          As fat festis and bankettis sausyd with glotony,
>          And that from mornynge to nyght contynually.
> (1461)  And on the holy day we dayly se that men
>          Soner to the taverne than to the churche ren.

Such couplets bear the stamp of true originality.[3]  So does the following stanza:

> (1462)  The taverne is open before the churche be,
>          The pottis ar ronge as bellys of dronkenes
>          Before the churche bellys with great salemnyte !
>          There here these wretches theyr matyns and theyr masse ! [4]
>          Who lysteth to take hede shall often se doutles
>          The stallys of the taverne stuffyd nere echone,
>          Whan in the churche stallys he shall se fewe or none.

Passages like these make us regret the more that the German original was not laid under contribution. Our priestly moralizer might have derived from it a wealth of concrete illustration.

151.—There is of course nothing like it in Watson. When we have read in his motto the astonishing expression:

> Who that kepeth not the sondayes
> And holy festes canonysed,

---

[1] P. Féret, *Histoire de la Faculté de Théologie de Paris*, iv (1900), 121 sq. ; Renaudet 90 sq.

[2] § 187.

[3] Many of Barclay's remarks throw an interesting light on the contention of Elizabethan writers—still repeated in books on English customs and manners—that the English drinking-habits were principally due to the military expeditions to Holland.

[4] An interesting rhyme, showing that, notwithstanding the Southern spelling, the pronunciation was Midland (W.S. mæsse = Merc. and Kent. messe).

and we see from the French original that he has connected his participle
with the wrong word :

> Qui les sainctz dimenches et festes
> Nobserve des canonisez
> Sainctz qui *etc.*,

we know that we must not expect much shrewdness from him.  He
has plenty of space, however, and so he can expand Drouyn's
French to his heart's content.  But his expansions are of the least
interesting kind.  The French ' Dieu donne . . . sa grace affin que lon
se puisse amender ' becomes ' Jhesu cryste . . . gyveth . . . hye grace
unto every synfull creature, lyvynge here in this wretched worlde, to the
ende that they may amende them.'  That is his way of filling out more
than two pages !

Drouyn's most interesting part is towards the end, where he leaves
his Riviere and gives us his own remarks.  But just here the Englishman
having nearly used up his space begins to leave out portions of a sentence.
Then we get incomprehensible passages like this : ' without the herynge
of a hole masse they wyll go to breke fast, saynge that two snuffes is
worthe a candel.'  The meaning of this proverb becomes clear only
from what is omitted : ' sans ouyr messe entiere yront desiuner, ou
*pour le plus brief orront deux demies messes,* disans que deux moucherons
valent une chandelle.'  Immediately after this proverb, however, the
English adds something original : ' and there they bruyle [1] the hye
masse and drynketh and shoteth theyr evensonge.'  A few lines further
there is a more interesting but less felicitously expressed addition : ' but
as for matyns, that is slepte, ye and oftentymes halfe the hye masse to.'

152.—Chapter 91 on TALKING IN THE CHOIR is an admonition
addressed to the priests in particular.  Its contents are more slender,
however, than might have been expected.  Brant does not mention
the priests directly ; he simply speaks of the people in the choir and says
that they talk ' von dem welschen krieg ' and other news, from the
Matins down to the Vespers, and that many attend only to earn their
money.  Such people usually go out as soon as they can, but they had
better stay away altogether.  He does not want to give offence :

> (27)  Aber von den dar ich nit drucken,

but does tell these ' fools ' that a man does not properly earn his stipend :

> (34)  So man dem roraffen zu gyent.[2]

Locher is somewhat more outspoken than his master.  He mentions
some more topics of clerical conversation : ' Quo narragonia fluctus
Pervolet Ionios,' that which ' agitur totum rigido Mavorte per orbem,'
the wars ' in regione Britanna,' and ' a Thurco pontica gesta.'  He says
that the ' dormentarius ' [3] runs about with his white staff spreading all

---

[1] *bruyle,* Mn.E. to broil, then retained still the meaning of the French *bruler*
as appears from Caxton's ' That he myght be brente and bruyled ' (NED.).

[2] This expression occurs also in chapter 92.  See § 37.

[3] Locher draws special attention to this by a note, ' nota dormentarium.'  The
position of this official may be best understood from a quotation from the *Stat. Cap.
S. Thom. Argentin.* fol. 42 in Ducange : ' Quia Dormentarius quilibet pro tempore
existens, est generalis servitor et pedellus ac nuncius capituli.'

the news throughout the choir, beginning with the Matins.  He also
speaks of those who attend only for their stipend, who ' ob nummos
carmina rauca canunt ' and had better stay at home.

This criticism of his own profession was enjoyed by the English cleric.
He speaks of ' dyvers toyes and iapis varyable ' (1388) and says that
canonical decrees are forgotten

> (1390)   Nat in the chirche so moche as in the quere.

The ' prestis in the quere ' tell each other all the news.

> (1391)   Full lytell advertynge howe the servyce goes.

Barclay knows all the technicalities of the Church Service better than
Locher, and the following satirical stanzas are written with all the zest
of almost complete originality :

> (1392)   The batayles done perchance in Small Brytayne,
>          In Fraunce or Flaunders or to the worldes ende,
>          Ar tolde in the quere, of some, in wordes vayne,
>          In myddes of Matyns in stede of the Legende ;
>          And other gladly to here the same intende,
>          Moche rather than the servyce for to here.
>          The Rector Chori [1] is made the messenger ;

> (1393)   He rennyth about lyke to a pursuyvant,
>          With his whyte staffe movynge from syde to syde,
>          Where he is lenynge, talys ar nat skant ;
>          But in one place nat longe doth he abyde.

> (1394)   And in the mornynge whan they come to the quere,
>          The one begynneth a fable or a history,
>          The other lenyth theyr erys it to here,
>          Taking it in stede of the Invytory [2] ;
>          Some other maketh Respons, Antym and Memory,
>          And all of fables and jestis of Robyn Hode,
>          Or other tryfyls that skantly ar so gode.

Locher could not have written anything like it.  Barclay even improves
upon Locher's saying about those who attend for money only :

> (1396)   The peny them prycketh unto devocyon.

But, in however lively a manner all this is expressed, the purpose remains
exalted and serious throughout :

> (1399)   It is convenyent our Lorde to magnyfye
>          With parfyte prayer, love, reverence and honour,
>          And nat with iapys and talys of no valour.

153.—Nothing so lively and so reserved is to be expected from
the French versions.  Riviere keeps close to the Latin, rendering the

---

[1] Rector Chori = Cantor = qui Scholae Cantorum praeest.  Honorius Augustod.
l. i, cap. 74 : Cantores ait capita pileolis operuisse, et *prae manibus baculos gestasse*
(Ducange).  It was part of the cantor's duty to move about the choir when it was
necessary to regulate the singing.  See Abbot Gasquet, *English Monastic Life* (1904),
59, where his office is described in detail.
[2] The Invitatorium, the opening Psalm of the Matins.  The other technical
names are still in living use.  The Memory is now usually called Commemoration.

' dormentarius ' by ' ung bastonnier.' [1]  But Drouyn has some notable additions, betraying a more acrimonious spirit, or rather echoing the diatribes of the French popular preachers.[2]  It begins already with his introductory invitation ' Lubryke foles preestes of the Chyrche, come and lerne some doctryne in this chapytre [3] and habandone chambres apparaylled, burgeyses (= bourgeoises), ladyes, damoyselles, and maydens.'  As topics of conversation he mentions the wars ' en france, en bourgoigne, en picardie, et plusieurs aultres lieux ' which Watson changes into ' in Fraunce, in Almayne and in Scotlonde.'  The Englishman had probably no idea what was meant by a ' batonnier ' whom Drouyn made run ' par leglise ' instead of ' le chœur ' and so he wrote : ' The clerke renneth aboute in the chirche, tellynge newe tydynges.' At the end Drouyn leaves Riviere and begins to abuse the priests again after his own fashion : ' Ye be not ashamed to speke unto harlottes and baudes in the chyrche, in makynge them sygnes, they folowe you paas by paas. . . . Ye be no more ashamed than the sowe that lyeth her downe in the myre.'  The following brings a less universal and more concrete charge : ' Some there is that wyll be without syngynge masse '—Drouyn speaks only of ' chanter ' but Watson's supplying the word ' masse ' seems to be quite correct—' unto a leven of the clocke, abydynge that some sholde gyve them money for to synge masse, for yf they have no moneye gyven them they wyll synge no masse.'—He alludes to some special classes only *per transennam* : ' Of mandyens,[4] or other, as well monkes, as abbottes, chanons,[5] as pryours, nothynge I speke, but they may be in the nombre with the other.'

Drouyn concludes with one of his well-worn phrases : ' Ils sont tenebreux, car perdus ilz ont leurs vies ordes et abhomynables.'  Watson had some more space to spare and turned this into : ' They be more obscure than many of the seculars, and commytte mo vyces and abhomynable synnes, in gyvynge ryght evyll examples unto the poore folkes and parysshynges.' [6]

154.—Chapter 73 speaks of RASH ORDINATION and Brant here lays bare the root of the greatest ecclesiastical abuses of the time. Historians quote this chapter as one of the most eloquent testimonies to confirm and illustrate what historical records reveal about the religious disintegration then increasing throughout Germany [7] :

Every peasant, says Brant, now wants his son to become a priest with the sole purpose that he may support the family, though he has no talent and does not

---

[1] The words are equivalent, for ' *bastonnier* = bedeau, concierge d'une église ' (Godefroy).

[2] Such denunciations occur in Olivier Maillard's sermons, quoted e.g. in A. Meray, La Vie au temps des libres prêcheurs (2me éd. Paris 1878), i, 146.

[3] The French has again ' satyre.'

[4] French ' mendians.'  The word is used in English also in a legal document of the year 1535 : ' Fryers mendyantes have littell or nothinge to live upon.'—NED.

[5] This word is not in the French.  Its insertion in this context shows that Watson had only a vague idea of the drift of this passage.

[6] In this last word we have a somewhat disguised survival of the ME. word used by Chaucer when describing his ' povre Persoun ' :

His parisshens devoutly wolde he teche (A. 482).

[7] Cf. Janssen-Pastor, i, 743 sqq.

even follow a regular course of study. That is why there are so many ignorant
clergy. It is the bishops that are to blame for ordaining such intruders. These
people without vocation often repent when it is too late. They have invented all
sorts of pretences to get ordained, but they often feel

> (49)　Keyn ärmer vych uff erden ist
> 　　　　Dann priesterschafft den narung gebrist.[1]

The unworthy should never touch the altar,[2] as we are taught by Moses and by
the examples of Oza, and of Core, Dathan and Abiron.[3]　Many also join religious
orders without a proper call ; parents foolishly put their children there, who afterwards curse them for it.　Only few—the strong statement is repeated twice over—
join the orders now at a reasonable age and from proper motives.　Brant seems to
make an exception, however, for the so-called Observants, for he adds :

> (89)　Vor usz in allen orden gantz
> 　　　　Do man nit halttet observantz

The last lines say that it is better not to enter a religious order than not to
observe its rules.

Brant's crushing indictment, which is so full of proverbial and
idiomatic expressions that only the barest of outlines can be given,
becomes a string of platitudes in Locher's short chapter, which holds up
the priests of Numa Pompilius as the highest models.　Only in the
second half does he make any attempt at pointed language.—The monks
he calls ' fratres subductis colla cucullis gestantes,' and he singles out the
followers of St. Augustine for particular criticism.—I need not remind
the reader of the piquant fact that Erasmus was then one of them, and
that Luther was to join them shortly after.

　　155.—The best of Locher's remarks are even better and more forcibly
expressed in Barclay [4] :

> (1087)　Everyman laboures nowe with all theyr myght
> 　　　　　Unto the order of prestehode to promote
> 　　　　　His sonne, howe beit he be a very sote.

> (1088)　If he be folysshe, or of his wyt unstable,
> 　　　　　Mysshapyn of his face, his handes or his fete,
> 　　　　　And for no besynes worldly profitable,
> 　　　　　For the holy Churche than thynke they hym most mete.

Only the ideas of Stanza 1087 are indicated by Locher, as are the first
two of the following :

> (1091)　The order of presthode is troublyd of eche fole,
> 　　　　　The honour of religion every where decays ;
> 　　　　　Suche caytyfs and courters that never were at scole
> 　　　　　Ar firste promotyd to presthode nowe adays.

---

　[1] Enumerating their miseries Brant, Zarncke 416 suspects, was probably alluding
to the anonymous ' Epistola de Miseria Curatorum ' which had appeared in 1489 in
the *Directorium Statuum* (described in Pellechet 4343 and BMC. i, 122).
　[2] Here occurs the passage (ll. 58–62) which Professor Lea (see quotation, § 1)
called the ' most significant ' remark of the whole Ship of Fools !
　[3] Zarncke 416 finds a difficulty here, but the story of Oza is in 2 Kings (Samuel)
vi 7 ; that of the three others in Num. xvi.
　[4] Rey 52 sqq. thinks that his version of this chapter may have inspired
Skelton's *Colyn Cloute* ; but this has already been contradicted by Koelbing 115.

The last two lines are original, and so it would appear that in this respect
at any rate the author felt his own person perfectly safe.  Numa is
conjured up of course.  But immediately after, Barclay again vents
his personal sentiments :

(1092)   But nowe blynde folys, nought knowynge save the cup,
         Falshode and flatery, ar brought out of the stable
         Streyght to the auter.
(1093)   From the kechyn to the quere and so to a state,
         One yester day a courter is nowe a prest become !
         And than have these folys theyr myndes so elevate,
         That they disdayne men of veɪtue and wysdome ;
         But if they have of golde a myghty some,
         They thynke them abyll a man to make or marre,
         And ar so presumptuous and proud as Lucifarre.

These stanzas are expressly marked as *Addicio translatoris*, and their
somewhat grating sound [1] is perhaps the symptom of a personal grudge.
But nearly every stanza contains original touches :

(1095)   To foles and to boyes presthode is nowe solde.
(1097)   O, where is chastenes and dame humylyte ?
         Alas, they ar dede and nat with us acquayntyd,
         But flaterynge falshode hath our facis payntyd.

This is sincere and open, and the last line is a good metaphor.

(1098)   Alas, the shepherd is lewder than the shepe ; [2]
         This great disorder causyth my herte to wepe.
         Alas, what lewdness is cloked under cowlys !
         Who can express the foly of these folys ?

156.—The last two lines are mere padding, to cover the transition
to another idea.  For he now begins to tackle the monks, not confining
himself to the Augustinians, as Locher had done, but as he states on the
margin : ' Monachi et ceteri regulares arguuntur.'  The three stanzas
may be quoted in full for what little documentary value they contain :

(1099)   O holy orders of monkes and of freres
         And of all other sortes of religion !
         Your straytnes hath decayed of late yeres,
         The true and perfite rule of you is done,
         Fewe kepyth truly theyr right profession
         In inwarde vesture, dyet, worde or dede.
         Theyr chefe stody is theyr wretchyd wombe to fede.

(1100)   O holy Benet, with God nowe glorifyed,
         O glorious Austen, O Francis decorate !
         With mekenes the placis that ye have edefyed,
         Ar nowe disordered and with vyces maculate.[3]
         Envy, Pryde, Malyce, Glotony and Debate
         Ar nowe chefe gyders in many of your placis,
         Whiche grace and vertue utterly out chasys.

---

[1] See also Stanza 468 in § 161.
[2] Contrast with this Chaucer's ideal Parson, C.T., A. 477 sqq.
[3] It may be of some interest to know that in Barclay's diocese of Exeter there
were sixteen Benedictine abbeys or priories, eleven Augustinian and three
Franciscan houses (R. J. E. Boggis, A History of the Diocese of Exeter (Exeter 1922),
64 sq.).

> (1101)    Those holy faders rehersyd afore by name,
> Composed rules holy and laudable
> For men religious to lyve after the same,
> Whiche nowe but lytell to them ar agreable,
> But in theyr lyfe from them moche variable.
> O holy Benet, Francis and Augustyne,
> Se howe your children despyseth your doctryne !

If such stanzas can be quoted for anything, with all their big words they might be adduced for the defence rather than for the prosecution. There is nothing paradoxical in the author's joining afterwards two of the religious orders here taken to task.

157.—In a long Envoy of four stanzas he speaks of priests in general again, and the language in which he expresses himself here is rather wary and reserved, so that we get the same impression that the ecclesiastical conditions in England, as far as Barclay knew them, were not nearly as bad as in Germany. He exhorts the pastors to instruct their flock and to set a good example :

> (1105)    Expell covetyse and desyre of dignyte ;
> Beware of Venus, hir dartis are damnable ;
> Take nat on you the order and degre
> Of presthode, without that ye be somwhat able.

A favourite and somewhat peculiar idea of his is expressed in the next stanza :

> (1106)    The greattest note of all mysgovernaunce,
> That nowe is usyd amonge the comonte,
> Procedith of folysshe prestis ignoraunce.[1]

And in the last stanza he makes his last and shrewdest hit :

> (1107)    The cause why so many prestis lackyth wyt,
> Is in you, Bysshops, if I durst trouth expresse,
> Whiche nat consyder what men that ye admyt
> Of lyvynge, cunnynge, person and godlynes ;
> But who so ever hym self therto wyll dresse,
> If an angell be his brokar to the scribe (!)
> He is admyttyd, howe beit he be wytles ;
> Thus solde is presthode for an unhappy brybe.

Simony is a very common charge against the clergy. It occurs also in Brant-Locher. But not in this chapter, and nowhere of this particular species. Was it an abuse peculiar to England ? Or is Barclay merely developing a *locus communis* ?

158.—Befoie we hear his other criticisms of the clergy, we must turn to Watson, to see what he has made of this chapter. He has plenty of space and so he can expand his text. This he does, but at the same time he unaccountably leaves out important parts of sentences. In the introductory invitation he inserts the queer phrase ' As I sate musynge all alone.'—Riviere's *rustic* is misprinted *ruste* in Drouyn, so that the peasant ( = Barclay 1087) is quite forgotten in the English : ' a lusty

---

[1] The ignorance of the clergy was a ground of much complaint on the Continent, especially in Germany (Janssen-Pastor i, 757). But when the Humanists speak of it, we must never forget that they had their own ideal of learning. See Locher's and Barclay's versions of chapter 27, §§ 248 sqq.

galaunt the whiche is replete with grete vyces.'—Literally from Drouyn
and almost equally literally from Riviere is : ' They founde themselfe
under dame pecune that at this present tyme is a grete pryncesse.'
Numa Pompilius becomes *Pompom et Numa* in Riviere, and in Drouyn-
Watson, *Numa Pompon*.  The following exclamation is quite Watson's
own and is typical of the man : ' O blessyd lorde Jhesu Chryst thou
endurest many wronges and offences in this vale of mysery ' !  Better
are his insertions in the following sentence, in which I shall put Watson's
own contributions in italics : ' The holy and blessyd Augustin gave
his rule unto his felowes and brederen, that they sholde in all calamyte
and myserye, and debonayrte *and humylyte* be in this worlde, lyvyng
solytaryly, but at this presente tyme, ye maye se *how well it is kepte,
and how straytley*, it is full rudely observed *God wote !* '—This little touch
of irony and the exclamation at the end is Watson's best contribution.
In the passage about *debonayrte* there is a mistake however.  Drouyn
wrote ' que en toute meschance et misere et debonnaire fussent,' wrongly
dividing Riviere's words :

> Que en toute meschance et misere
> Fussent au monde et debonnayre
> Vivans en vie sollitaire *etc.*

Watson's emendation, turning the adjective into a substantive and
adding to it, probably by way of a synonym, *and humylyte*,[1] does not
give an intelligible sense to the phrase.

Drouyn thus concludes his paraphrase (in Watson's words), ' of
whiche I holde my pease for this presente tyme ' ; but after this he adds
a long quotation from St. Jerome's well-known address to Priests :
' O priestes . . . Howe maye ye stratche forthe your handes unto
vyllaynous thynges the whiche oftentymes holdeth the body of our
Lorde, the whiche the blessyd aungelles may not do ' *etc.*, ending with
' for thou ought not to receive the ordre withoute consyderynge of dyvers
thynges.'

159.—Chapter 30, of PLURALITIES, is also highly interesting from
an ecclesiastical point of view.  Zarncke introduces his Commentary
with a long note tending to prove that Brant was singularly prejudiced
in not attributing these and similar abuses of the time to the pernicious
interference of the Pope ; and in order to get a more unbiassed judgment
of the question the Professor quotes George von Heimburg and Luther.
Present-day historians will prefer to listen to the testimony of an inside
critic rather than to that of professed partisans, especially where national
as well as religious passions can only obscure our vision.  This does
not mean that Brant was unprejudiced.  Few are the characters that
do not react, positively or negatively, to the stimulus of popular clamour.
And never was popular clamour stronger in Germany than at that time
of growing nationalism.  Class grievances were then easily turned into
popular causes, and represented by skilful agitators as cases of flagrant

---

[1] The two substantives are also combined by Caxton in his *Vitae Patrum* :
' Pacyence, humylyte, debonarete, and wylleful obedience.'     See NED. s.v. de-
bonairty.

injustice.—Brant does not mention the collation of benefices by the Pope. He simply states the problem of the great abuses then prevalent, realizing, no doubt, that it was too intricate to admit of such a simple solution ; that part of the responsibility rested on all classes of society ; and that the direct interference of Rome as often as not protected the interests of the people against the nobility.[1]

Brant puts his criticism into a short but very sententious chapter. Taking so many ecclesiastical benefices that a man cannot properly fulfil all the obligations entailed by them, is like overloading a donkey. It would make a man blind with care. It is like a bag which has no bottom, or like driving a man to his grave.[2] But many are seduced by so-called dispensations, and without being able to hold one decently, they possess various benefices and trade with them. Thus they sometimes get so many that they can hardly count them ; but they quietly live on there at ease, until they find death in them ; for in these dealings Simon and Giezi play an active part. (Act. VIII and IV Reg. 5.) Then follow the last four lines of grim sarcasm :

(31–34)  Merck wer vil pfrunden haben well
Der letsten wart er inn der hell.
Do wurt er fynden eyn presentz
Die me dut dann hie sechs absentz.

Locher translates a great part of this chapter. He expands the introductory comparisons, and says of the bag :

Saccum hic circumfert in quo non fundus habetur
Sed ieiuna fames : atque cupido vorax.

Then he inserts some remarks of his own on the ignorance of the clergy, their lack of virtue, and the obligation they are under to give the surplus of their income to the poor. After this he makes use of Brant's remarks anent trading in benefices, mentioning Giezi and Simon, and concludes with the first of Brant's closing ironical sentences :

Plures quisque igitur prebendas possidet : ille
Extremam expectet cum Iove tartareo.

160.—Watson's version of this chapter is again of more philological than of literary or historical interest. He leaves out the comparison with the donkey, because the printer had no cut available.[3] He writes ' all affusked ' to render ' tous aveugles,'[4] and speaks of ' to confydere the benefyces ' for the French ' conferer les benefices '[5] and ' men that be not propyce therto ' for ' gens qui ne sont point propres,' and ' moyennynge[6] some pryse ' for ' moyennant quellque pris.'

[1] On this aspect of the question there is a remarkable paper by Mgr. Moyes in *The Tablet* 144 (1924), 5 sq.—Geiler and others attributed the plurality-scandal largely to the right of patronage exercised by the aristocracy (Janssen-Pastor i, 751 sq.). Cf. Barclay's Stanza 473.
[2] The words are not very clear, but this is the general meaning and all we need for the interpretation of Locher.
[3] Perhaps Wynkyn did not know what cut to take, because Drouyn here inserts the woodcut of chapter 63, which also represents a donkey ; but this donkey is laden with a beggar's children instead of with a miller's bags !
[4] See § 137.
[5] There is no such word in the NED.
[6] The NED. quotes one example of this bold participle from Copland (1520).

Most other curiosities are due to additions or omissions in Drouyn's text. From the introduction he translates: 'The dyscrete men be without benefyces dyenge for hungre, and the foles ben in the syeges cathedrall.' In the comparison of the bag without bottom Riviere had written :

> En leur main portent sac sans rive
> Sans fons et partout *etc.*

Drouyn paraphrases away the bottomlessness of the bag, and so it becomes 'They bere theyr sacke in theyr hande and demandeth ever for to take' *etc.*—Riviere adds some objects on which the money from the benefices is spent instead of upon the poor :

> en cages
> En oyseaulx et pour les nourrir
> Chevaulx pour vous entretenir
> En robbes et divers ouvraiges
> Improffitables durs oultraiges.

Drouyn adds ' chiens ' and Watson turns the ' oyseaulx ' into ' hawkes ': ' in haukes, houndes, horses and gownes lyke seculars.' Towards the end Riviere mentions some more dishonourable practices: ' All this wyll saye bryefly that it is for to upholde theyr estates, playes, and for to maynteyne theyr harlottes with, and they doo many other evylles without comparyson.' Drouyn was not content with this and adds without Riviere's authority : ' But at this present tyme it is not so, for he that is moost ignoraunt shall have it, and gyve to every body a pece ( = pour en donner a chascun un lopin). Ye and that worse is they wyll be mytred without eleccyon and have the pastorall staff.' One can hear that Drouyn remembers some peculiar grievances which have only a distant connexion with the contents of this chapter, but he has not succeeded in giving intelligent utterance to his memories. Locher's final irony appears in Riviere as

> En ce faisant plusieurs au monde
> Actendent la prebende immonde
> De plato pour ie desservir
> Car œuvres font pour la servir.

There must be two misprints in these lines, for Drouyn rightly changes *plato* into *pluto* and the last *la* into *le*.[1] The prose version, filled out by Watson's additions (italicized in the following quotation), becomes :

> And in thus doynge in *this wretchyd* (!) worlde, they be worthy and deserveth to have the brebendes vyle *and abhomynable* of Pluto god of the infernall palus, for such folkes ben *commysed* for to serve hym, and [the rest is all Watson's own, showing that he has caught the spirit of his French original]—*and for theyr good and true servyce he shall exalte them unto inestymable payne in the profounde pytte of helle, there to remayne with hym perpetually.*

161.—These are not bad phrases to fill the allotted space ! And

---

[1] The correction supposes some sagacity in Drouyn of which I can hardly hold him capable. Did not he really use another, now lost, edition ?

yet—with a sigh of relief we turn to Barclay. Here at any rate we find Locher's thoughts in a readable form :

> (466) The folys whose hertis unto this vyce ar bounde,
> Upon theyr sholders bereth aboute a sacke
> Insaciable, without botome outher grounde.

The final irony is all the better for its concise expression :

> (477) But he that in this lyfe wyll alway besy be
> To get dyvers prebendes, shall have the last in hell.

But there is a great deal more in Barclay's version than Locher's thoughts. The greater part in fact is quite original.

> (461) And namely suche that lowest ar in degre
> Of byrth and cunnynge, of this condycion be,

is a typical remark of the somewhat pedantic churchman. But his best additions are of a more picturesque character :

> (465) Howe be it they thynke therby great welth to fynde,
> They gape yet ever, theyr maners lyke the wynde,
> Theyr lyfe without all terme or sertaynte :
> If they have two lyvynges, yet loke they to have thre.
> (466) The more that they have, the more they thynke they lacke :
> What devyll can stop theyr throte so large and wyde ?
> (467) Courters become prestis, nought knowynge but the dyce ;
> They preste [1] not for God but for a benefyce.
> (468) The Clerke of the kechyn is a prest become [2] . . .
> The stepyll and the chirche by this means stand awry !

Instead of Locher's three lines on trading in benefices and on Giezi and Simon, Barclay writes five stanzas which are all worth quoting, but from which I can find room only for the more striking expressions :

> (472) Some lyveth longe in hunger and in payne
> And in the somer day skarsly drynketh twyse,
> Sparynge monay therwith to by a benefyce.
> (473) Some for no wages in court doth attende
> With lorde or knight, and all for this polecy,
> To get of his lorde a benefyce at the ende.
> (474) Than if this lorde have in hym favoure, he hath hope
> To have another benefyce of gretter dignyte,
> And so maketh a fals suggestyon to the Pope
> For a *Tot quot* outher els a pluralyte [3] ;
> Than shall he nat be pleased with .ii. nouther thre,
> But dyvers wyll he have, ay choppynge and changynge ;
> So oft : a fole all, and a gode clerke no thynge !

This man evidently knows what he is talking about. He is apparently not referring to any case in particular, but to the general impression

---

[1] The substantive used as an intransitive verb occurs before Barclay, though it seems very rare. See NED.

[2] See Stanza 1093, § 155.

[3] *Tot quot* in this meaning has never been a technical term of the *stilus curiae* and does not seem to have been known on the Continent at all. But the expression became a favourite among English satirists of the sixteenth and seventeenth centuries to indicate a so-called Papal licence to hold an unlimited number of benefices. See the quotations in the NED.

made by some intriguing practices of the time upon those who were conversant with them.   His testimony, therefore, may be quoted as that of an eye-witness.

> (475)   The cure of soulys of them is set asyde ;
>           And no mervayle !   For howe sholde they abyde
>           To teche their parysshynges [1] vertue, wysdom or grace,
>           Syns no man can be atonys in every place ?
> (476)   Alas !  these folys our mayster Criste betray
>           Of mannes soule wherof they have the cure,
>           And settynge in their stede Syr John of Garnesey,
>           They thynketh themselfe dischargyd quyte and sure.

The mention of this proper name in this solemn passage can hardly be meant to indicate an individual.   Perhaps it was a somewhat proverbial appellation for those poor priests whom more successful pluralists for a small fee employed as their substitutes in rich livings, but the name does not seem to occur elsewhere.

162.—With greater asperity even than in chapter 30 Brant becomes more directly personal in his own long addition to Locher's Latin version, entitled ' De singularitate quorundam novorum fatuorum.  Additio Sebastiani Brant ' (e) and in reality satirizing the BEGHARDS AND BEGUINES.   On account of the unique interest of this treatise, hidden away under a camouflaged title in a rare Latin book, it may be desirable to give a fully detailed summary.

It is written as a poetical epistle to Jacob Locher on receiving the MS. of the Latin translation.   The more general part, which refers to the work of the translator, will be discussed in a later section.[2]

Brant calls the subjects of his satire ' Lolhardos Beguinasque ' or ' Beguttas Begardosque ' or ' Lolhardi, Beguinae sive Beguttae.'   They think that man on earth can attain the highest degree of perfection, in which he is beyond the reach of mortal sin.   And great is the number of fools who hold this doctrine.   They often shut the eyes of dead or dying people, so they may well accompany the crew of this Ship of Fools destined to be wrecked.   They were not included in the German original, lest simple readers should condemn the good with the bad.   And they themselves do not like to be numbered with the common herd, although they do not belong to the clergy.   Their ' sect ' is very numerous in Germany and in every German town.   The author protests, and he emphasizes his protest in a marginal note, that his satire is not directed against the good brethren, who follow faithfully approved rules, but only against the unlearned group who do not want to learn anything and yet like to walk about in long gowns for fear that they might otherwise have to earn their living by manual labour.   They like to live at their ease, not in order to do penance like Magdalen but that every ' lena ' may find ' bufonem suum.'   Their laziness makes them an easy prey for the devil.   They hold that everything is permitted to them, and that they need not live under any authority, saying that the Spirit is free and has no need to obey.   They live together and without a head, like locusts, so that no one can correct their errors and vices.   The brethren sometimes even go so far as not to confess their sins to a priest but simply to each other.   They say that kisses are mortal sins, but that fornication is only venial.   Hence— this *hence* (Latin *hinc*) is particularly malicious here—the brethren everywhere seek

---

[1] The same word, the same form, as in Watson.  See § 153.
[2] See § 321.

the sisters and console them and knock at their doors, making signs by snapping their fingers until they are admitted. Then the Lolhards throw down their cloaks and hoods and appear in short clothes, and the Beguines,

> Grandibus exutis sotularibus atque cothurnis [1]

dance [2] with them in their stockings.

> Tunc opera incipiunt communia : tunc labiorum.
> Hos operit labor : et facta sororia agunt.

If there is a chaste sister among them who refuses to take part in these vile acts, she is rebuked and called a transgressor and shunned, and in spite of her prayers she is accused of having broken a vase [3] or even of a worse crime and punished accordingly at the discretion of the brother. This is what I call, says Brant, ' perversum Lolhardum seu Goliardum [4] qui ventri vivit et umbilico.' Such I want to expose, but I shall ever praise the good ones, approved by Apostolic decrees or by their own life and labour. But sometimes they produce papal bulls exempting them from all work and giving them leave to indulge in all excesses without fear of punishment ! They like to have the outward appearance of real nuns and canons, wearing a habit as a wolf might wear sheep's clothing. Many, says Ovid, enter the room as heavenly beings, and retire incestuous. Who could explain all the wicked crimes that are done under a specious pretext ? Hypocrites can so easily deceive the simple. A Clodius may feign to be a Curius, a fiend may assume the appearance of Christ. You are a cursed crew that only adopt the name of religion and not its life. Doing the works of Satan you are his offspring. For those that are from God fulfil God's commandments, and they that are earthly embrace the pleasures of the earth. He who has once assumed the insignia of a fool will hardly ever lay down his dress. Hence I pray and beseech all who may find themselves in this Ship of Fools, that they should exert themselves and make haste to quit it *etc.*

163.—Here the reader will see Brant is already abandoning the Beghards and viewing his work as a whole.—The historical value of this chapter is not easy to determine exactly. There is a tone of gossip about it all, and the repeated asseveration that the author does not want to condemn the good with the bad, does not take away this impression. Two historical facts may partly account for this attitude of hesitation and uncertainty. In Brant's native town, Strassburg, there were two quite different houses of Beghards, as a local historian has shown.[5] The one was ' zum Trübel am Weinmarkt ' and its inhabitants had joined the Third Order of St. Francis and made temporary vows of chastity, poverty and obedience. These are probably the good ones meant by Brant. The other was ' im Thomanloch,' where there was also a house of Beguines. It is this second house with its twenty-four brethren that seems to have been in very bad repute, at least with

---

[1] I do not know for certain the meaning of these words. *Sotularis* or *subtalaris* is given by Ducange as ' pedulium genus quibus maxime monachi per noctem utebantur in aestate.' And from the statutes of St. Victor at Paris he quotes ' subtalares majores, id est Cothurnos, vel etiam minores cotidianos.' So I suspect that Brant is referring to such wooden sandals (Dutch *trippen*) as are still worn in some religious communities.

[2] This I take to be the meaning of ' incedunt calceolosque movent.'

[3] The Latin has ' urnam haec fregit et urceolum.' It sounds like a proverb, but I have not been able to identify it.

[4] Probably a mere term of abuse here, just as in Chaucer applying the name to the Miller (C.T., A. 560).

[5] C. Schmidt, Die Strasburger Beginenhäuser im Mittelalter, in *Alsatia*, N.F., I. (Mülhausen 1858–60), 149–228, esp. pp. 208, 222.

Brant and his circle. In his original German Narrenschiff he had
already grouped its inhabitants among the most disreputable beggars : [1]

> Der sytzen vier und zwentzig noch
> Zu Straspurg in dem dummenloch (ch. 63, 33).

Brant may really have known something definite about the victims
of his satire. But there is one disturbing factor that makes us doubt
the objectivity of his evidence. About 1497, the year in which Locher's
Navis appeared, Brant edited at Basel *Clarissimi viri juriumque doctoris
Felicis Hemmerlin cantoris quondam Thuricensis variae oblectationis
opuscula et tractatus*.[2] The first five treatises in this curious volume are
all directed against the Beghards : 1. Contra validos mendicantes ;
2. Recapitulatio ejusdem ; 3. Contra Anachoritas Beghardos Beginasque
silvestres ; 4. Lollhardorum descriptio ; 5. Glosa bullarum per Beghardos
impetratarum.[3] They are composed of very cleverly woven biblical texts.
In the first treatise, which takes the form of a dialogue between *Beghardus*
and *Felix*, he calls them e.g. 'insuper inobedientes, vaniloqui, seductores,
qui universas domos subvertunt, docentes quae non oportet, turpis
lucri gratia, semper mendaces, malae bestiae, ventres pigri' *etc*. In
the *Lollhardorum Descriptio* there occur the words often quoted : [4] ' In
tota Germania superiori non est contra fidem catholicam haeresis intro-
ducta nisi per vulpeculas illius sectae Beghardorum, Lolhardorum et
Beginarum maliciosissimae, absque eo, quod quam plures latrones et
sodomitae sunt in eorum habitu reperti.'

It is very difficult to say how much, or how little, objective truth
there is in these sweeping statements by the clever and zealous but
eccentric ' Cantor ' of the collegiate church of Zurich,[5] but Brant has
probably looked at the Beghards very much through Hemmerlin's spec-
tacles. So probably did Geiler and Wimpheling and Thomas Murner.[6]
But as long as the history of the Beghards, especially in the fifteenth
century, remains so obscure,[7] we cannot safely neglect the testimony of
such well-meaning men.

164.—Turning to the French and English versions of our text, we
have to bear in mind a few other historical details. In France the
original Beghards and Beguines, called Turlupini by Gaguin, had been

---

[1] Zarncke's explanation of these words (p. 402), taken from Strobel, is inadequate.
[2] More detailed descriptions in BMC. i, 172 ; Hain 8424.
[3] There is a summary of these treatises in J. L. a Mosheim, De Beghardis et
Beguinabus Commentarius ; fragmentum ex ipso MS. auctoris libro ed. G. H.
Martini (Lipsiae 1790), 469 sqq.
[4] Mosheim l.c. p. 451 ; Gieseler, Text-book of Church History (New York 1868)
iii, 375. Zarncke 447, with a mistaken indication of the place.
[5] See the article on Hemmerlin by J. P. Kirsch in the Catholic Encyclopedia
vii, 214. Mosheim expresses unfavourable opinions pp. 401, 403, 468, 476 *etc*.
[6] Quotations are given by C. Schmidt l.c. p. 226 sqq. The most humorous ones
are of course from Thomas Murner's Narrenbeschwörung ; cf. also ib. p. 222 note.
[7] Mosheim's posthumous work, quoted above, is still the principal authority on
the subject. The most complete article that I know of is by Herman Haupt in
Herzog-Hauck, Realencyklopädie für protest. Theologie und Kirche ii (Leipzig
1897).—Dr. Jos. Greven, Die Anfänge der Beginen (Vorreformatorische Forschungen-
Finke viii. Münster 1912), p. 17, still considers Mosheim as the ' einzige streng
wissenschaftliche Behandlung.'

all but completely suppressed in the fourteenth century [1] after their condemnation in the Council of Vienne. A great many of them had then joined the Third Order of the Dominicans or the Franciscans, so that in the fifteenth century the religious Tertiaries in France were commonly called ' beguini ' and ' beguinae.' This transfer of the name is the reason of much confusion in the history of the Beghards.[2] In the ' Beguinage ' at Paris there were only two Beguines left in 1471, and the house then became a convent of Poor Clares.[3]

In England the Beghards had never been known at all. And yet we have to note the very curious fact that on no language has their name left a deeper impression than on English. For an everyday word like *beggar* (and *to beg*) is, in all probability, nothing but the Old French *begard, begar* (and *beguigner*).[4]

The name of the Beghards in its full technical sense does not appear in English before the seventeenth century.[5] But the pseudo-Chaucerian Fragment C of *The Romaunt of the Rose* used *Beggers* already to render *Beguins*. And just as Brant places the inhabitants of the ' Dummen-loch ' at Strassburg among the real beggars, so here the context shows that there was but one step from the old meaning to the new :

> But Beggers with these hodes wyde,
> With sleighe and pale faces lene,
> And greye clothes not ful clene,
> But fretted ful of tatarwagges,
> And highe shoes, knopped with dagges,
> That frouncen lyke a quaile-pype,
> Or botes riveling as a gype.[6]

Since then the word *beggar* has penetrated into the very marrow of the language, but its original meaning has become entirely obscured.

165.—We may well wonder, therefore, what our translators can have made of this chapter.

To take the Drouyn-Watson version first, the beginning is harmless. As Brant had prefixed no motto to this chapter, there is none in Riviere either. But Drouyn has taken Riviere's first lines instead :

> Pource que devons avoir soing
> En nostre nef soit pres ou loing
> Non delaisser aucuns folz mectre
> En composant cy nostre mectre
> Il nous est pris a souvenir. . . .

---

[1] Mosheim l.c. 413.　　　　　　　[2] Haupt l.c. 519.

[3] L. Le Grand, Les Béguines de Paris in Mém. de la Soc. de l'Hist. de Paris et de l'Isle-de-France xx (1893), 334.

[4] The NED. derives *to beg* directly from *beguigner*. More probable, however, is Skeat's opinion that it is a ' back formation ' from *beggar*. Kluge derives it from OE. *bedecian*.

[5] The first quotation in the NED. is from H. More in 1656 ; other quotations are from 1764 (Maclaine) and 1826 (Southey), all treating of foreign history. The last mentioned is from the *Life of Sir Thomas More* ii, 329: ' Both Beghards and Beguines, throughout Germany, very generally became Lutherans.'

[6] See *Chaucer*, ed. Skeat, i, 202, *Romaunt* 7256 sqq. Skeat thinks it probable that the term Beggars (Beguins) is here used derisively ; the people really described seem to be the Franciscan Friars.

After these lines Riviere goes on :

> Ung tas de folz y convenir
> Begars de tiers ordre et beguines
> Hommes et femmes aians mines
> Dordeuse vile hipocrisie
> Et rempliz de vaine heresie.

But Drouyn felt that here the character of a motto was getting lost, and the main subject itself had already been entered upon.  And so he replaced them by

> De plusieurs folz faire venir
> En noz barques hastivement
> Pour gouverner diligement.

Watson translates these vague generalities :

> Bycause that we sholde be besy
> In our shyppe be it ferre or nere
> And take in other fooles by and by
> Whiche asprely [1] brynge in theyr gere
> Thynkynge with us to go in fere [2]
> And helpe us here for to governe
> Both at the purse [3] and at the sterne.

After this motto Drouyn combines his introduction with the first words of Riviere's text quoted above and so we get in Watson : ' I thought the other daye that a grete multytude of natural foles sholde come unto our shyppes, begared—[Drouyn has *begars* like Riviere ; so Watson is off the track already ; his Shakespearean participle can hardly have any meaning]—begared of the thyrde ordre with begyns as well men as women full of ypocrysye and heresye.'  Watson probably did know something of *begynes*, for they are also mentioned in Caxton's Golden Legend, and their name was soon to become a term of abuse in Bale's mode of speech.[4]  But the *thyrde ordre*, placed behind his *begared,* must have been a mere transliteration from the French.

166.—The word Lollard, a Middle-Dutch nickname, had spread over England as well as over Germany and France, but it seems to have become a generic appellation for all sorts of heretical and abnormal persons.  As such it is used by Barclay in chapter 38, where he says :

> (579)   Poule the apostyll doth boldly say and preve
>         That they whiche to such wytches wyll assent,
>         Ar heretykes, Lolardes and false in theyr byleve.[5]

---

[1] = roughly, fiercely.  The same form occurs in Elyot 1531.  See NED.

[2] in fere (=OE. ȝefēr) became a phrase in ME. in the meaning of *together*, and occurs as such in Layamon, in Chaucer, and is revived in Thomson's Castle of Indolence :  ' Much they moraliz'd as thus yfere they yode.'

[3] The meaning probably is ' the bow of a ship,' but I cannot account for the word.  See NED.

[4] See NED.

[5] The Latin has ' Qui vetulis credis [? credit] malesanis : credit anili Consilio,' and the margin quotes *I Thimo. IIII*, probably meaning v. 7.  Barclay has evidently not looked up the quotation.—A similar vague idea may have been present in his mind when in the opening stanza of this chapter (quoted below) he spoke of ' ypocrytis nat parfyte of byleve.'

The word must have had a very vague meaning in France as well.[1]  For Watson it had hardly any meaning at all.  In the beginning Riviere and Drouyn had corrupted it into *Lohardes* : ' Lohardes begutes venes, beguines discoures et begars, car on dit que vous faictes aller lesperit,'[2] and afterwards they had used it in a strange combination : ' O lolhart gormant et villain.'  Watson has simply skipped it in the first instance : ' Come on begynde[3] fooles, for it is sayde that you make the spyrytes to goo ' ;—and in the second he has changed it into ' O lorell gloton and vyllayne.'[4]

Such corruptions show that in the beginning of the sixteenth century the popular mind can hardly have associated the term Lollard with any technical meaning.[5]

From the rest of Watson's work one quotation will suffice ; it describes the articles of dress and the ' cothurni,' but Riviere's text must be given first, to have at least something of the sense :

> Ung manteau avez vilement
> Et dessoubz celle couverture
> Une courte et briefve vesture
> Affin que ie ne faille en riens
> Ce sont vous les lolhardiens
> Apres voz beguines sen vont
> Lesquelles grant soulliers avont
> Et les chaussent sans avantpiedz
> Moyen quilz sont si large aux piedz (!)
> Et voz beguines et lolhars
> Selon toutes voz loix et ars
> Faictes vos vies sororines
> En plusieurs vilitez sorines.

After Drouyn's prosifying, this becomes in English : ' You have a mauntell and under that mauntell a shorte cote to the ende that I fayll not (!), it is you grete lolardes after you begynde you go with large shone and [here Watson—not Drouyn—skips all about the ' avantpiedz '] after your lawes you lyve in delites vyle and abhominable.'

This may serve as a sample of what the rest is like.  The Frenchman knew only half of what it was all about, and the Englishman was entirely at sea.  No wonder that he made a somewhat precipitate conclusion : [6]

---

[1] The Marnef-translator, in his introductory explanation, speaks of ' ung tas de bigotz que lacteur de ce livre appelle lalhars [sic !] ou goliardz.  Les femmes de leur ordre beguines ou beguttes qui sont des ordres nouvelles.'

[2] This is supposed to render Brant's ' spiritus ire iubet '—i.e. a favourable wind is blowing so that we must weigh anchor !

[3] Watson uses the word *begynde* more than once in this chapter.  Professor Swaen suggests to me that the writer in his blundering fashion may have thought of some compound of *gin* in the meaning of *snare*.

[4] For *lorell* cf. Barclay 1921 : ' To lorellys often the lorde moste lowt ' ; a common ME. word, cognate with *losel*.

[5] In most of the chronicles of the time ' heretykes ' appears as a synonym of ' Lollers.'  See Extracts in A. F. Pollard iii, 238.  Cf. J. Gairdner, The English Church in the Sixteenth Century (1902) xi, 59 sq.—It is simplifying things a little too much to speak of ' Our Lollard Ancestors ' (W. H. Summers, London 1902) and of ' The Lollards and English Bible Reading ' just about 1500 (Mary Deanesly, The Lollard Bible, Cambr. 1920, p. 351 sqq.).

[6] The same as in ch. 24, § 115, and ch. e, § 322.

' for as it is sayd comynly all aboute, the man purposeth and God dysposeth.'

167.—Barclay's treatment of this chapter is very peculiar.—He begins in a tone of condescension and ironical satire :

> (1927)    Here maketh myne Autour a specyall mention
> Of ypocrytis nat parfyte of byleve,
> And suche as abuseth theyr relygyon,
> But I shall nat so sharply them repreve ;
> I am full lothe relygious men to greve
> Or discontent ; for if I so do wolde,
> A myghty volume coude nat theyr vyces holde !

He then takes the vaguest of Brant's expressions, leaving out the more concrete charges, and quietly applies them to all religious in general ; and at the end pretends to be

> (1940)    Levynge my actour for his prolyxite
> And to playne speche and eke to lyberall
> For to be drawen in langage maternall.

This air of mystery and this rather amusing fear of prolixity is probably nothing but a ruse to hide his own lack of comprehension. For it is evident that he does not want to mince matters at all :

> (1928)    I leve theyr pryde, I leve theyr covetyse,
> I woll nat touche theyr malyce nor envy,
> Nor them that Venus toyes exercyse
> I woll nat blame nor touche openly.
>
> (1929)    The maners rude, ungoodly and vylayne
> And assys erys clokyd under cowlys
> Knowynge no thynge, contemnynge yet the scolys.
>
> (1930)    I wyll nat say that they use any syn,
> Yet oft, forsoth ! they folowe nat the way
> Of the relygyon that they have entred in. . . .
> But often at ende it proveth evydent
> That under floures lurketh the serpent.
>
> (1931)    The wolfe or foxe is hyd within the skyn
> Of the symple shepe pore and innocent (= Brant).
>
> (1932)    Hange up the scapler, the amys,[1] cowle and frocke
> Or other habyte of eche relygyon
> Upon a tre clene dede or rottyn stocke.
>
> (1933)    And if that one lyve well and vertuously
> In way of grace, lyke as he ought to go,
> The remanent assayle hym with envy (= Brant).

It is all very lively and evidently written with a keen interest in the subject. But more concrete expressions than these do not occur in it. Wherever he leaves Brant it sounds like an admonition of Thomas à Kempis transposed to the tone of direct satire. He professes again and again, however, that he will not criticize the good but only the bad :

> (1938)    A hevenly lyfe is to be monke or frere,
> Yet is it nat ynoughe to bere the name.

---

[1] This is the canonical so-called *grey amice*, the same, and probably even the same word, as the Italian *mozzetta*. Not to be confounded with *amice* from the Latin *amictus*. See NED.

He wants only to emphasize the time-honoured suspicion of hypocrisy. And when he does not find enough in Brant, he produces the support of an even more unimpeachable authority :

> (1940)　Of suche a vyle and wretchyd ypocryte,
> 　　　　And of his maners playnly as they be
> 　　　　At this conclusion brefly shall I wryte,
> 　　　　As it is founde in good auctoryte.

The ' good auctoryte ' is quoted on the margin : ' Nota Bernardum contra ypocritas super cantica. Volunt esse humiles sine despectu, Pauperes sine defectu, Bene vestiri sine sollicitudine, Delicate pasci sine labore, Aliis adulantes, Aliis detrahentes, Aliis invidentes, Mordaces ut canes, Dolosi ut vulpes, Superbi ut leones, Exterius ut oves, Interius ut lupi rapaces, Sine auctoritate iudices, Sine visu testes, Sine processu doctores, Postremo falsi accusatores, Et omni virtute carentes.' [1] The paraphrase of these words affords him matter for half a dozen stanzas more, and by way of conclusion he adds :

> (1949)　But these wretchys have moche gretter hede,
> 　　　　Theyr wombe to fede, tyll they be full as swyne (!) ;
> 　　　　As for theyr soule they labour nat to fede
> 　　　　With godly wordes or holsome discyplyne ;
> 　　　　The greattest part to glotony inclyne,
> 　　　　Which is the rote of Venus insolence ;
> 　　　　Nowe juge ye, where is theyr continence.

St. Bernard's words are stronger than anything that Barclay has added, except for the implication contained in the last two lines. But though we might think that such cases as that of the rival poet, who was then rector of Diss, must have been notorious enough, yet there is nothing in Barclay, neither here nor elsewhere, but vague suspicions and generalities.

168.—Dean Colet preached to the Members of the Convocation of 1512 a very eloquent sermon which, for its enumeration of abuses to be corrected, has been regarded as an act of great intrepidity, and which seems to be one of the main reasons why he has been honoured with the title of ' Oxford Reformer.' [2] This sermon is, perhaps, the most valuable account of the Church in England at that time ; [3] but there is nothing stronger in Colet than in Barclay, and neither reaches St. Bernard's standard of severity. The great ecclesiastical complaint of the time in England appears to be besides the worldliness and ambition of such prelates as Wolsey, the ignorance of a great proportion of the clergy, and the abuses connected with ' Pluralities,' where not Papal

---

[1] St. Bernard's *Sermones super Cantica Canticorum* had been published at least eight times before 1501 (Peddie i, 97), once in Paris in 1494 (Pellechet 2097). I have not been able to identify Barclay's quotation ; but St. Bernard repeatedly denounces the abuses of the clergy in even stronger terms.

[2] F. Seebohm, The Oxford Reformers John Colet, Erasmus and Thomas More (3rd ed. 1887), 230 sqq. Carnal excesses are just alluded to on p. 242. See also the outline in J. H. Lupton, A Life of John Colet (Bell 1909), 181.

[3] F. A. Gasquet, Henry VIII and the English Monasteries I, 25.—Lupton l.c. p. 178 calls this same sermon ' the overture in the great drama of the English Reformation ' !

interference, but court intrigue, assisted by 'the dire pestilence of Simony,' as Colet calls it, was the cause.[1]

Barclay's criticism of friars and monks is too vague to have much value. Satire and criticism were in the air then, and had been ever since the 'Waning' of the Middle Ages; but before the Reformation this sort of criticism does not seem to have had firm root in England.— Since the publication of the Episcopal Registers and of the most confidential reports of Visitations the life and observance of the English monasteries have become known in detail. But even with the most complete documents before us, it has proved difficult to form an opinion that is not deeply tinged by personal feelings.[2] One thing seems unquestionable however. If the undoubted abuses and corruptions are grave and numerous enough to be interpreted as symptoms of degeneration, this can never have reached the same critical stage as in Germany. Human nature does not change much with time and place, and the ideals in England cannot have been very different from or far below those on the Continent. Whenever there is a widespread falling off from common ideals, one of two things will happen : either there will be a reaction to restore the observance or the ideals themselves will be changed. Both happened in Germany. The Alsatian Humanists and their friends did not only criticize, they strenuously worked for a restoration. At the same time, however, things had come to a head elsewhere, and outside the circle of the Humanists, in Saxony, a storm was gathering which was soon to sweep the old ideals away. England had neither the one nor the other. The 'Observance' was introduced from France and the Burgundian countries, but it remained a plant of foreign import and could only thrive under careful royal protection.[3] And the Protestant Reformation in England under Henry VIII, in so far as it was a religious movement at all, has never pretended to be otherwise than made in Germany.[4]

The satirist satirized because it was his business. Real life is somewhat different from literature. When given the choice Barclay himself saw no objection to swelling the ranks of 'Holy Benet and Francis decorate.' His substitution of the monks and friars, whom he was soon to join, for the original Beghards, of whom he knew nothing, has not enhanced the literary value of this chapter and has spoiled it as a document of historical interest.

[1] Gasquet ib. p. 21 sqq. See also the interesting literary debate between Chr. Saint Germain and Sir Thomas More in the same author's Eve of the Reformation (1900) 115–146, and the summary of More's ' Dialogue ' in J. Gairdner, Lollardy and the Reformation in England i (1908), 543–578.

[2] G. G. Coulton, lecturer in English literature in the University of Cambridge, has formed a very unfavourable opinion. But by giving a complete list of all the abuses found in about 180 communities of English Benedictine monks and nuns Mr. Egerton Beck has laid a very strong foundation for the opposite view. The Month 138 (1921), 128–143 ; 139 (1922), 112–121.

[3] For this statement see A. G. Little, Introduction of the Observant Friars in England in Proceedings of the British Academy xi (1923).

[4] J. Gairdner op. cit. p. 289 calls the corruptions of the Church in England ' somewhat less obtrusive than in Germany.' This would seem to be too weak an expression in view of the fact stated in the immediately following phrase 'it was not from any protest against real abuses that the Reformation here took its origin.'

169.—As a set-off against what precedes we have in chapter 105 a DEFENCE OF THE CARTHUSIANS or a satire of those who try to attack and revile them.

Fools, says Brant, hate the wise and all who do good, because they want the whole world to be as foolish as they are (1–16). And so when they see a wise man retire from the world, they say : ' Look at that Carthusian, that hypocrite ! Cannot we get into heaven in our worldly occupations as well as he with all his fastings and prayers (17–28) ? God has not made us to become monks, and we will not, for they are mere fools and could do more good outside. The monk lives in idleness but without pleasure (29–42). If everyone became a Carthusian like him, who would take care of the world ? His selfishness cannot be in accordance with God's will (43–49).'—Such is the foolish talk of those who love the world better than their own soul. There are plenty of fools on the earth, but if all men thought as they think, no one would find the way to heaven (50–56). The way to hell is easy enough, and if I had two souls I might risk one. But as it is I must take the greatest care, because God can have nothing in common with Belial (57–65).[1]

This chapter originated probably in one of Brant's many visits to the monastery of St. Margaret's near Basel. There one of his most intimate friends lived, John Heynlin, born at Stein near Speyer, and therefore often called Johannes a Lapide.[2] He was one of the most venerable figures in the Early Renaissance movement. As Rector of the University of Paris he had co-operated with Guillaume Fichet to introduce the printing press there in 1470 ;[3] he had subsequently taught and preached in the Universities of Tübingen, Bern and Basel. In this last town he was the centre of a whole group of *literati* and University men and continued to be so even when in 1487 he became a Carthusian,[4] in fact until his death, which took place on the 12th of March 1496, and at which Brant had received permission to be present.[5]

It must have been mainly his irritation at the obloquy to which this great friend of his was exposed, that inspired Brant to write this chapter.[6]

170.—When Locher's translation was published, John Heynlin had been dead for more than a year. I do not know if this may have

---

[1] There are Protestant editions of the Narrenschiff (Frankfort 1553, 1555, 1560, 1566, Basel 1574, Frankfort 1625) in which the second part of this chapter has been left out. This is quite intelligible. They have overlooked, however, that the criticisms in lines 17 to 49 are put on the lips of the fools. Zarncke thinks this oversight quite pardonable, ' da die hier dem narren in den mund gelegten äusserungen höchst verständig sind ' !

[2] M. Hossfeld has written his biography in Basler Zeitschrift für Geschichte und Altertumskunde 6 and 7 (1907, 1908).

[3] Cf. Renaudet 83 sq.     [4] Renaudet 94. Janssen-Pastor i, 143.

[5] Schmidt i, 209. Janssen-Pastor 144. The *Varia Carmina* contain two poems on Heynlin.

[6] His admiration for the Carthusians found also expression in a Latin *Carmen Sapphicum* in *Varia Carmina* F. iiii, used as an introduction in *Divi Brunonis Vita* n.d. n.pl. [Cologne ± 1510]. Procter 10498.—The Carthusians were universally noted in the fifteenth century as the ' ordo non lapsus.' They were praised by the severest reformers. See e.g. John Busch's testimony in his *Liber de Reformatione Monasteriorum* (ed. Grube, 722), Geert Groote's words quoted in the *Chronicon Windeshemense* (Grube 264) and Thomas à Kempis holding them up as models (*Imit.* i 25, v 103) *etc. etc.* Cf. Schoengen, *Schule von Zwolle* 6 A. 3 ; Janssen-Pastor i, 775 s. In England they were with the Observants the strongest opponents of Henry VIII's policy (Gasquet, Henry VIII and the Engl. Monast. 45 sqq. ; J. Trésal, Les origines du Schisme Anglican (Paris 1908), 116).

influenced his version of this chapter; but the original is hardly to be recognized in it.   It has been reduced to an ordinary short one of thirty-eight lines, but only fifteen lines of Brant's original are somewhat vaguely rendered in it.   They all belong to the beginning; the name of the Carthusians is entirely left out, and the last part contains nothing but Locher's own commonplace sermonizings.   The idea seems to be to say nothing more concrete than is justified by the vague title *Retractio a bono*.

In Barclay's version of this shadow of a chapter there is hardly anything worth quoting.   Here is the passage where Locher comes nearest to mentioning the Carthusians:

(1660)   Therfore if any whiche hath that gyft of grace,
        For to despyse this worldes wretchydnes,
        Withdrawynge hym selfe to some solytary place,
        Anone this fole lyvynge in viciousnes
        Cryeth out . . . :
(1662)   ' He loveth nat to come in open ayre
        But lorketh in cornes by fals ipocrysy,
        But we with our felawes lyve alway merely
        And though we in erth oft tymes do amys,
        Yet hope we hereafter to come to hevyns blysse.'

In Drouyn-Watson there is naturally nothing better.   The passage corresponding to the above is only:

' And yf he chese a delectable place to do good in, this foole shall put hym in the waye to make perturbacyon.'

171.—Chapter 98 on INFIDELS is hardly more than a sarcastic list of those whom Brant considers to be outside the pale of Christianity; they are not worthy even of his satire, because they are hopelessly

(4)  Gebunden uff des tufels schwantz.

They are:  the Moors, the Turks, Pagans, Apostates, the 'kätzer schul' of Prague which has corrupted all Moravia, and all those who do not adore the Holy Trinity.   Further the over-timorous who despair of themselves; witches, harlots, profligates, suicides and infanticides.

Locher's version begins with a more detailed explanation of the title, so that half his space is used up before he gets to the list.   He then mentions:  the Turks, Saracens, and Tartars, who are all Mohammedans, the Sarmatian Scythes (!), the 'Secta Bohemorum' that has corrupted the Moravians, among whom the 'Pragensis schola' has fallen from its degree 'fulguris instar.'   Then he speaks of those who hold false doctrines ('heretics' he explains on the margin) and who hold our holy religion to be untrue, and finally those who stab or hang themselves.   This last fills the page, and all the rest is left out.

Comparing the French and English versions with this Latin extract, it appears that in one passage, and in one passage only, Barclay must have followed Riviere rather than Locher.   The beginning is all Locher though very freely or rather loosely paraphrased.   The *externi* become ' fals forayns ' (1497).   Coming to the list, he says, he is not going to

waste words on the ' blynde Bestis ' that follow the doctrine of ' diceyt-
full Mahumyte ' (1499) ; but he will mention ' their sectis,'

    (1500)   For brevyte levynge theyr first invencyon.—
    (1501)   The cursyd jewes despysynge Christis lore,
                For theyr obstynate and unrightwyse cruelty,
                Of all these folys must nede be set before.

This giving pride of place to the Jews (from the context it would
almost seem that he considers them as a sect of Mohammedans [1]) is
without precedent in Locher and Riviere, where they are not even mentioned. Then follow the Turks, the ' Sarrazyns ' (1501), ' the houndes
of Tartary,' and then :

    (1503)   The Scithians and also they of Sarmatyke
                And they of Boeme by fendes fraudolent
                Ar led and blyndyd with an errour lyke,
                Despysynge the lawes of God omnypotent.
                Many ar the londes and iles adiacent,
                Whiche with lyke errour ar blyndyd and infect.
                The owgly Mauryans ar also of this sect.

    (1504)   These with other lyke ar folys and blynde dawes,
                Havynge the chefe shyp of foly and errour,
                For that they folowe vayne doctryne and fals lawes ;
                But namely they that be of suche furour
                Wylfully to forsake God theyr Creatour,
                On fals enchauntement whyle they theyr myndes set
                In the develysshe scoles of Praga and Tolet.

    (1505)   Nygromancians and fals wytches also
                Ar of this sort, folowynge lyke offence ;
                Not onely they that wytche craftis do,
                But they also that gyve to them credence
                Or them supportyth with favour or defence.

After this he mentions idolaters and heretics and last of all, just as Locher,
the suicides ; and to show his contempt of them all he concludes :

    (1507)   But of these mysbelevers more to wryte or tell
                Or to them envoy, theyr errour to counsayle,
                It were but foly and payne without avayle.

The omission of the usual Envoy at the end of this chapter is, therefore, meant as an expression of contempt !

172.—But what to think of the three stanzas just quoted ? The
beginning of Stanza 1503 is evidently written in imitation of Locher.
We can easily forgive the Englishman for not knowing what the humanist
meant by his ' Sarmaticos Scythas.' But he does not even seem to
know what the ' secta Bohemorum ' stood for ; for in the same breath
he adds ' the londes and iles adiacent ' and changes the ' Moravi ' into
the ' owgly Mauryans.' Shakespeare's countryman may have had no
clear ideas about the site of Bohemia, but it is rather striking that an
educated Englishman and an ecclesiastic of about 1500 should have
been ignorant of the identity of the Moravian Brethren, who were the

---

[1] Professor Swaen informs me that such a confusion was very common in
English Literature even later. The dramatists never hesitate to call Solimus a Jew.

lineal descendants of his own Wycliffites.   He seems not to have known
at all what Locher could mean by his *Moravi*, and being at his wits'
end he turned to Riviere for enlightenment.   There he found *Moravi*
on the margin changed into *Moriani* and in the text :

> Et si nostre nef tous les porte
> Saramaticque ausi deporte
> Scithe boeme qui democquent
> Nostre loy et si tous convocquent
> *La gent morians en leur secte*
> Qui est par trop vile et infecte.

This bad example must have influenced him.[1]   In itself it is quite con-
ceivable that both the Frenchman and the Englishman independently
misread Locher's *Moravia* into something meaning Moors.   But the
unusual expression ' ar also of this sect ' sounds like an echo of the
' morians en leur secte.'   And so I suspect that Barclay turned to Riviere
only because he did not know what Locher's *Moravi* were.[2]   If this
suspicion is correct, the explanation of Stanza 1504, which makes a
very puzzling impression, becomes rather easy.   For the ' develysshe
scoles of Praga and Tolet ' is undoubtedly taken from Riviere :

> Et ceulx qui sont si mal apris
> Densuivir prageuse lescolle
> Tholette laquelle recolle
> Mainte cherme et dyableries.
> Et qui toutes ces orderies
> Est du grant fouldre sa semblance.[3]

As Riviere has exactly the same marginal note as Locher here, viz. the
name *Praga* and nothing else, it is difficult to imagine a reason why
Barclay should have turned to Riviere and taken over the abnormal
name of ' Tolet,' unless he had already consulted him about the meaning
of ' Moravi.'—The names of Prague and of ' Tholette ' together with
the ' cherme et dyableries ' may also have suggested Stanza 1505 about
' Nygromancians and fals wytches,' for which there is no support either
in Locher or in Riviere.   That such a suggestion was perfectly natural
we shall presently see in Watson's version.

173.—So the only difficulty to be solved here is, where did Riviere
get his ' Tholette ' from ?   It is immediately preceded by the curious
adjective ' prageuse lescolle,' whereas the only forms known are *pragois*
or *prageois*.[4]   The author may have been thinking of the well-known

---

[1] That the Moravians were very imperfectly known in France is also evident from
a similar transfiguration of their name in the literal Marnef-translator, who is otherwise the best-informed of this whole company : ' Apres vient la secte de bohesmes
laquelle traicte les ludibres et mocqueries de la foy et a donne au *maures* les sonnetes
de follie et incitations derreur.'

[2] On the margin he retained Locher's *Moravi*.

[3] In the last line we have a comical transformation of Locher's ' fulguris instar.'

[4] No other forms, at least, are given by F. Godefroy.   I must add, however, that
the more correct Marnef-translator uses a similar adjective : ' Principalement
lescole pragense qui de son gre et science a la semblance de fouldre cheue est du
souverain degre.'   Or is even he simply transliterating the incomprehensible Latin
adjective, and did the marginal *Praga* not tell him anything ?—Riviere may also
have meant to write *pragense* ; *u* and *n* do not differ much.   But Drouyn copied
the word with a *u*.

anti-national league of the nobility, known by the name of ' La Praguerie,'
which, although half a century had elapsed since its failure, might have
left its traces and traditions in Riviere's native town, for Le Poitou had
been the centre of its activity. It had specially disturbed the South, and
somewhere in the South there was also ' la gent morians ' and ' Tholette '!
—Toledo was traditionally associated with magic in the Middle Ages,[1] and
it still retained its reputation in the fifteenth[2] and sixteenth centuries,
in Poitiers even long after Riviere's death ; for a bookseller of the town,
Guillaume Bouchet, wrote about 1584 : 'Eussent ces sorciers prins leurs
desgrés et estudié en l'escolle de Tolette.' [3]—It must have been a similar
association that led Barclay to speak of ' Nygromancians ' in the very
next stanza (1505). For we find the same idea in Watson. I shall give
one quotation only from his version, but it is a good specimen of the whole,
and the readers will now easily recognize in this hodge-podge the detached
morsels of the French or of the more distant Latin original :

> I shall specyfye unto you here of theyr sectes. The fyrste be the Turques, with
> the Sarasyns and the men of the londe of tartary, these vyllayne mathematycyens
> [!! Drouyn had still ' mahumetiens.'—Well, from Mahomed to Mathematics there is
> but one step !], of whome yssueth all errour. All these regyons ensueth them, that
> I shal declare unto you. Affryke. And the lymettes.[4] Asy a londe ryght puyssaunt,
> and the moost gretest parte of Europe, Samarytyque (!), Sythe, Boeme and the
> Monans.[5] Al our shyp is full of suche folke, for they honour the evyle ensygne-
> mentes, and dysprayseth the good. They be of them—

and here follows the passage to which I wish to draw attention. But
Drouyn's French must be given first : ' Ilz sont de ceulx qui ensuyvent
la mauvaise escole prageuse de tholette laquelle enseigne les chermes de
dyableries [6] qui est du grant fouldre sa semblance.' Now mark what
Watson substitutes for ' prageuse de tholette ' : ' They be of them that
folowe the cursed scole of Nygromancye the whiche enduceth them in
charmes dyabolyke, the whiche is of grete tempest his semblable.'
*Tholette* means *nygromancye* in some way or other. And Barclay has
needed no other inspiration for his Stanza 1505.[7]

174.—After the chapter treating of the Infidels there follows
immediately chapter 99 on the TURKISH DANGER. In this case
the order is not accidental as elsewhere, but intentional. For Brant

---

[1] D. Comparetti, Virgilio nel Medio Evo ii (1872), 974 ; (1896), 106 ; Engl.
transl. Benecke (1895), 320 sq.

[2] As such it is quoted by St. John of Capistran in his ' Responsio facta . . .
Apostillis per fr. Berbegallum ' (Archivo Ibero-Americano x (1923), 314) and by
Luigi Pulci in ' Il Morgante Maggiore,' canto 25, stanzas 42 and 259. See quotations
in M. Menendez y Pelayo, Historia de los Heterodoxos Españoles i (1880), 575, also
on the famous ' magician ' Michael Scott.

[3] I take the reference from La Curne de Sainte Palaye, Dictionnaire historique
de l'ancien langage françois, ed. L. Favre–M. Pajot, tom. x (1882), where the quotation
is given as *Bouchet, Serées II*, 287. There are several editions of this licentious
medley ; I have in vain tried to verify the quotation in the edd. Lyon 1584 in-4⁰
and Paris 1608 3 vols. in-12⁰.

[4] Just as in Drouyn. Riviere had ' toute Affricque et *ses* limites ' !

[5] *Morians* wrote Riviere ; but Drouyn had changed this into *Monans*, although
he copied Moriani on the margin : it comes to the same !

[6] First ed. has ' chermes et dyableriez ' ; second ed. ' Chermes de dybleries.'

[7] That Brant also mentions witches is evidently a mere coincidence.

this chapter was the most emotional and most important of all. In it he explained Dante's great ideals, which were kept alive among the Alsatian Humanists with great fervour :[1] the One, Holy, Catholic and Apostolic Church spreading over the whole world, with the Roman Emperor as its universally acknowledged worldly ruler and the source of all right.[2] Of Brant's very militant Catholicism no evidence need be adduced.[3] His passionate worship of the Sacred Person of the Emperor is best illustrated by his *Elegiaca exhortatio contra perfidos et sacrilegos Flamingos.*

In 1488 [4] the citizens of Ghent and Bruges had dared to imprison Maximilian. This was an outrage that hurt Brant's feelings so much that the strongest words were too weak to express his indignation. He addresses the criminals as 'latrones Cymbri, flamingica monstra,' he wishes 'Sanguine stagna fluant' and 'aequeturque solo terra nephanda suo,' and he calls upon all the nations of the world 'Perdite flamingos, Gandavos perdite diros.'[5]

A natural consequence of this religious imperialism was his vivid perception of the great danger which threatened Christian Europe from the Turks. About the time when he wrote and published the Narren-schiff, he was preparing a Latin work on the history of Jerusalem. It appeared in 1495, at Basel under the title *De Origine et conversatione bonorum Regum : et laude civitatis Hierosolymae cum exhortatione eiusdem recuperandae.*[6] By way of Epilogue to this prose-work he wrote a sort of extract in Latin Distichs *Ad Divum Maximilianum Romanorum Regem,* containing, towards the end, a fervent appeal to Maximilian to undertake a crusade, assuring him that the whole of Europe would certainly follow him :

> Nec tibi defuerint Belgae Hungaricique paratus
> Audiet et Gallus classica (crede) tua *etc.*[7]

---

[1] Stintzing 453.    [2] Schmidt i. 280.

[3] See especially chapters 11 and 103. Goedeke's contrary opinion (p. **xxiv**) requires no further refutation.

[4] Schmidt i, 281 says it was in 1482, but this is surely a misprint. The occurrence itself is described in all historical handbooks. One of the very oldest pamphlets in the Royal Library at The Hague is a 'Correptorium Flamingorum' referring to the same event, and printed at Antwerp in 1488. See W. P. C. Knuttel, Catalogus van de Pamfletten verzameling i (Hage 1889), 1 sq.

[5] *Varia Carmina* e iiii. The most abusive parts are in Zarncke 186 and Schmidt i, 281. There is so much humanistic display, however, of fine-sounding geographical names with fitting adjectives, that to modern ears the passion does not seem to ring quite true.—See also J. Knepper, Nationaler Gedanke 88.

[6] In the British Museum 166. e. i. Description of the book in BMC. iii, 792, and in Pellechet 2819. See also J. Knepper, Nationaler Gedanke 95.

[7] It is also in the *Varia Carmina* of 1498. The appeal is more fully elaborated in a later separate edition, Argentor. 1518 (British Museum 11408, e. 8) :

> Nec tibi defuerint Itali Hungaricique paratus,
> Anglici et Hispani Gallia et armipotens
> Sponte sua multos Reges populosque valentes
> Invenies tecum qui procul ire volunt.

That he did not feel quite safe in making this optimistic statement appears from its sequel, where he adjures the kings and princes 'per membra et viscera Christi' to live in peace and concord and in the holy faith.—The last poem of *Varia Carmina,* entitled *Thurcorum terror et potentia,* is an expression of the same haunting fear.

These religious political ideas, that agitated his spirit at the time, found also expression in the Narrenschiff, and he managed to make them fit into this environment of fools, by a felicitous turn of speech in the motto and a cleverly planned woodcut. A 'fool' is on his knees with a fool's cap in his hand before the high ecclesiastical and political authorities, and the author prays them in his own name :

> Lont mir myn narrenkapp alleyn.

175.—The chapter itself is a very long one of 215 lines, so that a detailed summary would lead us too far. The following are the leading ideas.

I cannot help weeping, says Brant, when I see the ever-increasing ruin of Christendom (1–9) caused by the heretics (10–14) and by the Mahommedans who have conquered one part of Europe after another (15–54). They will soon endanger Italy, Rome and us all (55–64). The four Eastern sisters of Rome have already fallen (65–70). The fault is our own selfishness (71–83), the discord and carelessness of our rulers (84–94). Rome received an emperor to rule its pride and has had him these 1500 years (95–106) ; but the moon is losing its light (107–112) because every one tries to pull down the Roman Empire (113–124). Each cares only for his private profit (125–139)[1] so that the whole is threatened with ruin (140–154). You have a noble king in Maximilian (155–164), and if you will be ruled by him, all may yet be saved (165–175). But no time is to be lost (176–184). O God, make our Princes see the danger, and let them all agree to avert it (185–211). I shall never tire of admonishing them, and whosoever will not listen, I shall give him my fool's cap (212–215).

In Locher's version this chapter covers as many pages (8) and contains as many lines (215) as in the original. But the sequence of the ideas is entirely different. The introduction is twice as long, the conquests of the Turks are enumerated in different order. Among the places endangered Locher manages to bring in his own native country :

> Ister et indomita Suevorum ab origine natus.

After an appeal to 'sancta Rhodos' he speaks of Bajazit's new sanguinary plans, and the carelessness of European princes. Then follow Rome's four sisters, then the European heresies and discords, and the beginning of the Roman Empire ; the Kings of Europe and the Pope are admonished to make peace, and Maximilian is praised as a Hercules, an Achilles, a Pompey, a Sylla and a Camillus. The German Princes are specially admonished and the chapter concludes with a new and longer eulogy of Maximilian, which in its grandiloquent verbosity never reaches the pathos of Brant's simple reference to

> (159)　Der edel fürst Maximilian.

176.—Evidently and naturally the greater part of this pompous chapter did not appeal very strongly to the translators.

Barclay's introduction is the best of all. He says that he is so grieved :

> (1509)　That with wete chekes by teres thycke as hayle
> 　　　　I am constrayned this harde chaunce to bewayle.
> (1510)　My doleful teres may I nat well defarre
> 　　　　My stomake strykynge with handes lamentable.

---

[1] How literally true this complaint was in Germany, see Janssen-Pastor i, 624 sqq.

Of the passion of the original, extinguished in Locher's stiff Latinity, there is nothing left but the ashes of this doleful rhetoric.

From the long list of geographical riddles set by the Latin I shall quote only two that have found the most curious solutions.

> pontium nunc habet Ionium.
> Bosphorus at Thracie : septem quoque regna Trionis :
> Nec fuerant Thurco regna paterna satis.

Barclay is the wisest. He omits the difficult ' pontum Ionium ' and the Bosphorus, and writes :

> (1521)    The londe of Trace, large in a marveylous wyse
> With the royalmes of Semptemtrion echone
> Longynge to his fader coude nat his mynde suffyse.

Riviere found no difficulty here :

> Ilz ont tant fait que bien a pont
> Ont pris de ionine le pont [1]
> Bosphore aussi la grant tracie
> Et sept royalumes de trionnie
> Bien amples grans et paterneulx !

Drouyn thought he might as well change ' Bosphore ' into ' beschore,' and Watson substituted ' Tarcye ' for ' Tracie,' and so impressed upon his English readers the fearful conquests of the Turks : ' They have taken the brydge of Ionyne Beschore, and the grete Tarcye and seven realmes of tryonnye.' Who would under these words have discovered the Ionian Sea, and the Bosphorus and the countries north of it ?

177.—In the second example Barclay allows himself to be caught very badly. The names and allusions *are* somewhat bewildering :

> Non satis Istricolas, Styriosque, et Pannona rura
> Tutari a Thurco gens modo nostra valet.
> Illyrici trepidant : insultus Appula rura
> Thurcorum metuunt : Itala terra tremit.
> Vix se defendet fumantibus Aetna cavernis :
> Enceladi cervix sentiet illud onus.
> Ister et indomita Suevorum ab origine natus :
> Thurcorum metuit nunc tolerare iugum.[2]

The marginal notes elucidate the meaning. In the first line he means *Istria, Pannonia* ; in the third *Illiria, Apulia* ; in the fourth *Italia* ; in the fifth and sixth *Sicilia* ; and in the last two *Danubius*.

This was enough for Riviere.

> Combien que ayent par leurs escolles
> Stirie pannone istricolles
> Toutes ces belles regions
> Royaulmes et grandes nations.

---

[1] Even the Marnef-translator speaks of ' le pont yonien.'

[2] Almost correct seems the Marnef-translation : ' La terre de italie aussi a grant peine se deffendra contre les turcs. La montaigne de Ethna avecques ses fumantes cavernes et apparcevra la teste de la montaigne Encelade icelle charge. Maintenant le fleuve de Ister né de lorigine des Suysses qui iamais ne fut domptez craint tolerer le iouc des Turcz et cheoir en leur subiection.'

He knows what he is talking about !

> Tellement la gent diliricques
> Tremblent et pour ces turcs iniques
> Toute la terre dytalie
> Compris avecque apulie
> Qui sont insultez et pillez
> Aux champs com pauvres exillez.

Here he must have taken his courage in both hands :

> Les ancelades es poternes (!)
> Au pres dethna aux grans cavernes
> Semblablement sont prosternez
> De cecille suevere nez (!)
> Et danubie tous ses gens
> En grans douleurs et pleurs ingens *etc*.

Watson simply transliterates Drouyn's paraphrase :

They have Pavonye [Drouyn had read *uu* instead of *nn* [1]], Istryce et Tyre [Drouyn reads *Itire* for *Stirie*], that is so fayre regyons, so that the Diriliques (!), Italyens and Apylyens trembleth for fere. With greate payne may the monte of Ethna defende hym, with the profounde cavernes, And the Ancelades feleth it. Semblably be prosterned they of Suevere, Cycylle and Danubie.

178.—We might expect something better from Barclay. And in the beginning he *is* a great deal better, evading the more difficult words and displaying some independent geographical knowledge :

> (1529)  The noble Cecyle is dayly in great dout,
> Istria, Pannony and also Lumberdy
> And dyvers other nacions there about,
> As Sycyll, the Stiryans, Venyce and Italy ;
> These ilys and regions quakyth contynually ;
> The royalme of Naplys lyveth also in dout
> Of the fals Turke besegeynge it about.

This seems to be as good as any ; though it is not quite clear what he means by mentioning *Sycyll* by the side of *Cecyle*. But then he suddenly plunges into the most laughable of absurdities :

> (1530)  The royalme of Denmarke with his hyll Ethnay,
> As men sayth, brennynge alway with flamynge fyre,
> Scantly escapyth the jeopardous affray
> Of these fals Turkes and theyr cruell impyre.

We are left to guess how he devised this geographical monstrosity. It is barely possible that Locher's *suevorum* suggested Sweden, and that this associated itself with Denmark. But another element has certainly contributed to the misapprehension. None of the translators seems to have understood that *Danubius* was the same as *Ister*, but although Riviere and his followers speak of *Danubie*, on Barclay's margin alone do we find *Danubia*. And *Danubia* standing over against the line in which

[1] And Watson knew all about ' Pavonye ' as it had already occurred in chap. 92 ! See § 38.

*Suevorum* occurred, must of necessity mean Denmark ! And as it was immediately preceded by a description of the Etna, it was quite natural to transport the mountain thither.

179.—But enough of these geographical freaks. We must now study the much more interesting patriotic element in this chapter.

First there is Locher's appeal to the countries of Europe :

> O Proceres latii : tuque o Germania fortis :
> Vos rigidi Galli : Pannoniusque ferox :
> Et tu papa sacer : Christi defendite nomen.

Riviere has not changed this much. He only left out the *Pannonius* and put ' france trespuissante ' instead, by the side of ' les Gaules roydes.' Drouyn emphasized his nationalism a little more and omitted the ' Gaules.' ' O princes barons et rommains. O france trespuissante et redoubtee entre les crestiens. O alemaigne la forte. O toy pape et pere sainct ' *etc.* Such expressions were not quite agreeable to the English taste however ; and therefore Watson, not less patriotic than Drouyn, wrote : ' O prynces and barons Romayns, O noble France, O Almayne the stronge, O excellente Englonde imperyall, so endued with fortytude. O thou holy fader the pope,' *etc.*

In Barclay there is nothing of these petty expressions of national vanity. He was reserving his patriotism for a better occasion, and now simply addressed :

> (1555)   O worthy prynces and lordes Italyen,
> Ye stoberne Flemynges [1] and ye of Pannony,
> O subtyle Lumberdes, Spanyardes and Frenchmen,
> And o holy Fader the Pope moste specyally, *etc.*

180.—Locher's flattery of Maximilian in true humanistic fashion put the national feelings of the translators to a severe test.[2] Riviere began by taking a very simple course. He changed *Maximilianus* on the margin into *Carolus christianissimus rex franciae* and applied all Locher's

---

[1] Does he leave out ' Germania fortis ' on purpose ? And does he know the stubborn inhabitants of the Low Countries better ?

[2] Even the ' literal ' Marnef-translator seems to have had his feelings hurt here. He omits the last part altogether and fundamentally changes Locher's first eulogy of Maximilian. He speaks of ' le treschrestien roy de France a present vivant [that is good for ever !] dont les tres redoubtez princes antecesseurs ont tousiours eu la saincte foy catholique bien a cueur,' and he supposes that he ' supportera nostre Maximilian vray chevalier de la foy. Comme ainsi soit que celluy francoy par antho- nomasie soit seul sans plus appelle franc quicte et exempt de toutes servitutes ou hommages, non tenant que de Dieu, de leglise et de soy.' After this he begs the Pope to exhort his clergy to greater zeal, so may he and all his people win the glory of Paradise. There our translator stops ! The last part of the words quoted is an echo of the principle which was considered fundamental in France—viz. that ' le Roi ne tient que de Dieu et de son épée ' (Thuasne i, 80 note). Drouyn uses a similar expression in his own chapter (f) on the Corruption of Right, where he addresses his king : ' tu es oing de saincte huylle : et couronne de larchevesque de reims. Tu nes point en rien subiect a lempire de romme.' Watson could not apply this to his Tudor King, but he had something better : ' Ye shal be exalted in the sempyternall courte with the rose fyrste stocke of your generacyon.'

expressions to his own hero, only with a much stronger emphasis upon the probable opposition of the envious :

> envieux tous maulditz.
> Cueurs desloyaulz cueurs interditz *etc.*

and with two notable additions. First a reference to the Italian wars :

> Considerez lagrant bataille
> Les puissans gens les legions
> Dhommes et grandes nacions
> Quil subiuga na pas long temps.

And towards the end he warns the envious again with a story (as the margin says) : *De imperatore Carlo Calvo . . . cui penas inferni deus demonstravit.*

> Lempereur Charles est le chauve
> Auquel monstra dieu sain et saulve
> Les grandes peines des dampnez
> Visez quil dit des condampnez
> Combien estoient de vostre sorte.[1]

Drouyn must have felt some misgiving whether Riviere was really rendering Locher faithfully. He looked into the Latin text and found the name of *Maximilianus* on the margin. That was all he wanted. He now eased his conscience by inserting a protest against the enemy of Charles VIII : ' O noble empereur Maximilien ou est ta force ' *etc.*[2] He had another difficulty. Charles VIII had died in the spring of 1498 and Louis XII had mounted the throne. Never mind. The marginal note became : *Ludovicus cristianissimus rex Franciae duodecimus,* and the address was directed to ' O toy Loys trescrestien roy des francys, toy qui a plus que iamais roy neust en France ' *etc.* He retained the glory of the old king however : ' Considerez comment Dieu a aide au feu roy Charles huytieme en toutes batailles, il a este crain des villains turcz luy qui menoit guerre contre les crestiens (!) Donc pour raison plus eminente Dieu vous aydera contre ces chiens.' He added a contemptuous reference to the King of England : ' Vous aultres roys que songes vous que vault garder ? Angleterre ny Escoce. Rien. Haban-

---

[1] This reference is so short that I have not been able to identify the legend referred to. Hincmar of Rheims tells the story of a Vision (Visio Bernoldi) in which Charles the Bald occurs lying in Purgatory (J. Sirmondus, Hincmari ep. Rhemensis Opera ii (Parisiis 1645), 28–31 ; reprinted in Migne, Patr.-Lat. 125, 1115–1120 ; cf. F. Kampers, Mittelalterliche Sagen vom Paradiese (Köln 1897), 62). I owe this reference to F. Bon. Kruitwagen, but I do not know if this is what Riviere means.

[2] Curiously enough, however, a little further down he speaks with respect of the same man without however mentioning his name : ' O puissant roy des rommains sage et prudent qui tiens le sceptre royal de lempyre rommaine quelque envie quon eut sur toy tu es puissant et digne de gouverner telle couronne. Je ne scay prince plus iuste, vertus domine en toy tu ayme paix ton honneur croist.' There is not a trace of this in Riviere. Why, then, did Drouyn insert it ? Did not he know that the King of France had no stronger opponent of his Italian ambitions than Maximilian ? I think we need not speculate very deeply. He had just written down an idea caught somewhere else, he is now culling some fresh ideas from Locher's Latin. The actual state of affairs did not (perhaps : not *yet*) ruffle the smoothness of his mind, and a feeling of inconsistency did not prevent him from picking the flowers where he found them. Happy man ! But as an actual witness we shall have to dismiss him from the court.

donnes ces isles, laisses dames et damoiselles, selles chevaulx : prenes
vos harnoys et faictes sonner vos trompettes iusques en Turquie.'—
After the story of Charles the Bald, he goes on with a very outspoken
original addition which naturally makes the impression of being part
of the story : ' Regardes quil dit de ceulx qui estoient comme vous
estes ( = R)   Vous enrechisses voz parens ' *etc.*

181.—After these remarks we are in a position to understand and
enjoy Watson's version.   Here at any rate there was a call to produce
something better than a mere string of detached words and expressions.
And he rose to the occasion.   The chapter is too long to give more than
the vital parts ; to let everyone have his due those passages that are
original in English have been italicized.

> O noble Emperoure Maxymilien, where is thy force, where is thy strengthe ?
> Wherat holdeth it that thou employeth it not upon these vyllayne Turkes ? . . .
> Alas thou purpenseth[1] not [tu ne pense] but for to make warre upon the crysten
> men, and leveth the infydeles that dystroyeth thyn empyre.   It were better for the
> to be a symple erle, than for to take suche a charge upon the, and not to do thy
> devour.   O thou *ryght puyssaunt kynge of Englonde,* the whiche hathe more rychesse
> than ever kynge of *Englonde* hadde, employe nowe thy puyssaunce upon the Turkes,
> and mescreauntes.   Thou art florysshynge in honour amonge the crysten kynges
> . . . O dukes, erles, barons *and knyghtes* of *this redouted realme of Englonde, whiche
> is the floure of crystendome* and tryumphaunte treasoure of bounte. . . .
>
> O noble lordes domynatours of Almayne, awaken you, for you be stronge and
> myghty, and sheweth it nat. . . . Shewe you in polysshed armes.   And go with
> the *Englysshmen and* frensshe men on the Turkes with a grete hoost. . . . Consyder
> how God dyde helpe kynge *Henry the Fyfte* agaynst the crysten men, the whiche by
> reason sholde helpe you soner agaynst the infydeles. . . .
>
> You other kynges what dreme you, what avaylleth the kepynge *and lourynge in
> your countrees* (!) ?   nothynge, habandone them and leve ladyes and gentylwomen,
> sadle your horses, take your harneys, and make sowne your trompettes in to Turkye.
> O you envyous and cursed hertes . . . you empesshe our good kynge of *Englonde*
> for to make warre, for the sustentacyon of the fayth. . . .
>
> I fynde of Charles Chauves, that reygned in fraunce, after Charlemaigne, and was
> the fourthe of that name, to whome God shewed the paynes of helle [Fr. des dampnez],
> Beholde there what he sayeth unto them that were as you be.   You enryche your
> frendes *the whiche ben yssued out of a poor lygnage,* in gyvynge theym the offyces
> of prudent gentylmen, and so by flaterynge *the chorles is promoted, and the gentylmen
> remayneth in extremyte.*   You desyre warre, but you kepe you ever ferre from *the
> strokes.*   In cytees and townes where as ye passe, the wyves and maydens ben
> vyoled, the poore men beten and robbed.   Who hath done it ?   My lorde and his
> men.   And then they dare not speke. . . .

In the conclusion Drouyn is paraphrasing Riviere again :

> O noble kynge . . . Reygne peasybly, and *whan* all *Englonde* is *in tranquylyte*
> [Drouyn did not make such a condition : ' et *puisque* toute france aille dessus '],
> then go upon the sarasyns and myscreauntes.   And recover that the whiche they
> have conquered.   And after your deth you and yours shall be lyvynge in the realme
> of paradyse.   But and ye do ony thynge agannst your God, and agaynst the comyn
> welfare, God shall hate you and your people also.   For whan a lorde is not belovyed
> of his subgectis[1] it is an evyl sygne and token.

182.—Barclay lifts us again into a more serene atmosphere.   In the
beginning he simply adapts Locher's expressions to his English king,

---

[1] Watson's 2nd ed. prints ' parpenseste ' in the first example, ' subiectis ' in the
second.

but he does it openly and honestly. For on the margin he writes *Mutatur laus Maximiliani Romanorum regis in laudem Henrici octavi Anglorum regis.* And he begins in a clear tone :

> (1557)    One hope we have our ennemyes to quell,
>             Whiche hope is stedfast if we ourself do well ;
>             For Henry the eyght, replete with hye wysdome,
>             By iust tytyll gydeth our septer of kyngdome.

He applies all Locher's classical names [1] to his own king ; he does not even shirk the name of Hercules for an eighteen-year-old boy ; though he has to add a qualification :

> (1558)    He passyth Hercules in manhode and courage,
>             Havynge a respect unto his tender age.[2]

He adds various little touches which show that he kept his object in view. He understood the difference between the old regime and the new :

> (1559)    Covetyse hath left behynde hym his ryches
>             Unto the hyghe possession of lyberalyte,
>             Which with the same shall kepe our lybertye.

He replaced the ' victrices aquilas ' of the German emperor by a more British emblem in fine-sounding alliteration :

> (1561)    There shall no Turke be abyll to indure
>             His rampynge Lyons rorynge in theyr rage ;

And the ' celica turba ' is completed by a British protagonist :

> (1562)    For God and his sayntis shall helpe hym for to fyght,
>             Saynt George our Patrone shall eke augment his myght.

Then comes the appeal to the ' Englysshe States ' but in a different tone from Riviere :

> (1563)    But, o Englysshe States, I humbly you requyre :
>             Unto your kynge of hert and mynde be true.

Thus he goes on to the end of Locher's chapter where he simplifies the fine-sounding names :

> (1569)    Obey to hym, Prynces, than trust I ye shall se
>             That by his manhode and counsell soverayne
>             All that is [3] lost we shall soone wyn agayne.

183.—He has not done yet, however. For he writes on the margin : *Addicio Alexandri Barclay. Jacobi Scotorum regis strenuissimi a magnanimitate laus summa.* And the six stanzas that follow are remarkable

---

[1] Ramsay lxxxviii is inclined to think that Skelton meant to parody this passage by comparing his Prince to thrice as many heroes !

[2] Some ten years earlier Bernard André, an Augustinian friar and Henry VII's Poet Laureate, had compared Hercules' twelve labours to *Les Douze Triomphes de Henry VII.* Text in J. Gairdner, Memorials of King Henry the Seventh (Rerum Brit. medii aevi scriptores 1858), 133 sqq. ; English translation, p. 307 sqq.

[3] The 1st ed. misprints *his* ; Cawood has the correct reading.

indeed. The preceding eulogy might be called obligatory. The translator could not very well do without it. It would have been a positive
omission. But these stanzas on James of Scotland are a quite voluntary
contribution, not called for by the context :

> (1570)   And ye christen Princes, who so ever ye be,
>          If ye be destytute of a noble Capytayne,
>          Take Iamys of Scotlonde for his audacyte
>          And proved manhode ; if ye wyll laude attayne,
>          Let hym have the forwarde ; have ye no disdayne
>          Nor indignacion, for never kynge was borne
>          That of ought of warre can shewe the Unycorne.

The Turks will retreat before his courage ; for—and Stanza 1572 is an
Acrostic on the name of Iacobus—' this most comely kynge ' is prudent
and strong and magnanimous and bold. Only he is poor ; and the
following lines, prosaic as they are, show something of a personal concern
about Scotland and the Scottish King :

> (1573)   Mars hath hym chosyn, all other set asyde,
>          To be in practyse of batayle without pere,
>          Save ryches lacketh his manfull myght to gyde ;
>          He hath nat plentye of all thynge, as is here.
>          The cause is that stormes in season of the yere
>          Destroyeth the corne, engendrynge so scarsnes,
>          Whiche thynge moche hurteth this Prynces worthynes.

The pride of the Turk will decay and fall if England and Scotland will
unite their strength :

> (1575)   If the Englysshe Lyon his wysdome and ryches
>          Conioyne with true love, peas and fydelyte
>          With the Scottis Unycornes myght and hardynes,
>          Than is no dout but all hole christente
>          Shall lyve in peas, welth and tranquylyte,
>          And the Holy Londe come into christen hondes,
>          And many a regyon out of the fendes bondes.

These lines were written three or four years before Flodden Field. In
an Englishman they would have betokened a breadth of outlook such
as we can hardly expect at that time of narrowing patriotism. So that
these stanzas provide the most conclusive argument for the writer's
Scottish birth. We must not ask whether it was dangerous to write
them or not ;[1] such lines are not written out of considerations of
prudence, but only out of strong personal feeling, and—national blood
is thicker than water.

184.—Taking the different versions of this chapter as a whole, we
can see reflected in them some of the principal factors which dominated
the political and ecclesiastical development of the late fifteenth and
early sixteenth centuries. Out of Brant's beseeching prayers we hear
his deep regretful feeling that the Holy Roman Empire in Germany is
breaking up into independent states, that the imperial power of the

---

[1] Jamieson xxx, lxxxix.

Middle Ages is waning, that the Christian commonwealth is a thing of the past. At the same time and more directly his appeal makes us realize what treasures of mental and spiritual energy were diverted from positive action by the perennial nightmare of the Turkish danger, which paralyzed the forces of Christianity just at a period when they were most needed.—Locher's Latin is a good example of how the real Humanists turned the gravest concerns of Church and State into themes for writing their literary exercises.—Riviere's and Barclay's substituting, as a matter of course, for Maximilian's name those of their own sovereigns, and applying the same epithets to them and entrusting them with the same work, can only be accounted for by the fact that to them, as to men of a later epoch, the word Emperor is only another title for a King, that national pride and patriotism are rising, and kingly power is growing to absolutism.

Brant is the religious idealist, Locher the pedantic humanist, Riviere the touchy royalist. Drouyn has not yet formed an opinion of his own ; perhaps he lives among the Burgundian ' Real-politiker ' who do not quite see their way here. Barclay is the cool peaceful ecclesiastic, who reasons about his patriotism ; Watson the humble printer's devil, loyal to his king of course, but with his own little axes to grind !

Patriotism is in them all. In Germany it has the enthusiasm of youth. It was a product of Humanism there and had hardly found expression yet outside the circle of Brant.[1] In France it betrays its origin and growth in the midst of continual wars. The struggle with England had first awakened the feeling of national unity.[2] And in the safety of the English isles themselves patriotism was accepted as a matter of course.—They were possibly all quite honest in summoning the Christian nations to repel the common enemy. But the very appeals to avert the danger betray also the cause why so little was done to avert it. All nations were willing to fight the Turks, but only under the leader-ship of their own king, and only after they were sure that their own interests are safe. On the other hand Barclay's naive reference to Denmark with its Etna being threatened by the Turks may well be taken as a symptom of how little the islanders understood the actual danger. For Barclay this chapter was only an occasion to vent his patriotic or royalist feelings. He can never have meant a real military expedition, when without the least misgiving he recommends first Henry of England and then the Scottish King as its chief leader. Minor men such as Drouyn thought a prospective expedition against the Turks the best opportunity to stammer their wail, that ' it is an evyl sygne and token whan a lorde is not belovyd of his subiectes.' His English translator finds his own ground of complaint in the fact that ' the chorles is promoted and the gentylmen remayneth in extremyte.'

The Turks need dread no danger. Lepanto is still far off.

---

[1] J. Burckhardt 94 sq. J. Knepper, Nationaler Gedanke 26 sqq., 81 sqq.— Jakob Wimpfeling 69 sqq.

[2] J. Burckhardt l.c.; C. Schmidt i, 17, 31 sqq.; Rashdall i, 556. Abel Lefranc, ' Le Patriotisme en France au temps de la Renaissance ' in *Foi et Vie* Dir. P. Doumergue 1915, 234 sq.

185.—The last chapter of this category in the Narrenschiff is the satire on HERETICS in chapter 103, under the ominous title of *Vom Endkrist*. Brant enumerates various symptoms here which make him fear that the end of the world is not far off.

There are a great many that pervert the true sense of the Scriptures (1–16) although they have so many opportunities of knowing better (17–24). They try to wreck the ship of faith (25–28). They are the false prophets who live with scorpions. See Ezechiel ii, 6 ; xiii sq. (29–40). They are the hired messengers of Antichrist (41–54). But they will come to a sorry end and Truth will prevail (55–62). St. Peter's ship is now in great danger (63–66), because the Scriptures are wilfully distorted (67–71). False doctrines are being sown by the messengers of Antichrist (72–76). Printers who work only for profit help them (77–80), and they produce very badly printed and badly corrected books by which they ruin others and themselves as well (81–91) !—The time of Antichrist is near at hand (92–93). Our faith mainly rests on three foundations : on indulgences, on books and on good doctrine (94–97). Of books we have so many that they are no longer valued (98–104). Sound doctrine is to be had in our numberless universities (105–109) but the scholars are despised rather than honoured (110–125). Nor do people nowadays care for indulgences although formerly they went on long pilgrimages for them, even as far as Aix-la-Chapelle (126–133). Our people are like the Jews who grew sick of the manna (134–141). The abundance of indulgences, therefore, seems like the last leaping up of a flame before it dies out altogether (142–145). So that I fear the day of doom is near, the light of grace will be extinguished and the ship of faith is going to be wrecked (146–152).

These are the contents of this famous chapter which has been quoted time and again by friends and enemies of the Protestant Reformation.[1] But it need not here occupy us very much. For Locher has reduced its 152 lines to 88 and some of the most interesting passages he has left out. He takes mainly lines 1–24, 29–34, 41–56, 63–74, 95–104, 112–113 ; and he concludes with the prophecy of 92–93. So he leaves untranslated everything that Brant says about printers, and about schools and scholars, and about indulgences !

186.—Barclay follows Locher faithfully. He also speaks mainly of :

(1621)    Such as varys the true sence
          Of Goddes lawe, expoundynge other wyse
          Than it in the text clere and playnly lyes.

And he improves upon the Latin figure of speech by the comparison :

(1622)    Such counterfayte the kayes that Jesu dyd commyt
          Unto Peter, brekynge his shyppis takelynge.

Brant's pathetic prophecy, which has become a calm statement of fact in Locher's final couplet, is diluted in the last stanza :

(1641)              Alas, the tyme is come
          That false prophetis our holy fayth distayne [2] ;
          They all shall turne, if favour them meyntayne ;
          And if they that preche for mede and vyle rewarde
          Shal them supporte,[3] our case shall be full harde.

But even here we feel that coming events cast their shadows before.

---

[1] See Janssen-Pastor i, 799 sq. ; Zarncke 450 sqq.
[2] The full form *distain* and the aphetic for *stain* appear both at the same time, viz. in Trevisa, Chaucer, Gower etc. See NED.
[3] First ed. has supportyth ; a misprint corrected by Cawood.

We hardly get the same feeling from Watson's conclusion : ' The tyme is comen that the fayth is subverted to dysdayne. And the prophets have advertysed (Fr. disverty) (!) dyvers men. The tyme is comen that these false prophetes converteth (Fr. subvertissent) the worlde by seduccyon and cautellous artes.' Most of this version is again a mere string of words without much sense, and hardly worth quoting. It is all translated literally from the French. Drouyn becomes interesting only when he adds something of his own to Riviere's paraphrase. This happens in two places. Towards the end he inserts : ' The bokes that be made in Englysshe (the French has of course ' en françoys ') touchynge the secretis of fayth causeth dyvers errours, and especially to women and symple men.'

187.—In the middle he gives us a piece of information of historical importance. In Riviere there is nothing ; the lines swing on very calmly :

> Seminateurs de zizannie
> Et gens rempliz de zizannie,
> Trois chose ie veulx cy bouter *etc.*

But in the middle of this passage Drouyn inserts a story of his own experience :

> Ils sont seminateurs de zizanies. Moy dernier translateur ay vey a Paris desgrader coupper la langue et puys bruller ung prestre qui tenoit quasi telles erreurs, et ny avoit sy grant docteur qui le peust mettre hors de la follie. Il disoit et fasoit de grans choses desquelles ie me tais pourc quil nest pas licite dire telles choses. Plusieurs sont a present qui ont aussy desservye la mort que cestuy la, donc ie vouldroye pour ma part que le createur du monde les eust pugnys de telle pugnition que toutes erreurs fussent hors de leurs teste. Je veulx icy mettre troys choses *etc.*

Here he goes back to Riviere and becomes dull and almost incomprehensible again. We could wish he had given us some more details. The question is : does he know much more ? He says the victim ' tenoit quasi telles erreurs,' although no special errors have yet been mentioned. But he is sure to have known what the ' grans choses ' were like, which he keeps secret only ' pourc quil nest pas licite dire telles choses.' We are left wondering what he can mean. But he goes on to say that there are several more such heretics and that they all deserve capital punishment. Heretics were the revolutionaries, the Bolshevists of that time ; their punishment was considered fully deserved, and the cruelties of the judicial procedure did not cause much excitement.

The particular case to which he is referring is not difficult to identify. The Inquisition, as a bitter modern critic [1] expresses it, had sunk to a subordinate position in France, although the spirit of inquiry and independence was spreading. The only execution for religious offences that seems to have occurred in Paris in the second half of the fifteenth century was that of one Jean Langlois, and the Inquisition had nothing to do with it. He was a Priest of St. Crispin's at Paris who had long lived abroad. On the 3rd of June 1491 he assailed the Priest who was

---

[1] H. C. Lea, History of the Inquisition of the Middle Ages ii (New York 1906), 142.

saying Mass in the cathedral, threw him to the ground in the presence of the whole congregation, upset the chalice and trampled the Holy Eucharist under foot. He was, of course, at once taken prisoner, and then he denied the Real Presence. He showed no signs of repentance, and on the 21st of June, after a solemn procession, he was degraded in front of Notre-Dame and handed over to 'the secular arm.' The executioner cut off the hand that had upset the chalice, and he was heard to cry that he had sinned and that he wanted to die in the Catholic Faith. Standonck, the pious director of Montaigu College, attended him till his death on the pyre.[1]

There can be little doubt that this was the case witnessed by Drouyn. A man in the crowd may well have thought that the tongue was cut off instead of the hand. But the real cause was probably alluded to in his 'disoit et fasoit de grans choses' and his 'Il nest pas licite dire telles choses' probably meant to say that the outrage committed was too bad to be described.

188.—The unwary reader of the English version might think that Watson himself had witnessed the affair. For he translates his French model with only one slight deviation :

> They be sowers of zizanies. I the laste translatour (!) have sene at Parys dysgrade, cutte the tongue, and after brenne a preest, that helde almoost suche erroures, and there was no doctour so grete [—this must be Standonck—] that myght put hym out of his foly [—we now know that this is not quite correct—]. He sayde and dyde grete thynges of whiche I holde my peas for dyvers reasons. [Here is the only alteration that Watson has introduced into his text ; and a very sensible alteration it is ; one can always allege ' dyvers reasons ' for not speaking of a thing one does not know !] There is dyvers at this present tyme that hathe as wel deserved the dethe as he, for the whiche thynge I wolde that the Creatour sholde punysshe them so, that all errours were expulsed out of theyr hedes. I wyll put here thre thynges *etc.*

I need not quote anything of the rest.

In the original German and Latin editions this chapter is preceded by a magnificent woodcut, which has been called ' the highest achievement of German art before Dürer's Apocalypse.'[2] In Barclay's translation an attempt has been made to imitate the original. Drouyn and Watson, or their employers, have left it out altogether, and inserted a ridiculous schoolboy's drawing instead. An apt symbol of their own work.

189.—At the end of the second and following editions of Locher's Navis Stultifera Brant has added a very long chapter of nineteen pages, preceded by a clumsy woodcut containing an astrological diagram.

---

[1] The story has long been known only from the *Chronicorum multiplicis historiae . . libri xx* of the Cambray Priest Christ. Massaeus (Antverpiae 1540), p. 268. This notice has been copied by Ch. du Plessis D'Argentré, *Collectio judiciorum de novis erroribus I* (Lutet. Paris. 1728), ii, 323. H. C. Lea o.c. ii, 144 misrepreesnts the story. A. Renaudet, *Préréforme* 110 sq., brings some further details taken from two MSS. in the Bibl. Nat. From Massaeus it was not even clear that the criminal was a priest. He is there only called Magister, and from the words used it would appear that the case had happened ' in sacello sancti Crispini.' But I have adopted Renaudet's emendations.

[2] Dr. W. Weisbach, Der Meister der Bergmannschen Officin (Studien zur Deutschen Kunstgeschichte vi, 1896) 36.

It does not appear in the principal translations, so I need not give a long summary. Its double title expresses the idea that DISORDER RUINS ALL (f).

Disorder first ruined the hierarchy of the Angels, followed by Adam's fall. God then resolved to keep the ruling of mankind in His own hands; but Cain usurped His power and after the deluge Cham founded worldly kingdoms. First came the monarchy of the Assyrians. It was supplanted by the Medes. The Hebrews also wanted to have their own kings, but their power was destroyed by the Medes and Persians. The kingdom of the Persians was absorbed by the conquests of Alexander the Great, and Alexander the Great's territory fell into the hands of the Romans. When the kingdom of Christ was established the Romans tried to suppress it, but Constantine the Great made the Kingdom of Christ and the Roman Empire into one, which we might hope would endure for ever, but the constellation of the three principal Planets, Saturnus, Mars and Jupiter, forebodes a fatal conclusion in the year 1503. The seat of the empire was once transferred from Rome to Constantinople, but Charles the Great brought it back to the West, and the Roman Empire of the Teutonic nation was to stand for ever. But the Turks are now threatening it with disaster and ruin. We hope and pray that the diet of Worms may bring about the indispensable concord to repel the common danger and the threat of the Planets.

190.—None of the translators has attempted anything like a translation of this sweeping view of the history of the world. Riviere [1] and Barclay leave it out altogether. The Marnef-translator gives in one short column some musings of his own. Drouyn looked into the Latin, but instead of translating or imitating it, he found in it the inspiration for writing two original chapters, both translated by Watson. Just as Locher had done for his ' Concertatio ' (b), he takes much more space for these productions of his own than for any of his paraphrases of the Ship of Fools. And in this case they undoubtedly deserve it. For they are readable throughout, and that is more than we can say of the rest of his work. I cannot give proportionate extracts, however, for though a fifteenth-century schoolboy's compositions may be very interesting nowadays, especially when the schoolboy calls himself ' bachelier es droits,' they are too loosely connected with the subject of this study to occupy much of our space. Comparing it with Watson's translation I shall just indicate the principal contents.

191.—The first is supposed to deal with the CORRUPTION OF RIGHT. Right means Roman Law, which was ' kepte full derely by the Romayns ' and exposed by various classical authorities and by the later Italian school, from Accursius and Cino da Pistoia to Antonio de Butrio and Nicolaus Panormitanus (names which Watson did not understand).—After the introduction the author first addresses the Pope (Alexander VI), ' the general vycayre of God also well in the thynges temporalles as spyrytualles,' saying : ' thou lovest better to sustayne warre than to put pease where as thou sholde,' and ' thou gyvest so many dyspences,' which is ' the woundynge of ryght the whiche is odyous.'—Then various abuses are enumerated, as for ' a relygyous man or an hermite to leve his habyte of relygyon and take a secular

---

[1] Riviere must have worked from the *first* Basel-edition, as appears also from his more scanty marginal notes, and from his omitting altogether those accompanying the woodcuts.

habyte . . . and to have thre or four cures.' This is especially very
bad because 'the good studyentes have nothynge . . . but the asses
shal be honoured.'—Maximilian of Austria is said to be 'lorde and
mayster almost of all the worlde' but 'the empyre is at the moost lowest
that ever it was sene' for 'he sholde nourysshe peas in chrystendome,
and he kepeth warre.'—All kings 'pardon the ryche and punysshe the
poore' and they 'make bysshoppes, abotes and pryours within oure
realmes and yet certaynly you may not.' Worse is that they exact
very high taxes : ' In the tyme passed the vylagyens were wonte but
for to pay unto the emperoure XXVI. pens (deniers) for theyr heedes
(pour chief dostel !), but nowe they ar so sore pylled that it is pyte
for to here theyr clamoure.'—The greatest abuse of the nobility are theyr
'justes and torneymentes' for 'knowe you not well that he the whiche
is slayne there ought not for to be buryed in holy grounde ; and that
he the whiche gyveth the stroke ought for to do penaunce.' And then
their swearing ! They should be punished as 'the good kynge Henry'
did (Drouyn had said 'le bon roy de france saincte loys).—And you
'men of the chyrche,' you must not bear 'harneys, staffe or swerde,
save for daunger of theves . . . nor longe here nor berdes' ; you must
not run 'from one towne to another playnge the ryotours' nor 'kepe
hawkes and houndes and grete nombre of horses . . . nor a woman
in your houses where as suspecyon myght be. . . . You defyle and
hurte ryght by your symonyes wherwith you are replete.'

There is nothing like the Law ! Especially for thee O King ! 'Thou
ought for to knowe what ryght (droit) is, to the ende that whan they
demaunde the some countree londe or rente that thou mayst answere
them *after ryght and reason*.'—These last four words are Watson's own
idea, for the Frenchman had mentioned the Salic Law (que fille ne succede
point au royaulme de france), to be upheld against 'les anglois qui
disent avoir droit au noble et puissant royaulme de france' and in the
case of 'la noble duche de bourgoigne.' Instead of this Watson of
his own accord feebly protested that 'the poore people . . . can have
no ryght without gyvynge of large money ; thus avaryce hath banysshed
ryght out of this countree.' But immediately afterwards he joins
Drouyn again, when, turning one of Brant's ideas upside down,[1] he
addresses the men of his own profession : 'Advocates . . . you are
equipared to the knyghtes, for by you as knyghtes is the lyfe and the
patrymony defended. Your offyce is necessary and lovable.'

I think it is evident that the author has simply been writing together
some thoughts that had struck him from the different chapters of his
handbook on Roman and Canon Law, and from bits of conversation
which he had picked up here and there. He concludes his chapter with
some pious admonitions, and then begins again under a new heading,
professing to blame THOSE THAT DO ALL THINGS WRONG.

192.—It is the last chapter in Drouyn and Watson, just before the
final Prayer to the Virgin (i), and in French it consists largely of an
explanation of the woodcut prefixed to Brant's chapter f ; but by way

---

[1] Ch. 79, see § 199.

of introduction it is preceded by a general complaint containing some
reminiscences of Locher's chapter 108.—Watson begins with the introduction all right : ' We se dyvers traversynge this see without ores, or
sayle, they be without lawe and without ordre, the whiche in passynge
have recountred some of the perylles *of the mareswyne* [1] that is for to
knowe scyllam syrtes, and charybdin. . . . The lytel ought to observe
and obeye to the greter, but at this tyme the contrary is done.   Almoost
all thynge is done contrary ' !—After this the real chapter begins in
Drouyn.   But Watson had no more room for it, and so he breaks off
suddenly with the reflection : ' *Wherfore but yf that we kepe better ordre
we are lyke to be punysshed eternally.*'

[1] The romantic *mareswyne* owes its origin to the mistaking of an adjective for a
substantive, for Drouyn speaks only of *des perils marins.*

## IX

### CHAPTERS RELATING TO LAWYERS AND PHYSICIANS

193.—The last chapters of the preceding category have already brought us into contact with legal authorities and questions. Brant was a lawyer himself and knew the temptations and abuses of his own profession. Chapter 2 may perhaps be called a satire on LAWYERS, but mainly on account of the French and English translations. Brant speaks in general of those who want to ' kumen in den rot ' or as the Latin has it ' civilem intrare senatum.'

He says there are so many ignorant persons among them. A faithful Chusai (2 Kings xvii) must often give place to a false Achitophel. Justice and nothing but justice should govern one's vote and voice in the Council. For if we are not inspired by justice, we shall receive no justice from God. With what judgment we judge we shall be judged (Mt. vii 2), and if one cast a stone on high, it will fall upon his head (Eccli. xxvii 28). The unjust will meet with a harsh doom for there is no wisdom nor prudence nor counsel against the Lord (Prov. xxi 30).

In Locher's Latin very few of these ideas are to be traced. Perhaps, besides the motto, only the first four lines and line 15. All the rest is his own. He quotes Sallust to praise the Roman Senate. Wise men should have their own opinion, he says, and not merely repeat what others say. Therefore they must study, and this point is insisted upon at some length ; and those who do not are threatened by the sentence of Aeacus in the Styx (!) and by God's judgment at the day of doom.

No wonder that the translators did not quite know what to make of this. I am not now referring to the puzzling motto and the woodcut of which I shall speak later on.[1] The body of the chapter was no less bewildering. But as Locher spoke of a Praetor and of Aeacus and of judgment they naturally thought that judges and lawyers were the principal persons spoken of.

194.—There is no trace of any influence from Riviere on Barclay ; so we may take his English version first, as it brings out the new character of this chapter best by its many original additions. Even in the first stanza the new note is struck.

(49) Right many labours nowe with hygh diligence
For to be lawyers the comons to counsayle,
Therby to be in honour had and in reverence ;
But onely they labour for theyr pryvate avayle ;
The purs of the clyent shal fynde hym apparayle,
And yet knows he neyther law, good counsel nor justice,
But speketh at aventure, as men throwe the dyce.

---

[1] See § 361.

In ancient Rome all was beautiful :

> (51)　But nowe a dayes he shall have his intent,
> That hath most golde ; and so it is befall,
> That Aungels worke wonders at Westmynster Hall.
> (52)　None can the mater fele [1] nor understonde
> Without the Aungell be weyghty in his honde.
> (54)　There is one and other alleged at the barre,
> And namely suche as chrafty were in glose
> Upon the lawe ; the clyentis stande afarre,
> Full lytell knowynge howe the mater goose ;
> And many other the lawes clene transpose,
> Folowynge the example of lawyers dede and gone,
> Tyll the pore clyentis be etyn to the bone.

The rest is mostly as in Locher ; including even ' Eacus as poetis sayth.' But the Last Judgment is described in the last stanza with some good additional detail :

> (59)　There shall be no bayle nor treatynge of maynpryse [2]
> Ne worldly wysdome there shall no thynge prevayle ;
> There shall be no delayes untyll another syse !
> But outher : Quyt, or : to infernall gayle.

The Envoy addresses the ' yonge studentes of the Chauncery,' adding between brackets :

> (60)　I speke nat to the olde, the cure of them is past !

and admonishes them to deliver ' the lady Justyce ' from her long bondage :

> (61)　That pore men and monyles may hir onys se !
> But certaynly I fere lyst she hath lost hir name,
> Or by longe prysonment shall after ever be lame !

The early countryman of Dickens may be trusted to follow his own inspiration on such topics. But all passion dies away in this humorous irony.

195.—A juridical character is also given to Riviere's version of this chapter and in Drouyn's paraphrase it is enforced even more distinctly. Watson translates literally

> But at this present tyme *in many places* be some counsellers *and governours of courtes as well seculers as ecclesyastykes*, that can not eschewe some evyll passage.

The words that I have italicized here are in Drouyn but not in Riviere. The rest is in both. They do not forget Aeacus of course :

> Wherefore truste me, for yf thou wylte kepe the regle of egall jugement and shewe good counsayle, it is expedyent that whan thou hast ony grete processe, cyvyll, crymynall, ecclesyastyke, or of excesse, or touchynge herytages, ye must demande counsayle of the most dyscrete and wyse men, for semblably as thou jugeth another thou shalt be juged and tormented by Eacus juge of helle.

It is surprising that a ' bachelier es droits ' such as Drouyn should not have inserted more of his own. He has only added two little

---

[1] See note to § 197.

[2] The two words ' bail and mainprise ' usually go together. See NED. s.v. mainprise.

sentences at the end : ' For who that wolde gyve all the golde and chevaunce [1] of the worlde shall not escape.  For He is the grete juge eternall and imperyall above all juges.'

196.—The folly of continual LAWSUITS is the theme of chapter 71, and here (as in chapter 79, to be mentioned next) Brant writes one of his best satires.  Lawyers have always stood in bad repute among moralists and among the people at large.  But never more so than in the fifteenth and sixteenth centuries.  At that time the historians of Germany speak of a popular rage against the practitioners of the law. In France the people called them ' grippe-deniers, escumeurs des bourses, harpies.' [2]  At the root of this general hatred lay probably the supplanta- tion of the old Germanic customs by the new Roman law, by which the people felt themselves deprived of their long-cherished rights, but which the princes and lawyers introduced more or less forcibly towards the end of the fifteenth century.[3]

The protests of the people found one of their best expressions in Brant's chapters 71 and 96,[4] though Brant himself does not seem to have grasped the real cause at issue, for by a strange irony of fate he was one of the staunchest promoters of the Roman Decretals.[5]

Chapter 71 is too sententious or too proverbial to be summarized. It would have to be quoted in its entirety.  He speaks of those who will always go to law, in order to shirk the duties of justice.  But they forget that they are only enriching solicitors and lawyers, who like long lawsuits, and who can make a tremendous case out of nothing.  And people like to engage lawyers from distant countries, who can distort justice by their loquacity, and the clients lose a great deal more than they can ever dream of winning.  Such fools should be made to sit on a hackle !

197.—This general description is enough for our purpose, for Locher has adopted hardly any of Brant's metaphors and striking expressions, but the general ideas are the same—except the two last mentioned, for which there was no room left.

And Locher's ideas are in Barclay :

> (1061)   For small occasion, for lytell thynge or nought
> Unwyse men stryve, devysynge falshode and gyle . . .
> And onely the lawyers catchyth the avauntage.

He improves upon his Latin model with his idiomatic expressions :

> (1065)   But in the mean space the lawyers are [6] made ryche
> Levynge these folys and theyr mater in the dyche.

---

[1] Common in such combinations in Caxton and all through the sixteenth century. See NED.

[2] G. Steinhausen, Geschichte der deutschen Kultur (1904), 439 ; C. A. Schmidt, Die Reception des römischen Rechts in Deutschland (1868), 141.  Quotations in Janssen-Pastor i, 590 sq.

[3] This is the view of Janssen l.c.  Against this chiefly G. von Below, Die Ursachen der Rezeption des Römischen Rechts in Deutschland (Hist. Bibl. 19) (1905), 67 sqq.

[4] As such they are quoted in Janssen-Pastor i, 587.

[5] R. Stintzing, Geschichte der populären Literatur (1867), xxv.

[6] First ed. has a, corrected by Cawood into are.

Locher mentions the *calamus avarus* writing *in crasso codice*, and the English is not less picturesque :

> (1066)    Thou besy fole, intende unto this clause :
>           That every lawyer shall gyve more advertence
>           To money and gyftis than unto thy cause ;
>           For after he hath set thy wordes and sentence
>           In his *fat* boke, fyllyd with offence,
>           And there pryckyd with his *covetous* pen,
>           Thou never shalt thryve whyle thy name is therein.

*Juris custodes* is too vague a reference and Barclay therefore particularizes :

> (1067)    For howe be it that the lawes ought be fre,
>           Yet sergeaunt, at turney, promoter,[1] juge or scribe
>           Wyll nat fele thy mater [2] without a prevy brybe.

Locher's concluding remark about loquacious lawyers becomes much more forcible in the English popular expressions, where they are described :

> (1070)    And with theyr fayre and paynted eloquence
>           To glose our mater in wordes of no substaunce,
>           So that juge that by way of innocence
>           Gydeth the lawe in just and right balaunce,
>           Of suche pleders is led the blynde mannys daunce,
>           So that they playnly prove before his syght :
>           The right to be wronge and the wronge to be right.

198.—A contrast to this sinewy language is supplied by Watson's poetical motto :

>        Who hath aspecte to dame Justyce
>        Makynge complayntes dolorous
>        Askynge her ryght whiche is propyce
>        Of all men beynge vertuous
>        Pervers cursed or malycyous
>        But the fool blyndeth her vysage
>        By false sentence full of outrage.

It is useless trying to analyze this sentence, or even to understand it. Rhyme is a tyrant for poor Watson and very often succeeds in killing the sentence and even its sense. What he really meant to translate is Riviere's motto copied by Drouyn :

>        Qui au conspect de dame justyce
>        Fait plusieurs grans noises et crys
>        Demandant son droit tout propice
>        Celluy fol comme mal apris
>        Tend daveugler le hault pris
>        De dame iustice et ses drois
>        Contaminer en tous endrois.

---

[1] A *promoter* in its technical meaning was 'one whose business was to prosecute or denounce offenders against the law, a professional accuser, an informer' (NED.). Empson's and Dudley's principal agents, who were arrested at the same time, were known by the appellation of ' promoters.'

[2] *Fele the mater*, which occurs also in Stanza 52 (above § 194), seems to be a technical expression, but it is not mentioned in the NED.

This may be a clumsy and garrulous rendering of Locher's Latin, but the sentence is at least correct, and enough sense is left to understand the meaning.

Riviere has an interesting paraphrase of Locher's expression ' excludi ab ecclesia,' which was meant for Brant's ' verbannen ' (8) :

> Ou bien citer devant la pompe
> Dofficial ou de leglise
> Par sa meschante et vile guise
> Souferra parfournissement
> Des editz et banissement
> Pource que au iuge aller denye *etc.*

More need not be quoted, for Drouyn has prosified this out of all recognition, so that we find nothing of it in English. The parallel of our first quotation from Barclay runs as follows :

> They use fraudes, decepcyons, and dyssymulacyons, how well that the cause be but lytell, yet they wyll make a grete processe of it, thynkynge to have vengeaunce by theyr fyers courages. Ye wene to corrupte the fayre tytles of the lawes and the chapytres of dame Justice.

Let this suffice. The most voracious reader could not ask for more.

199.—Chapter 79 institutes a comparison between LAWYERS AND SOLDIERS, though by soldiers Brant means the vagrant robber hirelings of that time.

> They both live in the same way, he says. The one steals in secret, the other in public. The one exposes himself to all sorts of weather, but the other is more dangerous with his ink-pot ! The soldier sets fire to the farms, but the lawyer robs the farmer (1–10). Both *might* be useful, if they did not look after their own profit first, if the one kept to justice, and the other did not rob (11–17). But since they are what they are, Brant says, they must pardon him for placing them here among the fools. For have they not booked their seats ? (18–25). There are too many lawyers who live on violence like robbers (26–29). It is a shame that the public roads should still be so insecure and dangerous (30–32). But the reason is that safe-conducts and passports bring in a goodly sum of money ! (33–34).

Locher has faithfully rendered the greater part of this chapter, at least as far as line 17. But he expands his text so much that after this he has to skip all the rest, and has only space for the remark about the unsafeness of the roads : a remark which sounds rather incongruous without Brant's satirical observation about safe-conducts.

200.—The translators were evidently at a loss as to what Locher's pompous verbosity meant. The title did not tell them much. *De militibus et scribis*, or as the second marginal title runs : *De scribis et equitibus*.[1] Riviere meant to express the underlying idea somewhat more distinctly and he wrote : *Des chevaliers gensdarmes scribes ou practiciens*,[2] and it must have been this that Barclay had before him

---

[1] Locher must have felt the difficulty of translating Brant's *Rüter*. The Alemannian word is used by Brant ' ganz im sinne des nld. ruiter,' viz. as ' der berittene knecht in den Gegensatz zu Ritter, dem zu Ross kämpfenden Adlichen ' (Grimm-Heyne, *Deutsches Wörterbuch* viii (Leipzig 1893) s.v. *reiter*). To denote a vagrant soldier on horseback *miles* was not an adequate expression, and *eques* might suggest the idea of a knight, as it actually did to all translators.

[2] So also Drouyn and Watson : ' Of knyghtes, men of armes, scrybes, and practycyens.'

when he wrote at the head : *Of the extorcion of knyghtis, great offycers, men of war, scribes and practysers of the lawe.* In the chapter itself there is no trace of any influence of the French. No wonder. Already Riviere's motto is as tame as possible :

> Si les rusticz sont opprimez
> Des gensdarmes et practiciens
> Malingz sont aussi supprimez
> Silz ont avoirs qui soient siens
> Les despoueillen [1] de tous leurs biens
> Et cogent payer sans pitie
> Plus quil nest deu de la moytie.

This was nothing for Barclay. But poor Watson had to imitate it, and so he stammered out :

> If the rustykes be oppressed
> With men of armes and practycyence
> And be beten and dystressed
> In dyverse wyse by influence
> Without reason or sapyence
> In takynge more than theyr duyte
> Of the poore men without pyte.

Full stop !—But Drouyn never loses courage and he summons a large meeting to listen to his interpretation of the master poet. ' Advocats, procureurs, practiciens, chevaliers, scribes, notaires, et gensdarmes . . . vous orrez une belle satyre.' Watson leaves out the ' practiciens '; they might do for the rhyme in his motto, but as he probably did not know what they really were, he wisely does not extend his summons to them : ' Advocates procurours, knyghtes, scrybes, notaryes, and men of armes . . . ye shall here a fayre satyre.' [2]

The ' fayre satyre ' is unreadable. The first half is downright nonsense, the second half is at best a collection of platitudes. I can only quote one or two linguistic curiosities. Drouyn had prosified Riviere's ' a la grande nef follatique ' into ' en la nef stultifere.' But Watson summons all his audience ' in the shyppe of fragylyte.' ' Laultre pour escripre pille deca, dela ' *etc.* becomes ' The other for to wryte pylleth here and there in lesynge of theyr soules, and all for to wynne goodes.' This proves that *to pill* was really felt as an equivalent of the French *piller*, and that the two words were connected, at least by popular etymology.[3]

201.—No such pedantic questions need occupy us when reading Barclay. In this chapter he is surely in good form again. The first two stanzas keep fairly close to Locher. But he is always more concrete. Instead of ' equites scribaeque maligni ' he mentions

> (1155)   . . . knyghtes and scrybes, exchetours and constables
> And other offycers which have auctoryte
> Under the kynge as shryfs,

---

[1] Drouyn changes this into *despoilles*. I cannot say which is the better. There is not much to be spoiled.

[2] This is one of the very few times that Watson ventures to use the word ' satyre '; his French model uses it in nearly every chapter.

[3] The NED. admits the influence of the French, but supposes the OE. forms, pilian, peolian, to account for the doublet : *pill* and *peel*.

or, as the list runs in the following stanza :

> (1156)  Constables, scribes, lawyers and sowdyours,
>            Exchetours, sheryfs and knyghtes that have delyte
>            To abuse theyr offyces.

He then makes one whole stanza out of Locher's three words : ' mea navis abibit.' Riviere makes also seven or eight lines of it, but they are not half as good as the truly English :

> (1157)  Hast hyther I requyre, my navy is a flote ;
>            Longe tary hurtyth, for hawsyd is the sayle,
>            The anker wayed, within borde is the bote,
>            Our shyp decked after a homely aparayle !
>            By suche passyngers I loke for none avayle,
>            But fere displesour, bycause I shall be trewe.
>            Yet shall I so, ensue what may ensue !

202.—After this courageous resolve he leaves his model for a while, because, first of all, he would have his say about one particularly good knight, and one particularly bad scribe. The four stanzas must be quoted in full :

> (1158)  Good offycers ar good and commendable,
>            And manly knyghtes that lyve in rightwysenes ;
>            But they that do nat, ar worthy of a bable,
>            Syns by theyr pryde pore people they oppres.
>            My mayster Kyrkham for his perfyte mekenes
>            And supportacion of men in povertye
>            Out of my shyp shall worthely be fre.

> (1159)  I flater nat ; I am his true servytour,
>            His chaplayne and bede man, whyle my lyfe shall endure,
>            Requyrynge God to exalt hym to honour,
>            And of his Prynces favour to be sure,
>            For as I have sayd I knowe no creature
>            More manly rightwyse, wyse, discrete and sad [1]
>            But thoughe he be good, yet other ar als bad.

> (1160)  They shall unnamyd my shyppis have in cure ;
>            And other offycers, who so ever they be,
>            Whiche in extorcion and falshode them inure,
>            Hopynge by the same to come to dignyte
>            And by extorcion to augment theyr degre.
>            Mansell of Otery for powlynge [2] of the pore,
>            Were nat his great wombe, here sholde have an ore.

---

[1] The word *sad*, as is well known, has had an interesting development of meaning. It is the same word as Latin *sat(is)* and Dutch *zat*. In OE. and in Middle English until the middle of the fifteenth century the word was used in the meaning in which the Dutch word is still often used, viz. as *sated, weary of*. In the fourteenth century it developed the meaning of *steadfast, strong, serious*. It was still used by Shakespeare in this meaning, and occurs even now in the archaic expression *in sad earnest*. The modern meaning which arose out of the idea of *excessive seriousness* developed itself gradually since the time of Chaucer. See quotations in the NED.

[2] *To poll* in the sixteenth and even in the seventeenth century meant especially : to plunder by excessive taxation. A frequent combination was *to poll and shave* Like Barclay, Caxton spelled it *powl*. See NED.

(1161)    But for his body is so great and corporate
And so many burdens his brode back doth charge,
If his great burthen cause hym to come to late,
Yet shall the knave be captayne of a barge,
Where as ar bawdes, and so sayle out at large
About our shyp to spye about for prayes,
For therupon hath he lyved all his dayes.

203.—'My mayster Kyrkham,' of whose merits Barclay speaks
with such humble respect, is certainly an historical name and can with
some probability be identified with Sir John Kirkham who belonged
to the 'Worthies of Devon,' and whose arms were: 'Argent three
Lions rampant Gules, within a bordure ingrailed sable.' He is known
as a large and noble benefactor to the neighbouring town of Honiton,
where, when High-Sheriff of the County of Devon in 1523,[1] he very
generously endowed the chapel of All Hallows.

He must have been a great benefactor also of our poet. Of what
nature were the benefits he rendered, is less clear. It has been supposed [2] that Barclay had the honour of being appointed by the worthy
gentleman to the office of Sheriff's or private Chaplain or to some similar
position of confidence. This would explain the poet's respect and
gratitude. But although according to this supposition Barclay could
call himself 'his true servytour, his chaplayne and bedeman' he would
scarcely have added 'whyle my lyfe shall endure.' Nor does it seem
to agree with the fact that in the Dedication [3] he considers his main
position to have been 'Chaplen in the College of saynt Mary Otery'
and 'capellanus humillimus' of its Warden Bishop Cornish. Had
Sir John procured him this benefice? Had he defrayed the expense
of his education or of his study? We do not know.

204.—We know even less of Mansell of Ottery, who is gibbeted as
a terror to the people in a way which would form a sufficient ground
for an action for libel in these degenerate days.[4] What sort of position
did the man hold? Was he a tax-collector? A catspaw therefore of
Empson and Dudley? At any rate he was a knave, and he was laughed
at for his broad back and his stout body, and he was even twitted with
being fond of 'bawds.' We need not take the case too seriously. Tax-
collectors and such like people must often hear that they 'spye about
for prayes' and are often accused of 'powlynge the pore.' And under
Henry VII they would certainly have been dismissed at once if they
were not very severe.

I have not been able to ascertain whether the name Mansell occurred

---

[1] J. Prince, Damnonii Orientales Illustres or the Worthies of Devon (Exeter
1701), 434 sq.—The author mentions also another knightly family of this name
without adding any details. The John Kirkham, who was High-Sheriff in 1507,
may possibly have belonged to it. He can hardly have been identical with the
above-mentioned Sir John, as his arms were quite different, viz. 'Or on a bend gules
three Mullets argent.' See Rich. Izacke, Remarkable Antiquities of the City of
Exeter, ed. Sam. Izacke (3rd ed. London 1731), where at the end on unnumbered
pages there is 'A perfect catalogue of all the sheriffs of the County of Devon.'
Jamieson xxxvii, vaguely referring to Prince and Izacke, makes the two persons
into one.
[2] Jamieson xxxvii.          [3] See § 346 sqq.          [4] Jamieson l.c.

at that time at Ottery.  Jamieson (xxxviii) positively asserts that no such name appears in any of the Devonshire Histories, implying that he has instituted a methodical search.  Of course the culprit was not a nobleman, and therefore his name is not so easy to trace as that of Kyrkham.  In the best-known 'Histories'[1] I have not come across the name of Mansell; the *Episcopal Register of Edmund Lacy, Bishop of Exeter (1420-1455)*, published in 1909 by the Rev. F. C. Hingeston-Randolph, strangely enough, contains no alphabetical list of persons; and R. Granville and W. E. Mugford have not yet completed their *Abstracts of . . . Parish Registers of Devon.*[2]  But the name was certainly not unknown in the county, for during the reign of Henry VI one John Mansell was witness to a contract for the abbey of Buckland near Taunton,[3] and the name occurs twice in A. B. Prowse's *Index to Personal Names in Westcote's View of Devonshire in 1630, ed. 1845.*[4]

This is no proof that Mansell was the real name of the criminal. It may have been his nickname.  But the readers must have known who was meant.  These satirical stanzas, immediately preceded by the eulogy of Kyrkham, are undoubtedly aimed at an historical, real personage.  Otherwise the satire would be not only harmless but futile.

205.—After having thus set apart the good knight and the bad scribe, Barclay goes on paraphrasing Locher, following him step by step.  Both the knight and the scribe will oppress 'the pore chorle,' but if there is any difference, it is that the knight 'in warre' is said to be

> (1163)   Robbynge and spoylynge by feldes prevely,
> But the scribe oppressyth the pore men openly.[5]

It is not certain what 'scribe' can have meant then.  The word was used for various public functionaries performing secretarial duties. Palsgrave vaguely translates it by *greffier*[6] and so Barclay's definition is not without interest:

> (1169)   The scribe is ordeyned hymself to exercyse
> To wryte with his pen iust lawes and verytable
> And shewe by his craft the rule of right iustyce.

---

[1] The reference is to J. Prince and R. Izacke, just quoted; R. Polwhele, The History of Devonshire (Exeter 1793-97); G. Oliver, Historic Collections relating to the Monasteries in Devon (Exeter 1820); G. Oliver, Ecclesiastical Antiquities in Devon (Exeter 1840); G. Oliver, History of the City of Exeter (Exeter 1861); G. Oliver, Lives of the Bishops of Exeter (Exeter 1861); Thom. Wainwright, An index to the names of persons in the Monumental Inscriptions found in . . . Devonshire Churches (Reports and Transactions of the Devonshire Association vol. 36, Plymouth 1904).

[2] The first volume appeared at Exeter 1908, containing the parishes whose names begin with *A* to *Br*.  Nothing further seems to have appeared yet; and this first volume has no list of persons.

[3] Tristram Risdon, The Chorographical Description . . of Devon (London 1811), 229.

[4] Reports and Transactions of the Devonshire Association, vol. 27 (1895), 443.

[5] The contemporary writer of the 'Italian Relation' also noticed 'there is no injury that can be committed against the lower orders of the English, that may not be atoned for by money.'—Quotation in A. F. Pollard ii, 222.

[6] See quotations in NED.

The following stanza adds something original about knights :

(1170)   By suche oppresion they increase theyr estate,
And by successyon of all theyr hole lynage.
Alas, the childe oft forgoys his heritage
Without right, longe or he be of discression,
And all by fals knyghtis spoylynge and oppression.

The idea of injustice being committed in relation to inheritances, and the infidelity of executors recurs so regularly under Barclay's pen (see §§ 92 and 121), that I cannot help thinking that he must be speaking of his own sad experience.[1]

Other men of the law are, by way of summing up, mentioned at the end :

(1172)   What shall I wryte of powlynge customers,
And spoylynge serchers, baylyfs and constables,
Sergeauntis and catchpollis, and other offycers,[2]
Whiche with others plate garnysshe gay theyr tables,
Theyr howsys stuffed with brybes abhomynables !
Suche by oppression become thus excellent,
Continuynge in falshode, for lacke of punysshement.

Barclay had mentioned these same personages with almost the same adjectives in an earlier chapter (9) Stanza 173.[3] And we can very well imagine that during the reign of Henry VII the people must have suffered much from them. But surely the eulogist of Henry VIII did not mean to say that after the accession of the new king those ' catchpollis ' could be long

Continuynge in falshode for lacke of punysshement.

And so it sounds more natural when in the Envoy he addresses the ' unjust offycers ' in a softer moralizing tone :

(1173)   Avoyde your extorcion done by cruelte,
Avoyde this desyre mad and myschevous lust,
Whiche ye have in spoylynge of the comonte.
Better is for you to lyve in povertye,
So plesynge God, with undefyled name,
Than by oppression to come to hye degre,
And than after deth be damnyd for the same.

206.—The PHYSICIANS get their turn as well as the lawyers. Chapter 55 compares the two professions, and it is difficult to say which of the two appears in the more unfavourable light. Especially in Barclay's version, as we shall see. Here is Brant's lecture :

A Doctor who diagnoses a serious case and then has to consult his books first, is a fool, because the patient may die before his return (1–6). Many call themselves

---

[1] One of the principal charges first brought against Empson and Dudley referred to extortions from heirs. See e.g. J. Lingard, The Hist. of England iv⁶ (1855),169.

[2] A *searcher* was an officer of the custom-house, a *customer*. The two words are used as synonyms in an Act of Henry VII. *Bailiff* is used by Langland in the same meaning as *catchpoll*, viz. a sheriff's officer, who arrests for debt, or also as tax-gatherer. A *sergeant* must have held a similar position. For the Promptuarium Parvulorum of the middle of the fifteenth century explains the word ' seriawnt, under a domys mann, for to arest menn, or a catche-pol.'—See NED.

[3] See § 279 ; cf. also Stanza 1152, § 121.

physicians without knowing more than what they have learned from a ' kruter büchlin ' [1] or from some old woman (7–10). They then have the pretension of curing everything, without making any difference between ages, sexes and characters (11–15). One herb is applied to all diseases, as the barber heals all wounds with one plaster (16–20). ' Her Cucule ' is their assistant. Whoever knows only one salve for all diseases of the eye, whoever

(24)  Purgyeren will on wasserglasz,

he is a fool like Zuohsta,[2] he is like an ignorant lawyer or like a confessor who knows nothing of the means for avoiding sin (22–32). Many are deceived by such fools and brought to ruin before they are aware (33–34).

Locher has paraphrased most of these ideas, expanding the first six lines into ten, and the next four also. In this second part he brings in the names of Podalirius (the son of Aesculapius), of Mesve,[3] of Avicenna and Galenus. After Brant's line 15 his page is nearly full, and so he begins to summarize. Instead of the barber he mentions a ' Thessalian witch,' [4] addresses the foolish doctor as *Cucule*, compares him to an *indoctus patronus consultus*, and concludes with a clinching distich :

> Aut te non medicum dicas : aut disce mederi :
> Aut si vis medicus : sis fatuusque simul.

207.—Barclay follows this Latin version at a considerable distance. For he brings in a new element at once, saying :

(776)  But nought they relefe of those paynes harde
       But gape alway after some great rewarde.[5]

The doctor tells the most serious patients that their disease ' is no thynge incurable ' but he does so only to get a good fee, and when he has got it he lets the patient die. Such doctors know nothing :

(779)  A herbe or wede that groweth upon a wall
       Beryth in it these folys medycyne !
       None other bokes have they nor doctryne.

Then appear Podalirius, Mesve, Avycen, ' Ypocras [6] and parfyte Galyen ' (780), and the ' bokes that speke of herbes only,' [7] and the

---

[1] Fischart mentions ' Die Bockischen, Mathiolischen, Reifischen, Fuchsischen Kreuterbücher ' ; Zarncke 390.

[2] This name has not yet been explained.

[3] The name occurs also in Brant, cp. 21, l. 21.   There are two Arabian physicians of this name.   The elder died *c.* 857 ; the younger, also called Mesua of Damascus, was an obscure personality of the eleventh century.   The latter seems to be meant here, as he was for centuries a standard authority on the composition of drugs, and his works were printed in twenty-six editions in the fifteenth century and later. See the article on the *History of Medicine* by J. F. Payne in The Encycl. Brit., and Sir William Osler, Incunabula medica (Bibliogr. Soc. Monogr. 19, 1923), 17 sq., with the bibliographical descriptions by V. Scholderer, ib. p. 44 sqq. (nn. 9, 10, 36, 90, 93, 153, 160, 162, 172, 176).

[4] *Thessala saga* ; possibly Brant's *Zuohsta*.

[5] Chaucer's ' Doctour of Physik ' shared a little of this habit,
       For gold in phisik is a cordial
       Therefore he lovde gold in special (C.T., A. 443 sq.).

[6] The name was so common (see e.g. *Canterbury Tales* A. 431) that its insertion as a stopgap has nothing striking.   I certainly cannot agree with Fraustadt 9, who attributes it to the influence of Riviere, who omits *Mesve* and corrupts *Podalyrius* into *Pollidarus*.

[7] I wonder if Barclay knew the real character of what Locher calls ' herbarum libri.'   Still they must have been as common in England as in Germany.   Out of the library of Peterhouse, Cambridge, Macer's *De virtutibus herbarum* was in daily

'old wives.' *Thessala saga* is rendered by ' faythles wytche ' (784) and the *Cuculus* as ' folysshe Surgyan.' Before he comes to Locher's final distich—which he elaborates in Stanza 790, the last one—he feels himself inspired by the comparison between a lawyer and physician [1] to write four original stanzas, distinctly marked as *Addicio Alexandri Barklay*. They elaborate at the same time the idea inserted in the beginning, and their virile expressions, sometimes clenched together by alliterations, are better than anything else in this chapter.

> (786)   A lawer and phesician ar both lyke
> Of theyr condicion, and both ensue one trayne ;
> The one begyleth the pacyent and seke,[2]
> Takynge his good for to encreas his payne ;
> The other labours and cauteles oft doth fayne,
> To clawe the coyne by craft from his clyent,
> Castynge hym of, whan all his good is spent.

> (787)   If he have money than hath he his intent,
> And if the seke have store ynough to pay,
> Than shall the cure be dryven from day to day.

> (788)   So if the lawer may any avauntage wyn,
> He shall the cause from terme to terme defarre ;
> The playntyf for a player is holde in,
> With the defendaunt kepynge open warre.
> So laweyers and phesicians thousandes do marre,
> And whan they no more can of theyr suers have,
> The playntyf beggyth, the seke is borne to grave.

Is not the last line, in its cutting conciseness, one of admirable satirical force ?

208.—No such original contributions appear in Drouyn-Watson. Riviere had little to inspire them. In this chapter he is even particularly weak. In Locher's very first line he mistakes *aegris* as *agris*, ' the sick ' as ' the fields,' and still makes bold to translate the sentence :

> Qui use dart de medicine
> Et es champs prent la congnoissance *etc.*

And Watson meekly follows him :

> Who that useth the arte of medycyne
> Takynge his knowlege in the felde
> He is a foole full of ruyne
> So to take herbes for his shelde
> Wenynge theyr vertue for to welde
> Whiche is not possyble for to knowe
> All theyr vertues bothe hye and lowe.

---

use, while the thirteen other volumes on medicine were kept in chains for reference only, according to the still preserved catalogue of 1418 (Cambr. Hist. ii, 364). In English the first *Grete Herbal* seems to have been printed only in 1516—see Rob. Watt, Bibliotheca Britannica iii (Edinburgh 1824). The oldest Herbals in the British Museum date from 1525 and 1526. These medical *Herbals* were quite different from the later botanical *Herbals*, such as John Gerarde first compiled (see Jusserand, Lit. Hist. ii, 310).

[1] The bracketing together of the legal and medical professions occurs also in Stanza 1152.

[2] The rhyme *lyke* : *seke* may illustrate the development of ME. ī and ē.

This is nearly the opposite of what Locher meant !—The death of the patient before the doctor comes back is long drawn out by the French rhymer, and this is reflected in the curious sentence :

> And then he cometh to the seke man more quycker than an urchyn [Riv. plus esveille qung erisson ; Dr. herisson], and the meane whyle the pacyent is almost deed, for or he be in the house the seke man is deed.

The one original idea in Riviere is that the Herbals were written in the mother tongue : ' Ou il ne gist point de latin.' Drouyn says more distinctly ' en francoys.' And therefore Watson felt obliged to write the following sentence :

> The artes of Pollydare, of Galyen, and of Ypocras suche folkes seketh not, but a grete sorte of bookes arborystes [1] that be *in englysshe* or in frensshe for to understand them the better, and in lyke wyse they folowe the medicynes of the same, wherby they slee and murdre many one.

It may be doubted whether the addition of *in englysshe* had any other origin than a patriotic determination not to be outdone by any Frenchman. One ' Arbolayre ' and one ' Grand Herbier ' at least had already been printed in French (Pellechet 1101, 1102), but I do not know if anything like it had appeared in English before 1516.[2]

With the *Thessala saga* and the *Cucullus* some confusion was inevitable. Riviere was wisely wary and left the dangerous words unchanged :

> Ainsi ces foles estourdies
> Guerissent de ces maladies
> Comme tessala saga faisoit
> Qui mesme se contrefaisoit.
> Cuculle dy moy cirurgien
> Qui ta apris faire ce bien, *etc.*

Drouyn thought it more prosaic and natural to speak of *tessala le saige*, and as he put no stop in the phrase *qui se contrefasoit Cuculus*, Watson translated literally : ' They hele and quarysshe al maladyes and sekenesse as tessala the wyse that counterfetteth Cuculus. Tell me surgyen ' *etc.*

One really original contribution there is in Drouyn, viz. at the very end of the chapter, and as Watson's page was not yet quite full the Englishman added to that one little phrase of his own :

> There be some physycyens that knoweth also well the water of a seke man [une urine] in the bottom of a morter [au cul dung mortier] as in an urynall. The other sayth in lykewyse that they shall knowe it in the uryne of a henne, or of a sowe '— no wonder that after this Watson exclaimed : ' *and yet they have as moche scyence as a calfe !* '

209.—Not only the Doctors but also the PATIENTS get their whipping. Chapter 38 is devoted to them.

---

[1] Riviere has ' ung livre arboliste ' ; Drouyn ' livres darboliste.' In English as well as in Old French there were two forms *arborist(e)* and *arbolist(e)*, now refashioned as *herborist(e)*. One form stood probably under the influence of *arbor*, the other of Spanish *arbol*. See NED.

[2] See note 7, p. 172.

He is a fool, Brant says, who will not follow his Doctor's advice, who will not keep to his diet, who instead of the wine prescribed insists on taking water or other things that are bad for him but happen to please him. The end will be that he dies (1–8). He who wants to recover soon must withstand in the beginning, for later on the cure will take him long (9–12). The patient desiring to get well again ought to show his wound to the doctor and to suffer it to be sounded and washed and dressed (13–17), even though the skin be scraped by it, if only his life can be saved (18–20). A good doctor does not abandon even a dying patient, but a patient must always submit to his treatment in the hope of recovery (21–24). He who tells lies to his doctor or to his confessor or to his lawyer, deceives himself alone and will bear the consequences (25–30). A fool is he who will not take his doctor's advice, but rather listens to an old wife's tale (31–33) and accepts the blessing of an amulet or some charmed herb that will bring him hell instead of health (34–36). I cannot mention all the superstitions that are being practised. People do not hesitate to invoke the devil, but it is the greatest folly to seek health against God's will (37–54). Many diseases are brought about by sin. So confess your sins first and seek the health of your soul before the health of your body (55–62). But many a fool says : First the body and then the soul, with the result that he loses both (63–68). Many have died in body and soul, who if they had turned to God and His grace first of all, would have been saved (69–74). Thus Judas Machabeus.[1] But quite otherwise Ezechias and Manasses (75–84). Jesus said to the infirm man who had been made whole : ' Sin no more, lest some worse thing happen to thee ' (85–88). Many make good resolutions in their illness, but when they have recovered it may be said of them, that they have grown worse instead of better (89–92). But God cannot be deceived, and they will not escape due punishment (93–94).

It is a great pity that the second part of this chapter, which would have appealed very strongly to some of our translators, has been entirely omitted by Locher. What he really translates and fills out with fine classical expressions, is only the first thirty-three lines (omitting, however, lines 11–12 and the reference to the lawyer in line 27). The space of a short chapter is then nearly full, and he summarizes all the rest in two lines :

> Moralem sensum nostro si carmine sumes :
> In vitiis aegrum te mora nulla premet.

An interesting expression, which may explain his *Thessala saga* in chapter 79, occurs in his explanation of the old wife's tale (*consilium vetulae*) :

> et herbas
> Quas in thessalico littore saga coquit.

210.—Barclay's paraphrase follows the Latin version throughout. The deviations are mostly called for only by the requirements of the rhyme.—One thing which he never misses and which shows that the Englishman always remains alive is that he never forgets to mention *ale* together with Locher's *wine*.[2] Here he says of the disobedient patient that he is

> (569)    Receyvynge colde water in stede of ale or wyne,
>          Agaynst read and counsell of crafty medycyne.

---

[1] Why ?

[2] Similar cases occur e.g. in Stanzas 267, 275, 290 etc. etc. The ' Italian Relation ' under Henry VII also observed the English preference for ale and beer, even by ladies of distinction.—Quotation in A. F. Pollard ii, 225.

The *Thessalico littore* [1] is left out, but Locher's last two lines receive the following rendering :

> (580)   But if thou to thy mynde and reason call,
> And of this wrytynge perceyve the sence morall :
> Whan thou art fallen seke and in dedely syn,
> Seke helpe betyme and byde nat longe therein.

It is perhaps these last words, it is no doubt also Locher's (and Brant's) comparison between a doctor and a confessor worked out in Stanza 576, that made Barclay think of attaching to this chapter by way of Envoy a little sermon on Confession in the true metaphorical vein of fifteenth-century Scholasticism :

> (581)   Thou man or woman, that lyest seke in vyce,
> To Goddes vycayrs confesse thy syn holly ;
> So shalt thou from thy goostly yll aryse,
> For thy soule fyndynge helpe and remedy ;
> Without leasynge shew hym thy synne playnly ;
> Let nat for shame, nor fall nat thereto agayne ;
> Better shewe thy  ore there to one secretly
> Than after openly and byde eternall payne.

> (582)   Ensewe the counsyll of a wyse confessour ;
> Take nat colde water in stede of vermayl wyne :
> For moche swetnes endure thou a lytell soure.
> Kepe well the dyet and threfolde medicyne,
> Ordayned for synne by spirituall doctryne,
> That is : confessyon, the next contrycyon
> With satisfaccion ; these thre with grace devyne
> Ar salves parfyte for all transgressyon.

Barclay is no doubt well grounded in moral theology.  But we do not often meet with moral theology in rhyme, fortunately !  Barclay will rhyme you anything.  If he had been among the Canterbury pilgrims, we should have had the Parson's ' merry tale ' in rhyme !

211.—In Watson's translation there is one exceptionally good improvement upon his French model.  When the patient is dead, says Drouyn, ' ne feront plus de molestations pour eulx mediciner,' and Watson changes this into ' and shall not nede no more playsters nor medycynes.'  This is almost Barclay's concrete style.  But one has to read many pages in Watson before meeting with anything like it.— There are several original *words* in his version, as he has plenty of room. He expands especially the passage about confession.  The French insists upon the necessity of confessing ' maints grand pechez lesquelz tu as faits ' ;  this is not long enough for Watson, and so he speaks of ' many grete and abhomynable synnes that thou hast commytted here in this world.'  And instead of ' car tu mettroyes ton ame en dangier ' he puts ' elles thyne absolucyon is of none effecte, and yet thou puttest thy soule in grete ieopardy and daunger.'

Like Barclay, Riviere has fought shy of the ' thessalico litore ' :

---

[1] The stanza (579) in which it should occur is quoted in § 166.

> Tu crois plus tost a une vielle
> Que lui et a ses raisons veille
> Quest une grande enchanteresse
> Une sorciere ou sinderesse
> Qui donne ung brevet ou proverbe
> Ou son fait gist tout en une herbe.

It is doubtful whether Drouyn understood the last two lines, when he prosified them into 'ung brevet ou tout son fait en herbe vive.' But this phrase must have given great difficulty to the Englishman, as appears from his brave effort : ' Thou wylte byleve soner an olde enchaunteres, or whiche the whiche gyveth a lytel brevet or a quycke herbe, wherin lyeth all her dede or fayte.'

In Early Modern French the word *brevet* was commonly used to denote an amulet or talisman, and in this meaning it is still found in Corneille :

> Et pour gagner Paris, il vendit par la plaine
> Des brevets à chasser la fièvre et la migraine.[1]

But in English the word has never been used in this sense. That is why Watson added by way of explanation ' or quycke herbe ' !

---

[1] See Dict. Larousse s.v.

# X

## CHAPTERS RELATING TO WOMEN AND MARRIAGE

212.—Ever since Juvenal's famous sixth satire the vices of women have been a favourite subject for (male) satirists.—Brant, who shortly before his marriage in 1485 wrote a poem on the perfidy of women,[1] was not likely to forget them in his Narrenschiff. They get their full due in chapter 64 on BAD WOMEN.

He begins by declaring that he does not want to say anything against good women. A good woman may bring her husband to reason as Esther and Abigail did (1–12). But a bad one gives bad advice, as Ochozias' mother and Herodias and Solomon's wives (13–17). A woman often becomes as loquacious as a magpie, like the Pierides (18–24). She then complains and talks and lies and slanders and allows her husband no peace even when 'barefooted friars are asleep' (25–30). Many a husband is married to strife, because his wife knows everything better than he (31–36). Such women bring ruin upon men, as Amphion experienced, as Calpurnia did and Joseph's mistress (37–44). No anger is like a woman's anger, she is like a lioness, or a she-bear, as Medea and Progne (45–50). No herb can be bitterer than a woman, and a woman's heart is like a trap to catch fools (51–54). There are four things the earth can hardly bear : a servant become a master, a drunken fool, a vixen of a woman, and a maid who inherits the goods of her mistress (55–62). Four things can never be satiated : a woman, hell, the earth, and fire (63–68). There are four things I cannot trace : the way of an eagle through the air, of a serpent over a rock, of a ship over the ocean, and of a grown-up man behaving like a child (69–74). Equally incomprehensible is the way of a woman, who on the point of committing adultery can ingenuously declare ' I have done no harm ' (75–78). A quarrelsome woman is like a roof dropping through (Prov. xix, 13). He who is yoked together with such a one, has a hell on earth (79–82). Vasthi has been imitated by many (83–84). Not to speak of murders like those committed by Poncia and Agrippina, the Belides and Clytemnestra, and the wife (Thebe) of (Alexander) Phaereus (85–90). Rare are wives like Lucrecia and Cato's Portia (91–92), but many are the lascivious like Thais (93–94).

Here the chapter breaks suddenly off as the page was full. As this is one of the three longer chapters in which Locher has an equal number of lines with the original[2] we may expect to find most of the above ideas back in his translation. And we do find them indeed. In the first sixty lines he omits only a few details, viz. the reference to the Prologue in 1 and 2 ; Ochozias and Herodias (14–16), the *Barfuszer* in line 30 ; and the strife in the next line ; Joseph's mistress (43–44) and the heart of a woman as a trap (58–59). After line 62 he omits

---

[1] C. Schmidt i, 209 sq.
[2] The others are ch. 6 (on the duties of parents) and ch. 99 (on the Turkish Danger).

a great deal more.　In fact he omits everything from line 63 as far as
line 84 (including the last two ' Priamels ' and the picturesque expressions
of 75–78).　So he jumps at once to line 85 and then follows Brant to
the end.　As a substitute for what was lost he presents us with several
original contributions.　The most remarkable among them are : (1) No
good woman, no ' Gracchorum mater ' should read this satire ; (2)
a prayer to deliver us from bad women ; (3) a reference to Juvenal's
satire ; (4) eight lines about the utter corruption of a bad woman ; and
at the end (5) a reference to a ' casta Sabina ' and the good fortune of
having a faithful wife.

213.—This rather elaborate textual comparison was necessary on
account of the literary interest of the chapter.

The interest is not exactly in the French versions or in Watson,
although some passages are worth quoting.　Best of all is Watson's
motto, which in this case is quite original :

> Who that in his mynde doth compasse
> To rule his wyfe after his wyll
> He maye also soone make an asse
> Renne a wallap [1] over a hyll
> For she always wyll have good skyll
> And also soone do after them
> As dryve a snayle to Jherusalem.

And then to think that of this he found nothing in Drouyn !—Our
moralists felt at home here.　No wonder !　' I must wryte a chapytre
(Fr. une satyre) of the women, for of theyr cursednes I can not hold
my peas.'　Riviere provided them with abundant material, for he draws
out Locher's stories as far as he can, so that he uses 421 lines for Locher's
(and Brant's) 94.　Instead of ' always ' he says ' en la vive et morte
saison ' with the result that the prose text became ' en morte saison elle
replendist en la maison,' and the English : ' In dethe tyme she
replendysshed in her house.'　Poor Watson was not so much to blame
for this as Drouyn.　If the latter had not skipped the most essential
lines in Riviere, Watson would never have written : ' Salomon the
whiche was condysyoned better than ony wyse man that ever was, for
his renowne is sprede over all the unyversall worlde.　And al for gyvynge
counsayll unto a woman vyle and dyshonest.'　As an alleviating circumstance for these absurdities we must take into consideration that
Drouyn *had* to omit much from Riviere's long drawn out lines.　But
then why did he turn Riviere's allusions to historical facts into general
truths ?

> She wyll brewe a daungerous drynke for to make hym be put in a darke pryson,
> saynge that he hath iniuryed the kynges persone by evyll reporte [Fr. quil a dit mal
> du roy], or that he hath stolen some thynge, or murdred and wyll pretende to make
> hym be slayne—brevely there is nothynge so daungerous unto a man as to have
> a cursed wyfe!

---

[1] This is the ME. form of *gallop*, derived from an ONF. form *walop*, whose
existence is proved by its adoption in old Flemish and MHG.　In the sixteenth
century it was superseded by a new loan from F. *galoper*.　See NED.

One more passage may be quoted, viz. the prose-version of the one
' Priamel ' preserved in Locher.

Ther is thre thynges that excedeth all other, and the erthe susteyneth them all
thre, but it apperteyneth not that the fourthe be susteyned.  The fyrst is the
servaunt that becometh mayster.  The seconde is the servaunt that is always dronke.
The thyrde is a wyfe that is furyous and full of debates.  And the fourth is the mayden
full of pryde, that is herytour of her lady or maystresse.  Suche a mayden thou
ought to eschewe and flee, for she gyveth often tymes drynke for to drynke wherin
reposeth venym (!!), and in conclusyon ever beware of the femynyne gendre !

214.—Passing on to Barclay's more important version, it should be
noted that Riviere changes the name of the *Belides* into *Danaides*,
taking his cue from Locher's marginal note, to which, however, he adds
a quite correct reference to Boccaccio : *Danaides de quo ponitur per
bocacium .i. de genealo. l. ii c. xxii.*  Of course Barclay has seen this
tempting note, and the text proves it.  Instead of Locher's single line :

> Belides occursu terrent modo corda virorum,

the Frenchman tells the whole story ; correctly, as far as I understand
it.  This must have been the inspiration of Barclay's four lines :

> (947)    What shall I wryte the cursyd cruelte
> Of the susters of Danaides echone,
> Fyfty in nomber, whiche by iniquyte
> Slewe all their husbondes, reservyd one alone.

Though Barclay has not copied Riviere's note, this passage is an
undoubted loan from the French, though the only one.  In all the rest
of the chapter Riviere's many fully-told stories have not left the slightest
trace upon the English version.  Locher continues to be followed, and
Locher exclusively.  Yet it strikes us from the very beginning that this
chapter is the only one in the whole work which is entirely written
in the Monk's Tale stanza.  Elsewhere this stanza is reserved for the
Envoy only and for some personal effusions.  The octave everywhere
marks an avowed contribution to the original.  Everywhere, except here.
It looks as if Barclay here wants to emphasize his personal interest and
prepossession for the subject.  And certainly he shows great freedom
of movement.  In many places the choice of expression is so good that
several stanzas deserve to be quoted in full.  But I can pick only a few
flowers from this prickly hawthorn.  The best of all is this lively
description of a curtain lecture, the details of which are all his own
invention :

> (931)    The pore husbonde with some is so bested,
> That he no rest hath one hour of the day,
> Nor in the night whan he is in his bed ;
> There she hym techyth a brawlynge Crede to say (!).
> And if he there ought unto hir denay,
> She gronyth grutchynge with hir complayntis styll ;
> Ye, foure dayes after, let hym do what he may,
> He shall hir nat asswage, tyll she hath chid hir fyll.

When Locher compares an angry woman to a tiger ' raptos dum catulos
sequitur ' Barclay makes a detailed picture of it :

> (936)   The cruell tyger to woman is nat lyke
>         Whiche whan hir whelpis from hir den taken be,
>         Rangyth about in furour them to seke,
>         For madnes gnawynge and terynge stocke and tre ;
>         A wrathfull woman is yet more mad than she.

After this there is Locher's reference to Juvenal (937), and his drastic
expressions about the corruption of women (938–941), in which the
' grande supercilium ' is elaborated to :

> (940)   Yet kepeth she a solem countenaunce,
>         As none were lyke hir in Englonde nor in Fraunce
>         In all vertues and knowynge nought of syn.

215.—After this there occur stanzas which at first sight seemed
extremely puzzling.

> (942)   I fynde in the worlde that there be thynges thre
>         Right harde to knowe, the fourth that no man may
>         Knowe nor perceyve ; first whan a byrde doth fle
>         Alonge in the ayre, no man can spye hir way ;
>         The way of a ship in the se, thoughe it be day,
>         Harde is to se whiche way the shyp hath gone ;
>         The thirde harde thynge, as I have oft heard say,
>         Is the way of a serpent over a stone ;
> (943)   But the fourth way that of all hardest is,
>         Of yonge man is in youthes lustynes.
>         A vycyous womans way is lyke to this,
>         Whiche after hir synne and great unhappynes
>         Fedyth hir with mete of blynde delyciousnes,
>         Than wypyth hir mouth and sayth in audyence,
>         With mynde assured and past all shamefastnes :
>         ' I have nat commyttyd yll, synne nor any offence.'

These ideas are not in Locher, Riviere, Marnef, Drouyn-Watson ;
they are only in Brant himself (69–78) :

> Dry ding ich nit erkennen kan
> Des vierden weisz ich gantz nütz von,
> Wann in dem lufft eyn Adler flüht
> Eyn schlang die uff eyn velsen krücht
> Eyn schiff das mitten gat im mer,
> Eyn man der noch hat kyndesch ler,
> Des glych der weg eynr frowen ist
> Die sich zum eebruch hat gerüst
> Die schlekt, und wüscht den munt gar schon
> Und spricht, ich hab nüt böss geton.

Is it possible, is it in accordance with the first principles of psychology
that Barclay should here suddenly have turned to the German, to translate these few lines, and then unconcernedly have gone back to the so
much weaker Latin version ?  For the following stanzas, of which the

helpless parallel in Watson has already been quoted, and which in Brant *precede* the passage just quoted, are undoubtedly from the Latin:

> (944)  Thre other thynges on erth I fynde certayne,
> Whiche troubleth the grounde and also the see,
> The fourth nouther see nor londe may well sustayne ;
> The firste is a churle that hath a bonde man be
> And so by fortune come unto hye degre ;
> The seconde is a fole whan he is dronke and full ;
> The thirde a wrathfull woman, full of cruelte ;
> He that hir weddyth hath a crowe to pull !

> (945)  Yet is the fourthe wors and more elevate :
> That is a hande mayde lowe of hir lynage,
> Promotyd from a beggar and so come to estate,
> Succedynge hir lady as heyr in herytage.
> Of such——

the rest is original, like the last line of the preceding stanza :

> Of such procedeth moche malyce and outrage,
> Disdayne, great scorne, vilany and debate ;
> For the Frenche man sayth in his langage :
> No thynge is wors than a churle made a state.

And then he goes on with Agrippina and Poncia, the Danaides, Lucrece, Clytemnestra, Cato's Portia and the 'chast Sabyn' (946–949), all as in Locher (and Riviere, see above).

The application to Brant seems incredible—and is not true.  Locher's one 'Priamel' is taken from the Bible, and the margin gives the exact reference: *Proverb.* xxx.  And there Barclay found everything.  The English translation of the Vulgate, used by Barclay as by his contemporaries, runs as follows :

18. Three things are hard to me, and the fourth I am utterly ignorant of. 19. The way of an eagle in the air, the way of a serpent upon a rock, the way of a ship in the midst of the sea, and the way of a man in youth.  20. Such is also the way of an adulterous woman, who eateth, and wipeth her mouth, and saith : I have done no evil.  21. By three things the earth is disturbed *etc.*

And here follows the 'Priamel' of Stanzas 944 and 945.  On comparing the Stanzas 942 and 943 both with Brant's German and with these Biblical texts, there can be no manner of doubt, that Locher's marginal note and nothing else has been the source.

216.—In the rest of this chapter there are not many remarkable passages.  After having exhausted Locher's chapter he adds two stanzas of his own invention.  They begin like an apology, but the first is more rhetorical than any :

> (950)  Ye gentyll wymen and other, great and small,
> Be nat displeasyd with these true, cours sentences,
> For certaynly I have nat wryten all
> The vyce of wymen, theyr synnes nor offences ;
> If I had red all the lyberall sciences,
> And all my lyfe shulde there about intende,
> Yet coude I never wryte all inconvenyences
> By wymen done nor theyr malyce comprehende.

The last stanza is somewhat more conciliatory, though there is some humorous sarcasm in the remark that he will ever praise the good :

> (951)    I may have leyser ynoughe therto tyntende
> Syns of them is no plenty but great geason.[1]

In the two stanzas of the Envoy all satire dies away, however, in a well-meaning exhortation to all ' wrathfull wymen ' and others.

217.—More scathing but less interesting is chapter 32 on HUSBAND AND WIFE, in which Brant sets out to prove that it is no use keeping wives under strict observation. A theme for Ben Jonson ! But there is no touch of humour in Brant.

> A bad woman will always escape, he says, and he quotes Danaë as an example. That a good woman will remain faithful without being jealously guarded is proved by Penelope (1–16). He who has a faithful wife may well call himself happy. One cannot plough straight furrows with a deaf horse, nor live straight with a fair but foolish wife (17–24). A well-behaved woman must be modest and not listen to every stranger. The danger is proved by Helena and by Dido (25–34).

Locher draws out the first sixteen lines so much that there is little room for the rest. Of 17–24 he has nothing. He changes the first part of 25–34 and his page is full after the name of Helena.

Barclay naturally paraphrases this truncated version. Hardly anything is worth quoting. One striking passage there is. Locher introduces the story of Danaë [2] :

> Non turris Danaes potuit servare pudorem.

This becomes in English :

> (497)    The toure of bras that callyd was Darayne
> Coude nat the damsell by name Danes defende.

He makes the same mistake as Riviere, making Danes into a nominative. But where did he get the name of that tower from ? It is not in Locher nor is there anything like it in Riviere. And yet he must have taken it from some French source of information. For there is no such name in classical mythology, but the French *d'airain* means the same as English *of bras* ! Towards the end, after mentioning the story of Penelope, he takes up the suggestion of one line in Locher, to write two stanzas about the ' folysshe jelowsy of men ' and ' mannys unkyndnes.' He then finishes his chapter. But while elsewhere the Envoy contains always a little sermon of his own, he here uses Locher's last six lines for it, so that we get Helena at the end of the Envoy (503).

218.—Drouyn is in this chapter more diffuse than his guide Riviere. He begins with a longer invitation than usual, in which occurs the curious sentence (derived from the motto and from the woodcut) : ' It is more facyle *and more easy* to kepe a basket full of fleene in the sonne than for

---

[1] *Geason* (< OE. gæsne = barren, scarce) is very rarely used as a substantive, but common in ME. and Early MnE. as an adjective. As such Barclay uses it in his fifth Eclogue : ' a good man is geason, not easy to be found.'—NED.

[2] The comparison is used for nobler purpose by Brant in his *Contra judeos hereticos, conceptionem virginalem fuisse possibilem argumentatio* in *Varia Carmina*, reprinted by Zarncke 176 sq.

to kepe one wyfe *alonely* from doynge evyl.' The italics are Watson's own additions. And pathetically he declares : ' I amytte [1] all to the jugement of God.'

The story of *Danes* is more detailed than in Riviere. The last sentence runs : ' et fut par Jupitur ceste pucelle defloree en ceste tour ' ; in English : ' And by this Jupyter the vyrgyn Danes was deflored in the toure *of Brasse.*' This last addition of Watson's is important in connexion with Barclay's Darayne. Where did Watson find this piece of classical learning ? Did both translators use some sort of French encyclopedia, which Watson understood and Barclay did not ?

One sentence is entirely original in Drouyn-Watson : ' Certainly it is a vylaynous reproche unto a woman whan she wyll not obeye unto her husbande ' ; and at the end, after the story of Helena he adds a long conclusion which in English, thanks to the abundance of space, becomes even longer. It contains an amusing bit of natural history, taken from some *Bestiaire* or other.

She hadde better to have stopped her eeres than to have beleved suche wordes. Wherfore, women, never abuse you with the *vayne* wordes of men, but do as the serpent dothe whan the enchauntour wolde take hym, *for* he layeth one of his eres to the erthe, and with the ende of his tayle he stoppeth the other, *to the ende* that he here not the enchauntementes *and charmes of the enchauntoure,* and on this wyse he scapeth *and is not taken. Loke that ye* have regarde unto this *example,* wyves *and maydens* that desyreth to lyve wel, and ye shal wynne you good renown.[2]

219.—One more chapter falls under this category, viz. chapter 52, on MARRYING AN OLD WOMAN FOR HER MONEY.

There is no fat in an ass, says Brant, and whoever marries an old woman must not expect much pleasure nor any children, but he will always be reminded of the money-bag that has deceived him (1–10). Little happiness comes from looking to fortune alone and forgetting honour and virtue (11–14). All domestic peace is lost in this way, so that the man would rather live in a desert, but he repents too late when he has sold his youth for money (15–22). He who has done so much for the ass's fat, would probably go much farther yet, but would never find more than dirt (23–26). Many are on the look-out for Achab's daughter,[3] but they will always be put to shame (27–28). Asmodeus the demon spoils many a marriage (29–30). Rare is the Booz who values a Ruth (31–32). Hence so many regrets and *criminor te, kratznor a te* (33–34).

Locher elaborates the beginning of this chapter and has no room left for the examples at the end nor for that curious piece of quasi-Latin that became so famous in German sixteenth-century literature.[4]

---

[1] The French has : ' a dieu le jugement doit remettre.' Does *amytte* stand for *admit* ? But according to the NED. the word has no meaning that would suit here.

[2] Drouyn probably found this wisdom in *Le Bestiaire damours* printed about this time in Paris (Hain-Copinger 3010, and K. Burger 616). As there is no copy in the British Museum, I have not been able to verify my suspicion, but the interesting item itself belongs to the stock-in-trade of every good Bestiaire. To quote one of the most famous : ' Et lo serpente vedendo che l'omo viene per levarli quello ch'elli guarda, sì si thura l'uno de li orecchi cola coda et l'altro percuote tanto in terra che se li enpie tutto de terra si che lo sono dell'arpa non lo po fare adormentare.' M.S. Garver-McKenzie, Il Bestiario Toscano (Studi Romanzi-Monaci viii ; Roma 1912), 38. Further references and medieval sources in M. Goldstaub-Wendriner, Ein Tosco-Venezianischer Bestiarius (Halle 1892), 298.

[3] Brant probably means Achab's *wife,* Jezabel.

[4] See Zarncke 388 sq.

He had to stop with Brant's line 25 or 26.   His most notable addition is the introduction of the woman's father inquiring after the financial status, and nothing else, of his prospective son-in-law.

220.—Barclay follows the Latin version at first faithfully, towards the end very freely.   Then he inserts good idiomatic expressions like this :

> (739)   For if a woman be foule and full of vice
> And lewde of maners, nought both to man and lad,
> Yet good shall hir mary, be she never so bad.

For the following stanzas the Latin contains only a suggestion in a word or two :

> (742)   Forsoth, it is an unmete maryage
> And disagreynge and moche agaynst the lawe
> Bytwene fresshe youth and lame unlusty age ;
> The love bytwene them is scantly worth a strawe,
> So doth the one styll on the other gnawe ;
> And oft the man in mynde doth sore complayne,
> His sede to sowe upon a grounde barayne.
>
> (743)   Than muste he have another prymme [1] or twayne,
> With them to slake his wanton yonge cowrage ;
> But in that space must he endure great payne
> With hir that he hath tane in marryage ;
> Hir bablynge tunge which no man can asswage,
> With wrathfull wordes shall sle hym at the laste ;
> His other prymes his good shall spende and waste.

221.—Riviere's French rhyming of this chapter, which is a great deal weaker than the English, cannot certainly have influenced Barclay, but it is of importance for the understanding of Watson's version ;  and the importance is heightened by the fact that it was inserted in the *Boke of three Fooles*, once ascribed to Skelton.[2]   The interpretation is indispensable already in the motto-stanza.   Watson writes here :

> The man the whiche dothe wed a wyfe
> For her treasour and her rychesse,
> And not for lygnage femynatyfe,
> Procureth doloure and dystresse
> With infynyte payne and hevynesse
> For she wyll do hym moche sorowe,
> Both at evyn and at morowe.[3]

The meaning of this curious stanza only becomes clear from Riviere :

> Celuy qui espousse une femme
> Pour son tresor et sa richesse,
> Non pour lignee avoir, infame
> Est, toute noyse a luy sadresse
> Tousiours elle luy courroux dresse
> Pacience perdent : couraige
> Et le prouffit du mariage.

---

[1] This is the first recorded occurrence of the word.   G. Harvey still uses it about 1573.   Afterwards it seems to have survived long in the Yorkshire dialect. The origin is obscure, but its meaning is pretty clear from the context.   Cf. NED.

[2] See §§ 47 and 57.

[3] The Pseudo-Skelton only changes *the whiche* in the first line into *that*, and *treasour* in the second line into *goodes*.   See A. Dyce, The Poetical Works of John Skelton, i (Boston 1856), 221 : ' The Boke of three Fooles M. Skelton, Poete Laureate, gave to my lorde Cardynall.'

The origin of Watson's *lygnage femynatyfe* becomes still clearer when we see that Drouyn in copying Riviere has forgotten the comma in the third line, so that Watson could combine *infame* with *lignee*, and then form an association between *infame* and *femme*!

After this Drouyn begins with his usual introduction: 'Laves vos yeux de leau satyrique vous pouvez trouver en ce present livre. Folz pecunieulx que pour avarice et pour avoir bon temps' etc. Watson does not dare to use the word *satyrique*, but he has plenty of space available and so he writes:

> Come and wasshe your eyen in the water of this chapytre *folysshe fooles without wytte or understondynge*. Pecunyous fooles, that bee avaryce, and for to have good tyme and to lyve joyousle, weddeth these olde wyddred women, whych hathe sackes full of nobles,[1] claryfye here your syghte, and ye shal know what goodnes commeth therby, and what joye and gladnes.[2]

In the passage about the enquiring father-in-law, Watson mixes up all Drouyn's pronouns, using *he* instead of *she*, and *her* instead of *his*. This makes it entirely unreadable, so that it is not even worth quoting as a curiosity.

222.—The last two lines of this chapter were written by Locher only to fill the page; so it is no wonder that none of the translators understood the connexion with what precedes. Barclay came very near to it when he wrote:

> (745) And so these folys subdue them to bondage.

But he felt this as rather unsatisfactory, and so he added:

> They wast theyr good, and so, whan that is spent,
> And nought remayneth theyr bodyes to relefe
> Theyr disputacion is nought but: hore! and thefe!

Riviere never made the attempt to get at Locher's idea and planned a conclusion of his own. But as he had no such lively language as Barclay at his disposal, he gives us only this:

> O amis considerez
> Et vos ardans cueurs moderez
> Et les aultres quonques ny fustes
> En ce lieu et qui ne beustes
> De ce bruvage nen beurez
> Et vous serez les bien eurez.

Drouyn prosified this so that he preserved all the words, *bruvage* probably by a misprint becoming *breuvavige*. But at the end he added a sentence of his own:

> Nonobstant que je ne deffens pas se marier mais dys que celluy qui se marriera preigne femme avec laquelle il puisse vivre en ioye de corps et dame et acquerir la gloire de paradis.

---

[1] Herford 352 quotes this phrase as typically Skeltonian; but it is literally from the French: 'ces vieilles ridees qui ont des escutz ung plein sac.'

[2] The Pseudo-Skelton changes only the first dozen words, eliminating the *washing*: 'Come hyther, and take this boke, and rede therin for your lernyng with clere iyen, and loke in this boke, that shewyth you folysh fooles' etc.; the rest is all like Watson, except that he reads *meryly* instead of *joyousle*.

Watson did not understand the word *breuvavige* and skipped it, and, probably mistaking *preigne* for an adjective, fashioned the conclusion as follows :

> My frends, whiche be not in that bande, put you not therin, and yee shalbe well happy. Notwithstandynge, I defende you not to mary, but I exhorte you to take a wyfe *that ye may have progeny by*, and solace, bodely and gostly, and therby to wyn the ioyes of Paradyse.

And this was regarded as an original paraphrase by a Poet Laureate or a sermon by an English parson on the Narrenschiff ! [1]

---

[1] See Dyce and Herford l.c. The most important difference between Watson and the Pseudo-Skelton is that the latter wrote (or it became so in print) *bodyly and goostly* instead of *bodely and gostly*.—Jamieson (lxxxii) must have admired Watson's language more than any, for, writing under the impression that Skelton was the author, he says that these passages ' are dashed off with his usual racy vigour ' !

## XI

## CHAPTERS RELATING TO VARIOUS CLASSES OF PERSONS

223.—First under this category may perhaps be grouped chapter 6 on the DUTIES OF PARENTS. A long double and serious chapter in Brant.

Parents ought to correct their children when young, for a vase retains the odour of its first contents and a slender twig can be easily bent (see Horace) (1–19). Punishment is beneficial to children, else they become like Heli's sons (20–28). Because this is forgotten, we see so many Catilines (29–30). Formerly it was otherwise, when parents provided their children with good teachers. Then Achilles had a Phœnix, Alexander an Aristotle, Aristotle a Plato, Plato a Socrates (31–40). At present parents take foolish teachers who make their children more foolish than they are (41–45). Old Crates rightly said : Parents should take more care of their children than of their riches (46–54). The parents will see the consequence when the child grows up to be good-for-nothing, extravagant and a spendthrift. For true honour springs only from good education (55–72). Noble birth is not your own, riches are a gift of fortune, fame is fickle, beauty and health are perishable ; but immortal are the effects of a good education (73–88). Socrates replied to Gorgias' question about the king's happiness : ' I do not know if he has learned the duties of virtue,' as if to say : Riches and power are nothing in comparison with virtue (89–94).

Locher, like his master, feels obliged to devote a double chapter to this treatise. Thus he was able to elaborate most of the above ideas. In 20–28 he has substituted the sons of Priam and of Tarquinius Superbus for those of Helen. In 40 he leaves out Socrates, he reduces 41–45, and changes 55–72 altogether. But he expanded the first half of the chapter so much that there is no room for the fine passage from 73 downwards. He mentions noble birth in four lines and then suddenly adds :

> Sed pater in culpa est : qui non vult esse severus
> Dogmaque nec gnatis vivendi suggerit aprum.

And there he stops, because the page is full ! The marginal notes in this chapter also appear unsatisfactory. For while there seems no doubt that from line 31 onwards Brant took nearly everything from Plutarch,[1] this source is not once mentioned in Locher's version ; Homer, the Bible, Canon Law and Juvenal [2] only are referred to.

224.—In Barclay there are two more references, viz. *Tarquinius*

---

[1] See the quotation in Zarncke 312 sq.

[2] Locher's text, printed in front of Barclay's English version, breaks off in the middle of the story of Tarquinius and in the middle of a sentence, just where in the original Basel editions the end of a page was reached, and where Wynkyn de Worde's page also happened to be full.

*de quo Valerius* and *Catelina de quo Salustius*. This looks suspicious. And indeed in Riviere we find the same reference to *Valerius*, though *Salustius* seems to be peculiar to the English version. The note proves that Barclay here must have looked into the French. But he did not find much there. In spite of the note, Riviere has added hardly anything to the story as told by Locher, except that Lucretia killed herself 'dung grant couteau.' And this detail is *not* in Barclay. Moreover he makes 'Tarquyne the proude' himself commit violence against 'Lucres' (123), while Riviere says even more clearly than the Latin, that it was his son. So : there is no influence of the French text here. But some little trace of Barclay's consulting it may, perhaps, be found in the preceding story of Priam, which is more complete in Riviere than in Locher, and in which the English text inserts the name of ' the fayre Helayne ' (122) and

> The cyte of Troy unto the grounde clene brent,

just as the French had spoken of Priam :

> Qui vit destruire sa cite

and of

> La noble et belle dame Helayne.

But these are trifles. On the whole he follows Locher faithfully, but he elaborates the ideas at more than usual length.[1] Some lines are very good renderings. So e.g. the Horatian comparisons :

> (118) But fyll an erthen pot first with yll lycoure,
>  And ever after it shall smell somwhat soure.
> (119) A lytell twygge plyant is by kynde,
>  A bygger braunche is harde to bowe or wynde.

Instead of simply mentioning the extravagance of young men, as Locher does, Barclay mentions the most obnoxious games :

> (134) Some theyr londe and lyvelode in riot out wasteth
>  At cardes and tenys and other unlawful gamys ;
>  And some wyth the dyce theyr thryft away casteth.

Of notable deviations from Locher there are none, not even proverbs [2] as far as I can see.

> (137) Without dout noblenes is moche excellent
>  Whiche oft causeth youth to be had in great honour,

is somewhat more emphatic and therefore more truly English than ' decorare pusillos Quae solet.'

225.—Watson opens his chapter, after the invitation, with the statement : 'The fader shall be alwaye myserable and gretely affusked (Fr. aveugle) that hathe not some aspecte unto his chyldren.' [3]

---

[1] Ramsay lxxxvi thinks that the dissertation of the sins of fathers and children in Magnyfycence is in all likelihood based on this chapter and on ch. 90.

[2] The proverbs mentioned by Seifert 11 are in the Latin.

[3] The French has ' qui naura aulcune cure de ses enfans.' This usage of the word *aspecte* seems almost peculiar to Watson. See NED. On *affusked* see § 137.

Although he has to abbreviate his text here and there, this chapter is on the whole fairly readable.   In the story of Tarquin he leaves out the ' grant couteau ' and one or two other words, so that we get :

> And more over have we not another example of proude Tarquyn the kynges sone of Rome [1] that ravysshed the faire Lucrece, the whiche for pure sorowe slewe herselfe *before all her frendes*.  It happened afterwards that bothe his fader and he were chased out of Rome vylaynously, and bycause of this there was never kynge of Rome sythe.

The slaying ' before all her frendes ' is added by Watson, perhaps to make it more tragical.   That the chasing-out *happened afterwards*, independently of the rest, however, is owing to Drouyn's prose.

The above Latin quotation (corresponding to Barclay's Stanza 137) is literally in Riviere :

> De noblesse est assez grant chose
> Dont sont decorez les pusilles.

Drouyn has hardly changed these words :  ' Cest grant chose que de noblesse, car les pusilles en sont decorez.'   Nor does Watson change them very much, but just enough to make it into a joke :  ' It is a grete thynge of nobles, for the *pucelles* ben therewith decored ' !—A great many deficiencies can be made up for by one good expression, and Watson gives us such a one in his translation of ' Souvent dune doulce beste naissent de mauvais chiens '—' Oftentimes a mylde bytche bryngeth forth shrewd whelpes.'   This is more idiomatic than Barclay's parallel passage :

> (138)   But this forsothe oft tymes fynde I true
> That of a goode beste yl whelpes may we shewe.

226.—Chapter 49 rebukes PARENTS who give a bad example to their children, because these will undoubtedly imitate them.

Locher leaves out the names of Brutus and Cato and Catiline and the last four lines, but translates the rest with remarkable fidelity, so that even the proverbial sayings are retained.—So they appear also in Barclay's translation :

> (701)   The monkes thynke it lawfull for to play,
> Whan that the Abbot bryngeth them the dyce.
> (703)   And no mervayle, for it hath never ben seen,
> That of a wolfe a shepe hath be forth brought.
> (704)   The yonge crab bacwarde doth crepe or go,
> As doth the olde, none can hir cours redres.

The Englishman adds some others from his own store, the best of which is :

> (697)   The yonge cok lerneth to crowe hye of the olde.

But on the whole Barclay keeps close to the Latin, closer than Riviere, who in the beginning of this chapter is much severer than Locher and towards the end becomes particularly tame and weak in his paraphrase.

---

[1] This is surely a bolder compound-genitive than the Chaucerian ' The Wyves Tale of Bathe,' *if* Watson means to reproduce the French ' Tarquin lenfant filz dung roy romain nomme Tarquin lorgueilleux.'  But perhaps he did not take in the meaning very clearly.

He can hardly have influenced Barclay's English,[1] but some of Locher's proverbs have through Riviere and Drouyn got into Watson's translation : ' Semblably yf an abbot be a player at the dyse or at the cardes, all the hole covente wyll do as he dothe.' ' The fader is lyke unto a crevyce the whiche goth more/backwarde than forwarde ' !

227.—Chapter 90 refers more directly to CHILDREN, but in the first twelve lines we find some peculiar views of the folly of parents who give away their property to their children. They get what they deserve, says Brant, when they are left in the lurch, or when the children wish them dead, or even assail them with sticks !—This bourgeois wisdom seems to have been typical of the popular morality of the time.[2] But the second half of the chapter expresses a more Scriptural opinion on the behaviour of undutiful children, taken from the Decalogue and from Prov. xx 20 ; Brant here points to the fate that befell Absolom and Cham and Balthasar and Sennacherib's sons and he commemorates the nobler examples of Tobias, Solomon, Coriolanus and the Rechabites. The conclusion repeats the fourth commandment.

Nearly the whole of this chapter is in Locher's Latin, except that he tones down the crudity of the first part somewhat, that Sennacherib is mentioned before Balthasar, and the conclusion is left out.

Barclay follows this Latin version, making it only a great deal more diffuse by writing a whole stanza for every two lines. In the first part he even goes farther and instead of Locher's two lines

> Si nimium vivax pater est : sibi tristia fata
> Exoptat natus : mortis et exitium,

Barclay uses two stanzas :

> (1370)   And where as he ought his father to honour
> To worshyp and love by dyvyne commaundement,
> The unkynde caytyf wyl do hym no socour,
> But suffreth hym abyde both pore and indigent ;
> And often this caytyf with handes violent,
> As past all grace shame or godly fere,
> With strokes doth his father hurt and dere,

> (1371)   Or suffreth hym utterly to dye for lacke,
> Or else hym dryveth unkyndly to the colde
> With a cowpyll of croches, a walet on his backe,
> Whan he hath spoyled hym of that he wolde ;
> So whan the father is tedyous and olde,
> His children thynke he lyveth alto longe,
> Oft wysshynge hym to be drownyd outher honge.[3]

There is nothing of Brant's crudity here, but the concrete expressions of the second stanza seem to contain a reminiscence of Geoffrey of Monmouth's story of King Lear.

---

[1] This is said against Fraustadt's assertion (p. 44), whose comparison, though he calls it ' interesting,' is far from convincing.

[2] See Zarncke's notes, p. 433.

[3] The weak form of the verb occurs in Stanza 1376, where Absolon is ' hangyd by the here.'

Locher's idea appears in a much weaker form in Watson :

Folysshe fader wherfore gyvest thou al thy fynaunce unto the sone.   O how thou arte folysshe to gyve unto thy sone, the whiche after the gyfte will wysshe the deed.   And thou sone *etc.*

Though the rest of the chapter makes all fairly good sense, there is nothing striking that deserves quoting.

228.—Chapter 5 is devoted to a satire on OLD FOOLS in a tone of rude sarcasm.

In the first 24 lines the old fool is speaking in his own person.  ' I am old and yet a fool ; I give my children all freedom, and make a will of which I shall be sorry after death.   I do as I have been taught, and glory in my own shame.   I have deceived many people and defiled many springs, and only regret that infirmities prevent me from doing as I used to do.   But I hope my son *Heyntz* will walk in my footsteps.   He is a chip of the old block, and one day people will say that he was a true son of his father.   He will be the real rogue and make one of the crew of the Ship of Fools, so that I shall enjoy it even in my grave.'—Such is old age nowadays, that is the reflection of the concluding six lines.   The old fools are like Suzanna's judges, they never think of their own souls, for it is difficult to get rid of old habits long acquired.

In Locher's classical expressions the tone of this chapter is less grating on the ears.   The ideas are all there, except Suzanna's judges and *Heyntz*, but the concrete drastic sayings have all been generalized, so that the satire has become quite respectable, polite and dull.

229.—Watson's rendering is equally dull.   Three little specimens of his best sayings will suffice.  ' I am a foole for of my foly I desyre to have lovynge and praysynge ' ;  this is the French ' ie desire louenge avoir.'—' Alas olde foole wherfore hast thou no shame that thy foly hathe surmounted the so longe ? '—And the last sentence :  ' Whan one abydeth to longe for to remedye his causes (a son *cas* !), with grete payne may he detray the meurs that ben roted in the herte '—*detray*, used to render the French *oster*, was good English then, as it also occurs in Hawes' Pastime of Pleasure and in Wolsey's letters,[1] but whether anyone not familiar with French could understand the word *meurs* seems rather doubtful.[2]

230.—Barclay has fortunately brought a little more life into it. He writes the whole chapter in the first person [3] and reserves the final reflections for the Envoy.   What he has enjoyed most is the idea of the foolish father instructing his son in his own roguery.   He will enumerate to you the situations where in his opinion the greatest roguery is committed.   And instead of being rude, his sarcasm becomes delightful and humorous.

---

[1] See NED. s.v.
[2] There is no such word in the NED.   Watson uses it even in his titles.   See Appendix under chapter 9.
[3] In Stanza 100 there is one little deviation in the expression :  ' Lame ar his lymmys.'   This must be due to an oversight and the *his* has been rightly changed into *my* in Cawood's edition.

(105) I shall infourme and teche my son and heyre
To folowe his fader and lerne this way of me ;
The way is large, God wot, glad shall he be,
Lernynge my lore with affeccion and desyre,
And folowe the steppys of his unthryfty syre.

(106) I trust so crafty and wyse to make the lad,
That me his father he shall pas and excel !
O that my herte shall than be wonder glad,
If I here of, may knowe, se, or here tell,
If he be false, faynynge, sotyll or cruell
And so styll endure !—I have a speciall hope
To make hym scrybe to a Cardynall or Pope.

(107) Or els if he can be a fals extorcyoner,
Fasynge [1] and bostynge to scratche and to kepe,
He shall be made a comon costomer
As yche hope, of Lyn, Calays or of Depe [2] !
Than may he after to some great offyce crepe,
So that if he can onys plede a case,
He may be made juge of the Common Place.

231.—Here is some real satire, such as Brant himself has never written. In Stanza 106 with its telling stroke at the end the very rhythm of the lines is expressive. The dialectical *yche* in the next stanza, a form at that time in common use in Devonshire, but occurring nowhere else in the *Ship*, is used to enhance the realistic effect.—We know already that Barclay had no high opinion of the honesty of custom-house officers. They have never been very popular. One only wonders why by the side of Calais and of Lynn, also Dieppe should be mentioned. Calais, the last English stronghold on the Continent, appealed to popular imagination. King's Lynn, long the favourite rendezvous of Norwegian ships, which carried on a lively trade with the Hansa towns,[3] must also have opened tempting prospects for unscrupulous ' customers.' But Dieppe had long been lost to England. Is it possible that the town was still famous among sailors, and that Barclay or his ' Old fool ' had caught up its name in their circle ?

' Juge of the Common Place ' seems to represent the acme of possible extortion. The Court of Common Pleas or Common Place [4] which had to decide civil actions at law brought by one subject against another, was held at Westminster, and the author of London Lickpenny had already had one of his sad experiences there :

> Unto the Common Place I yode thoo
> Where sat one with a sylken hoode *etc.*

Barclay has turned the unpopularity of such legal professions to the best satirical account.

---

[1] *To fase* or *to face* was a synonym of *to boast*, ' shew a bolde face ' as the Prompt. Parvulorum explains it. Shakespeare uses the word in another meaning.—NED.

[2] Cawood modernizes the spelling into : Lin, Callis, Deepe.

[3] H. G. Leach, Angevin Britain and Scandinavia (1923), 33, 41.

[4] The two words were confused in the sixteenth century. In the beginning of the seventeenth century judicial authorities made a distinction. ' The Common Place which dealeth properly with common Pleas.' See NED.

232.—Chapter 63 introduces us to the miscellaneous company of BEGGARS. Unfortunately it is a chapter that has suffered badly at the hands of the Latin interpreter. Beggars were a plague of the time [1] and Brant mentions a great many categories.

'Pfaffen mynchs örden' are the first, with relic-mongers who at every fair practise on the credulity of the people with their pretended relics : straw from the Bethlehem manger, a bone from Balaam's ass, a feather from St. Michael's wing, the bridle of St. George's horse, or the sandals of St. Clare (1–21). Healthy young men go begging when they are too lazy to work (22–26), and they teach their children the same, and do not hesitate to maim them for the purpose (27–32). The twenty-four Beghards at Strassburg are not forgotten, nor the colony, or beggarly free state, on the 'Kolenbergh' near Basel (33–38). They have their own jargon 'Rotwelsch' and Brant inserts a passage full of Rotwelsch words (39–52).[2] The old heralds, minstrels [3] and pursuivants have also degenerated into beggars (53–60). And they all deceive the people with false pretexts. They want a silver chalice, or they make believe to be lame, or to have the falling sickness ; they borrow children from each other to make a piteous show, or they pretend to be going on a pilgrimage to Compostella, or to be suffering from some bodily distortion (61–77). The number of beggars is continually increasing, they all seem to like the trade except the really poor (78–82). They eat the finest bread and drink the best wine, and do whatever they like, for their life is the freest of all (83–92). Many go abegging, who are richer than you and I ! (93–94).

Locher has only 36 lines for this chapter, and he barely takes the leading ideas of lines 1–32. Instead of Brant's concrete examples he inserts some pious reflections about almsgiving. He refers the reader to the German original ; for the various deceptions of the beggars, he says, can more easily be read in the 'theutona scripta,' and a marginal note repeats the reference. He himself cannot devote more space to it, for 'pagina deficiet'—and his page is just full ! !

What a pity ! Locher's mutilation of this chapter is a loss to English literature. The description of roguery, which is an important link in the development of the picaresque novel, was in great favour in the first half of the sixteenth century. If Barclay had known more of Brant, he might have contributed to Copland's compilation much more than he really did,[4] and Awdeley and Harman

---

[1] See the Basel Chronicle by J. Knebel, Seb. Franck's Proverbs, the Liber Vagatorum, and Geiler's opinion quoted by Zarncke 400 sq.

[2] Most of the words can be explained from the Rotwelsch Grammar, Francfort 1755, Zarncke 403. Various Rotwelsch vocabularies were already printed in the fifteenth century, e.g. in the third part of the Liber Vagatorum, which owes much of its inspiration to this chapter. See Zarncke cxxi.

[3] See § 287.

[4] The Hye Way to the Spyttel House. In the Prologue Robert Copland calls himself 'Compyler and prynter of this Boke.' It was printed after 1530. See W. C. Hazlitt, Remains iv (1866), 17 sqq. Some of the descriptions, e.g. on p. 37, resemble Barclay. Herford 360 sq. thinks that the main portion is suggested directly by the German original. In many respects, however, it is much more like Robert de Balsac's Le droit chemin de l'Hopital et les gens qui le trouvent par leurs œuvres et manieres de vivre (among the works of Symphorien Champier. See M. P. Allut, Étude . . . sur Symph. Champier, Lyon 1859, p. 119 sqq., who notes that Brunet mentions three other editions. See also Copinger ii, 1583). Curiously enough the author is also mentioned in Bale, Catalogus ii (1559), p. 63. The Dutch version 'Den rechten weg nae tGasthuys,' to be found in Veelderhande Geneuchlycke Dichten p. 126 sqq., is, at least partly, translated, and literally translated, from the French. The subject deserves closer study than I have been able to devote to it. The notes given by G. Kalff i, 123 are very incomplete.

might have found much more material to elaborate their character sketches.[1]

233.—Barclay has now to make the best of a bad job. He repeats Locher's curious statement that beggars are inclined

(905)　　　　　for all theyr poverte
　　　　　To kepe with them of children great plente.

He does not improve the pious reflections, and shortens the description of the begging monks :

(909)　The abbot, the pryour and also theyr covent
　　　Ar so blynded with unhappy covetyse,
　　　That with theyr owne can they nat be content,
　　　But to have more they alway mean devyse.

Riviere had reproduced the Latin more faithfully, and even heightened the effect of the description by a comical comparison :

　　　Et chacun deux est incite
　　　Porter ung sac ou une poche
　　　Et taster si chacun huys loche
　　　De porte en porte en la sepmaine
　　　Comme le porc de sainct anthoine !

But there is another addition which the Englishman did not find in the original :

(909)　Ye, in so moche that some have founde a gyse
　　　To fayne theyr bretherne tan in captyvyte,
　　　That they may begge so by auctoryte.

This can hardly be directed against some common frauds of the time but seems to be a satirical hit at the Trinitarians or Mathurins, as they were called in Paris, who professed to ransom Christians from captivity, in particular from the Moors. If so, and if we remember that the central figure of the Renaissance at Paris was none other than the Minister General of this order, Robert Gaguin, that Gaguin was one of the promoters of restoration and reform and had given new statutes to his own order,[2] and if it is true that Barclay had at one time been a friend or at least an acquaintance of this eminent man,—these satirical lines must be taken as a good-natured, though rather peculiar, joke.

One joke he omits :

　　　Spirituum vendunt pennas saepe aethereorum,

which represents Brant's sarcastic list of pretended relics. Instead of this Barclay speaks only of ' some fayned pardon ' (910), ' byldynges, relyques newe, fals bonys.' Perhaps he did not understand the Latin. Perhaps the old anecdote had lost its zest.[3]

---

[1] J. Awdeley's Fraternitye of Vacabones 1561 is little more than a catalogue of rogues. Th. Harman's Caveat or Warening for Commen Corsetors vulgarely called Vagabones (shortly after 1561) is a collection of real Characters and deserves the name of the standard work on its subject. Both edited by E. Viles and F. J. Furnivall, The Rogues and Vagabonds of Shakespeare's Youth (London 1907).

[2] Renaudet 204, 233.

[3] Did not Boccaccio invent it ? Riviere still enjoys it and even improves upon it :

　　　Et vendent les elles et plumes
　　　Du sainct esperit lassus des cieulx.

234.—He goes on immediately with Locher's ' validi mendicantes,'
the common beggar-folk, whose tricks are so graphically described, that
Harman's Counterfete Cranke [1] is clearly anticipated :

> (912)　(They) gyvyth theyr bodyes fully to slewthfulnes,
> The beggars craft thynkynge to them moost good ;
> Some ray theyr legges and armys over with blood,
> With levys and plasters, though they be hole and sounde,
> Some halt as crypyls, theyr legge falsely up bounde.

> (913)　Some other beggers falsly for the nonys
> Disfigure theyr children, God wot, unhappely,
> Manglynge theyr facys, and brekynge theyr bonys,
> To stere the people to pety that passe by ;
> There stande they beggynge with tedyous shout and cry,
> Theyr owne bodyes tournynge to a strange fassion,
> To move such as passe to pyte and compassyon.

The ideas of this last stanza are nearly all in the Latin.　They are
here followed by the reference to the ' theutona scripta.'　Barclay omits
the reference in the text, but puts it in the margin : ' Plura notantur
in libro teutonico.'—Here, if anywhere, we should say, Barclay ought
to have consulted the original *Narrenschiff*.　But instead of this he
gives us an invention of his own.　He will speak of ' yonge laddys '
and ' wymen wanton ' (914).　The beginning is not very successful ; but
soon his literary vein grows richer :

> (915)　They paciently theyr povertye abyde,
> Nat for devocion of herte or of mynde,
> But to the intent that at every tyde
> Other mennys godes sholde them fede and fynde ;
> But if they a whyle have ron in the wynde (!),
> And in theyr hande the staf some hete hath caught,
> They never after shall leve the beggers craft.[2]

These last lines are excellent.　Barclay in his best form.　And he
keeps it up in the two following stanzas, full of shrewd observation ; the
first lines of which give a delightful picture of the glories of gypsy-life :

> (917)　If the begger have his staf and his hode,
> One bagge behynde and another before,
> Than thynkes he hym in the myddes of his goode,
> Thoughe that his clothes be raggyd and to tore,
> His bode nere bare, he hath no thought therfore ;
> And if some man cloth them well to-day,
> To morowe it shall agayne be solde away !

> (918)　And if these caytyfes fortune to begge or cry
> For mete or money on woman or on man,
> If one of them that that they aske deny
> And so depart, anone these beggers than,
> Whan he is gone, doth wary,[3] curse and ban ;
> And if another gyve them ought of pyte.
> At the next alestake dronken shall it be !

---

[1] Viles-Furnivall, p. 50.

[2] Note the instructive rhyme : *caught : craft ;* similarly in Stanza 533 *nought :
brought : soft.*　This points to a dialectical pronunciation such as has been adopted
in the standard pronunciation of *laughter.*　The more usual rhyme sequence is
e.g. in Stanza 38 : *sought : brought : thought,* or Stanza 101 : *thought : nought :
brought.*　See V. Dalheimer.

[3] A common Middle English synonym of *curse.*　Cf. OE. wyrgan.

We are almost glad, after all, that the author has not paraphrased the German. He has now given us a truly English contribution to vagabond-literature, and with more light humour than Brant was capable of.

235.—How this sort of literature coincided with popular taste in France as well, is evinced by Riviere's additions to this chapter.[1] Most of them are to be found back in Watson, who could allow himself ample space for this chapter, more than two and a half pages. And his language and his style are remarkably good and intelligible, so that we can give a longer quotation without wading through linguistic eccentricities. Drouyn has added very little to Riviere's ideas, only one rough joke, which I have put between brackets. The italicized passages and expressions are Watson's own ; though mostly intended as mere padding, they are here the best of all, the last especially, which completes Barclay's and Harman's description.[2]

I fynde grete fautes in the abbottes, monkes pryours, chanons, and coventes for all that they have rentes tenementes and *possessyons* ynough, yet as folkes devoyde of sence *and understondynge*, they be never satysfyed with goodes. They goo *from vyllage to vyllage and from towne to towne*, berynge grete bagges upon theyr neckes, assemblynge so moche goodes, that it is grete mervayle, *and whan they be in their relygyous cloysters they make theym byleve that they have had lytell gyven them, or nothynge, for God knoweth they maken heven chere in the country*. And by this occasyon the poore nedy hathe none almesse, or elles it is but small. There is another sort of pardoners,[3] the whiche bereth relyques about with them in abusynge the pore folke, for and yf they have but one *poore* peny [ung denier] in theyr purses they must have it. They gadre togyder golde and sylver in every place lyke as yf it grewe. They make the poore folkes byleve moche gaye gere. They sel the feders of the holy Ghoost. They bere the bones of some deed body aboute, the whiche paraventure is damyned. (They shewe the heer of some olde hors saynge that it is of the berde of the Innocentes.) *Ther is an innumerable syght of suche folkes, and of vacabondes in this realme of Englonde*, the whiche be hole of all theyr membres and myghte wynne theyr lyves honestly. Notwithstondynge they go beggynge *from dore to dore*, bycause they wyll not werke, *and patcheth an olde mauntell or an olde gown with an hondred colours, and byndeth foule cloutes about theyr legges, as who say they be sore*. And often tymes they be more rycher than they that gyveth them almesse. They breke theyr chyldren membres in theyr youth, bycause that men sholde have the more pyte of them. . . . They be well at ease to have grete legges and bellyes eten to the bonis, for they wyll not put noo medycynes therto for to hele them, but soner envenymeth them, and dyvers other begylynges of which I holde my pease.

He concludes this little treatise, like his models, with an exhortation

---

[1] It is somewhat striking, therefore, that the Marnef-translator in his little preface to this chapter should have found it necessary to mention that ' lacteur avoit bien congneu lusaige *des almans* qui ont povrete voluntaire et peregrination perpetuelle.'— The Frenchman evidently thought that the contents of this chapter were not quite applicable to his own country. See notes on the Beghards § 164. But such a casual observation raises the question again : how much real observation was there in such descriptions ?

[2] It is quoted by F. W. Chandler, The Literature of Roguery i (1907), 50. The author barely mentions Barclay's name, and calls Watson's work a ' prose version of the German original.' On p. 75 sq. he adds that ' Barclay translated his Shyp of Folys (1508) from the German of Brandt.'

[3] See a very discriminating paper by Herbert Thurston on The Medieval Pardoner in *The Month* 142 (1923), 522–532, mainly based on Dr. Nik. Paulus, Geschichte des Ablasses im Mittelalter ii (1923), 265–291 : Die Quästoren oder Almosensammler als Verkündiger von Ablässen.

to the ' fools ' to remember the real poor ' auncyent men, poore wedowes, lazars (Fr. ladres), and blynde men.'  For they must not forget : ' Ye shall gyve accomptes byfore hym that created us.'

236.—An important group of people at a time when the Penny Post had not yet been invented, were the MESSENGERS or ' Pursuyvauntis ' as Barclay calls them.  Their negligence and carelessness must often have annoyed people even less punctilious than Sebastian Brant, who devotes chapter 80 to their ' folly.'

> Our Ship must have a messenger, he says.  And our foolish messenger must carry his letter in his mouth to prevent it from becoming wet ; he must walk very slowly and bring messages other than he has been told or forget them entirely through drunkenness. / He must meet as many people and spend as much money as possible ; he must try to find out the contents of his letters and tell them to every one and after a drinking bout he must come back without a reply (1–21).—Such are our real foolish messengers, who will run after our Ship between Basel and Aix-la-Chapelle, and who will never forget their bottle as a medicine for their dry liver (22–28).—Here the irony stops, and in biblical words the last six lines praise a good and faithful messenger (29–34).

Locher has turned the irony of lines 1–21 into the usual form of a complaint, and the second part (where he has of course dropped the names) is put between the biblical words of the conclusion.

So the difference between the translators and the original should not be a real but a literary one.  It is only the liveliness that is gone, so that the chapter conforms better to the monotony of the rest.  As such it appears both in French and in English.

Barclay's best description is in Stanza 1179 :

> They range about to eche alehouse and taverne,
> With the swete wyne theyr great hete to asswage
> Till he be brought into the dronken rage.

Such niceties as a transition from the plural into the singular, or from the third person into the second or reversely, we cannot notice, for they occur regularly in every chapter.  It is in pithy proverbial sayings that Barclay shows his strength, as when he describes the ' folysshe messangers ' :

> (1182)   More tendynge to theyr botell full of ale or wyne
> Than to theyr message, for this is provyd playne
> That : sende a fole forth and so comys he agayne.

No need to observe that the ale is English ale, and that the last line is quite original, as is the conclusion :

> (1183)           But we dayly proved se
>        That wyse wyll do wysely and folys as they be !

The Envoy seriously exhorts the messengers to be careful, steady, diligent, true and secret, and then the humorist suddenly pushes the preacher aside :

> (1184)   If ye do nat, I, Barclay, shall certayne
> For eche of you my folys lyveray dres,
> That is a hode to kepe you from the rayne !

237.—Drouyn has cut out much of Riviere's verbosity, and Watson in his turn abbreviates his French model. On the whole he does it rather skilfully so that no absurdities result from it. Some of Riviere's amplifications appear in a shortened but quite intelligible form :

They be longe in gyvynge of theyr letres, and is nothynge expedyent, the whiche causeth somtyme infynyte dommage, they to whome the lettres hathe be gyven can not make no dylygence, for the delayenge that hathe ben made. . . . And yf they go on message in somer they do nothynge but slepe, and hasteth them not.

Riviere adds quite a long passage about political ambassadors but Drouyn has almost entirely omitted it. So that in English we find only one sentence which by some oversight has been turned upside down : ' These imploratours or embassatours be not somoned to our shyp.' And then to think that Riviere had reserved a prominent place for them ! Even a political man such as Drouyn had said that they ' ne sont point exemps destre en nostre navire.'—Political considerations can hardly have influenced poor Watson ; he had probably not taken time to consider the meaning of ' exemps.'

238.—COOKS AND BUTLERS never go out of fashion, and are always a favourite subject for complaint. Brant expresses it in his lightest manner in chapter 81. He introduces them speaking in their own name :

Keller und köch, medge, eehalt, knecht,

we wanted to send a drunken messenger before, but he has suddenly disappeared, and so we arrive without being announced (1–11). We prepare rich dinners without scruple, because it is not we that have to pay for them. Especially when our master has left the house, we have a good time of it with our friends (12–20). And when he is asleep we tap the largest barrels of his best wine, and when we finally go to bed we put on two pair of socks not to awake him ; and if he hears something creak he thinks it is the cat! (20–29). But when after some days he goes down into the cellar, the barrel is almost empty and

So macht der zappf dann glunck glunck (29–36).

We prepare his dishes in so many different ways and season them so strongly, that they make him sick, and he must make use of a purgative or a clyster! (36–46).—We never forget ourselves but take the best of everything. For we know we have a bad reputation, and even though we were starved to death, people would say we had died from extravagance (46–52). The butler gives wine to the cook, and the cook will broil a sausage for the butler. He is accustomed to the fire ; that is why he has no fear of hell (53–58). Cooks and butlers are busy fools (59–61).

There are three more lines to fill the page, but the meaning is very obscure :—Joseph was adopted by the prince of cooks and Babuzardan took Jerusalem (62–64).[1]

Locher has reduced these sixty-four lines to a single short chapter of thirty-six lines, but with very little of Brant in it. He allows the *cellarii et coqui* only four lines of direct speech, for which he uses lines 12–14 ; he then applies to them the expressions of lines 21–25 and 30–36. The rest is nearly all classical words, words, words, with some vague reminiscences of the German original. And though he solemnly

[1] The reference is of course to Gen. xl and 4 Kings xxv ; but the first quotation is biblically wrong, and the second has nothing to do with the contents of this chapter.

declares : *sordida gesta cano*, he has really made a muddle of it.　His greatest absurdity is in the last two lines, which must be meant as an echo of lines 51–52 :

> Inde fame si quis coquus aut cellarius unquam
> Deperit : at crapula dicitur usque mori.

Here his translation is almost on a level with the work of bunglers such as Drouyn or Watson.

239.—Barclay has considerably improved upon Locher's work.　The short passage in which the cooks and butlers speak for themselves has almost become a convivial song of boon companions :

> (1187)　Be mery, companions, and lusty of cowrage,
> We have our pleasour in deynty mete and drynke,
> On whiche thynge only we alway muse and thynke.

> (1188)　Ete we and drynke we therfore without all care,
> With revyll without mesure as longe as we may !
> It is a royall thynge thus lustely to fare
> With others mete !　Thus revell we alway !
> Spare not the pot, another shall it pay !
> Whan that is done, spare nat for more to call ;
> He merely slepys the whiche shall pay for all.

He realizes the possibilities that Brant's ideas afford, few though Locher has transmitted of them.

> (1190)　By galons and potels they spende without care
> That whiche theyr lorde for his owne mouth did spare.

They even call in other ' glotons ' :

> (1191)　And strange dronkardys to helpe out theyr vylany,
> By whose helpe they may the vessellis make dry,
> And he that hath way to drynke at eche worde
> Amonge these caytyfs is worshyppyd as a lorde.

In these last lines he must be referring to some typical English drinking bout.　For the competition ' who may drynke best ' occurs also in Stanza 901,[1] and elsewhere (1739).

> He brastyth a glasse or cup at every worde,

is said of the man who rules the board.　The sound of the empty barrel which is in Locher :

> Bombo vasa sonant evacuata gravi,

is at least equalled by Barclay's

> (1193)　The vessyll empty shall yelde nought but : bom, bom !

This is almost as good as Brant's *glunck*.

The ' sordida gesta cano ' becomes a little less solemn but more natural in

> (1194)　I thynke it shame to wryte in this my boke
> The great disceyte ; gyle and unclenlynes
> Of any scolyon or any bawdy coke.

---

[1] § 286 ; Stanza 1739, § 297.

Barclay knew but too well that he was not singing ! He did not even want to, and was quite satisfied with preaching. Why should Locher make any higher pretensions ?

The absurdity of the Latin final distich was too obvious to be rendered in English. By a slight alteration the sense could be restored ; Barclay makes that alteration and with a fitting couplet he brings the chapter to a better conclusion :

> (1197)   In every dysshe these caytyfs have theyr handes,
> Gapynge as it were dogges for a bone ;
> Whan nature is content fewe of them understandes,
> In so moche that as I trowe of them is none
> That dye for age, but by glotony echone !
> But suche folys, were nat theyr hasty lokes,
> To my folysshe Shyp sholde chosen be for cokes.

240.—Watson speaks in this chapter of ' cookes ' (cuisiniers), ' caters ' (despensiers) and ' kepers of sellers ' (gardeurs de caves),[1] but to save space he omits parts of his French text. And so we look in vain here for the empty vessel. It was still in Riviere :

> Et le vaisseau frapper se on presse
> Bonbon crie sans fin et sans cesse
> Sa substance sen est allee
> Les servans lont tout avallee.

Drouyn must have felt rather lively paraphrasing this : ' Quant le maistre cuide trouver le bon vin en sa cave il ny a rien et crye le vaisseau, car les serviteurs luy ont tyre loreille.' Here is quite a new idea ! But Watson did not see the fun of it and simply skipped it all. Locher's conclusion is there, but it has become transformed out of all recognition : ' the whiche thynges nouryssheth your bodyes in grese, and kepeth you from longe lyvynge.' Drouyn has added to it, however, two more ideas. One a curious observation, the other a threat.

Ye put pynnes in the hennes hedes, and saythe that they be deed of some sekenes. And after ye ete them in makynge grete chere whan your maysters is on slepe. Kepe you well that in the laste ende ye be not at the table of helle, where as ye shall be served with todes and snakes, with the whiche the poore soulis is fedde ! !

241.—The very next chapter (82) speaks of PEASANTS and is quoted by historians[2] to illustrate the social conditions in Germany so shortly before the ' Peasants' Revolt.'

Not long ago, says Brant, peasants were simple and honest people (1–5), but now they drink wine, and though they earn much, they do not pay their debts nor their rent (6–12). They do not care now for plain coarse clothing, but it must be Leiden or Mechlin cloth, parti-coloured and embroidered, and adorned with fur and showy sleeves (13–18). Country people now set a bad example even to townsfolk, so that all simplicity has disappeared (19–23). They have plenty of money and still they lay in great stores of wine and corn to make them more expensive—until a thunderstorm destroys it all (24–29). There are many others that will over-reach themselves,

---

[1] Among Harman's *Vagabones* we also meet with ' katers, butlers and cooks.'
[2] Janssen-Pastor i, 256 sq.; cf. 384 sqq.

a citizen will be a knight, a knight a count, and a count wants to be a king (30–38). Peasants wear silk and gold, and farmers' wives are dressed like countesses ; riches makes them emulate the state of nobility (39–47). Those women wear more on their body than their whole property is worth, and so they reduce their husbands to poverty (48–59). All people nowadays shamefully try to surpass their own station in life, they all forget their forbears, they are all fools trying to accomplish the impossible (60–65).

This summary gives very little of the proverbial sayings in which this chapter abounds (especially 48–59). It would have served no purpose—for Locher has again refashioned this chapter in his own way. He changes lines 1–5 into a declamation of fourteen lines on the Golden Age. After this he takes his inspiration from lines 13–20 to write ten lines on the excesses of rustic dress and the bad example to townspeople. Then his page is nearly complete, and he fills the rest with reminiscences of lines 23, 24, 30, 31, 60, 61.

242.—The one valuable feature of this ' translation ' is the passage about rustic dress, and this is also what has appealed most to the French and English translators.—The trite generalities about the Golden Age have no interest. But the last stanzas in Barclay form a welcome contribution to peasant literature, of which there is so very little just at this period.[1] They follow Locher very freely, so that they may well be adduced to prove that the social conditions of the peasantry cannot have been very bad towards the end of the reign of Henry VII. One passage is entirely original :

> (1209)    Nowe carles ar nat content with one grange
>                Nor one ferme place, suche is theyr insolence ;
>                They must have many to support theyr expence.

The rest is more or less an echo of the Latin. But the main interest attaches to the passage on rustic excesses of dress. Unfortunately Barclay has not indulged here his inclination to expand, so that we get only one stanza, and in this one stanza, only the second line and the humorous reflection at the end are original.

> (1206)    Theyr clothes stately after the courters gyse,
>                Theyr here out busshynge as a foxis tayle,
>                And all the fassions whiche they can devyse
>                In counterfaytynge they use in aparayll
>                Party and gardyd [2] or short to non avayle
>                So that if God sholde theyr bodyes chaunge
>                After theyr vesture, theyr shape sholde be full strange.

From this description we might infer that the English peasant at that time must have been less guilty of extravagance in dress than of want of taste.

---

[1] P. Meissner, *Der Bauer in der Englischen Literatur* (Bonner Studien xv, 1922).
[2] *Party* renders the Latin *vestes partitas* ; *gardyd* must do duty for three lines in Locher, in which he speaks of *scutula, varius color, fimbria picta*, and *In manicis sculptas externo more figuras*. The word *garded* has the somewhat vague meaning of ' ornamented, as with lace, braid, embroidery,' and the first example given in the NED. dates from this time. Jamieson 341 gives a somewhat arbitrary explanation.

243.—More curious is Riviere's French peasant :

> Et porter ces cheveux enflez
> Crespes com de vent soufflez
> Emplumees leurs folles testes
> Et soit a dimenches ou festes
> Ses robes en facon toutes rondes
> Mesparties a grandes frondes
> Bordee de nouvelle bordure
> Collouree rouge ou verdure
> Et oultre plus bas que les anches
> Ont leurs robes et larges manches
> Et plus que grans sacz plantureuses.

Partly supplemented, partly abbreviated we find Riviere's description in Watson. None of the supplements, however, come from him ; they have been added by Drouyn, and as such they are bracketed in the following quotation :

None dyde were clothynges but after theyr estate. (But at this present tyme the labourers ben garded [1] lyke men of armes.) And brevely all the lyvynge men is so . . . you were heere longe, and busshed, curled and full of vanytees. O foles rustykes ye be federed (lyke pecockes), your gownes is ample with grete sleves half parted and brodred with bandes of dyvers coloures, (ye be at this present tyme more fyne and cautellous [2] than they of good townes).

---

[1] The French has *bigarres* ; the meaning is almost the same.

[2] *Plus fins et cauteleux.* Watson is probably again a slave of the French words; *fin* is ' fine,' and *cauteleux* is ' cautellous ' ; but in the expression *fin et cauteleux* the two words are used as synonyms ; and there is no indication that the English ' fine ' has ever had that meaning.

# XII

## CHAPTERS RELATING TO FOOLISH LEARNING

244.—The first and foremost place in his Ship—chapter 1—Brant has reserved for foolish BOOK-COLLECTORS. One would hardly have expected symptoms of bibliomania at a time when the printing-press was still in its cradle. But here the patients are. One of them speaks for all:

> I am the foremost fool, because I collect a library of books; and without understanding them, I love them dearly and protect them from flies (1–8). When people speak to me about some learned question, I always say: 'I have got all that at home' (9–12). Ptolemaeus considered his great library his greatest treasure, and still remained a pagan (13–17). I have also many books, but I will not read them, lest I should lose my wits and become an idiot (18–22). I can hire another to study for me (23–24). I am content with my German but I know just enough Latin to move freely in learned circles; for I know *vinum, gucklus, stultus,* and I know I am called *domne doctor* (25–32). I cannot see my ears, and I do not know that I am an ass (33–34).

The greater part of this chapter has been turned into Latin very skilfully. The first twenty-four lines can be recognized almost one by one in as many hexameters. There are a couple of additions that have some interest. Whereas the German fool is simply driving off the flies (8), his Latin colleague cleans his books with a feather duster (*plumatis flabellis*), which, in fact, he also wields in the woodcut; and he likes to look at the 'green binding' (*viridi tegmine*) of his books. The last part of the chapter is changed altogether. The Latin fool does not know Latin, and therefore replies 'yes' to all questions, but he is a great man 'Theutonicos inter balbos' (among the stammerers of German—Brant would hardly have used such derogatory words about his native language). The last five lines are a solemn exhortation to the 'Doctores' to look back to the ancients—because the common herd have all asses' ears.

Thus the very last line vaguely echoes Brant's conclusion.

245.—The French version does not add anything of interest to this chapter. The 'flabella' have been paraphrased away [1] and the 'green binding' receives only transitory notice—

> Et en passe mon appetit
> De veoir seullement la verdure
> Dont est taincte la couverture—

---

[1] It seems that only the Marnef-translator has taken note of it, when he speaks of 'celluy grand fol qui est en son estude pleyne de livres bien parez lequel tient une esmouchere ou verge en sa main pour en abatre les pouldres.'

and it has disappeared altogether in prose owing to Drouyn's manipulation. So that in English we get nothing more concrete than this :

> I doo my besy cure for to kepe them honestly frome poudre and dust. I make
> my lectrons and my deskes [the two words stand for the French pulpyctres] clene
> ryght often. My mansyon is all replynysshed [1] with bokes. I solace me ryght
> often for to se them open without ony thynge compylynge out of them. . . . It sholde
> be grete foly to me to applye by excessyve study myne understandynge (unto so
> many dyvers thynges, where through I myghte lese my sensuall intellygence), for
> he that procureth too knowe over moche and occupyeth hymself by excessyve
> studye, is in daunger for to be extraught from hymself [destre incense]. Also every-
> chone is dyspensed, be he a clerke [Fr. bien lettre] or understande he nothynge yet
> he bereth the name of a lorde.

The ' dyspensed ' hangs somewhat in the air, but this is Drouyn's
fault, not Watson's. In Riviere it was still one whole sentence :

> Aussi bien est dispense
> Soit bien lettre scavant ou non
> De porter de seigneur le nom.

246.—Barclay's version is rather more interesting and the whole
of it has been quoted as the best description in English of Bibliomania
in the Middle Ages.[2] No wonder. His College must have possessed
a considerable library,[3] and as according to the instructions of its founder
the ' capellanus beatae Mariae habeat curam et custodiam librorum '[4]
the librarian was presumably none other than our Author.

He pays no special attention to the ' flabellum.' His fool is only
' Savynge them from fylth and ordure by often brusshynge ' (36) ; nor
does the ' green binding ' appeal to him. He simplifies it into a ' fayre
coverynge ' (39), but elsewhere he gives us something much better of his
own accord :

> (36)    Full goodly bounde in pleasaunt coverture
>         Of domas,[5] satyn, or els of velvet pure.

*Domas* or *damas*, or as we should say *damask*, though now used to denote
a sort of linen, originally meant a rich silk fabric.[6] And indeed silk,
satin and velvet are known to have been very often used for costly
bindings in England at that time ;[7] velvet especially, though rarely
used in France and still more rarely in Germany, was in great favour
in England among the wealthier book-collectors. Examples still exist
that were made in the fifteenth century for Henry VII, whose library
was in all probability entirely bound in this material.[8] And the favourite
colour was not green but red.[9]

---

[1] The 1517 edition has *repylnysshed*, but this is an obvious misprint.
[2] F. S. Merryweather, Bibliomania in the Middle Ages (London 1849), p. 204 sqq.
[3] G. Oliver, Monasticon Diocesis Exoniensis (Exeter 1846) 261. Various dona-
tions and bequests of books are mentioned.
[4] See the letter of foundation in G. Oliver l.c. p. 265 ; cf. § 346.
[5] Cawood prints *damas*.                 [6] See NED.
[7] C. Davenport, The Book, its History and Development (1907), 148.
[8] C. Davenport l.c. p. 149.
[9] In the Wardrobe Accounts of Edward IV in 1480, entries show that the bindings were in ' cremysy velvet figured.'—W. Y. Fletcher, English Book Collectors
(1902) 2. Thomas Berthelet, Pynson's successor as royal printer and binder, supplied to Henry VIII a ' Psalter . . . covered with crimoysyn satyne.'—W. Y.
Fletcher on English Book-bindings in *Some Minor Arts practised in England* (1894) 12.

Barclay had an eye for detail ! But at the same time he satirizes all such costly bindings.   It is his ' fool ' who collects them and preserves them carefully :

> (36)  I kepe them sure, ferynge lyst they sholde be lost,
>         For in them is the connynge wherein I me bost.

Barclay himself would most probably have none of them.   He preferred a more solid material for practical use, and then of course he took his good English brown goat or sheep skin.[1]

247.—Barclay throws in four stanzas that have very little to do with bibliomania, and whose insertion is only partly justified by the context, but they are all the more valuable for it.    The first particularly on account of its proverbial character :

> (41)  Eche is nat lettred that nowe is made a lorde,
>         Nor eche a clerke that hath a benefyce ;
>         They are not all lawyers that plees doth recorde ;
>         All that are promotyed are nat fully wyse.
>         On suche chaunce nowe Fortune throwys hir dyce,
>         That thoughe one knowe but the Yresshe game,[2]
>         Yet wolde he have  a gentyllmannys name.

The other three stanzas fall under the category of ecclesiastical chapters, because they mention various vices of the clergy :  love of pleasure, avarice, ignorance, flattery of the nobility.   In the beginning of the first stanza the book-fool is still supposed to be speaking, but gradually Barclay seems to forget his puppet, and we hear him vent his own feelings—somewhat in the tone of personal animosity.

> (43)  I am lyke other clerkes whiche so frowardly them gyde,
>         That after they ar onys come unto promocion,
>         They gyve them to plesour, theyr stody set asyde,
>         Theyr avaryce coverynge with fayned devocion ;
>         Yet dayly they preche and have great derysyon
>         Against the rude laymen, and al for covetyse,
>         Though theyr owne conscience be blynded with that vyce.

Surely our honest chaplain is making exaggerated statements here. If it were only for the ' dayly they preche,' it is evident that this is not the language of dispassionate objectivity.   The ' clerkes ' described cannot be expected to have done more than their duty, and if they preached once a week they had fulfilled their obligations.[3]  If his reproaches remained equally vague and impersonal they would not hurt anyone.   But he does seem to have some individual clergyman in view and to cherish a personal grudge :

> (44)  But if I durst trouth playnely utter and expresse,
>         This is the special cause of this inconvenience :
>         That gretest foles and fullest of lewdnes,
>         Havynge least wyt and symplest science,
>         Ar fyrst promoted and have greatest reverence ;
>         For if one can flater and bere a hawke on his fyst,
>         He shal be made Person of Honyngton or of Clyst.

---

[1] C. Davenport, Thomas Berthelet (Chicago 1901) 13.
[2] A sort of backgammon.   See NED. s.v. Irish.
[3] F. A. Gasquet, The Eve of the Reformation (1900) 282 sqq.

On the river Clyst in the neighbourhood of Ottery there were several little benefices bearing the same name. Six of them are known : Clyst-St. Michael, Clyst-Hydon, Clyst-St. Gabriel, Clyst-St. George, Clyst-St. Laurence, and Clyst-St. Mary,[1] and so it is difficult to know which of them is meant. There can be no misunderstanding the other name. Honiton is known to have been a good living in the district, and Sir William Courtenay Knt. was its patron, and the incumbent from 1505 till 1517 was the Rev. Henry Ferman or Feyrman.[2] This priest, therefore, is the object of Barclay's indignation—or envy. It is clear from his words that this successful rival must have been out hawking with his patron, Sir William, and that Barclay considered himself more worthy and more learned. But we can hardly infer more from his words, although he does not hesitate to place the Rev. H. Ferman among the ' gretest foles and fullest of lewdnes.'

It is a pity that no more details about the biography of this ' fool ' are known. As there is doubtless some personal disappointment lurking in this stanza, we may see Barclay's own self-portrait, idealized no doubt, in the following stanza :

> (45)  But he that is in stody ay ferme and diligent
> And without al favour prechyth Chrystys lore,
> Of al the comontye nowe adayes is sore shent,
> And by Estates thretened to pryson oft therfore.

This must have been written in a fit of despondency, when he fancied himself a very unpopular man. But his own lively language proves that he can never have been the morose grumbler he here pretends to be ! He cannot have been quite serious about it. Else he would never have added

> (45)  Thus what avayle is it to us to stody more,
> To knowe outher Scripture, trouth, wysedom or vertue,
> Syns fewe or none without favour dare them shewe.

For many years to come Barclay is to go on translating one work after another. It would not be surprising if after all it should appear that, even while writing these stanzas, he was on the most friendly terms with the Parsons of Clyst and Honiton !

248.—Chapter 27 is a short but very important one on USELESS STUDY.

It opens with a common complaint. Students are fools, and their wide gowns with trailing tassels may well serve as a fool's costume. For they waste their time in rioting ; they don't care for real knowledge but only for useless trifles (1–9). But the masters themselves—and here the chapter rises to the value of a document in the history of education—do not understand the value of real knowledge, they rather indulge in barren chatterings about which was first, day or night ; whether

---

[1] F. C. Hingeston-Randolph, The Register of Edmund Lacy, Bishop of Exeter (1420–1455) (1909), Index, p. 404.

[2] G. Oliver, Ecclesiastical Antiquities of Devon ii (Exeter 1840), 77. A. Farquharson, The History of Honiton (Exeter 1868), says Ferman was appointed by Sir John Kirkham and E. Hardinge as one of the original trustees of Allhallows Charity. As he quotes no other authority than Oliver, however, I have hesitated to adopt this reading.

a man has made an ass ; whether Sortes[1] or Plato ran (10–15). That is the wisdom schools sell nowadays. Are they not fools, torturing themselves and their pupils, and not appreciating real learning (16–20) ? Origen[2] rightly compared them to the frogs and gnats that tormented Egypt (21–24). Thus we pass our youth. We go to Leipzig, Erfurt, Vienna, Heidelberg, Mainz and Basel,[3] and come home with disgrace (25–28), and when all our money is spent we are glad to get a situation in a printing office or a wine-cellar ! We then live on as boon-companions, and the student's hood has become a complete fool's cap (29–34).

Locher's version of this chapter is perhaps even more interesting than the original. Only it is not a translation, except to some extent the introduction about idle students. Instead of lines 10–15 Locher gives his own ideas. People, he says, are now always studying trivial grammars. They despise the fine volumes of Priscian's Grammar[4] which has been badly mauled by Alexander Gallus.[5] With words and garrulous syllogisms they try to solve the knots of Logic.[6] They give endless silly examples like : *Sortes clamat, Plato stat.* Thus Logic makes difficulties instead of solving them, and clear things become obscure by these wordy principles of Logic, which are repeated continually like the croaking of frogs.[7]—After this Locher takes the passage from lines 25–28 but altering some of the names. He mentions : Vienna, ' great ' Erfurt, Basel, the ' barbarous town ' of Leipzig, places beyond the sea, Spain, France and the ' great walls ' of Rome.—Finally, instead of the last six lines he says only ' pro stultoque respondere studente Possunt,[8] ' and that they wear their proud hoods, but have spent their youth in vain.

249.—We must refrain from comment until we have heard Barclay's version of this chapter, for which he has certainly not consulted Riviere, but which deserves being studied in detail. He summons to his Ship the Students

> (417)   Of this our royalme and from beyond the see.

He simplifies the long trailing garments mentioned by Locher (and Brant) to

> (417)   With theyr proud hodes on theyr neckes hangynge.

Was the Oxford or Cambridge full dress different from that used on the Continent ? But even on the Continent the *magna caputia* were the

---

[1] An abbreviation of the name *Socrates* very common in medieval hand-books. See below.

[2] The quotation is not directly taken from Origen, but from the Decretum Gratiani, Zarncke 356 sq. By gnats are means the *ciniphes*, mentioned in Exod. viii 16 sqq. and Ps. civ 31.

[3] These are the principal German Universities with which Brant was acquainted. But he omits Cologne and Tübingen, Zarncke l.c.

[4] He speaks of ' Grammatices Priscae sincera volumina,' but I suppose he only means Priscian.

[5] This I take it is the sense of ' Cuius Alexander gallus praecordia turbat.'

[6] We shall presently hear a better translation from Barclay ; I am endeavouring to state the ideas as simply as possible.

[7] The ' frogs ' are here introduced in a sense quite different from that of Brant. Still the margin gives the reference to the Decretum Gratiani from which Brant had taken his quotation. The passage is quite characteristic for Locher's attitude towards scholasticism.—Hehle ii, 26.

[8] The text really has *Possint*, but this seems a printer's error.

most conspicuous part of that dress, and the one specially ridiculed by the Humanists.[1]

Instead of simply ' in plateis,' the English students

> (419)     wander in every inconvenyence
> From strete to strete, from taverne to taverne.

On the study of Grammar and Logic we get more detailed information than from Locher, so that now the chapter gets its full educational interest :

> (421)     But most I marveyll of other folys blynde,
> Whiche in dyvers scyencis ar fast laborynge
> Both daye and nyght with all theyr herte and mynde,
> But of Gramer knowe they lytyll or no thynge,
> Whiche is the grounde of all lyberall cunnynge ;
> Yet many ar besy in Logyke and in Lawe,
> Whan all theyr Gramer is skarsly worth a strawe.

Here we have the first humanistic objection against the old school clearly stated. They do not study Grammar enough, although theoretically Grammar had always been the portal of all the Liberal arts.[2] They study day and night ' in dyvers scyencis,' they are busy ' in Logyke and in Lawe,' but the New School despises their labours because their Grammar ' is skarsly worth a strawe.'—Sound doctrine in bad Grammar was impossible ! It is mainly on this assumption that the ' Viri obscuri ' could bury their adversaries under their ridicule.

> 250.—(422)     If he have onys red the olde Dotrinall
> With his diffuse and unparfyte brevyte,
> He thynketh to have sene the poyntis of Grammar all ;
> And yet of one errour he maketh two or thre ;
> Precyan or Sulpice disdayneth he to se.
> Thus many whiche say that they theyr Grammar can,
> Ar als great folys as whan they firste began.

The old and the new jostle each other in this stanza. Priscian was a contemporary of Boethius and wrote his *Institutiones grammaticae* somewhere about 500. This work was in such favour during the Middle Ages that there are about a thousand Manuscripts still in existence. Since the thirteenth century it was, however, gradually supplanted by the work of Alexander de Ville-Dieu,[3] also known as Alexander Gallus or Alexander Grammaticus. The *Doctrinale Puerorum*, though meant to be an introduction to the *Institutiones*, became a rival, carried the day, and made the old work fall into oblivion. Grammar got largely merged into Logic.[4] Even the Universities, such as Paris[5] and Oxford,[6]

---

[1] Cf. Epistolae Obscurorum Virorum, ed. Ed. Böcking, Ulrichi Hutteni Equitis Operum Supplementum (Lipsiae 1864) i, 5 : ' magna caputia cum liripipiis ' ; p. 39 : ' Est autem habitus magistrorum nostrorum, sicut scitis, caputium magnum cum liripipio.'

[2] J. E. Sandys, History of Classical Scholarship i[3] (1921), 670.

[3] Sometimes, but without sufficient reason, called a Franciscan Friar.

[4] E. Norden, Die antike Kunstprosa ii[3] (1918), 721.

[5] H. Denifle-Chatelain, Chartularium Universitatis Parisiensis iii, 145.

[6] H. Rashdall, The Universities of Europe in the Middle Ages (1895) ii[2], 603 ; Lupton 38. Cambridge did not follow suit until 1480 (Mullinger i, 515).

though long clinging to their old Priscian, felt themselves obliged in the fourteenth century to introduce Alexander in his stead.  The *Doctrinale* remained the favourite handbook down to the time of the Humanists. Its modern editor [1] has described about two hundred and fifty MSS. and more than two hundred and sixty early impressions.  But towards the end of the fifteenth century there came a change, as all things human change.  The Italian Grammarians opened the attack, and one of the first among them was Giovanni Sulpizio from Veroli in the Roman Campagna,[2] himself author of an *Opus Grammaticum* which appeared in Rome before 1480.  After that new Grammars appeared by scores, but Sulpitius, Alexander and Priscian remained the outstanding names. For from the reaction against Alexander the old Priscian was restored to favour again.—The German Humanists of Brant's circle took up an attitude of compromise.  They did not condemn the *Doctrinale* so much as the thick layer of commentaries that had gradually settled upon it. Louis Dringenberg retained it in his famous school of Schlettstadt.[3] Wimpheling would not have it despised and meant his epoch-making *Isidoneus*, printed in 1497, to be a faithful interpretation of Alexander's principles.[4]

So we can understand that we do not find a word of disapprobation in the German version of chapter 27.  But Locher had studied in Italy and probably never felt much sympathy for the grammatical ideas of his master.[5]  That is why he mentioned Alexander Gallus as a disturber of the old classical Grammar.

In Barclay we get the view of an English pupil of the Humanists. The conflict of opinion was as strong in England as elsewhere.  The first master of Magdalen School, John Anwykyll, advocated an innovation of grammatical teaching, and was probably the author of the *Compendium totius Grammaticae*, printed at Oxford about 1483.[6]  But the very first printed book issued by Pynson's press in 1492 was again the *Doctrinale* [7] and there was so much demand for it that it was reprinted even after 1500, e.g. by Wynkyn de Worde about 1503, and by Pynson himself in 1505, 1513 and 1516.  The 1516 edition was, however, the last that ever appeared in England.[8]  Sulpitius had become a competitor, and was printed by Pynson in 1494 and 1498, and by Wynkyn de Worde

---

[1] D. Reichling, Das Doctrinale des Alexander de Villa Dei in Monumenta Germaniae Paedagogica xii (1893) ; see p. cxxi sqq., clxix sqq.

[2] D. Reichling l.c. p. lxxxv.

[3] Renaudet 422.

[4] J. Knepper, Jakob Wimpfeling 74 sqq.; cf. E. Norden, Die Antike Kunstprosa ii [3] (1918), 712.

[5] He is also said to have written a *Grammatica nova* of his own (Zapf 61 ; Hehle i, 20), but the work must be lost.  We have only his *Epitome Rhetorices* of the year 1496 (Zapf 62 ; Hehle i, 20).

[6] E. G. Duff 28.  What Lupton (23) writes about John Holt's *Lac Puerorum* as the earliest Latin Grammar in England must be a mistake.  The Brit. Museum Catal. of Early Engl. Books (1884) ii, 827 ascribes it to the year 1520.

[7] E. G. Duff 23 ; also Oxford n.d. and Pynson 1498 (Duff 22, 24).  Latin works for English consumption were, however, mostly printed on the Continent, so that probably thousands of copies came to England from Badius' press.  See Badius' edd. in Ph. Renouard i, 119.

[8] D. Reichling l.c.

in 1499, 1504, 1511, 1512, 1514, 1527.[1] No wonder! Sulpitius stood in high favour in Paris where Badius Ascensius issued one edition after the other,[2] and William Lily had personally attended Sulpitius' lectures.[3] —Barclay did not think much of Alexander's 'diffuse and unparfyte brevyte,' a judgment that sounds like the 'tedious brief scene' in A Midsummer Night's Dream.[4] He criticizes his fools for not honouring Priscian enough, and on the same level with Priscian there stood Sulpitius!

Poor Barclay! His great Sulpitius' fame was more short-lived than that of any of his rivals. Within less than a year after the publication of the Ship of Fools, Colet, Lily and Erasmus wrote a new Grammar for Colet's St. Paul's School,[5] and this new authority swept all the others away. Before the end of the century it was made compulsory throughout England, and has even survived, after further emendation, until the present day under the name of the *Eton Latin Grammar*.[6]

251.—Not only on the study of Grammar, but also on that of Logic, Barclay has his own opinions. The first four lines are paraphrased from Locher, with a very good sharpening of the metaphor in the beginning: the rest is all his own:

> (423) One with his speche rounde tournynge lyke a whyle [7]
> Of Logyke the knottis doth lows and undo
> In hande with his Sylogysimes, and yet doth he fele
> No thynge what it menyth nor what longeth therto.
> Nowe *Sortes currit*, now is in hande *Plato*,
> Another comyth in with *bocardo* and *pheryson*
> And out goeth agayne a fole in conclusyon.

> (424) There is nought else but *est* and *non est*,
> Blaberynge and chydynge as it were beawlys wyse [8];
> They argue nought els but to prove man a beest!
> *Homo est asinus* is cause of moche stryf!
> Thus passe forth these folys the dayes of theyr lyfe
> In two syllabis, not gyvynge advertence
> To other cunnynge, doctryne, nor scyence.

Here are some interesting allusions. Barclay is said to have studied in Paris University at some date between 1490 and 1500. Besides the circle of the Humanists, two schools of Scholastic Philosophy were represented there, called the Ancients and the Moderns. The Ancients

---

[1] E. G. Duff, n. 388-390; Westminster and London Printers 133; Renouard ii, 262 sqq.  [2] Renouard l.c.
[3] J. E. Sandys, A History of Classical Scholarship ii (1908), 229.
[4] I should add that on the margin he annotates: 'Sulpicius in Alexandrum. Est brevis ille nimis, fuscus et ille nimis.'
[5] F. Seebohm, The Oxford Reformers [3] (1887), 216. Shakespeare quotes from Lily's Grammar in *Twelfth Night* II, 3.  [6] Cambridge History of Lit. iii, 11.
[7] A striking spelling for ME. whele (wheel). Does Barclay recognize the sound change? And is the rhyme *whyle* : *fele* a symptom of the conflict between traditional spelling and new sound?
[8] I do not know what is meant by 'beawlys wyse.' I suspect a misprint of the word *baylys*, a form that occurs in Stanza 173, where Cawood (1570) has altered it into *bayliffes*. Jamieson explains *beawlys* by 'roaring out,' probably connecting the word with MnE. *to bawl*. This etymology, however, seems impossible, not only on account of the meaning (see NED.) but also because no substantival form from *bawl* is known.

or Realists upheld the traditions of St. Thomas and Scotus, the Moderns, also called Nominalists or Terminists, derived their inspiration mainly from William of Ockam and John Buridan. Since John Heynlin had left the University, Thomism had lost its strongest supporter and seemed powerless,[1] so that practically the two opposing parties were that of the Scotists and that of the Nominalists. Their protagonists were respectively Pierre Tateret or Tartaret[2] and Thomas Bricot;[3] these two were certainly the most prominent men in Scholastic philosophy during the last decennium of the fifteenth century.[4] It is probably their works, and perhaps their lectures that Barclay is satirizing here. Some quotations from their books may prove—not that Barclay was hitting the mark, but that he was aiming at it.

In Tartaret's *Commentationes in Libros Logicae Aristotelis*, published in 1494,[5] he may have read the following :

Propositiones de impossibili in quibus nulla ponitur negatio convertuntur per conversales negative ex parte modi. Ut ista. Omnem hominem impossibile est esse asinum. Si convertitur : ergo omnem asinum impossibile est esse hominem. Secundum dictum. Propositiones de impossibili in quibus negatio ponitur ad modum tantum convertuntur sicut illae de possibili quibus equivalent. Ut ista. Hominem non impossibile est esse asinum, convertitur sicut ista : hominem possibile est esse asinum. Sic videlicet asinum non impossibile est esse hominem, *etc. etc.*

In the same year 1494 Tartaret had another work of his printed, viz. his *Explanationes Summularum Petri de Hispania*[6] 'secundum subtilissimi doctoris Scoti doctrinam ac conformiter ad mentem Stephani Pruliferi[7] fidelissimi Scoti interpretis doctoris theologi ordinis minorum.' Here occur some passages that are perhaps even more to the point. Among the examples are : 'Sortem non possibile est non currere. Sortem non contingens est non currere. Sortem impossibile est non currere. Sortem necesse est currere,' *etc. etc.* And when explaining the laws of a good Syllogism he gives as an example of a bad one : 'Utrumque animal est asinus ; uterque homo est animal, ergo uterque homo est asinus,' and he adds the reason : 'Dicitur quod non est in *barbara*[8] cum subiectum maioris non distribuat distributione complexa et perfecta,' *etc. etc.*

We can sympathize with poor Barclay listening to all this, and quite naturally sighing : 'They argue nought els but to prove man a beest ! '

But the other school could not have been any more to his taste. In 1493 Thomas Bricot had printed his Commentary on the Philosophy

---

[1] Renaudet 94 sq., 247.    [2] Renaudet 247.    [3] Renaudet 96.

[4] John Mair, the Scotchman (see Renaudet 269, 308, 311), who afterwards became the principal nominalistic philosopher and theologian, published the first-fruits of his labours only in 1503 (Renaudet 404).

[5] British Museum I.B. 14218 (described BMC. 695 ; Hain * 15337), sign. L iii.

[6] British Museum I.B. 14216 (see BMC. 695 ; Hain * 15334 ; and cf. Renaudet 95 note 4). My quotations occur under sign. C and D iii.

[7] Brulefer had been the most famous Scotist of Paris before 1490, when he left France to go to Germany. A few years afterwards he was offered a chair in the University of Toledo. But he died in his native Brittany in 1499 (Renaudet 95, 260, 370).

[8] See next section.

of Aristotle ' secundum viam Modernorum ac secundum cursum magistri Georgii.' [1]

It was reprinted several times in Paris, Lyon, Basel, and Venice.[2] I quote from the 1496 edition, published at Friburg,[3] but as the work is a heavy folio-volume in two columns and small print, and full of abbreviations, I may be forgiven for having looked only at the last page. It is quite sufficient, however, for our purpose.

Manifestum est autem quod hominem esse animal, et hominem esse asinum sunt distincta enunciabilia, quia distinctis orationibus sunt significabilia. . . . Item hominem esse asinum est impossibile, quia hominem esse non est hominem esse asinum . . . ergo homo non est hominem esse et hominem esse asinum. Ultra hominem esse non est hominem esse asinum. . . . Ut omnis homo currit, ergo sortes currit, tenet in virtute istius cathegoricae sortes esse homo, et ad eam non sufficeret conditionale . . . bene sequitur nullus existens currit, ergo sortes non currit. . . . Sortes currit, ergo aliquod existens currit.

This is the last line of the book, which ends here with ' Finit feliciter metaphysica.' I am afraid that many a reader will feel like Barclay's fool :

> tournynge like a whyle . . .
> and yet doth he fele
> No thynge what it menyth nor what longeth therto . . .
> There is nought else but *est* and *non est*.[4]

252.—The *bocardo* and *pheryson* of Stanza 423 are still to be found in every modern hand-book of Scholastic philosophy.[5] They belong to a set of mnemonic made-up words formed to impress upon the memory the nineteen valid moods of a syllogism. As their form has been changed more or less in course of time, they may be quoted here from a handbook which Barclay must have used in some edition or other, namely from the then widely circulating *Summulae logicales* or *Tractatus Petri Hispani*,[6] of which the British Museum has ten editions and Hain-

---

[1] About George of Brussels, although called 'nominalium interpres acutissimus,' we know almost nothing.—Renaudet 97.

[2] Hain 3967, 3968, 3969, 3973, 3974, 3975, 3976.

[3] Brit. Mus. I.B. 14211 (BMC. 696 ; Hain * 3975).

[4] Barclay was at the same time thinking of Virgil, for on the margin he annotates : ' Virgilius. *est* et *non*, cuncti monosyllaba nota frequentant *etc*. His demptis nihil est hominum quod sermo volitet. Qualis vita hominum quam duo monosyllaba versant *etc*. Virgilius.'

[5] The mnemonic lines are e.g. in G. H. Joyce, Principles of Logic [2] (1916), 180, with full explanation ; also in P. Coffey, The Science of Logic i[2] (1918) ; Reinstadler, Elem. Philos. Scholast., i (1911), 94, who calls them 'admodum subtilia et usu spectata, fere nullius momenti, attamen . . non aspernanda.'

[6] Petrus Hispanus is no other than John XXI, who was Pope from 1276 to 1277. He was not the inventor, however, as they occur already in a Commentary of Psellus' Compendium written by William Shyreswood, who is recorded by Le Neve as treasurer of Ailesbury Lincoln in 1258 and 1267, and who is praised by Roger Bacon as greater than Albertus Magnus and without equal in common philosophy (see DNB.). C. Prantl, Geschichte der Logik im Abendlande iii (Leipzig 1867), 10 sqq., quotes the work from a Parisian MS. (Cod. Sorbonne 1797), and the mnemonic verses occur in it just as given above (except only that in the third line it has *campestres* instead of *camestres*), introduced, however, in such a way—' Modi autem et eorum reductiones retinentur his versibus'—that Prantl thinks Shyreswood cannot possibly be the first inventor. F. Bon. Kruitwagen calls my attention to the fact that the words in each line must originally have been placed in alphabetical order. This observation may, perhaps, one day lead to the discovery of the first source. Prantl's suggestion of a Greek origin does not seem very likely.

Copinger mentions more than a dozen others, all belonging to the fifteenth century.  In the edition of Basel ± 1485 [1] the mnemonic lines occur about the middle of the *Quartus Tractatus* :

> Barbara celarent darii ferio baralipton
> Celantes dabitis fapesmo frisesomorum
> Cesare camestres festino baroco darapti
> Felapton disamis darisi bocardo ferison.

In these words every vowel and nearly every consonant signifies something ; they have been called ' magic words . . . more full of meaning than any that ever were made.' [2]  But what was that to a Humanist ? What to a poet like Barclay ?

> Another comyth in with *bocardo* and *pheryson*
> And out goeth agayne a fole in conclusyon !

That is what he thought of it.  And many other Humanists thought the same.[3]

253.—But Barclay is not quite a Humanist of Locher's stamp. Locher condemns Logic unconditionally:

> Ars logicae falso nodos et retia cauta
> Nectit, et explicitum tenebras deducit in atras.

This was too sweeping an exaggeration for the English moralist, and he tones it down by saying the opposite first :

> (425)    I wyll nat say but that it is expedyent
> The to knowe of Logyke the chrafte and connynge,
> For by argument it maketh evydent
> Moche obscureness, somtyme enlumynynge
> The mynde and sharpynge the wyt in many a thynge ;
> But oft yet by it a thynge playne, bryght and pure
> Is made diffuse, unknowen, harde and obscure.

Thus he manages to maintain his equilibrium.  He uses the same caution again in his Envoy.

---

[1] BMC. 761 (cf. p. 272).   In the edition Cologne 1499 (BMC. 291) they are separated from each other.

[2] De Morgan, quoted by J. N. Keynes, Studies and Exercises in Formal Logic (2nd ed. 1887), 215.

[3] See Epistolae Obscur. Virorum (ed. Böcking, Lipsiae 1864), p. 203.  ' Bartholomeus Kuckuck ' writes to Ortuinus :  ' Et credo quod non scit unum punctum in libris sententiarum.  Nec ipse posset mihi formare unum Syllogismum in *Baroco* et *Celarent* quia non est logicus ' ; and ' William Stork of Deventer ' rhymes on Jacob de Hochstrat :

> Tandem fuit graduatus, et in Theologia qualificatus ;
> Quia ibi subtiliter disputavit, et multos sillogismos formavit
> In *Baroco* et *Celarent*, ita ut omnes admirarent (ib. p. 228).

—The editor quotes as books where the lines are to be found ' Hieron. Savonarola, Compend. Logices, Venet. 1534 ; Georgii Trapezunti de re dialect. libel. c. scholiis Joa. Noviomagi, Colon. 1545 ; Joa. Caesarii dialectica, Lugd. 1556 ; Melanchton, Dialectica, Wittenb. 1520.'  As they occur in every treatise on Logic, the list could easily be extended to a long catalogue.  One of the best known is George Reisch, Margarita Philosophica (ed. 1496, 1503, 1508, 1512, 1535), in the last edition on p. 166 sqq. (divided).

> (435)   Leve of suche stody as is unprofytable
>         Without fruyte outher godly discyplyne,
>         And gyve your myndes to scyences lawdable,
>         Where ye may your herte set and inclyne :
>         To Arystotyls or Platoys doctryne,
>         And nat alway on Logyke or Sophestrye.
>         I wyll nat say but it is a thynge dyvyne
>         And moche worth, to knowe Phylosophy.

The last two very lame and tame lines are characteristic of his own hesitation.—If we were sure, however, that Barclay had studied in the University of Paris, this stanza might be adduced to prove that he had attended the lectures of Jacques Lefèvre d'Etaples after 1494, or of Aegidius van Delft a little before that time.—But this is not the place to discuss the matter more in detail.[1]

254.—We have not yet heard Barclay's version of the second important part of Locher's chapter, that referring to the Universities. There again the English standpoint is brought out distinctly :

> (428)   One rennyth to Almayne, another unto Fraunce,
>         To Parys, Padway, Lumbardy or Spayne,
>         Another to Bonony, Rome or Orleance,
>         To Cayne, to Tolows, Athenys or Colayne,
>         And at the last retournyth home agayne
>         More ignorant, blynder and gretter folys,
>         Than they were whan they firste went to the scolys.

Spain is probably inserted only because Locher had added the ' gentes Iberas ' ; and there were three names in the Latin to represent ' Almayne.' Most of the Universities mentioned are those usually visited by English students.[2] Padua and Bologna and Rome in Italy ; Paris, Orleans, Toulouse in France. The Englishman could not forget the University of Caen, founded by his own countrymen after the fall of St. Joan of Arc, and, although it had been completely gallicised since the middle of the century,[3] it is just possible that shortly after 1500 some English students went there, as they certainly did a little afterwards.[4]—Athens is probably only a classical reminiscence. It had been in the hands of the Turks for over fifty years, and of course there was no University.—The mention of Cologne is remarkable. It is the only German University referred to by Barclay, and just one that had been omitted by Brant. The name had even to be refashioned to

---

[1] See Renaudet 129 sqq., 145 sqq. I need hardly add that Humanistic circles were not the only opponents of far-fetched scholastic subtleties. There is something ironical in the fact that the quotation from Geiler given by Zarncke 354 has been found to be borrowed from Hugo of St. Victor (Norden 721).

[2] See J. H. Lupton, A Life of John Colet, new ed. (1909), 46.

[3] See Ch. Fierville, Contributions à l'histoire de l'Université de Caen—Guillaume de la Mare (Extr. des Mém. de l'Acad. Nat. . . . de Caen, 1893), 9 sqq.

[4] H. Prentout, La Vie de l'étudiant à Caen au XVe siècle (Extr. des Mém. de l'Acad. Nat. . . . de Caen, 1905), 53. One might feel tempted to ask if Barclay himself could have studied there. But this seems out of the question, because no signs of Humanistic revival were apparent at Caen before the rectorship of Guillaume de la Mare. See L. Delisle, Catalogue des Livres imprimés ou publiés à Caen avant le milieu du XVIe siècle (Caen 1903, 1904), especially the *Tableau chronologique* vol. ii, 117.

suit the rhyme with *Spayne* and *agayne*, where another name would have
fitted in much more naturally.   Louvain was not only one of the scientific
centres of the North, it also took a leading part in humanistic studies,[1]
and must have been very well known in England.   John Skelton was
not content to be a ' Poet Laurate ' of Oxford and Cambridge but wanted
the same degree from Louvain [2] and Sir Thomas More had his Utopia
printed there.—The omission of Louvain is therefore as striking as is
the mention of Cologne.   Did Barclay write Louvain after all, and has
the printer only corrupted the name ?   Or had the author himself some
hidden motive for inserting ' Colayne ' instead of that University which
was a great deal better known to him ?

255.—Immediately after the University passage he inserts a stanza
of which he found only the idea for the second line in Locher :

> (429)   One bostynge the name of Lawer or Devyne,
>         His proude hode hye upon his stately necke ;
>         Thus muste a goode clerke unto a foul enclyne,
>         Lowt [3] with the body and with obedyence becke.

This looks again like a hit at some persons in particular, but here too
the reference is too vague to draw any conclusions as to the nature of
the slight which the writer may have felt.   The obvious inference would
be that Barclay himself was not ' bostynge the name of a Lawer or
Devyne,' and that he considered himself as a simple ' goode clerke.'
But other allusions stand in the way of this supposition, and one of them
occurs in this very chapter.   At the end before the Envoy he adds an
' Addicio Alexandri Barkley,' three stanzas, all in octaves :

> (431)   The great foly, the pryde and the enormyte
>         Of our studentis and theyr obstynate errour
>         Causeth me to wryte two sentences or thre
>         More than I fynde wrytyn in myne actoure.

After this prosaic introduction comes the autobiographical confession :

> (431)   The tyme hath ben whan I was conductoure
>         Of moche foly, which nowe my mynde doth greve ;
>         Wherfor of this Shyp syns I am governoure,
>         I dare be bold myne owne vyce to repreve.

We cannot imagine our moralist to have been ' conductoure of moche
foly,' unless he refers to his wasting his time on what a Humanist understood by ' unprofytable stody.'   But he who wrote these words must
certainly have been a student, and very probably a student at some
foreign University.—The two stanzas that follow are full of humorous
or at least good-humoured by-play.

> (432)   Howe be it I knowe my wordes shall suche greve
>         As them selfe knoweth fawty and culpable ;
>         But if they be wroth take they me by the sleve,
>         For they shall bere the hode and I wyll the bable !

---

[1] H. de Yongh, L'Ancienne Faculté de Théologie de Louvain (1432–1540),
Louvain 1911), 107 sqq. ; see also L. Delisle op. cit. p. 16.

[2] A. Rey, Skelton's satirical poems (Dissert. Berne 1899), 7 ; A. Dyce xi, xii,
v.  Oxford before 1490 ; Louvain before 1493 ; Cambridge in 1493.

[3] See note to § 166.

Who could be 'wroth' after this delightful warning?

> But firste ye studentis that ar of mynde unstable,
> Ye wasters and getters [1] by nyght in felde or towne,
> Within my navy wolde I set you a cable,
> If I not fered lyst ye your selfe wolde drowne!

This is quite harmless; the following stanza is more malicious, but the allegory of the ship maintains the playful spirit of light satire:

> (433)  Also I fere lyst my shyp sholde synke for syn,
> If that Cupido and Venus servytours
> On the unsure se my shyp entred within,
> Or all the folys promotyd to honours;
> I none receyve can of hye progenytours:
> My shyp is nat dressyd for them convenyent;
> And so I fere lyst theyr cruell rygours
> Sholde rayse to my shyp some tempest or tourment.

256.—There is no playfulness in Watson's version. But part of the passages corresponding to the three main points of the Latin, as we found them in Barclay, may be quoted.—First about the students. He mentions their 'longe gownes and hoodes' and calls them 'incessyve fooles' (folz insciens):

for whan ye sholde be at your lessons and in your studyes, *ye be at the taverne or amonge noughty packes* [2] [Drouyn is less descriptive: 'vous suivez mondanitez' which stands for Riviere's 'tous ieux et tous mondains plaisirs'], passynge your youthe in vicious operacyons, thay amagyne newe reasons, saynge that they be not subiecte to ryght and reason, for theyr flesshe is frayle!

Riviere and Drouyn have the same high estimation of grammar as Barclay.

There be dyvers fooles that wyll lerne foure or fyve scyences without havynge perfyte intellygence of theyr Grammar, that is the foundacyon of all scyences. They go rennynge unto Logyke and maketh a grete sort of argumentes and of croked sophyms [Fr. de syllogismes cornuz] and have ever in theyr mouthe Sortes or Plato, how well—[and here again the Frenchmen come nearer to Barclay in their direct contradiction of what Locher said]—how well that by Logyke and subtyll argumentes an obscure thynge maye well be claryfyed.

To the names of the Universities Riviere had added no other name than that of Paris, but Drouyn enumerates a great many more; Watson copies the whole list faithfully, changing only the name of the last-mentioned town:

They that renne to many townes, as to Vyenne, Arfonde [*sic* [3]: Drouyn has Erfonde; Riviere Erforde], Orleaunce, Parys, Poytiers, Pavye, Padoue, Toulouse, Lovayne, Montpellyere. In Basyle were they nourysshed. They can tell somthynge of Barbrye [that is what 'Lyps barbara tellus' has been reduced to! It is

---

[1] *getter* or *jetter* has the sense of Latin *jactator*, a braggart, so that *to jet*, though connected with Old French *getter*, *jetter*, MnFr. *jeter*, is probably a back-formation. For none of its typical English senses is recorded in continental French. See NED. s.v. jet.

[2] The first example of this expression given in the NED. (s.v. pack) dates from 1526.

[3] Watson cannot have known what was meant. The more striking is his persuasion that French *er* must be English *ar*.

Riviere's fault; he had understood only : ' et de barbarie scavent dire '], of the see, of Gaule. And they have sene the cyte of Rome, of London, of Naples, of Myllan, of Avygnon, and of *Yorke*.—[This last name is Watson's substitute for Drouyn's Amiens.[1]]

Besides the insertion of all these names, Drouyn has added two quite original passages. The first occurs in the middle of the chapter.

Folysshe legystes and decretistes that studyeth in codice and in Institutes [Fr. en code digeste et en Instituts] and that redeth the lessons of doctours, ye wene to be more experte than a grete advocate, and yet ye can nothynge bycause of the grete vaynglorye that holdeth you by the heed.

A ' bachelier es droits ' likes to lecture his fellow-students !—The other original addition is appended at the end :

They have long gownes full of plytes [2] and hodes [the French had : ' robes cornetes ou chapperons '] semynge grete clerkes, yet they are but beestes. They go to dyners and bankettes where they be set moost hyest wenynge to the assystentes that they be grete clerkes. The other ben players at tenys [in French : ' ioueurs de paulmes '], at cardes, at dyce, burdellers, and pyllours of taverners, rennynge nyght and daye, for to breke doores and wyndowes, and doynge other evylles infynyte (!). And theyr frendes [les parens] hathe grete payne for to assemble goodes for them, wenynge that suche ryotoures [gaudisseurs] be good clerkes, but they sell all to go on ryotynge [pour gaudir].

The unruly behaviour of the students at Paris is well known. But if this rebuke was not to be found in Drouyn's French text, it might have been written with an eye on Oxford, where such riots were not less common than elsewhere.[3]

257.—Chapter 65 (at least in the translations) satirises ASTROLOGY. —Brant speaks of all sorts of superstition here.

Fools, he says, pretend to be sure of future events from the stars and from planets and from God's own secret counsels (1–10), as if the stars ruled the world, as if God could not make a Saint out of a child of Saturn, as if the sons of Jupiter and of the Sun were not often very wicked (11–20). It is a heathenish habit to decide by the stars what we should do every day ; a Christian should only think of God's plans (21–28). And he who distinguishes between lucky and unlucky hours and days, has not sufficient trust in God (29–36).—Whoever has not thought out a new anecdote, or does not go about carolling about New Year's time, or does not decorate his house with fir's branches, or does not receive a present from his friends then, foolishly thinks it a bad beginning of the year (37–44). There are all sorts of such superstitions, soothsaying and augury, formulae, incantations, explanations of dreams, moonshine-plants and black magic (45–50). Everyone thinks himself blameless but he is not (51–52). People do not simply want to explain the course of the stars, they want to make them responsible for the smallest trifles (53–60). The whole world is full of this folly, and the printers are largely responsible (61–68).

---

[1] At least in the second edition. The first edition stopped after the name of Avignon.

[2] The word *plight* (plyte) was formerly used in the sense of *fold*. See NED. and cf. *pleat, plait*.

[3] To quote two examples. In 1502 some students of law made a great disturbance in the streets on the night of Trinity Sunday, and did much mischief to the doors and windows of Brasenose Hall. In 1506 there was a regular fight between Northerners and Southerners, in which the Principal of Hart Hall and two others were killed and many were wounded (H. C. Maxwell Lyte 380). In 1494 Fabyan (Chron. vii, 616, quoted by NED., s.v. jetter) records : ' This yere . . . was a great affray in Flete strete, atwene the getters of the Innys of court and the inhabytauntes of the same strete.'

If people only tried to learn the art of Moses and Daniel, it would be laudable (69–74). But nowadays they prophesy the death of cattle, or the blight of corn and wine, rain and snow, fair weather and foul ; that is what the farmers ask for in order to make corn and wine dearer ! (75–82). Abraham received no light from the stars among the Chaldees, but from the Lord in Chanaan (83–86). It is folly to force the decrees of God, but because the love of God is extinguished, people practise the arts of the devil, just as Saul did (87–94).

Of this long miscellaneous chapter Locher has not only made a short one, but he has translated literally nothing ! He has written a new little satire on astrology, with perhaps here and there an idea derived from the German.

He summons astrologers, mathematicians,[1] soothsayers [ariolos], ' planetists,' augurs, aruspices, who want to explain every minute detail by the stars. They pretend to understand every sign of the planets ; the threatenings of sad Saturn, the meaning of Mars, of cheerful Venus, of ' Atlantis nepos [meaning Mercury], of pious Jupiter. They say that the children of Saturn will be thieves and criminals, though Fate [Fata] can make them blameless. They say that the sons of Mars are born for warfare, but we often see them live in peace. The wise man is above the stars ; God rules everything. You pretend to know God's plans, O foolish mathematician, as if He reveals them to everyone. Let us rather leave all to His Providence. When God defends us no stars can bring us harm. What calendars [ephimerides] foretell is all vanity. There is no power in birth-constellation [' genesis ' Juvenal's expression], nor in forecasts, nor in fate.

The page is full, the chapter is finished. It is quite a dignified little effort, much more so than Brant's rambling treatise, in which the title and the main theme were often forgotten. But at the same time nearly all the interest and curiosity are gone. What at first sight looks a bit striking, the passage about the planets, is little more than a collection of commonplace remarks with which anonymous astrologers had been ridiculed or which poets had used for embellishment scores of times before.

258.—The whole interest of this chapter would seem to centre in one line :

Juste age : nec dubita, sapiens dominabitur astris.

The history of this one line is almost a summary of the whole history of the medieval attitude towards Astrology,[2] an attitude of curious wavering and inconsistency.

It used to be said that Petrarch's attack upon Astrology was an act of great courage, and that the Humanists continued the struggle against this superstition inspired by his glorious example ;[3] what Erasmus and Rabelais have written against it has been called an act of great cultural importance.[4] The truth is almost the reverse. The Church authorities had always warned against astrological superstition.

[1] In the 1493 verdict of the University of Paris quoted below (§ 258) *Astrologi* and *Mathematici* are used as synonyms, and *mathematica ars* is the same as *astrologia divinatoria*.

[2] See the interesting study by Th. O. Wedel, The Medieval Attitude toward Astrology, particularly in England (Yale Studies in English lx, 1920).

[3] Thus almost literally G. Voigt, Die Wiederbelebung des klassischen Altertums i, 75. As a matter of fact Petrarch's treatise consists of little more than pious admonitions culled from St. Augustine.

[4] H. Schoenfeld in Publications of the Modern Language Association of America viii (Baltimore 1893), 28, 30.

Brant's lines 21–28 are almost literally taken from the thirteenth-century Decretales.[1] And as late as 1493 the Theological Faculty of Paris, condemning the astrological writings of Symon de Phares, had given the general verdict: 'praedictam Artem . . . si modo Artis nomine digna est . . . prorsus vanam immo nullam esse . . . fallacissimam, superstitiosam . . . iudicaremus.'[2] The doctrine of the Church was clear enough, but the Poets and Humanists themselves were always getting entangled in this alluring speculation. Brant condemned astrology theoretically, but practically he wrote his *De Corrupto Ordine* (f) preceded by an astrological diagram, foretelling great disasters for the year 1503.[3] Brant's story is the story of many Humanists.[4] Chaucer is the principal example in England. His theory is to be found in the prose Treatise on the Astrolabe (II. 2. 60 sq.) when he speaks of 'rytes of payens, in which my spirit ne hath no feith,' but in his poetry he returns to astrology repeatedly, not only for an ingenious *jeu d'esprit* as The Complaint of Mars, but as an intimate conviction, as in The Man of Law's Tale:

> For in the sterres, clerer than is glas,
> Is writen, God wot, whoso coude it rede,
> The deeth of every man, withouten drede.[5]

And his following stanza was imitated closely from Bernard Silvestris, the first medieval champion of astrology.[6]

To make a compromise between their Christian theory and their superstitious practice the would-be enlightened of the Middle Ages used to encourage themselves by the saying: 'Sapiens dominabitur astris.'

259.—The origin of the saying has not yet been discovered, but it is quoted for the first time in the Summa Theologica of S. Thomas Aquinas (p. I$^a$ q. 115, art. 4 ad 3$^{um}$), where after setting forth the philosophic and theological point of view from which astrology or astronomy could safely be studied, he adds: 'Unde et ipsi astrologi dicunt quod sapiens homo dominatur astris.'—Gower prefixed it to his discussion of astronomy in the Confessio Amantis:

> Vir mediante Deo sapiens dominabitur astris

and again in a variant form in the Vox Clamantis:

> In virtute Dei sapiens dominabitur astra.

This doctrine had found its chief popular embodiment in Jean de Meung's *Roman de la Rose* [7] and it was a source of frequent inspiration for Gower's contemporary Eustache Deschamps.[8] The doctrine or at least the

---

[1] ii, 26. 5. 3 ; the quotation in Zarncke 406.     [2] D'Argentré i, 2, 325.

[3] In 1504, and again in 1520, he changed the dates (Schmidt i, 281). He had astrologers among his correspondents (ib. 232). See also his theory in a letter to Peutinger written in 1504, in Schmidt i, 262.

[4] See Burckhardt 380 sqq. ; Fr. von Bezold 129 sqq., 195 *etc.*

[5] C.T., B. 194-196.  Cf. The Knightes Tale, C.T., A. 1087 sqq.:

> Som wikke aspect or disposicioun
> Of Saturne, by sum constellacioun
> Hath yeven us this *etc.*

[6] De Mundi Universitate, or Megacosmos, composed between 1145 and 1153 (ed. C. S. Barach and J. Wrobel, Innsbruck 1876).  See Skeat's note v, 147, from Tyrwhitt.

[7] Wedel o.c. 137.          [8] Quotations in Wedel 135, 139.

phrase was still in favour in the fifteenth century. Lodovico Moro used it as an inscription for a cross,[1] and Gaguin wrote in a letter to William Hermans of Gouda in 1496 : ' Quin et Ptholomeus peritia astrorum illustris, dominari astris posse hominem non negat.' [2] Riviere does not seem to know the expression, for he paraphrases it entirely away.[3] But Barclay does. With much greater emphasis than Locher he writes :

> (981)    Thus it aperyth both playne and openly,
> That it is foly to gyve great confydence
> To the unsure science of Astronomy ;
> Wherfore have done, just man, note this sentence :
> A man of wysdome, vertue and science,
> If he the wayes of vyces set asyde,
> Shall gyde the sterris and they shall hym nat gyde.

Drouyn knows the expression also, for at the end of his paraphrase he appends an original sentence :

> Aulcuns escripvent les naissances des enfans comprenant estoilles et planettes lesquelz on voit souvent faillir et nest pas tousiours vray ce que lon cuyde. *Car nous avons que le sage domine aux estoilles.*

Or as Watson's English has it :

> Some wryteth of the natyvytees and byrthes of chyldren comprehendynge sterres and planettes, the which is sene fayle oftentymes, and all is not true that they thynke. For we have that the wyse man domyneth above the sterres, *and planettes.*[4]

260.—There is hardly anything else of importance to be found in any of the translations. Barclay keeps quite close to Locher's Latin, writing ' folys ' or ' mad men ' (974, 982) instead of *mathematicos*. He omits the *ephimerides* but in the Envoy he speaks of the vanity of writing Prognostications, which must have enjoyed some popularity in England,[5] at the same time betraying his own hesitation :

> (986)    Unto the sterris gyve nat *to* great credence,
> For many one therby hath ben abused ;
> And many one have stodyed sore and musyd
> To wryte Pronosticacions whiche have be founde
> Of none effect and than falsly excusyd.

---

[1] Burckhardt 382. The cross is still preserved at Chur in Switzerland.
[2] Thuasne ii, 27. Also Locher's margin quotes *Ptolomeus*. So does Deschamps. But the editor of Deschamps (Œuvres Complètes ii, 148) says that after a diligent search of Ptolemy's work he is unable to locate the quotation concerning the *vir sapiens.*—Villon names Solomon as the author. Thuasne l.c. annotates that the expression has also been ascribed to Virgil.
[3]          Seras des haultz constans et sages
         Chemineras par leurs passages
         Ou passerent et aultres dieux.
         Je te veulx dire *etc.*
Opposite this passage the margin refers to *Tholomeus.*
[4] Watson must have added the last two words to show that he does *not* know the expression.
[5] Two such Prognostications, printed before 1501, by Pynson and by Wynkyn de Worde, have been preserved. They contain mostly forecasts for weather (E. G. Duff, n. 349, 350). Prognostications were paid for from the Privy Purse of Henry VII in 1492 and 1496 (A. F. Pollard ii, 227, 230).

One little quotation will suffice to characterize the main part of Watson's version. Instead of all those classical personages mentioned in the beginning of the Latin version, and which Barclay had all replaced by 'witches,' Riviere had put

> Et ceulx qui tiennent les escolles
> Tous ceulx honorans les estoilles.

Drouyn thought he knew those who 'tiennent les escolles' and wrote *regens* instead. Watson altered this word a little bit to make it some-what better fit the context, and so he translated : 'the regyons of al them that honoureth the sterres'!

261.—In chapter 66 a contemporary of Columbus holds forth on the folly of GEOGRAPHY. It is one of the six longest chapters of the book, numbering no less than one hundred and fifty-four lines, and it reflects the sensation and commotion caused by the recent startling discoveries among the various classes of society. Geography became a hobby of cranks.

They are fools, says Brant, who with the assistance of a pair of compasses strive to know all about the earth, its dimensions, the depth and extent of the Oceans, and what supports the universe ; how it is that the sea does not drop off it ; whether it would be possible to sail round the earth, what the antipodes are like, and how they manage to walk upright, how people can measure the earth with a rod ! (1–18). Archimedes knew very much about it, he would rather be killed than have his circles disturbed, and yet he could not describe the end of his own life (19–28). Dicearchus, an expert in mountains, found Pelion to be the highest of all—but he never knew the Alps nor had he measured the depth of the pit in which he him-self fell (29–36). Ptolemy had ascertained the degrees of longitude and latitude, 180 degrees of the former, 63 of the latter near the equator, but only 25 round the Poles,[1] and Pliny reckoned this out in yards, and Strabo in miles (37–48). But since then many more countries have been discovered beyond Norway and Thule, such as Iceland 'Pylappenlandt,' and the Portuguese and Spaniards have found the Golden Isles with naked inhabitants ! (49–56). Marinus mistook the dimensions of the earth (57–58). Pliny wisely says that it is absurd to calculate the outside measure-ment of the earth without knowing its contents, and without even knowing the size of one's own mind (59–68). Hercules placed two pillars to mark the borders of Africa and Europe and yet he did not know that he was to fall through a woman's guile (69–76). Bacchus went through the world spreading the habit of drinking wine or beer or mead and Silenus and many other dissolute companions went with him (77–88). But even without them people would have learned drunkenness, but they are certainly nowadays corrupting a great many young people (89–94). But Bacchus has now in hell more thirst than joy, although the pagans worship him as a god, and our people still go about 'umb bächten,'[2] honouring him who only brought them evil (95–104). Evil habits last long, for the devil wants to keep his servants (105–108). But to return,—why do people aspire to things greater than themselves, without ever thinking of the approach of death ? (109–116). Though knowledge in itself may be true, yet it is folly to study other things before knowing oneself, to seek for vain glory and to forget the kingdom of heaven (117–127). Fools are dazzled by earthly joys ; many discover strange countries, with-

---

[1] Zarncke 907 observes that Brant's presentment of Ptolemy's geography is quite exact.

[2] An allusion to a popular custom of young people running about at Christmas-time begging and rioting. Grimm suspects that the word is derived not from Bacchus but from 'frau Berchta.'

out discovering themselves (128–132). A wise traveller such as Ulysses who gathered true doctrine everywhere or Pythagoras from Memphis,[1] or Plato who travelled from Egypt to Italy in search of wisdom, or Apollonius who sought out all wise men to make himself more wise, such a traveller, whose main object would be real wisdom, might be forgiven (133–151) ; though even this is not quite sufficient, for those who are fond of travelling will hardly serve God whole-heartedly (152–154).

A curious side-light upon the grim severity of this satire, especially in its first part, is thrown by the fact that in the same year in which the Narrenschiff appeared, Brant was probably the first to popularize in Germany Columbus's letter to Raphael Sanchez *De insulis nuper inventis*.[2] It was probably one of his friends, Matthias Ringmann Philesius, who induced Martin Waldseemüller at St.-Dié to publish in 1507 the famous Latin translation of the Quatuor Navigationes of Amerigo Vespucci.[3]

262.—Brant's work has again fared very badly at the hands of Locher. He paraphrases the first six lines, and then leaves his model to dilate in eighteen long lines upon the sort of knowledge that a foolish geographer or geometer seeks. To fill the rest of the page he takes an idea from Brant's lines 35–56, viz. that Pliny and Ptolemy have made mistakes because unknown countries have been found since, in particular by Ferdinand, King of ' Hesperiae occiduae.' Then Locher had enough of it, and stopped !

This is typical of the true Humanistic attitude. Burckhardt[4] has already alluded to the fact that Humanism has done much harm to the study of physics and a modern scientist has shown that the development of the science of Roger Bacon, astronomy and geometry and physics, is mainly due to the much cried-down Nominalists and Terminists. Buridan and Nicolas Oresme and many others in England and France appear to be the ancestors of Copernicus and Galileo and Descartes.[5] And the *Imago Mundi* and the *Meteora* of a Nominalist like Pierre d'Ailly had been of great help to Columbus as well as to his rival who gave the New World its name.

Humanists of the stamp of Locher never took a great interest in such

---

[1] This place of origin is mentioned by no classical author.

[2] Schmidt i, 253 ; ii, 357 : *In laudem . . Ferdinandi Hisp. regis. Bethicae et regni Granatae obsidio victoria et triumphus. Et de insulis in mari Indico nuper inventis.* 1494 Basel. Bergmann, 4°. The last part was also published separately in 8° by Jac. Wolff at Basel (BMC. iii, 777). The first German translation appeared in Brant's native town—Strassburg (B. Kistler) in 1497 ; a copy is preserved in the Brit. Museum (BMC. i, 163). See S. Ruge, Gesch. des Zeitalters der Entdeckungen 264.

[3] The original was written in Italian in 1504 and sent to René II of Lorraine, who had it translated into French. It is upon this French translation that Canon Basin based his Latin version ; it was printed as an appendix to Ringmann's Cosmographiae Introductio. Waldseemüller was a native of Friburg. See Schmidt ii, 113 sqq.; and bibliographical description ii, 398 ; K. Goedeke, Grundrisz zur Gesch. d. Deutschen Dichtung i² (1884), 434.

[4] P. 213.

[5] P. Duhem, Etudes sur Léonard de Vinci i (1906), 10 ; iii ; Les Précurseurs Parisiens de Galilée (1913), xi, xiii. Even Tateret upheld the traditions of Buridan, and Albert of Saxe and Marsile d'Inghen (ib. iii, 96 sqq.). Nicole Oresme is called the discoverer of analytic geometry ; but the foundation seems to have been laid by the Oxford School of Swineshead (ib. iii, xi, 375). Cf. the same author's articles in Revue Générale des Sciences 1909 and in Archivum Franciscanum Historicum vi (1913), 23 sqq.

things, except perhaps in so far as they lent fresh attraction to fine-sounding geographical names.

Locher adduces some in the eighteen lines above referred to. There he mentions the four points of the compass as *Eous, calor australis, occiduus tepor, axis hyperboreus*, and the *ursa minor*. Besides Europe and Asia he commemorates: *Graecos, Aeolios, Cappadocas, Cylices*, the *Lybiae gentes, Atlas* and *Calpe*, and *Herculis fretum*. Of course he does not omit the one classical name he found in Brant, *semotam Thylen*, but he adds moreover the *Brytannos* ' in orbe extremo,' and the *Theutona claustra*, and far-off islands, and the tides, and finally after mentioning that a geographical fool will even study the works of Strabo, he exclaims as though in despair :

> Intactum toto nil sinit orbe quidem !

263.—Riviere did not appreciate all this very much. He bungles through all those proper names without caring much what they really mean, e.g.

> Athlante les hercules calpee
> Se monte et toute la thelee (!)
> Bretaigne es fins de la monarche
> Aupres du mer et sur sa marche
> Langurgite et profundite *etc.*

Small wonder that Drouyn should have been at a loss what this meant. So he skipped ' la Thelee,' and ' Bretaigne ' as well. But to make up for it he inserted some names that were more familiar to him :

> il mesure ursie pour comprendre le pays et peuple, asye, apulye, cilice, grece, atlante, calpee, les herculees, *thessalie, france, bourgoigne, picardie, naples*, et es fins de la monarche, de la profundite et ingurgite de la mer *etc.*

Watson had not much space for this chapter, and so he did not cudgel his brains to find out why this list of curiosities should have been inserted, and what was to be found ' es fins de la monarche.' He retained only one name, the most curious of all, viz. that into which the Lesser Bear had been transformed ; of all the rest he made short work : ' He mesureth Ursye, for to comprehende the countree and people *with all the regyons of the worlde*. And the profoundyte of the see ' *etc.*

264.—The passage in Locher which has more actual interest is the conclusion about newly discovered countries and about King Ferdinand. Only vague rumours, however, must have penetrated to Riviere in 1498 :

> La terre qui fut incognue
> Des prisces que hom navoit cogneue
> Fut ell pas magestee
> A loueil combien que avoit estee
> Long temps dom sans estre apparcue
> Or maintenant et elle sceue
> Sans molestacion de cueur.
> Et si aucun hom ne ly cueur
> Ne tira voil a desarroy
> Avant ferdinandus le roy
> Sur mer neantmois sont astables
> Et gens quasi innumerables.

Drouyn seems to have known a little more about it. But he made some small mistakes or misprints in paraphrasing the first part, *terre* becomes *tierce*; *prisces* is misprinted *pristes*, and in the sixth line the word *molestacion* has dropped out. And so the Englishman innocently translated literally: 'The *thyrde* whiche is unknowen. Of *preestes* that never had ben manyfeste, was she nat founde with the eye, and *not with the herte* [sans de cueur!].'—In the concluding lines, however, Drouyn leaves Riviere altogether, evidently alluding to the story of Columbus:

> Il fut ung qui congneut que es isles despaignes avoit gens habitables. Il vint au roy nomme ferdinandus lequel luy bailla ayde tellement quilz trouverent aulcunes isles de gens qui nentendoient riens touchant dieu le createur. Et navoyent reigles ne loix, mais vivoient comme bestes.

Lack of space may have forced Watson to summarize this, but from the way he does it, it would seem that he had not yet heard in 1509 of the discovery of America: 'There was one that knewe that the yles of Spayne was enhabytaunt. Wherfore he asked men of kynge Ferbynandus [*sic*], and wente and founde them, the whiche lyved as beestes.' Columbus gained only posthumous glory!

265.—Barclay is somewhat better informed than his naive countryman. He follows Locher's version quite independently, interspersing his paraphrase with various little reflections of his own. Thus after mentioning the investigations in the West, North and South he muses:

> (990)  thus all the worlde wyde
> By these folys is meated by ieometry,
> Yet knowe they scant theyr owne unwyse body.

He also enumerates most of the names that he found in Locher:

> (992)  Than with his compace drawyth he about
> Europe and Asye, to knowe howe they stande
> And of theyr regyons nat to be in dout.
> Another with Grece and Cesyll is in honde,
> With Apuly, Afryke, and the newe fonde londe,
> With Numydy and where the Moryans do dwell,
> And other londes, whose namys none can tell.

The fifth line, adducing countries *bien étonnés de se trouver ensemble*, is an original contribution. The last one also, but it is not meant as a convenient makeshift, for the author goes on with nearly all the names in Locher, and not a few of his own:

> (993)  He mesureth Athlant, Calpe and Cappadoce,
> The see of Hercules, Garnado and Spayne,
> The yles there aboute shewynge all in groce,
> Throwynge his mesure to Fraunce and Brytayne,
> The more and lesse, to Flaundres and Almayne;
> There is no yle so lytell that hath name,
> But that these folys in hande ar with the same.

It is rather disappointing to find that none of our translators busied themselves much with the 'Semota Thyle.'[1] Only Riviere made a guess at it saying 'toute la thelee,' but his prose-companion threw it overboard. This reminds one of a story told of Richard of Bury. When this learned bibliophile met Petrarch at Avignon in 1330, the latter seized the opportunity to enquire as to the exact position of the ancient Thule, and was disappointed to find the English Envoy perfectly indifferent to this interesting topic.[2]

266.—After mentioning the 'Doctrynes of Strabo' (994) Barclay adds:

> (995)  Whiche wrote in bokes makynge declaracion,
> Somtyme hym groundynge upon auctoryte
> How eche royalme and londe had sytuacion,
> Some in brode feldes, some closyd with the see.

This is a vague enough description of the contents. But it is not impossible that Barclay was really acquainted with Guarino's translation of Strabo's Geography.[3]

Finally there is the concluding passage about recent discoveries:

> (998)  For nowe of late hath large londe and grounde
> Ben founde by maryners and crafty governours,
> The whiche londes were never knowen nor founde
> Byfore our tyme by our predecessours;
> And here after shall by our successours
> Parchaunce mo be founde wherin men dwell
> Of whome we never before this same harde tell.

These lines betray a lively personal interest, more so than Locher's casual remark, or Riviere's obscure genèralities, more even than Drouyn's more detailed information. It is only a pity that in the next stanza Barclay repeats the same idea in a weaker form, and concludes with a superfluous, though quite natural, moral:

> (999)  Ferdynandus, that late was Kynge of Spayne,
> Of londe and people hath founde plenty and store,
> Of whome the bydynge to us was uncertayne,
> No Christen man of them harde tell before.
> Thus is it foly to tende unto the lore
> And unsure science of vayne geometry,
> Syns none can knowe all the worlde perfytely.

The first part of this stanza is probably meant only as a translation from the Latin. And as the Latin was some dozen years old, Barclay thought he might safely put in that Ferdinand 'late was Kynge of Spayne,' although as a matter of fact that sovereign was still alive and would be for another half-dozen years. Spain and the political world evidently lay beyond Barclay's horizon.—The second part resembles Brant's moralizings, though it cannot have been taken from the German. It is simply a natural reflection of the translator, who has understood

[1] And yet in 1502 Henry VII had paid five pounds 'to men of Bristoll that founde Thisle.'—Quoted from Bentley's Excerpta Historica by A. F. Pollard ii, 345.

[2] 1 Epp. Fam. iii, 1 in J. E. Sandys, A History of Classical Scholarship ii (1908), 219.

[3] J. E. Sandys, ib. p. 50.

the drift of the whole chapter.  The same may be said of the Envoy,
in which a Brantian idea is successfully developed :

   (1000)   Ye people that labour the worlde to mesure
              Therby to knowe the regyons of the same,
              Knowe firste your self ;  that knowledge is most sure,
              For certaynly it is rebuke and shame
              For man to labour onely for a name,
              To knowe the compasse of all the world wyde,
              Nat knowynge hym selfe nor how he sholde hym gyde.[1]

---

[1] This is one of the very few Envoys in a seven-line stanza instead of in an octave.

## XIII

## CHAPTERS RELATING TO MANNERS OF THE TIME

267.—In this last category of chapters the translators found the freest scope for their own powers of observation—and of imagination. Brant devoted nine chapters to denouncing the folly of some popular manners and customs he had observed. Two of them occur in the beginning of his work ; five about the middle, and two others were not written until the book had been completed, so that they were only inserted in the second edition of the year 1495.

First we have chapter 4 on NEW FASHIONS.

Formerly, says Brant, meaning the period covered by the Old Testament, men wore beards, but now they resemble women (1–4). They use cosmetics, and wear rings and gold chains round their bare necks, as if to represent St. Leonard [1] (5–8). To make their hair fall in wavy ringlets, they use sulphur, the white of eggs and a sort of basket ; they try to make it fair by heat and sunlight—and it becomes nothing but a breeding place for lice! (9–14). Lice have a good time of it in their clothes full of folds. Their gowns, cloaks, shirts, slippers, boots, hose, shoes, cowls, and mantles [2] with their fur coverings are all very wide so that people in them resemble Jews (15–20). The fashions change continually, a sign of the fickleness of our characters (21–24). The jacket, short and cut out, hardly covers the navel ; this is a great shame for the German nation, so to uncover what nature wants to hide (25–29). Thus we fall from bad to worse, but he who gives scandal to others will one day get his deserts (30–34).

There is a full explanation of all the details of this chapter in Zarncke, pp. 306–311.[3] But our concern is more with the Latin version. Locher has paraphrased very freely. He uses fourteen lines, almost half his available space, to dilate upon the disappearance of the beard, which was such a glory, he says, to Socrates and the philosophers. Next he speaks of the hair ; it is curled like that of Sicambers and Ethiopians. Men bare their painted breasts, to tempt the women. They wear chains round their necks and rings on their fingers. Their clothes are too short and painted so as shamelessly to expose their pudenda. What shall I say, Locher exclaims, of their various tunics and cloaks with yellow borders and their outrageous footwear! We resemble the

---

[1] St. Leonard was the patron saint of prisoners, and the ex-votos offered to him by rescued prisoners usually consisted of chains. Lydgate has ' A Prayer to St. Leonard, made at York ' (ed. J. O. Halliwell, Percy Society ii, 1842, p. 205), in which he prays especially :

Remembre on hem that lyn in cheynes bounde.

[2] These are presumably the nearest English equivalents of the German technical terms, but I do not pretend to understand them all.

[3] See also Janssen-Pastor i, 259 sqq.

Assyrians and the Turks and the Jews (recutitorum ritibus). And he appeals to 'Germania' to expel those shameful customs, else she will lose her fame. But God will certainly punish those who lead criminal lives.

268.—Although anything but a translation, and though there are only a few points of contact between the German and the Latin, enough details about the articles of dress are retained to appeal to the translators.

We are naturally interested in the Frenchman's view first, whom we may expect to express a great many ideas of his own on the subject. Indeed in the beginning, before mentioning the beard, he philosophizes on the different forms of sleeves then worn :

> Mais ie ne puis pas bien penser
> En mon cueur ne contrepenser
> Lequel est le plus fol des deux
> Usant du nouveau rit et vieux
> Ou cil qui prent les grans condetz
> Comme font ung tas de lourdetz
> Ou cil qui porte manches larges
> Comme font maintenant les paiges
> Si non de dire quil me semble
> Que mectre se peuent ensemble
> Comme deux folz car cest tout ung
> Si lung est bien noir lautre est brun
> Se lung est fol lautre lest plus
> Si lung boiteux lautre perclus.

That is the philosophic attitude ! Old fashions are as foolish as the new !—It is doubtful whether Drouyn has quite understood the passage, for he throws together the 'grans coudetz' of the 'lourdetz' and the 'manches larges' of the 'paiges,'—but at the end he adds a sentence of his own in which he clearly distinguishes the 'grans coutieres' from the 'larges manches.' Watson has done his best to express Drouyn's meaning in English :

> I can not well conspyre [penser] in my herte the whiche is the moost foole of theym twayne that use the olde or the newe customes, or he the whiche wereth grete sleves with grete bordures [grans manchez a coustierez—and here he skips ' comme font ung grant tas de lourdaulx et de paiges,' rightly thinking, perhaps, that it would not do to place a slouching *lourdeau* and a page on the same level !], or they the whiche bereth large sleves. Save that me thinketh it is all one thynge, and that the one is as folysshe as the other. For he thynketh that hathe the bordured sleves [les grans coutieres] that he is as honestly clothed, as he the whiche hath the large sleves [les larges manches].

269.—Riviere did not quite share Locher's enthusiasm about the beard. So he begins by reversing the statement :

> Honteux sont et honte les prant
> De porter grant barbe au visaige
> De peur de monstrer leur vieulx aage
> Mais leurs corps et viz si bien gardent
> Si bien les acoutrent et fardent
> Que iamais ne deviennent vieulx
> Se semble.

Drouyn thought that a man with a beard could not very well use paint to improve his complexion ; and so in the fifth line he leaves out the word 'fardent.'  Watson's translation is quite literal : 'Some bereth grete berdes for fere that they seme not more auncyent.  They araye [ilz acoutrent] theyr bodyes and vysages in such a facyon that they seme yonge, but yet they be olde.'

Regarding the hair, Riviere adds nothing to the Latin.  But Drouyn inserts a curious reference to the German hair 'longz iauniz et fardez,' which becomes in English : ' The other bereth theyr heere as Sycabryens [Drouyn's spelling], or longe, yelowe and trussed lyke Almaynes, or as Ethyopyens cryspe and curled, the whiche is combed ten tymes a daye.'

270.—For the description of the articles of dress one longer quotation from the French poet must be given :

> Leur habitz sont si dissoluz
> Quilz monstrent prez que leurs corps nuz
> Pour decevoir les pauvres filles
> Par leur facons tresinutiles
> Et sont comme chevaux maliers
> Leurs colz chargez de gros coliers
> De grosses chesnes et chesnettes
> De bagues dor et de baguettes
> Les doiz rempliz de gros anneaux
> Larges bonnetz et grans chapeaux
> Robes courtes iusques aux hanches
> Pleines de pliz et larges manches
> Pourpoins decoupez entaillez
> Manteaux divers et fretaillez
> Robes courtes de divers draps
> Voire qui sont a deux rebras
> Lung derriere lautre devant
> Les autres qui sont pleins de vent
> Portent les chemises brodees
> A grans manches toutes bordees
> De fin lin. que pourray ie escripre
> Si non de crier et de dire
> Que nous suivons par noz meffaitz
> Les mescreans et turcz infectz
> Desquelz portons les vestemens.
> France *etc.*

Drouyn has changed this description a little here and there, and at the end he has appended some more details of his own.  The English translation is very faithful on the whole :

Some hathe theyr habytes soo shorte that one maye almoost se theyr ars.  There be some that have theyr neckes all charged with grete chaynes, and ben al repylnysshed [*sic*] with golden jewelles, theyr handes full of gemmes and rynges.  Ample bonettes with lowe neckes and garded [larges bonnetz a grans rebras et dehachez] lyke as it were for dyspyte, and therupon the small [1] hattes, that is set all upon one syde.[2]  Theyr gownes longe full of playtes, and the sleves large as a

---

[1] The French has : ' avec cela de *grans* chapeaux quon porte sur loreille.'— Watson must have discovered his mistake, for the second (1517) edition changes *small* into *grete*.—This is the most important difference between the first and the second edition which I have observed.

[2] Cf. Barclay, Stanza 171, § 179.

sacke. Theyr doublettes is garded endlong and overthwarre [pourpoins decouppez en taillades], bordred with velvet or with sylke.  Clokes bended with dyvers colours. There is dyvers clothes worne at this present tyme, the gownes have double re-braced colers.  Theyr shyrtes ben fronced *with golde or sylke, ye and that is* of the fynest clothe *that can be founden.*[1]  It is the guyse of the infydeles, or the turkes and sarazyns vyle and abhomynable.  The grete shone rounde as a boule,[2] and after them the squared, buskynnes all to cut [brosequins decouppes], slyppers bygared [pantouflez dehachees], the hosen garded [chausses biguarrees] and bended with velvet or satyn [this is less strong than the French 'nervees de drap dor ou de velours'], the purses as sachelles [comme panetieres], with gyrdylles of taffeta. What lacketh there more. nothynge. save the fayre swerde or hanger [la belle espee ou rapiere] by theyr syde.

The only thing that appears to be original in Watson's version is the toning down of a few expressions.  We know that men's fashions were extremely luxurious at that time all over Europe.[3]  But in England the reign of King Henry VII and the example set by the court must have exercised some sobering influence.[4]  That is probably the reason why Watson has not applied his usual method in changing the final appeal.  Riviere changed the *Germania* of the Latin into *France*, and Drouyn repeated the word twice over.  Watson, however, does not substitute the name of his own country but very sagaciously appeals to : ' O chrystendome, chrystendome ' *etc.*  That will always hold good.

271.—Quite different is Barclay's treatment, who writes here one of his most powerful chapters.[5]  Like Riviere, he has left out the most offensive parts, but except in the first five stanzas (77–81) he has entirely changed the whole plan of this chapter, so that in a truer sense than the French, it may be called wholly original.  Even in those five stanzas the greater part is original.  In the beginning he summons his audience :

> (78) Drawe nere ye Courters and Galants disgised,
> Ye counterfayt caytifs, that ar nat content
> As God hath you made.[6]

And all stations of life are included :

> (79) Mannys fourme is disfigured with every degre,
> As knyght, squyer, yeman, jentilman and knave
> For al in theyr goynge ungoodely them behave.

---

[1] The 1517 edition misprints *fobe unden.*

[2] On the origin of the broad *becs de cane* see the note to § 121.  R. J. Planché (A Cyclopaedia of Costume i, 460 ; ii, 140) says these broad shoes began in Flanders about 1470.

[3] F. v. Bezold, 149.

[4] F. W. Fairholt, Costume in England, ed. Dillon (1885), i, 218.  See also A. Abram, Social England in the Fifteenth Century (1909), 150.

[5] Perhaps imitated, but feebly, in Skelton's Magnyfycence.  See the quotations in Ramsay lxxxii.

[6] This expression, not in Locher, occurs in Riviere :

> Tout le monde se contrefait
> Et veullent ce que dieu a fait
> Par presumpcion contrefaire.

I do not think, however, that this is an indication of Barclay's having consulted the French.  It was a sort of commonplace idea of the time (see Fr. von Bezold, p. 111).  Barclay uses it several times, e.g. also in Stanza 85 and 1761, and in the passage corresponding to this latter stanza even Locher shows himself familiar with it (ch. 110[b]) :

> Abscondunt faciem, quam Deus ipse dedit.

The beard is just mentioned, but with fine alliterative emphasis :

> (81)  At that tyme was it reputed to lawde and great honour,
>        To have longe here, the beerde downe to the brest,
>        For so they used that were of moste valour.[1]

272.—After this, leaving his model almost entirely, he speaks first of gentlemen and courtiers, then of women, and finally of clerics.—He begins with a sort of introduction, in which, like a practical Englishman,[2] he lays stress upon the financial side of the question :

> (82)  Fewe kepeth mesure, but excesse and great outrage
>        In theyr aparayle, and so therin they procede,
>        That theyr goode is spent, theyr londe layde to morgage
>        Or solde out right ; of thryft they take no hede,
>        Havinge no peny them to socour at theyr nede ;
>        So whan theyr goode by suche wastefulnes is loste,
>        They sel agayne theyr clothes for half that they cost.

This standpoint is taken up again and again.  Sometimes in an amusing little remark, as when he complains that the clothes

> (84)  [Are] wyde without mesure, theyr stuffe to wast thus gothe ;
>        But other some they suffer to dye for lacke of clothe !

Sometimes we get a more serious view, as, when the courtiers have difficulty in maintaining their state :

> (86)  Than stele they or robbe they ; forsoth, they can nat chuse !
>        For without londe or labour harde is it to mentayne,
>        But to thynke on the galows, that is a careful payne !

And this gives us a glimpse at a grisly London scene :

> (87)  But be it payne or nat, there many suche ende ;
>        At Newgate theyr garmentis are offred to be solde ;
>        Theyr bodyes to the jebet solemly ascende,
>        Wavynge with the wether, whyle theyr necke wyl holde.

273.—Some of the descriptions are in Barclay's best style : as e.g.

> (83)  A fox-furred [3] jentelman of the fyrst yere or hede [4]
>        If he be made a bailyf, a clerke or a constable,
>        And can kepe a parke or court and rede a dede,
>        Than is velvet to his state mete and agreable—
>        Howbeit he were more mete to bere a babyl !

---

[1]  The long beard had become the exception in the fifteenth century.  F. Hotten-roth, Trachten der Völker ii (1891), 139.

[2]  Just as Hoccleve had done in his ' Of pridd and of waste clothyng of Lordes men.'—Early Engl. Text Soc., Extra Ser. viii (1869), 105 sqq.

[3]  Compare Skelton's Bowge of Court, l. 234 :
     Methoughte his gowne was all furred with foxe.

[4]  For this *hede*, rhyming with *dede*, I have found no suitable meaning in the NED.  Barclay always rhymes *dede* (W.S. æ, Angl. ē) with other words in which ME. narrow ē occurs.  Dalheimer has counted 23 cases.  This rhyme *hede* : *dede* would be the only exception.  I suspect there is a mistake or misprint here.

It is not picturesque description, however, he intends to give, but severe criticism. He calls ' another sort ' almost as bad

> (84)    As yonge jentylmen descended of woithy auncetry,
>          Whiche go ful wantonly in dissolute array,
>          Counterfayt, disgised and moche unmanerly,
>          Blasinge and garded, to lowe or else to hye.

> (85)    Some theyr neckes charged with colers and chaynes,
>          As golden withtthes,[1] theyr fyngers ful of rynges,
>          Theyr neckes naked almoste unto the raynes,
>          Theyr sleves blasinge lyke to a cranys wynges.

This was probably written partly under the influence of the Latin. But golden necklaces had really become common among men since the fourteenth century ;[2] their ' gowns ' could be very wide with sleeves that might very well be compared to cranes' wings.[3] It is also known that just about 1500 low necks were fashionable among men.[4]—To a moralist we must allow the licence of exaggeration, considering that he saw (with Locher) a danger for morality in these low necks :

> (89)    To tempt chast damsels and turne them to your mynde,
>          Your brest ye discover and necke. Thus your abusion
>          Is the fendes bate, and your soules confusion.

> (90)    Ye garded galantes, wastinge thus your goode,
>          Come nere with your shertes brodered and displayed
>          In fourme of surplys.

If the arrangement of the chapter was not so totally different one might be tempted to think that Barclay had read Riviere's description. But the slashed upper garments displaying the embroidered shirts could hardly anywhere have been more conspicuous than in England,[5] so that Barclay might well venture a comparison with ecclesiastical surplices.

274.—The women come in for their share of the satire in two stanzas. The first is written in a somewhat derisive tone :

> (91)    And ye jentyl wymen, whome this lewde vice doth blynde,
>          Lased on the backe, your peakes set a loft,
>          Come to my Shyp ; forget ye nat behynde
>          Your sadel on the tayle, yf ye lyst to sit soft ;
>          Do on your decke, slut, if ye purpos to come oft,
>          I mean your copyntanke ; and if it wyl do no goode
>          To keep you from the rayne, ye shall have a foles hode.

I do not pretend to understand what all this means. The ' lased on

---

[1] This must be Old English wiðig, MnE. withe or withy ; but surely an Orm-like spelling !

[2] Viollet-le-Duc, Dictionnaire du Mobilier Français (1874) iii, 260.

[3] See the pictures e.g. in Viollet-le-Duc iv, 344 sqq., 456, 194 sqq.

[4] Viollet-le-Duc iii, 257. Cf. also the above description by Riviere. Authorities on costume quote Barclay's stanza to prove that the fashion in England was not less offensive than elsewhere.—J. R. Planché, A Cyclopaedia of Costume ii, 154 ; Idem, Hist. of Brit. Costume, 3rd ed. (1907), 239.

[5] See Planché i, 458, extracts from Henry VIII's inventory of apparel.

the backe' occurs also in a satirical ballad of the time, *The Maner of the World now-a-dayes.*

> Of wymen kynde
> Lased be hynde
> So lyke the fende
> Say [ = saw] I never.[1]

'Your peakes' are probably the same as 'your decke'[2] and 'your copyntanke.' But what they really are, is difficult to say. The last word occurs here for the first time in English, and during the reign of Elizabeth and James I it was always used to indicate the 'sugar-loaf hat' worn by men.[3]  Perhaps Barclay meant to satirize the steeple-caps or hennins, which were a fashionable headdress for women in his youth both in England and in France, and which, though out of fashion at the beginning of the sixteenth century,[4] may still have been much worn in country places. What 'your sadel' is, I cannot even make a guess.[5]

The second stanza brushes all play and detail away, and with eloquent severity denounces all indecent clothing :

> (94)   By the ale stake knowe we the ale hous,
> And every inne is knowen by the sygne,
> So a lewde woman and a lecherous
> Is knowen by hir clothes, be they cours or fyne,
> Folowynge newe fassyons not graunted by doctryne ;
> The bocher sheweth his flesshe it to sell :
> So doth these women, dampnyng theyr soules to hell.

This severity impressed the early Puritan writer of *Pryde and Abuse of Women*, Charles Bansley, who evidently took a hint from this stanza when between 1540 and 1550 he wrote

> For lyke as the jolye ale house
> Is always knowen by the good old stake
> So are proud Jelots sone perceaved, to
> By theyr proude foly, and wanton gate.[6]

---

[1] MS. Sloane 747, fol. 88, quoted by F. W. Fairholt, Satirical Songs and Poems on Costume (Percy Society 81, 1849), 66 ; A. Dyce, The Poetical Works of John Skelton i (1856), 434. For the custom itself see Viollet-le-Duc iv, 74.

[2] Jamieson 340 explains *decke* as *trimmed*, and *slut* as an *apron* ; 'used by Barclay,' he adds, 'as synonymous with Copyntanke.' Mr. Jamieson has missed the meaning altogether. See the words in the NED.

[3] J. R. Planché, A Cyclopaedia of Costume i, 258 ; NED. s.vv. copintank, copataine (Shakespeare's spelling) ; 'capotaine' is used by Scott for a woman's headdress (Kenilworth).

[4] Viollet-le-Duc iii, 242. England may also have been a little behindhand (F. Hottenroth, Trachten der Völker ii (1891), 139). The satirist can surely not mean the diamond-shaped hood, which became the fashion in court circles during the reign of Henry VII, and gave quite a conventual appearance to the face (Fairholt, Costume in England i, 226). Perhaps Barclay means the horned headdresses similar to those mentioned by Brant in his Prologue line 120. See § 314.

[5] Of all the different meanings of *saddle* given by the NED. not one is quite suitable here.

[6] I take the quotation from a reprint by J. Collier (n.d.). See also W. C. Hazlitt, Brand's Popular Antiquities of Great Britain i, 5 ; on Bansley see Cambridge History of Lit. iii, 97.

275.—Finally Barclay laments the intrusion of worldliness into clerical dress :

> (93)   The clenlynes of Clergye is nere also decayed,
> Our olde apparale, alas, is nowe layde downe
> And many prestes asshamyd of theyr crowne.
>
> (94)   Unto laymen we us refourme agayne,
> As of Chryste our Mayster in maner half asshamed ;
> My hert doth wepe, my tunge doth sore complayne,
> Seeing howe our state is worthy to be blamed.

The author is certainly not afraid of telling the full truth, but what he weeps over here is not anything like similar abuses in Germany.[1] But of course when the old clerical ' apparale ' is laid down, when ' many ' priests do not wear a tonsure, then they are ' worthy to be blamed,' and as the faults of some reflect upon all, it may be said that ' The clenlynes of Clergye is nere also decayed.'

He concludes his chapter with the obligatory address to England :

> A Englonde, Englonde, amende ! or be thou sure :
> Thy noble name and fame can nat endure.

This is Locher in English. Barclay was not troubled with those little patriotic qualms of conscience that inspired Watson's extension of ' Germania ' to ' Christendome ' at large.

276.—But the preacher has not done yet. The Envoy to this chapter consists of three stanzas, and the first two are of great interest.

It is a well-known fact that at the accession of Henry VIII France was still the ' arbiter elegantiarum ' in the world of fashion,[2] and an authority on historical dress asserts that especially men's apparel was completely under French-Burgundian influence since the second half of the fifteenth century, so that every new fancy that arose in France was promptly imitated in England.[3] This is fully borne out by Barclay :

> (96)   Reduce, courters, clerly unto your rembrance
> From whens this disgysyng was brought, wherin ye go ,
> As I remember, it was brought out of France ;
> This is to your plesour, but payne ye had also,
> As French Pockes, hote ylles, with other paynes mo :
> Take ye in good worth the swetnes with the sour,
> For often plesour endeth with sorowe and dolour.

The French pox or ' morbus Gallicus,' the ' fashionable ' disease of the time,[4] is first mentioned in England about this time, and very

---

[1] See Janssen-Pastor i, 721.

[2] J. R. Planché, Cyclopaedia of Costume ii, 155. See also the Treatyse of a Galaunt, quoted § 40. In Stanza 1808 Barclay mentions ' Almayne ' by the side of ' Fraunce ' ; see § 108.

[3] F. Hottenroth ii, 138. Even in Italy French fashions were imitated (Burckhardt 273). Bansley found another origin of course :

> From Rome, from Rome, thys carkerd pryde,
> From Rome it came doubtless.

[4] Many Humanists, Locher among them, fell a prey to it (Fr. von Bezold, 391). The earliest, or certainly one of the earliest writers about it was Brant in his De Scorra pestilentiali sive Mala de Franzos, published in 1496 and translated into German by Jos. Gruenpeck. See C. H. Fuchs, Die ältesten Schriftsteller über die Lustseuche in Deutschland von 1495 bis 1510 (n.d.), pages unnumbered, and the bibliographical descriptions in Hain *8094, *8095 ; Schreiber v, 4129, 4130.

probably came from France. It is not clear what is meant by the
'hote ylles'; perhaps the Sweating-sickness, which had appeared just
then and which became so famous in Elizabethan literature. If so,
the French origin is less authenticated; when the epidemic afterwards
spread over the Continent, the name 'English sweat' was not a
misnomer.[1]

277.—Barclay's grim taunt is in the true moralist's taste. But
with a sudden transition he becomes the courtly poet and points to the
king as a model of decency for his country:

> (97)  But ye proude Galaundes [2] that thus yourself disgise,
>        Be ye asshamed! Beholde unto your Prynce;
>        Consyder his sadnes,[3] his honestye devyse;
>        His clothynge expressyth his inwarde prudence;
>        Ye se no example of suche inconvenyence
>        In his Hyghnes, but godly wyt and gravyte.
>        Ensue hym, and sorowe for your enormyte.

This stanza must have been written before April 1509. King Henry VII
did set an example. But when the work was printed after the accession
of the new king, Barclay wrote on the margin: *Laus summa de gravitate
eximia henrici anglorum regis VIII.* Henry VIII could not so soon have
abandoned the traditions of his father's household.

The last stanza of this chapter is more of a curiosity:

> (98)  Away with this pryde, this statelynes let be!
>        Rede of the Prophetis clothynge or vesture,
>        And of Adam firste of your ancestrye (!),
>        Of Johnn the Prophete; theyr clothynge was obscure,
>        Vyle and homly; but nowe what creature
>        Wyll them ensue? Sothly; fewe by theyr wyll;
>        Therfore suche folys my navy shall fulfyll.

278.—Brant was a very punctilious educationalist; he had already
written several rhyming treatises on good manners [4]; he loved decorum
in everything; and in chapter 9 he writes a peculiar treatise on
INDECOROUS MANNERS.

Many people proudly strut about in their cloaks, moving their head this way and
that, and now walking with quick steps and now very slowly (1–5). This is a sign
of unlawful levity (6–8). A well-mannered man is approved of by the wise (9–12).
Real wisdom first is chaste, then peaceable, modest, consenting to the good and full
of good fruits—Jac. iii. 17—(13–16). Good manners are better than riches, for
manners show the inward man (17–20). Many have not been well educated and
have the manners of 'a cow,' whereas good manners are the highest ornament
of man (21–26). Noah had an ill-mannered son, but he who has a wise and well-

---

[1] The first outbreak occurred in England in 1485; a less fatal one in 1507;
severer again in 1517, and a very terrible one in 1528, when it spread over Eastern
and Northern Europe. The last outbreak happened in 1551 (Encycl. Brit. xxvi,
186). Its fame lingered on much later.

[2] Barclay uses different spellings for the same word: *galants* (78), *galantes* (6),
*galauntes* (89); and here is *galaundes*.

[3] On the meaning of sadness, see note to § 202.

[4] See § 293.

behaved child may thank God for it (27–32).　Albinus, who had been badly educated, bit his father's nose [1] (33–34).

Locher's version of this chapter has borrowed only a few ideas from the German and never in the same order.　From its Latin verbosity the following list of ill manners can be made out : Curled hair, moving one's hands, immodest faces, irregular gait, ludicrous contortion of one's features.—The rest are all generalities, with echoes of Brant's lines 6–16 [2] and nothing more.

279.—In the first three stanzas of his English version, Barclay imitates Locher's pretty closely.　But then, when some details are mentioned, he begins to move more freely :

> (171)　Some are busshed, theyr bonetes set on syde [3] ;
> Some wave theyr armys and hede to and fro ;
> Some in no place can stedfastly abyde,
> More wylde and wanton than outher buk or do ;
> Some ar so proude, that on fote they can nat go,
> But get [4] they must with countenaunce unstable,
> Showynge them folys frayle and varyable,

> (172)　Some chyde, that all men do them hate ;
> Some gygyll and lawgh without gravyte.

The rest of this stanza and the two following are entirely original. The thoroughly English sound is at once to be heard :

> (172)　Some thynkes hymselfe a gentylman or state,
> Though he a knave, caytyf and bonde churle be ;
> These folys ar so blynde, them self they can nat se ;
> A yonge boy, that is nat worth an onyon, (!)
> With gentry or presthode is felowe and companyon.

A bad thing that proper distances should not be observed !　And now that he is speaking of ' pride,' Barclay thought he might as well give the various men of the law another piece of his mind :

> (173)　Brybours [5] and baylyes that lyve upon towlynge
> Are in the world moche set by nowe a dayes ;
> Sergeauntis and catchpollys that lyve upon powlynge,
> Courters and caytyfs, begynners of frayes
> Lyve styll encreasynge theyr unhappy wayes ;
> And a thousande mo of dyvers facultyes
> Lyve avauntynge them of theyr enormytees.

---

[1] This is a curious version of Aesop's well-known fable about the thief and his mother (Zarncke 318).

[2] Locher camouflaged the reference to the Epistle of St. James, and added between brackets *ut docti referunt*, which appears in Barclay 177 ' As wyse men sayth.'

[3] See Drouyn-Watson in § 270.

[4] The word, printed *jet* by Cawood, occurs again in Stanzas 651, 652, and 902. It denotes a swaggering gait.　See the explanation, § 255 note.

[5] In the Envoy to chapter 19, addressing ' Ye bablynge brybours,' Barclay used the word in its more popular and general sense of ' rascal, wretch.'　Here, however, it seems to have the special more or less technical meaning of ' extortioners ' ; as Cranmer in his Catechism speaks of ' Extorcioners, brybers, pollers, and piellers, devourers of widowes houses.'　See NED.　On the other words used in this stanza see § 205.

When you come to think of it, indeed, all men are arrant fools :

> (174)   Within the chirche and every other place
> These folys use theyr lewde condicions ;
> Some starynge, some cryeng, some have great solace
> In rybawde wordes, some in devysyons,
> Some them delyte in scornes and derysyons ;
> Some pryde ensueth, and some glotony
> Without all norture, gyven to vylany.

After this effusion Barclay walks in Locher's steps again :

> (175)   Theyr lyfe is folysshe, lothsome and unstable,
> Lyght brayned, theyr herte and mynde is inconstant *etc.*

It is these undiscriminating exaggerations and pedantic generalizations that robbed all such satires of their intended effect, and turned them into mere literary pastimes.

280.—But Barclay rides his hobbies with far greater dexterity than Riviere.  As a rule the Frenchman follows Locher much more blindly.  Only in one passage in this chapter does he strike out on his own :

> Les ungs sont mignons perruquetz
> Les aultres portent les bouquetz
> Les ungz se iactent de leurs mains
> Les aultres se monstrent haultains
> Les ungs siblent les aultres chantent
> Les aultres a tous propos dancent *etc.*

Watson limits the expressions which he found in Drouyn's prose-version to the ' yonge folkes.'  Did he feel something of the exaggeration ?  I think that abundance of space here as elsewhere influences the translator much more than abundance of thought.  Some of his additions, however, italicized in the following quotation, are not without interest :

*But the yonge folkes ben so replete with pryde and other vyces that is ryght tedyous to here recounted, for some be foure or fyve houres in pyckynge them*[1] *or*[2] *they can be redy, in behavynge them as hye prynces,* the other have theyr bodyes inconstante, the other bereth *odyferous* floures (bouquetz) aboute them *for to be swete,* the other be past shame.  Some whysteleth, the other syngeth *vytuperable songes,* some be movable as the wynde, the other ben as lyght as a fether, some be soone angrye, and some be appesed in an instante, the other kepeth scylence when it is no nede, the other speke to often, the other be not contente with nothynge *etc.*

281.—Chapter 61 is a sermon against DANCING.

Those who enjoy dancing, says Brant, are mere fools for they make themselves dizzy and tired and dusty (1–4).'  But it is worse.  It has been invented by the devil when he made the Hebrews dance round the golden calf (5–10).  And it really causes licentiousness and impurity, so that I know no play more harmful than dancing (11–19).  When banquets are held on the occasion of a churchale[3] or of a first Mass of a newly ordained priest, even priests and monks dance in their habits (20–22).  At those balls the women sometimes spin round so that the bare legs can

---

[1] *To pick* = to deck, adorn.   A common meaning of the word at that time. NED.

[2] *or* = before.                    [3] German *uff kilchwih.*

be seen (23–25). When Jack dances with Jill he thinks it as sweet as figs, he never feels hungry and easily gives ' eyn bock umb eyn geisz ' (26–30). If that is called playing, I call it fooling (31–32). Many wait long for a dance but will not rest satisfied with that (33–34).[1]

Locher has paraphrased about one half of this chapter, viz. lines 5–19. As an equivalent of lines 20–22, he says that dancing has spread everywhere, so that even the churches are hardly (vix) free ; and everyone dances : boys and girls, fresh youth and decrepit age, the clergy and the monk in his cowl. For lines 26–30 he substitutes a *rusticus* with his *amica*, and the end at the bottom of the page is :

> Non sitis hunc tota nocte dieve premit.

All the rest he has left out, but in the beginning of the chapter he refers to the Bacchanalia (*furiosa Thyas*), to the priests of Cybele (*Druydae galli*) on Mount Ida, to the *Salii* of Rome, and again to the festivals of Cybele (*Cybeleios choros*).

282.—Most of this ' humanized ' chapter does not seem to have made an impression on Barclay. He follows it nearly all very faithfully without giving us much of his own. ' Bacchus sacryfyce ' (875) and ' the Druydans ' and ' the hylle of Yde ' and the rest are all there with ' theyr servyce detestable ' (876).—Only towards the end, where Locher has most mutilated some of Brant's ideas, he gradually makes himself more free.

> (884) What place is voyde of this furyous foly ?
> None ! So that I doute within a whyle
> These folys the holy churche shall defyle.

This is still entirely Locher. But now he begins to modify :

> (885) Of eche sort some ar gyven unto the same ;
> The prestis and clerkes to daunce have no shame ;
> The frere or monke in his frocke and cowle
> Must daunce in his dortor, lepynge to play the fole.

The idea of the friar or monk foolishly dancing in his dormitory is quite original and a good one indeed. Such sport, however, was far from harmless in Barclay's eyes.—He continues with children, maids, wives, ' olde queans,' and a picturesque paraphrase of the dancing *decrepiti senes*:

> (886) And the olde dotarde thoughe he skantly may
> For age and lamenes stere outher fote or hande,
> Yet playeth he the fole with other in the bande.

The almost incomprehensible conclusion of the Latin he leaves out entirely and adds instead in the last stanza :

> (888) That whan they ar departyd from the daunce,
> On lust and synne contynually they muse.

He appends a more outspoken Envoy :

> (889) And who that suspectyth his mayde or wyves talye,
> Let hym nat suffer them in the daunce to be,
> For in that game, thoughe sys or synke them fayle,
> The dyse oft renneth upon the chaunce of thre.

---

[1] The meaning of the last two lines is very obscure. Zarncke 398.

283.—Just as Barclay, Riviere follows the Latin fairly closely, but his version is much more prolix and full of misunderstandings, not of sufficient interest to be reproduced here. The only part of Watson's prose version worth quoting is the end.

And for to dysporte them the more they go in to every place soo that with grete payne the temples is excepte. And for thes unhappy daunces cometh grete myscheves, and inconvenyentes. Not alonely to the laye people, but also unto the clerkes, and them of the chyrche, for they daunce also, how well that theyr thoughtes be vertuous,[1] yet they be beten downe with mundanytees and ben sene reygne in maladyccyon. . . . Yonge maydens be nothynge endoctryned as they were in tyme paste, they can no more vertuousnes nowe, nor honour, nor amyable speche [doulx parler], in the worlde is nothinge but synne. All men as well on werke dayes as on holy dayes ['jours ouvries que festes' says Drouyn ; Riviere had 'iours de festes ou ieunes'] daunseth, ye and they that by so auncyent that they maye scarcely susteyne themselfe, enrageth for to daunce. . . . More than a thousande myllyons of evylles is done at the daunce [Drouyn and Riviere spoke of only 'cent millions'!]. . . . Amonge you younge maydens that putteth al your curyosyte therin, yf ye wyll lyve without vyce, flee that thynge.

End of the chapter ! And Watson has translated everything from Drouyn, and Drouyn has changed very little in Riviere's text.

284.—SERENADING is the subject dealt with in the next chapter (62), which must have been written by Brant when he had been disturbed in his slumbers by a party of students singing and playing at night under the window of a fair one in his vicinity.

I wish to commemorate, he says, the serenaders who, instead of going to bed, stupidly run about the streets at night and knock at people's doors to attract the attention of the girls (1–8). They should be driven away with stones or with 'eyn kammer loug' (9–11). What pleasure do they find in being frozen of a winter's night while serenading a foolish woman (12–15), or while jumping over the logs in the timber market ?[2] (16). Students do that, clerics as well as lay people, crying and shouting and roaring and bawling as if they were being murdered (17–20). One fool tells another, and then they appoint musicians, who keep the secret so well that it is proclaimed from the house-tops[3] (21–26). Even husbands leave their wives in bed to behave thus foolishly, never thinking of the upshot of it all (27–30). I will not mention here those who run about in foolish disguises ; many would take offence, if I were to call them fools (31–34).

Locher leaves out lines 16, 21–26 and the end 31–34. In their place he gives us :

Nocturni lemures stigiis de fontibus orti,

and the *Eumenidum cohors,* and the *Ismaria lyra.* In lines 17–20 he mentions *proceres, clerus, monachi atque sacerdos* and in lines 27–30 he elaborates the probable result.

---

[1] Riviere had :

Combien que la pensee saine
Devroient avoir et grant vertuz.

This became in Drouyn, probably by a misprint, ' Combien que la pensee detesoient avoir vertueuse.'

[2] This line shows that Brant is thinking of not serenading only but all sorts of nightly riot.

[3] This is probably the meaning of :

Die vischers uff den küblen schlagen.

See Zarncke 400.

285.—Barclay somewhat simplifies Locher's classicism, and speaks only of :

> (893)     The Furyes fereful spronge of the flodes of hell.

The following is an almost literal translation, but it may be quoted for its idiomatic expressions :

> (893)     More wyldly wandrynge than outher bucke or doo,
> Some with theyr harpes, another with his lute,
> Another with his bagpype or a folysshe flute.

> (894)     Than mesure thay theyr songes of melody
> Before the dores of theyr lemman dere,
> Yowlynge with theyr folysshe songe and cry,
> So that theyr lemman may theyr great foly here ;
> And tyll the yordan ¹ make them stand arere,
> Cast on theyr hede, or tyll the stonys fle,
> They nat depart but covet there styll to be.

As partakers in this sort of nightly riot Barclay does not enumerate quite the same people as Locher ; he especially mitigates the statement about the clergy :

> (896)     But folysshe youth doth nat alone this use,
> Come of lowe byrth and sympyll of degre,
> But also statis them selfe therin abuse,
> With some yonge folys of the spiritualte ;
> The folysshe pype without all gravyte
> Doth eche degre call to this frantyke game :
> The darkenes of nyght expellyth fere of shame.

The description of the foolish husband and the conclusion (898–899) are the same as in the Latin.   But after that he adds three more stanzas before the Envoy, marked on the margin as *Addicio translatoris Alexandri barclay.*

> (900)     Thoughe I have touchyd of this enormyte
> In Englysshe tunge, yet is it nat so used
> In this royalme as it is beyonde the se.

286.—This is a valuable piece of historical information, which we are sure must be quite correct.   For elsewhere he never expresses any misgiving as to the applicability to his English public of Brant's or rather Locher's satire.   Everything that deserves criticism in Germany or Switzerland is considered to exist in an equally or even more objectionable form in England.   Only here does he make an exception.   Not out of patriotic pride.   On the contrary :

> (900)     Of great nyght watchynge we may nat be excusyd,
> But our watchynge is in drunken glotony
> More than in syngynge or other melody.

---

¹ On the obscure origin of this word see the NED.   The Latin has *urina* and *olla.*

(901)   Whan it is nyght and eche shulde drawe to rest,
Many of our folys great payne and watchynge take
To prove maystryes and se who may drynke best [1]
Outher at the taverne of wyne or the ale stake.
Other all nyght watchyth for theyr lemmans sake,
Standynge in corners lyke as it were a spye,
Whether that the weder be hote, colde, wete or dry.

(902)   Some other folys range about by nyght,
Prowdely jettynge [2] as men myndeles or woode,[3]
To seke occasyon with pacyent men to fyght,
Delytynge them in shedynge mennys blode
Outher els in spoylynge of other mennys gode.

There is nothing flattering or romantic in this picture of English night-life.

287.—A little touch of romanticism is found in Watson's introductory motto :

Who gothe aboute every nyght
Playenge on instrumentes swetely
And syngynge songes by the lyght
Of the mone melodyously
Before his ladys doore truely
He is a foole endurynge colde
Which he shall fele whan he is olde.

The moonlight idea is not in the French. Watson probably inserted it as it was a convenient rhyme-word taken from some commonplace in the ballads or romances.—In the body of the chapter he does not betray any personal interest, he is only translating his text omitting such difficult words as 'aubadeurs.' Two samples may illustrate this. Riviere did not understand the *Lemures* and *Eumenides* very well :

Et aucunesfois leur sourvient
Paricion de nuyt qui vient
Deumenides la grant furie
Les deturbe fort les arie.

Drouyn simplified this into : 'Aulcunesfois leur vient des aparitions de nuyt deumenides la grant furie.'—Watson puzzled by the word *deumenides* seriously writes that those 'juters on instrumentes [4] . . . have vycyons by nyght that be ryght horryble' !

In the passage that corresponds to Barclay's Stanza 896 Watson changes only 'Les mecaniques' into 'the mynstrelles,' which shows that the old word had entirely deteriorated in meaning : [5] 'The *mynstrelles* be not alone doynge so. But the yonge and joyous men, gentylmen, preestes, relygyous men, and monkes, doynge on the nyght all thynges dysordynate.'

---

[1] Cf. Stanza 1191 (ch. 81) in § 239.
[2] *to jet*.   See notes to § 278 and § 255.          [3] Wood = mad.
[4] This is Watson's version of the French ' joueurs dinstrumens.' The word *juter* is not recorded by the NED.
[5] Compare Brant's statement in chapter 62, § 232. See E. Eckhardt, Die lustige Person (Palaestra xvii, 1902), 221.

288.—Chapter 74 is a little satire on HUNTING.[1]

This sport is not without folly, because it involves great expense. Hounds must be fed and hawks are expensive, so that every hare or grouse costs a pound. And what a waste of time and labour in driving the game and seeking it among mountains and forests. More game is scared away than shot, and many a sportsman brings home a hare which he has bought in the market ! Many others want to show their courage and go hunting lions and bears and wild boar or else chase the chamois but they find only danger.—And now farmers are encroaching upon the rights of the nobility. They go out in the snow and have already secretly sold the game while the nobleman is still searching for it.—Nemrod, the first hunter, was abandoned by Heaven, and Esau became a huntsman because he was a sinner. There are few such hunters now as St. Hubert was and St. Eustachius, who left their hunting to serve God.

The chapter is in its first half so full of technical terms, that Locher probably found it too difficult to put into Latin, and in Juvenal's satires there is nothing resembling it, so that he could not very well write an original composition on a classical model. At all events he has simply skipped the chapter with the result that no translator of the Narrenschiff has ever had any idea of its existence.[2]

289.—A similar fate awaited chapter 75 in which Brant ridicules ARCHERY.

If I were to hold a contest of archery for fools, says Brant, many would have to take part in it. He who would be nearest the mark, would be the hero. To do this he must aim deliberately, neither too low nor too high. In such contests it often happens that some have their bows or strings broken, or they are disturbed, or their crossbows go off too soon, or the target seems to have got out of place ; others always shoot wide of the mark so that they never get a prize.—But they always find some excuse for their missing ; if this had not happened or that, they would have won the prize !—I know several archers who always go to a contest at some far-off place where only the most skilful people meet. They will always try their luck, but have the expenses to pay and even lose their stakes. Many will try a shot at wisdom, but they never hit the mark, because they do not take deliberate aim. Most people miss like Jonathan. He who will always be successful needs the arrows of Hercules, who always shot what he wanted. A man ought to be careful to shoot well, for otherwise he is a fool, and he will only get the last prize, a sow ! He who will shoot and hunt and handle the crossbow has little profit and much outlay.

This curious chapter is less difficult and Locher *has* translated it ; but only for the third edition, where the translation appears towards the end, without the woodcut, in an uncommon metre, and on unnumbered pages. As it was the second edition that was reprinted in Paris and Lyons,[3] this chapter remained unknown in France and was never translated into French or English.

This is indeed a pity, for the chapter is one of the most successful

---

[1] On Brant's and Geiler's opinions about this subject see A. Schultz, Deutsches Leben 521.

[2] H. Schönfeld (in Modern Lang. Notes vii, 1892, 346) suggests that it may have influenced the satire on hunting in the Encomium Moriae, and that the immediately following ridicule on erecting large buildings has undoubtedly been taken from Brant : ' Es kann keinen Zweifel unterliegen dass die Quelle für den Gedanken in Brant cap. 15 zu suchen ist.' His argument is unconvincing, however.

[3] See §§ 11, 24 sq.

that Locher has done. It is at the same time one of the most faithful. Nearly all Brant's ideas are in it with even better application ; only the contest at some far-off place, the name of Jonathan and the very last reflection are left out. The whole is couched in a delightfully lilting metre in stanza-form of a favourite medieval pattern.—So many heavy classical passages from Locher have been quoted that we are glad to see him here for once from a less humanistic but more human side. The first three and the last three stanzas may serve as fair examples of his more sprightly workmanship.

> Si non vultis indignari
> Et poetam criminari
> Boni sagittarii
>   Io. Io.

> Ludos fingam pharetrales
> Atque pugnas sociales
> Festivo dictamine
>   Io. Io.

> Signum ego collocabo
> Atque metam designabo
> Prope littus equoris.
>   Io. Io.

And the conclusion :

> Raro bene sagittare
> Scimus : telum et vibrare
> Lyppi nam sunt oculi
>   Io. Io.

> Pauci habent herculeas
> Nunc sagittas et pharetras
> Cuncta quibus tetigit.
>   Io. Io.

> Stultus ergo iaculator
> Et ignarus sagittator
> Porcum fovet sordidum
>   Io. Io.

290.—Chapter 77 on GAMBLING is in all the translations and was, of course, of universal interest.

Many fools, says the German, play day and night at cards and at dice, without sleeping, without eating, but drinking the whole time (1–11). And the following morning one has the face of ' die guten byeren,' another is vomiting, a third has the colour of a corpse, or else of an unwashed blacksmith (12–18). Their heads are so upset that they are yawning all day as if to catch flies, and they could not listen to a sermon for an hour, even if their fortune were at stake, yet as long as they are at the game, they never think of sleep (19–28). Even women forget them-selves so far that they freely mix with men sitting at the same table, gambling and playing instead of plying the distaff (29–38). In playing, like should stick to like, as Alexander said to his father when bidden to run in a match : ' I should not like to disobey my father, but he ought to make me run with kings only ' [1] (39–50). But nowadays all stations are mixed ; priests, nobles, middle class ; good and bad

---

[1] Where is this anecdote told ? asks Zarncke 422

(51–54). The clergy especially ought to remember that playing with laymen often leads to quarrelling and envy, and that all play is forbidden them by Canon Law (55–62).—If anyone could play by himself there would be no danger of anxiety and of loss and of swearing (63–66). If I were to enumerate the qualities of a good player, I should quote Virgil [1] : ' Despise gambling, for it stirs up avarice and envy, and it destroys your mind and your honour ' (67–76). A player must have money and courage, and bear his losses patiently, and wait his chance ; for many a one comes in full and leaves empty (77–82). Whoever plays to win only, hardly ever obtains his wish. Not to play at all means peace, playing means risking (83–86). He who goes to every tavern and tries his luck at every game, must have much to stake and often go home penniless (87–90). If anyone has three plagues and still tries to catch me, we shall be as four fatal sisters to him [2] (91–92). Since playing can hardly ever be free from sin, players are not God's friends, but children of the devil (93–95).

Instead of this long chapter Locher gives us a short one, not by way of a summary but as an original production with some leading ideas only taken from Brant. After the introduction he gives just one line from the Pseudo-Virgil, and then follows with a long but very vague description of the abuses inherent in playing dice. In about twenty lines he introduces the *tres bene currentes*, and the *senio*, the *canicula*, *Venus* and a quotation from Juvenal. The players are said to be regularly swearing and (in direct contradiction to Brant's first lines) not to feel any hunger *nor thirst*. After this description he fills up the remaining space with two lines about women (Brant 29 sqq.), two lines about the different stations in life (Brant 51 sqq.) and four lines containing confused reminiscences of Brant 39 sqq., 93 sqq., 61 sq., and then concludes with a distich :

> Nam mala proveniunt ex ludo crimina multa :
> Ludus opes minuit : et bona cuncta terit.

291.—Barclay paraphrases only this preposterous Latin version, without showing a trace of any other influence. The ' Furyes thre ' (1125) appear and the ' thre dyse rennynge square all of one sort ' (1127), Venus and Juvenal (1129), ' thyrst nor hunger ' (1131), swearing (1132), women :

> (1133) The wymen and maydes, which is abhomynable,
>      In game and other to men ar even semblable,

the different ' maners of degre ' etc.

Perhaps Barclay did not understand the *senio* and the *canicula* (six and nought) ; at all events he omits them, but gives us instead the best and most interesting stanza of this chapter :

> (1128) Suche folowe this game stryvynge nyght and day,
>      Tournynge the dyse somtyme by polecy,
>      Them falsely settynge, assaynge if they may
>      Some vyle avauntage for to obtayne therby,[3]
>      But than if they nat set them craftely,
>      Anone begynneth brawlynge and debate,
>      Blasfemynge and other, the pot about the pate !

---

[1] Brant means the spurious poem *De Ludo*, in his own Virgil edition (Strassburg, Grüninger 1502, fol.), sign. bb. 1 *r*. ; Extracts in Zarncke 423.

[2] This sentence seems due to a misunderstanding of the (Pseudo)-Virgilian :
> Initio furiis ego sum tribus addita quarta.

[3] The *for to* in this line is either dependent on ' assaynge ' or simply due to an anacoluthon.

It appears that coney-catching was known long before Greene and Peele.—The whole stanza must have been drawn from life, but the last line contains an exquisite thumbnail picture, a Jan-Steen scene cleverly represented with one stroke of the pencil.[1]

In the Envoy the author insists that all gains must be given back :

> (1138)     And that small lucre that gotten is therby,
> Though thou about the same hast moche payne,
> Thynke well that it is gotten wrongfully ;
> The lawe the byndeth it to restore agayne.

And he adds a piece of sound businesslike wisdom, vigorously expressed :

> (1139)     Wherfore me thynke that man doth surest play,
> That with this madnes medlyth nat at all,
> But in his cofres his moyney kepis alway,
> For that is sure howe ever the cardes fall
> Or other game, as tables,[2] dyse or ball ;
> And better a lytell sure than moche in fere and dout :
> Better have one birde sure within thy wall
> Or fast in a cage than twenty score without.

292.—Watson is not capable of such good proverbs nor possessed of such a stock of common sense.   He does add a few words to Drouyn's text to fill his abundance of space, but they are little more than synonyms and repetitions of the ideas already expressed before.   There is more originality in Drouyn himself.   He often appends a reflection of his own at the end of the chapter.   So he does here.   Locher had warned against puritanical exaggeration ' *Quem decet* ' etc.,[3] and through Riviere this warning had appeared in prose as : ' I wyll not saye but that a lytell playe to men of a sorte, the whiche is but by maner of recreacyon, it is well done.'   And it was probably this warning that Drouyn wanted to emphasize a little more strongly when he added : ' The playe of dyce is no worse of itselfe than the playe of sabot.   There is no dyfference save only for the evyll that ensueth.'   I doubt whether the English readers understood this declaration.   The ' jeu du sabot ' is the French term for a boy's spinning a top.   But *sabot* in English can hardly have been a common name for this pastime, as it appears nowhere else.[4]

---

[1] This stanza is quoted by F. G. Stokes in his edition of the Epistolae Obscurorum Virorum (London 1909), 13, to illustrate a passage which may vice versa be adduced as an illustration of Barclay : ' Et fui commotus in ira mea, et accepi cantarum et percussi ei ad caput.   Tunc ille poeta fuit iratus super me, et dixit quod fecissem rumorem in domo sua, et dixit quod deberem exire de domo sua in nomine diaboli.'

[2] A sort of backgammon.   Or rather the game of backgammon, as now played, is one of the games played on the tables (Th. Wright, A History of Domestic Manners (1862), 219).   It is probably the oldest game of all.   Whereas cards were not introduced into Western Europe until the fourteenth century, the Anglo-Saxons already borrowed the ' tables ' from the Latins, as appears from the words *tæflstanas* (=dice), *tæflan* (= to gamble), etc.   The game is also mentioned by Chaucer and Shakespeare ; cf. The Frankelyn's Tale 900 ; L.L.L. V, ii, 326.   A backgammon table is represented on the woodcut of chapter 49.   The woodcut for this chapter (77) gives only playing cards and dyce and (see Brant as against Locher) pots of drink.

[3] More distinctly in Barclay (1135) :
> I wyll nat say but it is commendable
> For recreasion somtyme to use suche sport
> So it be done in season and tyme laudable *etc.*

[4] At least the NED. does not mention it.

After this warning Drouyn concluded with a curious example of medieval symbolism, literally translated by Watson : ' The fyrste poynt of the dyce is made in despyte of God. The seconde in despyte of God and the vyrgyn Marye. The thyrde in despyte of the Trynyte. The fourth in despyte of the Trynyte and of the vyrgyn Marye. The fyfte in despyte of the fyve woundes. The syxte in despyte of al the courte celestyall, *as it is written.*' The last words have been changed in English. For the French had only ' comme lon dit ' appealing to a popular saying or perhaps to a sermon rather than to any written text.

293.—We have reached the two important chapters which Locher found in the second edition of the Narrenschiff. The first (110ª) deals with BAD MANNERS AT TABLE, a subject in which Brant took a good deal of educational interest. Already about 1490 he had translated in German rhymes the so-called Disticha Catonis,[1] and also the Moretus and Facetus, two didactic treatises on manners written in Latin by one Reinerius Alemannus, whose Phagifacetus [2] he also translated freely under the title ' De moribus et facetiis mensae : Thesmophagia.' [3] The last-mentioned work is very nearly related to our chapter 110ª, and as the German rhymes are divided into short sections by Latin titles, which give a fairly good idea of its contents, some of the most characteristic may be copied here :

> Pauci servant mores mensae.
> De manibus lavandis.
> De discumbendi ordine.

[1] Concerning the earlier German translations see the monograph of Professor Zarncke, Der deutsche Cato (Leipzig 1852). Caxton had printed the English version ' full craftily made . . . in ballad royal ' by Benedict Burgh, rector of Sandon (Cambr. Hist. iii, 290), and one made by himself ' out of frensshe ' (E. G. Duff 76–79). See further note to § 298.

[2] Reinerius was a twelfth-century monk, but that is practically all we know of him. The Phagifacetus has been edited by H. Lemcke, Reineri Phagifacetus, addita versione Sebastiani Brantii (Stettin 1880). The name is there (p. 10) explained as ' vox hibrida, quam recte perspiciens glossator codicis stetinensis interpretatur : est fagifacetus a fagin graece, quod est comedere latine et facetus, quasi liber tractans de facesia comedendi.'—*Facesia* is also used in the second or marginal title of this chapter in the Latin : see Appendix ; it is the Late Latin word for *urbanitas* or ' courtesy.'

[3] All these poems are reprinted by Zarncke : Catho in Latin durch S.B. getütschet (667 lines), pp. 131–137 ; Facetus im latin durch S.B. getütschet (522 lines), pp. 137–142 ; Liber Moreti . . noviter translatus (516 lines), pp. 142–147 ; Thesmophagia (748 lines), pp. 147–153.—See also Schmidt i, 319.—Professor Zarncke (p. 471) seems to have planned a comparative study of the many medieval treatises on table manners written in Latin, Romance and German. But as far as I know the plan has never been carried out. On p. 461 he suggests that nearly all such treatises can be traced back to one common source in the thirteenth century, viz. Der welhische Gast by Thomasin of Zerclare, the German-writing Italian ecclesiastic. This work, which now ranks among the Middle High German classics, was published by Dr. H. Rückert, Der Wälsche Gast des Thomasin von Zirclaria (Bibl. der deutschen National-Lit. xxx, Leipzig 1852), with full apparatus, but in a very unattractive and almost unreadable form. A convenient summary, however, with extracts is given by E. Oswald, Early German Courtesy-Books, in Early Engl. Text Soc. Extra Series VIII (1869), ii, 97–140. A very discriminating appreciation in A. E. Schönbach, Die Anfänge des deutschen Minnesanges (Graz 1898), pp. 35–78 ; some further details in Fr. Ranke, Sprache und Stil im Wälschen Gast des Thomasin von Circlaria (Palaestra 68, Berlin 1908), 1 sqq., 169.

Non sepe conspicienda sunt fercula.

Manus non inmittenda capiti.

De pediculis providendis.

De impletione buccarum.

De flatu in cibum.

De tussi et screatione in mensa.

Non sunt olfacienda cibaria.

De convivatione cum mulieribus.

Non totum esse comedendum quod in disco ponitur.

294.—The following bare summary will show that all these subjects (even the pediculi) are also in our chapter, besides a great many more.

I must add here some fools, Brant says, whom I had forgotten before, because it is no real sin they commit but only indecent behaviour (1–14). They do not wash their hands before meals (15–16). They take the best and highest places (17–23) ; they begin without saying grace (24–26) ; they serve themselves before all others (27–32) and fill their mouths excessively (33–36). They take out of their mouths what they do not like (37–40), or hanging over the table let things drop from their mouths into the dish (41–46). Others smell everything first (47–50), and throw away what they do not like (51–56), or survey all the dishes to choose what is best without thinking of the others (57–74), or to eat as much as they can (75–85). They drink with their mouths full in such a hurry that they defile cups and people (86–95). They have never enough to drink and do not wipe their lips before taking their glasses (96–99). They make a noise in drinking with their teeth or their throat (100–105). They propose to drink to and before every one else (106–119), and want to have all the conversation to themselves (119–126). Others will catch their vermin,

Mit sechs füsz und eym ulmer schilt,[1]

and kill them on their plate (127–132). They blow their noses or clean their fingers (133–134) or put their arms and elbows on the table (135–137) so that the table is shaken or even a worse thing happens, as occurred to the bride of Geyspitzheym ![2] (138–146). Others again put ‘ pfeffer bry ’ on their bread with dirty hands (147–150), or they pick and choose, leaving the worst to others (151–169). I could mention many another abuse as whistling in the bottle (170–173), or taking salt with our fingers, although this is better than doing it with the knives which we bring with us and which perhaps we have used for some dirty purpose (174–182). It is also considered bad manners to split the eggs, but this belongs to more refined etiquette, of which I cannot speak now (183–189). So I will not insist either upon the various ways in which something that has dropped in your glass can be removed (190–209). But at the end do not forget to say grace, for he who neglects this duty may truly be called a fool (210–216).

295.—Locher uses 94 lines for these 216, or together with the motto and the woodcut four pages instead of Brant’s eight. After an introduction, somewhat answering to Brant’s lines 1–14, he speaks of washing the hands and face (cf. 15–16), of saying grace (24–26), and of something resembling lines 41–46, but so that the six lines become nearly a whole page ; Ceres and Bacchus and the Falernum appear in it with ‘ Curius frugi.’ After this long digression he touches Brant’s lines 17–23 and 51–56 for a moment and then again begins about Bacchanalia, about loud clamouring and singing, the breaking of all the vessels and about

---

[1] The Ulm coat of arms bears a cross.

[2] The bride of Geyspitzheym seems to be a figure from the popular Carnival plays. Brant gives the whole story, which is as stercorous as that of Neidhart.

Sardanapalus ! After this he says he cannot mention everything, because the standard of manners differs with the countries (he mentions the Graii, the Latins, the Germans (whose country he calls ' theutona terra '), the Sauromatae, the Turks and the Ethiopians). But all must say grace (a reminiscence of Brant's conclusion), and we all do not live to eat but eat to live. And we must drink, because our soul lives in the blood and cannot live in the dry ! But we must observe due measure, as more people have died by excess than by violence. The mansions of the great used to set an example of good manners, but they are now all corrupted, and decency has died out.

It is really incomprehensible how Locher has ever dared to call this a translation, and even more incomprehensible how Brant could have calmly put up with such a mutilation of all his favourite ideas.

296.—Riviere has paraphrased this chapter even more thoughtlessly than usual. The Latin says that an invited guest sometimes calls in others to share the meal and the wine, but as the meal is called ' sortem Cereris ' and the wine ' donum Lyaei,' Riviere thinks that harvest time is meant and he paraphrases :

> Et si maint bruvage ont receue
> Ceste gent ou temps de moysson
> Labandonnent et a foyson etc.

' Curius frugi ' becomes ' le begnin curieux ' ; the ' theutona terra ' was evidently an unknown region to the Frenchman, as the country of the Sauromatae naturally was, for he confidently writes :

> Ou bien *en tantine* et cheri
> Et tient ses coustumes et ritz
> Ou aultre qui vivre a appris
> Ou pais et *la sauromate.*

The theory about the soul in the blood becomes a downright joke.

> Toutesfois nous avons actende
> Que pour fort boyre et vivement
> Nous vivons et plus longuement
> Que vin nous rende affectueux
> De bon sang et fort vertueux
> Nostre esperit et cest nostre ame
> Et laquelle comme estant dame (!)
> En nostre cueur et sang se tient
> Et si iamais ne se contient
> Ainsi que disons en sec lieu.

Then, as if suddenly becoming aware that he is writing rank nonsense, he adds :

> Toutes fois cecy ne dit dieu—
> Ains y a ordonne mesure *etc.*

297.—Barclay understands his subject a great deal better, and his method is far superior. He loses no time in adopting a typically English point of view :

> (1725)   They spare no coyne, no coste, nor yet expence
> But brede and mete, dayntyes, bere, ale and wyne
> They drynke and devour lyke wyse as it were swyne.

He explains more in detail what has to be done first, for he blames those who begin to eat :

> (1726)  Or theyr face be wasshyd or handes ; and the same
> Do they or they say theyr *Ave* or theyr *Crede* ;
> As for theyr *Pater Noster*, of it take they no hede.

There is a suggestion of a drinking match in Locher, just where his pedantic *donum Lyaei* occurs.[1]  Barclay wisely omits the latter altogether, but makes the bout a great deal more lively :

> (1729)  Some drynkes, some quaxes [2] the canykyn halfe full
> And some all out, chargynge hym in suche wyse,
> That the wyne semyth for to ryve his skull,
> That he hath no power from the borde to ryse.
> (1730)  Than drynke they about, every fole to other,
> In order ; but he that doth forsake the pot
> Shall no more be taken as felawe, frende and brother,
> But cast out of company, callyd fole and sot ;
> The other stryve drynkynge, echone by lot.

And better even and more graphically than in Stanzas 1191 and 901 (§ 291) :

> (1739)  Some synge and revell as in Bacchus sacryfyce . . .
> And loke, whome this sort most ungoodly can fynde
> He shall the borde have ruled by his mynde ;
> He brastyth a glasse or cup at every worde,
> So that the drynke overcometh all the borde.

298.—*Curius* and the rest are almost literally from the Latin :

> (1732)  Where is Curius and abstynence soverayne ?
> Where is olde persimony wont to be so gode ?

So is the ' soul in the blood ' :

> (1746)  Our soule is a spyryt, as Scripture doth expres,
> Wherfore it may nat rest in place of drynes,
> So must we our blode norysshe and meyntayne,
> For in the same our spyryte doth remayne.
> (1747)  But in every thynge is ordre and mesure.

The habits of the different countries are mentioned with less classical names but with more common sense than in Locher :

> (1741)  For every nacion at table hath his gyse,
> Some we commende and other some despyse.
> (1742)  The Grekis, Latyns and the men of Almayne
> In theyr behavour many other thynges use
> Agaynst the use of Englonde, Fraunce or Spayne ;
> The Turkes and Paynyms have also in them misuse,
> And men of Ynde these wayes afore refuse,
> Havynge other maner, yet other them despyce ;
> Thus every nacion lyvynge hath his gyse.

---

[1]  Inque vicem Bacchi madido certamine sese Sollicitant.

[2]  The NED. suggests with a query, that *to quax* is a variant of *to quass* ( = to quaff), but the verb has been found nowhere else.  Cawood changes *quaxes* into *quafes*.

This is a good explanation of, and even an improvement upon, the Latin text.—More familiar names are mentioned instead of the 'Sauromatae,' and 'men of Ynde' is just what Locher meant by his 'Aethiopus.' [1]

The Envoy brings a good old proverb, the application of which, however, to the subject in hand seems a bit far-fetched :

> (1750)    It is an olde saynge, that man ought of dutye
> Behave hym on hyll as he wolde in hall,
> Usynge and accostomynge hym to honestye.

It is not of general good manners that this chapter treats. After Locher's re-handling it does not even treat of good manners at table. It has simply become another treatise on gluttony and drunkenness.

The English public was provided with the necessary instruction for table-etiquette by those manuals that are known under the title *Stans puer ad mensam*, such as the one ascribed to Lydgate, published by Caxton,[2] or such as the grammarian Sulpitius had written, which enjoyed great popularity in England.[3]

299.—The prose paraphrase of Riviere's very clumsy version is of some interest on account of its additions, and, sometimes, its omissions. The additions are bracketed in the following extracts from the English translation and Watson's own contributions are italicized.

> They set themself at the table without *sayenge ony graces or* wasshynge theyr handes, (save in theyr soppes [4] and or the morsell is downe they drynke without remyssyon and swaloweth the morselles all hole for hast, theyr trenchours is laden lyke mountioyes,[5] and theyr cappes [6] full of wyne *and ale*), whan they have dyned they ryse from the table without gyvynge ony thankes unto God for his goodes *etc.*—And thus they spyll by excesse bothe the body and the soule (After that they have well dronken, they fyght lyke beggers,[7] fallynge in the fylthe and myre lyke swyne) *etc.*

Riviere has drawn out Locher's list of countries into seventeen lines, from which I quoted four above. But the *tantine* and the *Sauromate* have been left out by Drouyn, as well as many of the other verbosities, for which he has substituted an amusing saying of his own ; 'How well that the one is of Grece, the other latyns (or hebrews), eche hath his

---

[1] 'Men of Ynde' is Barclay's name for Negroes, as appears from Stanza 89, where the hair of the 'galauntes' is said to be 'curlynge as men of Ynde.' And as this appellation was very common in ME. (see quotations in NED.) there can be no allusion to Vasco da Gama's discovery of the sea route to India in 1498, as Fraustadt (p. 44) suggests.

[2] E. G. Duff, 269. Reprinted in W. C. Hazlitt, Remains of Early Popular Literature i (1866), 23–28, where other works of a similar nature are mentioned. Hazlitt's remark that Lydgate may have derived his work from Sulpitius Verulanus must be due to some chronological confusion. F. J. Furnivall published a similar treatise from Ashmole MS. 61 in Early Engl. Text Soc. Extra Series viii (1869), 56–64, with very convenient marginal notes. The poet appeals to Grosteste and Dr. Paler, but his precepts are very much like Brant's.

[3] Renouard ii, 271 sqq. enumerates the various editions ; the second, third, fourth and fifth are all from Wynkyn de Worde's press.

[4] Fr. souppes.

[5] This is simply the French word *montioyes*, used in the 2nd ed. of Drouyn ; the 1st ed. spelled *mongoyes*.

[6] Fr. *verres* ; so *cappes* is probably a misprint for *cuppes*.

[7] French : 'Ilz se battent comme coquins.'

maner to lyve.  (The one is fatte the oter [1] is lene, after the maner of
theyr countrees.)  Some be symple, the other gracyous and honest.'
It sometimes happens that Drouyn forgets the negative particle and then
we get in English :  ' Alas Jhesus, thou haste made us for to drynke
wyne and ete mete in this world.' [2]

300.—Locher, as we saw above, concludes by saying that the mansions
of the great are as corrupt as the others :

> Perdidit atque vetus nomen famamque fidemque
> Amplius in toto nec viget orbe decus.

Barclay paraphrased this so as to offer no excuse for the ' symple
comontee ' :

> (1749)  Theyr olde name and fame of honestye
> Ar under fote ; so worshyp is exylyd
> Nat onely from the court and men of hye degree
> But also from the symple comontee ;
> Both yonge and olde usyth suche excesse
> At tables without maners of honest clenlynes.

But an entirely different idea is conveyed by the prose-version.  First
Riviere had been led astray by the *vetus nomen*, probably thinking
that this must refer to classical authors.  And then Drouyn broke a
lance for the learning of the ' pouvres vertueux,' amongst whose number
he probably reckoned himself.  Watson was literally translating his text
when he concluded :

> The workes of the auncyent men appetyteth [3] by the holy lawes that they have
> wryten and dyvers other bookes.  And now they knowe nothynge no more than
> wylde beestes (and scyence is governed by the pore and vertuous men elevate in
> honour, and be oftentymes preferred afore the noblenesse). [4]

301.—The popular festivities at Shrovetide or Carnival are intimately
connected with the fundamental conception of the Narrenschiff, which
professes to be printed ' *uff die Vasenacht*.'  Yet the CARNIVAL-
FOOLS are taken to task only in the additional chapter (110b) of the
second edition of the German original.  To judge from this satire—and
Brant's testimony is borne out by that of his friends and some later
satirists [5]—all sorts of extravagance must have been committed in
Brant's country of the Upper Rhine.

---

[1] Misprint for *other*, as the word is regularly spelled elsewhere.
[2] Locher's *divinus conditor* became in Riviere :
> Helas Jesus le roy divin
> Ne nous a faiz pour boyre vin
> Et viande prendre au monde *etc.*

[3] Drouyn has *appetent*, which is probably a misprint, for the word is used to
represent Riviere's *apparoisent*.  A typical example of the way in which Watson
translates only words without caring for the sense.  *To appetite* occurs already in
Chaucer and all through the sixteenth century, but it makes no sense here.

[4] Drouyn writes :  ' et est science gouvernee par les pouvres vertueux que
science eslyeve en honneur sont souvantesfois preferez devant les nobles.'  A stop
has probably dropped out after *pouvres*, but Watson took it as belonging to the
following word.

[5] See Zarncke's notes 463–467.

Carnival-fools, he says, also deserve a fool's hood, for they often continue their excesses when Lent has already begun (1-4). Some blacken their faces and disguise themselves like scarecrows [1] (5-8). They pretend to hide their identity, yet they wish to be recognized as great men, though they mean only to commit immoral actions (9-20). They are given cakes in many houses though they should be rather driven away for divers reasons (21-24). That Shrovetide should be chosen for excesses is the height of folly (25-32). They run about noisy and dirty, and the greatest fool is king (32-36). Gluttonously they devour what they can get even till midnight (37-39). The devil has invented this game to ruin souls (40-42). They eat as if they had to live upon it for a whole year, and have not yet done when the Matins are sung (on Ash-Wednesday), but continue to eat forbidden food till daybreak (43-48). Jews, Pagans and Tartars observe the rules of their faith better than Christians (49-53). Those who have their heads full of Carnival-foolery on Ash-Wednesday weaken the effect of Lenten fasting and may be called fools for the rest of the year (54-59). Only few receive the Ash-cross with due devotion ; most prefer their blackened Carnival faces, the devil's sign, to Christ's insignia (60-67). The women like to show themselves so that they can also be blackened, which sometimes happens even in the churches (68-73). The wild mob carries an ass through the streets (74-75) [2] and then dancing begins and a popular tournament by mechanics and peasants who have never ridden a horse (76-81). Many a one is wounded there or breaks his neck—and that is what they call play ! (82-84). Then the wine-drinking begins, and fasting is forgotten (85-86).—In some places [3] these excesses continue for a fortnight or even the whole of Lent and into the Holy Week, so that repentance and confession do not come before Maundy Thursday.

Wann man die hültzen tafflen lüt [4] (87-92).

And as soon as Easter is over—Easter-cakes are not to their liking—these fools like to go to Emmaus [5] (93-96).—Women then hasten to lay down their mantles and veils, because they prefer a fool's hood to a decent mantle (96-105).—I conclude : Carnival disturbs devotion, a bad life often ends badly, a fool's cap is dangerous and yet is often worn during Lent and the Holy Week (105-115).

302.—The extraordinary interest of this chapter justifies a full summary of Locher's ' translation.' In German this is the only chapter without a woodcut and without a motto, but Locher has a bad woodcut representing Diogenes and Democritus, and a motto in which he mentions them as Democritus and ' Cynicus.' [6]

If Democritus and Crassus (who laughed only once) lived at present they would laugh to see the

Larvatos fatuos : stultiloquosque viros (1-6).

---

[1] I here adopt Goedeke's explanation instead of Zarncke's.

[2] What this ass means is not clear. The context does not permit us to think of Palm-Sunday festivities. Perhaps Carnival was connected with the Festum Asinorum. But no such connexion is recorded in Kirchenlexicon iv, 1403 sqq.

[3] an ettlich enden. Evidently Brant did not know this from his own experience. But a satirical preacher sometimes wants an appeal to the vague country of Elsewhere. Some people, however, seem to have resented Brant's exaggerations, and an eighteen-year-old Humanist felt called upon to write a defence of Carnival. Dietrich Gresemund was the son of a Mayence doctor, and so he called himself Podalirius (the son of Aesculapius) in his curious little pamphlet ' Podalirii Germani cum Catone Certomio de furore germanico diebus genialibus carnisprivii dialogus : editus per Theodoricum Gresemundum Juniorem Maguntinum,' s. l. et a. [Mayence, Friedberg 1495]. Description in BMC. i, 47. A full summary of its contents by H. Heidenheimer in Zeitschrift für Kulturgeschichte, N.F. iii (Weimar 1896), 25-35.

[4] When the rattle is used instead of the bell. The custom is still observed in Catholic churches.

[5] On Easter Monday the Gospel reading was—and is—taken from Luke xxiv 13 sqq. ; and the festivities on that day got a popular name from that Gospel.

[6] The lines are numbered in the following summary without counting the motto.

No crime is too bad for them (7–8). As soon as the limbs of the Druids (*Gallorum*) are moved by holy emotion to celebrate the wild feasts of Cybele, as soon as the Bacchantes (*Maenades*) celebrate their orgies, and the foolish crew commemorate the bad shades of the dead (*Lemures*) (9–12), one takes a mask, another some indecent dress and defiles his face with paint ; one wears hired hair on his head,[1] another takes bought teeth or a white gown (13–16). Some will be dressed as Parthians, others like Getae or Sarmatici, and others again stain their faces so that they are almost as repulsive as Cerberus (17–20). They bring musical instruments and sing for their girls to hear, and they spend whole days bawling before the doors of their lady (21–24). Happy the girl who can defend herself from these masked fools. They stick at nothing, and seduce the chaste. In their face they wear a devil, who tears the hearts of young maidens and of wives with his nails (25–30). For crimes that are never done in the course of the year, are committed at the time of the masked (*larvatorum tempore*). The mask often enters your houses as a wily fox to steal your hens, and by carelessness you often defile your own marriage (31–36). What shall I say of their manners and scurrilous words and jokes ? (37–38). The mask represents the old Saturnalia [2] or the naked Salii and Mamurius the brass worker, or I rather believe them to be the manes of Pluto (*Ditis lemures*) and the terror-bringing gods sent back at that time, for the fatal hydra-hair hangs on their heads (39–43). They hide the face which God Himself has made ; they defile nature, cover their true clothes with others and stain their faces with paint (44–46). One pretends to be lame, another proclaims himself blind (47). The mask hides nobles and gentlemen (48). Worse still : these masked sports and dances and excesses are continued until Easter. At a time when Christ's Passion is commemorated, we put on masks and eat every forbidden food. We are regretfully late in rising with Christ, and we continue in our usual criminal ways (49–56).—But now we pray those *lemures* cordially that they may at last be wise and leave off their sin. For that it is a sin when we change our faces and our nature, who can doubt ? Depart from us, wild error (57–60). Rumour has it that once a masked man was killed, and that the devil straightway carried off him and his mask to hell ; and rightfully so, for he whose image he bore might justly claim his own (61–64).

303.—We have now before us the contents of Brant's German chapter, and the same *in latinum traducta eloquium* by Locher. It appears that the only points of contact between the two are : Locher 13–16 and 44–46 with Brant 5–8 ; Locher 49–56 with Brant 87–92. It is just possible that Locher 25–30 has been suggested by Brant 21–24 and 40–42, Locher 48 by Brant 9–20. But not a single line has been really translated. We have met with other such cases before, and we always find Brant approving of such 'translations' and decorating them with his marginal notes. It is the phenomenon that Professor Huizinga has observed in Gaguin and his school : [3] whenever those early Humanists write in their vernacular they are true medievals and natural and readable, but as soon as they draw their Latin cloaks about them, their only care is for good form, and they forget truth and naturalness, and their highest ideal is a deceptive imitation of classical expressions.— What proves more fatal for the French and English translators is that the real subject of this chapter can hardly be discovered from Locher's

---

[1] ' in fatua fronte ' ; perhaps a false beard is meant.

[2] The theory about the Saturnalian origin of Carnival, which is still held by many, probably dates from the time of the Humanists. It was also held by Geiler ' procul dubio.' See A. Schultz, Deutsches Leben, 406. On its value see H. Thurston in The Month, 1912, 225–239.

[3] J. Huizinga, Herfsttij der Middeleeuwen, 546 sq.

fine words, although lines 49–56 clearly show that he, like his master, means to speak of the same Fastnacht.  But when you do not know the master, it is difficult to find out what the words of the pupil imply, and if you have never known what Carnival-fools are—it becomes practically impossible.

304.—I have not been able to ascertain whether Barclay's country had much more than its ' Pancake Day ' and its ' Pancake Bell ' at Shrovetide, whether the Italian custom of celebrating the occasion with masquerades had become popular across the Channel.  I hardly think it had.[1]  At any rate neither Barclay nor Riviere has understood the meaning of this chapter.  As we have seen the occasion is directly pointed at by Locher only in one word.  ' Carnival ' is no classical Latin, so he said ' larvatorum tempore ' (32).  When Barclay had proceeded with his paraphrase as far as this expression, he cleverly extricated himself out of the difficulty by a literal translation which remained as vague as the Latin : ' whan this disgysynge is ' (Stanza 1759).  The Frenchman was not half so careful.  Finding the expression preceded by a *hoc*,[2] he helplessly blunders into :

> Toutes les griefue et dures forme**s**
> Qui sont quasi faictes au monde
> Et qui *a present* tant habonde
> Les font et tous grans pechez ors *etc.*

Surely Riviere was not the man to assist Barclay as an interpreter of Locher !  Some common misinterpretations of so difficult a text are but too natural.[3]  In the motto *Cynicus* is mentioned by the side of *Democritus*, and the following stanza is a faithful enough paraphrase :

> (1751)  Democritus laughed to scorne and dyd despyse
> These folysshe games and worldly vanyte,
> And such folys as oft [4] them selfe disgyse
> By counterfait vysers, expressynge what they be ;
> But other wyse Cynicus a man of gravyte
> Oft tyme bewayled the bytter and harde chaunce,
> Seynge in the worlde of folys suche abundaunce.

---

[1] The best authorities I have consulted do not mention it.  Only P. H. Ditchfield, Old English Sports, Pastimes and Customs (1891), 19, and again Old English Customs extant at the Present Time (1896), 59 sq., says that the same kind of festivity was practised in England as in Germany, and he quotes ' an old writer ' :

> Some run about the streets like monks and some like kings ;
> They counterfeit both bears and wolves and lions fierce in sight
> And raging bulls ; some play the cranes with wings and stilts upright.

As, however, he does not give any explanation as to the identity of the ' old writer,' the value of this testimony remains problematical.  Cf. note to § 307.

[2]        Quicquid enim sceleris totus non perficit annus
>                 Hoc larvatorum tempore conficitur.

[3] Fraustadt 8 and 9 sees Riviere's influence on Barclay in the cases mentioned above.

[4] The insertion of *oft* here is a little but significant indication that the real meaning of this chapter was entirely lost sight of.

Similarly Riviere-Drouyn :

> Democritus le sapient . . .
> Fut de la chose non polye
> Mais au contraire se deslye
> Cinicus et pleure le monde
> Qui en grant vanite se fonde.[1]

But this is no proof of any influence of Riviere's text upon Barclay. For how was either of them to know that *Cynicus* was only an adjective, and that the person really meant was Diogenes ? [2]

305.—Locher's learned apparatus of classical names offered unsurmountable difficulties to both. First the Druids, Bacchantes and Lemures of lines 9–12. Riviere simplifies the list, but amplified the description, saying that the fools

> ressemblent les pretres
> Du dieu Mars en leurs divers estres
> Qui faire sacrifice veillent
> En grant fureur et sappareillent
> Et faisant ce vil sacrifice
> Remuent leurs corps et office
> Par une maniere de dance *etc.*

How much more skilfully Barclay sets about to solve the difficulty ! With an amusing stroke of humour he writes :

> (1754)  They wander ragynge more madly in theyr vyce
> Than doth suche people as forsake goddes [3] lawe,
> Whan to theyr ydols they make theyr sacrifyce,
> *Whose names to tell as for nowe I despyse* !

Another difficulty lies in lines 17–20, where the Parthians occur and the Getae and Sarmatici and Cerberus. Riviere tries to render all this, except the Cerberus, and speaks of ' la vesture des parture ' and ' du pais des geticque ' and ' des gens saramaticques.' [4]  Barclay does just

---

Watson's translation of the motto does not improve it :
> Democrytus the sapyent
> By this that he sawe so grete foly
> Of fools that were neclygent
> He laugheth fast and that on hye
> Bycause they coude no polycye
> And Cynicus wepeth ryght fast
> Bycause that the worlde is not stedfast !

[2] The words *Diogenes* and *Democritus* are in the woodcut of the Latin text ; the Basel editions have them in Gothic letters, the Paris and Lyons editions in ordinary type.  But in Riviere's and Drouyn's French, as well as in Barclay's and Watson's English texts, the words do not appear.  In Badius' *Collectanea* the names are *Democritus* and *Heraclides* (this name being probably due to a confusion with *Heraclitus* !).

[3] Both Pynson and Cawood print *goodes*.  But this must be a misprint.

[4] Drouyn omitted the last name, but the other two had become so obscure that Watson may have intended a literal translation when writing : ' the other have party clothes [here go the Parthians !], and the other have theyr gownes of getyque [that is what the Getae have come to !], and thus they make theyr pompes ' !

the opposite; he keeps Cerberus, or rather represents him by a more familiar personage—and dismisses all the others:

> (1756) And other some *in straunge londes gyse* (!)
> Aray them selfe, eche after his delyte;
> And other some besyde theyr vayne habyte
> Defyle theyr faces, so that playne trouth to tell,
> They ar more fowle than the blacke devil of hell.

With a similar clever device the Englishman avoids the third difficulty where (in lines 39–43) besides Saturnus the Salii are mentioned and Mamurius and Pluto. Barclay gives the same idea in plain straightforward language:

> (1760) These folys that them selfe disgyseth thus
> In theyr lewde gestis doth outwarde represent
> The frowarde festis of the idoll Saturnus
> *And other disceytfull goddes and fraudulent,*
> Or els rather, forsoth, in myne intent,
> That they ar wyckyd spiritis, I byleve,
> Sende out of hell to erth, mankynde to greve.

306.—With one important exception all the rest is in Barclay just as in Locher. He shortens a little the sequel of the serenading-scene in lines 25–30:

> (1758) which I wyll nat expres
> Lyst that, whyle I labour this cursyd gyse to stynt,
> I myght to them mynyster example of lewdnes.

What he omits is very little, however, viz. only the metaphorical lines 29 and 30; and yet he adds:

> (1758) And therfore in this part I shall say les
> Than doth my actour, and *that in dyvers clauses* (!),
> Whiche is nat done without suffycyent causes.

The most natural and most attractive passage in Locher is the medieval legend [1] with which he concludes his chapter. Barclay translates it very neatly:

> (1767) I have harde that a certain man was slayne,
> Beynge disgysyd as a fowle fende horryble,
> Whiche was anone carryed to hell payne
> By suche a fende, which is nat impossyble;
> It was his right, it may be so credyble,
> For that whiche he caryed with hym away,
> Was his vysage and his own leveray.

This is a great deal more intelligible than Riviere's intricate verbosity:

> Aussi certainement vous iure
> Que une dissimulee inivre
> Fit aucun et sans nulle fable
> De labit quil print de dyable

---

[1] Such a legend is told by the Augustinian monk Gottschalk Hollen; see A. Schultz 405 sq. F. Bon. Kruitwagen informs me that there is nothing like it in any edition of the Speculum Exemplorum.

Fut pugni ainsi quil le porte
Car a bas en enfer lemporte
Et ainsi porta le loyer
Diceluy du quel semployer
Voulut et porter son ymage
Toustes fois greveux et oultrage.

Drouyn understood so little of this French that he reduced it to one sentence, which appears in Watson as : ' They oughte to do iniuryes unto them that wereth the habyte of devylles, for certaynly they shall bere them unto hell at the laste.' The legend has left behind a very scanty relic !

307.—The one important exception where Barclay positively deviates from the Latin text is to be found in Stanzas 1763 and 1764, corresponding to Locher 49–56 ; or rather only 49 and 50, for Barclay paraphrases the others faithfully, apparently unaware of the fact that they should be taken together ; in line 50 the continuation of the scandal until Easter is mentioned, and in line 53 during Lent and the Holy Week (' Passio quo Christi meditatur tempore ').

Riviere equally disturbs the unity (and the meaning) of these lines :

Toutesfois et plus ie complains
Ces simulacres deceptifz
Et sainctes festes inceptifz
Comme *au sainct noel* ou a pasque
En lieu de servir a dieu pas que
Ne font . . .
Et en la sainte passion
Ou chacun benediction
Doit recepvoir du createur *etc.*

The *sainct noel* is not in Locher, of course.   It confuses the whole context. And the writer had probably no better reason for inserting it here than that Christmas belongs to the *sainctes festes* as well as Easter.[1] Barclay misunderstands Locher as much as Riviere, but what he changes and inserts is evidently taken from his own conscious observation :

(1763)    Some goeth on four disfourmed as a bere,
          Some payne them croked, and some impotent,
          Some with theyr fyngers theyr iyen abrode blere ;[2]
          And yet that is wors and worthy punysshement :
          These folys disgysed moste set theyr intent
          On hyest dayes and most solemne also
          In suche disfigyred maner for to go ;

(1764)    As is Christis feste or his Natyvyte,
          At Easter and moste speciall at Wytsontyde,
          Whan eche creature sholde best disposyd be,
          Settynge all worldly vanytees asyde.

---

[1] Drouyn thought he might put in another feast-day, and he added *sainct iehan*. And Watson thought he might as well omit them all and insert the Virgin Mary : ' these symulacres deceptyves in holy festes, for in place to serve God *and the vyrgyn Mary*, they are at daunces ' *etc.*
[2] The meaning of this line is not very clear.   *To blear the eyes* is a common expression.   But how could people *blear their eyes abroad with their fingers* ?

*Easter* is in Locher, so its presence here proves nothing. *Christmas* can hardly be taken from Riviere, and *Whitsuntide* is undoubtedly original. Both Christmas and Whitsuntide have always been occasions of typically English celebrations. And some of the more objectionable forms of celebration are probably indicated in the first three lines of Stanza 1763, which are equally original.[1]

308.—From Watson's version some extracts have already been given. They were among the best. Most of the rest is too childish to quote. The childishness is partly due to Riviere, partly and mostly to Drouyn, but partly also to Watson himself. One little sentence suffices to prove this. Of Crassus he says : ' Not withstondynge he wolde laughe at the obscure tempestes and to se the fooles garded and bordred and dysfigured.' This nonsense takes the place of Locher's

> Praecipue nostra si tempestate videret
> Larvatos fatuos : stultiloquosque viros (5, 6).

Riviere is responsible for the English ' tempestes,' Drouyn for the *obscure* ' tempestes ' and for the ' garded ' fools, while Watson himself has substituted his ' bordred ' instead of the *larvatos*, which are the real subject of this chapter.—The main cause of all the trouble is Locher himself. His manipulation of this chapter did make it very difficult. Barclay's very correct paraphrase of the distich shows it distinctly, for the seemingly harmless insertion of the word ' dayle ' in the third line shows that even the most acute translator would lose his way in this humanistic maze :

> (1753)   But namely sholde he laughe, if that he myght se
> The wayes of men in this our time lyvynge,
> Howe they with vysers dayle disgysed be,
> Them selfe difformynge almost in every thynge.

---

[1] Disguising like animals is also given as a prominent feature of the festivities meant by Ditchfield's ' old writer.' See note, § 304. It does not seem to have been characteristic of continental Carnivals.

## XIV

## INITIAL AND FINAL CHAPTERS

309.—For more than one reason the introductory and the concluding chapters will have to be taken together. It is not a question of ' les extrêmes,' for they are at opposite poles only in the printed book. In reality they must have been written about the same time, and some of the initial chapters, such as the long apparatus of the Latin text, and Barclay's Dedication, bear evident traces of having been written when the whole work was complete. They all view the work as a whole, and they are all of special historical, literary or bibliographical importance. Those that are derived from the German original deserve the first place.

The first edition had two chapters fewer than the second. Hence we find the first general review under chapter 110 where a PERSONAL DECLARATION is hidden away under a vague title *Hynderred des Guten.*

Many have profited by my work, says Brant, but many others, feeling their own guilt, have taken offence, and ascribed their own folly to me [1] (1-10). A scabby horse will not keep quiet under the curry-comb and a dog will whine when you hit him (11-14). I know the fools abuse me for the exposure of their folly ; but such abuse is self-accusation (15-21). If you do not like my book, you need not buy it, unless you wish at last to get rid of your own folly (22-27). But do not blame my book before you have read it (28-30). Everyone likes his own business best ; that is why fools like their own folly and always object to the truth (31-34).

Locher paraphrases the first eight lines only, amplifying them so that they occupy eighteen lines, more than half his space. Then he asks the reader's clemency for his own work : he is only a youth translating the writings of his master. The critics may be envious, he says, but they may spare at least this useful work ; and if they feel themselves offended by it, it is no use grumbling. And if they deride it, I am comforted by these simple poems. I pray only that they may be useful and I do not care for carping fools. Hence, O readers, smooth the severe wrinkles

---

[1] The German has

er schyltet das gedicht
Und henckt der katzen die schellen an
Die im uff beyden oren stan.

The second line is also used in the motto and serves to explain the woodcut. Locher here translates *ligans nolam gutture murilegi*. This novel adaptation of the story of ' belling the cat,' afterwards imitated by Thomas Murner and Hans Sachs, is probably Brant's own. See Zarncke 460. Barclay translates it from Locher's motto in Stanza 1707, where he says that those who slander and despise the just, ' about the cattis necke suche men a belle doth tye.' This interpretation can hardly have been current in English.

of your brow ; read my work, cease from abusing it, and be pleased with
it now that it is finished.

*Placeat quod modo finit opus.* But the Latin does not end here.
Unlike the first German edition Locher's translation has at least nine
chapters to follow.

310.—Barclay paraphrases this chapter so freely, especially the
second half, that nearly all the expressions may be called original. The
apology

    (1712)    They shall my youth pardone and unchraftynes,
                Whiche onely translate to eschewe ydelnes,

is still an echo from Locher, except for the conventional thought,
expressed in the second line.[1] But a real personal feeling must have
prompted the translator's

    (1713)    Requyrynge pardon if I have ben to large !

The whole following stanza, based on two lines in the Latin, is worth
quoting for its idiomatic English and its delightful pedantry :

    (1714)    To wryte playne trouth was my chefe mynde and wyll ;
                But if any thynke that I hyt hym to nere,
                Let hym nat grutche but kepe hym coy and styll,
                And clawe were it itchyth,[2] so drawynge hym arere ;
                For if he be hasty, it playnly shall apere
                That he is fauty, gylty and culpable,
                So shall men repute hym worthy of a bable.

The rest of this chapter, of which parts have sometimes been quoted
to show Barclay's great courage in denouncing the vices of his countrymen, and to prove how dangerous such outspoken language then was,
is equally largely imitated from the Latin. It is of importance mainly
for the good English expressions :

    (1717)    But if my warke be nat moche delactable
                Nor gayly payntyd with termys of eloquence,
                I pray that at least it may be profytable . . .
                I care nat for folysshe bacbyters ; let them passe :
                The swete cymball is no pleasour to an ass.

---

[1] The same idea is expressed in The Argument (k). See § 341.

[2] On this very graphical expression Jamieson (p. l) annotates ' The use of this, it
occurs again in the Eclogues, might be regarded by some of our Southern friends, as
itself a sufficient proof of the author's Northern origin.' In Barclay's Egloge iv
(Cawood's edition C iii 3) the expression runs :

         I clawe oft where it doth not itche
         To see ten beggers and half a dosen riche.

There is nothing typically Northern here, for exactly the same expression occurs in
such good English writers as John Heywood and Puttenham. See NED. I may
here correct an error of Jamieson's which has misled several readers, even a
philologist like V. Dalheimer. On p. xxx he gives a list of ' Scotch words ' in
Barclay ; they are : ' *gree, kest, rawky, ryve, yate, bokest, bydeth, thekt* and *or* in its
peculiar Scottish use.' Afterwards he seems to have had some misgiving, for in the
notes (xc) he adds that they were ' stated in popular fashion to be Scotch ' ; but he
continues to think that ' so many words of northern usage must form at least a strong
corroborative argument in favour of northern origin.' As a matter of fact *not a
single one* of those words was specifically Scotch at Barclay's time. Most of them
were standard English ; and in as far as they were dialectal they occurred in Devon
as well as in the North. This is not the place to demonstrate this in detail ; but a
reference to the NED. and to J. Wright's Dialect Dictionary will convince any
reader.

This last line is literally in Locher. But Barclay enjoyed it so much that he inserted an original stanza to paraphrase the idea :

> Melodyous myrth to bestis is uncouthe,
> And the swete graffis of wysdome and doctryne
> Savoureth no thynge within a folys mouthe,
> Whiche to the same disdayneth to inclyne.
> Cast precious stones or golde amonges swyne,
> And they had lever have dreggis, fylth or chaffe ;
> No mervayle l for they were norysshed up with draffe.

The chapter concludes in a more subdued tone, more subdued even than Locher's final excuse :

> (1720)  Be pleased withall, and if that ye ought fynde
> Nat ordered well and as it ought to be . . .
> Unto your correccion all hole I do submyt :
> If ought be amys it is for lacke of wyt.

The heroic attitude of the Humanist did evidently not exclude the traditional writing-humility of the Middle Ages.[1]

311.—Riviere inserts a great many more original ideas than Barclay, without, however, assuming much of an heroic attitude. He appeals to the

> Gens lectrez discretz saiges testes

praying them :

> Ne nous inferez nulz molestes
> Et si cause sommes trop ieunes
> Car nous disposasmes tous ieunes
> Le composer fest et feriers
> Ensemble tousiours les ouvriers
> Et a tresgrande diligence.

He has worked at it, not only on weekdays, but even on Sundays and holy days and usually before breakfast, if this is the meaning of the second *ieunes*.—Of one thing he seems sure now, namely that his metre is correct :

> Nostre indiscrete rethoricque
> Conterez comme on fait musicque
> Si les vers sont bien mesurez

And so he may well exhort the reader :

> Si lisez a dimenche ou feste
> Noz ditz ne soyez debiles
> Desperitz ou obnubilles.

Drouyn was rather pressed for space when prosifying this. So was Watson, who leaves out whole sentences in consequence. It is possible that he thought part of it not quite applicable to his own case, and therefore dropped Drouyn's ' car nous ieunes avons ce dispose, nous avons compose iours ouvriers et festes.' But the result of this double process of condensation is that very little remains worth quoting. The best sentence is this : ' If that ye wyll not se our booke, go elles where.'

---

[1] Huizinga 544.

A very sensible piece of advice! And the conclusion : ' wherfore you lectours I beseche you to take the good documentes and leve the evyll.'

312.—In the first German edition this chapter was immediately followed by chapter III, in which Brant writes an APOLOGY.

It is foolish, he says, to reward a labourer before he has done his work (1–8). So it would have been folly to offer me money in order not to write this book ; for the money would have been gone ere now, and I should not have been silent long, for everything on earth is folly (9–15). If I had written this work for money, my reward would have been very little, and I should never have finished it ; but witness Heaven ! I have done it only for God's glory and the welfare of man (16–23). Still I shall be criticized, I know, and if the wise must censure me, I shall gladly submit to it, for I should not like to write anything against God's doctrine or against the faith or anything dishonourable. So I pray everyone not to put a wrong inter-pretation upon my words (24–38). But just as spiders draw poison from flowers that yield honey to the bee, so it will be with me ; fools will for ever remain what they are and they only will complain of me (39–51). I have seen many a fool rise very high, but eftsoon he had fallen and was nowhere (52–59). I must not say more, for fools often condemn precipitately (60–65). Everyone that reads this book may say to me : ' physician, heal thyself, for thou art a fool as we are ' (66–70). I know I am, and I confess to God that I have done many a foolish thing and that I cannot get rid of my folly (71–75). Yet I have been trying, so that I know many sorts of fools (as you may see), and I hope with God's grace to become a better man (76–81). Let everyone strive not to remain a fool, and let not the bauble grow old in his hand (82–85). Thus do I, Sebastianus Brant, conclude, that every one may aspire to wisdom :

Keyn gut werckmann kam nye zu spatt (86–89).

Instead of translating this chapter Locher writes his own *Excusatio* in sapphic strophes, all (except the last) ending with the burden *Plaudite musae.* The ideas may be summarized as follows :

I have translated this into Latin verse, but the reader ought to thank my master for it. I have not done it for glory or praise or for gold ; I am not ambitious, I do not aspire to the Laureateship.[1] All the praise is due to Brant, the great poet, who rivals the classics. For myself I must ask the pardon of the gods, because I feel myself still a fool. Some will like my work ; others will disapprove of it. I ask also their pardon, because I have not studied enough in my youth. I should have written in prose, but song comes spontaneously to my lips, and so I have become a barbarous poet ! If there is anything good in it, I owe it to my master. We have no reason to envy the Greeks or the Latins now, for the frozen waters of the German Rhine have produced famous poets everywhere, and we have even our own Virgil ! And so, O friendly reader, look with favour upon the songs ; and to the rude pictures of this work and to my youth be indulgent.

Very few of the ideas will be recognized as borrowed from the German ; in fact, I think, only lines 16–26 and 71–75.

313.—Riviere has abstained from paraphrasing this chapter, which he must have felt as having too narrow an application. So it does not appear in Drouyn or Watson either. Barclay has the Latin text inserted just before his own final Prayer to the Virgin (i), but without translating it. It has partly inspired, however, his own introductory chapter,[2] in

---

[1] But when he got it from Maximilian shortly after finishing his work, in the same year 1497, he was immensely proud of it, and had himself represented on the fly-leaf of his later works with a huge garland round his head ! See also Hehle i, 28.

[2] Cawood has printed it at the end, immediately after the Latin text (fol. 260).

which he professes to be ' excusynge the rudenes of his translacion.'
This takes the classical and traditional form of an address to the book :

> (1)   Go, boke, abasshe the thy rudenes to present
>        To men avaunced to worshyp and honour
>        By byrthe or fortune or to men eloquent.

The whole chapter consists of four stanzas only, and the form is kept up
throughout ; he continues to address the book :

> (1)            thou ought to quake for fere
>        Of tunges envyous whose venym may the dere.

> (2)   For to the redar thou shewest by evydence
>        Thy selfe of rethoryke pryvate and barayne,
>        In speche superflue and fruteles of sentence.

' Many will blame thee, especially the bad, but the vertuous will defend
thee '—in such passages we may hear an echo of Locher.   The echo is
very faint indeed in Barclay's best stanza :

> (3)   But if thou fortune to lye before a state,
>        As Kynge or Prince or Lordes great and smal,
>        Or Doctour Divyne, or other graduate,—
>        Be this thy excuse to content theyr mynde withal :
>        ' My speche is rude, my termes comon and rural,
>        And I for rude peple moche more convenient
>        Than for estates, lerned men or eloquent.'

As with nearly all the other chapters there is an Envoy at the end, in
which the author speaks in his own name to the readers, exhorting them
to amend their lives :

> (5)   And yf ye so do and ensue vertue and grace,
>        Wythin my shyp ye get no rowme ne place.

314.—There is one more chapter that goes back to the German
original, BRANT'S PROLOGUE (L).

All countries, he says, are now full of good and useful books, especially of Bibles
and editions of the Church Fathers (1–4), and still the world is not growing better
and the number of fools will not decrease (5–12).   One Ship cannot hold them all,
but they want a great number of all sorts of ships and of carriages (13–23).   I have
drawn their pictures, and he who cannot read may still find his image here (24–30).
For this is a mirror in which everyone can recognize himself, for everyone has some
folly in him (31–40).   He who sees his own folly may soon become wise, but he
who thinks himself wise is the real fool and should certainly read this book (41–46).
For here he will find all sorts of folly described (47–60).   Real fools will never
recognize their own picture, but I seek only the approval of the wise (61–72).   Truth,
as Terence says, will always bring hatred, but I do not care for backbiting and
criticism, if only people will return to honour and virtue (73–87).   This work has
cost me no small labour, and many a night have I spent in vigil poring over it while
the fools were sleeping or gambling and drinking, driving in sledges over the snow,
or committing excesses or calculating and preparing their deceitful trade (88–106).
—This is a mirror for all people, not for men only, but also for women (107–113).
Girls are especially foolish, they wear shameless clothes like men ; they have pointed
shoes and very low dresses and they do up their hair like the horns of an animal
(114–122).   I do not want to give offence to good women, but the bad are in my Ship
of Fools (123–128).   Everyone can find himself here, and if anyone does not find
himself, let him wait till I bring him back a fool's cap from Frankfort market !
(129–136).

Locher reduces this rambling introduction to one hundred lines ;
and he does it on purpose, for he calls it a *Hecatostichon*.  But for his
first eighty lines, he takes about fifty lines from the original (skipping
lines 24–30), ornamenting Brant's ideas with classical details.  The
end is entirely Locher's own.  In it he refers the critics to the German
original, says that he follows the examples of the *Satyrici poetae*, and
apologizes for calling the readers all fools !

315.—Barclay paraphrases this Prologue in his usual way without
borrowing a single idea directly from Brant, or, as far as I can see, from
Riviere.  But he inserts a great many quite original thoughts, usually
tending to make the Latin expressions more concrete and thoroughly
English.  Locher's ' spernuntur leges ' becomes :

> (15)    Lawyers are lordes, but justice is rent and tore,
>         Or closed lyke a monster within dores thre ;
>         For without mede or money no man can hyr se.

Instead of ' fools think themselves wise,' the Englishman says :

> (18)    No goodnes they perceyve nor to no good aplye,
>         But if he have a great wombe and his cofres ful,
>         Than is none holde wyser betwene London and Hul.

He wisely leaves out the passage concerning the carriages, which badly
disturbs the allegory, but he adds a great many details to the description
of the ships, showing that he is perfectly familiar with nautical terminology.
He mentions ' barke, galay, shyp and bote ' (19), and says that his fools
strive

> (20)    For to be chefe as Purser and Capytayne,
>         Quarter mayster, Lodesman or els Boteswayne,

Of the three following stanzas only the first two lines may be called
a translation :

> (21)    They ron to our shyp, eche one doth greatly fere,
>         Lyst his slacke paas sholde cause hym byde behynde ;
>         The wynde ryseth and is lyke the sayle to tere ;
>         Eche one enforseth the anker up to wynde ;
>         The se swellyth ;  by planettes well I fynde :
>         These obscure clowdes threteneth us tempest ;
>         All are nat in bed whiche shall have yll rest !

> (22)    We are full lade, and yet forsoth I thynke
>         A thousand are behynde whom we may not receyve ;
>         For if we do, our navy clene shall synke ;
>         He oft all lesys that coveytes all to have !
>         From London rockes Almyghty God us save !
>         For if we there anker outher bote or barge,
>         There be so many that they us wyll over charge.

> (23)    Ye London galantes, arere, ye shall nat enter ;
>         We kepe the streme and touche nat the shore ;
>         In Cyte nor in Court we dare nat well aventer,
>         Lyst perchaunce we sholde displeasure have therfore ;
>         But if ye wyll nedes, some shall have an ore,
>         And all the remenaunt shall stande afar at large
>         And rede theyr fautes paynted aboute our barge.

The allegory remains confused, of course, but there is that light stroke of humour which in Brant always becomes more bitter and sarcastic.— He laughs at the fool :

> (26)  Thoughe he be nought, he thynketh al is well ;
>        Suche shall in this barge bere a babyll and a bell.

He mentions a few more of the crew than Locher :

> (29)  Here ar prodigal galantes with movers of debate,
>        And thousandes mo, whome I nat wel dare name ;
>        Here ar bacbyters whiche good lyvers dyffame,
>        Brakers of wedlocke, men proud and covetous,
>        Pollers and pykers with folke delicious.

And then follows a delightful and interesting stanza :

> (30)  It is but foly to rehers the names here
>        Of al suche foles as in one shelde or targe,
>        Syns that theyr foly dystynctly shal apere
>        On every lefe in pyctures fayre and large
>        To Barclay's stody and Pynsones cost and charge ;
>        Wherfore, ye redars, pray that they both may be saved
>        Before God, syns they your folyes have thus graved !

The relation between the author and his printer must have been quite intimate. And it was regarded as a quite equitable division of the burden : the writer did the study, and the printer bore the expense.[1]  No wonder, that

> (310)  The charge Pynson hathe on me layde,
>        With many folys our navy not to charge.[2]

Whether there was also a division of profit after the sale of the book, or whether the author received any fee for his work, there is no mention.[3]

In the conclusion of the Prologue Barclay leaves out Locher's reference to the German original and changes the *Satyrici poetae* into ' noble poetes

> (32)  Afore my dayes a thousande yere ago.'

Instead of the Latin's more general apology he concludes more definitely and more to the point :

> (33)  But if I halt in meter or erre in eloquence
>        Or be to large in language, I pray you blame nat me ;
>        For my mater is so bad : it wyll none other be !

316.—Riviere's version of this Prologue takes that peculiar form of the *Chant palinodique* which was fashionable among the French rhétoriqueurs from the fourteenth to the end of the fifteenth century.[4]

---

[1] The same expression is used in the Postscript to the Dedication ' By Rycharde Pynson to hys coste and charge.' See § 349.

[2] § 114.

[3] Pynson's contracts with Harman for his *Vulgaria*, and with Palsgrave for his French Grammar, have been preserved and are in Brewer's *Calendar of State Papers Henry VIII*, vol. iii, 118 (n. 337), 1522 (n. 3680), iv, 16 (n. 39), 2403 (n. 5459), and reprinted with annotations by F. J. Furnivall in a pamphlet for the Philological Society 1868. An interesting illustration of Erasmus' difficulties with his printers. See B. Kruitwagen, O.F.M., Erasmus en zyn drukkers-uitgevers (Amsterdam 1923).

[4] It is used e.g. by G. Alexis, Michaut, Taillevent, Pierre Chastelain, Robert Gaguin *etc*. See H. Chatelain, Recherches sur les Vers français au XVe siècle (Paris 1908), 144.

It is a seven-line stanza with the rhyme-scheme of what is known in England as the Chaucerian stanza (a b a b b c c), but usually consisting of eight-syllable lines, and ending with a proverb. If the proverb is connected with the contents of the stanza, the result is not unpleasing to modern ears. In Riviere's first stanza it would hardly strike us as very uncommon :

> Par tout le monde et regions
> Resonent les scientifficz
> Denseignemens a legions
> Faiz par nos peres deificz
> Et le monde en est tout confiz
> Que nous disons saincte escripture
> En nostre loy gist grant droicture.

But the effect often becomes more cacophonous ; e.g. in the nineteenth stanza :

> Aussi mest il bien necessaire
> Car y a tant dinnumerables
> Follatis de pervers affaire
> Qui font des maulx irreparables
> En mes vers qui sont numerables
> Ne peuvent estre tous descriptz
> Qui ayme dieu tient ses escriptz.

And in Stanzas 61 and 63—Riviere surpasses himself in prolixity—he applies the same trick to some communications about his own work :

> Et ce fut dans le temps dautonne
> Proprement que ie commencay
> Ainsi que rasins on entonne
> Et descripre ie mavencay
> Dont me fut estrange lessay
> Juc fuz dedens et difficile
> Il fait tout qui scet le stile.

In the last stanza it seems quite natural again :

> Tant continuay mes escriptz
> Que finay en moys de decembre [1]
> En la grant cite de paris
> De france le principal membre
> Et fut lan comme me remembre
> Mil quatre cens nonante sept
> Dont soit loue dieu qui tout scet.

317.—In some cases these proverbs have left traces on Drouyn's prose, as e.g. for the first stanza : ' Maintenant est le monde plain de science et denseignemens faitz par noz peres anciens tellement que la saincte escripture est en plus grant vigueur que iamais : car en elle est tout droicture.' But in most cases he has left out the disturbing proverb. In this early chapter he was still quite fresh, and he could write a really good paraphrase like the one just quoted, so that this whole chapter is

---

[1] The printing and the writing must have followed each other very quickly, for the colophon says ' imprimee . . . lan de grace M.CCCC.XCVII.,' though this may also mean the beginning of 1498, for the year did not end until the 25th of March.

remarkably free from eccentricities.   But the ideas are so commonplace
that they are not worth quoting.   The last three stanzas he does not
paraphrase at all, but gives his own apology instead.   I shall quote
Watson's translation of the conclusion as well as of the beginning :

> ' Nowe is the worlde ful of scyence and documentes made by our auncyent faders,
> in suche wyse that the holy scripture is in gretter vygoure than ever it was, for in
> her is all ryght.'—' Pardon me you oratours yf ony thynge be evyll couched [mal
> couche] and you lectours that occupyeth the tyme in this lecture, yf you fynde
> ony faute, please it you to excuse the capacyte of me and the yongthe that I am
> yet in [la ieunesse ou suis encore], consyderynge that there is none so welle shodde
> but that they may slyde somtyme [il nest sy ferre qui ne glisse].'

318.—Next in dignity to the chapters taken or imitated from the
German—and a place of precedence might even have been granted
them—are Brant's own contributions to the Latin version.

First there is one of more general import, a short piece of about a
dozen distichs, which he calls a *Celeusma* (I).   It consists of several
disconnected ideas, but the principal part is a CALL TO THE FOOLS,
serving to bring out the allegory.

> Come along, men, Brant says, the east wind is blowing, we must leave for the
> land of fools, for Narragonia.   Cut the cables and we are off.   We are overwhelmed
> by numbers ; one ship cannot hold them all—(another idea begins to disturb the
> allegory)—not only men are coming, but a great many women as well.   He who has
> collected us, believe me—(the two ideas are struggling with each other)—has watched
> whole nights.   And justly so.   For none of us cares for the present, or the past, or
> the future.—(Now the original allegory is dropped altogether.)—In this mirror
> everyone can see the life and the ruin of mankind.   He who compares his own life
> with what he sees here will not easily call himself faultless.   For he who holds
> himself always wise, is always a fool.   When I wanted to find a place for myself
> among the fools, I found that I had often been a fool in all places.—I must speak
> the truth :   it is to the benefit of the fools themselves, and their idle chatterings
> shall not move me.

Here Brant breaks off at the end of a page.   The tyranny of space
has probably crushed the last lines together.   On comparing the ideas
with those contained in the Prologue, the reader will find that they are
exactly those left out in Locher's *Hecatostichon*.   We may, perhaps,
interpret this as a sign that the old master was, after all, not so very
much pleased with the Latin version as he professed to be, that he
allowed himself at least a little protest against Locher's mishandling of
his text.[1]

319.—No French translator has dared to tackle this little *Celeusma*
with its somewhat technical beginning.   But the Englishman knew a
great deal more than Brant about the technicalities of navigation.   He
takes some ideas from the Latin, but assimilates them so thoroughly
and gives them such an original idiomatic turn, that he may well claim
this chapter as all his own :—' Barclay the translatour to [2] the Foles.'

---

[1] The marginal texts by the side of the woodcuts (§ 10) should probably be
interpreted in the same sense.   See § 321.

[2] Misprinted *tho*, corrected by Cawood.

(6)  To Shyp, galantes, the se is at the ful,
     The wynde us calleth, our sayles ar displayed ;
     Where may we best aryve ? [1]   At Lyn or els at Hulle ?
     To us may no haven in Englonde be denayd !
     Why tary we ?   The ankers ar up wayed ;
     If any corde or cabyl us hurt, let, outher hynder,
     Let slyp the ende or els hewe it in sonder.[2]

(7)  Retourne your syght, beholde unto the shore ;
     There is great nomber that fayne wold be aborde ;
     They get no rowme, our shyp can holde no more ;
     Haws in the cocke,[3] gyve them none other worde !
     God gyde us from rockes, quicsonde, tempest and forde !
     If any man of warre, wether or wynde apere,
     My selfe shal trye the wynde and kepe the stere.

In the other four stanzas of which this chapter consists, he drops the
allegory nearly as much as Brant had done.   He only claims to be ' chefe
mayster and captayne ' of his ship, adding a very good reason :

(8)  Though some thynke them selfe moche worthyer than he,
     It were great marvayle, forsoth ! syth he hath be
     A scoler longe, and that in dyvers scoles,
     But he myght be captayne of a Shyp of Foles !

In the next stanza he paraphrases part of Brant's last lines, and then
adds ' But this I leve,' meaning probably that he found no more in
his original and so had to continue by himself :

(9)  But this I leve, besechynge eche degre
     To pardon my youthe and to bolde interpryse,
     For harde is it duely to speke of every vice.

He adds with great rhetorical emphasis that he cannot ' touche the
vyces all,' and if there had been fewer vices in the world,

(10)  I cowde nat have gathered of fowles so great a nomber.[4]

320.—There are two contributions by Brant, which are more directly
addressed to his pupil and translator.   The first (H) is inserted in the
beginning, and is called an EXHORTATION TO LOCHER.   Here
it is the second part that elaborates the allegory, so that it must have
been written just as it stands, immediately before the ' Celeusma.'

Some time ago, he says, I have described the fools in the vernacular, and my work
is well known everywhere.   When I had finished my Ship of the Narragonians in
German, I intended to translate it into Latin for the benefit of the learned, and I
made a beginning.   But then I was distracted by so much business, that my
work was retarded, and I had to give it up, break my pen and leave my ship in

---

[1] He cleverly evades the ' Narragonia.'
[2] This is a remarkable rhyme, pointing to a pronunciation *sinder*.   Dalheimer
thinks it a Scotch form.   But the umlauted sound seems to have been Scotch only
in the adj. or adv. *synder*, not in the prepositional phrase *in synder*, which occurs
± 1400 in ' Minor Poems from the Vernon MS.' 716 (3), while a Scotchman like
Douglas uses ' in sownder.'—NED.
[3] Two words, *hawse* and *cock*, instanced here for the first time in literature.
Both were common technical words in the sixteenth century.   See NED.
[4] The idea is perhaps taken from Locher's Introductory Epigram (B) (§ 333).

mid-ocean.  There I handed over my work to you, my dear James, in preference
to all others.  So raise the mast, weigh anchor, and the wind will fill the sails.  You
hold the helm, appoint the fools to their places, give the signal for the rowers, throw
out the cables and the ship is under way.  But avoid the sunken rocks, the Scylla
and its opposite ; when necessary cast your anchor to prevent the winds and waves
from wrecking your vessel.  Take care lest you should perish by whirlwinds or
tempests.  And so farewell.

This is mainly important to show the relation between the master
and his pupil.  Brant's distracting business, which prevented him from
doing the translation himself, has become a loss for French, but
principally for English literature.  How Barclay would have revelled
in the proverbial, pessimistic, sarcastic moralizings of the old jurist.
Unless, indeed, the stiff brocade of the Latin vestments would have
made the master walk with the same measured step as the pupil affects.
But he would not at least have left out so many of the central ideas of
the principal chapters.—These are vain regrets.  It is Locher's version that
we have to accept, as all the translators and Brant himself accepted it.

321.—We have a more direct testimony for this in the LETTER
TO LOCHER, which forms the end of the chapter (e) on the Beghards.

Here after writing one of his most withering satires,[1] he prays all the fools to
leave his ship as soon as possible, because he is going to enter the harbour !—You
have all the merit of this translation, he says to Locher, I like your work well enough
(*sat placet !*),[2] and on the margin I have annotated the authorities from whom I have
collected my extracts.  But I hope the reader will excuse the printers, who are
always in a hurry.  I have tried to correct all the misprints but their precipitancy
has left many mistakes.  The critics will now laugh at them, I am sure ; but I write
only for the benefit of the wise ; I can never satisfy the fools, who will censure
everything and yet know nothing and like their own selves best.  But those aspiring
fools will soon have a fall and lose the nest and the birds.[3]  Nothing, not even the
best, can please all.  You have persuaded me, O brother, to look through and
correct your translation.  I have done what I could, your master is proud of your
talent.  And together with your friend Joannes de Olpe I bid you go on with what
you have so well begun, that you may live long and happy.  Farewell.

The most interesting passages in this letter, besides the complimentary
expression of satisfaction, are those referring to printers and printers'
errors, and to the marginal notes.  Locher's text is indeed fully equipped
with references to biblical and classical authorities.  But when Brant
pretends that they are the sources from which he has derived his text,[4]
we must give a very wide interpretation to his words.  Hundreds of

---

[1] See § 162.

[2] The very next line does sound like a remonstrance :

Nota magis fuerat nobis inventio nostra.

But as the context is somewhat obscure, I dare not press it.  See note [4].

[3] This refers to the original woodcut, a bird-nesting fool, the same as for the
original German chapter 36.  For the second edition, reprinted in France, a new and
different woodcut was made.

[4] The words do not seem to be very clear :

Nota magis fuerat nobis inventio nostra :
  Quo quaeque excerpsi dicta decora loco :
Idcirco ascripsi loca concordantia : lector
  Noscere quo valeat : singula quaeque cito.

texts are quoted that cannot possibly have influenced either the German or the Latin version, and on the other hand he very often omits mentioning his real sources.[1] This has long been recognized. But the importance of the texts quoted in the second [2] edition of Locher's version beside the woodcuts would seem to have been unduly overlooked. In a great many cases these texts have very little to do with Locher's version, but they give a faithful interpretation of the meaning of the German original. As they have left no trace of influence, however, on the English versions, no more details can be given here.[3]

322.—Riviere has translated the beginning of this letter together with the rest. Instead of Brant's *Apostropha ad Philomusum*, however, he annotates *Excusatio ad lectores*, and tones down the harshness of the judgment on the printers :

> Pardonnez aux bons imprimeurs
> Doulx et loyaulx cueurs et terreurs
> Nayez contre moy *etc.*

He then speaks of the critics and ends with the touching, truly medieval prayer :

> Ne vueillez lire ces versez
> Que nayez vos doulx yeulx versez
> Au ciel en loyalle amitie
> En disant ayez pitie
> De cueur ainsi que lexprime
> Qui translata ce livre en rime.
>             Amen.

Drouyn paraphrases the beginning faithfully, but after a few lines, finding his space nearly filled, he suddenly breaks off and brings his chapter to a rather abrupt conclusion with one of his favourite proverbs which seems to be a sort of stopgap or cliché.[4] Watson's translation is perfectly literal :

> Pardon more over the prynters loyall and amyable, yf that you fynde ony faute by them. For there is none but that he may fayle somtyme, and yf he be never so cunnynge nor wyse. You fooles have none indynacion upon me for my scryptures and wrytynges, yf that you fynde ony thynge evyll couched or ordred this notwithstondynge it is pleasaunt unto them that wyll lyve vertuously, for as it is sayd comynly all aboute, the man purposeth, and god dysposeth.

---

[1] Zarncke has identified the majority of the sources. They are : (1) Classical authors : Plutarch, Horace, Juvenal, Ovid, Persius, Terence, Boethius, Cicero, Pliny, Sallust, Disticha Catonis, and Pseudo-Virgil ; (2) the Bible : Psalms, Proverbs, Ecclesiastes, Sapientia, Eccli., Jeremias, Ezechiel, Matthew, Mark, Luke, Rom., Corinth., Hebr., James, John, and Apoc. ; (3) Canon Law : Decretum Gratiani, Decretales Gregorii. See the full list Zarncke 483 and cf. 296.

[2] A very few are to be found already in the first edition, used by Riviere.

[3] Cf. § 318. They would seem to have been the principal source for the quasi-learned apparatus of prose-notes with which Jodocus Badius has provided his Latin verses on Brant's woodcuts. They must also have provided material for the commentary which accompanies Guy Marchand's *Der zotten ende der narrenscip* §§ 12, 29. Even the titles of these marginal texts, which are given as ' second titles ' in the Appendix, seem to have enjoyed some special favour, and it is worth while to compare them with the titles of Badius given by Renouard i, 281–284.

[4] See § 166.

323.—There is no toning down in Barclay's version :

> (1956)  Let nat the redar be discontent with this
> Nor any blame agayne me to obiect,
> Though that some wordes be in my boke amys ;
> For though that I my selfe dyd it correct,
> Yet with some fautis I knowe it is infect,
> Part by my owne oversyght and neglygence
> And part by the prynters nat perfyte in science.

> (1957)  And other some escaped ar and past,
> For that the prynters in theyr besynes
> Do all theyr workes hedelynge and in hast ;
> Wherfore if that the redar be wytles,
> He shall it scorne anone by frowardnes,
> But if the redar wyse, sad and discrete be,
> He shall it mende, laynge no faut to me.

Though in all this the Englishman keeps fairly close to his Latin model, he seems to have assimilated all the ideas much more perfectly than in the greater part of his translation.  Nearly every stanza contains original expressions of his own.  When Brant says that it is impossible to satisfy everyone, Barclay quotes as examples ' Virgyll a poet excellent ' and ' Jerome with other Doctours ' (1961), and in his final stanza he leaves Brant and Locher altogether.  With the typical self-satisfaction of a moralist he writes about the popular tales of the time and about the frivolous writings of John Skelton his rival :

> (1962)  Holde me excusyd, forwhy my wyll is gode
> Men to induce untò vertue and goodnes ;
> I wryte no iest ne tale of Robyn Hode,
> Nor sowe no sparcles ne sede of vyciousnes ;
> Wyse men love vertue, wylde people wantonnes ;
> It longeth nat to my scyence nor cunnynge
> For Phylyp the Sparowe the dirige to synge !

324.—This is the most unambiguous reference to Skelton in all Barclay's works.  *The boke of Phyllyp Sparowe compyled by mayster Skelton Poete Laureate* was published by Rychard Kele at an uncertain date.  Barclay's contemptuous allusion shows that it must have been before 1509 [1] and at the same time that there was no love lost between the moralizing chaplain and the eccentric Rector of Diss.  John Bale, whose bibliographical data have proved to be trustworthy on the whole, has even recorded the fact that Barclay had written a whole book *Contra Skeltonum* ; [2] but it is rather remarkable that there is no trace of any retort from the quarrelsome Rector. [3]  Various little allusions in Barclay's

---

[1] Cambr. Hist. iii, 71.

[2] It is mentioned in the *Scriptorum illustrium Brytanniae . . Catalogus*, i (Basel 1557), p. 723, not in the earlier *Illustrium majoris Britanniae Scriptorum . . . Summarium* (Ipswich 1548 ; Wesel 1549), additio, fol. 254 v.  The name occurs in Bale's manuscript notes (ed. R. L. Poole and M. Bateson, in Anecdota Oxoniensia 1902 ; see p. 19), but not in the first entry.  He seems to owe the information to *Nicolaus Brigan et alii*.  Nicholas Brigham is a noted antiquary † 1558, and his testimony has undoubted value.—Be it noted, by the way, that he is the builder of Chaucer's tomb in Westminster Abbey (DNB. vi, 330).

[3] The often quoted reference to a ' frownyng countenance ' in the *Garlande of Laurell* is too vague to be called a reply.—Ramsay lxxxviii.

works seem to be directed against his contemporary, but the real nature of the quarrel remains entirely in the dark. Skelton prided himself— as so many Humanists did—on his title of *Poet Laurate*, which he had received from the Universities of Oxford and Louvain and Cambridge.[1] There are some little allusions to the empty glory of that name in Barclay's poems, but nowhere does he go farther, and nowhere does he give a more direct detail than in the stanza just quoted. Among the boasters he mentions 'some other crowned as Poetis Lawreate' (Stanza IIII, see § 36). Elsewhere (Stanza 808, see § 127) he asks :

> Where (ar) the Phylosophers and Poetis Lawreat ?

The fourth Eclogue contains what Jamieson (lxxx) has called 'an onslaught evidently levelled at the abominable Skelton,' but there is no more evident reference in it than :

> And to what vices that princes moste intende
> Those dare these fooles solemnize and commende.
> Then is he decked as Poete laureate,
> When stinking Thais made him her graduate.

We should not forget that on the Continent the Poets Laureate could be counted by the dozen at that time,[2] and that we have no proof that Barclay is always thinking of his English contemporaries and not merely following the literary fashion.

325.—It is certainly not impossible that the whole of Stanza 1962 is meant as a sneer at Skelton, because there is some probability that he was the author of a Robin Hood pageant [3] and because he might perhaps be said to have been sowing the 'sede of vyciousnes' and to love 'wantonnes' even then. But it is also possible that only a more general and vague allusion is meant. 'To tell a tale of Robin Hood' seems to have long been an expression for gossiping or telling worthless tales. As such it occurs already in *Piers Plowman* (B-text, passus V), where the figure of Sloth is represented as saying :

> I can nougte perfitly my pater-noster, as the priest it syngeth :
> But I can rymes of Robyn Hood and Randolf Erle of Chestre.

Various popular ballads on Robin Hood still exist, which go back to the fifteenth century.[4] In the beginning of the sixteenth century (1521) John Mair [5] wrote in his *Historia Majoris Britanniae* : 'Rebus hujus Roberti (Hudi) gestis tota Britannia in cantibus utitur,' and one or two years after the translation of the Ship of Fools had appeared, Wynkyn de Worde published the famous *Geste of Robyn Hode*.[6] Barclay did

---

[1] See above, § 254.
[2] G. Voigt, Die Wiederbelebung des class. Altertums ii³ (1893), 278.
[3] See Fr. Brie in Englische Studien 37 (1907), 35 ; Ramsay xcviii ; Cambr. Hist. iii, 68.
[4] As early as the first half of the fourteenth century they seem to have become known in Holland.—J. de Vries, Robin Hood en Mijn Here van Mallegem in Tijdschrift voor Nederl. Taal en Letterk. xxxvi (1917), 11–54.
[5] Quoted in Encyclopaedia Britannica s.v. Robin Hood.
[6] Reprinted by A. W. Pollard, Fifteenth Century Prose and Verse (1903), 35 sqq.

not consider it a very obnoxious or offensive story. It is simply ' a folysshe yest ' [1] and the pity is only that many ' thynke . . . no Scripture . . . so true nor gode ' (Stanza 198) and that the priests should tell such stories in the choir,—although these are not of the worst ; for sometimes they tell ' other tryfyls that skantly ar so gode ' (Stanza 1394). When there is a fitting occasion the author has no objection to the story at all ; as he wrote later in his Eclogues,—at some festive banquet :

> Yet would I gladly heare some mery fit
> Of mayde Marion, or els of Robin Hood.[2]

But his translation of the *Ship of Fools*, of course, is a much more serious occupation ! This is worth an honest moralist's while, and so he may well sigh at the end of his work :

> I wryte no iest ne tale of Robyn Hode.

326.—There are several additions to the Latin version which do not go back to Brant at all, either in Latin or in German. Only two of them have been translated into French and English, but the others, which do not seem to have recently attracted any attention, are perhaps even more interesting from a bibliographical or literary point of view. A brief summary of each will bring out the more important points.

First there are different complimentary addresses to the generous ecclesiastic—who brought out at his own expense all those beautiful editions with fine illustrations of the works of Brant and his friends at Basel, John Bergmann from Olpe.[3]

327.—In the beginning there are just TEN LINES TO BERGMAN (G), in which Locher congratulates the printer, because, he says,

you exalt the Muses, you make our poets famous, and give an eternal name to Brant. You are worthy to be praised by all the Muses themselves, especially for the new expressive figures.[4] Rome itself cannot equal us. Farewell.

328.—At the end there are other addresses, in which Locher tells as much of his own work and ideas as of the printer's glory. He begins there with a LETTER TO BERGMAN (c) in high-flown prose.[5]

I have many critics, he says, but supported by Brant I fear nothing. Is it a shame for a young man born in Swabia and fed on acorns, to write poetry ? Apollo will protect me. I know my work is not perfect, but even Cicero and Virgil were criticized. And if the critics are not perfect themselves they should not abuse my work. The gods may help me that my labours may grow in the faith and that I

---

[1] It is worthy of note that just about this time the word *Gest* or *Jest* passed from its original Chaucerian sense into the modern meaning. See E. Eckhardt, Die lustige Person (Palaestra xvii, 1902), 221.

[2] Quoted by Jamieson lxvii.

[3] What little is known about him is collected by Dr. C. Chr. Bernoulli in P. Heitz, Basler Büchermarken bis zum Anfang des 17. Jahrhunderts (Strassburg 1895), xviii. See also BMC. iii, 795.

[4] *argutis dictata recentia signis.* I do not know whether this refers to the wood-cuts or to the letterpress.

[5] It was usual for the Humanists to reserve their finest writing for such addresses and dedications. And fine writing always meant an abundance of pseudo-classical hotch-potch.—Huizinga 540.

may give beautiful editions of literary monuments.[1] You especially, John Bergman, by your kindness and your munificence, help to raise literature in Germany out of its deep-sunk neglect. For you bear all the expenses of having excellent books well printed. The writers' glory but enhances yours. Hence it is that I want to have this letter printed at the end as a testimony to your kindness and friendship. From Friburg 1497.

329.—By way of postscript he appends three distichs, containing little else than ' kind regards to Brant,'[2] and then writes a longer poem of two pages as an ENVOY TO BERGMAN (d).

He says that with the protection of Bergman and of Apollo he fears nothing, not even the Turks and the ' Getae.' My song, he asserts, will penetrate into fortresses and palaces ; the fighting soldier, the common people and the learned scholar will all read it and cherish it. It is not as presumptuous and sublime as the great epics, but simple and unassuming. It may go to Bergman, and he may show it to Brant, who will certainly be pleased with it, and protect it as his own work !

330.—It is for his master that Locher naturally reserves his most exalted praise. It is contained in two contributions. First a LETTER TO BRANT (C) in high-flown prose.

O most melodious poet and my most beloved master—these are the principal ideas—I should like to dedicate this work to you because of your kindness and because of the pleasant lessons I enjoyed in which you inspired me with the love of poetry just as Callistratus inspired Demosthenes (!) All the reeds of the Nile and all the papyri of Egypt would not suffice to express my gratitude. You will approve of my translation from the German. I need not be ashamed of it. My famous master Philip Beroaldo, whose lectures I heard at Bologna, did not think it beneath him to translate the Italian works of the celebrated Petrarch and of Boccaccio.[3] I feel myself in my relation to you, as Isocrates and Plato did to Socrates, and Theophrastus to Aristotle. I have proclaimed your fame throughout Germany and in the schools of Italy. Witness Hubertinus Crestentinas, the official poet of the Margrave of Montferrat and Piedmont,[4] whom I have told that you were

---

[1] Is he alluding to his preparations for the edition of Horace, which followed shortly after the Navis Stultifera, Hehle i, 30 ?

[2] He strangely calls him ' noster Thaedigena,' translating the word Brant into Latin (taeda) with an ending similar to Brant's own ' Olpigena ' (in chapter f).

[3] Filippo Beroaldo (1453–1505), a Humanist professor of Bologna and for two years also at Paris (Thuasne i, 282–283 n. ; Renaudet 116). His Duae Historiae ex Boccaccio conversae were published separately at Bologna in 1492 (K. Burger 355). The translation of one of Petrarch's Cantos is contained in the Orationes, perhaps first published in Paris about 1490 (Pellechet 2215 ; Burckhardt 184).

[4] This ' poeta stipendarius ' was probably one of those masters of Locher who, together with Beroaldo and Brant and the Venetian grammarian Franc. Niger (see Hain 11858–11884) and the Paduan Professor of Classics John Calphurnius, had already repudiated their pupil, when Barclay read these lines. In 1503 there began a very passionate controversy between Locher and the old theologian George Zingel, afterwards continued by James Wimpheling. It developed into something resembling the Reuchlin controversy. As it does not seem to have been known in England, however, and as Barclay appears to have been wholly ignorant of it, its story falls outside the scope of this study. But just at the time when the English translation was published Wimpheling wrote a book entitled Contra turpem libellum Philomusi. Defensio theologiae scholasticae et neotericorum, and it contained a distich under the name of Locher's masters of poetry : Ph. Beroaldi, Ubertini clerici, Jo. Calphurnii, F. Nigri, Seb. Branti :

> Theologos semper dileximus, haud Philomusus.
> Talem discipulum nos habuisse pudet.

Ch. Schmidt i, 234 ; Hehle ii, 9 sqq. ; Dr. J. Knepper, Jacob Wimpheling 1450–1528, p. 219. The origin of the quarrel was perhaps a financial question. Dr. G. Bauch, Die Anfänge des Humanismus in Ingolstadt (Histor. Bibliothek xiii, München 1901), 72.

our Ovid ! So I hope you will favour this work with your protection. For some
critics will censure it severely, but under your protection I feel safe. I have also
a higher buskin, I can write tragedies and pleasant poetry and I am a worshipper
at the altar of Mathesis.[1] So help me with your favour and pray for a favourable
wind. Farewell. Friburg, February 1st, 1497.

331.—This letter, in which the bombastic language covers rather
prosaic contents, is followed by a still more high-flown SONG TO
BRANT (D) in elegiacs, to express the following ideas.

If this were a piece of fine lyric poetry I should dedicate it to you. Nothing
rude and simple is worthy of your name, because you are yourself a great poet and
orator. Germany may be glad that the Muses have come to her. We live so far
away from Helicon. Apollo could easily penetrate into Italy, but we live in a
climate where genius cannot easily thrive, and our language is Sarmatian (!) and
guttural and coarse. But since Brant has commenced to cultivate poetry, our
country has produced quite a number of poets and prose-writers. There is nothing
more excellent than to devote one's life to learned recreation [docto ludo] ; study
brings fame and noble titles, and the poets are well rewarded. So old and young
may rejoice at Brant's glorious leadership. O my friend, I often kiss the paper on
which I find your poems. I wish I could always enjoy your company, for you
always speak melodiously and you are equal to the poets of antiquity. But I need
not praise you, as your own writings are your most eloquent praise.

332.—None of these pieces have been translated by Riviere or
Barclay, but they were all, including the eulogies on Bergman, inserted
by Pynson in his edition of Barclay's translation, as they had been faithfully reproduced by the French printers. It was probably only for
lack of space that he omitted BECCADELLUS' EPIGRAM TO
BRANT (g). This Thomas Beccadellus says of himself that he was
a student at Bologna, that he was still 'impuber' and that he was
a Fleming.[2] But he has so completely concealed his, no doubt, honest
Flemish name under the fine Latin dress, that his identification has
probably become impossible.[3]

His praise of Brant is even more exaggerated than that of Locher.

It says, that Italy and Greece may now cede the palm to Germany, because
of her flourishing studies of Law, of Astronomy, of the doctrines of Pythagoras and
Plato, and of Medicine. Also the Muses have come to her, and many heads are
laurelled. But there is one great poet, who combines poetry with the study of Law,
the glory of the country and of our people [*Nostre* quoque gloria gentis !]. O Brant,

---

[1] I do not quite see the meaning.—As early as 1495 Locher had already published
one of his 'tragedies.' It is a series of dialogues to deprecate and ridicule the
French expedition to Italy.—His other works before the 'Navis Stultifera' are :
(1) A number of lyrics, *i.a.* six erotic Elegies addressed to 'Panthia' ; (2) a
'Grammatica nova' (now lost, it seems ; see § 250) ; (3) an 'Epithome Rhetorices' ;
(4) 'Theologica emphasis sive dialogus super eminentiam quatuor doctorum
ecclesiae' ; (5) 'Oratio de studio humanarum disciplinarum . . in publico auditorio
studii Friburgensis.'—Hehle i, 19–22 ; cf. ii, 58.

[2] He says this in an 'Egloga' addressed to a friend of his who was also a friend of
Brant's, the Strasburg canon Thomas Wolf. This Egloga is really a dialogue about
the Italian expedition of Charles VIII, and expresses the hope that the Emperor
Maximilian may repel all future invasions. It was inserted in the Basel-edition of
1498 on the unnumbered sheets before *De corrupto Ordine* (f). See a summary in
C. Schmidt ii, 65.

[3] One Thomas Beccadellus published at Bologna in 1489 a dialogue called
*De precendentia intra el Cavaliere Dottore et Conte*, described by Hain 2726. Our
Thomas Beccadellus calls himself 'Bononiae studens.' Is he the same person ?
But how, then, can he still be 'impuber' in 1498 ?

I am astonished that you have never visited Italy, and yet you are an expert in Law and in poetry !

The little Postscript to Bergman exhorts him to print Brant's ' divine ' poems, as he has preserved so many writings for posterity.

333.—Besides these professedly personal addresses, Locher has about half a dozen introductions for the benefit of the general reader. First three little poems. The INTRODUCTORY EPIGRAM (B) apologizes for the trivial, simple songs contained in the book.

> I could produce something more polished, he says, if I were to write tragedies.[1] But I have now preferred a more plain style of writing for the fools. May Jupiter grant this Ship a safe journey. If it were still the *aetas Saturnia* or the Golden Age, there would not be so many fools in it.

334.—LOCHER'S APOLOGY (E) takes the form of a poem in sapphic stanzas, fifteen in number.

> The famous poets of old could soar high and sing of great subjects, of kings and wars and tragedies—such are the contents of the first nine stanzas. The last six say :—I am a humble poet, and so I must apologize for my shrill piping. Let others sing of legends and wars, I am content with my humorous (*iocoso* !) little song and I believe you will be satisfied with my weak Muses, born in a ' slow climate.' They will certainly please my master.

335.—His EPIGRAM TO THE READER (F) is in the usual elegiacs.

> The famous Brant, he says, has fashioned this Ship of Fools. I may call it a satire, for it praises virtue and censures vice ; a thing which Homer could hardly have done. O my master, you were born under a favourable constellation. I shall translate your vernacular witticisms (*lepores* !) into simple Latin. All those who will embark in our ship must run, for we are starting for the western sea ; some will row and others will attend to the sails. Run, for we are launching out into the deep !

336.—Of greater significance than these little poems, which the translators did not think worthy of their efforts, are the prose Introductions. Professedly there is only one in Locher, viz. the PROLOGUE (K), but what he calls the *Argumentum* (M) is only a continuation of the same ideas. The first may be summarized as follows.

> The world is full of errors that bring mankind to ruin, and hence the wise have always tried to cure them better than Aesculapius did. In the Greek gymnasia Socrates expounded his principles about the highest good. Then came Plato, who constructed a model republic and stirred the people to the practice of virtue. Meanwhile the poets wrote heroic or bucolic poetry or treated of the stars or of love— the *Elegiaci*—or of the fall of princes—the *Tragici*. Others cultivated the old Comedy with great liberty of speech. Chief among these were Aristophanes, Eupolis and Cratinus. From this old Greek Comedy the Latins derived their Satire. The first satirist was Lucilius.—The Latins were really the first to write satires. As Fabius says in his *Institutiones Oratoriae* : instead of our satire the Greeks had their old Comedy. After Lucilius came Horace with more polished style, and

---

[1] On his tragedies see § 330 ; Creizenach ii, 30 sqq. A full list in Dr. P. Bahlmann, Die lateinische Dramen von Wimpheling's Stylpho bis zur Mitte des 16ten Jahrhunderts 1480–1550 (Münster 1892), 12–17. There are seven of them, written between 1495 and 1513. One of his last has been analyzed by L. Geiger in Zeitschrift für vergleichende Literaturgeschichte und Renaissance-Litteratur N.F. i (1887), 72–77. Some others by Herford 74 sqq. The real Latin drama worth the name did not begin before George Macropedius from Gemert, whom Herford (p. 84) calls ' a man of great eminence, probably of all modern Latin dramatists the one whose talent had the largest measure of genius.'

Persius.   And last and chief of all Juvenal.—Why do our people not give greater honour to such poets ?   Their only aim was to teach virtue and to correct vice. Nowadays the number of fools is infinite, so that it is fortunate that a poet has arisen to expose the vices of fools and to satirize their abominations.   Our master Brant has undertaken this task in the vernacular for the benefit of all mankind, following the example of Dante and Petrarch, heroic poets who have written wonderful poems in the Etruscan tongue.   As the Narragonia or the Ship of Fools, which we might aptly call a satire, seemed necessary for all nations, I thought it worth while to translate it into Latin, so that it could be understood by the French, the Italians, the Spaniards, the Pannonians and the Greeks.—But the readers must forgive me if on account of the mediocrity of my talent, I have made mistakes, for this book is written to teach wisdom and to censure folly.   Hence let everyone look in it as in a mirror to see his own life, and to live more happily.

337.—Barclay has translated the greater part of this Prologue almost literally into good English.   Here and there he adds a little note of his own.   After the name of Esculapius he adds : ' which was fyrst inventour of Phesyke and amonge the gentyles worshypped as a god.' *Ob dicendi fingendique iucunditatem* is rendered by ' And that for theyr eloquent retoryke and also for theyr mery ficcions and invencions.' *Comoedia quam Greci archaeam vocarunt* becomes ' which comedies we cal Interludes,' reminding us that Barclay lived at the time of the Interludes, but at the same time showing that he did not understand the Greek word *archaeam*, which he, indeed, leaves entirely out in the quotation from Fabius.—When speaking of the later contempt for poets he adds a whole sentence : ' Shulde theyr writyng that suche thinges disprayse and revyle be dyspised of many blynde dotardes that nowe lyve, whiche envy that any man shulde have or understonde the thynge whiche they knowe nat.'   Such a sentence shows that the Englishman had some experience or at least some feeling of his own on the subject.— Brant's *lingua vernacula* is ' playne and comon speche of Doche in the contrey of Almayne.'   The name *Narragonia* is left out, probably because the Englishman did not understand the pun.—The entire conclusion from this passage downwards is refashioned and instead of contenting himself with the rôle of interpreter he now says something on his own account :

But amonge divers invencions composed of the sayde Sebastian . . . one called James Locher his disciple translated the same into Latin. . . . Than another, whose name to me is unknowen, translated the same into Frenche.   I have oversene the fyrst invencion in Doche and after that the two translations in Laten and Frenche whiche . . . agreeth in sentence, threfolde in language.   Wherfore wylling to redres the errours and vyces of this oure royalme of Englonde . . . I have taken upon me, howbeit unworthy, to drawe into our Englysshe tunge the sayd boke, named the Shyp of Folys, as nere to the sayd thre langages as the parcyte of my wyt wyll suffer me.

After this he returns to the Latin text, changing the name of *Jacobus Philomusus* into ' Alexander de Barklay ' and adding to ' folysshe people ' : ' of whom over great nombre is in the royalme of Englonde ' !

338.—This quotation brings us face to face with the whole problem. The expression that the German and the Latin ' agreeth in sentence ' is evidence enough that Barclay has never compared the two texts, and even when applied only to the Latin and the French it requires a very wide interpretation.   Our comparison has shown that Barclay always follows Locher, except occasionally [1] where he prefers Riviere's para-phrase. But not a trace of any real influence of the German original is to be discovered. On the contrary. Almost every chapter of the English version compared with the originals proves decisively that there are only two possibilities : either Barclay had never seen the German text or he did not understand a word of it.

A few considerations make the latter supposition the more probable one. First because it exculpates the author from telling a deliberate lie in this Prologue. Secondly on account of the few names mentioned in chapter 92.[2] Thirdly because he does not seem to have understood the German pun contained in the word *Narragonia* which occurs in several chapters. And finally because he has fairly displayed his linguistic knowledge in his *Introductory to wryte and pronounce French*, printed by Copland in 1521.[3] In this work he shows that he must have been in several parts of France, as he mentions the pronunciation of 'many' (p. 805), 'dyvers' (807), 'some,' 'certayne' (809, 812) 'countres of Fraunce,' and of 'pycard or Gascoyne' (809), but on p. 812 there is the following remarkable passage : ' In *language, qui, que,* u is wryten not soundyd. Nevertheless in dyvers countres after the foresayd letters (q. g. s.) they sounde w doubled as *quater, quare, quasy.* Englysshe men and Scottes alway sounde u after the letters both in Latyn and in theyr Vulgayre or common langage. In lyke wyse do dutche men, and almayns. As *quare, quatuor, quart, quayre, qwade,* and such lyke.' From this statement it would appear that the author knows not only English, French and Latin, but also Scotch, and Dutch *and* German (he clearly distinguishes the two languages here). But he quotes no other Dutch or German word than *qwade.* And though this word occurs in Middle High German at an earlier period,[4] about 1500 it was Dutch and not German. And this single word—he quotes no others in a treatise evidently meant to impress the reader with his wide knowledge of languages—may have been picked up either at Louvain or in the North of France.[5]

---

[1] All the cases are collected together in § 377.

[2] See § 40. Fraustadt quotes this chapter in a footnote on p. 45 to argue against Seifert that ' anschluss an Brant is zwelfellos.' Besides this ' undoubted ' example he adduced one ' probable ' case, viz. the name *David* in chapter 13 (see § 45). No other point of contact has ever been so much as hinted at. These two passages, therefore, constitute the sole foundation for Koelbing's assertion that Barclay ' used the German original.' See quotation in § 7.

[3] Its principal parts have been published from a rare copy in the Douce Collection, Oxford, by A. J. Ellis (Early English Pronunciation iii (1871), 804 sqq.). It is immediately followed by Copland's own *Maner of dauncynge* with the following justification : ' These daunces have I set at the ende of this boke to thentent that every lerner of the sayd boke after theyr dylygent study may reioyce somewhat theyr spyrytes honestly in eschewynge of ydelnesse the portresse of vyces ' !!

[4] See Grimm's Wörterbuch and M. Lexer, Mittelhochdeutsches Handwörterbuch (Leipzig 1876) s.v.

[5] Palsgrave, the writer of *L'eclaircissement de la langue francaise*, published by Pynson in 1530, accuses Barclay of shameless plagiarism : ' I have sene an olde boke written in parchement in manner in all thynges like to his sayd Introductory : whiche, by coniecture, was nat unwritten this hundred yeres.'—See the ed. by F. Génin in Collection de Documents inéd. sur l'Hist. de France (Paris 1852), and Ellis l.c.—But this seems only the spiteful language of a competitor whom his contracts prove to have been a business man (see § 315).

These considerations lead to the conclusion that when Barclay says 'I have oversene the fyrst invencion in Doche' he is consciously using an equivocal term; not, as Seifert [1] said, to escape the censure of pedantic critics—for pedantic critics cared much more for the Latin translation than for the German original—but as a mere pretence of his own pedantry, and because Brant was the famous man and Locher was only his prophet.

339.—Riviere has also translated this Prologue, but his translation is in several places inferior to Barclay's. He drops the Greek word *archaeam* altogether and he leaves out the name of Dante, saying that Brant is 'ensuyvant florentin et francoys pethrarcque.' The omission may be due to an oversight, for in the French text the word *ensuyvant* stands at the end of a line. But this makes it evident that Barclay has not used Riviere. Drouyn has copied him literally but no English translation appears in Watson, who probably thought one Prologue amply sufficient.

340.—Immediately after his Hecatostichon (J) (§ 314) which para-phrases a part of Brant's Prologue, Locher writes (under M) in prose a SECOND PROLOGUE, which he calls an *Argumentum in Narragoniam,* but which apparently serves no other purpose than to fill a blank page.[2] Its greater part contains little else than big words and repetitions of ideas expressed before.

> He says : this Ship is for the welfare of mankind.  It might have been called a Satire,[3] but the Author liked the novelty of the title (*sed auctorem novitas tituli delectavit*).  In all respects it is like the old satires : a mirror to hold up to the eyes of man.  My translation is not word for word, but gives only the sense [*would to heaven this were true* !] in simple Latin.  So the readers will pardon my presumption, remembering my small talent and my youth.  I have omitted poetical digressions and the obscure legends [*he has done almost the opposite*] and done my work in un-adorned words and straightforward constructions.  So I hope the reader will reward it with his favour.

The 'unadorned words and straightforward constructions' may be conceded when we compare the body of the book with the high-flown verbosity of Locher's own introductory contributions.

341.—Barclay introduces the translation of this 'Argumentum' by the solemn declaration : 'Here after foloweth the boke named the Shyp of Foles of the world, translated out of Laten, French and Doche [his conscience now prompts him to give the last place to that mysterious book, which he may have cherished with reverent looks, as Petrarch did his Homer] into Englysse in the Colege of saynt Mary Otery by me Alexander Barclay.'

---

[1] P. 10.

[2] Owing to this 'Argumentum' the typographical arrangement of the Latin version has become fundamentally different from that of the German original. The ideal of the German, faithfully observed at least in the first half, was to have the woodcut on the left-hand page, so that the whole chapter (unless it was a double one) lay at once before the reader. The Latin ideal, equally observed in the first half, is just the reverse. The woodcut is on the right-hand page, and the chapter usually ends on the back of the same sheet. See further § 362.

[3] The same idea as in the Epigram to the Reader F (§ 335) and in the Prologue I (§ 336).

He translates *satyra* by ' the Satyr ' and adds the explanation :
' that is to say : the reprehencion of foulysshnes.' He applies all Locher's
expressions to himself,[1] also ' the scarsnes of my wyt and my unexpert
youthe ' [2] and the ' poetical digressions ' and adds only that in his translation he is ' some tyme addynge, somtyme detractinge and takinge away
suche thinges as semeth me necessary and superflue.'—We have seen
that he has ' detracted ' very little, but that even his printer had to
interfere to prevent him from adding too much.[3] The only thing that
he omits in this ' Argumentum ' is Locher's last little sentence. But
instead of it he writes a whole page beginning : ' But the speciyl cawse
that movethe me to this besynes is to avoyde the execrable in-
convenyences of ydilnes, whyche, as Saint Bernard sayth, is moder of
al vices ' *etc.* This statement is nearly the opposite of what he said in
his Dedication : ' Tametsi crebris negociis varioque impedimentorum
genere fatigatus ' *etc.*, but he is again translating ; not from the Latin,
this time, but from the French.

342.—Riviere begins his work with a PROLOGUE DU TRANS-
LATEUR (J). After a few sentences, in which he quotes ' Ysidore en
son petit traicte du souverain bien ' [4] he goes on : ' Pour eviter les
dommagables et importables ennuytz de oysivete qui est (ainsi que dit
sainct Bernard) mere de tous vices ' *etc.* It is all almost literally as in
Barclay, who omits only two sentences. The first is a quotation from
Lactantius, which gives a very apt definition of folly in the sense in which
Brant understood the word : ' Car ainsi que dit lactance en son livre de
vraye iustice : Stulticia est in factis, dictisque per ignorantiam boni
atque recti erratio ' [5] of which only the translation is somewhat free,
not to say incorrect : ' Folie est en dictz et en faitz devier de bien et de
droit par ignorance.'—The second sentence omitted by Barclay is the
last one in which the Frenchman sympathetically writes : ' En suppliant
humblement a tous lecteurs que ilz nayent regard au langage maternel
et groz stille couche en ceste translacion qui a seulement este faicte pour
gens rudes et non lectrez mais que benignement pardonnent au translateur
qui est ieune.'

Instead of this the Englishman writes his second original sentence
in this long Argument : ' And to the entent that this my laboure may be
the more pleasaunt unto lettred men, I have adioyned unto the same
the verses of my Actour with dyverse concordaunces of the Bybyll to

---

[1] Jamieson xviii quotes these *literal* translations to prove that Barclay was
' actuated by patriotic motives ' *etc.* |

[2] Though he was well over thirty then, being born, according to Jamieson's
calculation, about the year 1476, and he is credited (but see § 347) with having
published his first translation from the French in 1503.—Locher was twenty-six when
he wrote about his *teneros lanuginis annos*.

[3] See Stanza 310, §§ 114, 315. It was a much more truthful confession which
he made to Bishop Cornish in his Dedication : Fateor equidem multo plura adiecisse
quam ademisse.

[4] *St. Isidori de summo bono* had already appeared in several editions (Hain 9281–
9292), one of them at Paris in 1495. Proctor 8121 mentions an undated Marnef-
edition. This may have been used by Riviere in 1497.

[5] ' De Justitia ' is the title of the Fifth Book of Lactantius' *Institutiones Divinae*,
which were published repeatedly since 1465. See Hain 9806 sqq.

fortyfy my wrytynge by the same, and also to stop the envyous mouthes (if any suche shal be) of them that by malyce shall barke ayenst this my besynes.' Of his ' concordaunces ' he speaks also in his Dedication (A).[1] But the parenthesis is very significant as throwing an illuminating side-light upon the many rhetorical passages concerning the envy and malice and cruelty of all authorities civil and ecclesiastical. In moments of forgetfulness the heroic attitude is abandoned and the prosaic truth appears.

343.—Drouyn has copied Riviere's translation of the ' Argument ' (M), and Watson has translated it, drawing several sentences out at greater length so as to fill the allotted space. I shall quote only the more important passages :

> Wherfore this present bok may be called satyre [Fr. satyre], notwithstandynge that [ne fut que] the fyrste auctoure dyde delyte hym in the newe intytulacyon of this present boke. . . . Nevertheles thynke not you lectours that I have worde for worde dyrecte *and reduced this present boke out of Frensshe in to our maternall tongue of Englysshe* [redige ce present livre dalemant en latin], for I have onely (as recyteth Flaccus) take *entyerely* the substaunce of the scrypture [le sens de la lettre], in esper-aunce that my audace presumptious [audace presumptueuse] sholde be pardoned of the lectours havynge aspecte unto the *capacyte* [la paucite] of my tendre yeres and the imbecylyte of my lytell understandynge in levynge the egressyons poetyques and fabulous obscurytees *etc.*

It is always difficult to see what Watson means, *if* he means anything. Practically he has done the opposite of what he says here, for if ever translation was ' worde by worde ' it is Watson's in most of his chapters. But has he changed ' la paucite ' on purpose into ' the capacyte,' feeling that his first youth had passed ? The insertion of the incongruous word *entyerely* proves the uselessness of all speculation as to Watson's real meaning.

344.—Riviere's *Prologue du Translateur* has not been copied by Drouyn, who writes his own Prologue instead, explaining the reasons that moved him to turn this book ' de rime en prose.' The principal reason, supported by quotations from Terence (' tot capita quot sensus ' !), Virgil and Aesop, seems to be (in Watson's literal transla-tion) ' that the one delyteth hym in latyn, the other in Frensshe, some in ryme and the other in prose.' The following passage has been left out by Watson ; the poetical version deserves all praise ' avec sa rethorique, laquelle me semble digne de louange. Sy en aulcuns lieux iay adioute quelque chose [this must principally refer to the invitation with which he introduces nearly every chapter [2]] ie ne lay pas fait par arrogance, mais pource quil venoit a propos.' Then follows this sentence in the second edition of 1499 : ' Et avec ce iay adjouste despuis ma premiere translation plusieurs satyres pour parfaire le livre au long, lesquelles ne sont point au premier livre que iay translate, pour quoy ie appele la petite nef des folz, et cest est la grant nef stultifere.' This state-ment does not appear in the first edition of 1498. Nor is it found

---

[1] See § 348.
[2] And to the conclusion of many chapters, which often wind up with a sentence or two of Drouyn's own invention.

in Watson's translation. Zarncke (226 note), who had already drawn attention to this sentence, deduces from Watson's omission, that the 1498 edition must have been the model for the English translation.— There is very little difference between the two editions. A careful comparison, however, from cover to cover [1] has shown that if by ' la petite nef ' the 1498-edition is meant, the addition of ' plusieurs satyres ' is nothing but bluff.[2] There are misprints in 1498 and other misprints in 1499, there are small deviations here and there, of very little actual importance, but just enough to show that Watson has not used the first edition but the second ; [3] but no new chapter, we may almost venture to say : no new sentence, has been added. Even the two original chapters with suspicious titles, serving for chapter f, which are called ' addition nouvelle ' and ' addition,' figure already in the first edition. So that the sentence quoted above is probably nothing but a printer's advertisement to recommend his goods. Drouyn's version must be as much due to the initiative of an enterprising printer as Watson's.

345.—Watson has also an addition of importance here, for which he has probably left out the praise and the advertisement of his model.

I Henry Watson indygne and symple of understandynge have reduced this present boke into our maternall tongue of Englysshe out of Frenshe, at the requeste of my worshypfull mayster Wynkyn de Worde, thrughe the entysement and exhortacyon of the excellent prynces Margarete, countesse of Rychemonde and Derby, and grandame unto our moost naturall soverayne lorde kynge Henry the VIII whome Jhesu preserve from all encombraunce. If that I have added *etc.*

the rest as in Drouyn.—This statement is perhaps best explained by the colophon at the end of the book :

Thus endeth the shyppe of fooles of this worlde. Emprynted at London in Flete strete by Wynkyn de Worde prynter unto the excellent pryncesse Margarete, Countesse of Rychemonde and Derbye, and grandame unto our moost naturall sovereyne lorde kynge Henry the VIII. The yere of our lorde M.CCCCC.ix. The fyrste yere of the reygne of our soverayne lorde kynge Henry the viii. The vi. daye of Iulii.

Lady Margaret Beaufort, Countess of Richmond and Derby, that pious and munificent patroness of learning, who had translated the Fourth Book of the *Imitation of Christ* from the French, and who was sixty-eight years old in 1509, probably never knew our poor Watson and certainly never ' entysed and exhorted ' him. But just as she established and endowed many institutions of charity and religion and learning, mostly at the suggestion of her confessor Blessed John Fisher, she also gave liberal grants to the printing-press, and Wynkyn de Worde was one of her *protégés.*—Watson must have written his Prologue between the 22nd of April, the date on which Henry VII was succeeded by his son, and the 29th of June, when Lady Margaret died. Wynkyn

---

[1] Bibliothèque Nationale Rés. Yh 2 (Pellechet 2828) and Rés. Yh 3 (Pellechet 2830).

[2] The copy Rés. Yh 3 in the Bibl. Nat. wants the first two sheets, containing the Prologue. But Zarncke's transcription of it entirely conforms to the text in the British Museum copy, IB. 41795.

[3] See e.g. §§ 109, 134, 299.

completed his printing a week after her death, but still retained his title of honour ' prynter unto ' etc.

346.—Barclay's version did not appear until nearly six months later, as appears from the Postscript appended to its DEDICATION (A) to Bishop Cornish, from which some extracts must now be given.

It is entitled ' *Venerandissimo in Christo Patri ac domino : domino Thomae Cornisshe tenensis pontifici ac diocesis badonensis suffraganio vigilantissimo, suae paternitatis capellanus humilimus Alexander Barclay sui ipsius recommendacionem cum omni summissione et reverentia.*' In the text the following personal relations are mentioned : The translation of the Ship has been promised to the Bishop,[1] who had ordained Barclay [2] and bestowed several benefits on him.[3] The Bishop had also advised him to print the Latin of ' the author ' by the side of his own translation ; [4] for some reason or other Barclay called himself a disciple or pupil of his illustrious Warden [5] and in the English subscription he adds that he was ' at that tyme Chaplen in the sayde College of saynt Mary Otery in the counte of Devonshire.' [6]

These relations become partly clear from the various stipulations made by the founder of the College. Bishop Grandisson of Exeter must have been a very punctilious man and in his foundation-letter contained in, and confirmed by, a bull of Pope Clement VI dated from Avignon 27 June 1342, he lays down very many detailed instructions.[7]— The College is to consist of eight Canons, the first of whom is to be called *Custos*, or Warden, of eight *Vicarii Chori*, one of whom was to be called *Capellanus B. Mariae* (on a salary of eight pence weekly and twelve shillings per annum ! [8]), of *octo clerici qui secundarii vocantur* [9] etc. ; and the *prefatus capellanus beatae Mariae habeat curam et custodiam librorum et ornamentorum ejusdem capellae* etc. As none of the others had the title of *Capellanus* I suspect that our translator of the Ship of Fools was *Capellanus Sanctae Mariae* and therefore also the librarian of his College, which is known to have possessed a considerable collection of books.[10]

Thomas Cornish was Suffragan Bishop of Bath and Wells and titular Bishop of Tyne and, according to the ' List of the Wardens of the College ' extracted from the Registrum by Oliver,[11] he was collated

[1] Stultiferam classem, ut sum tuae paternitati pollicitus, iam tandem absolvi.

[2] quia sacros ad ordines per te sublimatus et promotus.

[3] multisque aliis tuis beneficiis ditatus.

[4] Atque ut tua consuluerit paternitas, autoris carmina cum meis vulgaribus rithmicis una alternatim coniunxi.

[5] tu venerande Presul discipuli tui exiguum munusculum hilari fronte accipito.

[6] See § 349.

[7] The letter is given *in extenso* by G. Oliver, Monasticon Diocesis Exoniensis (Exeter 1846 in fol.), pp. 264–268. It is followed by the *Statuta*, in which e.g. directions are given about spring-cleaning (cum lancea longa et alis aucarum, ita quod non nocent picturis, p. 271) and for the collegians to be at home at curfew-time (pulsacione ignetegii finita, *ib.*). See above, § 118.

[8] But this must have increased very much since the preceding century, for the head of the Grammar School was granted the same salary by Bishop Grandisson ; but at the time of the dissolution in 1545 Sir John Chubbes, the then Master, received £10, a maximum salary. A. F. Leach, The Schools of Medieval England (The Antiquary's Books n.d., 1914), 194. Opposite this page there is a picture of the church as it still exists.

[9] See § 118.     [10] Oliver, p. 261.     [11] Ibid.

to the wardenship on 1 December 1489, resigned this office in June 1511 and died in 1513. So he was Barclay's immediate ecclesiastical Superior.

347.—There are some other noteworthy passages in the Dedication. The author calls this work ' meorum primicias laborum qui in lucem eruperunt '—the firstfruits of his published work.—And yet !—Bale [1] has enumerated among Barclay's works *Castellum laboris lib. i* ; and the translation of Pierre Gringore's *Le Chasteau de Labour*, universally attributed to Barclay, had been issued by Verard at Paris as early as the year 1503, and had been reprinted in England by Pynson about 1505, by Wynkyn de Worde in 1506, and was still in demand, as appears from the new edition which Wynkyn de Worde published about 1510.[2] It is not likely that Barclay could have forgotten this work of his. Nor need he have ignored it, for although even the French original was an egregious failure as a work of art,[3] there was nothing in the translation for Barclay to be ashamed of. Why then did he call the Ship of Fools the firstfruits of his published labours ? There is no reason to doubt Bale's statement, says Mr. A. W. Pollard,[4] but have not Barclay's own words to the contrary been overlooked ? [5] Is the authorship of *The Castell of Labour* so very certain ? And is not it remarkable that an author who in his Ship of Fools appears so egotistical that he mentions his own name nearly on every page, should have edited his first work anonymously without ever claiming it as his own ?

348.—Concerning his method of translation, the Dedication contains the confession already quoted : ' Fateor equidem multo plura adiecisse quam ademisse' and he adds two reasons : first a patriotic consideration : ' partim ad vicia quae hac nostra in regione abundantius pullulant mordacius carpenda,' and then a remarkable acknowledgment : ' partimque ob Rithmi difficultatem.' Modern readers will appreciate the difficulty of fashioning every two or four lines of the Latin into a Chaucerian stanza ! He goes on to say : ' Adieci etiam quasdam Bibliae aliorumque autorum concordancias in margine notatas quo singula

---

[1] Catalogus 1557 (cit. § 324), p. 723. Not in the Summarium. According to the MS. (cit. ib.) he took the information at the last moment *ex Museo Joannis Alen.* John Allen (b. 1476) was archbishop of Dublin from 1528 to 1534. See DNB. i, 305.

[2] Two editions are described in detail by Jamieson xcvii. All four by A. W. Pollard in his Introduction to ' The Castell of Labour translated from the French of Pierre Gringore by Alexander Barclay, reprinted in facsimile ' (Edinburgh, Roxburghe Club 1905), p. lii ; cf. p. xlvi. Our knowledge of the first English edition is due to the discovery and identification by Mr. E. Gordon Duff of a single leaf of it among the Bagford fragments at the Brit. Museum (Harl. 5919, No. 215), and subsequently of a few more leaves in the library at Lambeth Palace.

[3] See H. Guy, Histoire de la Poésie Française au XVIᵉ siècle, i (Paris 1910), 288. Hardly less severe is the opinion of Ch. Oulmont, Pierre Gringore (Biblioth. du XVᵉ siècle xiv, Paris 1911), 103 sqq.

[4] o.c. p. xxxvi.

[5] They have certainly been overlooked by T. H. Jamieson, who in a note appended to his *Life and Writings*, p. xc, adds : ' It ought to be noted that the modesty of the young Author prevented him from affixing his name to his first production. . . . Bale, Pits, Wood, etc. all include it in the list of his works without remark.'—Pits, Wood, etc., simply copy or paraphrase or corrupt Bale's list. One of the corruptions found its way through Pits into Sbaralea, Supplementum et castigatio ad Scriptores trium ordinum S. Francisci (Romae 1806), 13.

magis lectoribus illucescant ; [1] simul ad invidorum caninos latratus pacandos ' *etc.* The rest is all about the fury of the critics in the same strain as Locher's Letter to Bergman (§ 328) and the conclusion of his Hecatostichon (§ 314).—He has not added many notes however. Besides the hundreds of quotations copied from Brant's notes to Locher's text [2] (and a dozen or so from Riviere) hardly more than two dozen are quite original. Very often, however, especially in the later chapters, he gives the full text instead of the simple reference.

349.—The date of the Dedication must also be noted. The Latin text ends with : ' Ex impressoria officina Richardi Pynson. III. Idus Decembris,' without the year ; that is the 11th of December. The English Postscript says : ' This present Boke named the Shyp of Folys of the worlde was translated in the College of saynt Mary Otery in the counte of Devonshyre : out of Laten, Frenche, and Doche [3] into Englysshe tonge by Alexander Barclay Preste, and at that tyme [4] Chaplen in the sayd College. Translated the yere of our Lorde God .M.ccccc.viii. Inprentyd in the Cyte of London in Fletestrete at the signe of Saynt George. By Rycharde Pynson to hys coste and charge : [5] Ended the yere of our Saviour. .M.d.ix. The .xiiii day of December.'

This shows that the bulk of the translation must have been done in 1508 before the accession of Henry VIII, so that the various panegyrics on ' the rede Rose redolent ' were originally written for Henry VII and were only at the last moment supplied with a new inscription. [6] The Dedication was written on the 11th of December 1509, a few days before Pynson had completed the printing, [7] and as the author was then in the printing office, we may suppose him to have been there all the time seeing his work through the press and making the necessary alterations and corrections. [8]

350.—Last to be mentioned is the PRAYER TO THE VIRGIN (i) with which the French and English translators conclude their books. Riviere puts it in decasyllabic stanzas rhyming a a b a a b b c c, and invokes her as ' O Vertuz . . . O Raison . . . O Pallas . . . O Minerve . . . O Castaldie,' but he always means the same for he adds :

> Je me prosterne et metz icy davent
> Vous suppliant me impartir vostre grace.

---

[1] Cf. the quotation § 342.    [2] See § 321.

[3] On this misleading statement, which may be due to the printer here, see § 338.

[4] Had he resigned his chaplainship even before the printing was completed ? His later works were all published while he was a Benedictine monk at Ely. See A. W. Ward's article in DNB. It is usually assumed that he left St. Mary's College only after the resignation of Bishop Warden in 1511 (Jamieson xxxix ; Pollard o.c. xxxviii). Shortly after 1521 he joined the Franciscan Observants of Canterbury.

[5] The same expression as in Stanza 30 (§ 315).

[6] But a few changes must have been made. Think of the Hercules ' Havynge a respect unto his tender age ' in Stanza 1558 (ch. 99, § 182).

[7] The statement (found e.g. in A. W. Pollard o.c. p. xxxvi) that the MS. of the Ship of Fools was dedicated in 1508 to Bishop Cornish, must be due to an oversight. The text itself clearly says : ' Stultiferam classem, ut sum tuae Paternitati pollicitus, iam tandem absolvi *et impressam ad te destinavi.*'

[8] See Stanza 1956, § 323.

and again

> O Dame, o Pallas . . .
> Impetre moy doulce dame benigne
> Le haultain bien et mansion divine
> . . . Puisque ie suis par ton moyen a fin
> De ce livret si tresnet et si fin
> Te suppliant impetrer a ton filz
> Que ie puisse . . .
> . . . te obeyre o tres doulx crucifix

and that all the fools may repent and reach heaven at last :

> Et ton manteau de vertuz nous assourbe
> Moyen duquel es haultz cieulx perviendrons
> Sa ton filz plaist et celle part viendrons.

351.—Drouyn has taken only some phrases from this poem for his prayer, which is almost entirely original. Watson's translation is quite literal : ' Moder of God vyrgyn invyolate, the whiche hathe borne the fruyte of lyfe, to the I yelde me, and put me entyerly in to thy savegarde, to the ende that thou be advocate towarde thy swete sone that he defende me from this folysshe company in the whiche I have regned longe tyme.'—Then he thanks Pallas and Minerva for ' the eloquence . . . moyennynge [1] the whiche I have fynysshed my boke.' In one sentence he invokes the Holy Trinity and then returns to Our Lady again : ' O gloryous sterre of the see . . . advocate of the gendre humayne . . . thou hast implored for me towarde the verbe incarnate.' Towards the end the prayer suddenly changes into an address to the readers : ' Pardone me al that redyth this boke yf that you fynde ony thynge that is not well, for the fragylyte of my yougthe holdeth me in such mobylyte that myn understondynge can not comprehende ony morall sence.' The last words differ from the French ' mon entendement ne peult pacifique-ment se incomber aux lettres.' Then Watson leaves the French altogether and concludes with one short sentence : ' but also well as God hathe gyven me grace I have applyed my symple wyt, praynge all lectours to have me excused. Thus endeth the shyppe of fooles of this worlde.'

Drouyn has a much longer conclusion, in which he says that he has added ' aulcune satyre que iay translate de latin en francoys et un aultre que de moy mesmes ay faicte.' This must refer to the two chapters mentioned under f.[2] And the second of them he calls a translation !— He goes on to say that he has written at Lyons ' at the request of the publisher Guillaume Balsarin.'

352.—Barclay may have taken a hint from Riviere but certainly nothing more. In a more rhetorical style than usual he writes a dozen octaves all ending in the refrain :

> Direct our lyfe in this tempestuous se.

It is a Litany of invocations such as must have been quite familiar

---

[1] See § 160.    [2] See § 190 sqq.

to the Churchman. The best stanza, containing a reminiscence of a famous passage in St. Bernard, is also the most personal one :

(1972)    Thou art the Sterre, blasynge with bemys bryght
Above these worldes wawes so violent,
Our synnes dark enclerynge with thy lyght,
Mannys mediatryce to God omnipotent.
Wherfore to the, o Lady, I present
This symple boke, thoughe it unworthy be,
But pore and symple and moche ineloquent,
Rudely composyd in this tempestuous se.

And by way of conclusion [1] the end of the Prayer :

(1974)    And after whan my soule is separate
From this mortall body and clot of clay,
With thy holy presence, O Moder immaculate,[2]
From me expell the ougly fende away,
O Moder of mercy, syns thou well may ;
Thy Sonnes presence purchase for me
By thy ayde and socour, that I may say,
That I have escapyd this stormy se.

---

[1] The concluding Chaucerian stanza (1975) is quoted in § 374.
[2] No writer of that time, who was in any way connected with the school of Brant or Gaguin, was likely to forget the Immaculate Conception.

XV

## THE ELEMENTS OF UNITY IN THE SHIP OF FOOLS

353.—In the preceding pages the Ship of Fools has been treated as a collection of detached sermons. In reality Brant had made little else of it. Each chapter is complete in itself and has little or nothing to do with the rest. Stray thoughts, prompted from time to time by some petty annoyance, or met with in the course of his reading, or suggested whenever his sense of decency and order was outraged, would mould themselves almost unconsciously into tetrameters. These he would piece together for his chapters which he finally without reference to any logical sequence placed within the covers of his book.[1] The principal unifying factor is the idea—prevalent among most of Brant's friends and one that had become very popular in France—that all was FOLLY.— The tale of how Brant came by it has often been told.[2] Attention has been called especially to the German Carnival-plays and to Felix Hemmerlin's *Doctoratus in stultitia* in which he promotes his adversary ' Andreas ' to the degree of Great Fool in a parody of withering satire, ' datum anno iubileo (1450) die kalendis Januariis.'—But special facts and writings are only symptoms. The idea had become common property in the second half of the fifteenth century. It is all folly ! They are all fools ! The whole world is a lunatic asylum !—Such are the ideas that underlie a great part of the popular literature of that time. The ' Order of Fools ' became a favourite form of popular organizations [3] and nowhere more so than in France and Burgundy where ' La mère folle ' of Dijon about 1450 was only the first of a long list. ' La Sottie ' became a peculiar French species of literature and it remained in favour until the beginning of the following century.[4] It is all folly—is the underlying idea of ridicule and satire, and the spirit of satire had lived throughout the later

[1] C. Schmidt i, 298 ; K. Goedeke, Grundrisz i, 383.

[2] Most concisely and fully in C. Schmidt i, 294. Some of the data are more fully described by W. L. Schreiber, Manuel de l'Amateur de la Gravure ii (Berlin 1892), 318 sq.

[3] The very first example is probably the one solemnly approved by Count Adolphus of Cleves in 1381 ; not till about 1450 were there many similar clubs. Lydgate turned the idea to moral purpose in his ' Order of Fools,' ed. Furnivall in Early Engl. Text Soc. Extra Series viii (1869), 79–84.

[4] See Em. Picot, Recueil général des Sotties (Paris 1902). The earliest example (p. 1) dates from about 1420, but the majority belong to the second half of the century (pp. 11 sqq.). See also E. Picot, La Sottie en France, in Romania vii (1878), 236–326. The Dutch *sotternie* is said to owe its name to the French *sottie*. The English *sotelty* is quite different ; so are the *Narrenspiele*. Only Denmark seems to have developed a species very similar to the French type.

Middle Ages. There was a good deal that provoked satire of course. But when is there not ? A Juvenal will always grin ' Difficile est saturam non scribere.' That cannot be the only explanation.

354.—Since the rise of the Third Estate satire appears as a natural reaction against the idealisms of chivalry.[1]     In the beginning it worked only as a safety-valve. But the fifteenth century was a century of decline and disintegration ; it was barren of great popular ideals ; chivalry became a form without a substance, and satire won what idealism lost. In the twelfth and thirteenth centuries the wandering Goliards had catered for the occasional outbursts of a Bank-holiday spirit, and they had discovered the Land of Cockayne and founded the Order of the Ass, the *Novus Ordo Brunelli*.[2]     In the thirteenth century Reynard the Fox became the official representative of a loyal opposition-party, and his importance and influence and maliciousness grew with the strength of his supporters. When the perfection of their organization made them conscious of their own majority, all pretence was brushed aside. Failing in their attempts to obtain political ascendancy, they openly ridiculed the governing classes and their ideals and adherents.[3] The popular literature of the fifteenth century is like a long Carnival-procession of fools. The procession grows longer as the century proceeds, until at last all ranks and stations of life are forced to take part. Grave moralizing preachers point to the grim shadow of Death. But Death, too, is compelled to swell the number of the Fools, and the foolish procession becomes a ' Danse Macabre ' to the incessantly repeated tune of *Stultorum infinitus est numerus*.

355.—*Stultorum infinitus est numerus* is also the motto of Brant's Ship of Fools, as it is the text of every one of Geiler's sermons. But their conception of folly was not one of ridicule. Classical satirists had dwelt on the identity of vice, imprudence and madness, but it was not worldly wisdom that the moralists of the fifteenth century wanted to inculcate, they did not want to ridicule anything, they wanted to correct. They took a one-sided view, as professional moralizers are always apt to do, but to assert that Brant's conception of folly was not Christian but Greek [4] is a misinterpretation either of Brant or of Christianity. The Ship of Fools was not written under the influence of Lucian and of the new Italian Renaissance, as the *Encomium Moriae* was. Brant knew his Bible, and had found hundreds of texts to support his thesis.

The conception of folly embodied in the Ship of Fools is the *stultitia*, defined by Lactantius in Riviere's quotation,[5] and those who indulged

---

[1] G. L. Petit de Julleville, La Comédie et les Mœurs, 287.

[2] An Englishman seems to have been the founder. I am referring to the Speculum Stultorum by Wireker, a precentor of Canterbury under King John.— Herford 325 sq. ; Alden 6 ; Schmidt i, 324 ; Cambr. Hist. i, 192 ; Baumgartner, Weltliteratur iv, 406.

[3] See Lenient, La Satire en France au Moyen-Age, p. 13 : ' La Gaule ou la France, comme on voudra l'appeler, a toujours médit de ses maîtres. Esclave, elle tremble et obéit, mais se venge par la satire de ceux qui lui font peur. Elle conserve ses rois pendant quatorze siècles, en se reservant le droit de les chansonner ; et l'on a pu dire d'elle avec raison qu'elle était une monarchie tempérée par le vaudeville.' Cit. in Alden 7. Cf. Petit de Julleville o.c. p. 208.

[4] Kalff i, 220.          [5] § 342.

in the parody and ridicule of the Carnival-plays were held to make the greatest fools of themselves (see chapter 110[b]).[1]

356.—This conception of folly was common to all the moralists of the time. They were kindred spirits. But Brant's own satire is much severer, not to say crueller, than that of his English imitators. The constant repetition of all the synonyms of the word fool [2] was moderated a great deal, and the scathing taunts that are to be found in nearly every chapter of the original have become very rare in Barclay.[3]

I do not think this happened from any set purpose ; it is entirely due to the interference of Locher. The Humanist pure and simple revelled in classical names and classical quotations, but when he had reached the passages emphasizing the folly of mankind, his page was usually full and the chapter was at an end.—Barclay has not weakened the central idea of folly any further. On the contrary. In nearly every Envoy he preaches to the ' Fools ' and never gets tired of it. In his own way he resembled Brant rather than Locher. He was much less of a Humanist than of a Late Medievalist. It is to be regretted all the more that the kindred spirits never met, and that Barclay was not able to work directly from the German original.

357.—Another element of unity in the Ship of Fools, and the second in importance, are the WOODCUTS. Every chapter is preceded by a woodcut, and these woodcuts form an essential part of the book.—They are on the whole admirable little pictures. What their real origin is does not concern us much here. But the principal results of recent investigations [4] must be briefly mentioned.

It is certain that they have not been drawn or cut by Brant himself, but he has probably indicated to the illustrator for which passages he wanted pictures. He can hardly have done more. There is more humour in one woodcut than in the text of all the chapters of the Narrenschiff. The majority of the pictures [5] have been composed, drawn and cut by an unknown artist of genius, who cannot be identified with Albrecht Dürer,[6] but who will henceforward be called by the name of Master of the Bergman Printing house.[7] Three or perhaps six others have co-operated with the great master.[8] In Locher's Latin version

---

[1] § 301.      [2] See the list in Zarncke xlvii sqq.      [3] See e.g. Stanza 96, § 276.

[4] R. Muther, Die Deutsche Bücherillustration i (München 1884), viii, 64 sqq. ; Dr. W. Weisbach, Der Meister der Bergmannschen Officin ; Idem, Die Baseler Buchillustration des XV Jahrhunderts ; W. L. Schreiber v, xxxix, 123–134 ; Maria Wolters, Beziehungen zwischen Holzschnitt und Text bei Sebastian Brant etc. passim.

[5] Weisbach, Der Meister, p. 23, has ventured to give the exact list. See below, note 8.

[6] This is against the thesis of Daniel Burckhardt, Albrecht Dürer's Aufenthalt in Basel 1492–1494 (München 1892). See especially pp. 27 sq., where all Bergman's best woodcuts are ascribed to Dürer.

[7] There is only one man among all his contemporaries whom Weisbach (p. 63) calls the equal or even the superior of the Unknown Master, and that is the equally anonymous ' Master of the Amsterdam Cabinet.'

[8] An attempt at grouping is made by Weisbach, Die Baseler Buchillustration, p. 69. The short list of these groups may be acceptable to the privileged few who possess a copy of the original Basel editions in German or Latin.—Group A : chaps. 11, 25, 28, 66, 75, 76, 98, 99 ; Group B : chaps. 3, 4, 60, 77, 97 ; Group C : chaps. 9, 49, 67 (these three groups are very nearly related to each other) ; Group D :

issued by Bergman, the woodcuts were printed from the same blocks that had served for the original, but a few new ones were added,[1] augmented by two others in the second edition.[2]

358.—The story of the woodcuts as works of art begins and ends at Basel.[3] The Paris and Lyons printers tried to imitate them as well as they could, but what they produced were little more than curiosities. Pynson took as his models those which he found in Riviere's translation, published at Paris in 1497.[4] He succeeded remarkably well, but naturally he did not surpass his model, and no one will pronounce them to be of any artistic value. Wynkyn de Worde never had cutters who could emulate the workmanship of his Westminster colleague ; [5] what they produced for Watson's translation are worse than curiosities, they are caricatures. That is at least the impression of a modern reader. The contemporaries thought differently perhaps.

359.—Pl. I. and II. give a photographic reproduction of the obverse and the reverse of the title-page of the original German.[6] The first is a work of the unknown Master, and although it has no place in the Latin [7] nor in any of the later translations, it is not only of artistic but also of sufficient literary importance to deserve a prominent place.[8] The second picture was also used for chapter 108, and there it was retained

---

Title-page *verso* (= chap. 108), chaps. 1, 2, 5, 12, 17, 18, 19, 21, 23 (?), 24, 26, 30, 33, 51, 74 ; Group E : chaps. 78, 80, 86.—The others are by the great master. Note, however, that Locher's edition contains a few new woodcuts not determined by Weisbach. See following notes.

[1] Viz. title-page, chapter 83, 110[b], concertatio (b, three very bad ones).—Schreiber, Manuel v. 1, n. 3567.—It is really not fair of Jusserand (A Literary Hist. of the Engl. People ii (1906), 115) to quote these last, the worst of the whole book, to show that the ' curious engravings . . are, like the text, worthy of the Middle Ages, not of the Renaissance.'

[2] Viz. De singularitate (e), and De Corrupto Ordine (f, a bad one).—Schreiber l.c. 3571 sq. The first ed. contained chapter e, but it was preceded by the woodcut of Brant's chapter 36. See §§ 22, 23.

[3] The same blocks went, however, from one printer to another. Bergman handed them over to Nicolaus Lamparter at Basel, who used them for the 1509 edition of the German (Zarncke cii sq.), and they appear for the last time in 1512 in the edition produced by Mathys Hupffuff at Strassburg (Zarncke ciii sq.). The year before the same blocks must have been used for the Strassburg-edition of Geiler's Navicula Fatuorum in 1511 (Proctor 9995, British Museum C. 64, d. 5).

[4] I have compared all Pynson's woodcuts with the Basel and with all the French editions, the two Latin ones of Lyons and Paris (Pellechet 2824 and 2825), the French of Riviere (Pellechet 2827 ; n. 2829, the Marnef-translator repeats the same woodcuts) and of Drouyn (Pellechet 2828 ; 2830 repeats the same) ; it would take too long to enumerate all the details, but, although there remain some small difficulties, there can be little doubt that the above statement is correct. Decisive is e.g. the picture belonging to chapter 11.

[5] E. G. Duff, The Printers . . of London, 62 sq. Cf. A. W. Pollard, Introd. to the Roxburghe Club ed. of ' The Castell of Labour,' p. lvii. On the low state of English art at that time see K. Woermann, Geschichte der Kunst iv[2] (Leipzig 1919), 68 sq. ; and Walpole, Anecdotes of Painting, quoted ib. and p. 1551. See also C. de Mandach, La gravure à l'époque de la Renaissance in Michel's Histoire de l'Art, p. 403.

[6] They really are the facsimile of a facsimile, for the photo was taken from Koegler's reproduction. See § 20. The British Museum possesses only one loose leaf of the first Basel editions, representing the cut belonging to chapter 18. See Campbell Dodgson, Catalogue of Early German and Flemish Woodcuts in the British Museum i (1903), 222.

[7] Nor even in the third Basel edition of the German original. See § 368.

[8] See § 367.

ℜoꝛ place befoꝛe:condigne foꝛ his degre
In this great Carake nowe ſhall he rowe with me

Gaudeamus oés

ℕere ſhall Iacke/charde/my bꝛother Robyn hyll
with ℳyllers and bakers that weyght and meſure hate
All ſtelynge taylers:as Soper:and ℳanſhyll
Recepue theyr rowme:bycauſe they come to late
The fouleſt place is mete foꝛ theyr eſtate

PLATE III.—Woodcut belonging to Chapter 108 in Barclay's translation, 1509.
See § 359.

.

Bothe in the flodes and wawes tempeſtcous
Wherfore you ought to be gladde and Joyous
Seynge that you are of the myghty ſtocke
Of fooles peruers whiche is ſo grete a flocke

PLATE IV.—Woodcut belonging to Chapter 108 in
Watson's translation, 1509.  See §§ 359 sq.

by the Latin version and its successors. It is of course inferior to the first,[1] but there can be little doubt that it was imitated from the lower portion of the ·work of the Master.—The two others are English productions. Pl. III comes from Pynson's printing office and illustrates Barclay's text.[2] It is a fairly good specimen of his average work, which is not much inferior to that of his French colleagues. Pl. IV is Wynkyn de Worde's masterpiece for Watson's translation.[3]

360.—It is really his masterpiece. On comparison it appears to be the most successful of all, and the printer must have thought the same, for he used this cut also to illustrate the title-page. What will be considered more strange by modern readers is that none of all the pictures in both Pynson's and Wynkyn's editions has had greater success in English literature than this amusing ship. For it is this picture and little else that has inspired that remarkable fragment known as *Cocke Lorelles bote*,[4] which has always been quoted as a product of the literary relations of England and Germany.[5] It was produced by Wynkyn at an unknown date but probably shortly after his edition of Watson's Shyppe of Fooles, and it is fully illustrated. But its illustrations are nothing but repetitions of the same woodcuts that had served for Watson. There are four of them. Why he chose these, I cannot say ; they do not bear the slightest relation to the text. Perhaps the choice was mainly determined by the fact that they were about the most amusing of the whole collection. They belonged originally to chapters 18, 19, 77 and 108. The last is the one reproduced here, and it is repeated twice, just as in Watson. The compiler of this malicious list of various London trades cannot have needed much other inspiration.—His production remained popular all through the Elizabethan age.[6] But it seems far-fetched indeed to attribute any part of it to German influence.[7]

361.—There is another aspect of the woodcuts, and one of literary importance. In what sense have they influenced the text ?—The question can be viewed from two different sides. First of all: the explanation given to the woodcuts. In the German original we can hardly speak of influence in this sense. In at least the majority of cases the text is primary, the picture secondary. It is only in those

---

[1] It belongs to Weisbach's group D. See § 357.
[2] From the copy in the British Museum G. 11593.
[3] From the Bibliothèque Nationale Vélins 2. 368.
[4] The original is in the British Museum C. 21.2.12. Reprints : London 1817 (facsimile) ; Edinburgh 1841 (text without woodcuts) ; Percy Society 30, 1843 (no cuts ; ed. by F. Rimbault, who in his short introduction speaks only of Brant and Barclay) ; Aberdeen 1884 (by an anonymous editor who reproduces the ideas of F. Rimbault).
[5] See Professor Herford 341 sqq. (summarized in Cambr. Hist. iii, 61, 83). The observations on the woodcuts on p. 342 note are, of course, written under the same mistaken impression. Also Alden 21 sq.
[6] Allusion by Awdeley in 1575 (Herford 362), by Ben Jonson (Cambr. Hist. iii, 482) and many others.
[7] Professor Herford's is a very clever book, written in a brilliant style and displaying a detailed knowledge of German and English literature. But the author sees nothing but Germany and England, and has thus created a mistaken notion of the currents of international influence.

nine cases in which the same picture is repeated for a second chapter that one of the two probably owed its inspiration to the woodcut.[1]

In the translations the importance becomes different.  Locher had all the pictures before him, and so had his followers.  The meaning of most of them is so obvious that the explanation required no great ingenuity or was even superfluous.  But in several cases the woodcut does not serve to illustrate the real contents of the chapter but only some particular passage or allusion.  Locher sometimes leaves out exactly those allusions, and then there is no explanation and the matter remains where it was.  But sometimes he does give a Latin translation of a German proverb, and then the efforts of the translators become interesting to watch.

The example in chapter 57 has been mentioned.[2]  There are several others of a similar kind.  It might be instructive to go through them all, but one more is sufficient.  In chapter 2 Brant speaks ' Von guten reten ' *de bonis consultoribus* [3] and in the motto he says that those members of a council who do not follow the dictates of their own conscience but simply approve what the majority or the authorities propose, make themselves into mere tools.[4]  This last idea he expresses in a German proverb :

> Der selb die suw inn kessel stoszt,

meaning literally :  he himself pushes the pig into the cauldron.—The picture then represents this proverb :  two fools are busy pushing a pig into a big cauldron.  Locher translates the proverb into Latin :  Ille agit inque scrobem trudit ubique suem.  *Scrobis* is not a cauldron, but a ditch or a grave, and his translation therefore is so free as to become unintelligible.  It was unintelligible to the translators.  Riviere-Drouyn render it by :

> Et besche dung pourceau la fousse [5]
> Et par apres dedens le pousse.

They must have written this with an eye on the picture, for the fools really work from behind.  Watson did not pay attention to such details and boldly rhymes in his inimitable poetic style :

> For he bryngeth the hogge unto the pyt
> And afterwarde reverseth hym in it.

Barclay, on the contrary, worked quite independently of the Latin ; he looked at the picture only and coined a bran-new proverb of his own :

> (78)          Suche is as wyse a man
> As he that wolde seeth a quycke sowe in a pan.

362.—The pictures have influenced the text also in another way—

---

[1] See M. Wolters' careful study, pp. 21–27.     [2] See § 147.     [3] See § 193.
[4] I have adopted the very plausible explanation given by Karl Goedeke, Das Narrenschiff (Deutsche Dichter des 16ten Jahrhunderts vii, Leipzig 1872) ; cf. also Zarncke's notes, p. 302 sq.
[5] *fousse* is *fosse* adapted to the rhyme.

they have mechanically determined the exact length of each chapter in the German and also in the Latin version.—The co-operation between the printer and the author as well as the first translator was very close. Each chapter had to consist of a motto (numbering three lines in German, four lines in Latin), a picture, four lines of text on the same page and then either one or two or three exactly full pages of thirty lines.[1] So all the chapters had to be thirty-eight or sixty-eight or ninety-eight lines long (in the German one line less). Locher, as we have seen, preferred the thirty-eight lines. But he could not write less, nor a little more. The length of each chapter is fixed unalterably beforehand. That is why the German text often becomes prolix. Having once transgressed the limits of the first page, the following had to be filled as well. That is also the reason why Locher's translation very often breaks off abruptly.

In the editions issued in France the original arrangement was no longer observed. The chapters there usually end in the middle of a page, so that the Procrustean treatment to which they had been subjected was no longer apparent. The translators never had a suspicion of the truth. They regarded every chapter as a well-considered whole [2] and they all felt themselves much freer in their poetical, or other, inspiration. In Drouyn's text, however, some influence of the printing-press is discernible, especially in the second part. It is difficult to prove this without entering upon very uninteresting details which would take up a great many pages, but one can feel it in his process of condensation or expansion : he works within the printing office, and certain mechanical limits must be observed. In Watson's case this is even much clearer. Attention has been drawn to it in the preceding pages more than once. He must have done his work sitting next to his compositor, and he inserted superfluous or omitted necessary words by dictation. It was all one to him ! Is it not people like Watson, and perhaps Drouyn, that Brant alludes to in the conclusion of chapter 27 ? [3]

363.—Last of all, and least in original importance, is that element of Unity that has preserved a popular fame for the Ship of Fools up to the present date : the idea of THE SHIP. It is perhaps this idea more than anything else that made the great success of the book outside Germany. Brant's masterpiece has no doubt exercised an enormous influence on German Literature. The whole of the sixteenth century is full of it, and not until Opitz became the new German law-giver in the seventeenth century, did the Ship of Fools lose its hold upon popular imagination. But it was always the fools that came to the foreground. Of all the long list of works written under the direct influence of Brant, which are enumerated by Zarncke,[4] and of which the last dates from the eve of the Thirty Years' War, there is hardly one that lays any stress

---

[1] There are some slight deviations in the second part of the German text. Zarncke lii gives more exact details. On the fundamental typographical difference between the German and the Latin see note to § 340.

[2] So does Fraustadt, who used the last reprint (Basel 1572).

[3] § 248.

[4] Pp. cxvi–cxxxvii : more than twenty pages, with many extracts.

on the ship-idea.[1]  Even professed and evident imitators of the original
preferred the Folly to the Ship.[2]  It is always Folly or later her twin-
brother, the Devil.[3]

364.—In France a different choice was made.  It is the motive of
the Ship which was never forgotten there.  The first was probably
Badius's Stultiferae Naves, of which the French translation (by our well-
known friend Drouyn) was published before the Latin in 1498 [4] under
the title of La Nef des Folles, a sort of continuation of the Ship of Fools
for the benefit of women.  Then Badius's own interpretation of the
woodcuts (and of Brant's marginal notes [5]) in the ' Navis Stultiferae
Collectanea.' [6]  In most other works the fools disappear altogether, at
least in the title, and Symphorien Champier writes his ' Nef des Princes '
and his ' Nef des Dames vertueuses,' to which Robert de Balsac adds
' La Nef des Batailles ' (Lyon 1502).[7]  In 1507 and 1508 and again in 1511
Verard published a work by Nicolas de la Chesnaye entitled ' Nef de
Sante.'[8]  Et cetera.  These are only some random examples, but a long
list could probably be made of French Nefs, all suggested by Brant's
or rather Locher's ship-motive.  Brant's fame in France rested on his
Ship and was always connected with the Ship-idea.  When in 1512
the writer of the ' Contreblason des faulces amours ' [9] gives one of the first
places among the most celebrated French writers to Brant, it was in all
probability only because he knew him to be the original writer of a Nef.
Jean Bouchet wrote a French satire, partly inspired by a Latin poem in
Brant's Varia Carmina, [10] but his publisher Antoine Verard did not think
Bouchet's name famous enough to be an advertisement for the book ; he
suppressed the name of the real author altogether and one fine day early
in the sixteenth century he surprised the French public with : *Les regnars
traversans les perilleuses voyes des folles fiances du monde, composees par
Sebastien Brand, lequel composa la nef des folz derrenierement Imprimee*

---

[1]  The exceptions are only the Narrenschiff von Bundtschuh (E. Weller, Repertorium typographicum [Nördlingen 1864], 96), from a literary point of view a very
trifling little pamphlet (Zarncke cxx), and the title, but hardly more than the title,
of Geiler's Collections of Sermons (Navicula *sive speculum* fatuorum ; Navicula
Penitentiae ;  Das Schiff der Penitenz ;  Das Schiff des Heils ;  Bibliography in
C. Schmidt ii, 381 sqq.).  Brant's Prologue and even Locher's Argumentum are still
hesitating between the allegories of a ship and of a mirror !

[2]  This is especially clear in Murner's works, which contain a great many verbal
imitations of the Ship of Fools, but which never adopt the allegory.  Cf. the titles
of his works :  Der schelmen zunft ;  Narrenbeschwerung, Die geuchmat ;  Von dem
grossen Lutherischen Narren (Schmidt ii, 422 sqq.).

[3]  See Zarncke cxxxvi sq.

[4]  The original Latin appeared in 1500.  See Renouard ii, 67 sqq. ;  cf. i, 10,
157 sqq.

[5]  See § 321.

[6]  The first edition 1505 had the same title as Locher's version, a fact which has
misled many writers to call it a translation of Brant's German original, and (probably
for no other reason than that Badius is better known than Locher) even a more faithful
translation than Locher's.  On the fallacy of this statement see Renouard i, 160.

[7]  See M. P. Allut, Etude . . sur Symphorien Champier (Lyon 1859) 109, 115,
131.  Cf. Ch. Schmidt i, 315 ;  Dr. Th. Süpfle, Gesch. d. deutschen Kultureinflusses
auf Frankreich i (1886), 33.

[8]  J. Macfarlane, Antoine Verard (Bibliographical Society vii, 1900), 41, 89, 120.

[9]  Piaget-Picot, Œuvres poétiques de Guill. Alexis i (Paris 1896), 278-81, cit.
H. Chatelain, Recherches sur le Vers Français (1908), ix.

[10]  *De spectaculo conflictuque vulpium, alopekiomachia*, is the characteristic title.

*a Paris et autres plusieurs choses composees par autres facteurs*, and the
name proved an attraction so strong that at least four editions were sold
within two years.[1]

365.—It is not, however, for any mysterious anthropological or
geographical reason that the French cherished the Ship-idea more than
did the Germans. We find the same from the Humanists all over the
world. When they speak of Brant, they will always commemorate the
Ship. Ulrich von Hutten will tell you of him :

> Pulchre illi latum classis deducta per aequor
> Convehit insipidos quolibet orbe viros.[2]

The witty parodist of the *Epistolae Obscurorum Virorum* makes
' Philippus Schlauraff ' write to Ortwin Gratius :

> Venit Sebastianus Brant, der nam mich bei der hant,
> Dicens mihi sequere : nos volumus navigare
> Ab hinc in Narragoniam propter tuam stulticiam.[3]

The well-read Italian critic Lilius Gregorius Gyraldus knows the names
of two works by Brant : ' Rosarium divae virginis matris sapphicum,
et Navis, que stultifera vocatur.' [4] The opponents of the Immaculate
Conception inveigh against Brant ' et omnes suos complices in furibunda
nave secum fluctuantes.' [5] When Germain de Brie, the Greek scholar,[6]
who was as much a nationalist as the others, had written a Latin poem
to celebrate an episode of the Anglo-French war, the burning of a vessel
called ' La Cordeliere,' under the title *Chordigerae Navis conflagratio*,
printed by Badius in 1515,[7] Sir Thomas More, his English friend, felt
his patriotism so much offended by it, that he must needs send the
offender some contemptuous epigrams ; and from one of them it appears
that he, too, knew that there was a book called ' navis ' or ' ratis
stultifera ' :

> Brixius en Germanus habet sylvamque ratemque,
> Dives opum terra, dives opum pelago ;
> Utraque vis illi quid praestat scire ? vehuntur
> In rate stulticiae, sylvam habitant furiae.[8]

The same fame was perhaps responsible for the introduction of the

---

[1] Ch. Schmidt i, 261 sq. Other editions in K. Burger 631, 632 ; Macfarlane,
n. 149, 182. It was reprinted again in 1522 and 1530, and was even translated into
German (Hamon, Bouchet 21, 400 sq.). Bouchet kept up a life-long protest against
this pilfering, calling himself Le Traverseur ever afterwards. A lawsuit had not
helped him. See Macfarlane p. xxvii, and especially E. Picot, Une Supercherie
d'Antoine Vérard in Romania xxii (1893), 244–260, with a note by A. Piaget (Hamon,
Bouchet, 23 sqq.).

[2] Böcking, Opera (1862) iii, 79, Elegia X ad poetas germanos.

[3] Böcking i, 198, lines 104–106.

[4] De Poetis Nostrorum Temporum, ed. K. Wotke (Lateinische Litteratur-
denkmäler des XV. und XVI. Jahrhunderts, Berlin 1894), p. 65.

[5] *Defensio Bullae Sistinae* n.d. fol. 1, in St. Ignatius College, Valkenburg, F. m. ii,
14 ; cf. Schmidt i, 220.

[6] Baumgartner, Weltlitteratur iv, 606.

[7] Renouard ii, 225. It was provided with a Preface by Erasmus (Allen i, 447 sqq.;
A. Tilley 206).

[8] Herford 324. Th. Mori Epigrammata, ed. Basil. 1518, p. 114.

ship-motive in Skelton's Bowge of Court.[1]  All the Humanists knew
the ' Ship.'—Erasmus forms an exception.  He was not a German and
could still write about Brant without mentioning the Ship.[2]  But he
is an exception that proves the rule.  For he was one of those who had
had personal intercourse with the old master.

The reason of the striking difference between Brant's fame in
Germany, which rested mainly upon his collection of ' Fools,' and that
same fame outside Germany where it was always connected with the
idea of the Ship, is quite simple.  The Germans knew the German text,
and the others did not.  In France they knew at best Locher's version
or Riviere's paraphrase.  And the development of the ship-motive is
quite remarkable.

366.—To Brant himself the idea came in all probability as an afterthought.  He had probably written more than half the chapters before
he realized the value of this new idea.  There is a clearly marked
difference between the first sixty-one chapters and the rest in length,
in style, and last not least in allusions to the ship-idea.[3]  In the first
half there are hardly half a dozen lines that have any reference to a ship.
In the woodcuts the ship is never once represented.  But in the second
half everything changes suddenly.  The ship is mentioned and drawn
again and again.  But it remains a secondary intrusive idea, and Brant
has never become clearly conscious of his own allegory.

The origin of this allegory in Brant's mind can perhaps be more
distinctly traced than the vague idea of Folly.  Here is something
definite and personal, which must have a definite origin.  It can hardly
be Brant's own invention, for Brant's was not an inventive genius, and
if he had invented it, he would have assimilated it more thoroughly.
Three works are known that *may* have influenced him.  There is a little
German poem of the middle of the fourteenth century, which had never
been printed, Heinrich Teichner's *Schif der flust* ; [4]  there is a long Dutch
poem which was very popular all through the sixteenth century, Jacob
van Oostvoren's *Die blauwe Schute* [5] written in 1413 ;  and there was a
Latin humoristic oration composed by one of Wimpheling's friends
Jodocus Gallus [6] entitled *Monopolium et societas vulgo des Liechtschiffs*,[7]
printed at Wimpheling's instigation in the anonymous *Directorium
statuum* at Strasburg at an uncertain date but probably in 1489.[8]
Zarncke [9] thinks the last-named work must have decided Brant's choice.

---

[1] It was probably written before 1509 (Cambr. Hist. iii, 74 ; cf. Ramsay lxxxix).
Herford 354 suggests that it is all inspired by Barclay.  More directly A. Rey 51.

[2] See his Phalegium Epigr. (Basel 1518), 349, quoted in Zarncke opposite p. 1.

[3] It would lead me too far to demonstrate this in detail, although it is an
extremely interesting subject.  The materials are nearly all given by Zarncke
li–lxxiii.  It is perhaps owing to the very fulness of his exposition, that it has drawn
less attention from critics than it really deserves.  See § 367.

[4] Reprinted Zarncke lxi.

[5] Reprinted ib. lxvii ; cf. Kalff, Westeuropeesche Letterkunde i, 73, referring to
Gesch. d. Ned. Lett. ii, 102.

[6] C. Schmidt ii, 40 ; Zarncke in Haupts Zeitschrift ix, 1, 123 sqq.

[7] Reprinted in Zarncke lxvii ; some extracts in Herford 331.

[8] Pellechet 4343 ; BMC. i, 122.  See above § 154.

[9] P. lxxiii.  Herford 331 sqq. adopts his explanation.

367.—His reasoning is not quite convincing, chiefly because he must suppose and does suppose that more than half the chapters had been written at least five years before the book was published.—Perhaps none of the three works has had any decisive influence. Brant may have got his felicitous thought nearer home. Mary Wolters has shown [1] that he found the inspiration for some of his chapters in the woodcuts. Would it be presumptuous to suppose that he owed the conception of the Ship itself to the engraver ?

We know that the title-page was cut by the unknown Master,[2] who was a creative genius and who by far surpassed Brant in humorous conception and in composition.[3] He cannot have been inspired much by the rambling moralizations of the old Humanist. He may have been acquainted with the *Blauwe Schute*. Who knows but he may have become familiar with naval imagery at a more likely place than Basel ? Had he not watched the ships in some busy seaport of the Low Countries ? [4]

He did not care about the allegory of course, but his work was imitated by his weaker colleague who produced the second picture. And this second picture has become the direct inspiration of chapter 108, the only chapter of the whole book in which Brant has attempted to sustain the allegory. Both pictures were probably cut when Brant had finished his 61st chapter, for the beginning of the next chapter seems to indicate that the author had originally planned to make a conclusion here :

> Jetz wer schyer usz der nerren dantz
> Aber *etc.*

and then he holds forth about Serenading. In the following chapters there are continually expressions denoting that the author is conscious of writing a continuation to a work that had already been finished.[5] And it is just in these chapters that the ship-element becomes prominent, and that it begins to appear in the ordinary woodcuts.[6]—If the picture for the title-page was cut when Brant had thus half finished his work, there can be hardly any doubt but the realization of the Ship as an allegorical motif is due to the impression which the picture made upon the writer.—Once conceived it penetrated into the rest of the work, but it never lost the stain of its vicious origin, it remained an afterthought throughout the book.

368.—It was not an afterthought for Locher. He could not, however, change the character of the whole work. But he did what he could. In more than thirty places [7] he inserted a reference to the Ship where Brant had not thought of it. Brant himself assisted in this work of improvement by contributing the Exhortatio (H) and the Celeusma (I), in which the allegory is more marked than anywhere else except in chapter 108. The printer had a new title-picture cut, a very bad one, but it had the great merit in Brant's eyes that it omitted the cart and

---

[1] M. Wolters 21 sqq.    [2] See above, §§ 357, 359.    [3] M. Wolters passim.
[4] I wonder whether experts could not indicate some points of contact between him and the Master of the Amsterdam Cabinet, § 357.
[5] See Zarncke lii.    [6] See § 366.    [7] See Fraustadt 15.

represented only the ship.[1]—And thus the Humanists and the rest of
Europe outside Germany received a work which really deserved the
name of a Ship. They could no longer hesitate, as Geiler had done
(as well as Brant himself), whether to call it a Ship or a Mirror. And
the name secured the success of the book in France and elsewhere, where
it lost the support of the original woodcuts. Nothing but Locher's
own pedantry prompted him to express some disapproval in a for the
rest quite correct remark : ' Potuisset hic noster libellus non inconcinne
satyra nuncupari, sed auctorem novitas tituli delectavit.' [2] *Novitas
tituli* indeed, but if the author had followed this advice, if he had called
his book a ' Satire on Mankind in General,' all Locher's efforts would
have failed to carry its fame far beyond the German frontier.

369.—Barclay has again improved upon Locher. We have seen
how he developed the idea of the Call to the Fools (G).[3] There are no
fewer than forty places in which he inserts a reference to the allegory
of the title without the authority of the Latin. Still he is far from consistent. In the more serious chapters he does not think of the allegory
but only of his sermon. There are about fifty chapters in which even
the slightest allusion is lacking.[4] And in the majority of cases he merely
mentions ' this ship ' or ' this barge ' as a synonym for ' this chapter '
or ' this book,' without being quite sure whether his book is one ship or
a collection of ships or a whole navy.[5] Sometimes he bethinks himself
of a special place or a special office in his ship, and the allegory becomes
a little more vivid.[6] But in the most vivid passages the reader is never
sure whether the fools are already on board, or whether they are anxious
to get there, or whether they are compelled to embark. Some people
are dismissed because they are too good, others because they are too
bad or because they are too numerous.[7] The ship or navy is ready to
sail [8] or it is in mid-ocean [9] or it has just come back to port [10] or—I do
not know what he means ; as in

> (239)  The wynde is up, our navy is aflote,
> A bande of folys a borde is come yet more ;
> Theyr cursed maners *etc.*

and the sermon begins. Brant's confused allegory remains confused
in the Prologue,[11] but sometimes Barclay's own intrusion of the allegory
makes confusion worse confounded :

---

[1] Even in the next edition of the German original (1499) it was substituted for
the work of the great Master, to whom Brant owed so much.

[2] Argumentum (K). See § 340 sqq.       [3] See § 319.

[4] Viz. chapters 2, 5, 6, 7, 9, 12, 13, 15, 17, 18, 22, 23, 26, 28, 29, 33, 37, 39, 41,
44–47, 50, 53, 55–57, 64, 65, 67, 69–72, 76, 86, 88, 90, 95, 97, 99, 104–107,
110b, a.b.

[5] Such vague indications are to be found in Stanzas 5, 98, 194, 335, 374, 460,
500, 518, 595, 626, 734, 826, 875, 888, 905, 1086, 1150, 1160, 1198, 1440, 1973.

[6] Stanzas 62, 287, 386, 479, 531, 825, 837, 856, 874, 1161, 1197, 1350, 1877, 1900.

[7] Stanzas 20, 22, 146, 433, 835, 1124, 1158.       [8] Stanza 517.

[9] Stanza 1157.       [10] Stanza 904.

[11] See esp. Stanzas 23 and 24, § 315.

(1141)    Of folys I wot there is great company
          Within my boke in fygures and scripture,
          But in this Shyp namely ar there many
          Whiche theyr owne foly can by no meane endure,
          Suche in this barge shall of a rowme be sure ;
          Though they have rowme, I can graunt them no rest,
          For with the asse they rudely ar opprest !

Lines 3–6 are Barclay's own invention, but the last line was in Locher
and could not be omitted because it contained the explanation of the
woodcut !

The ' Ship ' never became a real allegorical motif, but it remained an
external ornament, as it had been for Brant.    Brant liked the ornament
of course.    He understood that the saying about good wine may be all
right as a proverb but that in practice the success of the wine often de-
pends upon the bush.    Locher as well as Barclay has managed to make
the bush a bit larger, but they never imagined that their ornament could
improve the contents.—Never are the ' fools ' summoned or anxious
to get into the ship for any better reason than to hear a sermon.    Brant
had never thought of a real voyage—until he had seen his own title-page.

370.—Inspired by the woodcuts he then made his highest allegorical
effort and produced his now famous chapter 108, which is meant to describe THE VOYAGE TO THE LAND OF COCKAYNE.    No better
illustration could be given of the confusion wrought by an intrusive
allegory in the mind of an author who had no taste for it, than an analysis
of this curious chapter.    By keeping very close to the text it is perhaps
possible to give an idea of it without altering or spoiling the allegory
too much.

In the beginning the crew (or passengers) of the ship (or ships) are
introduced as speaking personages, but now and then the author speaks
in his own name.

Recruited from every country our crew sails about from *Narbon* to *Schluraffen-*
*land,* calling at *Montflascun* and *Narragun* (1–8).    We seek harbours everywhere
but can find no landing place, aimless we rove about not knowing where we shall
arrive, without rest but content with our folly (9–16).    We have many companions
and followers who will even swim after our ship to obtain a berth in it (17–21).
Though we are care-free, our voyage is full dangerous, for none studies the chart
or the compass, or the hour-glass or the stars (22–29).    Our ship may crash through
the Symplegades, we shall venture through *Malfortun* but shall never touch land,
misled as we are by Scylla and Charybdis and the Syrtes (30–38).    We shall see
many monsters : Dolphins and alluring Sirens and the one-eyed Cyclops (39–46).
It was Ulysses who burnt out the other eye (47–54).    But seeing the fools it will
grow again and he will open his mouth wide to devour many of us (55–60).    The
others will become food for Antipathis and his Laestrygones.

Do würt der narren herberg syn (61–68).

Homer has invented this story to inculcate wisdom (69–71).    He has praised Ulysses
for his prudence in the many adventures of his ten years' voyage, as when he declined
Circe's potion, and even delivered his companions with the herb Moly (72–83).
Thus he escaped very often, until at last his ship was wrecked and all his companions
were drowned (84–91).    Wisdom then assisted him to swim to the shore ; but he
was killed by his own son, for when he knocked at his door, he was recognized by
no one except by the dog (92–101).—I return to *our* voyage (102).—We seek profit

in a deep morass but shall soon be badly stranded ; our mast and tackle will break and the wind and the waves will hinder our swimming (103–111). The Ship of Fools, once sunk, will never come back, and we feel little inclination to swim to the shore as Ulysses did (112–117).—We stand on a slippery deck washed by the waves, our many boats will soon be necessary both for the crew and for the master of the ship (118–122). The gale is shaking it wildly, and a whirlwind may soon wreck us all, ill-advised people that we are (123–128).—A wise man will profit by our fate and not venture on the ocean, unless like Ulysses he can battle with the winds and, if necessary, swim to the shore, for otherwise he will be drowned like a fool (129–136). One should always steer to the shore of wisdom, for the number of fools is already great enough (137–141). The wisest man is he who understands his own duty or who accepts the teaching of good discipline ; all the others are fools (142–149). If they are not in this Ship, they will soon find another, in which they will find goodly company to sing their *Gaudeamus*.

Oder das lied im narren don (150–154).

Although we have left many of our brethren behind, our ship is heavy enough to sink (155–156).

371.—Locher takes the first eight lines and elaborates them into thirty-four, mainly by mentioning quite a number of countries and nations, from which the fools are recruited. Amongst them is ' Gallia tota,' and ' ultima Thyle ' and ' Britain,' the ' Cymbri torvi ' [1] and the ' flavi Sycambri,' and of course also the indispensable ' Getae ' and ' Sauromatae.' As port of destination he mentions : ' Narragonum patriam,' and ' Stolidum solum.' Next he paraphrases lines 30–46, about the dangers of the sea-route and the monsters ; then he borrows some ideas from lines 9–16 (inserting Circe as ' dea stultitiae ') about the aimless voyage, and from lines 129–131 about the wisdom of remaining on land.

Here, having written sixty-eight lines and filled his third page Locher breaks off his chapter.

The explanation of the allegory is to be found only in those lines of Brant which Locher has omitted and in the title *Das schluraffen schiff*, which was clear to every German reader.[2] Locher's title is *Latina navis seu barca socialis*. The meaning of *barca socialis* is no doubt ' Ship of boon companions,' and *latina* probably indicates that the boon companions were mostly half-finished students who went through life with little else than some knowledge of Latin.[3] But we may well wonder how many readers understood this very veiled allusion.

372.—It offered of course no difficulty for the translators ! Riviere-Drouyn wrote *La nef latine ou barcque socialle* and Watson consequently *Of the shyp latyne or barge socyale*. As the Latin chapter is in its greater part little more than a collection of proper names, we can expect a great many curiosities in the French translators and their English interpreter. Riviere is still intelligible. And sometimes even malicious. The Latin

---

[1] In the *Egloga Thomas Beccadelli Cimbri*, which in the 1498 ed. of Locher's translation follows his *De fatuis sagittariis* (see § 332 note 2), there is an explanation : *Cimbri Flandrenses quos nunc mutato nomine dicunt* !

[2] On the popularity of the story of the ' Land of Cockayne ' in Germany, see § 147.

[3] Explanation given by Zarncke 457. See also the end of chapter 27 in Brant.

had mentioned among the crew ' Gallia tota ' but had forgotten the Germans.   Riviere will set this right.

> La terre et royaulme desperie
> Et quasi toute la germanie
> Et finablement de la gaulle !

' Ultima Thyle ' has not dropped out here but appears as ' la grant gent de thillie.'   Drouyn-Watson simplifies all this.   He just mentions : ' Esperyce, Almayne, Fraunce, Mausyrye, Thyllye, Brytayne, Flavye, Cymberyens, Syccambriens ' *etc.*   It would require too much space to explain the linguistic origin of all these peoples and countries.   The most interesting is Locher's *turba Getarum*, which becomes in Riviere ' La turbe de gecte vaillante.'   Drouyn retains this line, only changing *gecte* into *gette*, and then Watson translates : ' And the turbe of the watche valyaunt in armes.' [1]   This shows enough what this chapter must be like in Watson's English.   There are no two sentences in it which can be understood without reference to Drouyn, and from Drouyn to Riviere, and very often we have to go still further from Riviere to Locher.   Then we know at least what names are meant, but little more.

373.—In this chapter Barclay's workmanship is again infinitely superior to that of his fellow-translators, although he could not of course understand from Locher's text what was the meaning of it all.   But the very difficulty of the Latin makes him all the more independent of it.   Hence we find him summoning the crew in the first eight stanzas with perfect freedom of movement.   Locher's abstruse title is dispensed with and a rhyming one is placed instead :

> The unyversall shyp and generall barke or barge
> Wherin they rowe that yet hath had no charge.

Starting from an idea expressed in Locher's motto :

> (1876)   And if perchaunce some one hath had no ore
> Nor place before, condigne for his degre,
> In this great carake nowe shall he rowe with me,

he begins by reserving a special place for some of his nearest acquaintances :

> (1877)   Here shall Jacke, charde, my brother Robyn hyll [2]
> With Myllers and bakers that weyght and mesure hate,
> All stelynge taylers, as Soper and Manshyll,
> Receyve theyr rowme, bycause they come to late ;
> The foulest place is mete for theyr estate :
> A rowme for rascoldes hard by the pompe shall be,
> That stynkynge placis and knaves may agre.

They have one comfort, viz. that nearly the whole world is as foolish as they.   So their companions will be from ' many a straunge nacyon '

---

[1] OFr. *gette* or *gaitte* = watch in the meaning of sentry ; other forms of the word are *wette, waite,* whence MnE. *to wait.*

[2] The punctuation and the capital letters are those of the original.   I cannot guess what persons are referred to.—Herford 347 quotes this stanza as having had special influence on *Cocke Lorell's Bote.*

(1879), and these nations are those mentioned by Locher. But Barclay adds several more that were apparently less strange :

> (1881)   The Lumbarde nacion, untrue of dede and mynde,
> . . . the dwellers of Cecyle and Almayne,
> Of Italy, Fraunce, Flaunders, Grece and Spayne.
> (1882)   The Pycardes, Normans and Neapolytayns
> Come in great clusters our navy to augment,
> So doth Venycians, Gascowns and Romayns,
> And Lytell Brytayne is all of lyke assent,
> And also the Great, by ryches excellent,
> Which nowe is callyd plentyfull in Englonde,
> Comyth to our Shyp, with Wales and Scotlande.[1]

Here especially nobody must be forgotten :

> (1883)   The out-yles, all dyspersyd here and there
> In the mayne se, also come in one bonde ;
> So many comys, that certaynly I fere
> Within my shyp they al can nat well stonde ;
> Hyther comys also the dwellers of Irelonde,
> Denys and Mawrys, Patryke and Mackmure,
> In mantels preckyd for lacke of precious furre.

The author knows the typically Irish names, and he also knows that the people over there are much poorer than in England, ' by ryches excellent.' England itself will have to supply the greatest contingent.

> (1884)   In Englonde is no cyte nor shyre, towne,
> Boroughe ne vyllage, howe pore so ever it be,
> Nor noble palays of suche a great renowne,
> But some maryners sende must they unto me.[2]

Then the voyage begins, but at the same time Barclay goes back to his Latin original, without making another attempt to make the allegory somewhat more consistent. Only the first stanza of this part is original and therefore more concrete than the Latin and more English, but the central idea remains as vague as it was :

> (1886)   My folysshe felawes, therfore I you exort,
> Hast to our navy, for tyme it is to rowe !
> Nowe must we leve eche sympyll haven and porte
> And sayle to that londe where folys abounde and flowe,[3]
> For whether we aryve at London or Brystowe
> Or any other haven within this our londe,
> We folys ynowe shall fynde alway at hande.

374.—The rest is only of importance as showing that Barclay understood most of Locher's humanistic allusions. The ' Syrenes ' become the ' marmaydes ' whose ' songe dullyth our mynde ' (1892), and the Cyclops is called by his proper name Polyphemus (1893). Though the name ' Circe ' is left out, there is still ' the vyle and vayne goddess of

---

[1] Before a nasal-group the *a* sound must still have wavered between *a* and *o*. The two spellings are used promiscuously. A few stanzas further on (1886) there is *londe : hande*.

[2] The text misprints *unto come*.

[3] This is the best translation of Locher's *Narragonum ad patriam* which I have come across.

folysshenes and worldly vanyte' (1896). But some more far-fetched names, such as the 'Syrtes Lybicas' and the 'Neptunia monstra,' are turned into a more moralizing reflection without the least thought of the main allegory :

> (1890)  And some so wander without gyde or counsell,
> That in the hourlynge [1] pyttis of ferefull hell
> Theyr shyppis brake and there alway remayne
> Within that gulf in endles wo and payne.

These are the 'Syrtes Lybicas'; and in the last stanza (1848) the 'Neptunia monstra' become 'hell monsters' that 'by furyous violence Swalowe up thy soule to payne from ioy and blys.'

One feels from this that also for Barclay the allegory is an ornament and nothing more. What he really wanted was only to point a moral. He may pick up a flower by the wayside, but he will never forget his real purpose : the fools must be lectured.

That the allegory was never more than a flower is made palpable by the concluding stanza of the whole book, where he perplexes the artistically minded reader with the statement :

> (1975)  Our Shyp here levyth the sees brode
> By helpe of God almyght, and quyetly
> At anker we lye within the rode.
> But who that lysteth of them to bye,
> In Flete strete shall them fynde truly,
> At the George, in Richarde Pynsonnes place,
> Prynter unto the Kynges noble grace.
> Deo gratias.

[1] Cawood prints *hurling* ; the word was commonly applied in the sixteenth century to the roaring or blustering of the wind. See NED.

## XVI

## CONCLUSION

375.—The year of the accession of Henry VIII was the meeting-point in England of three periods of literature. The Middle Ages were passing away, and Stephen Hawes, who wrote his CONVERSION OF SWEARERS in 1509, was perhaps one of their last literary exponents. The new Italian Renaissance, which was conquered for Northern Europe by Charles VIII in the Italian wars, gave its first literary product to England when Erasmus wrote his ENCOMIUM MORIAE, which owes its very name to the fact that it was written under the hospitable roof of Sir Thomas More in 1509. And in between there is that curious Interregnum, known as the Early Renaissance, initiated by the Council of Basel and Aeneas Sylvius in Germany, by Fichet, Heynlin and Gaguin in France. By a strange coincidence it was just in 1509 that its chief literary production was translated into English. The vicissitudes which the Ship of Fools underwent in its various versions throw a most illuminating light upon the character of this period so difficult to analyze.— The Renaissance was indigenous to Italy alone, where it had been growing gradually and naturally since the twelfth century. But every now and then some of its seeds were carried across the Alps. Germany received it in the main half a century before the Narrenschiff was written. There was hardly anyone who cherished it more enthusiastically than Brant, and yet he did not recognize its vital qualities. He was determined to enrich his own ' barbarous language ' with this foreign classicism, which was to him as a costly spice from the Golden Isles. He felt that it would add a new flavour to his own medieval conceptions, but the conceptions remained what they were. They were never transformed as by a leaven, and Erasmus' refinement of taste was still far to seek.

Locher did not appreciate these seeds of the Renaissance, which he found in Germany. He had studied in Italy itself, and the whole story of his life proves that he was ready to sacrifice all medieval traditions in favour of an unconditional surrender to the charms of the classics. But his classicism was no improvement upon that of his master. On the contrary. He made Brant's moralizations subordinate to classical precedent and fine-sounding names ; and his Navis Stultifera, though professedly preserving the nourishing qualities of the original, is principally concerned with making the piquancy of the new Renaissance only more pungent.

This was what appealed most to the taste of many readers in France. France had the strongest medieval tradition, but during the whole of the fifteenth century there had been various attempts to start little clubs whose members could exchange fine-sounding letters on trifling topics full of classical allusions.[1] The ' Early Renaissance ' in the second half of the century represents the same sort of classicism which Eustache Deschamps affected in his poetical letter to Chaucer almost a hundred years before. Riviere was a disciple of the ' nobles rhétoriqueurs.' Hardly satisfied even with Locher's extravagant classicism, he must introduce into his work some more mythology from De Genealogia Deorum, from Dionysius Siculus and Valerius Maximus. But he was a ' rhétoriqueur ' and an ' orateur ' above all and could write scores of well-scanned lines to express his moralizing reflections.

Various Englishmen had studied in Italy and the classics were being taught at Canterbury and at Oxford and Cambridge.[2] But there had not been any humanistic Renaissance in England. The tradition of Lydgate was still unchallenged when Barclay translated his Ship of Fools. In 1509 he is still fully a late medievalist. He admires the literary fashions of France of course, but when following his own natural inclinations he elaborates all Locher's classicism into a moralizing sermon.

The whole Renaissance was *caviare to the general*. No better illustration of this fact could be given than what Drouyn and Watson have made of it. When the Humanists and even the Rhétoriqueurs took their classical delicacies outside the circle of the chosen few, it was the fashion to admire them, but real appreciation was out of the question, for nobody understood anything of it. The prose-paraphrases make it quite comprehensible that both in France and in England it took more than two generations to build a new period of vernacular literature on the ruins of the Middle Ages.[3]

376.—Looking at the Ship of Fools more in detail one can feel from the German that Brant must have been a man of confused metaphors but of stern convictions ; narrow and bitter, perhaps, without poetic inspiration, and sarcastic without humour, but a pillar of strength for his friends and admirers.—Locher was a man of a different stamp. He was nothing but a schoolmaster, if we are to take his translation as the measure of his character. The Narrenschiff was the product of a glowing indignation tempered with the pedantry of a Humanist. The Navis Stultifera exaggerates the pedantry and leaves the indignation only

---

[1] This period has been suggestively described by Professor Huizinga, whose work has just been translated into English under the title *The Waning of the Middle Ages*.

[2] See Maxwell Lyte 383 sqq. ; Gasquet, The Eve of the Reformation, 23 sqq.

[3] In Germany it took more than a century.—The zenith of Renaissance inspiration was reached by French poetry in the work of Ronsard during the sixth decade of the century. Only from the year 1579, when Spenser and Sir Philip Sidney gave earnest of their genius, did the stream of great literature flow in England continuously or with sustained force (Sidney Lee, The French Renaissance in England (1910), 5 sq.). Wyatt and Surrey were aristocratic spirits and as individualistic as Erasmus. Perhaps even more so. Their poems were only published after their death.

dimly discernible.—Stern moralists are often obliging friends.  This is perhaps the best explanation for the fact that Brant professed to approve and even to admire the work of his pupil.

But in judging the German as well as the Latin text we must never forget that both were written in the most intimate co-operation with the recently invented printing press.  The press had its own technical limitations and technical ideals and both Brant and Locher had to conform to its requirements.  The end of a page had to be the end of a chapter.  This is one of the principal reasons why the Latin differs so completely from the German.  For Locher nearly always preferred the shortest arrangement possible.  In the first eighty-two chapters there are only two to which he devotes more than two pages, viz. chapter 6 and chapter 64, although there were no fewer than twenty-two such in Brant (6, 13, 16, 19, 26, 33, 38, 46, 49, 56, 57, 63, 64, 65, 66, 67, 72, 73, 75, 76, 81, 82).  In the rest of his book he becomes a little more liberal, though he *always* makes the longer chapters (83, 85, 86, 92, 95, 102, 103, 104, 105, 107, 108, 110[a], 110[b], 111, 112) a page or two shorter.[1]— This cannot possibly be ascribed to the demands of the printer.  On the contrary, it would seem that the printer preferred the size of the original, for Locher's own Concertatio (b) and his other additional matter together with Brant's treatise on the Beghards (e) and (in the second edition) on Disorder (f) have brought the book back again to its original size.— But it is not a question of size.  Locher did not work according to any standard of thought.  It was just as the fancy of the moment struck him.  Sometimes he followed most of Brant's ideas, at other times, and more usually, he made a haphazard selection or paraphrased a few lines at the beginning.  But as soon as his page was full, he was ready to break off even though the main subject had hardly been touched upon.  It has been calculated that Brant wrote 7034 lines and Locher 5672,[2] but hardly a third part of Brant's ideas can be traced in the Latin, and certainly not more than a tenth part of his grimmest sarcasm.

And yet this travesty was palmed off on the public as a real translation.  And it was accepted as such.  It found an enthusiastic welcome in France, and from France it journeyed to all the countries that were under French literary or political influence.  It seems an amazing fact ; but yet one not entirely inexplicable.  It is still doubtful in how far the Humanists really admired it, or whether they knew more of it than the title and that it was ' written by Brant.' [3]  A rather significant fact is that the Latin was never reprinted after the year 1498.[4]—But the book was certainly admired by the people, who, no doubt, looked principally at the pictures, for the most nonsensical paraphrases, those of Drouyn and of Watson, had the greatest momentary success.  To the moralists of the times also it must have appealed very strongly, for it contained

---

[1] The only exception is chapter 99.

[2] Fraustadt's figures.

[3] See § 365.

[4] The 1572 edition was rather a revival ; its model was one of the French editions. See also § 365.

just enough of the spirit of the original to serve as matter for a sermon. That is how Riviere used it. Out of Locher's 5672 lines he made 17133,[1] although he did not understand all those classical allusions. But the sermon was honest and it fell in with the taste of large numbers in France.[2] Those were the days of preachers. The biographer of the well-known Franciscan, Olivier Maillard,[3] can repeatedly quote the *Nef des Folz* to illustrate the sermons that were most popular in Paris and in the Provinces.

377.—It must have been through Riviere's paraphrase that Barclay became acquainted with the Ship of Fools. For in the headings of the chapters, wherever the French title deviates somewhat from the Latin, the French rather than the Latin is reflected in the English translation.[4] And where the arrangement of the *Nef* differs from that of the *Navis* (chapters 20 and 21) the English version does the same. But the bulk of the translation is all done from the Latin, that is to say from the Latin edition published at Paris and reprinted at Lyons in 1498.[5] It is not impossible that Barclay has ' oversene ' a copy of the German original, but it was all Greek to him ; he did not understand a word of it.[6]— How he worked with the Latin and the French before him is not quite clear. He must have diligently scanned the marginal notes of the French edition, and this accounts for the deviations in chapters 6, 8, 10, 53, 64, 85, and perhaps also 33.[7] For chapter 98 we must assume some difficulty in identifying the ' Moravi.'[8] But for chapters M, 12, 13 and 25[9] the only reason is perhaps that he had already done these chapters, before the Latin text fell into his hands. This explanation is not satisfactory, but nothing better has ever been suggested.

378.—His paraphrase appears to be partly the drudgery work of a conscientious but clever translator, partly the well-meaning sermon of a good-humoured preacher, who is anxious to work for the benefit of his countrymen and takes a delight in riding some peculiar hobbies of his own. His knowledge of the classics is not so great as Locher's, but he knows much more of them than Riviere. Of his own language he has a perfect command,[10] and if his metre is halting and imperfect, it is partly, perhaps, due to the language itself and its rapid development,[11] and partly to the conventions inherited from Lydgate. The main reason was probably that he did not care much. He was not a poet. He had a great facility in fashioning Chaucerian stanzas out of every two or four lines of his original, and he surpassed Locher in concrete individual

---

[1] Fraustadt's figures.

[2] Renaudet 240 sq.

[3] A. Samouillan, Olivier Maillard, sa Prédication et son Temps (Toulouse 1891), 219, 272 etc.

[4] See chapters 14, 19, 21, 28, 29, 30, 31, 42, 51, 64, 66, 72, 79, 80, 81, 90, 110b. d in the Appendix.

[5] See § 130.　　　　　　　　　　　[6] See § 338.

[7] See §§ 224, 111, 102, 58, 214, 133.　　[8] § 172.

[9] §§ 341 sq., 81, 45, 94.

[10] It has been somewhat hastily assumed that there are traces of Scotch influence in his words and expressions. See §§ 310, 319.

[11] Some critics would attribute nearly everything to the language.

conception. But he only wanted to preach his sermon and he is usually at his best when he leaves Locher alone. Most of his original contributions can be easily recognized even without the help of the marginal notes, for the more original he is the more lively becomes his language. One can feel the quickening of his pulse when he is making his own attacks. The Chaucerian stanza suits him best. He adopts the Octaves chiefly for his Eulogies and for his Envoys, but they are both mostly very rhetorical, unless he uses them for a humorous purpose.[1] He has more humour than Riviere or Locher or Brant himself, but he has all the unbearable prolixity of an old-fashioned preacher. He makes Locher's text four times as long as it was, writing almost fourteen thousand lines.[2] This makes his work longer by half than the whole of *Paradise Lost*.—A comparison of his character with that of Brant is impossible. He has nothing to do with Brant and very little in common, except that they were both moralists. He has nothing of the clumsy ruggedness of the German, but neither do we feel from his paraphrase the imposing personality that made Brant the centre of a worshipping group of friends. He is not conscious of any originality in his mind, and there was very little initiative in his aspirations. He preferred the guidance of a youthful Frenchman to the inspiration of his own better genius.[3]

379.—Of Drouyn and Watson it is better to say nothing. They can have been little more than the colleagues of the compositors who printed their works. Especially Watson ; he is the more helpless of the two. He knows a little French, but that is all. He gets paid for his work, but he does not take the least interest in it. He will translate anything that he is set to do, whether nonsense or not.[4] The printer is responsible for everything he writes. And the printer had chosen Drouyn as a model, perhaps by accident, perhaps because he was shorter than Riviere, cheaper to print and easier to translate.—Drouyn has at least something original. He begins nearly every chapter with his own 'Invitation,' and at the end he often adds a reflection of his own, which sometimes takes an amusing or an interesting turn.[5] He has even managed to write two entire chapters of his own [6] and now and then he has consulted the Latin. But he, too, worked at command, and he no more merits a place in the history of literature than Watson. The name of the Ship of Fools has placed them on a higher pedestal than they really deserve.

---

[1] Cf. ch. 112, § 110 on John Bishop.

[2] According to my calculation exactly 13926 lines. Fraustadt (and Koelbing in the Cambr. Hist. iii, 59) says 14034 ; he has probably included the prose-introductions.

[3] A synthesis of the biographical elements contained in this study has been left out on purpose. They are perhaps sufficient to justify a new biography.

[4] He has translated at least three other works : *Valentine and Orson*, *The Church of Evil Men and Women*, and *The History of Oliver of Castile*. This last work has even had the honour of a fine edition for the Roxburghe Club (by R. E. Graves in 1898). In the 'Introyte' he uses the same expression as in the 'Shyppe' ; he is doing his work 'at the commandement of my worshypfull mayster Wynkyn de Worde.'

[5] See §§ 90 and 187.　　　　　　　[6] See § 191 sqq.

380.—The course of the Ship may be summarized in a table :

1. Brant First Edition 1494.
|
2. Brant Second Edition 1495.
|
3. Locher First Edition 1497.
|

---

| 4. Riviere 1497. | 5. Locher Second Edition 1497. |
| 6. Drouyn 1498. | 7. Locher Paris (and Lyons) Edition 1498. |

4. Riviere 1497.
|
6. Drouyn  1498.          7. Locher Paris (and Lyons) Edition 1498.
(With some in-
fluence from 7.)
|                  9. The Marnef-   (Badius      10. Barclay 1509.
8. Drouyn 1499.           translator   1498, 1500,   (With some in-
|                     1499.       1505.)      fluence from 4.)
11. Watson 1509.

|
(Cocke Lorel's Bote.)

381—The Ship of Fools is no instance of ' Early German Influence on English Literature.' If Locher had attempted to give a somewhat faithful translation of the German text, it would require only a little straining of the word to say that the French and English versions were due to German influence, although even then we could not speak of literary relationship. But the Latin has very little in common with the German original except the woodcuts. A third part of the ideas, a tenth part of the sarcasm [1] is only a rough estimate. But to this must be added that of all Brant's innumerable vernacular expressions and comparisons and proverbs hardly anything was translated by Locher. Classical patterns decided his choice, unless, as in some of the mottoes, the German expression was necessary to explain the woodcuts  And in such cases either Barclay did not understand the meaning or he spoiled his own allegory by a literal translation. [2]

Some dozen years ago it was shown that Erasmus's works had influenced Shakespeare's Jest-Books and Lyly's Euphues to an extent which had never been suspected before. [3] But nobody has drawn from it the conclusion that Shakespeare or Lyly stood under Dutch influence or that it proved the existence of literary relations between Holland and England. —Locher was in his own way as much of a Humanist as Erasmus was, with this small difference—that the first was perhaps talented while the second was undoubtedly a genius. No more than Erasmus did he ever write a word of his own vernacular. It was not German idiom and German imagery that coloured his language ; all his idioms and all his

[1] See § 376.
[2] See the ' Nithardus ' in § 56, the ' crinis ' in § 128, the ' dull asse ' in § 135, the ' assa columba ' in § 147, belling the cat in § 309, the ' quycke sowe ' in § 361, and the ' oppressing ass ' in § 369.
[3] H. de Vocht, De Invloed van Erasmus op de Engelsche Tooneelliteratuur der XVI en XVII eeuwen (Koninkl. Vlaamsche Academie Gent 1908), i, 49 sqq., 92 sqq.

images and even most of his ideas were borrowed from the classics. Such are not the men to form connecting links between one national literature and another.

382.—It would have been strange indeed if the German Narrenschiff had been translated into English. Ever since the Norman Conquest English civilization had been controlled by French standards. France gave the lead in literature as well as in customs and manners and dress. The whole story of the English Renaissance in the sixteenth century has been rightly described as the story of the *French* Renaissance in England, because all classical sources and Italian currents reached this country through French channels.[1]

Germany remained a *terra incognita* all through the Middle Ages. When her literature achieved its highest masterpieces in the thirteenth century no trace of their influence can be discovered across the Channel. And towards the end of the fifteenth and in the beginning of the sixteenth century no signs were visible of any turning of the tides. Caxton had perhaps become first acquainted with the printing press at Cologne. Wynkyn de Worde was a German himself. But neither of them introduced any German literature into England. The Anglicized German himself preferred a bad French version to the good original of the most famous work that Germany had produced in the fifteenth century.

If any country besides France may be said to have exercized any influence on English literature, it was Holland, when it had been brought to greater economical and cultural significance by the policy of the Dukes of Burgundy.[2]

383.—Quite recently the associate Professor of German in the University of Wisconsin, Bayard Quincy Morgan, published an exhaustive 'Bibliography of German Literature in English Translation.'[3] On p. 11 he writes : 'The appearance of translations follows closely on the development of the printing press into a successful and active business, and we have over a score of translations in the sixteenth century. The earliest one known to me is the 1509 edition of Sebastian Brant's Narrenschiff.[4] It is followed in 1525 by Hieronymus Braunschweig's treatise on surgery, in 1528 and 1530 by editions of the pranks of Eulenspiegel, in 1537 and 1538 (and again in 1548) by the comparison of the old and new learnings of Urbanus Rhegius.'

This statement presents the traditional view on the subject, but it creates a quite mistaken impression of the foreign influences that were brought to bear on the history of English literature in the beginning of the sixteenth century. Of the Narrenschiff no more need be said. A 'treatise on surgery' falls outside the scope of a student of literature,

---

[1] Sidney Lee, The French Renaissance in England (1910). Wyatt and Surrey form no exception. See ib. p. 111. North's Plutarch came from the French of Amyot, p. 156. The Pleiade may almost be said to have taught the Elizabethan lyrists their trade, p. 454.

[2] Caxton himself translated his Reynard the Fox from the Dutch. See E. G. Duff, n. 358.

[3] Studies in Lang. and Litt. xvi (Madison 1922), 708 pp. in royal 8vo.

[4] It is only fair to add that in a note on p. 60 he calls Barclay's translation 'a free rendering of the Latin version of Jacob Locher.'

but the colophon of the book may perhaps be quoted from the general catalogue of the British Museum : ' Thus endith the . . . Experyence . . . of surgery . . . whiche boke of late was translated out of speche of hye Almayne *into lowe Duche*. And afterwarde into our mother tong of Englys . . . B.L.' [1]—The pranks of Eulenspiegel were certainly not translated from the German, but either from the French or from Low-German [2] or from Dutch.[3] The first edition at any rate was brought out by the well-known Dutch printer at Antwerp, Jan van Doesborgh, probably about the year 1519.[4]

Only one item on the list remains : ' the comparison of the old and new learnings of Urbanus Rhegius.' [5] This places things in the true perspective.

Tyndale landed at Hamburg in 1524 and Roy and Barlow took Manuel's Die Krankheit der Messe as their model for their joint production ' Rede me and be not wroth ' or The Burial of the Mass in 1528.[6] This was the New Learning as Urbanus Rhegius understood it.[7] It had begun when, far away from the circles of the Alsatian and French Humanists, Luther affixed his theses to a church door at Wittenberg. The printing press did not establish any new literary relations. Both the Early and the Late Renaissance came from France, but the New Learning in a religious sense came from Germany.

[1] Ed. P. Treveris, at London, in Southwarke 1525. The earliest Dutch translation mentioned by Nijhoff-Kronenberg (n. 506) dates from 1535, but the British Museum possesses an imperfect copy which the General Catalogue ascribes to " [Amsterdam ? 1520 ?]."

[2] ' Low German ' is as different from ' German ' as English is.

[3] On the various theories see Fr. W. D. Brie, Eulenspiegel in England (Palaestra xxvii, 1903), 10 sqq.

[4] R. Proctor, Jan van Doesborgh, Printer at Antwerp (Bibliogr. Society Monograph II, 1894), p. 13 : ' n.d. (c. 1519 ?) 4°. Two editions printed by R. Copland are as regards the text almost word for word the same.'

[5] It was translated by William Turner.

[6] Herford 40 sqq. Arber, English Reprints 28 (1871), who calls it ' one of the worthiest satires in our language,' notes on p. 6 that it was written not earlier than February or March 1528. In 1529 there appeared a Low-German ' Burial of the Mass '; text in Jahrbuch des Vereins für niederdeutsche Sprachforschung xxi (Norden 1896), 147–155, but the editor says nothing about its relation to the other versions.

[7] Gasquet, The Eve of the Reformation 18 sq.

## A COMPARATIVE TABLE OF ALL THE CHAPTERS OF

| Chapter[1] | Brant's Title | Locher's Titles[2] | 2nd ed. fol.[3] | Basel 1572[4] page | Barclay's Title | 1st ed. fol. |
|---|---|---|---|---|---|---|
| A | | | | | Domino Thome Cornisshe | *u* |
| B | | Epigramma ad lectorem | i *v* | *u*[5] | | |
| C | | Epistola | i *v* | *u* | | |
| D | | Carmen | iii *v* | *u* | | |
| E | | Sapphicon | iiii | *u* | | |
| F | | Epigramma | v *v* | *wanting* | | |
| G | | Ad Joh. Bergmannum | v *v* | *wanting* | | |
| H | | Ad Jac. Philomusum | vi | | | |
| I | | Celeusma | vi *v* | | Barclay to the Foles | v |
| J | | | | | | |
| K | | Prologus | vii | | The Prologue of J. Locher | vi |
| L | Vorred | Hecatostichon | viii *v* | *u* | The Prologe | x |
| M | | Argumentum | x *v* | *u* | *no title* | xii |
| 1 | Von unnützen buchern | De inutilibus libris Inutilitas librorum | xi | p. 1 | Inprofytable bokes | xiii *v* |
| 2 | Von guten reten | De bonis consultoribus Judicis officium | xii | 3 | Of evyl counsellours. Juges and men of lawe | xv *v* |
| 3 | Von gytikeit | De avaritia et prodigalitate Avaritia | xiiii | 4 | Of Avaryce or Covetyse and prodygalyte | xvii *v* |
| 4 | Von nuwen funden | De novis ritibus | xiii | 6 | Of newe fassions and disgised Garmentes | xviii *v* |
| 5 | Von alten narren | De antiquis fatuis Inveterata fatuitas | xv | 8 | Of old folys that is to say the longer they live the more they are gyven to foly | xxii |

[1] The numbers are Zarncke's. The letters indicate chapters not found in the German, e

[2] The marginal notes are also provided with a title, which often deviates from that o only this secondary title.

[3] The Paris and Lyons reprints have the chapters on the same folio as the 2nd Basel edition d (cxxxviii *v*), e (cxxxix).

[4] I have added the pages of this late edition for the convenience of the readers of Fraus

[5] *u* is used to denote unnumbered pages or leaves.

[6] The first volume is meant as far as chapter 63 ; then follows the second volume.

P OF FOOLS IN THE DIFFERENT VERSIONS AND EDITIONS

| n° | Stanza | Riviere's and Drouyn's Title | Riviere fol. | Drouyn fol. | Watson's Chapter and Title | Contents | Section |
|---|---|---|---|---|---|---|---|
| | | | | | | Dedication | 346 |
| | | | | | | Introductory Epigram | 333 |
| | | | | | | Letter to Brant | 330 |
| | | | | | | Song to Brant | 331 |
| | | | | | | Locher's Apology | 334 |
| | | | | | | Epigram to the Reader | 335 |
| | | | | | | Ten lines to Bergman | 327 |
| | | | | | | Exhortation to Locher | 320 |
| 3 | 6 | | | | | Call to the Fools | 318 |
| | | Le prologue du translateur | u | ii | The Prologue of the translatour | Prologue du translateur | 342 |
| 5 | | Prologue de Jacques Locher | u | ii v | | Prologue | 336 |
| I | 12 | Prolude | u | iii v | Prolude | Brant's Prologue | 314 |
| 7 | | Argument | u | iiii | Argument | Second Prologue | 340 |
| 9 | 34 | Des livres inutilz | i | iiii v | I. Of bookes inutyle | Book-Collectors | 244 |
| 4 | 48 | De bons conseilz | i v | v v | II. Of good counsayll | Lawyers | 193 |
| 29 | 62 | De avarice et prodigalite | ii | v v | III. Of avaryce & prodygalyte | Avarice | 62 |
| 34 | 77 | Des nouveaulz ritz et nouvelles coustumes | iii | vi v | IIII. Of newe guyses and customes | New Fashions | 267 |
| 41 | 99 | De anciens folz | iiii | vii v | V. Of auncyent fooles | Old Fools | 228 |

Vorred.
pter. This title has become very prominent in the Paris edition. Renouard i, 281–284 gives
re are usually a few lines on the preceding page. Exceptions are the chapters c (fol. cxxxvii v),
sertation.

| Chapter | Brant's Title | Locher's Titles | 2nd ed. fol. | Basel 1572 page | Barclay's Title | 1st ed. fol. |
|---|---|---|---|---|---|---|
| 6 | Von ler der kind | De doctrina filiorum De eruditione puerorum | xvi | 10 | Of the erudicion of negligent faders, anenst theyr chyldren | xxiiii |
| 7 | Von zwytracht machen | De delatoribus et litigiorum promotoribus Procuratio rixarum | xviii | 14 | Of tale berers, fals reporters and prometers of stryfes | xxvi v |
| 8 | Nit volgen gutem ratt | Non sequi bona consilia Spernere consilia salubria | xix | 16 | Of hym that wyll nat folowe nor ensue good counsell, and necessary | xxix |
| 9 | Von bosen sytten | De incompositis moribus De corruptis moribus | xx | 18 | Of disordered and ungoodly maners | xxx |
| 10 | Von worer fruntschafft | De lesione amicitiae Violare amicos | xxi | 20 | Of brekynge and hurtynge of amyte and frendshyp | xxxi v |
| 11 | Verachtung der gschrift | De contemptu Scripturae Scripture contemptus | xxii | 22 | Of contempt or dispysynge of holy Scripture | xxxiv |
| 12 | Von unbesinten narren | De improvidis fatuis Non providere futura | xxiii | 24 | Of folys without provysyon | xxxvi v |
| 13 | Von buolschaft | De amore venereo Calamitas amatorum | xxiiii | 26 | Of disordered love and veneryous | xxxvii v |
| 14 | Von vermessenheit gotz | De peccantibus super dei misericordiam Peccare super mīa dei | xxv | 28 | Of them that synne trustynge upon the mercy of God | xli |
| 15 | Von narrechtem anschlag | De fatuis edificandi incoeptibus Incipere et non prius providere | xxvi | 30 | Of the folisshe begynnynge of great bildynges without sufficient provision | xlii v |
| 16 | Von fullen und prassen | De potatoribus et edacibus De epulonibus | xxvii | 32 | Of glotons & ronkardes | xliv |
| 17 | Von unnutzem richtum | De inutilibus divitiis Divitiarum sollicitudo | xxviii | 34 | Of ryches unprofytable | xlvii |
| 18 | Von dienst zweyer herren | De obsequio duorum dominorum Servire duobus | xxix | 36 | Of hym that togyder wyll serve two maysters | xlix |
| 19 | Von vil schwetzen | De nimia garrulitate Garrula lingua | xxx | 38 | Of to moche spekynge or bablynge | li |
| 20 | Von schatz finden | Invenire rem alienam et non reddere Invenire et non reddere | xxxi | 40 | Of hym that fyndeth ought of another mannys it nat restorynge to the owner | liv v |

| Stanza | Riviere's and Drouyn's Title | Riviere fol. | Drouyn fol. | Watson's Chapter and Title | Contents | Section |
|---|---|---|---|---|---|---|
| 112 | De la doctrine des enfants | iiii *v* | viii | VI. Of the documente of Chyldren | Parents | 223 |
| 141 | Des raporteurs detract- eurs et litigieux | vi | ix | VII. Of reportours and detractours | Backbiting | 104 |
| 154 | De non suyvir bon con- seil | vii | ix *v* | VIII. Of them that ensueth not good counsayll | Taking Advice | 111 |
| 168 | Des meurs incomposees | viii | x | IX. Of folysshe meurs and condycyons | Indecorous Manners | 278 |
| 179 | De lesion damitie | viii *v* | x *v* | X. Of the hurtynge of amyte | True Friendship | 102 |
| 196 | De contempner lescripture | ix *v* | xi *v* | XI. Of the contem- nynge of scrypture | Contempt of true Doctrine | 136 |
| 209 | Des folz impourveux | x *v* | xii | XII. Of foles unpur- vayed | Improvi- dence | 81 |
| 222 | Damour venerieuse | xi | xiii | XIII. Of vayne and transytory love | Lechery | 44 |
| 238 | De ceulx qui pechent sur la misericorde de dieu | xii *v* | xiii *v* | XIIII. Of them that syn on the mercy of God | Presump- tion on God's mercy | 80 |
| 251 | Des foulz faisans les edifices | xiii | xiiii | XV. Of fooles mak- ynge edefyces | Improvi- dence | 82 |
| 263 | De yvroignes et glou- tons | xiiii | xiiii *v* | XVI. Of dronkerdes and glotons | Gluttony and Drun- kenness | 71 |
| 282 | De richesses inutiles | xiiii *v* | xv | XVII. Of rychesse inutile | Avarice | 64 |
| 296 | De service de deux maistres | xv *v* | xvi | XVIII. Of the ser- vyce of two maysters | Two Mas- ters | 84 |
| 309 | De trop parler | xvi | xvi *v* | XIX. Of to moche speche | Loquacity | 114 |
| 334 | Laultruy trouver et ne le rendre. | xvii *v* | xvii *v* | XXI. For to fynde other mennes goodes and not to yelde them agayne | Finding | 92 |

| Chap-ter | Brant's Title | Locher's Titles | 2nd ed. fol. | Basel 1572 page | Barclay's Title | 1st ed. fol. | 2n |
|---|---|---|---|---|---|---|---|
| 21 | Von stroffen und selb tun | De eo qui in alios animadvertit et met peccat Medice cura te ipsum | xxxii | 42 | Of them that correct other and yet themselfe do nought and synne worse than they whom they so correct | lii v [1] | |
| 22 | Die ler der wisheit | De contione sapientiae Sapientiae praecepta | xxxiii | 44 | Of the sermon or erudicion of wysdome | lvi v | |
| 23 | Von uberhebung glucks | Iactatio et confidentia fortunae Fortune vanitas | xxxiiii | 46 | Of bostynge or havynge confydence in fortune | lviii v | |
| 24 | Von zu vil sorg | De nimia curiositate mortalium Cura inutilis | xxxv | 48 | Of the overgreat and chargeable curyosite of men | lx v | |
| 25 | Von zuo borg uff nemen | Mutuum accipere *same* | xxxvi | 50 | Of them that ar alway borowynge | lvii [2] | |
| 26 | Von unnutzem wunschen | De inutilibus votis et petitionibus Quid orandum | xxxvii | 52 | Of inprofytable and vayne prayers and peticyons | lviii | |
| 27 | Von unnutzem studieren | De inutili studio Inutile studium | xxxviii | 54 | Of unprofytable study | lx v | |
| 28 | Von wider gott reden | Temere loquentes contra Deum Corripere facta dei | xxxix | 56 | Of them that folysshly speke agaynst the workes of god | lxiii | |
| 29 | Der ander lut urteilt | Qui alios judicat Iudicare alios | xl | 58 | Of them that gyve jugement on other | lxiv v | |
| 30 | Von vile der pfrunden | De pluralitate beneficiorum Benefitiorum pluralitas | xli | 60 | Of pluralitees that is to say of them whiche charge them selfe with many benefyces | lxvi v | |
| 31 | Von uffschlag suchen | De eo qui exceptiones querit ad emendandum se Differens benefacere | xlii | 62 | Of them that prolong from day to day to amende themselfe | lxvii | |
| 32 | Von frowen huetten | De custodia mulierum Observare mulieres | xliii | 64 | Of hym that is Jelous over his wyfe and watcheth hir wayes without cause | lxviii v | |
| 33 | Von eebruch | De adulterio Lenocinii fatuitas | xliiii | 66 | Of avoutry and . . . of them that ar bawdes to their wyves | lxx v | |
| 34 | Narr hur als vern | Semper fatuus Stultitia gaudium stultorum | xlv | 68 | Of hym that nought can and nought wyll lerne . . . De octo secundariis | lxxii v | • |

[1] The Latin text follows the order of the original. The English (as the French !) places ch.
[2] After fol. lxi begins fol. lvii *etc.* again.

| Stanza | Riviere's and Drouyn's Title | Riviere fol. | Drouyn fol. | Watson's Chapter and Title | Contents | Section |
|---|---|---|---|---|---|---|
| 322 | De ceulx qui corrigent les aultres et eulx mesmes pechent | xvi v | xvii | XX. Of them that correcteth other and synneth themselfe | Fault-finding | 98 |
| 346 | De concione sapiencie | xviii | xviii | XXII. Of the conscyon of sapyence | Discourse of Wisdom | 107 |
| 360 | De iactation et confiance de fortune | xix | xviii v | XXIII. Of iactaunce and cunfydence of fortune | Suffering Fickleness of Fortune | 122 |
| 374 | De trop grant curiosite | xix v | xix | XXIIII. Of to grete curyosyte | Anxiety | 115 |
| 387 | De prendre a credit | xx v | xix v | XXV. Of them that taketh a truste | Usury | 94 |
| 399 | De peticions et veux inutilz | xxi | xx | XXVI. Of petycyons and vowes inutyle | Ill-advised Prayers | 140 |
| 416 | De lestude inutile | xxii | xxi | XXVII. Of studye inutyle | Useless study | 248 |
| 436 | De ceulx qui parlent contre dieu follement | xxii v | xxi v | XXVIII. Of them that speke folysshely agaynst god | Disapproving God's Works | 76 |
| 448 | De aultruy dire iugement | xxiii v | xxii | XXIX. To gyve iugement on another | Fault-finding | 99 |
| 460 | De ceulx qui se chargent de plusieurs benefices | xxiiii | xxii v | XXX. Of them that charge them with benefyces | Pluralities | 159 |
| 479 | De ceulx qui different de iour en iour eulx amender | xxv v | xxiii | XXXI. Of them that desyre for to amende them from daye to daye | Procrastination | 125 |
| 491 | De ceulx qui veullent garder femmes | xxvi | xxiiii | XXXII. Of them that wyll kepe wyves | Husband and Wife | 217 |
| 504 | De adultaire | xxvii | xxiiii v | XXXIII. Of advoutrye | Adultery | 48 |
| 516 | De celuy qui est fol en tous temps | xxviii | xxv | XXXIIII. Of hym that is alwayes folysshe | Fickleness | 116 |

and ch. 21. Cawood must have perceived the incongruity, for he omits the Latin text of ch. 21.

| Chapter | Brant's Title | Locher's Titles | 2nd ed. fol. | Basel 1572 page | Barclay's Title | 1st ed. fol. |
|---|---|---|---|---|---|---|
| 35 | Von luchtlich zyrnen | De iracundia ex levi causa Irasci sine causa | xlvi | 70 | Of great wrathe procedynge of small occasyon | lxxiv |
| 36 | Von Eygenrichtikeit | *wanting* | | | *wanting* | |
| 37 | Von gluckes fall | De fortunae mutabilitate Fortune mutabilitas | xlvii | 72 | Of the mutabylyte of fortune | lxxvi v |
| 38 | Von krancken die nit volgen | De egrotante inobediente Patiens impatiens | xlviii | 74 | Of them that be diseasyd and seke and ar impacient . . . | lxxix |
| 39 | Von offlichen anschlag | De nimium apertis consultationibus Aperte insidias ponere | xlix W. | 76 | Of over open takynges of counsell | lxxxi v |
| 40 | An narren sich stossen | Fatuorum damno sapientes nos fieri convenit Alienis periculis fieri sapientem | l | 78 | Of folys that can nat beware by the mysfortune . . . of others | lxxxiii |
| 41 | Nit achten uff all red | Nil curare detractiones hominum *same* | li | 80 | Of them that forceth or careth for the bacbytynge of lewde people | lxxxv |
| 42 | Von spott vogelen | De subsannatoribus et calumniatoribus Abstrahere a bono | lii | 82 | Of mockers, and scorners and false accusers | lxxxvii |
| 43 | Verachtung ewiger freyt | Contemptus aeternorum gaudiorum Transitoria praeferre eternis | liii | 84 | Of them that despyse everlastynge ioye and settyth thynges transytory . . . | lxxxix[1] |
| 44 | Gebracht in der kirchen | Tumultus et confabulatio in ecclesia Dehonestare ecclesias | liiii | 86 | Of them that make noyses . . . dishonest in the chirche of god | lxxxxi v |
| 45 | Von mutwilligem ungfell | De protervo ac spontaneo periculo *same* | lv | 88 | Of them that wyllynge and knowingly put them self to ieopardy . . . | lxxxxiii v |
| 46 | Von dem gewalt der narren | De potentia fatuitatis *same* | lxxiiii | 126 | Of the great myght and power of folys | cxxxiiii I |
| 47 | Van dem weg der sellikeit | De via foelicitatis et futura peccatorum poena De via felicitatis | lvi | 90 | Of the way of felycyte and godnes and of the payne . . . unto synners | lxxxxv v |

[1] Misprinted cclxv.

| Stanza | Riviere's and Drouyn's Title | Riviere fol. | Drouyn fol. | Watson's Chapter and Title | Contents | Section |
|---|---|---|---|---|---|---|
| 533 | De courroux qui procede de petite cause | xxviii v | xxv v | XXXV. Of angre that procedeth of a lytell thynge | Wrath | 61 |
| | *wanting* | | | *wanting* | The Self-opinionated | 43 |
| 549 | De la mutabilite de fortune | xxix v | xxvi | XXXVI. Of the mutabylyte of fortune | The Wheel of Fortune | 123 |
| 567 | De limpatient en maladie | xxx v | xxvii | XXXVII. Of the impacyence in sykenes | Patients | 209 |
| 583 | De consultacions apertes | xxxi | xxvii v | XXXVIII. Of consultacyons to openly | Keeping Secrets | 112 |
| 595 | Comment on doit estre saige par lexperience du mal | xxxii | xxviii | XXXIX. How one ought to be wyse, by experience of the evylles . . . | Misfortunes of Others | 119 |
| 608 | De non avoir cure des detractions . . . | xxxiii | xxviii v | XL. Not for to have cure of detraccyons . . . | Backbiting | 105 |
| 622 | De subsannateurs calumniateurs et detracteurs | xxxiiii | xxix | XLI. Of subsanatours, calomnyatours and detractours | Mockery | 103 |
| 636 | Du contempnement de la ioye eternelle | xxxv | xxx | XLII. Of the dyspraysynge of the Ioye eternall | Heaven and Earth | 85 |
| 650 | Du tumulte et parlement qui se fait en leglise | xxxvi | xxx v | XLIII. Of tumulte and ianglynge in the chirche | Irreverence in Church | 144 |
| 667 | De ceulx qui senclinent . . . a souffrir mort | xxxvii | xxxi | XLIIII. Of them that enclyne them to suffre dethe | Useless Prayers | 142 |
| 959 | De la puissance des folz | lvi v | xlii v | LXII. Of the puyssaunce of fools | Respecters of Persons | 69 |
| 681 | De la voye de felicite et peine a venir . . . | xxxvii v | xxxi | XLV. Of the felycyte and payne to come | The Two Ways | 87 |

| Chapter | Brant's Title | Locher's Titles | 2nd ed. fol. | Basel 1572 page | Barclay's Title | 1st ed. fol. | 2 |
|---|---|---|---|---|---|---|---|
| 48 | Eyn gesellen schiff | Socialis navis mechanicorum | cxxxix | 251 | The unyversall shyp of craftymen, or laborers | cclxiiii | 2 |
| 49 | Bos exempel der eltern | Prava maiorum exempla Mala exempla parentum | lvii | 92 | Of the yll example gyvyn unto youth | lxxxxvii | |
| 50 | Von wollust | De voluptate corporali Voluptatis incommoda | lviii | 94 | Of bodely pleasour or corporall voluptuosyte | lxxxxix v | |
| 51 | Heymlicheit verswigen | Archana esse recondenda Secreta tacenda | lix | 96 | Of folys that can nat kepe secrete theyr owne counsell | ci | |
| 52 | Wiben durch gutz willen | Uxorem ducere propter opes Nubere propter divitias | lx | 98 | Of yonge folys that take olde . . . wyves, for theyr ryches | ciii | |
| 53 | Von nyd und has | De livore et invidia Invidie proprium | lxi | 100 | Of envyous folys | cv | |
| 54 | Von ungedult der straff | De impatientia correctionis Non velle corrigi | lxii | 102 | Of impacient folys that wyll nat abyde correccion | cvii | 1 |
| 55 | Von narrechter. artzny | De fatuis medicis et empericis Medicus indoctus | lxiii | 104 | Of folysshe fesycyans that onely folowe paractyke | cix | 1 |
| 56 | Von end des gewaltes | De saecularis potentiae exitu Potentatus seculi finis | lxiiii | 106 | Of the end of worldly honour and power | cxi | 1 |
| 57 | Furwissenheyt gottes | De praedestinatione Prescientia dei | lxv | 108 | Of predestynacion | cxiii v | 1 |
| 58 | Syn selb svergessen | De oblivione sui ipsius Negligere propria | lxvi | 110 | Of folys that forget themselfe and do another mannys besynes | cxv v | 1 |
| 59 | Von undanckberkeyt | De vitio ingratitudinis De ingratis | lxvii | 112 | Of the vyce of unkyndnes and folys that it folowe | cxvii | 1 |
| 60 | Von im selbs wolgefallen | Sui ipsius complacentia Sapientiae proprie confidere | lxviii | 114 | Of folys that stande so well in their own conceit . . . | cxix v | 11 |
| 61 | Von dantzen | De choreis et saltationibus Choree fatuitas | lxix | 116 | Of lepynges and dauncis and folys that pas theyr tyme . . . | cxxii | 11 |
| 62 | Von nachteshofyeren | De nocturnis ioculatoribus Nocte ludere in plateis | lxx | 118 | Of nyght watchers and beters of the stretes playnge by night . . . | cxxiiii | 11 |
| 63 | Von bettleren | De mendicis et eorum vanitatibus Mendicantes improbi | lxxi | 120 | Of folysshe beggers and of theyr vanytees | cxxvi | 11 |

| son e | Stanza | Riviere's and Drouyn's Title | Riviere fol. | Drouyn fol. | Watson's Chapter and Title | Contents | Section |
|---|---|---|---|---|---|---|---|
| 3 | 1899 | De la nef socalle mech-anicque | cxv v | lxxvi | CXIIII. Of the shyp socyale mecanycque | Decay of the Guilds | 96 |
| 4 | 693 | Du maulvais exemple des plus grans | xxxviii v | xxxii | XLVI. Of the evyll example of the moost byggest | Parents | 226 |
| 9 | 708 | De voluptuosite corporelle | xxxix v | xxxiii | XLVII. Of the voluptuousnes corporall | Lechery | 46 |
| 3 | 721 | De ceulx qui ne peuvent celer leur secret | xl v | xxxiii v | XLVIII. Of them that not hyde theyr secretes | Keeping Secrets | 113 |
| 7 | 734 | De celui qui espouse femme pour ses richesses et avoir | xli v | xxxiiii | XLIX. Of hym that weddeth a wyfe for to have her rychesses | Marrying for money | 219 |
| 2 | 749 | De envie | xlii v | xxxiiii v | L. Of envye | Envy | 56 |
| 6 | 762 | De limpacience de correction | xliii | xxxv v | LI. Of impacyence in correcyon | Self - complacency | 33 |
| 0 | 775 | Des inscavens et folz medicins | xlv v | xxxvi | LII. Of folysshe physycyens | Physicians | 206 |
| 5 | 792 | Du douloureux depart de la puissance du siecle [1] | xlvi v | xxxviiv | LIII. Of the dolorous departynge of the puyssaunce of heven [1] | End of Worldly Power | 126 |
| 1 | 810 | De predestinacion | xlvii v | xxxvii | LIIII. Of predestynacyon | Predestination | 146 |
| 76 | 825 | De oublier soy mesme | xlviii v | xxxvii v | LV. To forgete hymselfe | Minding one's own Business | 120 |
| 0 | 837 | Du vice dingratitude | xlix | xxxviii | LVI. Of the vyce of ingratitude | Ingratitude | 97 |
| 86 | 856 | De soy mesmes la plaisance | l | xxxix | LVII. Of his own pleasaunce | Vanity | 34 |
| 91 | 874 | Des danses ioyeux et saltacions | li | xxxixv | LVIII. Of daunces and dysportes | Dancing | 281 |
| 96 | 890 | Des aubadeurs ioueurs dinstrumens | lii | xl | LIX. Of players of instrumentes | Serenading | 284 |
| 01 | 904 | Des mendicans et leurs vanitez | liii | xl v | LX. Of beggers and of theyr vanytees | Beggars | 232 |

[1] In Drouyn the last word is printed ciecle. This explains Watson's *heven* !

| Chapter | Brant's Title | Locher's Titles | 2nd ed. fol. | Basel 1572 page | Barclay's Title | 1st ed. fol. | 2nd fo |
|---|---|---|---|---|---|---|---|
| 64 | Von bosen wibern | De iracundis mulieribus Ira muliebris | lxxii | 122 | Of the yre immoderate . . . and great lewdness of wymen | cxxix | 12 |
| 65 | Von achtung de gstirns | De cura astrologiae Astrologiae vanitas | lxxv | 128 | Of the vayne cure of Astrology | cxxxvi$v$ | 12 |
| 66 | Von erfarung aller land | De geographica regionum inquisitione Mathematicae superstitio | lxxvi | 130 | Of the folysshe descripcion of dyvers contrees | cxxxviii $v$ | 12 |
| 67 | Nitt wellen eyn nar syn | De eo qui non vult esse fatuus Non velle stultitiam propriam recognoscere | lxxvii | 132 | Of hym that wyll not se his owne folyssheness and that stryve agaynst his strenger | cxl $v$ | 13 |
| 68 | Schympf nit verston | De non intelligentibus ludos Iocum non intelligere | lxxviii | 134 | Of folys that understonde nat game . . . | cxlii $v$ | 13 |
| 69 | Bos dun und nit warten | Malefacere et non expectare Multos ledere | lxxix | 136 | Of them that wylfully offende nat takynge hede to the ende . . . | cxliii $v$ | 13 |
| 70 | Nit fursehen by zyt | De improvidentia futuri Pigricie fatuitas | lxxx | 138 | Of foles without provysyon | cxlvi $v$ | 13 |
| 71 | Zancken und zu gericht gan | De litigantibus in iuditio De rixosis | lxxxi | 140 | Of great stryvers in the lawe for thynges of nought | cxlviii$v$ | 13 |
| 72 | Von groben narren | De obscaenis fatuis De turpiloquio stultorum | lxxxii | 142 | Of foles abhomynable in fowle wordes of rybawdry | cl $v$ | 14 |
| 73 | Von geystlich werden | De status spiritualis abusu Omnes modo cupiunt clericari | lxxxiii | 144 | Of the abusyon of the spiritualte | clii $v$ | 14 |
| 74 | Von unnutzem jagen | *wanting* | | | *wanting* | | |
| 75 | Von bosen schutzen | *wanting* [2] | | | *wanting* | | |
| 76 | Von grossem ruemen | De inani fastu et iactatione Se iactare | lxxxiiii | 146 | Of the prowde and vayne bostynge of folys | clv | 146 |
| 77 | Von spylern | De lusoribus Ludo intenti | lxxxv | 148 | Of carde players and dysers | clvii | 148 |
| 78 | Von gdruckten narren | De suppressis fatuis Multe fatuorum pressure | lxxxvi | 150 | Of folys oppressyd with theyr owne foly | clix $v$ | 150 |
| 79 | Ruter und schreiber | De militibus et scribis De scribis et equitibus | lxxxvii | 152 | Of the extorcion of knyghtis and practysers of the lawe | clxi $v$ | 152 |

[1] The pages of this and the following chapters are from the 2nd volume.

| on | Stanza | Riviere's and Drouyn's Title | Riviere fol. | Drouyn fol. | Watson's Chapter and Title | Contents | Section |
|---|---|---|---|---|---|---|---|
| 1 | 921 | De condicions courroux et grandes maulvaitiez des femmes | liiii | xli *v* | LXI. Of condycyons, murmurynges and grete unhappynes of wyves | Bad Women | 212 |
| 3 | 973 | De la cure dastrologie | lvii *v* | xliii | LXIII. Of the cure of astronomye | Astrology | 257 |
| 3 | 987 | De celuy qui veult descripre . . . toutes regions | lviii *v* | xliiii | LXIIII. Of hym that wyll wryte and enquere of all regyons | Geography | 261 |
| 8 | 1001 | De celuy qui ne veult estre fol | lix *v* | xliiii *v* | LXV. Of hym that wyll not be a fole | Avarice and Prodigality | 65 |
| 3 | 1015 | De ceulx qui nentendent ieux | lx *v* | xlv | LXVI. Of them that can take no playe | The Biter Bit | 101 |
| 8 | 1031 | De limpacience daucuns qui . . . veullent mal faire | lxi | xlv *v* | LXVII. Of the impacyence of some that . . . wyll do evyll | The Biter Bit.— Trusting People | 100 |
| 3 | 1045 | De limprovoiance du temps advenir | lxii | xlvi | LXVIII. Of unpurveynge for the tyme to come | Improvidence | 83 |
| 8 | 1059 | De litigans ou plaidoyans en iugement | lxiii | xlvi*v* | LXIX. Of lytygans or pleaders in iugement | Lawsuits | 196 |
| 3 | 1074 | Des folz abhominables en parolle | lxiii *v* | xlvii | LXX. Of fooles abhomynable in wordes | Obscene Language | 49 |
| 7 | 1086 | De lestat et abus spirituel | lxiiii *v* | xlviii | LXXI. Of the estate and abuse spyrytuell | Rash Ordination | 154 |
| | | *wanting* | | | *wanting* | Hunting | 288 |
| | | *wanting* | | | *wanting* | Archery | 289 |
| 4 | 1108 | De sote vaine et orguilleuse iactation | lxv *v* | xlviii *v* | LXXII. Of folysshe and proude iactaunce | Boasting | 35 |
| 9 | 1123 | De ioueurs | lxvi *v* | xlix | LXXIII. Of players | Gambling | 290 |
| 5 | 1141 | Des folz supprimez | lxvii *v* | l | LXXIIII. Of fooles surprysed | Difficult Positions | 121 |
| o | 1155 | Des chevaliers gensdarmes scribes ou practiciens | lxviii *v* | l *v* | LXXV. Of knyghtes, lawyers and soldiers, men of armes, scrybes, and practycyens | | 199 |

² Only in the third edition of the Latin, which was never reprinted.

| Chapter | Brant's Title | Locher's Titles | 2nd ed. fol. | Basel 1572 page | Barclay's Title | 1st ed. fol. | 2nd fol. |
|---|---|---|---|---|---|---|---|
| 80 | Narrehte bottschafft | De stulta nuntiorum legatione Nuncius inutilis | lxxxviii | 154 | Of folysshe messengers and pursuyvauntis | clxiii $v$ | 154 |
| 81 | Von kochen und keller | De cellariis et cocis Coqui et cellarii | lxxxix | 156 | Of folysshe cokes and buttelers | clxv $v$ | 156 |
| 82 | Von burschem uffgang | De rusticorum arrogantia Rusticorum ambitio | xc | 158 | Of the arrogance and pryde of rude men of the country | clxvii $v$ | 158 |
| 83 | Von verachtung armut | De paupertatis contemptu Paupertatis contemptus | xci | 160 | Of the contempt and dispysynge of povertye | clxx | 160 |
| 84 | Von beharren in gutem | Non perseverare in bono *same* | xciii | 164 | Of them that begin to do well and contynue nat | clxxiii | 164 |
| 85 | Nit fursehen den dot | De neglectu mortis Mortis neglectus | xciiii | 166 | Of folys that despyse deth makynge no provysion therfore | clxxvii[2] | 166 |
| 86 | Von verachtung gottes | Contemptus in deum Contemnere deum | xcvi | 170 | Of folys that despyse God | clxxx $v$ | 170 |
| 87 | Von gottes lestern | De blasphemiis in christum Contra blasphematores | xcvii | 172 | Of blasphemers and swerers by the name of God and his sayntis | clxxxii $v$ | 172 |
| 88 | Von plag und strof gots | De plaga et indignatione dei Flagella dei | xcviii | 174 | Of the plage and indignacion of God, and folys that fere nat the same | clxxxv $v$ | 175 |
| 89 | Von dorechten wechsel | De fatua permutatione Fatua permutatio | xcix | 176 | Of folys exchanges scorsynges and permutacions | clxxxviii | 177 |
| 90 | Ere vatter und mutter | Honorare parentes *same* | c | 178 | Of folysshe children that worshyp nat their fader and moder | clxxxx | 179 |
| 91 | Von schwetzen im chor | De cavillatione sacerdotum in choro Garrulitas chori | ci | 180 | Of the claterynge and bablynge of prestis and clerkis in the quere | clxxxxiii | 182 |
| 92 | Überhebung der hochfart | Superbiae ostentatio Superbia | cii | 182 | Of elevate pryde and bostynge (An exclamacion ayenst pryde) | clxxxxv | 184 |
| 93 | Wucher und forkouff | De usurariis et foeneratoribus Usurarii | ciii $v$ | 185 | Of usurers and okerers | clxxxxviii $v$ | 187 |
| 94 | Von hoffnung uff erben | De vana spe futurae successionis Optare aliorum mortem | ciiii $v$ | 187 | Of the vayne hope that folys hath to succede to herytage . . . | cc | 189 |

[1] Misprinted lxix.

| on | Stanza | Riviere's and Drouyn's Title | Riviere fol. | Drouyn fol. | Watson's Chapter and Title | Contents | Section |
|---|---|---|---|---|---|---|---|
| | 1174 | De folles legacions et messagiers | lxix | li | LXXVI. Of folysshe legacyons and messengers | Messengers | 236 |
| | 1185 | Des queux des panciers et gardeurs de celier | lxxi | li v | LXXVII. Of caterers and kepers of sellers in houses | Cooks and Butlers | 238 |
| 5 | 1200 | De lexcessive arrogance rustique | lxxii | lii ¹ | LXXVIII. Of the excessive arrogance rustyke | Peasants | 241 |
| 9 | 1212 | Du contempnement de pauvrete | lxxii v | lii v | LXXIX. Of the contempnynge of poverte | Despising Poverty | 67 |
| 8 | 1242 | De celui qui ne veult perseverer en bien | lxxiiii | liii v | LXXX. Of him that wyll not persevere in goodnes | Perseverance | 90 |
| 3 | 1258 | Du contempnement ou meprisement de la mort | lxxv v | liiii v | LXXXI. Of the dysprysynge of dethe | Death | 132 |
| 3 | 1293 | Du grant contempnement de dieu ou meprisement | lxxvii v | lv v | LXXXII. Of the grete contempnynge and dyspraysynge of God | Provocation of God | 77 |
| 8 | 1307 | Des blasphemes contre iesu-crist | lxxviii v | lvi | LXXXIII. Of them that blaspheme our lorde Jhesu cryste | Blasphemy | 78 |
| 6 | 1333 | De la playe et indignacion de dieu | lxxix v | lvi v | LXXXIIII. Of the plage and indygnacyon of god | God's Indignation | 79 |
| 1 | 1349 | De la folle ou sote permutacion | lxxx | lvii | LXXXV. Of the folysshe permutacyon | Heaven and Earth | 86 |
| 7 | 1367 | De honnourer pere et mere | lxxxi v | lvii v | LXXXVI. To honour fader and moder | Children | 227 |
| 52 | 1386 | De la cavillacion des prestres et du chœur | lxxxii v | lviii | LXXXVII. Of the cavyllacyon of preestes in the quere | Talking in the Choir | 152 |
| 58 | 1401 | De la grande demonstrance dorgueil | lxxxiii | lviii v | LXXXVIII. Of the great demonstraunce of pryde | Vainglory | 37 |
| 66 | 1429 | Des usuriers et fenerateurs | lxxxiiii v | lix v | LXXXIX. Of usurers and fenerateurs | Usury | 93 |
| 70 | 1442 | De la vaine esperance davoir et succeder | lxxxv v | lx | LXXXX. Of the vayne hope to have and succede | Waiting for Dead men's shoes | 135 |

² Misprinted clxxiiii ; one folio is skipped.

| Chapter | Brant's Title | Locher's Titles | 2nd ed. fol. | Basel 1572 page | Barclay's Title | 1st ed. fol. | 2nd fc |
|---|---|---|---|---|---|---|---|
| 95 | Von verfurung am fyrtag | Non observare dies festos *same* | cv *v* | 189 | Of folys that kepe nat the holy daye | ccii | 19 |
| 96 | Schencken und beruwen | Largiri et penitere Cum tristi vultu donare | cvi *v* | 191 | Of folys that repent of that they have gyven | cciiii | 19 |
| 97 | Von tragkeit und fulheit | De accidiae vitio Accidia | cvii *v* | 193 | Of the vyce of slouth | ccvi | 19 |
| 98 | Von uslendigen narren | De externis et infidelibus fatuis De extraneis fatuis | cviii *v* | 195 | Of straunge folys and infydels as sarasyns, paynems, and suche lyke | ccvii *v* | 19 |
| 99 | Von abgang des glouben | De fidei catholicae et imperii inclinatione De reipublicae christiane interitu | cix *v* | 197 | Of the ruyne of the holy fayth catholyke and dymynucion of the Empyre | ccxii | 20 |
| 100 | Von falben hengst strichen | De assentatoribus et parasytis De assentatoribus | cxiii *v* | 205 | Of flaterers and glosers | ccxviii *v* | 20 |
| 101 | Von oren blasen | De delatoribus et obloquutoribus Facile credere | cxiv *v* | 207 | Of tale berers and foles of lyght credence unto the same | ccxx | 20ç |
| 102 | Von falsch und beschiss | De falsariis et fraudulentia De falsariis rerum omnium | cxv *v* | 209 | Of falshode, gyle and disceyte and such as folowe them | ccxxii *v* | 21} |
| 103 | Vom endkrist | De Antichristo | cxvii | 212 | Of the falshode of Antichrist | ccxxiiii *v* | 213 |
| 104 | Worheyt verschwigen | Veritatem obticere Tacere veritatem | cxviii *v* | 214 | Of hym that dare nat utter the trouth for fere of displeasour | ccxxvii *v* | 216 |
| 105 | Hyndernys des gutten | Retractio a bono Retrahere a bono | cxix *v* | 216 | Of fools that with drawe and let other to do good dedes | ccxxix *v* | 218 |
| 106 | Ablossung gutter werck | Omissio bonorum operum Bonorum operum negligentia | cxx *v* | 218 | Of the omyssion or levynge of good warkes | ccxxxi | 220 |
| 107 | Von lon der wisheit | De praemio sapientiae De via felicitatis | cxxi | 220 | Of the rewarde of wysdome | ccxxxiii | 222 |
| 108 | Das schluraffen schiff | La ina navis seu barca socialis Societas fatuorum | cxxxv | 246 | The unyversall shyp and . . . barge, wherin they rowe : that yet hath no charge | cclxi *v* | 248 |

[1] Drouyn : De la saincte foy catholique de nostre mere saincte

| on | Stanza | Riviere's and Drouyn's Title | Riviere fol. | Drouyn fol. | Watson's Chapter and Title | Contents | Section |
|---|---|---|---|---|---|---|---|
| 4 | 1454 | De non observer les sainctz dimenches et festes | lxxxvi v | lx v | LXXXXI. Of them that observeth not the sondayes and other feestes | Non-Obser-vance of Holy Days | 150 |
| 9 | 1469 | Eslargir ses biens et sen repentir | lxxxvii v | lxi | LXXXXII. To gyve his goode and after repente hym | Almsgiving | 68 |
| 4 | 1482 | Du vice de paresse | lxxxviii | lxi v | LXXXXIII. Of the synne of slowth | Sloth | 97 |
| 8 | 1495 | Des folz infideles | lxxxix | lxii | LXXXXIIII. Of fooles infydeles | Infidels | 171 |
| 2 | 1508 | De la foy catholicque inclinacion et de lem-pire ¹ | lxxxx | lxii v | LXXXXV. Of the holy fayth catholyke of our moder holy chirche | Turkish Danger | 174 |
| 0 | 1577 | Des assentateurs blan-deurs . . . et escu-meux de court | xcii v | lxv | LXXXXVI. Of bland-ysshers and flaterers | Flattery | 42 |
| 4 | 1590 | Des delateurs et vains raporteurs | xciii v | lxvi | LXXXXVII. Of de-layers, and vayne re-porters | Backbiting | 106 |
| 9 | 1603 | Des faulsaires et fraud-uleux | xciiii v | lxvi v | LXXXXVIII. Of false begylers | Various Forms of Deceit | 95 |
| 24 | 1619 | De lantecrist | xcvii v | lxvii | *no title* | Heretics | 185 |
| 31 | 1643 | De celluy qui taise verite | xcix | lxviii | C. Of them that hydeth trouthe | Truth above All | 138 |
| 35 | 1655 | De retirer aucun bien faisant et de bien fait | c | lxviii v | CI. To withdrawe the good dede and what it is | Praise of the Car-thusians | 169 |
| 38 | 1667 | De lobmission de bonnes œuvres | ci | lxix | CII. Of the obmys-syon of good werkes | Good Works Persever-ance | 89 |
| 44 | 1681 | Du loyer de sapience | cii | lxx | CIII. Of the prays-ynge of sapyence | The Two Ways | 88 |
| 06 | 1876 | La nef latine ou barcque socialle | cxiiii | lxxv v | CXIII. Of the shyp latyne or barge socy-ale | Voyage to the Land of Cock-ayne | 370 |

¹ ination du sainct empyre rommain (literally in Watson).

| Chapter | Brant's Title | Locher's Titles | 2nd e. fol. | Basel 1572 page | Barclay's Title | 1st ed. fol. | 2nd e fol. |
|---|---|---|---|---|---|---|---|
| 109 | Verachtung ungfelles | Neglectus infortunii<br>Periculum non vitare | cxxii *v* | 222 | Of the despysynge of mysfortune | ccxxxv | 223 |
| 110 | Hynderred des guten | Detractio bonorum<br>Obloqui bene operantibus | cxxiii *v* | 224 | Of bacbyters . . . and of them that shal disprayse this wark | ccxxxvii | 226 |
| 110a | Von disches unzucht [1] | De immoderata mensae turpitudine<br>Facecia mense | cxxiiii *v* | 226 | Of immoderate vyleness in manners, usyd at the table | ccxli | 228 |
| 110b | Von fasnacht narren [1] | De larvatis fatuis<br>De gaudio larve | cxxvi *v* | 230 | Of folys disgysyd with vysers and other counterfayte apparayle | ccxliv *v* | 231 |
| 111 | Entschuldigung des dichters | Excusatio Jacobi locher Philomusi<br>Derisio boni operis | cxxxvi *v* | 249 | A. Barclay excusynge the rudenes of his translation | i *v* | 260 |
| 112 | Der wis man | Viri prudentis descriptio<br>Sapientia | cxxviii | 233 | The descripcion of a wyse man. (To syr Johnn Bysshop of Excester.) | ccxlvii | 234 |
| a | | In commendationem philosophiae<br>Bonorum hominum persecutio | cxxix *v* | 236 | Of folys that dispyse wysdome. . . . A lamentacion of Barclay | ccl | 237 |
| b | | Concertatio Virtutis cum Voluptate | cxxx *v* | 239 | A concertacion or stryvynge bytwene vertue and voluptuosyte | cclii | 239 |
| c | | Epistola Jacobi Locher Philomusi ad . . . Bergmann | cxxxix *v* | *wanting* | | | |
| d | | Ad numeros suos ut J. Bergmanum festine adeant | cxli | 255 | | | |
| e | | De singularitate quorundam novorum fatuorum. Additio S. Brant | cxlii *r* | 257 | A brefe addicion of the syngularyte of some newe folys | cclxix | 255 |
| f | | De corrupto ordine vivendi pereuntibus<br>Inventio Nova Sebastiani Brant. Quod inordinatio causa fuerit destructionis omnium rerum | cxlv | 263 | | | |

[1] These two chapters do not occur in the *first* German edition.  Hend

| Stanza | Riviere's and Drouyn's Title | Riviere fol. | Drouyn fol. | Watson's Chapter and Title | Contents | Section |
|---|---|---|---|---|---|---|
| 1674 | De deprisement de son infortune | ciii | lxx v | CIIII. Of the dyspraysynge of his fortune | Prudent Behaviour in Difficulties | 128 |
| 1707 | De la detraction des biens | ciii v | lxxi | CV. Of the detraccyon of goodes | Personal Declaration | 309 |
| 1722 | De limmoderee layde vile et orde turpitude de la table | ciiii v | lxxi v | CVI. Of the immoderate turpitude of the table | Bad Manners at Table | 293 |
| 1751 | De folz deffigurez et larves ou prenans dissimulee vesture | cvi v | lxxii v | CVII. Of foles dysfygured takynge straunge clothynges | Carnivalfools | 301 |
| 1 | *wanting* | | | *wanting* | Apology | 312 |
| 1769 | De la vraye descripcion dhomme prudent | cviii | lxxiii | CVIII. Of the true descrypcyon of prudent men | Praise of the Wiser Man | 109 |
| 1794 | De la commendacion philosophie | cix | lxxiii v ² | CIX. Of the recommendacyon of phylosophye | Praise of Wisdom | 108 |
| 1810 | Concertation de vertuz avecques volupte | cx | lxxiii | CX. Concertacyon of vertue with voluptuosyte | Strife between Virtue and Lust | 52 |
| | | | | | Letter to Bergman | 328 |
| | | | | | Envoy to Bergman | 329 |
| 1927 | De la singularite daucuns nouveaulx fols. addicion. | cxvi | lxxvii | CXV. Of the syngularyte of some newe foles | Beghards and Beguines | 162 |
| | | | | | Letter to Locher | 321 |
| | *Only Drouyn.* 1. De ceulx qui veullent corrompre le droit : addition | | lxxviii | CXVI. Of them that corrupt the ryght | Disorder Ruins All | 189 |
| | 2. De ceulx qui font toutes choses au contraire : addition | | lxxx v | CXVII. Of them that do all thynges contrary | | |

---

xcrescent numbers.                  ² This number occurs twice.

| Chapter | Brant's Title | Locher's Titles | 2nd ed. fol. | Basel 1572 page | Barclay's Title | 1st ed. fol. |
|---|---|---|---|---|---|---|
| g | | Epigramma Thome beccadelli Cymbri adolescentuli primarii et impuberis ad D. Sebastianum Brant. . . . | clvi | *wanting* | *wanting* | |
| h | | De fatuo mundano. (Paris and Lyons) | | *wanting* | Of folys that ar over-worldly | cclxv *v* |
| i | | | | | A conclusion . . . Balade of the translatour in honoure of the Blessyd Virgyn Mary, moder of God | cclxxiii |

| Stanza | Riviere's and Drouyn's Title | Riviere fol. | Drouyn fol. | Watson's Chapter and Title | Contents | Section |
|---|---|---|---|---|---|---|
|  | *wanting* |  |  | *wanting* | Beccadellus's Epigram to Brant | 332 |
| 1911 | *wanting* |  |  | *wanting* | Worldly Fools | 130 |
| 1963 | *no title* | lxxxi *v* |  | *no title* | Prayer to the Virgin | 350 |

# REGISTER

The figures refer to sections. Titles of books are between inverted commas. No capitals are used for words as such.

TO WAIT, 372
Waldseemüller M., 261
walet, 227
wallop, 213
'Wälsche Gast,' 293
wanhope, 90, 115, 119, 137
Warden, 346
Wars of the Roses, 66
Warton, 7
wary, 234
watch, 372
Watson H., 16, 36, 184, 345, 362, 375, 378
Watson's age, 343
Watson's works, 379
'Wealth and Health,' 78
Weariness, 85
Weisbach, 357
werke dayes, 283
Westminster, 117
Westminster Abbey, 324
Westminster Hall, 194
Wheel of Fortune, 123
whelpis, 225
Whitsuntide, 307
Wimpheling J., 163, 250, 330, 367
Wine, 95
Wireker N., 354
Wisdom, 107 sqq.
Wise Man, 109
Witches, 210
withy, 272

Woerden, 13
Wolf, 94
Wolters M., 367
Women, 114, 274, 290
wood, 286
Wood A., 347
Woodcuts, 172, 187, 192, 304, 327, 345, 358, 381
Wooden shoes, 112
Worldly Fools, 130
Wrath, 61
Wrong, 192
Wyatt, 375
Wycliffites, 171
Wynkyn de Worde, 345, 358, 382

YATE, 310
yordan, 285
York, 256
Youth, 319, 341, 351
yowlynge, 285
Ypocras, 207

ZACHONI J., 11, 25
Zarncke, 6, 99, 159, 293
Zerclare, 293
Zingel G., 330
Zomeren H. van, 149
Zuohsta, 206